Springer Texts in Business and Economics

For further volumes:
http://www.springer.com/series/10099

Peter Dorman

Microeconomics

A Fresh Start

Springer

Peter Dorman
The Evergreen State College
Olympia, WA, USA

ISSN 2192-4333 ISSN 2192-4341 (electronic)
ISBN 978-3-642-37433-3 ISBN 978-3-642-37434-0 (eBook)
DOI 10.1007/978-3-642-37434-0
Springer Heidelberg New York Dordrecht London

Library of Congress Control Number: 2014941109

Printed on acid-free paper

Springer is part of Springer Science+Business Media (www.springer.com)

Acknowledgements

Most introductory-level textbooks, at least in the U.S. market, are now the products of vast armies: not just the authors whose names you see on the cover, but hordes of reviewers, research assistants, design specialists, and others whose job is to help assemble, edit, shape and market the book itself and then all the ancillary items—the websites, test banks, instructors' slides, videos, and other enhancements that keep emerging from the development of new technology.

This book was written entirely by one person with just a tiny bit of assistance. There are costs to this approach, which I will get to shortly, but one big advantage: it is possible to offer a new, coherent vision of the subject matter, free from any pressure to conform to how things have been done in the past. In economics, I think this one plus outweighs all the minuses, but you can judge for yourself.

Of course, no book of this type is truly the product of just one individual. Just to be in a position to write it, I had to make my way to professional status as an economist, and that I owe above all to my dissertation chair, Herb Gintis. To say that Herb was an ideal advisor would be an understatement; he really took me under his wing and did whatever it took (including occasional childcare) to help me succeed. My debt to him cannot ever be repaid.

As a teaching professor of economics I have benefitted enormously from my colleagues at Evergreen State College, where I have worked for the past 15 years. Most teaching at Evergreen is interdisciplinary, undertaken in teams. I have taught economics in the context of biology, ecology, physics, history, sociology, philosophy, political science and cultural studies. This has been an invaluable laboratory for seeing the place of economics in the broad expanse of human knowledge and for augmenting my economist's skills with those honed by other kinds of training. Their impact on this textbook should be obvious.

In addition, Evergreen is one of the premier teaching institutions of higher education in North America. It has played a pioneering role in the development of learning communities, inquiry-centered courses, active learning strategies and other innovations. I have been honored to teach with colleagues who are master educators by any definition of the term, and most of what I have learned as a teacher I owe to them.

On the receiving end of my experimentation in the classroom have been my students. In more ways than I could document they have left their traces on this text, some by making specific recommendations, others simply by showing me what works and what doesn't. Their patience and goodwill, and above all their thirst for learning, has made it possible for me to develop new approaches to teaching economics through trial and error. And the more I took the plunge into rethinking how introductory economics could be refashioned, the more necessary a new kind of textbook appeared. The very idea of this book emerged logically from my interactions with students at Evergreen.

Once I realized I needed to write a textbook, the biggest challenge was getting started. Here I can credit Peter Barnes, who provided a month's glorious solitude at Mesa Refuge. By the time I left, about a third of the micro text had been drafted and I had discovered a smart, friendly and socially committed colleague. Several pages of the text bear his imprint and are much the better for it. Since then I have also benefitted from reviews of individual chapters, especially by Matson Boyd, Josh Mason and Sevinç Rende.

To be published, a book still needs a publisher (although this may be changing). I was fortunate that Barbara Fess of Springer saw value in the unfinished work I sent her, and she has kept me on track through the final revisions. When I think I am missing all the inputs that a more commercially-oriented publisher might provide, I remind myself how professionally satisfied I am working with Springer and how supportive Barbara and her colleagues are of my vision. It's well worth it.

But that brings me to the downside of working on my own. Economics is a vast subject matter, and no one can possibly encompass all of it. Although I have gone over it again and again, I am sure this text has its share of errors and omissions. Here I depend on you. Please make note of any flaws you discover and take the time to let me know. I will post them on the web and incorporate fixes in any future edition. Many thanks in advance!

Finally, the sheer time and effort that goes into a project like this places a strain on any relationship. I am deeply grateful that Heike Nolte has coped with understanding and generosity. I thank her for being wonderful in general and for putting up with my questionable American work habits.

Contents

Part IV Microeconomic Challenges

Part I

Foundations

Economics and the Economy 1

It would not be easy to avoid all discussion of economics in twenty-first century America. You would have to keep your distance from television, radio and newspapers, not to mention casual conversations on the job, over a beer, or at a family gathering. In fact, our society is saturated with economics, reflecting the great power that economic events have over our lives, even though the forces that produce them are often mysterious. Economics is like the weather, only more so: all around us, obviously important, subject to prediction but only slightly to control.

Unfortunately, much of the folk wisdom about economics—the assumptions behind casual discussion that are often reflected in the media—is *wrong*. It misrepresents what economics is and what it has to say to us. Since we get these messages, consciously and unconsciously, dozens of times each day, the first step in studying economics is to *unlearn* the assumptions we pick up in daily life. This is not easy to do. I will discuss a few of the more common myths in this chapter, but it is my experience that deeply ingrained ideas do not fade away easily. You will want to return to these myths later on, as we gradually build up a body of theories to replace them.

1.1 Myth #1: Economics Is the Study of How to Make Money

Economists are certainly interested in the strategies people employ in order to make money, but the purpose of economics is not to help anyone do this more successfully. The vantage point of economics is not any particular individual and their material goals, but rather society as a whole. *Economics is about what is beneficial for society in general.* What's good for any particular individual is not necessarily good for all of us as a group, and economics takes this distinction very seriously. Often economists are interested in interfering with the money-making plans of particular individuals or businesses in order to safeguard the interests of society.

A good example of this is the study of monopoly—a situation in which a single business controls all or most of a market. Monopoly can be very lucrative: get rid of your competitors and you can make higher profits. Economists are interested in the

P. Dorman, *Microeconomics*, Springer Texts in Business and Economics,
DOI 10.1007/978-3-642-37434-0_1,

ways businesses exploit the power of monopoly, whether they raise prices and restrict options for consumers, or whether they engage in pre-emptive innovation and even price-cutting in order to discourage future competition. In this sense, they do study the money-making process. But the goal is not to make monopolists rich, since that can easily happen at the expense of society. Instead, the purpose of economic analysis is to anticipate how monopolists will use their power, what effect this will have on the rest of society, and therefore whether action should be taken to restrict this power or limit how it can be used. In their studies of these questions, economists should be guided by the desire to promote the well-being of all members of society and not just those who hold a monopolistic advantage.

1.2 Myth #2: Economics Says that Supply and Demand in Free Markets Solves All Our Economic Problems

To be honest, there is a germ of truth here: economists, as a group, are far more supportive of free markets than just about anyone else. They tend to be more pro-business, regarding profits as largely justified and beneficial. They are more likely than other academic specialists to question the desirability of regulations that limit the freedom of businesses to make money as they see fit. This hostility toward government often translates into a belief that supply and demand should govern economic outcomes, or that these forces are so powerful that it is not a good idea to stand in their way.

Most people, for instance, think it's a good idea for the government to set a minimum wage, a bottom limit to the amount employers must pay their workers for an hour's work. They think minimum wages contribute to fairness and reduce poverty. (People disagree on what this minimum should be of course, but not as often on the need for *some* minimum.) A high percentage—perhaps as many as half—of economists, however, think there should be no such regulation of wages. In their view, if a worker is willing to work for a very low wage and an employer is willing to pay it, it would be unwise to interfere. The forces of supply (workers) and demand (employers) for labor should determine wage rates, and nothing else.

Nevertheless, it is much too sweeping to claim that economics is ever and always wedded to free markets. In situation after situation, economists are quite willing to support government or other forms of intervention in order to protect the interests of society from the actions of individuals in the marketplace. They do this because they believe that markets often *fail*; in fact, much of economic theory consists of a careful analysis of the causes and consequences of this failure. Economists are more likely to support the ideal of a free market, but they are perfectly willing to withdraw this support when markets misfire. We will see many examples of this over the course of this text.

1.3 Myth #3: Economics Is About "Economizing"—Holding Down Costs

This is a case of language playing tricks on us. The common meaning of economizing is to make do with less; it's a term we're all familiar with. It is natural, then, to think that this has something to do with economics as well. There is just enough truth to the idea to make it really insidious; economists, after all, look for ways to cut *unnecessary* costs. But, as we will see, costs alone have no meaning in economics—they matter only in the context of the benefits they make possible. "No pain, no gain" is as relevant to economics as it is to anything else: sometimes costs must be increased in order to take advantage of an opportunity. This is true for a business considering an investment possibility, or a student borrowing money to finance an education, or a country improving its infrastructure to stimulate new increases in productivity. Sometimes economizing is highly uneconomical.

There is another aspect to this myth that deserves mention. It is normal for businesses and individuals to look for ways to cut their costs by shifting them to others. Not every tax is paid or workplace injury reported; sometimes natural resources that belong to the entire society, such as clean air and clean water, are used without any compensation. When this happens, some people's costs go down, but not necessarily the full cost to society. Since the perspective of economics is that of society as a whole, cost-shifting is not cost reduction at all. In other words, individual economizing may not be the same as social economizing, quite apart from the problem that benefits need to be considered as well as costs.

1.4 Myth #4: Economists Want to Increase the Amount of Money Possessed by Individuals or Communities

Sometimes it looks this way. Economists often speak of the need for more economic growth, measured as quantities of money. (At the time of this writing, the most recent measurement of the size of the US economy is about 16 trillion dollars.) Certainly on an individual level, we are often concerned with increasing our income or savings. Isn't the goal of economics just to do this for everyone at once?

The problem with this view is that it mistakes the value of something for the units in which it is measured. Money in itself is meaningless: you can't eat it or live in it, and it provides just a tiny bit of heat if you burn it. The real value of money, of course, lies in the things you can buy with it—and it is these things that economics is concerned with, not money itself. The difference is important; as we will see, it is possible for the amount of money that people have to go up even when the real amount of "stuff" (actual goods and services) remains the same. (This is called inflation.) Moreover, many important economic costs and benefits are not measured in money at all. A worker who receives training on the job is receiving an important benefit (as is also, perhaps, the employer), but this may not take a monetary form. A business that pollutes the local water supply is generating a significant cost to society, but no money may change hands. Economics is concerned with "real" costs and benefits in this larger sense, not simply with the sloshing of money back and forth between people. Of course, flows of money are important and need to be kept track of, but this is only one part of what economics is about.

1.5 Is Economics the Study of the Economy?

No. There is no single discipline or body of thought that studies the economy in all its complexity. Economics studies certain aspects of the economy, and it studies them in certain ways.

To see this, it helps to agree on what we mean by "the economy". The concept is actually rather fuzzy; in fact, for most of human history people did not have this concept at all. The notion that some portion of our individual and collective lives could be set aside and labeled "economic" is a modern invention. Without going into the difficult theoretical issues that we would have to consider if we wanted an exact definition, we can speak generally about three aspects of economic life:

Economic institutions. These are systems of organization that play a role in the production, distribution or use of goods and services. Examples include corporations, government agencies (especially those that regulate the economy), markets (to be defined in Chap. 6), and families or other household groups (that distribute goods among their members, produce important economic services like child-rearing, and make decisions about who will provide what sort of labor in the paid labor market). Institutions that play a role in the economy also play other roles: they can be political or social institutions as well as economic ones. There is thus an important overlap between "the economy" understood as a system of institutions, and the other aspects of society. This is one reason economic reality is so difficult to see from the vantage point of just one field of study, such as economics.

Economic behavior. People and organizations engage in economic behavior when they participate in the production, distribution or use of goods and services. Some of this behavior takes the form of decision-making; other behavior involves carrying out decisions. You may decide to take a job, for instance; this act of choice is an example of economic behavior. So is the actual work you do once you begin the job. You might go one step further, and say that anything you do that affects your work, such as commuting choices or social connections established with coworkers, is economic behavior too. If you take this wider view (which is probably the most useful one), it is clear once again that much of our life is simultaneously economic and something else.

Economic outcomes. Economies have results. Things get produced, and resources are used in one way rather than another. People do certain types of work and receive pay in return. Goods and services find their way to specific consumers, who use them to greater or lesser advantage. The natural environment is preserved or degraded in the process. Health too is an economic outcome, as is education, and even peoples' choices over how many children to have, where to live, and how much time to devote to personal and community activities are economic to a significant degree. Once more, there is no clear dividing line between an economic outcome and an outcome that might be looked at from some other perspective, such as the family or the political system.

The closer one looks, the clearer it is that "the economy" is not a distinct thing walled off from the rest of life; it is really just one aspect of everything we are and do. It is far too diffuse and complicated to be captured by any single body of thought. Psychologists, sociologists, philosophers, geographers, political scientists, ecologists—all these and more have something to say. But this raises the question, what is the relationship between economics and the economy? If economics is not specifically "the study of the economy", what is it?

1.6 What Economics Is

There are two ways to describe what is distinctive about economics: it is a body of thought and an organized profession. Both are crucial to what we will be exploring in this book.

Economics is an intellectual tradition. It encompasses more than two centuries of research and speculation, recorded in books, journal articles, government reports, lectures, and other forms. This is a dynamic process, so new ideas do not simply sit side-by-side with old ones; the old ideas are often revised or pushed aside. At any point in time, economics is what economists of that era think and say. Some of this will reflect long-standing beliefs, but much of it will be new. It is important to look both backward and forward, to consider the roots of current doctrines but to keep abreast with their continuing evolution.

In particular, as we will see, economics is organized around a few core ideas, and these ideas distinguish it from other perspectives. Economists tend to be outcome-oriented (ends justifying the means), concerned with a tightly defined conception of efficiency, and disposed to thinking about the economy as a set of exchanges. Their theory is narrow in some respects and quite sweeping in others, but it is different from the theories you would find being discussed by practitioners of other social sciences. One of the purposes of this book is to make these core ideas available to you, the reader, so that you can make your own decisions concerning what is useful about the economic approach.

At the same time, economics is a profession. It is organized politically, sociologically and, yes, economically. It maintains professional organizations which help certify who is and is not a "real" economist. It organizes conferences and learned books and journals, which determine what ideas will be disseminated within the profession and to the larger public. It inhabits departments at colleges and universities which hire, fire and promote academic economists, determining which careers will prosper and which will be cut short. Finally, its leading practitioners are often given top positions in business and government, where their theories can be translated into action. While no academic specialty has as much power as the "practical" professions, such as law or management, economics has more power than most. It is common to find that high-level politicians, officials, and policy analysts rose through the ranks of the economics profession.

What this means is that economics is not just a way to think about reality; it is an important part of that reality. Even when they are wrong in their judgments, what economists think matters. As we will see, economists as a profession often adopt positions that are very different from those of the majority of the population. This adds to the visibility of economics within the political process. It would be difficult to be an active citizen today without a critical understanding of economic arguments.

From my experience, students are often disappointed by the study of economics. They come into economics courses eager to learn about the economy, and instead they are up to their ears in the abstract and often arcane theories of the economics profession. I empathize with their plight, but I urge them to keep at it. Economics as an approach to studying economic life has its shortcomings, but it has valuable insights to offer too. It is sometimes necessary to slog through quite a bit of preliminary explanation before these insights become apparent and are available for use. Moreover, economics is itself an important part of the world it studies. There is value to knowing where economists are coming from—or, as a famous economist, Joan Robinson, once said, the reason to study economics is to avoid being misled by economists.

▶ Terms to Define

Economics vs the economy
Economics vs economizing
Cost shifting
Economic institutions
Economic behavior
Economic outcomes
Money vs "real" economic goods and services

Questions to Consider

1. Before entering this class, did you subscribe to any of the four myths identified above?
2. Read through a recent comprehensive newspaper, such as *The New York Times*, the *Washington Post* or, in other languages, *Le Monde*, *Frankfurter Allgemeine Zeitung* or *El Pais*. How many economists are cited? In what contexts? What opinions did they offer?

2 Economics Yesterday and Today

As we have just seen, economics is not just an open-ended study of the economy, nor is it simply a collection of ideas and tools. It is an enterprise, with its own particular history, structure and values. We have sketched some of this very briefly, but we need to consider the economics enterprise in more depth before beginning the actual study of economics. After all, it is the deeper purposes of economic analysis that give meaning to the various definitions and models we will examine, and these purposes are the product of many generations of teachers, writers and researchers, each building on or reacting to the experiences of their predecessors. What economic ideas mean cannot be separated from what they mean to those who develop and use them.

In this chapter we will approach this problem from two directions. First we will pay a visit to the England of Adam Smith and his contemporaries in order to see what questions they were trying to answer when they set economics on its modern path. As we will discover, the concerns of these "founding fathers" have cast a shadow that still touches us today. But one difference between then and now cannot be avoided: the early economists considered themselves practitioners of philosophy, law, history and politics. They saw their main purpose as the persuasion of their fellows toward a particular brand of policy and institution-building. Most contemporary economists would call themselves scientists; their goal is to contribute to an expanding body of valid information and explanation. This entails a bit of juggling, since they, like their forebears, also want to influence events. This raises the difficult question of how to combine science and persuasion and even deeper questions of regarding the relationship between the two. This may seem to be something of a tangent, but how to draw the line between disinterested analysis and judgments of value and desirability—indeed, whether there even is such a line—will reappear frequently in the chapters to come. That's why some introductory observations are in order. But first the history.

P. Dorman, *Microeconomics*, Springer Texts in Business and Economics,
DOI 10.1007/978-3-642-37434-0_2, © Springer-Verlag Berlin Heidelberg 2014

2.1 The Historical Context

To a remarkable degree, economics (at least in the English-speaking world) is about the merits of a single, simple answer to a question people have been asking for over 200 years. The question is whether the unprecedented power to change the world wielded by modern economies can be allowed to operate free of any conscious, overall control. The possible answer is that a system of generalized competition can harness this power to socially beneficial ends. Economics has been mulling this answer for centuries, wondering whether or not it is true.

The story behind this question takes us back to the first modern economy, that of Great Britain in the eighteenth century. British society had deep roots in institutions and practices going back to the middle ages. Its government was in the hands of a landed aristocracy that could trace its lineage to the knights and noblemen of ancient times. About 95 % of the population consisted of common farmers and workmen, people with no political rights and few expectations of economic or social advancement. The moral order was under the control of an established church, which viewed its Christian doctrine as the basis for how life should be lived, from the vagabond drifting from village to village on up to the king himself.

In economic terms, this medieval legacy was highly conservative. There was little innovation from one generation to the next, much less from one year to the next. Boys had an obligation to assume the occupations of their fathers, and girls were raised to manage the same domestic responsibilities carried out by their mothers. There were rules stipulating how different sorts of work were to be carried out, how much sellers could charge for their products, what could be done with land and other property. Everyone saw themselves enmeshed in a web of responsibility, aware that the entire social order depended on this responsibility being fulfilled. The purpose of life was to see to these responsibilities, which meant accepting one's role in the system. Of course, there were rebels, but rebels were suppressed, often ruthlessly.

It is fair to say that, until the eighteenth century, most Britons lived and died in a world that looked identical to the one in which they were born. Technology changed gradually and hardly at all in the villages. Hardly anyone went from rags to riches or back again. Beliefs and customs were stable and predictable.

The dominant worldview, shared by aristocrats and commoners alike, was one of unequal reciprocity. No one could deny that some were rich and powerful and others poor and without recourse. God, it was thought, had created the world this way, and had assigned duties appropriate to each station. The poor owed their obedience and steady effort. The rich were responsible for the welfare of those beneath them; they were obligated to defend them in times of war, feed them during poor harvests, and see to it that they were not taken advantage of due to weakness or ignorance. (This last obligation was relative, of course, since the wealth of the nobility could hardly have existed without exploitation of the common people.) The great virtues espoused by the Church were loyalty and mercy.

This established order was increasingly shaken by events at all levels. On the local level, some aristocrats began running their domains more like capitalist farms, designed to make as much money as possible, than feudal estates. In the cities, merchants took advantage of improved trading opportunities to amass new concentrations of wealth, and they used this wealth to secure a higher social status that was formerly available only by birth. At the national level, England was engulfed in a revolution during the 1640s, and the balance of power between king and parliament shifted toward the latter 40 years later. But it was not until the eighteenth century that the older order could be seen to be crumbling before the eyes of contemporary observers.

The middle of the century witnessed the start of the "industrial revolution". New mechanized technologies appeared in textile production, coal mining and other industries, and this had profound social effects. Entire occupations (like that of the handloom weavers who supplemented their farming income with home production of cloth) disappeared. New occupations, especially mill work, demanded labor, and workers abandoned their ancestral homes to travel to the factories that were beginning to emerge. The new enterprises multiplied new wealth, and the notion that one should go through life simply carrying out inherited responsibilities seemed too limiting. Why not venture to get ahead, to seize some of this new wealth by starting a business, developing a new idea, or acquiring one of the new productive skills commanding greater pay and prestige? A society regulated by obligation was, within the space of just a few generations, mutating into an arena for competing ambitions. Individualism was openly espoused by a new breed of "romantic" artists and writers, calling for rebellion against the values of the church and the other pillars of tradition. (You can see the conflict between individual ambition and the traditional call to duty in the novels of Jane Austen. Rebellion reaches its peak in poets like Shelley.)

If England was something of a European follower at the start of the seventeenth century, behind more advanced regions of the continent in learning, the arts and the level of economic prosperity, it was the undisputed leader of the world at the close of the eighteenth. An explosion of production propelled England into the unprecedented position of global economic hegemony. Its manufactured goods undersold local competition from Lisbon to Bombay. Its wealth was used to build the world's most powerful navy, which in turn made the British Empire second to none. Travelers from other countries made their way to England to find out how this island on the fringe of Europe, with its grim climate and relatively undistinguished history, had conquered all comers.

But the English themselves were taken by surprise as well. How had such a dramatic change occurred? What could explain the spectacular increase in wealth, the ultimate source of the country's military and political dominance? Was it a particular natural resource, a characteristic of the population that made it more productive, or were there institutions and policies that fostered economic progress? And if it was the last of these, could these institutions be emulated, so that prosperity could spread around the world?

At the same time, pride and satisfaction with British economic growth was shadowed by a deep fear that this new era would come to a bad end. Children were rebelling against their parents, the church had lost its unquestioned moral authority, and unbridled ambition had taken the place of duty to one's community. What would hold society together in the absence of duty? Would England descend into Thomas Hobbes' fearsome "war of all against all"? By what alchemy could the lead of narrow self-interest be transmuted into the gold of social order? The responsibilities inculcated by traditional morality were the only social glue England had known; casting them off might make some people rich beyond their dreams, but wasn't there a price to be paid?

2.2 Adam Smith

Various answers were proposed to this question, but none could match the power and sweep of the one offered by philosopher and legal theorist Adam Smith. Smith was a leading figure in the "Scottish Enlightenment" of the mid-late eighteenth century. (A group of brilliant Scotsmen were revolutionizing philosophy, politics and science.) In 1759 he wrote *The Theory of Moral Sentiments*, a work arguing that the general desire to protect one's reputation, and the internalization of the views of others as a form of sympathetic emotion, provide a sufficient basis for morality. A world of individual ambition can be one of honesty and cooperation if a solid reputation is the precondition for success. Better still, people may internalize the imagined scrutiny of others, and this produces a sort of conscience. Once such feelings have been implanted, upright behavior will continue even if no one else is looking. A theory based on reputation within a fairly small community whose members interact repeatedly is not a bad hypothesis for "well-born" residents of Great Britain during this period. The number of noble and upper-class families numbered only in the thousands, and word of foul play could get around. (We will see later that a similar process, modeled by repeated game theory, applies reasonably well to many situations in our own day.)

But Smith was not satisfied. The process of rapid economic development was drawing in Englishmen (and Scotsmen) of all social classes. It was becoming common for people in the course of their daily business to make transactions with others they had never seen before and would likely never see again. Indeed, international trade was beginning to play a more important role, and the ultimate buyers of a good might have no idea who the original producer was, much less an expectation of doing repeated business. And, in any event, the theory of conscience-due-to-reputation had nothing in particular to say about *why* England's economy was growing so rapidly or whether such spontaneous and unregulated growth should be left alone or placed under some form of control.

After many years of study and reflection, including a pivotal trip to France, where he met with that country's leading economic thinker, François Quesnay, Smith unveiled a new approach in his major work, *An Inquiry into the Wealth of Nations*, in 1776. (For economists, the start of the American Revolution is the second most important event of that year.) This is one of the great achievements in world literature, and it is well worth reading even today. Smith's writing style is lucid and often elegant; his blending of observation and reflection is masterful.

(Smith's work is in the public domain, and full-text versions can be found on the Internet.) His argument is both simple and complex and not as easy to pigeonhole as is sometimes believed.

For our purposes, Smith's main point is that social order and prosperity alike are the products of vigorous, free competition. It is competition that, according to Smith, provides the incentives that power economic growth and that guarantee that growth will be in accord with the public interest. Since all mainstream economic theory since Smith has been concerned with these two claims, either endorsing or denying them, it is essential to be completely clear on what they entail.

Smith argued that the traditional society of obligation and inherited status cultivated unproductive attitudes on the part of rich and poor alike. If no one could get ahead—if your status at birth was unalterable—there would be no reason to work harder than anyone else. In such a world, good enough is good enough. Moreover, without rewards for innovation and risk-taking, progress in technology and business methods would be sporadic at best.

A competitive world would be quite different, he thought. Consider, for instance, the role of land ownership. Under the old system, still partially in effect during Smith's lifetime, extensive land holdings were a perquisite of nobility. You were an aristocrat because your family possessed a spread of land, and you possessed this land because your family was aristocratic. As an aristocrat, your obligation was to preserve this land and pass it on to future generations, so that the noble lineage would continue unbroken. The productivity of the land was secondary.

Those without land, meanwhile, were unable to acquire it. If the land is tied up in the hands of the aristocracy, then the common people can gain access only as tenants. This means they would have less freedom to make changes in how the land was being used, and any investments they might make, such as irrigation or drainage, would be lost to them if their tenancy were ended. Of course, there is no reason to suppose that hereditary aristocrats are any wiser in the ways of agriculture than their best tenants, so enormous potential human resources—the ingenuity of commoners—was simply lost to society.

Now consider the impact of the economic, social and legal changes taking place in the seventeenth and eighteenth centuries. An enterprising landowner might institute a change in crops or cultivation methods, even though this would lead to tenant farmers losing their livelihoods—a violation of his duty under the old system, but in many cases a step toward increased efficiency. Soon whole communities were uprooted, with families migrating to the new industrial towns, hoping to make ends meet by factory work. Lands open to everyone for grazing livestock or hunting in the winter to survive the lean times could be turned into private property, violating traditions extending back to the middle ages. A nobleman could even sell the land outright, choosing to embrace the aristocracy of money instead of feudal privilege and obligation. Modern property rights in land, and a free-market approach to agriculture ended centuries of rural stagnation, but they also exposed the majority of English country people to risks they had never known before. The *freedom* of those with wealth and ambition to compete became the *necessity* for all, however destitute, to compete as well.

Like many of his compatriots, Adam Smith viewed these developments with alarm, but he also felt that they were the only sure basis for England's current and future prosperity. Competition would be hard, he thought, but eventually it would lead to new efficiencies, so that the lot of even the poorest would be better than in the old days of ironclad tradition. Under the pressure of competition, people would develop their skills, so that they could earn a better living and improve the well-being of society at the same time. As more activities were put on a market basis, it would be possible for a small number of very efficient operations to serve the entire nation. Their efficiency would be based on a **division of labor**—breaking down production into small operations and permitting workers to specialize in just one—and achieving **economies of scale**. By breaking the chains of tradition, moreover, the most creative and enterprising individuals, whatever level of society they might come from, would be encouraged to bring about advances in technology. Competition would reward innovation, even while it separated the useful innovations from the useless. Even the least skilled workers would gain from competition, because their labor would be sought by a multitude of employers; if any paid lower wages or made the work more disagreeable than the rest, they would fail to assemble a workforce altogether.

Thus, for Smith, the problem—the spread of competition and self-seeking throughout society, unbridled by traditional customs or morality—was also the solution. It should be the policy of the government, he thought, to accelerate this process, removing as quickly as possible all restrictions on the use of property and all obligations inherited from the past.

The name for this new regime, as it appeared in the legal system, was **freedom of contract**. The doctrine has two parts. First, it claims that consenting parties should be free to negotiate any agreement they might agree to, whether or not outside observers approve. Workers and employers should be free to agree on any set of wages, hours and working conditions, unimpeded by regulations from government. This means, of course, that there could be no minimum wage laws (or maximum wage laws, as were common in pre-Smithian England, either), occupational safety laws, restrictions on permissible hours of work, etc. If the owner and the worker agree on terms, who should interfere? It would also mean the end to any regulation of financial or commercial agreements, and for the same reasons. The second claim was that no one should bear any obligation unless it was expressly agreed to, for instance in a contract. Hence *caveat emptor*—"let the buyer beware"—because sellers had no obligations to back up the quality of their wares unless buyers were able to wrangle from them a formal agreement. Owners of inns would no longer have the obligation to lodge and feed travelers; they could refuse service for any reason or no reason at all. Landlords would have no obligations to tenants other than those spelled out in contracts; without written protection people could be turned out at a moment's notice.

Freedom of contract was the legal form of the new free-market doctrine. It converted every interaction under its domain into buying and selling, and it permitted the markets it created to determine their own results. Of course, freedom of contract was a theory and not a reality. It took generations of crusading by jurists, politicians and intellectuals like Smith to gradually undo the shackles of the medieval system, and before the job was complete, demands for new types of regulation arose—but this is a story for later. Nevertheless, freedom of contract, and the free-market system it defined, provided a simple, powerful idea that many influential Englishmen rallied around. This ideal, never fully implemented anywhere, is referred to as **laissez-faire**, from the French for "let people do whatever they choose".

Aside from his practical arguments, Smith made a political case for laissez-faire. Imagine a "state of nature", he says, a world without artificial rules inherited from the past. People would soon begin to establish markets and trade with one another, because it is human nature to do so. Without any edicts from on high, a complete system of markets would emerge, and something like freedom of contract to sustain it. Thus, laissez-faire is the "natural" state toward which all societies would gravitate, were it not for the irrationalities of their own customs and laws inherited from the past. It is enough to remove these fetters for laissez-faire to emerge of its own accord. Moreover, Smith thought it was self-evident that freedom of contract was freedom itself; he therefore referred to a free-market economy as the system of "natural liberty". This political argument has never left the stage, and supporters of laissez-faire today are as likely to be moved by this vision of individual freedom as they are by more pragmatic economic concerns.

The main point in all of this is that economics is not a pure product of the intellect in the sense that, say, mathematics is. It has its origin in a specific time and place, and it came forth to make the argument that a system of free markets could surmount all the criticisms made of it. It could promote economic growth for the entire nation and also rising incomes for all social classes. It would prevent abuses through the discipline of competition, and it would achieve a more perfect morality than all the preachings of the priests and professors. It would render most government activities unnecessary and permit people to enjoy the maximum possible extent of personal freedom. To be a "political economist" (that was the term) in the generation following Adam Smith was to believe all this and to take it as a personal mission to prove it to the world.

Smith was one of the most influential thinkers of his era. His contemporaries felt he had demonstrated through examples and the force of reason that natural liberty and laissez-faire were to government and society what Newton's laws of motion were to planets and apple orchards. Nevertheless, it gradually occurred to careful readers that Smith had proved nothing. At crucial points in his argument he simply assumes that certain arguments are true, because they sound reasonable to him and he had the words to make them sound reasonable to others. Beginning with his disciple, David Ricardo, economists began to find flaws in the Master's intellectual system. Eventually, it became clear that the case for laissez-faire, if it existed at all, could not be universally applicable; it could only be true under certain conditions. Modern economics, even to this day, is largely about the analysis of those conditions, and the search for what to do if the conditions do not hold.

2.3 Economics in Other Languages

Meanwhile, other traditions were beginning to take hold on the European continent, and these should be noted, since they also contributed to the evolution of economic thinking.

In France, the Revolution (1789) and its Napoleonic aftermath instigated a new interest in the application of science to public affairs. A pivotal event was the creation of a national engineering corps (Corps des Ponts et Chaussées), and a national technical university (École Polytechnique), with responsibility for roads, bridges and other public works. The prestige of science was enormous, and many political leaders and intellectuals expected that a new era was dawning in which scientists and managers would organize all aspects of government and economy, bringing the fruits of reason and efficiency to society as a whole.

In this environment, several mathematically-trained theorists, above all the remarkable Augustin Cournot (1801–1877), worked on techniques to measure the benefits of private and public projects and to organize the collection of economic data. Cournot gave us the rudiments of formal supply-and-demand analysis and the first intimations of game theory. The image that emerges from their work is not that of the philosopher turning to practical affairs, like Adam Smith, but the dispassionate physicist or chemist writing equations for how many carriages will use a bridge using models derived from the natural sciences.

In principle, the models of Cournot and his contemporaries could be applied to the broad social questions raised by Smith, Bentham and Ricardo, but they also suggested, by their very precision, the perspective of the administrator who wants to replace seat-of-the-pants guessing with disciplined evaluation. This in fact was the actual use: the work of these post-Revolutionary French thinkers was not immediately recognized as "political economy". It was taught to engineers and future managers, creating a tradition of professionalized planning that was one of France's contributions to nineteenth century culture. Nevertheless, the spirit of this work lives on today at the heart of economics. Much of the theorizing and number-crunching economists do is still primarily for the purpose of designing programs, forecasting costs and benefits, and anticipating market responses.

Later in the nineteenth century, during the period leading up to and then following German unification (1871), a series of economists and historians emerged in that country with a quite different problem to place on the agenda: what sorts of institutions allow for sustained, long-run economic growth, and how does growth alter them in turn? Why have some countries jumped on the growth track, while others have remained stagnant? And why do some countries seem to burn themselves out, going through a phase of growth and then falling back?

The most prominent of these thinkers was Max Weber (1864–1920); typical issues for him were the role of accounting in the early development of capitalism, the role of religious belief, and the rise of bureaucratic forms of organization. Other practitioners of the "German Historical School" examined labor markets and the way job skills were passed down and acquired, the role of geography (an interest that goes back to Humboldt, the early nineteenth century explorer and author, in fact), and systems of land tenure. In the final decades of the nineteenth century, German economists also specialized in the use of economic research for social reform. They provided analysis that made for more effective legislation, as well as statistical methods for evaluating how well the reforms were working.

This perspective migrated across the Atlantic, where it appeared as "Institutional Economics" and flourished during the first half of the twentieth century. (The American Economic Association, the main professional organization for economists in the US, was founded in 1885 by institutionalists.) Institutionalism along these lines has almost disappeared from the profession, however, and one is more likely to find followers of Weber and his ilk in sociology or political science departments in modern American universities. Nevertheless, the questions have never gone away, and there has been a resurgence of interest in them, now based on techniques from game theory and regression analysis in statistics. In particular, the field of development economics—the study of economic growth and change, or sometimes the lack of it, in poorer regions of the world—is deeply influenced by this long tradition of thinking about institutions. We will return to institutional questions in considerable detail later in this book. Meanwhile, policy analysis—the use of economics to assess public policy options—is now a component of mainstream economics everywhere.

Pulling these strands together, you should see economics as the product of many ideas originating from many places—but the biggest piece is still the one first laid by Adam Smith in 1776. In the confrontation with the sweeping vision of an Invisible Hand, much of the theory you are about to encounter was conjured up.

2.4 Economics Today: In the Image of Science

A careful reader might be somewhat perplexed at this point. The invisible hand argument, and the larger questions of liberty, social benefit and social order that it attempts to answer, seem more like the stuff of philosophy than science. It is fine for people to talk about "natural liberty" and the "interests of society", but what place can such concepts occupy in a field of study like economics that aspires to a precise, testable account of how economies operate?

Whether, and in what way, economics can be regarded as a science depends, of course, on what you think a science is. In this second part of the chapter we will consider how economists have thought about this problem, even as they continued to wrestle with the legacy of Smith and freedom of contract.

To begin with, we need an idea of what we mean by "science". A good place to start is with the view held by most economists, since this influences how they do their work, whether justifiably or not. It is probably fair to say that, according to this view, science is the practice of adding, piece by piece, bits of information to the pile of society's "correct" understanding. The sequence involved is thought to go something like this:

First, we begin with an understanding inherited from the past. Earlier generations groped toward a practice of science, and they succeeded in creating a body of knowledge. But the knowledge they have passed on to us is incomplete and even inconsistent, and in any event the world keeps changing, so old ideas may no longer be relevant; hence the need for continuing research. The second step is the formulation of a hypothesis, an informed guess about what may be true concerning some aspect of the world. Hypotheses do not come out of thin air; they are deductions from or extensions of the wisdom passed on to us by previous generations of scientists. That is, we should identify that part of past knowledge that we believe to be correct, such that any new truth we discover in the future will have to be broadly consistent with it, and use it to devise new hypotheses. The third step is the experiment. This can take many forms, but usually involves either a logical test, such as the construction of a mathematical model, or an empirical one, such as a statistical analysis. Hypotheses that fail such tests are discarded; those that pass are placed before the profession in the form of articles in learned journals. (Books are assumed to play a smaller role in the process, because hypotheses are proposed and tested one at a time, and books because of their length usually juggle a great many hypotheses at once. As you advance in economics you read fewer books and more journal articles.) This begins a fourth stage, in which other researchers may try to find unnoticed problems with the hypothesis, perhaps subjecting it to new tests—new models or sources of data. Only if a hypothesis survives this scrutiny is it anointed with the blessing of science: it can now be added to the repository of accepted truth that the next round of research can take as a starting point. This sequence is sometimes called "the scientific method". The vast majority of economists think this is the way all sciences work, and they seek to emulate the process in their own discipline.

But there are academic specialties, based in disciplines like history, sociology and philosophy, that study in a rigorous way how actual sciences function. These researchers, drawing on theories of knowledge creation and validation, as well as historical studies of scientific advance, offer a much more complicated account. In fact, it would be more accurate to say that they offer *lots* of accounts that differ in many ways. It's a fascinating topic, but well beyond the scope of this text. For us, it's enough to explore a few common themes that are particularly relevant to economics.

The first big question is, what do sciences try to do? What is this "knowledge" that they try to build up? Is an equation knowledge? A specimen in a natural history collection? A speculation about the origins of time? The short answer is that different sciences produce different kinds of knowledge. Mathematics produces theorems and proofs. Physics does too, but it also conducts experiments that attempt to measure the quantitative dimensions of physical entities and forces. Chemistry is a bit like physics, but with more cataloging of knowledge about different chemical substances. On the other hand, some sciences, like geology, are mostly descriptive, pulling together lots of "small" theories about specific questions rather than a single "big" theory, and have somewhat less predictive power. (True, plate tectonics is a very big theory, but most matters of interest to geologists are not directly deducible from it, at least not through pure theory.) Very loosely, what they all have in common is that they try to answer the "why" and "how" of natural phenomena with materialistic explanations: they appeal to mechanisms that can be measured and observed (sometimes indirectly with complicated apparatuses) to explain why the world is the way it is.

Economics follows this pattern, up to a point. As we will see, economists propose a grand theory about human behavior in market or market-like situations that they hope can explain the world we live in. It is an open question, however, whether this theory is materialistic—observable and measurable—in the sense that the natural sciences are. Some of the fundamental forces invoked by economists will turn out to be psychological and invisible, assumptions about preferences people have for the things they buy and sell, so that attention tends to shift from processes, the mechanisms that explain economic events, to outcomes. In other words, economists put a lot of effort into testing hypotheses about which outcomes are likely to occur, rather than what mechanisms operate to produce these outcomes. (It is possible that this generalization will be obsolete in a few years, if the role of **behavioral economics**, which is based on observable aspects of psychological and social influences, becomes more prominent.) This is rather different from the usual approach of science. Maybe we should say that economics resembles an applied field, like medicine. Medical researchers perform trials to see whether a drug will treat an illness, and if the outcomes are positive, the drug will be prescribed even if the profession is unsure about the precise reason for its success. Economic policies may not be so different.

But that raises a second question: what constitutes "success" for experimental testing, whether of theories or pharmaceuticals? How certain does a scientific or professional field have to be before it puts its stamp of approval on a result and adds it to the storehouse of "known" facts? And what is the tradeoff between high standards of believability and the need for practicality?

We have a framework for thinking about this problem that makes it much easier to analyze—in fact, this is one of the most useful frameworks you can have for thinking about almost any question in a rational way, so take note. In any situation of uncertainty, when we propose a hypothesis, a course of action, a solution—anything—there are two ways we can go wrong. The first is **Type I Error**, the risk of thinking something is true when it is not; the second is **Type II Error**, the risk of not thinking it is true when it really is. The first is often referred to as the risk of a "false positive", where "positive" signifies that you think there is a basis for accepting a proposition, and the second is the risk of a "false negative", where "negative" means you think there is a reason to reject a proposition.

Here's an example. Suppose we want to know whether a particular pharmaceutical will speed up recovery from certain strains of influenza. We conduct a test on 200 people who have this disease, giving half of them the experimental treatment and the other half a placebo. (A placebo is something that looks the same as the treatment to the patient, but is neutral.) We find that, on average, the individuals who were given the treatment recover a bit sooner. We are not completely sure the drug is effective, however, because there is natural variability in how people recover, and it is within the realm of possibility that the treated half would have bounced back faster in any case. In this example, Type I Error would arise if we conclude that the medicine works, but in reality it doesn't—all we saw was random noise. We can eliminate this type of error completely by concluding that the medicine doesn't work, but in that case we are at risk of Type II Error if it actually does. It is easy to see that there is no avoiding the risk of *some* kind of error; we can choose only which kind we would rather live with.

Economists face this same conundrum. For instance, there are demands in several countries to raise the statutory minimum wage. What effect should we expect this to have on unemployment rates? Would unemployment go up, down or remain about the same? Research on this topic is inconclusive, and of course the answer will probably differ from one country or even region to another. It may also depend on how much the minimum wage is raised as well as the broader economic context. Suppose we rephrase the question in a simple yes-no fashion, for instance "Will an increase in the minimum wage in this location at this time result in an increase in unemployment?" An economist might say the answer is yes, but if she is wrong it's a Type I error. Or she can say that she doesn't think this will happen, and she could be wrong about that too: Type II. To study a problem and propose an explanation or prediction is to expose yourself to the risk of being wrong in one way or the other.

All of us go through life making judgments under cloudy circumstances. We think it's going to rain, so we leave the bike at home. We think the exam will be easy, so we study less. We think the party will be fun, so we accept the invitation. Or we take the bike, study more, and pass up the party. Either way, we face the unavoidable risk of either thinking something will happen when it won't, or vice versa.

In their day jobs, scientists take an extreme position on the question of risk: they minimize to the fullest possible extent the risk of Type I error, no matter how great the risk of Type II error. Science rests on the fundamental distinction between those things you know with virtual certainty and everything else. What we call "the scientific method" is actually a set of procedures for minimizing Type I error. This means things like validating all the equipment you use in an experiment, documenting each step, setting up the experiment to minimize the possibility that extraneous factors will interfere, and using very conservative statistical rules (low threshold *p*-values) to determine whether measured effects are "significant". Of course, given this obsession, scientists also want to reduce the risk of Type II error whenever it's also possible; the best-designed (most "powerful") experiment is one that has low risk of either kind of error. But there is no doubt which risk will be taken if there is any choice in the matter. In "real" sciences, committing Type I error—announcing to the world that you've discovered something, when in fact you haven't—is a very serious breach and can even be career-ending. Type II error—failing to identify a result that you've actually uncovered—means passing up an opportunity for success, but little more.

This is why it is reasonable to think of science as a process of accumulating bits of true knowledge, so that over time the explanatory power of science goes up and not down. When you think about it, there are no other social institutions that have this characteristic. Today's music is not necessarily better than yesterday's (just ask any of us older folks), nor are today's politicians better than those of the past, but today's science *is* better. The bias toward minimizing Type I error may slow down the progress of knowledge, but it also ensures that change really is progress.

The reason for stressing the role of Type I error minimization in science is that economists don't practice it. There are reasons for this, honorable and not-so-honorable. On the honorable side is the fact that economics is never far from policy, and in the pragmatic world of policy a single-minded approach to error, always minimizing one type at the expense of the other, is inadvisable. Consider again the issue of raising the minimum wage. From a scientific point of view, one should not take a position unless there is a very high degree of likelihood that the position is correct. This means our hypothetical economist should not predict an unemployment effect unless she is very, very certain of it. But in the real world, there are costs to making mistakes on both sides. If she says the increase will have no effect and it does, real people have to shoulder the consequences. A sensible approach would take into account how severe are the social costs of unemployment compared to the social costs of low wages, as well as the likely effects of a policy on both of them. In a policy field like economics there is risk on all sides, and one must try to find a practical balance. This is one reason economics is not "science".

Another reason is that, since economies are so complicated, and we keep finding ourselves in new situations that prevent us from simply extrapolating lessons from the past, tests of economic hypotheses are often of very low power. That is, they have lots of Type I *and* Type II error. If we adopt the conservatism of other sciences and only accept propositions that have extremely low risk of Type I error, we won't have much economic knowledge at all. There is no real alternative to setting looser standards.

On the less honorable side, we can mention that economists are often attached to their theories for personal or ideological reasons. A researcher's career can depend on the combat between ideas, so it is natural for economists to hang onto their positions until they are absolutely untenable. This is equivalent to saying that only an extremely large risk of Type I error is sufficient to make them change their minds. Also, economics is closely tied to political and financial interests: economic theories lead to economic policies from which some benefit and others lose. This too can muddy the waters and lead to too much credence in claims supported by too little evidence.

Be aware, however, that these generalizations about economics and its status, or non-status, as a science are just that, generalizations. Economics is an enormous field with a large number of practitioners. Some branches of economics are fairly close to scientific standards, and some economists are more assiduous than others about evaluating the evidence.

Meanwhile, we still have a large unresolved issue from our discussion of Adam Smith: what about the rather nebulous character of the invisible hand claim? How can there be a precise and at least somewhat scientific discipline that throws around terms like "best for society"? To put this question in a more modern context, it is first useful to make the distinction between positive and normative statements. **Positive statements** are those which describe, explain or predict. They may be true or false, but in principle they have the potential to be verified against the facts. **Normative statements** are those which express preferences; they are often marked by words like "should" and "better". In principle, normative statements cannot be held to a narrow factual standard, since personal values are partially independent of facts. (I cannot "prove" that your values are wrong.) Nevertheless, as we will see, fact and value are not completely separate domains either.

Much of economics is strictly positive in the sense above. Economists, for instance, have tools to predict how putting a tax on a product will affect its price. Will producers pass most of the tax along to consumers, or will they have to swallow most of it themselves? If the tax was introduced in the past and we already know how it turned out, these tools can provide a description of the process and an explanation for why it occurred. If we are thinking about instituting this tax in the future, the tools will help us anticipate its effects. This does not mean, of course, that the tools never fail, only that the job set for them is either a description of events, an explanation for them or a prediction of the future.

A very large portion of economics, however, is normative. Economics, as we will see in much greater detail in Chaps. 4 and 6, has an elaborate theory of when people are better or worse off. This rests on a set of assumptions about human psychology and what it means to be better off that can't be based solely on factual evidence, but once these assumptions are accepted it is possible to analyze well-being in an extremely precise way. This is the domain of "welfare economics", where welfare refers not to a government program, but to the study of well-being.

As you would expect, welfare economics is also where economists come to grips with the invisible hand argument: what it means, why it might or might not hold, and what conditions need to be satisfied for it to operate. Economists use these same concepts to analyze whether particular policies add to or detract from overall social welfare. Are the benefits from regulating a particular food additive greater than the costs? Would breaking up a particular monopoly make consumers better off? Would there be benefits to eliminating tariffs on agricultural goods, and if so, how large would they be? Proposing answers to questions like these is the bread-and-butter of most policy-oriented economists, especially in the realm of micro-economics. Their work shows it is possible to be extremely analytical and precise about matters of value—provided you begin with shared assumptions about what "value" means. Because of the importance of the welfare dimension of economics, Chap. 6 is entirely built around specifying and exploring its assumptions and implications.

Of course, people do not all agree on what constitutes value, and this raises an important issue: by predicating their work on one particular notion of what societies should strive for, are economists implicitly supporting one political ideology over the others? Is economics intrinsically "liberal" or "conservative", tilting left or tilting right? Does it tend to support the rich at the expense of the poor, or vice versa? How can one possibly take a position on economic policy, or the invisible hand as a general philosophy of how economies should be organized, *without* being tainted by ideology? To probe the matter further, we need some help from theories that have been developed to explain interplay between what people believe and where their interests lie.

The modern theory of this relationship begins with Karl Marx, the nineteenth century socialist thinker. Marx argued that cultural and intellectual factors were not the cause of historical change; rather, it was the material facts of history—the development of economic life—that provided the basis for science, religion, philosophy and other "mental" conceptions. Beyond this, he had a particular theory of economic development, in which all known societies, beyond the most primitive, are divided into a large class that produces most of the wealth through its labor and a small class that commands a "surplus" portion of that wealth for its own use—the exploited and the exploiters. Very simply put, the primacy of economic life over the life of ideas translates into the claim that each class is likely to hold beliefs that justify its particular interests. Each will see its own particular class interest as universal, the ideal that all would agree on if they only understood. He attached the word "ideology" to this interest-based set of beliefs. For Marx, the notion that God created the world pretty much as we find it was part of the ideology of the Middle Ages of European Christendom. It was believed by the ruling orders because it justified their position of wealth and power vis-a-vis the peasants under their command. When the peasants gained an awareness of their very different interests, they rejected this theology and replaced it with another, under which a social upheaval was required to achieve a second coming of Christ. Similarly, the wealthiest elites in the modern capitalist order adhere to an ideology in which making profits through business investment is natural and desirable; they believe this because it is in their interest to do so. (In other words, economics is capitalist ideology!)

Subsequent generations of thinkers have been intrigued by this Marxist formulation but also troubled by its limitations. The historical record is not nearly as clear as Marx would have it. Changes in ideas often preceded the economic changes that Marx pointed to as the true motor force, and the relationship between interest and belief is not so mechanical as the Marxist theory suggests. (Among other things, it doesn't explain Marx' own ideas, or those of his close collaborator Friedrich Engels, who was himself a factory owner.) The simple division of society into a few economic classes is, at best, overly simplistic, and we now recognize that there are many other bases for difference in interest in society: ethnic and racial divisions, gender hierarchy, national groupings, affiliations according to particular activities or beliefs. (Claus Offe, a German post-Marxist, has said that, in the modern world, a worker and a capitalist, both of whom own boats and like to go sailing, have more in common than two workers or two capitalists, one of whom has a boat and the other not.)

What these complications suggest is that an a priori theory of who is likely to believe what will not get us very far. Instead, a field of study has emerged called political sociology (which incorporates an older field called "the sociology of knowledge"). Practitioners of this field do research on the social factors that explain why different beliefs are common among different groups. They find that interests do play an important role, but not in a mechanical fashion. Ideas have logical connections to each other, and these may exert a force that contradicts simple economic interest. For instance, if business owners believe that a free-market system is socially desirable, this may commit them to particular policies, such as the freedom of workers to quit their jobs whenever they want, that fly in the face of their immediate interests. Also, business owners may have deep religious beliefs, or they may value outdoor activities and be environmentalists. We can't say who will believe what without first studying the evidence.

Despite the complexity of modern versions of the theory of ideology, one useful generalization can be made. The life situations people find themselves in typically pose particular kinds of problems, and people have a tendency to favor ways of thinking that help them solve these problems. This is similar to the idea expressed by the adage that, to a hammer, most of the world looks like a nail.

In the context of economics, this insight suggests that much of the disagreement over how the economy works can be traced to the different problems that seem important to different people. As we will see, for instance, inflation is a serious problem for holders of financial wealth, and many economists have devoted their lives to understanding the factors that make inflation more likely. Their particular views on inflation are not simple reflections of their or anyone else's interest in stable prices, but the intellectual framework that is useful for limiting the risk of inflation is not necessarily best for, say, combating unemployment or promoting economic growth. The same can be said for "competition". This concept plays a central role in explaining the openness of the system to new business formation, or the ability of existing businesses to change their markets or operating strategy. These are important problems which actual and potential business owners or managers have to solve every day. Labor unions, on the other hand, are in the business of *suppressing* competition among their members; competition is a problem they try to solve.

I doubt that this generalization can be carried very far. Often, what is attractive about a particular economic analysis has little to do with its direct problem-solving potential. The conceptual "fit" between economic theories and philosophical or political biases may be more important overall. Nevertheless, in the spirit of critical analysis, you should keep the potential for ideological influence in the back of your mind. Think about what problems particular theories seem to address, who tends to face such problems, and what other approaches might make sense to other groups in society whose problems are not the same. Above all, ask these questions of yourself: why do you gravitate toward some ideas and away from others?

The Main Points

1. England became the world's fastest-growing economy in the eighteenth century. At the same time, the traditional constraints of custom and religion were being shed, and Britons wondered what new force could or should control the vast economic powers being unleashed. Adam Smith's answer was that the force of competition, along with standards of behavior based on reputation and mutual respect, was a sufficient basis for organizing economic life. He argued that giving individuals maximum freedom to conduct business, whether as owners, workers or consumers, would result in the most prosperity—not only for England, but also for all other countries. This view is summed up in the expression "the invisible hand".
2. Intellectual currents in other countries also contributed to the emergence of economics. In France, planners and engineers developed methods for

calculating the economic benefits of public projects. German thinkers in the nineteenth century stressed the role of institutions in channeling economic life, ideas that continue to influence studies of economic development in the long run.
3. Contemporary economics presents itself as a science, understood as the accumulation of empirically tested hypotheses derived from a consistent body of theory. Nevertheless, economics does not prioritize minimization of Type I error (false positives) over Type II error (false negatives) as most true sciences do. To some extent, this can be attributed to the greater practical urgency of economic research: governments, businesses and civil society look to economics for advice on problems that cannot wait for the slow, skeptical progress of science. The result, however, is that much less confidence can be placed on economic doctrine than the bodies of knowledge found in chemistry, biology and other "hard" sciences.
4. Economics is also subject to ideological influence in a way that the natural sciences are not. This need not be fatal, however, since ideology is about why people believe one thing rather than another (the relationship between beliefs and interests), and not whether their beliefs are correct. Economists can also reduce the impact of ideology by distinguishing between positive and normative concepts, although there remains some overlap between the two. Ultimately, it is not possible to fully rise above ideological pressures, but economic analysis can increase our understanding of the effects of economic policies and institutions, especially if we keep the potential for bias clearly in mind.

▶ Terms to Define

Caveat emptor
Division of labor
Economies of scale
Freedom of contract
Ideology
Invisible hand argument
Laissez-faire
Positive vs normative statements
Type I versus Type II error

Questions to Consider

1. Economic life is about who does what kind of work, what goods and services are produced, how the methods of production are determined, and how goods find their way to those who want to acquire or use them. We have seen that many of these things were decided in a traditional way in England prior to the Industrial Revolution. Can you think of similar examples of traditionalism at work in the modern economy?
2. Do we still have a "social order problem" today? What are the main indicators that we do or do not? If we do, is greater competition (as in Adam Smith's theory) part of the problem, part of the solution, or both? Be as specific as you can about particular economic and social issues.
3. In 1960 a group of black students from the Greensboro campus of the University of North Carolina "sat in" at a drug store lunch counter. They deliberately went to a business that they knew would discriminate against them and when asked to leave, they stayed in their seats. The owners called the police, and the students were arrested. In response to events like this, the federal government eventually passed a series of civil rights laws that prohibited business owners from refusing to serve people because of race or certain other factors. Explain how these laws violate the principle of freedom of contract. What force did Adam Smith expect to regulate the social behavior of freely contracting businesses? Do you think this force was insufficient in a situation like Greensboro's? Are there some freedoms business owners should not have in any case?
4. Most geologists today believe that the earth is covered with plates (large pieces of its surface) that slowly separate and collide. If they are right, then nearly all geologists prior to the 1960s, when plate theory gained acceptance, were at least partly wrong about how the earth's crust was formed. Does this mean that their work was less "scientific"? What criteria are you using for "science" when you answer this question?
5. Economists spend more time talking about the positive-normative distinction than chemists. Why?
6. Is there any reason to suspect that ideological factors played a role in the development and rapid acceptance of Adam Smith's theory of free competition? Does your answer imply that his theory is less or more successful in explaining how economies work?

Four Building Blocks of Economic Theory 3

Economics is not sociology, psychology or politics, but it relies on assumptions about society, mental and emotional processes, and the political and legal environment. Until recently, however, these assumptions didn't come from the other disciplines which take them as their fields of study; instead, they were largely inherited from the eighteenth century worldview out of which Adam Smith and his followers fashioned their early renditions of economic theory. That is to say, they reflected the prejudices of the Enlightenment in England around the time of the American revolution. They are rationalist, individualist and concerned with subduing nature for the greater benefit of civilization. In this chapter we will look carefully at several of the most important conceptual building blocks, explaining exactly how they appear in modern economics and subjecting them to critical scrutiny.

3.1 Choice and Exchange: Metaphors for Economic Life

Think about a day in the life of anyone taking part in an economic system—a day in *your* life, perhaps. A list of economic activities might include:

- which consumer goods, like toothpaste or breakfast food, you use, and how much
- which household goods you use, and which you leave for others in your household
- commuting to work and getting there on time (or not)
- working
- studying and attending classes
- paying bills
- shopping
- housecleaning
- raising children

P. Dorman, *Microeconomics*, Springer Texts in Business and Economics,
DOI 10.1007/978-3-642-37434-0_3,

- borrowing money or buying financial assets as investments
- quitting old or accepting new employment
- searching for goods, jobs, housing or other items, without necessarily buying, renting, enrolling, etc.

All of these activities are economic in the sense that they involve the production, distribution or use of goods and services. If we added up this entire list for everyone in our society, the sum would look very much like "the economy" as a whole.

This is how the real world is, but so many qualitative differences make it impossible to do the sort of systematic analysis economics aims at. Somehow, we must simplify. There are many ways to do it, but economics selects just one: it treats every form of economic activity as a *choice*, and every economic interaction between people as an *exchange*. These are such shocking simplifications, with such profound implications for all that follows, that we need to examine them very carefully.

Choice and exchange in their economic usages are metaphors. A metaphor draws our attention to some aspects of a complex phenomenon by referring to something else that shares them. For instance, one famous metaphor is: Time is a river that flows endlessly through space. Time is a difficult concept to wrap one's mind around, but this metaphor does help somewhat. It points to the one-way movement of time as we experience it, and the water imagery reminds us that time can "carry" things along with it. On the other hand, time is not at all a river in other respects, nor is a river time. Time is not made up of a physical substance the way rivers are made up of water. Moreover, rivers can be dammed or even have their direction of flow reversed; try that with time! The point is that metaphors are helpful as long as we remember their limitations.

What about the metaphors used in economics? First consider choice. Much of what we do in the economy does involve choosing: we choose where to work, where to live, and paper or plastic in the check-out line. No doubt many of the choices we make are unconscious, but it might not be too far off the mark to think about them as if they were conscious and "rational" as we will describe in the following section. Nevertheless, the metaphor of choice can be misleading in some instances. There are two reasons for this.

First, many of the actions we undertake are governed by a process very different from conscious choice. In fact, quite often choices are made for us by others. Many goods are consumed institutionally, for example, such as lunch offerings in a work or school cafeteria. Often one member of the household purchases goods for other members. We are also subject to pressure, sometimes intense pressure, from people we are close to over questions like employment, major purchases, etc. In some cases the pressure comes from society in general, through judgments of what is fashionable or signals high or low prestige. In these cases, treating an economic decision as if it were a free individual choice may be a mistake. We will discuss this problem in greater detail in the chapter on consumption.

Second, many activities are not choices at all. You can choose whether to buy white or red potatoes, but cooking the potatoes is an act of (household) production, not a choice. Working, doing the actual tasks that make up a job, is not choosing; it is working. Spending days or weeks searching for a new house is not making a choice; it's doing a search. Of course, subject to the qualification we made in the previous paragraph, all these activities lead up to or follow from a choice. In other words, what the metaphor of choice is telling us is that what is deemed important about any economic activity is the element of choice connected to it. This is a simplification of great power, because it enables us to make general statements that apply to the many aspects of life through their common element of choice, but it downplays the economic importance of the non-choice element. For example, as we will see, economists until recently have reduced the experience of work to the moments at which a worker chooses to begin or quit a job. Other aspects of work entered in only to the extent that they provide information used in making this choice. Real jobs, however, are usually social situations in which individuals interact continuously; they have communication and power structures that play an important role in both the productivity of work and its impact on the worker. To use the metaphor of choice is to direct attention to the discrete moments in which workers decide whether to join or quit; it directs attention away from the ongoing interactions on the job.

Now consider the other metaphor, exchange. This one is, if anything, more elusive. In the view of economics, the market is the primary mechanism that governs economic life, and markets are the place where buyers and sellers exchange with one another. We think we know what an exchange is: I have something you want, you have something I want, and we exchange with each other. If it is a freely chosen exchange, each of us will be at least as well off as before, and at least one of us (the one who initiated the exchange) will be better off. Add that up over millions upon millions of exchanges each day in a large country like the United States, and you appear to have a recipe for continuous economic improvement. In addition, exchange has the added benefit of being fairly simple in structure and therefore not too difficult to analyze. A provides B with something; B provides A with something else. It happens in an instant, and then it's over. It can be fully described by listing the parties to the exchange, what they provided each other, and the exact place and time the exchange took place. As you might expect, it is easy to translate this into the language of mathematics.

The preceding discussion of choice should have already alerted you to a potential drawback with exchange as a metaphor for economic relationships: economic interactions can take place before or after moments of exchange, and something important is lost if we don't incorporate them. This is true of work relationships, household relationships, landlord-tenant relationships, and so on. A more complete economics (which doesn't really exist yet) would combine the aspect of exchange with the institutional, cultural and social structures that bring people together in economic life.

There is additional wrinkle, however. The simple model of exchange, instantaneous and unambiguous, is not characteristic even of most transactions economists call exchange. How can this be? I believe that here, as in so many other areas, the root of confusion can be found in language. We use the same word, exchange, to refer to many different types of transactions, similar in some respects but different in others. An exchange of the simplest type is a simultaneous trade of one good for another that completely exhausts the transaction. But most real-world transactions differ at least a little from this stylized type, either because they take place over a substantial period of time, or because the terms of the exchange are not simple "things" that can pass from one hand to another, or both.

Consider, for instance, the employment relationship. Economics speaks of labor markets, in which workers sell their labor, firms purchase it, and the two parties agree on the price (wage). But what do workers actually sell? They can't sell their labor in the sense of divesting themselves of it, since it is inseparable from them. In a sense, they are selling a promise to submit to the authority of the employer, but this is hardly an open-ended promise, and should they violate it there is usually no recourse for the employer other than severing the contract. But more fundamentally, how can any human being sell his or her own *future* submission? At each instant in time we remain not only capable of choice, but *forced* to choose what to do with ourselves. Whatever the formal trappings, short of selling oneself into slavery there is no way a worker can suppress his or her future freedom of choice in return for money. Of course, employment contracts are based on this fiction, and because they are people normally try to adhere to them as best they can. For our purposes, it is enough to point out that it is simply impossible to swap today's money for tomorrow's obedience in the same way we might swap used paperbacks in an instantaneous exchange at a flea market.

You might think that at least consumer markets display the simpler form of simultaneous exchange. In a sense they do, but in another sense they don't. Certainly something like an instantaneous exchange occurs when a good, like a pair of blue jeans, exchanges for money at a precise moment in time at a store's cash register, but there are aspects to this transaction that linger on into the future. On a mundane level, the consumer has the option of returning the blue jeans under certain conditions, voiding the sale, and the store owner faces the possibility that a check might not clear. Beyond this, however, more subtle maneuvering may be taking place. Most consumer goods like blue jeans are now branded; they are sold under a well-known brand name as part of a larger strategy to increase the sales of the brand in a variety of markets. Each purchase is a moment in a larger effort on the part of the brand to expand its share; so the price might be set, for example, to influence future behavior and not simply to make money at one point in time. To treat the transaction as if it were a single disconnected moment might be to miss the forces that really determine what goods are offered to the market at what prices.

For another example, consider an individual who takes out a loan from a bank in order to start a business. There is a sense in which the making of such a loan is an exchange according to the simple version used by economics: one party, the borrower, receives money in the present and offers in return a promise to pay back the original amount plus interest at some point in the future, perhaps putting up some of the business assets as collateral. (That promise, incidentally, is very much a "thing": it is a piece of paper, and the bank can sell it to interested buyers just as it can sell anything else it owns.) But unlike a "real" exchange (such as the exchange of paperbacks), the process does not come to an end at the moment the loan is made. The bank may have legal rights to monitor the way the new business is run. It may be able to veto business decisions it doesn't agree with, and it may have the right to shut down the business when it thinks it is in danger of not being repaid. This raises a host of difficult issues: just what rights should the bank have? What control should they have over the collateral? Under what conditions should they be free to call in the loan before its term expires? These questions have to be resolved somehow, and they may even be negotiated by the two parties (although often they aren't), but it would be stretching things to describe the entire process as an "exchange". There is clearly an *aspect* of exchange in a credit relationship, but there are other aspects as well.

One way to highlight the role of exchange as a metaphor for market activity is to imagine other possible metaphors. Perhaps the best-known alternative is the notion that markets are the site of *combat* between competing interests. Joseph Schumpeter, the Austrian-born economic theorist, was particularly fond of this way of thinking about markets, and his work is suffused with images of war and contest. According to this view, the most important thing that markets have in common is not consensual exchange but eat-or-be-eaten competition. Businesses are like armies: within their own walls they mobilize for combat, in the outside world they throw all they have at their competitors. To the victors go the spoils: profits and market domination. The losers must tighten their belts; they may even be driven out of the market altogether. Schumpeter scoffed at the notion that markets are efficient or even orderly. The thrust and parry of the marketplace does not tend toward an equilibrium, he argued; markets are constantly assaulted by new business initiatives designed to change supply and demand, not merely adapt to them. While the competitive process, in Schumpeter's view, generates waste and dislocation, it more than makes up for it by spurring entrepreneurs to discover new, more productive ways of meeting society's economic needs. We could spend many more pages investigating the strengths and weaknesses of the Schumpeterian approach to economic analysis, but for our purposes there is a much simpler point. The market mechanism as a form of warfare is as plausible a metaphor as that of market "exchange"; in fact, business schools are more likely to adopt the combative than the consensual interpretation of markets.

Another famous metaphor can be found in the writings of Karl Marx. For Marx, at the heart of any economy is labor. It is the work that people put into goods and services that gives them value. Even the machines that are used to improve the productivity of labor impart value only because they themselves are the product of previous work. Thus the economic system can be seen as something like a hydraulic network of pipes and reservoirs. Labor flows from workers to commodities. Commodities are sold for money, some of which is returned to workers, who then buy back a portion of their aggregate labor in the form of consumer goods. The difference between these flows—value created by labor and value returned to it—accumulates in "holding tanks" called capital, where it can be used to construct new equipment, employ new workers or simply gratify the desires of those who own these pools of value. The entire analysis is built up from this metaphorical account of the flow and accumulation of value (labor time). Nothing much is changed by the social rituals that accompany these flows; the fact that employment agreements are contractual (take the legal form of exchanges) is nearly incidental. You could do the same type of analysis if labor relations were dictated by a court or government agency. Here the metaphor built around the flow of labor value calls attention to aspects of the economy that are obscured by an emphasis on exchange, just as the metaphor of exchange highlights aspects (the role of worker choice) that Marxists tend to underplay.

It may be that, as linguistic creatures, we have no way to avoid the use of metaphor altogether. Nor can we switch every few moments from one metaphor to another without disrupting our train of thought. There is nothing fundamentally wrong with beginning with the metaphors of choice and exchange, so long as we keep in mind their limitations and remember to correct for them when they become glaring. Make a mental note that economics rests on metaphor; we will return to this fundamental insight many times.

3.2 Psychology: The Assumption of Rational Self-Interest

One of Smith's contemporaries was fellow-Scotsman David Hume. Hume elaborated a philosophy in which the human mind is divided neatly into two parts, the faculty of reason and the raw, uncontrollable force of emotions. Reason can tell us *how* to do something but never *why*, in the ultimate sense of "to what end?" Emotions alone provide the motive force of human behavior, the goals to strive after, but emotions are not governed by reason. Hence there is a sort of means-end dichotomy, where emotions, which are beyond the power of philosophy, provide the ends and reason the means.

This is also the framework for what is still the predominant economic view of psychology. People are said to have preferences which reflect their emotional makeup, but they have no control over these preferences; they simply are what they are. They are taken as given by the reasonable person, who then devotes his or her intellectual resources solely to the task of satisfying them. To be rational is to satisfy your preferences as fully and efficiently as possible.

To make matters easier, economists assume that all preferences adhere to self-interest. There is much confusion in the writings of economic methodologists on this issue. The question as it is most often put is this: by definition, do people ever act against their self-interest? After all, if I choose to do one thing rather than another, it must be because it is what I "want" to do; therefore it satisfies my own desire and responds to my self-interest. Even diving into an icy river to save a total stranger who is drowning is what I want to do if I do it and is therefore in my self-interest. Even doing this on an impulse when I don't know how to swim is acting in my self-interest. Putting aside all the hair-splitting, the matter comes down to a question of definition. If we define self-interest as whatever motivates me to do something, then the concept is purely tautological: it is true by definition. In that case, however, it doesn't tell us very much. The only interesting propositions are those that might be false; then there is a real question being answered. So in this case the relevant question is whether people are usually self-interested in another sense—whether they put their personal comfort and convenience ahead of the desires of others. This is an empirical question: we could examine the evidence, and the answer we get might be different for different people, different cultures, different times.

In point of fact, economists nearly always assume that people are self-interested in this second sense as well. They are thought to respond to what they, individually, will get out of a course of action and to pay no attention to the consequences for others. Because of this, the basic unit of motivation in economics is the **incentive**, the extra reward or harm that will come to an individual for making a particular choice. Economics is typically the study of incentives: what they are in any given situation and how people can be expected to respond to them. Most economists do not think it is very effective to persuade people through appeals to religion or morality; what works is to give them the proper incentives that will lead them to do what you want them to do.

A good example is crime—for instance, car theft. Most of us think about crime in moralistic terms. Certain acts are wrong and people should not do them. The purpose of punishment is to achieve a measure of justice, in the sense that it would be unfair if people benefitted from acts like car-theft and were never at risk of any loss, even if caught. If it is unacceptable for people to benefit themselves by violating the rights of others, then either they should be prevented from doing so in advance, or they should be punished in some way after the fact. Different people have different conceptions of justice, but generally they involve some balancing of the "badness" of the violation with the degree of retribution. Nevertheless, the main way we would expect to reduce crime is through education and social influence. Children should be taught not to steal from one another, and adults who commit theft should be subject to public disapproval. A society in which many people *want* to steal is already in trouble, whatever measures are taken to control them.

There is, however, a field called "the economics of crime", which is the application of standard economic concepts to the issues raised by various forms of crime. In the case of car-theft, the economist reasons like this: All people are self-interested, including potential thieves. They might choose to steal cars because of the prospect of personal gain, particularly the money they can make by stripping ("chopping") and reselling them. Thus, in the absence of any policy, they have an *incentive* to do this. An effective crime deterrent policy would be one that erases this incentive through some combination of greater resources spent in policing and prosecuting and greater penalties for those found guilty. The economic problem is one of devising the most efficient mix of these measures and choosing the most efficient tradeoff between the cost to society of having cars stolen and the cost of measures to change the incentives to steal them. Justice, in the conventional sense, has nothing to do with it, nor is any consideration given to the cultural and social factors that might make people want to steal cars in the first place. The entire problem is one of incentives: incentives for people to steal or not steal, incentives for society to spend money to prevent theft or absorb its costs.

In this example we can see that the assumption of self-interest is crucial. Since the economist assumes that all people are self-interested, the only policies available are those that alter the calculations people will make; criminals will have to consider the risk of doing time as well as the rewards of driving off with a new

Mercedes. Nevertheless, in most societies crime of this sort is not commonplace because most people are *not* self-interested in this narrow sense. Most people will not steal things just because they think they can get away with them; they will be inhibited by an inner voice that reminds them that stealing is morally wrong, or that gets them to see the situation through the eyes of the person whose car is stolen. In fact, some people may steal even though it is *against* their self-interest in the personal-comfort-and-convenience sense we are using. They may be hostile toward the individual or group they are stealing from, or may be acting in revenge of some earlier deed. Both possibilities point to limits to the economic approach to crime.

At the same time, we should not be so quick to reject the self-interest hypothesis altogether. Even if many people are not self-interested about crime, certainly some are, and altering their incentives may be a reasonable way to frame public policy. Moreover, few people are completely non-self-interested, and so an incentive-based approach may work up to a point even if it is not the complete answer. This is not a question that can be decided at the level of theoretical abstraction; the role of self-interest has to be looked at on a case-by-case basis, with an open mind.

3.3 Rationality and Uncertainty

It would seem that we have now tackled the hard part of the economic conception of rationality, and that the rest, the use of reason to pursue interests (self or otherwise) should be fairly straightforward. Not so. In fact, economists have a very precise notion of what it means to be a rational individual, and this has produced a complex and fascinating debate. In the coming pages we will investigate this concept of **rational choice**— what it requires, what it tries to explain, the limits it is unable to overcome.

Let's begin with a situation that calls for a decision. It's five o'clock: what should I make for dinner? Now, what's interesting here is not what I will actually make (if that's what you'd rather read about right now, I'd suggest putting this text down and picking up a cookbook), but how I will make my choice. First, we might take note of the fact that there is nothing preordained about eating a large meal in the early evening. Other cultures do this differently, and this suggests that **cultural norms**, which I will discuss in a later chapter, have a role to play. Second, I might not think about what to make at all, because I had already planned this meal some time ago. I went to the store, bought the ingredients and solidified my intention of cooking a particular dish. While I am perfectly free to reconsider this plan, of course, I might be on automatic pilot and follow the plan without thinking about it. Third, I might feel an urge to make something I have the ingredients for but haven't eaten in a long time, or that reminds me of friendly dinners I've had in the past. In other words, I might act on impulse. Or fourth, maybe I make the same thing every other Tuesday, and here I am: it's that other Tuesday and why change now? In this case I'd be a creature of habit. What all of these approaches have in common is what they are not: they are not rational in the sense that economists use the term. Some of them are unconscious—I am not aware of making any choice at all. Others may be governed by parts of my mind that are not particularly rational, such as my love of familiarity and repetition, my urge to imitate those around me and follow their cultural norms, or my sudden craving for mashed potatoes (which may vanish after the first forkful).

To be rational, on the other hand, is to calculate the costs and benefits of each course of action in light of a clearly defined set of goals. The goals in this case might be some combination of keeping to a healthy diet, eating something that tastes good, and using up the vegetables at the bottom of my refrigerator that are about to nurture new life forms. Whatever they are, I should, if I am rational, think through all my options and try to anticipate how each will help meet these goals. I must be fully aware of my choice (not unconscious) and must not give in to passing emotions that interfere with this systematic calculation.

This would be relatively easy if I knew with perfect certainty exactly what outcome would arise from every option. If knew in advance exactly how each dish would come out, how I would feel about having made it a week later, whether anyone else was likely to drop by unannounced, how long the leftovers would keep, etc. I would be capable of a high degree of rationality without much effort. Unfortunately, most choices in life must be made under conditions of **uncertainty**. We have some knowledge, but we don't know everything. We can say that, even if we can't predict the future, we have a reasonable idea of which outcomes are possible and which are not. If I boil a pound of potatoes for myself and eat them, I will not be hungry 15 minutes later. The point is that we can, if we think things through, reduce the infinity of potential outcomes for each course of action to a relatively small number of outcomes worth paying attention to. What we don't know is which outcome will occur for sure.

To make my example more specific, let's suppose I want to make a salad if the dinner is just for me, but I would rather have prepared a pasta dish if friends come over to visit. So we will focus on just two options, salad or pasta, and two possible outcomes, one if I eat alone, the other if I eat with friends. To make things even easier, let's summarize the outcomes by giving them numbers on a scale of zero to ten, where 0 is absolute misery and 10 is perfect bliss. My decision could be portrayed in the matrix (Fig. 3.1) that appears on the following page.

Clearly, if I am eating by myself, I'd rather have a salad, but the salad won't work very well for a crowd. I like pasta somewhat by myself, but it would be the best choice if there will be others joining me. If I had reason to think there was exactly a 50–50 chance that I would have friends over, I could do the calculation required by this version of rational choice:

$$\text{Salad} = .5 \times 6 + .5 \times 3 = 4.5 \tag{3.1a}$$

$$\text{Pasta} = .5 \times 4 + .5 \times 8 = 6 \tag{3.1b}$$

Aha! I should put the water on for pasta right now. I will be a little disappointed if it's just for me, but I will be very happy if friends drop by. This is a very simple example of an **expected utility** calculation. The numbers that represent the values

		Outcomes	
		Alone	Friends
Options	Salad	6	3
	Pasta	4	8

Fig. 3.1 A matrix for calculating the expected benefit of dinner. Each cell (intersection of row and column) represents the benefit from dinner under that condition (alone or with friends) and based on that food choice (salad or pasta)

of the outcomes are referred to as their utility; the calculation is expected because I don't know for sure what the future will bring, but I factor in the probability of each outcome. Equations 3.1a and 3.1b represent the closest I can come to a rational anticipation or expectation of the future.

Of course, the odds of friends arriving may be less than or greater than 50 %, and I might not know off the top of my head how desirable any of the outcomes are. We could rewrite Eqs. 3.1a and 3.1b to be more general, so that they can apply to any possible pair of probabilities and any valuation of the outcomes. This means moving into the realm of algebra, replacing specific numbers by unspecific letters. To do this, let's invent some terminology. Let's call the first possible outcome, the one that occurs when I'm alone, outcome 1 and its utility for me v_{S1} for "the value of outcome #1 when I make salad" and v_{P1} for "the value of outcome #1 when I make pasta". Then the utility for me when friends come over is v_{S2} or v_{P2} depending on what I make. Each outcome has a probability; call the probability of the first outcome (alone) p_1 and the second (friends) p_2. The formulas for my two options are now:

$$\text{Salad} = p_1 v_{S1} + p_2 v_{S2} \tag{3.2a}$$

$$\text{Pasta} = p_1 v_{P1} + p_2 v_{P2} \tag{3.2b}$$

For each of these, we could write it using the summation sign:

$$\text{Salad} = \sum_i p_i v_{si} \quad i = 1, 2 \tag{3.3a}$$

$$\text{Pasta} = \sum_i p_i v_{pi} \quad i = 1, 2 \tag{3.3b}$$

Now we are ready to graduate to the most general version of the expected utility formula, one which could apply to any option with any number of possible outcomes. It looks like this:

$$\mathrm{EU(B)} = \sum_i p_i v_{\mathrm{B}i} \quad i = 1, 2, \ldots., n \quad \sum_i p_i = 1 \tag{3.4}$$

The left-hand side reads "the expected utility of (option) B" and it equals the sum of the product of probability and value for every possible outcome. The middle part of Eq. 3.4 says that there are n possible out comes, and each one of them is calculated. The short equation on the right says that the sum of all probabilities is equal to 1; this means you are not overlooking any potential outcome. (Whatever eventually happens has to be one of the possibilities you calculated.)

This is how it looks for any single option B. What economists mean by "rational choice" is that individuals should select B so as to maximize Eq. 3.4. To do this, you would have to identify all the possible outcomes that might arise, assign a probability to each of them, determine the value of each outcome given a particular course of action, add up all probability/value products (p times v), and do this for *every* option that presents itself. It's not easy being rational, and by the time you're finished it's likely that everything has changed, and you'll have to do your calculations all over again.

Narrowly speaking, all of this is simply absurd, and spelling it out as I have just done seems to be enough to discredit it. Nevertheless, there is a fallback position that most economists would embrace. Yes, no one has the time or obsession for detail to make truly rational decisions as defined by Eq. 3.4, but perhaps most people, most of the time make decisions that are reasonably close to this standard, even if they don't know it. One version of this story is that we have rational compartments of our brains that are constantly cranking away, making calculations of this sort without any direct supervision by our conscious minds. Thus, we make decisions that are more rational than we realize. Another story says that we approximate Eq. 3.4 through trial and error. We make similar types of decisions over and over, and we learn from our experience what sorts of choices give us the greatest utility.[1] Thus we end up choosing *as if* we were rational, even if, at any moment, we aren't. As we will see in future chapters, "as if" plays a large role in economic theorizing. There is a third story: even if this isn't such a good description of how people actually act, it's the ideal model of we should think about the choices we face. By basing itself on this notion of rationality, economics, in this case, would be about how people should be even if they aren't—it would be a normative, not positive, theory of decision-making.

As we will see further on, however, there has been much interest among economists in recent years of other models of decision-making, typically drawn from cognitive and social psychology. This field of *behavioral economics* is growing rapidly and has applications to nearly every topic of economic research. It would take us too far afield to introduce it now, but the more general point is that the rigidity implied by expected utility as a depiction of ordinary, day-to-day

[1] Note that this argument is essentially the same as Darwinian natural selection, transposed to the realm of behaviors.

decision-making is breaking down. For later investigations of alternative theories of individual and organizational choice, however, we will need to have a clear understanding of expected utility, since the alternatives are normally defined as carefully specified departures from it.

Incidentally, there is a major alternative to the calculation of expected utility that is frequently employed in business and policy circles, even if economists largely ignore it: scenario analysis. Since this is a textbook on economics, I won't spend much time with it here. In general terms, however, scenario analysis involves four steps:

- Identify the key factors that are likely to influence future developments. At most, pick just handful of such factors; in many instances analysts pick just two. Examples could include whether new laws will be passed that alter the marketplace, whether public opinion shifts in one direction or another, whether new sources of energy are found, and so on.
- For each factor, pick a very small number of alternative developments to look at: a specific law will or will not be passed, public opinion goes in one particular direction or another, a new energy source with certain characteristics is or is not found. No attempt is made to incorporate all future possibilities; just a few representative ones are considered. Business gurus, for instance, like models with two factors and two possibilities for each, creating a 2×2 matrix of scenarios. This looks very nice in a slide presentation.
- Each combination of factor developments, such as each cell in a 2×2 matrix, constitutes a scenario. Analyze this scenario: what actions should be taken and what outcomes should we expect?
- Sum up all the scenario analyses. Which are the most desirable and which the least? Which scenarios are most likely? What actions taken today, before we know which scenario applies, will work best across different possibilities?

Scenario analysis does not try to boil everything down to a single number the way expected utility analysis does. It is purposely fuzzier. On the other hand, it makes fewer assumptions, such as attaching exact probabilities to each potential outcome, and it provides more "stories" that explain *how* outcomes occur and which factors may play the largest role, rather than just crunching numbers. The reason for bringing it up at this point is to demonstrate that the version of rational decision-making employed by economists is not the only one that exists, or even the one that decision-makers are most likely to use.

3.4 Individual and Collective Rationality

There is one more wrinkle in the theory of rationality that will play a large role in the chapters to come, the distinction between **individual** and **collective rationality**. Its most vivid representation is in a sort of game that goes by the name of Prisoner's Dilemma. This was created in 1950 by Merrill Flood and Melvin Drescher, who were working at the time for the RAND project funded by the US Air Force. It takes its name from a story that its authors told in order to flesh it out, although, as we will see, it is highly adaptable to a wide variety of stories. It goes like this: suppose a crime has been committed and the police take in two suspects, who are held in separate cells. The evidence against them is limited, and the prisoners know this. It is clear that the best chance for a conviction is for one or both to confess, and the prisoners know this too. What each doesn't know, however, is what the other will do. The police, being sensible, offer each a deal. If you confess, they say, we will take that into account in sentencing. In fact, if you confess and finger your partner, and if we use this testimony to convict him, we'll let you off completely free. On the other hand, if you hold out against us and your partner confesses, you'll get the maximum we can throw at you. If you both confess your time in jail will be less than this maximum. What the police don't say, but what the prisoners know, is that if neither confesses they will be able to plea bargain to get an even lighter sentence, since the evidence is so meager. The dilemma in the Prisoner's Dilemma is deciding whether to give the police what they want.

Let's see how this can be expressed algebraically. To do this, we need ways to represent the elements of the story. The first step is to identify the players. That's easy; we can call them A and B. Then we need to assign letters to represent the two possible choices of confessing or not confessing. The standard language used by specialists in the field is to refer to them as *defecting* and *cooperating* respectively. That is, by confessing a prisoner is turning against his partner; by sealing his lips he is continuing to act in a partnerlike manner. (Note: the game explores the strategic interaction between the prisoners, where the police are in the background. For this reason, the refusal to speak with the police is called cooperation, even though the police wouldn't see it that way.) We shorten these to D (defect) and C (cooperate). Next we need representations of the consequences for the prisoners of their choice of actions. A simple way to convey this is with numbers, as we might for scores in a game. In this way, the higher the score the better the result. The numbers themselves are arbitrary; to make things easy we will select the integers 1, 2, 3 and 4.

The characteristic features of a Prisoners Dilemma game are summarized in the **payoff matrix** of Fig. 3.2 on the next page. It shows the outcomes to both players resulting from each combination of choices. A chooses between row 1 (D) and row 2 (C); B chooses between column 1 (D) and column 2 (C). The pair of numbers tells us what happens to the two of them (A's payoff, followed by B's) when A and B have made their particular choices. For instance, the upper-left cell says that, if both A and B choose to defect, each player will receive a "2". In the upper-right cell, A gets a "4" and B a "1".

To keep things as simple as possible, we are assuming that the game is perfectly *symmetrical*, that the payoffs for each player are the mirror image of the payoffs for the other. Three more assumptions will make the point of the game inescapable. First, we will assume that the prisoners are selfish; they care only about what happens to themselves individually and are unconcerned about the fate of their partners. In doing this, we are simply applying the economist's typical first-approximation assumption of rational self-interest to the players in our hypothetical game. Second, we will take it as given that only direct benefits recorded in the payoff matrix influence their decisions; that is, they are completely outcome-driven

		B: D	B: C
A	D	(2, 2)	(4, 1)
	C	(1, 4)	(3, 3)

Fig. 3.2 Payoff matrix for a two-player prisoners dilemma. A and B are the players; C (cooperation) and D (defection) are the choices. There are four possibilities depending on which choices are made, ranked from 1 (worst) to 4 (best). Within each set of parentheses, the payoff for A is given first, then the payoff for B

and take no account of ethical principles, customs or other such considerations. Finally, we add the assumption that this is purely a one-time event: the police make their offer once, and then there is no further interaction between any of them. (This last restriction eliminates any possible influence of future "games" on this one.) All in all, this is a highly artificial world we have created, but, for now, its purpose is clarity of insight and not realism.

What then will our prisoners do?

Note that it is in the individual interest of each player to defect, no matter what the other one does. Suppose you are player A, for instance. Your opponent, B, will either cooperate or defect. If B cooperates you are better off by defecting, since $4 > 3$. If B defects, you will also be better off if you defect too, since $2 < 1$. So either way, you should choose D. (Formally, since D has a higher payoff than C for A whatever B does, there is no need to estimate the likelihood of B's choice, as we would if we were to use the expected utility formula in Eq. 3.4; $EU(D) > EU(C)$ for all values of p.) Since the same logic applies to your opponent's decision, however, the pair of you are likely to end up in the upper left-hand cell, each receiving 2 when, with some forethought and coordination, you might have been able to agree that both should cooperate, so that both would receive 3 instead.

Looking more closely, we see three distinguishing characteristics of the Prisoners Dilemma game. First, both players face a *cost to unilateral cooperation.* In other words, if you cooperate and the other player defects, you get the worst possible payoff. This is sometimes referred to as a "sucker's reward". (It is what baseball legend Leo Durocher no doubt had in mind when he said "Nice guys finish last.") Second, both face a *benefit to unilateral defection.* If the other player is cooperative but you defect, you get the best possible payoff. There is a reward in this type of game to those who prey on the trust of others. Finally, *mutual cooperation is better for both players than mutual defection.* It doesn't make sense for the players to end up defecting against one another, since they could both do better by cooperating instead. These three characteristics, in fact, define the Prisoners Dilemma as a particular type of game. (There are many other games that have been developed by economists and other social scientists to aid in the analysis of complex strategic interaction. Some are close relatives of the Prisoners Dilemma, created by altering one or more of the three characteristics described in this paragraph.)

Can a Prisoners Dilemma have more than two players? Yes: for convenience let player A remain an individual, and have player B represent "everyone else". From each player's perspective, they are A and the others are B; so as long as the payoffs remain the same, the decision-making and the outcomes remain unchanged. Additional complications can be introduced by tying the payoffs to the proportion of B that cooperate or defect, but we will not take them up now. They don't alter the essential characteristics of the game, although they do alter the prospects somewhat for arriving at mutual cooperation. (They tend to make explicit agreement more difficult, but also lower the cost to deploying cooperation as an individual strategy, as we will see in a later chapter.)

What makes the prisoners dilemma so interesting is its stark opposition of individual and social rationality. From an individual standpoint, the best choice is D, taking advantage of the benefit of unilateral defection or avoiding the cost of unilateral cooperation, depending on the choice taken by the other player. Since this is true for both, by following their individual self-interest, they end up in a state of mutual defection, each earning the inferior reward 2. It is in their collective self-interest, however to arrive at mutual cooperation, since in that case both would be better off with 3. In this respect, the Prisoners Dilemma represents a case in which the sort of self-centered calculation normally presupposed by economists is self-defeating.

It is important to underline this conclusion. Recall that, for economics, the governing metaphor for describing economic life is exchange. People are assumed to take part in exchanges based on their calculations of self-interest. If exchange is voluntary and sufficiently well-informed, at least one party will be better off for undertaking it, and no party will be worse off. Therefore all exchanges that meet these two conditions are "good", and a major purpose of economic policy is to facilitate them. This is what "free market economics" is all about. We have questioned whether the metaphor of exchange leaves something out and whether rational self-interest is the right account to give of why people make the choices they do, but the Prisoner's Dilemma poses a different challenge: *if a real-world situation has the characteristics summarized in Fig. 3.2, even perfectly well-informed, voluntary, self-interested exchange can lead to participants being worse off rather than better off.* To put it differently, the case for markets depends on there *not* being some aspect of the situation that rewards the sort of cooperation people engage in when they put the interests of others ahead of themselves. True, in many of the contexts in which markets function, they function well enough: there are minimal opportunities for cooperative gain. Nevertheless, it is important to be on the lookout for the exceptions, as we will see.

With the logic of the model under our belt, let's switch to real-world examples. Consider first the problem of insuring that corporations honestly report their financial condition. Corporate record-keeping is extremely complex, and outside observers may not be able to tell whether financial reports accurately reflect current business earnings and potential future liabilities. Businesses want to issue positive reports in order to make it easier to get new financing at low interest rates, and to keep their stock prices as high as possible. (We will look more closely at the incentive effects of financial markets in Chaps. 8 and 17.) But dishonest reporting complicates the problem of management and may squander whatever goodwill exists toward the company in the eyes of the public. To make things as simple as possible, assume there are only two companies and only two consequences of honest or dishonest reporting, stock prices and public image, with the first more important than the second. With just two companies and one stock market, relatively higher share prices for one company mean relatively lower prices for the other. We also (temporarily) assume that there are just two options, honesty and dishonesty, that the choice of which option to take is made independently by each company with no possibility of revision, and that there is no public regulation of corporate accounting.

For each company there are four possibilities:

(a) It is dishonest but the other company is honest.
(b) It is honest but the other company is dishonest.
(c) Both are honest.
(d) Both are dishonest.

How will they rank them? Given our assumptions, we expect (a) to be best, then (c), then (d), then (b). Here's why: (a) The best outcome arises when your own company is dishonest but the other is honest. This gives you a clear advantage in the stock market, which (by assumption) is more important than the risk of a negative public image if you are found out. (b) If both companies are equally honest or dishonest, their effects on the stock market cancel out, and the only difference has to do with public perception. In this case, mutual honesty is the better policy, since both companies enjoy more public approval. (c) Mutual dishonesty also preserves the status quo in the stock market, but comes at the cost of potential public disapproval. (d) The worst outcome occurs when you are honest and the other company isn't, since now your stock prices fall and theirs rise. Again, this is assumed to outweigh the benefits of potentially greater public approval.

This information can be displayed in a payoff matrix, as on the following page in Fig. 3.3, where dishonest reporting constitutes defection (D) and honest reporting cooperation (C).

As before, it doesn't matter what the other company chooses; dishonesty is preferred. If company B is dishonest, A can either be dishonest and receive (d) or be honest and receive (b)—but (d) is better than (b). Similarly, if B is honest, A can get (a) by being dishonest and (c) by being honest—and (a) is better than (c). So A does not have to read B's mind; it is better to fudge the accounting report in either case.

In the real world these assumptions are not entirely valid. Certainly there are more than two companies, and they have the opportunity to revise their accounting policies every time they prepare a new report. We will see in Chap. 10 that this moderates the collective action problem to some extent. If the reports are dishonest it is also possible that the financial markets will find out, and this could have devastating consequences for the company *and* its accountants. Nevertheless, despite all these qualifications, the historical record demonstrates that businesses,

		B: D	B: C
A	D	A gets (d) B gets (d)	A gets (a) B gets (b)
	C	A gets (b) B gets (a)	A gets (c) B gets (c)

Fig. 3.3 Payoff matrix for honesty in accounting as a two-player prisoners dilemma. A and B are two companies that can either report their financial condition honestly (C) or dishonestly (D). The ranking of outcomes is (a) > (c) > (d) > (b), based on the assumption that the effects in the stock market of differences in honesty outweigh the costs of dishonesty for potential public disapproval—if the dishonesty is revealed. Each company therefore has an incentive to choose D, even though the result is that they are both worse off than they would be if both chose C

if not closely regulated, will often produce misleading accounting reports. (These acts of dishonesty often start out as small exaggerations and omissions and then gradually expand until they are out of control.) This is why industrialized countries *do* have regulations that impose penalties on firms and their accountants if dishonest reporting is brought to light. The goal is to alter the incentives so that, with possible penalties taken into consideration, (c) comes out on top of the ranking.

Next consider an important issue of public policy, state incentives for economic development. Suppose A and B are states—New York and California, for instance. A private company plans to make a major investment, but is unsure which state to locate in. Each state wants to be chosen, since the investment will create jobs and expand the tax base. If we want to cast this in the form of a Prisoners Dilemma, we can designate defection as negotiating individually with the company, offering subsidies like tax breaks and subsidized state-provided services. Cooperation means refusing to enter into negotiations and offering no special incentives to the company. It is plausible, then, that Fig. 3.4 on the following page might reflect the payoffs to each pair of choices, particular if they are evenly matched as potential investment sites. If both states offer equivalent subsidies they are on an equal competitive footing, but whoever wins the contest will have to provide costly benefits to the company. On the other hand, if neither makes offers the competitive situation is unchanged, and the winning state avoids having to pay for subsidies. Mutual cooperation is therefore better for both states than mutual defection. Unfortunately, both the incentive to unilateral defection and the penalty for unilateral cooperation exist in this example, provided that, for each state, the benefit of gaining the investment exceeds the costs of the subsidies. If New York cooperates by refusing to negotiate, California can (quietly) cut a deal and come out ahead. Moreover, if California defects, New York is worse off if it cooperates than if it defects too. For these reasons, it will be difficult to ensure that both states adopt a cooperative strategy. In the real world, of course, there are 50 states, and the prospects for achieving cooperation are even worse; this is why most states spend millions or even billions of dollars in a dubious competition over investment and

		B: D	B: C
A	D	• costly subsidies offered • equal competitive chances ∘ costly subsidies offered ∘ equal competitive chances	• costly subsidies offered • high likelihood of winning the investment ∘ no subsidies offered ∘ little chance of winning the investment
	C	• no subsidies offered • little chance of winning the investment ∘ costly subsidies offered ∘ high likelihood of winning the investment	• no subsidies • equal competitive chances ∘ no subsidies offered ∘ equal competitive chances

Fig. 3.4 Payoff matrix for investment competition as a two-player prisoners dilemma. A and B are two states competing to have a private investment sited. D (defecting) means offering subsidies to lure the investment; C (cooperating) means not offering them. The four cells describe payoffs resulting from the four combinations of choices. The first payoff listed is A's; the second is B's

jobs. (Note that public investment incentives serve no legitimate social function in this example, since, by hypothesis, the investment will take place somewhere with or without subsidies. There might be a case for subsidies if the investment itself, and not just the location, is at issue.)

Now let's step back from these examples and take stock. For purposes of explanation (or perhaps shock value), I have emphasized the dilemma aspect of the Dilemma. Individual interest drives players into situations that are collectively irrational. Is there no escape then? In fact, the main direction of research into this game (theoretically, in controlled experiments and real-world case studies) is in solutions. There are several possible routes to a cooperative outcome, each with its costs and benefits:

- Coercion. An organization representing all the players can try to force them to cooperate by punishing defectors. This, of course, is one of the functions of organized crime in real life police scenarios. The prisoner who "sings" (confesses and implicates others) is in trouble.
- Inducements. Instead of punishments for defection, an organization can offer rewards (called "side payments" by game theorists) for cooperation. Some groups, for instance, enter the names of individuals who take on voluntary burdens into raffles, where they can win prizes.
- Reputation. If the game is played repeatedly by the same players (as it often is in real life), the players themselves can bring about cooperation by rewarding other cooperators and punishing defectors. "What goes around, comes around" is the

motto of such groups. Networks of cooperation and mutual support are common, in fact, in most stable communities that have been studied.

- Custom. Societies often promote social norms that require its members to cooperate. They are taught them ("socialized") at an early age, and the result is that most people go through life abstaining from chances to cheat and take advantage of others without even consciously considering it. Of course, not everyone is equally well-trained, and social customs seem to allow loopholes for situations in which defecting is permitted. Thus, there is a tendency in many societies to tolerate self-interested calculation when the other parties are unseen and unknown, or when they are outsiders or disparaged castes or classes.
- Intrinsic satisfaction. There is some experimental evidence that human beings, being social creatures, are genetically equipped to experience satisfaction in cooperation, at least in some contexts. Virtue, it seems, *can* be its own reward.

We will return to these potential escape routes later on as we apply the Prisoners Dilemma model to various economic issues.

At this point you may be wondering how common such applications of the Prisoners Dilemma actually are. The answer is that it is one of the most widely used theories, not only in economics, but in several other fields as well. The reason this game has captured the imagination of researchers is that, despite its simplicity, it seems to get to the heart of many problems in modern life. Once the model has become familiar, you too may begin to see hints of it everywhere. Of course, complicated real-world situations are seldom fit exactly into the format of this game, and it is a matter of interpretation and judgment whether the similarities outweigh the differences. This is something to keep in mind when we return to the Prisoners Dilemma in future chapters.

3.5 Equilibrium: People as Particles

Ask most people what they think "equilibrium" means, and they will tell you something like "balanced", "in the right place" or "satisfied". We talk about people achieving an equilibrium in their lives, in which their different interests are each given a proper role, and the result is a general feeling of well-being. To be in disequilibrium is to be out of balance: missing something important, dissatisfied, unhappy.

As in so many other cases, the technical use of the word "equilibrium" departs significantly from its popular use. For economists, no concept is more important; nearly every theory they use depends on equilibrium as its organizing principle, and so the potential for misunderstanding is very large. In this section we will look carefully at the economic version of equilibrium, and identify the features that differ from the everyday variety.

Economists take their notion of equilibrium from classical mechanics (Newtonian physics). In any physical state there are a variety of forces at work on each "body" or physical unit. A billiard ball is struck, and the force of the cue initiates motion. Momentum propels it forward at a decreasing rate, as the effects of gravity and friction take their toll. Eventually there is no force sufficient to cause the ball to change position, and it comes to a stop. Equilibrium is a state in which no existing force is sufficient to alter the system; it will remain in that state until a new force is applied.

This is also how economists think about equilibrium. Suppose I land a new job that pays twice as much as my old one. I now have lots more money, and I'm looking to spend some of it. My spending pattern—the amount I generally spend per month on food, entertainment, etc.—is now out of equilibrium, since a new force is bringing about a change. I will increase my spending until the level I reach is consistent (from my perspective) with my new income, at which point it will stabilize. Economists would say that I have reached a new equilibrium in my consumption, based on a change in income. This equilibrium is expected to continue until some new change—in income, prices, life circumstances, etc.—disrupts it.

To be very precise, equilibrium in its economics usage has two elements. First, it identifies a situation in which there is no "inner" tendency toward change. Once the people or institutions that make up the situation have achieved a common equilibrium (an equilibrium for each participant that takes into account everyone else's), there is no reason for any further change, unless some new event takes place. This is the "timeless" aspect of equilibrium: equilibrium as a cessation of time. (If time is motion, equilibrium, because it is motionless, has no time.) In the real world, of course, nothing ever stands still, and this means that equilibrium (in its economic sense) can apply only to models of things, not the things themselves. This is a limitation of models, but, as we have seen, limitation is the *point* of building models—they are conscious attempts to limit our vision in order to see particular things more clearly.

The second aspect of equilibrium is more subtle. Recall the example of my change in consumption after receiving an increase in income. Equilibrium occurs when the spending change is completed, but the story begins in a state a disequilibrium, before I change my spending. When the curtain rises, I have the extra money, but I am not spending it yet. In order for the concept of equilibrium to come into play, I have to make the transition from lower to higher spending. In the real world, this might take a bit of doing; spending requires effort. I might need to locate new stores or open up a new bank account. For the purposes of our highly simplified story, the exact process is not important. What is important is the *assumption* that I will manage it somehow, and go from a routine of spending less to one of spending more. In other words, for the concept of equilibrium to have any meaning in a world of disequilibrium, the must be a process—an impetus—that moves participants in the economy toward equilibrium when they are not in it.

Thus, every instance of equilibrium in economics has two components. First, it identifies a state at which the economy (in a model) comes to rest. Once this state is achieved it will persist as long as the conditions of the model persist. Second, it incorporates a story that describes why and how people, beginning in a state of disequilibrium, will move to equilibrium. In my spending example, the story might be one of unsatisfied desires when I had less money, a backlog of items on my wish list, etc.

This is exactly what equilibrium means in economics and nothing more. *It does not imply happiness, balance or perfection*. Indeed, we will see that it is possible for an economy to be in equilibrium (according to commonly used models) and for massive problems to exist: high levels of unemployment, great disparities in income and wealth, life-threatening pollution and the failure to provide essential goods and services to those who need and want them.

In principle, economics is concerned with improving social well-being. The strategy used by most economists is outlined in the box below:

The Economist's Strategy for Addressing a Social Problem

1. Create a model representing the essentials of the current state of the economy or some important part of it.
2. Determine the equilibrium of this model.
3. Demonstrate the reasons why this equilibrium falls short of solving the larger problem under investigation.
4. Propose changes to economic policies or institutions that mitigate the shortcomings of the equilibrium in Step 2. These can either be changes in the way the economy operates, so that a different equilibrium will emerge with fewer social deficiencies, or an adjustment to be administered after the original equilibrium is reached.

Suppose, for example, that problem is global warming, the buildup of greenhouse gases that threatens catastrophic changes in the world's climate patterns. This is due to many factors, one of which is that people who own cars are driving them too much and burning too much gasoline. The economist would begin by demonstrating that this excessive driving is not a temporary aberration, but an equilibrium that can continue indefinitely unless something is done. This part of the analysis would be couched in some form of supply-and-demand theory: estimating the demand for gas as affected by prices, the supply provided by oil companies, etc. The current situation is an economic equilibrium if consumers are buying the quantity of gas they want to buy at the going price, and oil producers are producing the amount of oil they want to produce at that price. Both are doing what they would like, given what the others are also doing. Hence there is no reason for anyone to choose differently.

The third step is for the economist to show that the equilibrium in the market for gasoline is not optimal for "society"—in this case, the world as a whole. This can be done by assessing the costs and benefits of reducing global warming or, more simply, demonstrating that some of the cost of burning gasoline is not being taken into account by consumers and producers in the model; their behavior is "defective" from a social standpoint. This leads to the final step, which might result in a proposal for a tax on gasoline at the pump, for example, in order to reflect the true cost of greenhouse gas emission, so that the new equilibrium (with the tax) would be better for society than the old one.

In this example, and in all the work that economists do, equilibrium is a concept whose only purpose is to facilitate modeling and other forms of analysis. It does not imply any normative judgment about whether the economy is doing what we want it to. It can be used normatively, of course, when economists employ models to help them devise solutions to economic situations they see as problems for society.

3.6 Systems of Allocation

As the previous sections of this chapter should make clear, economists regard the fundamental economic question to be that of choosing among alternative options available to us. This is typically done in the context of limited resources. Consumers do this when they decide what to buy (the resource being money), firms when they decide what to produce and how, and so on. In economics lingo, this is the problem of **allocation**. Any given economy offers us a system for making allocative decisions, but this system can vary dramatically depending on where and when we look.

Indeed, everywhere there are people there is an economy. Human economies have existed in all historical eras and on every continent. If we permit them to pass before us—the hunting and gathering societies, the irrigation-based civilizations of China and the Middle East, the native people of the Pacific Northwest and their potlatches, the early renaissance merchant economies of northern Italy and the Hanseatic League, modern industrial capitalism—it seems as though there is no common thread. (This is disconcerting: will future generations find anything in our own economic order that reminds them of their ways?) Yet, at a very high level of abstraction, we can say that only five types of economic decision-making have ever appeared:

1. Custom: we do it this way because this is how it is done. The basis for custom may be a religion, a body of traditional teachings, or simply the unconscious imitation of older generations.
2. Gift exchange: individuals or groups provide goods or services to others with no specified payment in return, but with the expectation that others will make similar gifts to them in the future. Some anthropologists might argue that gift exchange is really a form of custom, since the expectations that keep the system going are usually embedded in larger customary relationships. For instance a successful hunting party will share its bounty with others who were less successful, knowing that the roles may well be reversed after the next hunt—but this in turn depends on social norms regarding "proper" behavior that make it reasonable to assume that such reciprocity will actually take place.
3. Administration: one entity, either individual or collective, instructs another entity to do, or not do, something. Governments regulate modern economies according to this principle; this is also the basis for college admissions, where admissions officials decide which students can be enrolled.

4. Collective organization: the members of an entity decide on the actions of their *own* group. What distinguishes collective decision-making from administration is that a collective process is mutual—the decision-makers are the same ones who will have to abide by the decision—whereas administrators make decisions for others. (Administrators in one context, of course, can be collective decision-makers in another; think of a board of trustees. One moment they are collectively planning their own calendar, and then next they are making policy decisions for the university or other institution they are in charge of.)
5. Markets: individuals or groups enter into voluntary contracts with one another. Decisions in markets are made by decentralized agreement; each participant decides whether to accept the offers of others, and the choices are added up in the marketplace to produce a social outcome.

These are ideal types; in reality, most institutions are mixed. In fact it is not uncommon to find all five of these commingled in the same social nexus. Perhaps a very simple example will make this clear. Suppose I stop at a farm stand to buy some vegetables for dinner; what allocative mechanisms are at work? Certainly I am involved in a market, since I am offering to buy goods from a producer, but that is not all. The administrative mechanism of government regulation is there behind the scenes, determining, for instance, what chemicals the farmer was permitted to use in growing the food, and how much residue can be left on it. Even if I am willing to buy food with more chemical contamination for a lower price, I do not have that legal option. (Of course, the farmer might violate this law.) Custom also enters in. Am I permitted to "test" the produce before I buy it? Can I peel back the corn husks to look for pest damage? Can I sample the strawberries? This is entirely a matter of local custom. In some situations this behavior is expected; in others it would be taken as a violation of accepted practice. You probably won't see any signs posted telling you what's allowed; you just have to know. (Anyone who has shopped at farm markets in different countries will recognize how much customs can vary, and how this affects the quality and price of what is bought.) Finally, when I take the bag of fruits and vegetables home, the ultimate allocation is a combination of gift exchange and collective decision-making. A family, of course, is fundamentally a system of gift exchange; family members provide goods (like produce bought at a farm stand) and services (like cooking) without demanding immediate compensation, expecting that those who benefit today will make their own contributions tomorrow. There is also an element of conscious, collective decision-making. For example, as a family, we may discuss what to do with all those strawberries: should we just pile them into bowls and eat them as they are or use them to make a pie? So all five mechanisms are likely to come into play at some point, and all of them are "economic" in the sense that they help determine the production and distribution of food—a fundamental economic good.

To consider another example, we have already examined the ways that work in typical businesses has aspects of voluntary exchange (markets) and other aspects that do not fit so neatly into that framework. Certainly market allocation is involved when workers consider what job offer to accept, for example, or when wages are negotiated. But there is also a large role for administrative allocation, as in the day-to-day authority invoked by supervisors. Work teams sometimes have scope for collective decision-making, and custom (for instance, "corporate culture") is pervasive. It is also recognized that some businesses run on a type of gift exchange: employers make a "gift" of better wages and working conditions than the market requires, and workers respond with a "gift" of greater work effort and higher commitment. We could be justified in saying, then, that productive work in our society is not organized solely through markets, but also through the other four allocative mechanisms. Nevertheless, markets play a larger role in these aspects of the US economy than in most of Western Europe, and, as we will see in a later chapter, this role has continued to expand in recent years. Allocation is rarely left to just one process, but some processes may be more important than others.

The Main Points

1. Choice and exchange can be considered metaphors for economic life, in the sense that they foreground certain aspects of the economy—moments of personal choice, especially related to buying and selling—at the cost of giving less attention to other aspects. This is can be made clearer by comparing the conventional metaphor of economics (choice) to others that have sometimes been advanced, like Marx's view of the economy as the product of human labor or Schumpeter's emphasis on combat between businesses competing to conquer each other's markets.
2. Economists usually assume that individuals are rationally self-interested. This embodies two assumptions, that we tend to act on the basis of what serves our own personal interest (rather than taking into account the interests of others apart from how they affect us), and that our reasoning adheres to the model of expected utility maximization. To be rational in this sense is to consider all possible outcomes of every course of action, placing a probability and a value on each. The formula that expresses this is

$$\mathrm{EU(B)} = \sum_i p_i v_{\mathrm{B}i} \quad i = 1, 2, ..., n \quad \sum_i p_i = 1$$

where EU(B) is the expected utility of option B, p_i is the probability of outcome I arising, and v_{Bi} is the value of this outcome should it occur. The rational individual calculates this for all possible options and then chooses the one whose expected utility is greatest. An alternative approach to the problem of uncertainty is scenario analysis.
3. There is an important distinction to be made between individual and collective rationality, where the first refers to choices that maximize expected utility for individuals one at a time, while the second represents choices that people might make in a coordinated way that could yield even more individual utility. One powerful demonstration of this distinction is the prisoner's dilemma model. It is characterized by three features: the benefit of unilateral defection, the

disadvantage of unilateral cooperation, and the superiority of mutual cooperation to mutual defection, where cooperation refers to choices made by individuals that are in the interest of other players and defection to choices that are against the interest of other players. In a prisoner's dilemma it does not matter what other players do; each individual is better off defecting whether or not the other cooperates or defects. Nevertheless, by both acting in an individually rational manner, the players end up with the less desirable outcome of mutual defection. In practice, societies have evolved various mechanisms that sometimes steer individuals in the direction of cooperation in prisoner's dilemma-like situations.
4. As used by economists, "equilibrium" does *not* mean "desirable". Rather, it refers to a state of affairs in which there is no inbuilt tendency toward change, and to which individuals are likely to return if they deviate from it. The purpose of having such a concept is to facilitate prediction: by identifying a particular outcome as an equilibrium, economists are asserting that it is likely to arise, and the specific reasons why the equilibrium properties are believed to be met provide the basis for explaining this prediction.
5. Economists view economic systems as solving problems of allocation, determining how limited resources are devoted to competing uses. In general terms, there are five such allocative mechanisms—custom, gift exchange, administration, collective organization and markets. In practice, they tend to overlap.

▶ Terms to Define

Administration
Allocation
Collective organization
Cooperation vs defection (in a Prisoners Dilemma)
Custom
Equilibrium
Expected utility
Gift exchange
Incentive
Individual vs collective rationality
Markets
Payoff matrix
Prisoner's Dilemma
Rational choice

Questions to Consider

1. Make a list of all your economic activities (involvement with the production, distribution or use of goods and services) yesterday. Which of your activities could best be described as choices? Which were exchanges (money for goods and services)? To what extent were the non-choice and non-exchange activities foreseen and incorporated when you chose and exchanged? How close do the choice and exchange metaphors come to encompassing the factors that people other than yourself should take into account when trying to understand your economic life?
2. Increasingly, colleges and universities are being asked to regard themselves as businesses providing educational services to their student customers. In other words, students are viewed as exchanging money for a package of services including classes, student support, campus life activities, etc. This approach is then used to identify marketing, quality assessment and other initiatives for higher education modeled on management in the for-profit sector. Clearly, this vision depends on the appropriateness of the underlying metaphor of education as an exchange. What, in your view, are the advantages and disadvantages of thinking about education in this way? What aspects of the situation are captured in the exchange metaphor? What aspects are excluded or misrepresented?
3. How many decisions have you taken in the past week that were *not* based on self-interest? In other words, how often did you put the interests of others ahead of your own?
4. Look again at Fig. 3.1, with its utility matrix for the salad-or-pasta dinner choice. What is the break-even probability of friends coming over? That is, at what probability of friends dropping by is the expected utility of making a salad equal to the expected utility of making pasta? Can you show how this would be calculated using the expected utility formula represented by Eqs. 3.2a and 3.2b?
5. To what extent was your decision to take this economics course "rational" in the precise terms of expected utility theory? Did you consider all the alternative courses of action? Did you forecast the likelihood and desirability of possible outcomes resulting from this decision?
6. Do you think that rationality in the form of expected utility maximization (using the formula in Eq. 3.4) represents an ideal that we should aspire to, even if it is sometimes beyond our abilities? Should people be encouraged (or even taught in schools) to think this way?
7. One of the most-publicized problems in professional sports is the use of performance-enhancing drugs. Of course, not all such drugs constitute a problem, just those that are physically harmful, like steroids. (Steroids increase the risk of cancer later in life.) Try to fit the Prisoners Dilemma model to this problem. Assume a two-person contest (all other competitors can be folded into player B) and symmetrical payoffs. Crucially, assume that each athlete values winning so much that having a competitive advantage outweighs the future health costs of taking steroids. Construct a payoff matrix as in Figs. 3.2, 3.3,

and 3.4, and show that the three central characteristics of the Prisoners Dilemma apply. Show that the assumption that winning is valued above health is necessary for two of these characteristics. Do you think this assumption is warranted in real life? Which of the routes to cooperation sketched above is employed by sports organizations like Major League Baseball, FIFA (soccer) and the Olympic Games?

8. Most people in large cities live far from where they work or go to school. If a large proportion of them rely on cars for transportation, the result is rush hour traffic jams. Each driver presumably calculates the advantages and disadvantages of the various options available: drive or take mass transit, drive alone or carpool, leave and return during rush hour or travel on an off-peak schedule, etc. Driving every day, they are well-informed about the consequences. Under these circumstances, can daily traffic jams be an equilibrium outcome as we have defined equilibrium in this chapter? How could you find out? Suggest an approach using individual surveys, as well as one that looks at overall behavior (traffic flows) rather than individual statements. In each case, what would count as evidence of "equilibrium gridlock"? And why would it matter whether or not traffic tie-ups are equilibrium events? In other words, who might be able to use this information, and for what purposes?
9. In the household(s) you grew up in, what was the balance between the five systems of allocation? Which systems were employed for which goods or services? Do you wish the balance had been different? How?
10. Public libraries purchase books which are then made available to the community free of charge. There is little or no cost to acquiring a library card, and cardholders may borrow any books they choose. Of what system or systems of allocation is the library an example?

Values and Objectives

4

In the previous chapter we looked at several key elements of the framework used by economists to do positive analysis—explanation of the past and prediction of the future. Now we will sketch the framework for normative analysis. The central concept is **economic efficiency**. We will begin by taking a bird's-eye view of the topic and then move up close to study in some detail its underlying components, **economic costs and benefits**. These ideas are not complicated, but they differ subtly but significantly from the everyday use of the same words. It's important to remove any potential sources of confusion before moving to the model-building that lies ahead.

4.1 The Economy as a Machine

At the risk of oversimplification, we can depict the economy as an enormous machine, as in Fig. 4.1 on the following page. At the left is the intake pipe. Into it go all the inputs needed to make the economy go. These are *costly*, in ways we will describe shortly. In the middle is the mechanism itself: lots of production, processing, shipping, servicing, and everything else people do to create economic value. At the right is the final output ready for consumption, the goods and services for which we need an economy in the first place. These constitute the economic benefits produced by the system.

Of course, it's not quite that simple. Many of the outputs are also inputs. For instance, the computer on which this book is being written is a product of the economy. It produces personal benefits for me when I use it to communicate with family and friends, and it is also an input into the production of further goods (economics textbooks). A more accurate diagram would have pipes circling back from output to input, looping through and around one another. That would be a more accurate representation, but doesn't really add much to the main story. A second wrinkle is potentially more significant. Not everything that comes out the output pipe is beneficial to society: modern economies produce pollution, stress and other undesirables. They also produce weapons of mass destruction, as well as the

P. Dorman, *Microeconomics*, Springer Texts in Business and Economics,
DOI 10.1007/978-3-642-37434-0_4, © Springer-Verlag Berlin Heidelberg 2014

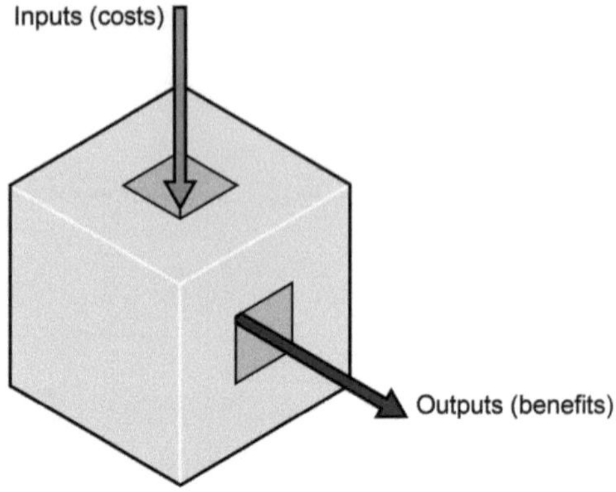

Fig. 4.1 The economy as a machine that transforms inputs into outputs. The economy is seen as taking in inputs such as labor, raw materials and equipment and producing outputs (goods and services) of benefit to consumers

less dramatic arsenals that cause daily carnage around the world. Without getting into the fine points of exactly which outputs cross the line separating benefits from costs, we can agree that at least some of what the economy produces makes us worse rather than better off. Economists refer to these things as **bads**—in contrast, of course, to goods. In principle, bads should be treated as costs of operating the economy in the same way inputs are. The only confusion is that they appear on the output side of the machine.

The diagram is also incomplete in key respects. Above all, it ignores nature, the ultimate source of all inputs and ultimate receptacle of all outputs. As drawn, there is no production process that produces the inputs; they simply fall out of the sky. Nor do outputs go anywhere after they come out the pipe. Presumably they vanish into thin air in order to make room for more outputs in the future. Neither of these ideas is very sensible. In Chap. 20 we will return to these problems to see what economists have to say about them.

For now, the simple point of the drawing is that the purpose of the economy is to convert costly inputs into beneficial outputs. Like any machine, we could give it an efficiency rating: its outputs minus its inputs. Translated into economic terms, this leads to the concept of **net economic benefits** as spelled out in Eq. 4.1:

$$\text{Net economic benefits} = \text{Total economic benefits} - \text{Total economic costs} \quad (4.1)$$

Producing these net benefits is the underlying purpose behind having an economy in the first place. The larger the net benefits, the more productive—efficient—the economy. In fact, the overriding goal of economics, as it is usually practiced, is *maximizing* the net benefit available to society; this is a slightly more elaborate version of the "viewpoint of society" referred to in Chap. 1. It may be that losses exceed gains for some individuals, but so long as the machine as a whole is producing the largest possible net benefit, it passes inspection. Very roughly, this is equivalent to the "greatest good for the greatest number" criterion of classical utilitarianism.

As a slight digression, you may be wondering, why maximize the surplus of benefits over costs, rather than the ratio between the two? The reason is that the ratio that really matters is net benefits per person: other things being equal, an economy that produces more net benefits for each of its members is regarded as superior to one that produces less. Since population changes relatively slowly, maximizing net benefits per capita is the same as maximizing them, period. To make the point clear, consider a simple agricultural economy with a given population. Would it be better to have a single small farm with a very high ratio of outputs to inputs or a great many farms, each with a less impressive ratio, but producing a lot more food overall?

So much for the top-level view. Now let's dig a little deeper: what are these things we have called costs and benefits, and how might they be measured?

4.2 Economic Benefits

All animals have economies, in the sense that all do some sort of work to transform available inputs into necessities like food and shelter. (Have you ever watched a bird building a nest?) There is simply no other way to survive. Humans too require these basics, but they also desire much more than the absolute minimum. In fact, history has not yet recorded a standard of living that most people were completely satisfied with, leaving them no urge to acquire more. Moreover, human society is a complex of networks and hierarchies that we all depend on to get our needs met, and the goods that position us in the social nexus cannot be neatly separated from the ones we get for being in that position: think of what it takes in the way of clothing and transportation, not to mention housing, education and other goods, to land a decently-paying job.

What I am getting at is this: there is no simple biological measuring stick to determine what goods or services provide benefit to us, or to measure the amount they provide. For better or worse, we must rely on more subjective conceptions of benefit and value. The most subjective of all is the value placed on a good by the person who acquires it, and this is the approach adopted by most economists (although we will later find a growing body of dissent). More precisely, economists normally say that the value of an item to any person is the maximum amount he would be willing to pay to acquire it. The self-explanatory term for this measurement basis is **willingness to pay**. Adding up the willingness to pay on the part of each end consumer for every good or service produced in the economy would yield the total benefits produced. Note, as we already saw in Chap. 1, that money serves as a unit of measurement in this process, but not the objective itself. We can speak of so many dollars worth of consumer benefit, but the benefit comes from consuming real goods and services, not from the money people spend on them.

Note that willingness to pay is normally not the same as the price actually charged for an item. Most people find that the price tag is less than the maximum they would spend; that's why they make the purchase. If the price were exactly the same as willingness to pay, the consumer would be on the borderline, not sure whether to buy or not. This happens sometimes, but it is not the general case. Because of the divergence between these two amounts, and since only the price is publicly observable, it is difficult to get an accurate measurement of willingness to pay. Economists have developed several techniques to do this, but they provide only an approximation. Still, the theoretical idea is clear enough, and we will refer to it in the future under the supposition that, in a pinch, we could put a number on it.

Also, it should be noted that people get for free some goods they would be willing to pay for. Most radio programming, for instance, is free, as are most roads and sidewalks, urban parks and the like. In some cases no price is charged because the government has made a conscious choice to subsidize the consumer; in others the barrier is the sheer impracticality of trying to make people pay. (We will return to this issue in Chap. 15.) The principle that the willingness to pay is generally different from the price actually paid applies here as well, the only difference being that the price is zero. If a parent is willing to spend as much as $10 to take his child to the zoo, it doesn't matter if they go on a free (no admission charge) day; $10 remains the monetary measurement of his benefit.

Even at this very abstract level, and with all the simplifying assumptions we have made, there is a crucial doubt that needs to be addressed regarding the concept of benefit. In an attempt to be careful, I have used the term *economic benefits*, since only some of the good things in life are products of our economy. Arguably, many of the greatest benefits to be had are not economic at all: love and friendship, inner peace and fulfillment, the pleasure from playing music or staring into the night sky. Economic well-being is only a part of a much larger whole, and not necessarily the most important part. The doubt is this: what if, in some circumstances or perhaps even in general, economic benefit comes *at the expense* of other good things in life? This is a very old doubt with an impeccable pedigree; nearly every religion and major philosophy claims it is true. If they are right, then more economic benefit does not necessarily signify more benefit overall, and economics' claim to speak on behalf of human well-being is undermined. In many instances, this problem probably does not arise, but it is too important to put aside and forget. We will raise it again from time to time in this book.

In essence, the economic conception of benefit is very simple: society consists of individuals, and individuals benefit from the economy as consumers of goods and services. The total economic benefit conferred to society is the sum of all the individual benefits individuals derive in their role as consumers. Nothing else is regarded as beneficial, at least in the narrowly economic sense. There may be political, cultural or other values, but these do not lie within the purview of economics.

4.3 Economic Costs

As we have seen, to an economist the economy is a giant machine that produces goods and services. More output from this machine is usually viewed as a good thing: economists want to provide more "stuff" for more people. On the other hand, this stuff comes at a cost, and costs must be taken into account. To be efficient, our economy should be able to produce the greatest value of goods and services for any given cost, or, more or less equivalently, to produce any given value of goods and services at the least possible cost. In order to ascertain whether this is actually the case, economists need a working understanding of "cost", but the definition they use differs substantially from the everyday version, and this is a possible source of confusion.

Let's begin with the everyday use. A cost is a price someone pays or a burden someone bears. If I buy a pair of shoes for $40, this amount is my cost. It represents something I had to give up, and it is mine and no one else's (unless they bought another pair at the same price). But a cost does not have to be monetary. If I say hurtful things behind a friend's back, it may come back to me in the form of a serious cost—a lost friendship or perhaps a guilty conscience. Again, whatever its form, it is *my* cost; how could I extract my own personal sense of guilt and transfer it over to someone else?

Economists use the concept of cost much more narrowly than this. As we will soon see, many of the things we normally think of as costly are not costly in the eyes of economists, and economists recognize costs that most other people do not notice (or perhaps agree with). Since cost plays such a central role in economic theory—it is what the value of goods and services are compared to—it is essential to be precise, even to the point of splitting hairs.

To an economist, a cost represents what "society" gives up in order to produce things. Of course, these costs are often experienced by specific individuals, but societies are made up of individuals, and so economists believe that individual costs, or at least some of them, can be added up to determine the aggregate, social cost. And what is it that societies give up? Economists recognize only two types of cost, disutility and opportunity cost. If anything is referred to in everyday language as a cost but does not fit into one of these two categories, economists do not include it.

(A) Disutility. Disutility is negative utility, but what is utility? In economics, utility refers to the satisfaction of preferences or desires and therefore implies a state of well-being. To have more utility is to be "better off" in some sense. Note that utility in this context does not imply usefulness. A vacuum cleaner can contribute to my utility by making it easier to clean my house, but so can a beautiful photo to hang on the wall. Disutility, by contrast, is a reduction in well-being, the satisfaction of fewer preferences or perhaps the "dissatisfaction" of them. If I can't stand the noise my vacuum cleaner makes, running it may give me more disutility than utility.

Disutility is a cost of producing things. Much of the labor performed in our society is directly unpleasant: boring, painful or even dangerous. Having people put up with such hardships is one of the costs of "doing business". Similarly, the ill health resulting from pollution may be another source of disutility connected with production. An efficient society would try to minimize the amount of disutility people must bear to produce any given value of goods and services.

(B) Opportunity cost. While disutility is an important cost of production, it is not the most important. In fact, many goods and services entail no disutility at all. Like (I hope) most teachers, my own work in the classroom is not at all unpleasant; in fact, I usually enjoy it. This is not to say I might not prefer to do something else instead of teaching (at least some of the time), but that is a case of getting less utility from teaching, not disutility. It is likely that a large percentage of the work people do is at least somewhat pleasant, in which case disutility does not figure in. Even in the case of unpleasant work, disutility is rarely the largest cost.

To see how economists look at the problem, recall that the economy is viewed in economics as a series of choices. At each moment, people are deciding whether to do one thing—buy or sell something, etc.—or another. To make one choice is to reject the alternatives; if I spend my afternoon fixing my broken vacuum cleaner, I am deciding not to spend the time reading a book or taking a walk in the woods. By giving up these alternatives, I am assuming a cost when I spend my time on the vacuum cleaner, even if I don't find this repair work unpleasant (no disutility).

Specifically, economists define the **opportunity cost** of a choice as the value of the best alternative foregone. If reading a book was my best alternative to an afternoon of repair work, then the value of this reading is the opportunity cost of repairing. Similarly, the opportunity cost of my time spent as a teacher is the value of this time in its best alternative use, and the opportunity cost of the classroom I teach in is the best use this room could have been put to if I and my students weren't in it. Expressed this way, it should be clear that opportunity costs comprise the largest share of economic costs in general. Except for the most dangerous or unpleasant work, the greatest cost associated with working to produce a particular good or service is the lost opportunity to spend the time on something else. Similarly, one must take into account the opportunity costs of all the other elements that go into production, such as natural resources and manufactured equipment.

In economics, these costs are generally assumed to be measured by the amount of money needed to compensate them. Take disutility, for instance. It is much more dangerous to weld I-beams on the upper floors of a skyscraper than at street level. Given the choice, most people would rather not risk life and limb hundreds of feet in the air. Economists expect, then, that employers will have to pay a higher wage to get welders to accept this more dangerous situation, and the extra money it takes to get a voluntary acceptance of this danger is the measure of its disutility. Of course, it may be the case that dangerous work does not earn a higher rate of pay; in fact, much of the really bad work in our society is among the *worst* paid. This represents a breakdown of the pricing system, in the sense that prices (in this case wages) are not telling us what the true cost of the disutility is. This interferes with our ability to measure disutility cost, but it does not change the true cost itself: unpleasant or dangerous work generates the same disutility whether it is compensated or not. The same can be said for the disutility caused by pollution, which is very rarely compensated in our society.

Opportunity costs are far more likely to be compensated, due to property rights. Suppose a plot of land can be used for one of two purposes, as a farm or for a shopping mall. The opportunity cost of either option is the value of the other. Assuming the land is privately owned, and that the owner is primarily interested in making as much money as possible (as we have seen, these are normal economic assumptions, and they are often true), whichever choice is made, the return must be at least as great as the opportunity cost. So, if it is decided to use the land for the mall, the payment to the landowner must be at least as great as what could be obtained by farming; it must compensate the owner for the opportunity cost—otherwise the landowner would not allow the mall to built and would farm instead. This is also true of employment: wages paid to a worker must be sufficient to compensate for the opportunity cost of the time involved—the value of the best alternative use of that time. If you can spend the time fishing instead and make the equivalent of \$6 an hour on the fish you catch, you must be paid at least this to induce you to give up fishing and go to work instead. (This example assumes you are interested only in money, but it could be extended to include the value of your enjoyment of fishing, or work.)

The relationship between opportunity cost and prices can be illustrated using a simple diagram. Before we try to represent an economy, it might be easier to begin with a universal problem: how to divide our time between waking and sleeping. There are 24 hours in a day, no more, no less. Any time spent being awake is time not spent sleeping, and vice versa. (I am assuming that people do not spend any time doing a little of each of these simultaneously.) We can say, then, that the opportunity cost of an hour of sleep is the value of an hour of being awake, and similarly that the opportunity cost of an hour of being awake is an hour of sleep. We can see this in the following diagram:

You could spend the entire day in bed or the entire day awake and active, but usually you will want to do some of each. Figure 4.2 on the following page illustrates two typical possibilities: 6 hours sleeping and 18 hours awake, or 6 hours awake and 18 hours sleeping. Of course, any other combination is possible, so long as they add up to 24. The thick line represents all those possibilities; any point on this line is a potential combination of waking and sleeping hours. You can't be to the right of this line, because the day is not that long, and you can't be to the left of it because the day is not that short.

Recall that the definition of the slope of a line is the change in its vertical component divided by the change in its horizontal component:

$$\text{slope} = \frac{\Delta y}{\Delta x}$$

In this case, the slope of our sleeping–waking line is the change in hours awake divided by the change in hours asleep as we move along the line, and it equals -1. The commonsense meaning of this is that for every additional hour of being awake, we give up one hour of being asleep, and vice versa. This is exactly the same as saying that the opportunity cost of an hour of one is an hour of the other. The slope depicts the tradeoff, which is exactly one for one—which is why the slope is -1. Another way we could say the same thing is that the *price* of an hour of sleeping is an hour of being awake, and vice versa. The slope of the line tells us what the price of one is in terms of the other—in this case simply 1. (The prices are equal, at least as measured in time.)

Fig. 4.2 A "production possibility curve" for dividing a day between being asleep and being awake. There are only two uses of time, and they must add up to 24 hours. Eighteen hours of waking time and 6 hours of sleeping time is one possibility, as is 18 hours of sleeping time and 6 hours of waking time. There is a one-to-one tradeoff between these two uses

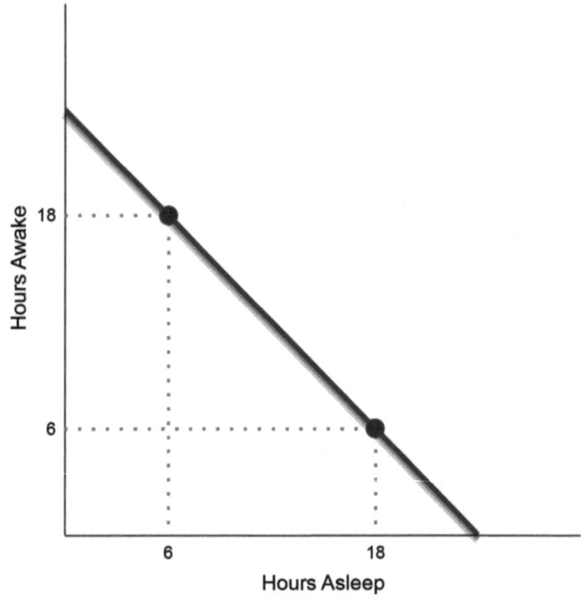

It is not a large step to consider a very simple economy that produces two goods, rice and beans, with a fixed amount of land. Some of this land is wet and is better suited to rice production; other land is dry and is more productive growing beans. The people in this society face the choice of deciding how much of each crop to grow. We might portray their production possibilities in the diagram on the following page:

Our mythical land could devote all its resources to rice and grow an amount equal to the point on the y-axis where the production possibility curve intersects it (just above R_A). It could also grow only beans, and have a bean crop equal to the point at which the curve intersects the x-axis. More likely, the population would prefer a combination of the two, and so they would consider possibilities along the curve between these two endpoints. Two such possibilities are depicted here, A and B. At A they can grow R_A bushels of rice and B_A bushels of beans. R_B and B_B reflect the corresponding amounts at B.

Suppose they begin at point B. They might decide that their diet is too bean-heavy and choose to move to A instead. In doing so, they would be giving up $(B_B - B_A)$ bushels of beans in order to increase their rice production by $(R_A - R_B)$. As a first approximation, we might say that the opportunity cost of increasing rice production by this amount is the amount of bean production given up. It is actually a bit different, however. Recalling that the slope of a curved line at any point is the slope of a straight line tangent to it at that point, we can see that the opportunity cost changes as you move from B to A. At B the slope is given by the line BB, at A by AA. BB has a steeper slope; there is more change in rice per change in beans than along AA. This means that the opportunity cost of beans is greater at

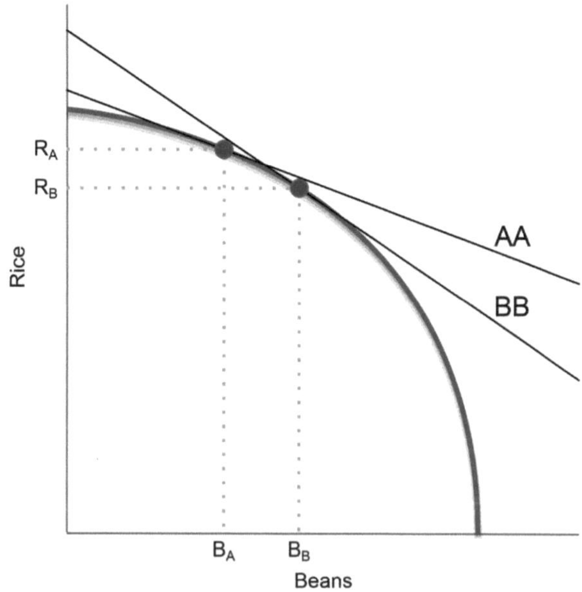

Fig. 4.3 A production possibility curve for a simple economy with two crops. Points A and B represent two potential production choices. To move from B to A is to increase rice production by the amount ($R_A - R_B$), but to decrease bean production by the amount ($B_B - B_A$). The slope of the line *AA* represents the tradeoff between the two goods at point A, and similarly for *BB* and point B

B than at A: you have to give up more rice to get more beans along BB than AA. The opposite is true for rice; its opportunity cost is less at B than at A.

Why might this be the case? We can imagine that, as you specialize in rice production, you are converting land more suited to beans to rice instead. This means you are giving up more beans to gain less rice—a higher opportunity cost of rice. The same story might be told about specialization in beans. Putting this all together, and assuming this is the only factor that might affect the productivity of either crop, we end up with a production possibility curve like that in Fig. 4.3, concave to the origin. The technical name for such a production system is that it exhibits **diminishing marginal returns**. We will revisit this concept when we discuss production costs in a future chapter.

One other point needs to be made. In Fig. 4.2 we were necessarily on the "sleep/ awake possibility" line, since a day has exactly 24 hours. In Fig. 4.3 it is not possible to be outside the line (by definition), but it is very possible to be inside it. After all, few economies produce at their maximum potential. Resources may be used inefficiently or not at all, especially if the economy suffers from unemployment. If we are at an interior point (not on the curve), it is possible to produce more of both goods, and so the concept of opportunity cost does not apply. We do not need to give up some of one thing to get more of something else. Moreover, through economic growth the production possibility curve is shifted outward, and this too permits more of some things without less of others (at least potentially). It is sometimes said that the most basic lesson of economics is that *there ain't no such thing as a free lunch*. Well, perhaps. But if the economy is functioning below its maximum potential, or if there are unrealized opportunities for growth, there are indeed free lunches to be had. We might even say that one of the main purposes of economics is to search out potential free lunches through improvements in efficiency and resource utilization—exactly the opposite of the familiar saying.

So far, we have been exploring aspects of disutility and opportunity costs, particularly the latter. It cannot be overstressed that these two types of cost are the *only* ones recognized in economics. They exclude some things we normally call "costs", and they include things we normally don't consider. Here are examples of each:

Economic costs but not personal costs. Our national parks and wilderness areas contain millions of acres of old growth forests, forests that have never been harvested for timber. In common usage, we would say that there is no cost to this state of affairs; after all, the forests have been there for millennia, and all we have to do to keep them wild is nothing. Indeed, it would be costly to send in teams of timber workers to cut down the trees. Nevertheless, the economist would say that maintaining these forests in their natural state is very costly: by choosing to retain wilderness, we are taking on the opportunity cost of their value as timber. That is, the value that these trees would have if we cut them down and sold them, net of the cost of cutting, is the opportunity cost of choosing not to do this. To say this is not to say that we *should* cut them down, of course, just that wilderness is costly. Note however that, if the trees are not privately owned, there is no group in society that perceives this opportunity cost as a personal cost in the everyday sense. It is purely hypothetical to say that the trees could be cut; in reality, no one currently has a claim on them or any expectation of receiving money from them. At most, we might say that the government bears this cost, because the trees are on public land. The point remains that there exists an opportunity cost, as economists understand this term, even though there is no single individual who bears this cost in the everyday sense.

Personal costs but not economic costs. Suppose you and I spend an evening playing poker, and you win $200 from me. This loss represents a cost to me, as we normally understand this word, but it is not an economic cost. No resources were used to create one thing instead of something else, and no payment was made to compensate people for any recognized economic cost. I end up with less money, and you end up with more, but there has been no cost to "society" for the production of anything. When money changes hands, but there is no economic cost incurred, economists say that a **transfer** has taken place. We will see in future chapters that transfers often play a large role in redistributing the costs and benefits of economic life, but their impact on the overall quantity of these things is less clear. (In the poker game there was no change at all in the total amount of money between us; the transfer simply moved some of the money from my pocket to yours.)

Finally, having surveyed benefits and costs as perceived by economists, we are now in a position to understand why *employment is a cost, not a benefit.* This seems paradoxical—in fact, exactly the opposite of how people usually think about it. Unemployed people want jobs, and when more jobs are created there is a tendency for wages to go up even for those who already have them. Politicians campaign on the promise to create more jobs. You would think that jobs would count as benefits, not costs, but you would be wrong. Jobs, except for those that are so pleasurable people would be willing to pay to work in them, fall under the category of costs. The wages workers receive have to be enough to compensate them for the disutility of work and the opportunity cost of their time; otherwise they wouldn't accept them. Meanwhile, benefits are reserved solely for consumers and are measured by willingness to pay.

Nevertheless, under most circumstances more employment *is* a good thing. Normally, the value created by the work people do is greater than the cost of this work itself, which is just another way of saying that the economy is productive. Some of this extra value goes to consumers in the form of goods that cost less than the benefits they confer, and some goes to workers in the form of wages that exceed the value of the time they give up by taking the job. (Some also goes to other groups, such as owners of companies, government tax collection, etc.) So it is ultimately true that creating jobs usually increases the net benefit available to society, but it also remains the case that the jobs themselves—the actual work—belong on the cost side of the ledger. This is an important distinction, because the goal of society, according to economics, should not be to create more work but more of the things that work can produce. Telling people to work slower or use less technologically sophisticated methods might increase the amount of work needed, but most economists would regard this as a step backwards, increasing the costs of production but not the benefits.

The Main Points

1. Economics regards the economy as if it were a giant machine transforming inputs into outputs. The inputs are costs, the outputs are benefits (unless they are undesirable byproducts like bads), and the goal is to maximize the net benefits of the machine's operation, according to the formula

$$\text{Net economic benefits} = \text{Total economic benefits} - \text{Total economic costs}$$

2. Economic benefits are measured according to the willingness to pay of consumers, which is normally greater than the amount they actually do pay. Economists generally put aside concerns that consumer demand may not register the "true" value of goods and services.
3. Economic costs take one of two forms. Most are opportunity costs, what we give up by using a resource for one purpose rather than its best alternative. Some are disutility costs, the harm or displeasure incurred in producing something, which, in a well-functioning market system, should also be compensated monetarily.
4. The production possibilities curve illustrates the concept of opportunity costs. In its two-dimensional form, it shows possible combinations of two goods that might be produced. The curve represents combinations in which the maximum amount of a second good is produced subject to various production levels of the first. Any point on this curve can be considered one of maximum

economic efficiency. The slope of the curve measures the opportunity cost—the amount of one that has to be given up in order to achieve a unit increase in the amount of the other. If the curve is a straight line, the slope is equal throughout, and the opportunity costs are unchanging. If the curve is bowed out from the origin, the production system is characterized by diminishing marginal returns—less increases in the output of a good the more one specializes in producing it. If the curve is bowed inward toward the origin, we would see increasing returns to specialization. In any case, the normal state of affairs is one in which society operates inside the curve: we are not producing at maximum efficiency and there are potential gains from improving our methods, organizations and policies.

5. Some economic costs are not personal costs. This is especially the case when resources that might be used are public property: there are opportunity costs to using them (and therefore economic costs) even though no particular individual bears a personal cost.
6. Many personal costs are not economic costs. This is especially the case when transfers take place: items of value are transferred from one person to another without any flow of goods or services in the opposite direction. The same things are available to the economy as a whole, but their distribution across individuals has changed.
7. Employment, since it is the use of a resource (human labor), is regarded as an economic cost, even though we usually think of increases in the number of jobs as "good". What makes employment beneficial is the prospect that the goods and services produced by workers will be of higher value than the costs, opportunity and disutility, of producing them. Simply increasing the amount of work performed without increasing the value created by that work, however, reduces economic net benefits.

Terms to Define

Bads
Disutility
Economic benefits
Economic costs
Economic efficiency
Economic vs noneconomic benefits
Net economic benefits
Opportunity cost
Willingness to pay

Questions to Consider

1. Many of the most remarkable engineering feats of the last century have been long underground or underwater tunnels, putting roads beneath mountains, rivers and seas. Unfortunately, it is common for workers to be killed in the construction of these marvels; health and safety in such conditions are an uncertain art. If the total amount of money needed to construct these tunnels, including all the wages paid to workers in view of their high level of risk, is less than the total that the general public would be willing to pay for the convenience of traveling through them, does this mean that they provide net economic benefits? Do you agree with the conclusion reached by economic analysis? Explain. If the construction of a tunnel provides net economic benefits, does this also mean that it is necessarily efficient in economic terms? Can you give a hypothetical example to explain your answer?
2. Look at this week's bestseller lists for fiction and nonfiction books. Putting aside differences in the cost of books, sales are a good indication of consumers' willingness to pay: presumably a book that sells 100,000 copies represents greater total consumer valuation than one that sells only 2,000. Do you agree with the argument that the bestsellers produce the most economic benefits? Do they produce the most benefit, economic and noneconomic, overall? If you think there are other sources of benefit, how might you measure them—or at least, how would you know whether one book provided more than another? You may find it easier to think about this question if you have the actual bestseller lists in front of you.
3. A survey found that Americans were more willing to support regulations to clean up oil spills if they thought the costs would be borne by large oil companies than small, owner-operated gas stations, even though the costs themselves, in monetary terms, were the same. According to the economic view of cost, should it matter who pays it for whether it is seen as too high or not? Why might it make sense to judge this policy on who pays the cost, as well as how large the cost is? What are the potential drawbacks of making distinctions on the basis of who pays?
4. According to the theory of disutility presented in this chapter, in general it doesn't matter if you don't spend your life working at a job you enjoy, so long as you make enough extra money to compensate you for the daily grind. Imagine two jobs, A and B. A pays $20,000 per year but is completely fulfilling, and it produces services valued by consumers at $40,000 a year. B is monotonous and oppressive; still you would be willing to take it at $30,000 a year, and it produces services valued at $60,000. Which job is "better" from the standpoint of economic efficiency? Does this analysis leave out any significant aspects of the problem?
5. Suppose the production possibilities curve in Fig. 4.3 were convex to the origin rather than concave, as in Fig. 4.4:

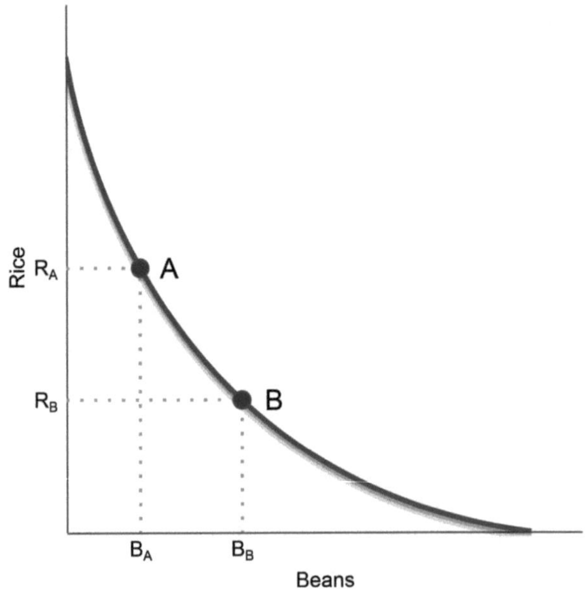

Fig. 4.4 The production possibilities curve is convex to the origin

What is happening to the opportunity cost of rice as this economy specializes in more rice? Is the same thing happening to the opportunity cost of beans as there is more specialization in beans? The concave curve was justified by a story about different types of land suited to the growing of different crops; can you think up a story that could justify a convex curve like the one above?

Analyzing Markets

5

5.1 Introduction: Crisis in a Cup

Mohammed Ali Idris is a coffee grower from Ethiopia. Interviewed in 2002, he had this to say about what was happening to his livelihood and life as a result of changes in the coffee market:

> Five to seven years ago, I was producing seven sacks of red cherry (unprocessed coffee) and this was enough to buy clothes, medicines, services and to solve so many problems. But now even if I sell four times as much, it is impossible to cover all my expenses. I had to sell my oxen to repay the loan I previously took out to buy fertilizers and improved seed for my corn, or face prison.
>
> Medical expenses are very high as this is a malaria-affected area. At least one member of my household has to go to hospital each year for treatment. It costs US $6 per treatment. We also need to buy teff, salt, sugar, soap kerosene for lighting. We have to pay for schooling. Earlier we could cover expenses, now we can't. . .Three of the children can't go to school because I can't afford the uniform. We have stopped buying teff and edible oil. We are eating mainly corn. The children's skin is getting gray and they are showing signs of malnutrition.[1]

In the early years of the century, plunging world coffee prices created an economic and humanitarian crisis in much of the developing world. Coffee is the world's second largest commodity trade behind oil; more than 25 million people are employed growing it, mostly on small farms. Coffee grows only in tropical and near-tropical regions, so the major producers are in Africa, Latin America and Southeast Asia. These countries are not rich to begin with. As the price small coffee growers can get in the market plummeted, malnutrition, disease and illiteracy were the results.

Figure 5.1 shows the long-term trend in prices earned by growers for Arabica, the most commonly traded type of coffee, during the period leading up to and following the crisis. (The other is Robusta, a lower quality bean that accounts for

[1] Gresser, Charis, & Sophia Tickell. (2002). *Mugged: Poverty in your coffee cup* (p. 10). Oxfam. www.maketradefair.com.

P. Dorman, *Microeconomics*, Springer Texts in Business and Economics, DOI 10.1007/978-3-642-37434-0_5,

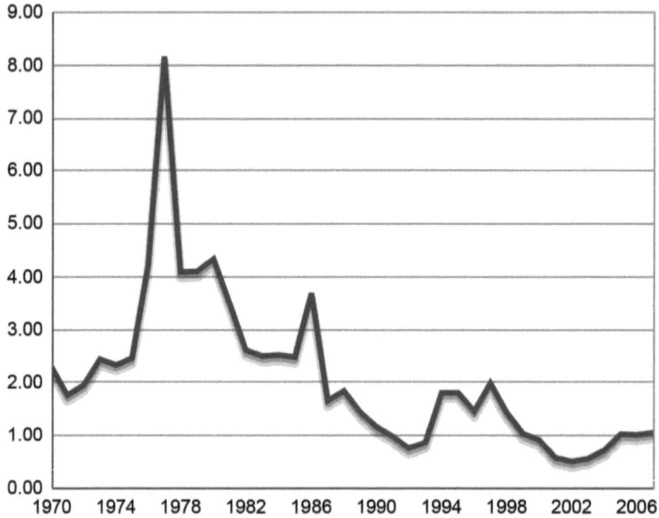

Fig. 5.1 NY price for Brazilian Arabica, 1970–2007, per pound in 2005 $US (Source: USDA 2008)

20 % of the market.) Specifically, it displays the price per pound received by shippers in New York City for Brazilian Arabica, adjusted for inflation. (The prices in each year were converted to an equivalent number of 2005 dollars.) Other coffees were somewhat higher or lower, but the general trend was virtually the same. The high point was a spike in the mid 1970s, when a drought in Brazil led to a global shortage. Since then the overall movement was down, and by 2002 the price had reached an all-time low—so low, in fact, that farmers could no longer even recover their cost of production, much less earn an income. After this the price recovered, but only slightly.

This disaster affected whole countries. Particularly in Africa, it was common for coffee to account for a large share of a country's export earnings. In Burundi, for instance, an astonishing 80 % of all foreign sales were for coffee; the number was over 50 % in Ethiopia and close to that level in Uganda. When coffee earnings collapsed, so did the ability of these countries to earn the precious foreign exchange (dollars and euros) with which they could keep up payments on their foreign debt and perhaps purchase a few imports. So the coffee crisis gripped entire populations and pushed countries further back in their pursuit of economic and social development.

Those of us who are fortunate enough to have witnessed this catastrophe from a distance should also be disturbed. We are the ones who drink the brew purchased at the cost of so much hardship. Moreover, we have the resources to make a difference in how the world coffee market operates—if we understand it. But what exactly is the problem? Why did prices drop to such a low level? Unless we can answer these questions, anything we might try runs the risk of doing more harm than good.

There are many *possible* reasons why coffee prices might fall. Perhaps it has become cheaper to produce the bean in some regions, and this puts pressure on everyone else. Or maybe consumers are buying less of it. Or maybe there is too much coffee being produced, or not the right kind. Or maybe the price is being manipulated by powerful special interests. How would we go about trying to figure out what the true story is? What information should we look for, and how can we analyze to separate reality from fantasy?

Economics offers a helpful tool, supply and demand analysis. This is a fairly simple but highly flexible way of depicting how a market works, and it guides users toward answers to questions like those we have asked about coffee. It doesn't take long to learn, and it has many "add-ons" that permit it to tackle more complex issues, such as those involving labor, natural resources and technology. This chapter is devoted to presenting this tool and explaining how to use it. After a brief look at the assumptions necessary to apply the supply and demand model, the following section introduces the model itself. After this, we will look more closely at the three main building blocks, supply, demand and equilibrium. We then put this model through some practice exercises and conclude by seeing what it has to say about the causes of the coffee crisis.

5.2 Some Simplifying Assumptions

Models require that we impose simplifying assumptions on complex, messy real-world situations. What follows are the most important ones for using supply and demand analysis. Some just make it easier to use, while others are necessary if the model is to be used at all. The line that separates convenience from necessity is not fixed; it shifts as economic theorists delve ever deeper into the logical underpinnings of the relationships that make up the model. There is a lot of prestige attached to being able to demonstrate that a model holds under slightly less restrictive assumptions than previously believed. The assumptions of interest to us here are:

1. There is a single homogeneous type of good or service that can be the subject of a market. You can have a market for running shoes, garden hoes, or haircuts, but first you have to assume that there is a generic item we can identify as a running shoe, a garden hoe or a haircut. More sophisticated models of markets can accommodate qualitative differences, but only in certain specific ways. Most supply and demand models you will see, in this text and elsewhere, simply assume that all goods in the market are identical. From a historical standpoint, this is an extraordinary assumption—one that could only have been made in relatively recent times. For most of human history, production methods were artisanal: each item was individually distinctive, and it wouldn't have occurred to people to treat them as identical. (There are some exceptions; for instance, evidence exists that grain, wine and other commodities were viewed as standardized goods in Roman times.) With the rise of standardization and especially mass production, thinking that similar goods are essentially the

same comes more naturally. We will have more to say about standardization in Chap. 7.

2. Producers produce goods with the intention of selling them, and those who want to use these goods expect to buy them. This should be obvious, but again it is a product of social evolution and has hardly been the case through most of human history. People have to accept and adopt the role of buyer or seller. One of the difficulties with establishing markets in human organs, for instance, is that there is great resistance to adopting these roles.
3. Market participants are self-interested. Sellers want to receive the highest price they can get, and buyers want the lowest price. Neither sacrifices her own interests in the market for the sake of others.
4. Market participants are rational. Here rationality is used in the sense of Chap. 3: people maximize their self-interest through the choices they make. In particular, sellers refuse to sell unless the price they receive is sufficient to cover their costs, and buyers refuse to buy unless the price they pay is less than or equal to the value they get from their purchases. No one is made worse off by entering into a market transaction; no one makes mistakes.
5. A corollary to the previous assumption is the "law of one price": in every market there can be only a single price at any moment in time. No one would agree to buy at a higher price if a lower price were available, and no one would agree to sell at a lower price if a higher price were available. Notice that this "law" is often broken in practice.
6. Other than their market interconnection, individual preferences are independent of one another. What I want to buy and the price I am willing to pay do not depend on what you buy and vice versa, except insofar as your choice affects the market price. The same goes for sellers. This assumption allows us to simply add up the independent demand curves of individuals to get the overall market demand curve, and the independent supply curves of different producers to get the market supply curve. It also guarantees that the supply and demand curves will be independent of one another, so that we can track changes on one side of the market (supply or demand) while holding the other constant.
7. There is a one-time-only interaction between buyers and sellers. Historical time as such does not exist in a supply and demand analysis; rather, we assume that the model represents a single, unrepeated instance. The choices of buyers and sellers may well depend on their expectations of the future, but their participation in the market is instantaneous. In making their choices, they do not take into account any effects their current decisions may have on future market transactions. Each moment in the market is its own universe, with no past or future. (In the language of game theory, a market is a one-shot game, not a repeated game.)

These may seem like very stringent and unrealistic assumptions. As in most aspects of economics, however, it pays to give the matter some benefit of the doubt. The simplifications necessary to employ market analysis are often not too far removed from reality, and experience shows that we can often learn a lot by organizing our thinking in terms of this model. As you will see, for instance, it definitely helps us understand the ups and downs of coffee prices. Moreover, the model provides a baseline, a reasonable starting point for analysis. When we encounter an aspect of real life that forces us to question one of these assumptions, we can then think about how this will alter the conclusions a simple supply and demand analysis would otherwise impose on us. You will see examples of this in later chapters. For now, we will make the assumptions we need to make in order for supply and demand to work as intended—but we will do it *knowing that we are making these assumptions.*

5.3 A First Look

Here is a "naked" supply and demand diagram. It is stripped to its bare essentials. What is being depicted is a market, which, in non-technical terms, consists of all the buying and selling of some particular good or service. Individuals do not appear in this diagram; rather, it represents everyone involved in this market collectively. At this extremely general level, only two kinds of information are recorded, the possible prices people may buy or sell at, and the possible amounts they may buy or sell. All other aspects of the situation—the thoughts or feelings of these people, their relationships to one another, the qualities of the goods being considered—are ignored. Note, incidentally, that there are few labels and no numbers in this diagram. We don't know what goods are being traded, how much or at what price. All we see are two curved lines intersecting in two-dimensional space, bounded on the left and below by measurement axes.

So this is it: the basis for nearly all ground-level economic reasoning. In a nutshell, you would read it in this way: The straight lines represent two axes; the vertical axis is price and the horizontal axis is quantity. Thus, the further "north" we go in this diagram, the higher the prices, and the further "east" we go the higher the quantities of goods being offered for sale or purchase. The supply curve represents the amount individuals wish to sell at various prices. (One assumption behind this curve, and the demand curve as well, is that there will be only one price for all the transactions taking place in this market at any moment in time. The price may change, but only over time, not between individual goods or people.) It is upward-sloping, which is to say that it travels from the southwest to the northeast. At lower prices there are fewer goods offered for sale, and as the price rises more goods are placed on the market. The demand curve represents the amount individuals wish to buy at different prices. It is downward-sloping, which means that at high prices there is less desire to buy, but more at lower prices. Here in a nutshell is the framework for thinking about markets (including coffee markets). Don't worry if Fig. 5.2 is still mysterious at this point: we are just making an initial acquaintance.

Before going further, consider an important point: even though we are drawing curves in a two-dimensional diagram, the relationships they represent are nearly always invisible in real life. That is, in general you don't see supply and demand curves. At any moment in time you see a specific price, or maybe a small range of prices, and a quantity of goods being bought and sold, but you don't see the full

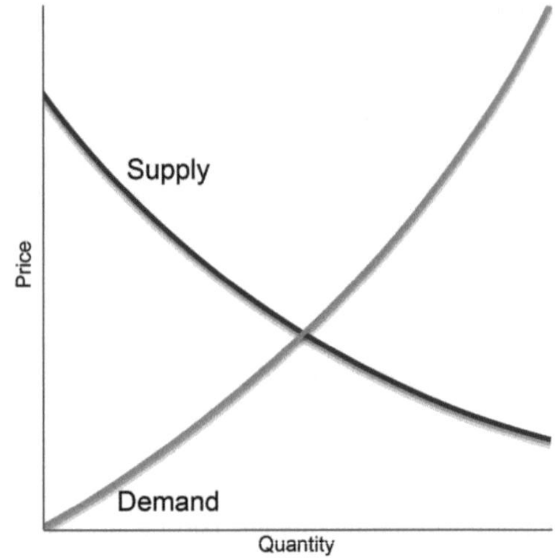

Fig. 5.2 A basic supply and demand diagram

range of *possible* prices and quantities represented by these two curves. True, you might see more price-quantity combinations over a period of time or across different regions, but, strictly speaking, these would not tell you about supply or demand curves at a moment in time and a specific place. (You would also have to use somewhat imprecise statistical techniques to infer separate supply and demand curves from observable trading data.) The closest you can come to actually seeing such curves in real life would be to perform a survey of buyers and sellers, asking them how much they would buy or sell at various prices. Market researchers sometimes do this, but in most cases to which supply and demand analysis is applied, there do not exist "real" curves corresponding to the ones we draw in our diagrams. What this means is that such curves are not real objects we can observe, but intellectual constructs that help us understand how markets work.

Having clarified that point, let's look under the hood. Where do these curves come from, and what shapes can they reasonably take?

(A) The supply curve. The amount of something that people are willing to sell depends on many things. The cost of acquiring this good is an obvious consideration. Perhaps the sellers are making this item themselves, in which case their supply will depend on the cost of materials, the cost and characteristics of labor, the technology, etc. Or they may be middlemen, like wholesalers or retailers, in which case they have to pay attention to the price they have to pay as buyers in some other market. The capacity of the sellers may also be a factor: how many of them are there, and how much do they have in the way of investments, like buildings, land, materials, equipment, etc.? Another influence might be the expectations that sellers have of the future—whether they expect prices to go up or down, for instance, which will persuade them to sell now or wait until later. And of course sellers will be interested in the price they can get if they sell today. For any given situation, the possibilities are almost endless. But the trick employed in economics is to suppose that all of these factors are assumed to be constant, fixed and unchanging, except just one: the current price buyers are offering to pay. This is the meaning of the supply curve. It says that, with all other factors held constant, there is a one-to-one relationship between the going price and the amount sellers wish to sell. (Remember that in a supply and demand diagram there are no individuals, just sellers as a group and buyers as a group.) Each point on the supply curve represents one such combination, and movement along the curve means seeing how a change in the price affects the amount offered for sale. If you go up (northeast) along the curve, the price is rising along with the quantity; the opposite holds for movement down (southwest) along the curve. The story is Pavlovian: flash a price and the sellers will respond with a perfectly predictable amount they want to sell.

There is one critical point to bear in mind: this supposedly predictable relationship between price and quantity depends entirely on the initial assumption that every other factor is being held constant. This assumption is important enough to merit its own name, *ceteris paribus*. The words are Latin, for "things [being] equal". In econospeak, people will say things like, "This relationship holds ceteris paribus." They are simply invoking the common, but sweeping, assumption that nothing else will change that might interfere with the one relationship being examined. In the case of the supply curve, each point along the curve, and the curve as a whole, depends on everything else in the whole world being exactly what it is and staying that way. If anything of significance changes, the whole curve moves. Read that sentence again: if anything of significance changes, the whole curve moves. Understanding why and how this happens is fundamental to understanding the use (and possible misuse) of the supply and demand apparatus.

Let's consider our original example, the global market for coffee. The supply side of this market consists of producers and processors who make coffee beans available to the ultimate consumers, such as most of us. One well-publicized event that occurred was that, during the decade of the 1990s, Vietnam became a major producer. Let us suppose (falsely of course) that this is the only thing that happened on the supply side of the market during the 1990s. We might represent this in the diagram on the following page:

Before Vietnam entered the market the curve might be drawn as S_1, after as S_2. The whole curve has shifted to the right. For any given price, say P*, the world's suppliers, including Vietnam, will produce more: Q_2 instead of Q_1. This is true for any possible price: the new supply curve is completely to the right of the old one. This shift in the supply curve underlines the original point: it was the assumption of ceteris paribus that enabled you to draw the curve in the first place. If this assumption is broken—if some factor of significance other than the market price changes—the whole curve must be redrawn. In this case, the change is rather obvious; the addition of Vietnam to the ranks of major producers leads to a rightward shift in the curve as a whole.

To summarize, we have seen two potential ways prices or quantities can change. Either can change as a result of a change in the other, as we saw represented by movement *along* a supply curve. But either can also change despite *no* change in the

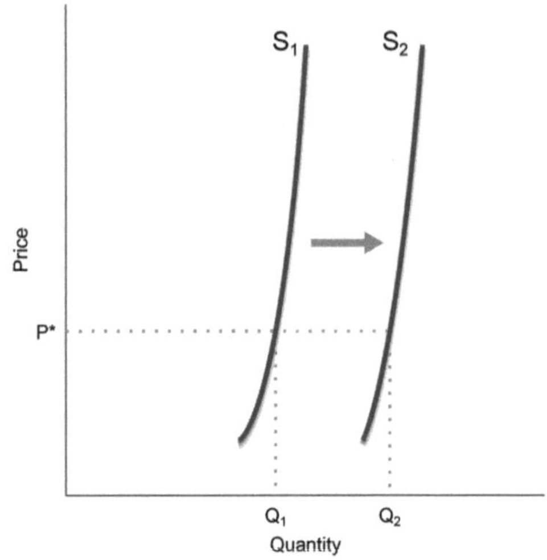

Fig. 5.3 Vietnam expands its coffee production; the supply curve shifts

other, as represented in movement *of* a supply curve. Knowing the difference between these two possibilities is 90 % of what you need to know about this topic.

Take a moment to consider some other hypothetical possibilities. (1) Because of a drought during a crucial phase of the growing season, there is a change in the amount supplied. This will look like a mirror-image of Fig. 5.3. Now the supply curve will shift to the left. Once again there has been a change in one of the factors normally held constant under the ceteris paribus assumption, in this case the productivity of coffee growers. At any potential price they will bring less to the market. (2) Caffeine is found to be a major cause of brain damage. This will *not* cause any shift in the supply curve, because none of the ceteris paribus factors have changed. From the supplier's perspective, the only thing that's changed is the amount consumers are willing to buy, which is to say the amount they will be able to charge if they want to sell their harvest. The supply curve stays put, but there is movement along it—in this case down and to the left. (3) Fair Trade importers offer growers a higher price than the going market rate. Once again the supply remains fixed, since it is the price sellers can get which is changing. The movement is up and to the right along the supply curve, at least for the fortunate growers who are able to qualify under Fair Trade rules.

If this makes sense to you, you are ready for the other 10 %. Take another look at Fig. 5.3. Notice how vertical the supply curve looks in this diagram, compared to the one in Fig. 5.2. Why did I draw it this way? The assumption behind the artwork (I'm being charitable) is that agricultural commodities like coffee have more vertical supply curves than average. The reason for this is that, in the relatively short run (within the growing and harvesting period of a year), the amount that will be produced is more or less what it is, no matter what the going price. Coffee plants don't yield more beans just because the price goes up. The decision to plant, combined with the weather and a few other factors, predetermines the harvest. On the other hand, the curve is not completely vertical, because there is still some discretion on the part of growers. They can harvest more or less intensively, put more or fewer resources into storage and processing in order to cut down on waste, etc. When prices are high, they will squeeze a few more beans out of their operation somehow; the reverse when prices are low. So the supply curve still slants, but only a little.

We have a name for highly vertical supply curves: they are called **inelastic**. There is a formula for calculating the elasticity of a supply curve:

$$\text{elasticity of supply} = \frac{\%\text{change in quantity supplied}}{\%\text{change in price}}$$

We speak of a supply curve as being elastic if the formula has a value greater than one—if the percentage change in quantity is greater than the percentage change in price. It is inelastic if it is less than one. The nearly vertical curves in Fig. 5.3 are highly inelastic. Imagine going from a low price to a high one on either curve. There would be a very large percentage change in the price, perhaps more than 100 % (double), but only a very small percentage change in the quantity, say 5 % or 10 %. So the value of the fraction, with quantity on top and price on the bottom, would be close to zero. A very horizontal curve would have an extremely high elasticity; it could easily be 10 or 20 or 100 (if it were very flat). Here is a tip for making sense of the word "elasticity": think of something elastic like a rubber band. It is highly stretchable; you pull on it and it gets longer. This is the same as the quantity supplied in an elastic supply curve. If the price goes up, the quantity stretches in response. The opposite is true for an inelastic supply curve. Price changes can pull and pull on it, but quantity stretches hardly at all. This may not be the most scientific approach to understanding elasticity, but you might find it useful anyway.

Visually, a supply curve is inelastic if it points downward toward the horizontal axis, which is the case in Fig. 5.3. If it points toward the vertical axis, it is elastic. Of course, unless the supply curve is a straight line, it will point in different directions depending on what part of the curve you look at. Recall from geometry that the slope of a curve at any point is determined by the straight line tangent to it at that point. We could then say that the supply curve is elastic at one point but inelastic at another, depending on the slopes of the corresponding tangents.

Why bother with this terminology of elasticity? One reason is that it gives us a language to talk about the geometry of curves without actually having to draw them. Simply by saying that the supply of coffee is inelastic, I am alluding to a curve such as the one(s) drawn in Fig. 5.3. Moreover, if the supply of coffee really is inelastic, this tells us something about the nature of the coffee industry. In the time frame represented by the diagram, the amount of coffee producers put on the market is not very responsive to the price: the amounts produced at a high price will be very similar to the amounts produced at a low price. This piece of information will prove useful later on when we attempt to unravel the mystery of the coffee crisis.

(B) The same sort of analysis can be applied to the demand side of the market. Many factors affect the amount that consumers want to buy—their desire for the product, the amount of income available to them, the prices of other goods they might buy instead, their expectations about future prices and availability, and certainly the price currently being charged for the good in question. In order to produce a demand curve, we make the assumption that all these factors, except the current price, are held constant, and then we can consider the relationship between price and quantity purchased. This relationship depends on the *ceteris paribus* assumption, just as the supply relationship did; change one of the factors being held constant and the whole relationship changes.

Let's imagine how this would work for the world coffee market. Suppose the buyers we are interested in are the volume coffee purchasers, the "middlemen" who buy from the actual growers and then resell to the companies that sell coffee to people like you and me. These buyers must keep in mind the amount of coffee consumers may be willing to drink, costs of marketing and distribution, and the need to stockpile supplies in times of low prices or draw down stockpiles if prices are expected to rise. But we can also assume that they will buy in larger quantities when current prices are low, and in smaller quantities when they are high. This gives rise to a demand curve such as we see in Fig. 5.4 on the next page.

As you can see from this diagram, at high prices buyers purchase somewhat less; as the price falls, the amount they purchase goes up. Nevertheless, the quantity varies just a little, even if price changes are substantial. That suggests that demand is **inelastic**, just as supply was. The formula for the price elasticity of demand is virtually the same as that for supply:

$$\text{price elasticity of demand} = \frac{\%\text{ change in quantity demanded}}{\%\text{ change in price}}$$

In this case, very large percentage changes in price have very little effect on the percentage change in the quantity demanded; hence the choice of an inelastic demand curve. Is this realistic? Both logic and experience suggest it is. The price of coffee beans is a relatively small part of the total cost of a cup of coffee, so coffee drinkers will tend to buy about the same amount whatever the price of beans. The number of coffee drinkers is generally independent of prices anyway, and wholesalers have little difficulty passing along increased costs.

Note that no change is assumed to take place on the demand side of the market. No events have transpired in the world to change the relationship between the price charged for coffee and the quantity purchased. The demand curve doesn't tell us what the price or the quantity demanded will be, just that if we know one we can deduce the other by finding the corresponding point on the curve.

(C) Equilibrium. So here we have two pieces of information, the supply curve and the demand curve. What do they tell us about events in the coffee market, or any other market? To answer this question, we need to add more assumptions about how buyers and sellers respond to one another.

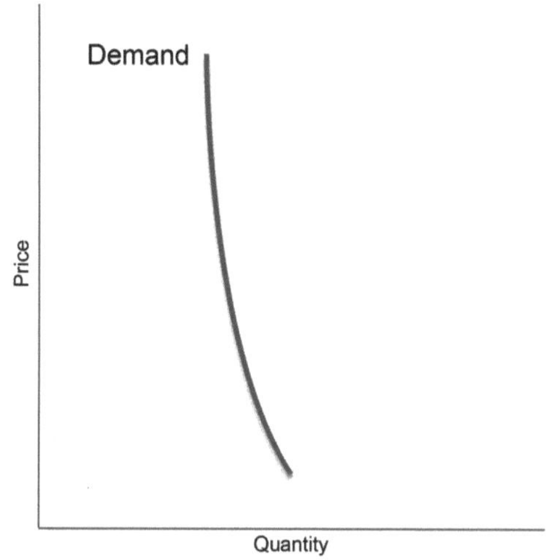

Fig. 5.4 World demand for coffee

Let us assume that buyers always prefer to be at some point on their demand curve rather than off the curve, and that sellers always prefer to be at some point on their supply curve. If this is true, then both can do this simultaneously if and only if their curves cross. The reason is that there can be only one set of prices and quantities for both groups: whatever price buyers are paying is also the price sellers are receiving, and the amount buyers are buying is also the amount sellers are selling. We can see this graphically in Fig. 5.5 on the next page.

At any point along the D curve buyers would be acting in accordance with their intentions. At any point along the S curve sellers would be acting in accordance with their intentions. They are both able to do this simultaneously at price P_2 and quantity Q_2. At any other price this would not be possible. Consider price P_3, for instance. At this price, buyers want to purchase an amount of coffee equal to Q_3, while sellers would prefer to sell Q_1. Both cannot be satisfied. The most likely outcome is that sellers will make Q_1 available, and that is all buyers will be able to acquire. The difference between what they want to buy and what they are able to buy, Q_3 minus Q_1, represents **excess demand**. Those who place their orders first may be able to make their purchases, but there will be other buyers who will be told that all the supplies are gone. An opposite situation would occur at P_1. In this case the amount that buyers wish to buy is less than the amount sellers wish to sell. Some suppliers would manage to make sales at this higher price, but others would be left with unsold stock. This would be a condition of **excess supply**.

Economists generally assume that both excess demand and excess supply are unstable. If either buyers or sellers are not able to make the transactions they wish (as represented by their demand and supply curves), they will have an incentive to change their response to the market. In the case of excess demand, suppliers who find themselves quickly selling out will be tempted to raise prices, and they may find buyers among shoppers who are trying to avoid being frozen out by a shortage. In the case of excess supply, suppliers who find their inventories piling up may try

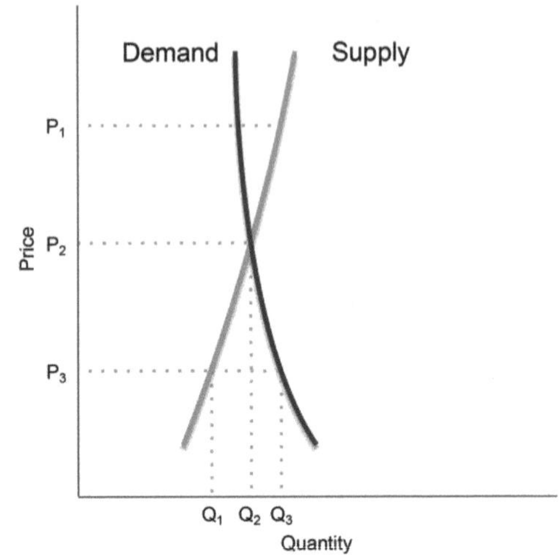

Fig. 5.5 Equilibrium in the coffee market

lowering their prices, and clever consumers will bargain aggressively to take advantage of the situation. Thus excess demand will tend to lead to an increase in prices, and excess supply to a decrease. As long as the price is below P_2 there will be pressure for the price to go up, and vice versa. Only at P_2 is the price at least temporarily stable.

This analysis explains why the term **equilibrium** is used to describe prices and quantities like P_2 and Q_2. A situation is in equilibrium if there are no forces internal to it that would lead to a change; change can come only from the outside. If the situation is in **disequilibrium**, however, change is likely to occur even if no outside factors play a role. In our analysis of demand and supply, the line that separates inside and outside is the ceteris paribus assumption. If this assumption holds—if all the factors that enter into the demand and supply relationships remain constant—then nothing is transpiring on the outside to alter the market. It will remain as it is if it is in equilibrium, which is to say if the market price is P_2. If this is not the price there will be pressure for readjustment, pushing the price toward P_2. The pressure will end only when equilibrium is restored.

It should be apparent that equilibrium is a powerful concept for explaining and predicting how markets will function—the purpose of positive theorizing in economics. Once we have the information that enables us to draw supply and demand curves, we can say with some confidence what prices we expect to see, and how much will be produced and sold. This is true even if the initial situation is not in equilibrium, since the pressures exerted by excess demand and supply will tend to move the market in the direction of equilibrium.

To see the power of this concept, consider a good that is *not* currently bought or sold on the market, such as individual solar-powered helicopters. The technology probably exists to produce this gizmo, and no doubt there are some people who would like to have one. Nevertheless, we don't see them for sale at the mall. Why not?

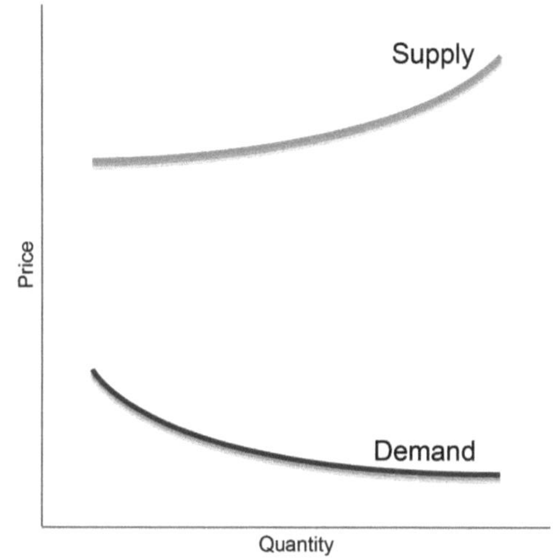

Fig. 5.6 Demand and supply for individual solar-powered helicopters

The market in all likelihood looks like that depicted in Fig. 5.6.

There are prices at which consumers would buy and prices at which producers would produce and sell, but there is no overlap between them: the cheapest price at which such a device can be made is still too expensive for the most rabid consumer. There is no equilibrium price in this market, and the only equilibrium quantity is zero. If the supply-and-demand model of the market, with its predictive notion of equilibrium, is correct, then *every* non-produced good must look something like this. Thus, equilibrium analysis can not only explain the prices we expect to find in the market, but also why there are no markets at all for many potential goods.

At this point it is only fair to mention three important limitations of equilibrium reasoning in economics. First, in the real world few markets are actually in equilibrium at any moment in time. If there are strong pressures pushing markets toward equilibrium, it is also true that the flow of outside events never stops, and this leads to changes in the equilibrium even before the market can get there. At best, equilibrium analysis is approximate; it is not a precise reflection of how markets function. Second, the assumptions we made about excess demand and supply do not always hold. Buyers and sellers may respond as we suggested, but they may not. There are many markets in which excess supply or demand can persist for months or years, with no apparent effect on prices. In those cases the notion of equilibrium as an intersection of demand and supply curves (no excess demand or supply) may be too simplistic. There are more intricate analytical devices (such as those offered by game theory) that can be used to represent more complex forms of equilibrium. (See Box 5.1.) Finally, equilibrium is a positive concept—it helps us explain or predict—but it has no necessary normative significance. Although we already considered this in Chap. 3, it is such an important point that it deserves another paragraph all to itself.

Language can play tricks on us. Words often mean different things in different contexts, and we can go wrong by failing to recognize the distinctions. Equilibrium can give rise to exactly this type of confusion. In normal speech, equilibrium is a desirable state of affairs. The word has connotations of balance and harmony. It is only reasonable to extend this warm, fuzzy feeling to economic equilibrium—reasonable but wrong. In fact, there is no presumption in economics that a market equilibrium is better than a disequilibrium. It all depends on the market. Here is an extreme example: the market in nuclear weapons. It is altogether possible that there are private individuals who have access to nuclear weapons at the present time. Some may have escaped military control during the collapse of the Soviet Union; it may also be the case that countries with secret programs have permitted a few of the weapons to enter the black market. No doubt there are other individuals, many of them terrorists or criminals, who would like to purchase such weapons. Insofar as sellers are motivated by the money they can make selling weapons and buyers are constrained by how much they can afford to pay, there are supply and demand curves, and therefore also a market equilibrium. At some price, the number of nuclear warheads underground arms dealers want to sell is equal to the number potential mass murderers want to buy. With luck, however, the market will *not* reach an equilibrium, and these transactions will never take place.

This is clearly an extreme example, and yet it is not so different in principle from more commonplace economic threats. Many of the goods produced in modern economies are harmful to the environment and to human health. Much of the work performed to manufacture and distribute these goods is hazardous, degrading or oppressive. We can explain why these problems exist using the apparatus of market equilibrium, but we should be clear at all times that explanation is not justification. Equilibrium is a positive, not normative, concept. In the next chapter we shall consider the conditions under which there may (repeat: may) be a connection between equilibrium and human betterment, but for now we should view them as entirely separate and distinct phenomena.

Box 5.1: Excess Demand, Excess Supply and Everyday Life in Market Economies

The standard representation of market equilibrium is where the demand and supply curves intersect: the amount sellers wish to sell is exactly equal to the amount buyers wish to buy at the equilibrium price. If there is either excess demand or excess supply, the price is out of equilibrium, and economists expect it to adjust.

If you think a bit about this, you will realize it does not capture the normal experience we have living in a market economy. The easiest way to see this is to consider what life is like in an economy *not* governed by markets. Much of the world was like this, in fact, until 1989, when the Soviet Union began to collapse and its allies in eastern Europe shed their Communist parties and embraced capitalism. In the old Soviet model, sellers were in a position of power and buyers had to struggle to be able to make a purchase. Stores

(continued)

Box 5.1 (continued)
seldom had enough inventory to meet demand, and there were frequently lines that formed so that scarce items could be distributed on a first-come, first-serve basis. There was no attempt to advertise goods, and sometimes you couldn't even locate where they could be found. The stores themselves often kept most of their wares in a back room: you went to the counter and asked the clerk to see if what you wanted was in stock. With shortages the norm, store employees could play favorites, deciding who to serve on the basis of friendship, gifts or sheer whim.

It is exactly the other way around in a market economy. In most cases there is chronic excess supply: sellers carry more inventory than they can expect to sell, and they knock themselves out trying to convince us to buy more of it. An extreme example is provided by grocery stores. A recent study found that about 10 % of all food items stocked by American groceries is never sold at all, but simply thrown away—in a world in which hundreds of millions of people do not get enough to eat. But this is just a more visible instance of a pattern that holds in most parts of the economy. Hardware stores stock more tools than they can sell, and office supply stores stock more paper. In most restaurants there are more tables than are likely to be filled on all but a few nights, and the remainder bins of bookstores remind us that more books are printed than readers are usually willing to buy.

The point is that much more effort goes into sellers courting consumers than consumers seeking sellers. The advertising industry is built on this fact. It is so fundamental to how we live in market economies that it is easy to lose sight of. Nevertheless, it is worth pondering: why is excess supply so typical of most markets? Is it because of too little competition or competition that is especially intense? Why is it profitable to offer a larger quantity of goods and services than you can expect to sell? One way to approach these questions is to think about markets where excess supply is *not* the norm, such as sales of new cars (where there are wait times for popular models) and medical services (where patients are much more likely to wait for doctors than doctors are to wait for patients). How and why are these examples different?

Whatever answers we give, the fact remains that the simple supply and demand model, with its image of equilibrium where excess supply is zero, is at best an approximate representation of the real world. Economic life would be very different if sellers needed buyers no more than the other way around.

Before leaving the topic of equilibrium, we should consider what the concept means in a world of many markets, all of them interlinked. There are markets for shoes and markets for socks, markets for cars and buses, markets for the goods farmers buy and the goods they sell. What happens in one of these affects the others. When the pressure to get to equilibrium leads to adjustment in one part of the economy, this is experienced as an "outside" force in other markets. A chain reaction is set off, and the effects may ultimately rebound on the market that set the process in motion in the first place. We can make economic analysis much simpler by focusing on just one market at a time, but to do so is to overlook the interconnectedness of real-world economies.

To address this problem, economists have developed the concept of **general equilibrium**. This is a situation in which all markets are in equilibrium simultaneously, each taking the others into account. Economists spent decades investigating the mathematical basis for the hypothesis that economies might have such a general equilibrium. By the mid 1950s it had been proven that this was a logical possibility, although more recently theorists have found new grounds for skepticism. They have shown that economies typically have many potential general equilibria, a problem from the perspective of explanation and prediction. (If an analysis shows that, say, 12 combinations of prices and quantities could all be in equilibrium, how do we know which one is likely to occur?) They have also shown that the adjustment process sparked by excess demand and supply can shift the equilibrium itself, making it more difficult to use the supply-and-demand model to make predictions. We will have more to say about general equilibrium in the final chapter; for now, the main point is that, in using demand and supply curves, it is important to keep in the back of one's mind the possibility that there may be important effects that extend beyond the confines of a single diagram.

5.4 Using Supply and Demand

The best way to get a feel for the supply and demand apparatus is to use it. Let's imagine various situations that might arise in an economy and see how they could be approached with the three building blocks of supply, demand and equilibrium.

(A) Ice cream. Suppose you open a home-made ice cream stand specializing in vegetable flavors—spinach, zucchini, turnip, etc. After the initial burst of demand (because people have been waiting all their lives to try these new taste sensations), you settle into a predictable level of sales. We might ask how various events would affect the amount of ice cream you sell per week and the amount you are able to charge for it. For instance, suppose that global warming produces a month-long heat wave during the late spring. People are looking for cooling, refreshing snacks, like cucumber-cilantro swirl. The result may be depicted as in Fig. 5.7 on the following page.

By shifting the demand curve from D_1 to D_2, we are reflecting the increased desire of consumers to buy ice cream at any price. Even after demand shifts, it is still the case that more ice cream will be bought as the price falls (the curve is downward-sloping), but the quantity is greater. If you pick one price in particular (identified as a vertical distance up the P axis), you can find out what the sales will be by tracing a horizontal line over to the demand curve. First you will reach D_1, which tells you how much will be bought if this is the demand curve, and then you will reach D_2. Since D_2 is to the right of D_1, more ice cream will be bought during

Fig. 5.7 The effect of a heat wave on ice cream sales. Before the heat wave, the demand curve was D_1, resulting in price P_1 and quantity Q_1. After the heat wave, the demand curve shifts to D_2, producing the new equilibrium price P_2 and quantity Q_2

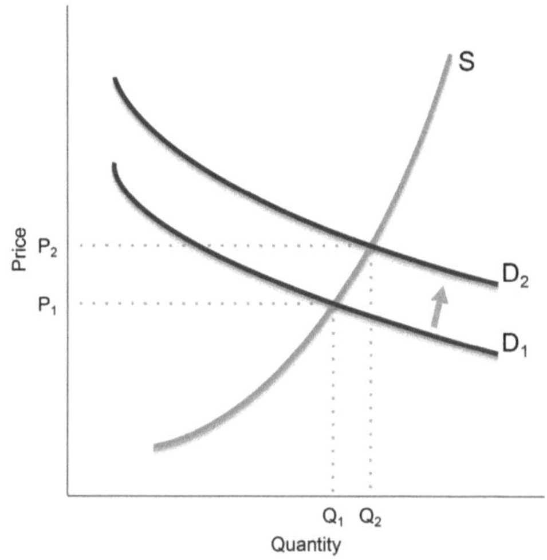

the heat wave than before it. Alternatively, you could think of D_2 as being *above* D_1: for any potential quantity of sales, a higher price can be charged during the heat wave. Note the thought process that led us to shift the demand curve. Because of the higher temperatures, consumer preferences, which are one of the factors normally held constant in conjunction with the *ceteris paribus* assumption, have changed, and this shifts the entire curve. On the other hand, nothing has transpired to change the *ceteris paribus* factors on the supply side; this curve remains where it was.

Applying the concept of equilibrium permits us to make a prediction. We expect that, in the absence of any outside change (like the weather), the market would settle at a price of P_1 and a sales level of Q_1. Due to the heat wave, these will change to P_2 and Q_2. In other words, the price will go up *and* so will the sales. The process has been instigated by a change in the demand curve. Although there has also been a change in the amount of ice cream sold, there has been no change in the supply curve. *We see movement **of** the demand curve and movement **along** the supply curve.* Knowing which curve to move and which to keep in place is 90 % of the art of applying the supply-and-demand framework.

Now suppose that, rather than a change in the weather, we see a change in the tax laws. What happens if the city decides to raise money by placing a tax on ice cream vendors for each scoop they sell? We can picture the result in Fig. 5.8 as shown on the following page.

If ice cream sellers such as yourself have to pay a tax, this increases your costs and means that you now need to charge a higher price than before. In other words, your supply curve will shift upward (or to the left). On the other hand, nothing has changed to alter the relationship between the price and the quantity consumers want to buy, so the demand curve stays put. The equilibrium quantity sold will fall from Q_1 to Q_2, while the equilibrium price will rise from P_1 to P_2. Note that the increase in price per scoop is substantially less than the amount of the tax per scoop. (You can read the size of the tax increase from the vertical distance between S_2 and S_1,

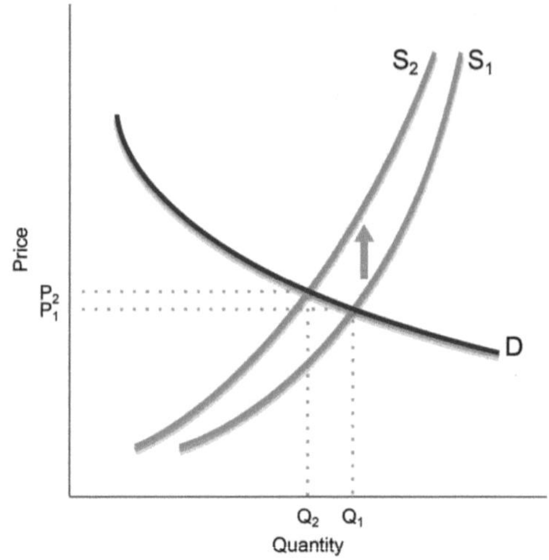

Fig. 5.8 The effect of a tax increase on the ice cream market. The original supply curve is S_1, resulting in equilibrium price P_1 and quantity Q_1. After a tax is placed on ice cream sellers, the new supply curve is S_2, with equilibrium price P_2 and quantity Q_2

which indicates how much the cost per scoop has risen for sellers.) This means that sellers are able to pass along some of the tax increase, but not all of it. By looking closely at this diagram, you can see that the portion that can be passed on to consumers depends on the slope of the demand curve, loosely related to the price elasticity of demand. As drawn, the demand curve is rather elastic: relatively small changes in price induce consumers to make relatively large changes in their ice-cream eating habits. What if the D curve were inelastic—more nearly straight up and down? If you try this out on a piece of scratch paper, you should find that the price increase becomes larger and the quantity decrease smaller. At the limit, with a perfectly inelastic (vertical) demand curve, all of the tax increase could be passed along to the consumer. At the other limit, with a perfectly elastic (horizontal) demand curve, none of the tax could be passed along, and all would be absorbed by the seller.

This gives us one clue toward why economists think about the elasticity of demand and supply. As demand becomes more inelastic, suppliers gain more power over buyers; they can increase prices with relatively little concern about lower sales. But what determines the elasticity of demand? Many factors are relevant, but the most important ones are tied to a single word: substitutes. If consumers have ample opportunity to substitute other goods for the one being considered, their demand will be elastic. This was the assumption that led to the fairly elastic demand curve in Figs. 5.7 and 5.8; presumably most consumers of ice cream have alternative ways to spend their money that are almost as satisfying, and so they will be sensitive to relatively small price changes. An opposite case would be cigarette smokers, whose tobacco consumption is relatively insensitive to price shifts. (This is not to say that prices have no effect at all, just less than for ice cream, because of the addictive quality of nicotine.)

(B) Housing in a college town. Here our example will be the market for apartment rentals in a college town. To simplify matters, we will overlook all the differences in size, quality and location that affect prices and assume that there is a single "standard" apartment available at the same rent everywhere. (This is only for the purpose of keeping the analysis within a single diagram; in principle we could incorporate all these differences if we were willing to draw a separate diagram for each type and location.) What does the demand curve look like? It is probably moderately inelastic. There are substitutes for renting an apartment—doubling up in existing units, living with parents or other relatives, or finding some other town to live in and commuting—but these are not always convenient. (The reality of homelessness in our communities demonstrates that many of our neighbors can find neither an affordable apartment nor a satisfactory alternative.) As for the supply curve, it is almost completely inelastic in the short run. In other words, within the next few months the supply of housing is nearly fixed; it can only be augmented or diminished slightly by decisions involving repairs to marginal units or potential subdivision. Only in the long run, over a horizon of several years, is it possible to greatly increase the amount of housing available through new building or to remove a large number of units through demolition or conversion to new uses. So let us stick with the short run for now. As a first exercise, imagine how the market will change if the local college expands to take on more students. This is shown in Fig. 5.9 on the next page.

As more students move to town to attend the college, the housing market becomes saturated. If no measures are taken to anticipate this, the supply will increase only marginally, from Q_1 to Q_2; meanwhile, the equilibrium rent will shoot up from P_1 to P_2. Only in the long run, as more apartments are built and the supply curve shifts to the right, will rents moderate.

We could well imagine that, if rents skyrocket as in Fig. 5.9, there will be pressure to hold them back politically. One way to do this is rent control. Rent control laws can take many forms, but they all have in common a legislative prohibition of rent increases above a certain percentage or in the absence of certain types of investment. If rent control is adopted in our hypothetical town, the immediate result might be a situation like that in Fig. 5.10 on the following page.

A new controlled rent, P_c, might be established, higher than the original level (P_1) but below the level that would otherwise result in the market after the influx of students (P_2). Fortunately, in the short run, there would be almost no visible effect on the number of apartment units available for rental. (There isn't room in the diagram to depict a Q_c between Q_1 and Q_2.) The danger, however, is that a poorly drafted rent control law could have damaging effects in the long run. This can be seen in Fig. 5.11 on p. 89.

Once again, rent control reduces the rent students and others have to pay, but now there is a bigger difference in the number of apartments available. The more the demand curve shifts to the right, the greater the gap, over time, between the apartment supply at market rents and at controlled rents. Meanwhile, with a shortage of apartments, opportunities open up for black market-type activities. Renters can sublet their apartments for a considerable profit, and landlords can charge "finder's fees" and other dubious charges to take advantage of the scarcity. These and other stratagems are commonplace in cities with rent control laws. On the other hand, a well designed law can mitigate most of these effects if it

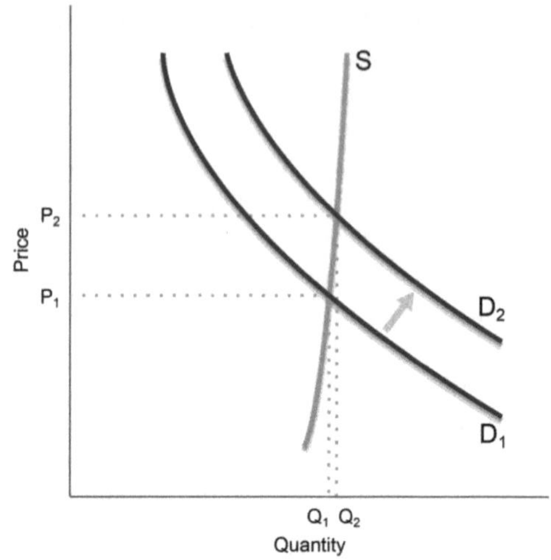

Fig. 5.9 The effect of a college expansion on the local apartment market. The initial demand curve is D_1, producing the equilibrium price P_1 and quantity Q_1. After the college accepts more students, the demand curve shifts to D_2, and the new equilibrium price is P_2 and quantity Q_2

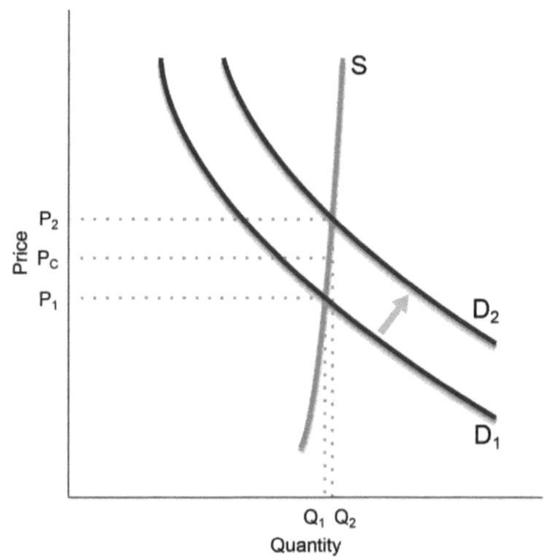

Fig. 5.10 The short run effect of rent control on a local apartment market. In the absence of rent control, a shift from D_1 to D_2 would result in an increase in the equilibrium rental price from P_1 to P_2. To prevent this, a rent control is imposed, restricting the rise in price to P_C. The result is that the price rise has been limited, with hardly any effect on the number of apartments offered—in the short run

incorporates incentives for new building. It is scarcity, not intervention in the market per se, that leads to the worst aspects of rent control.

5.5 Another Cup of Coffee

Keeping the supply and demand apparatus in mind helps us decipher the changes that roiled the world coffee market. We have already considered the reasons why both the supply and demand curves for coffee are likely to be highly inelastic. (The shapes of these curves could be measured using real-world data, but the technical

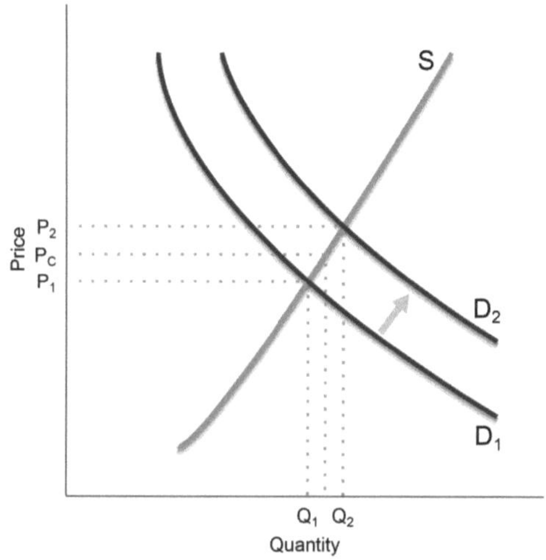

Fig. 5.11 The long run effect of rent control on a local apartment market. In the long run, supply is more elastic. Now the effect of imposing rent control at P_C is to reduce the number of apartments supplied to the market well below Q_2, the number that would be supplied with demand curve D_2 and without rent control

aspects of that procedure would take us away from the subject matter of this chapter.) How about the fluctuations of price and quantity?

The most important single fact to know about coffee is that, until 1989, the major producing countries collaborated on an International Coffee Agreement. This arrangement established export quotas, limiting supply in order to bolster prices. The agreement fell apart in that year, and each country was then free to produce as much as it wanted. It takes about 5 years from the time of initial planting to the first harvest, so it was not until the mid 1990s that the full effect of this change was felt. In 1994/95 world production was about 90 million bags; this total rose to about 115 million bags in 2001/02. The biggest increase came from a new kid on the block, Vietnam. Partly in response to World Bank advice (backed up by loans), Vietnam increased its production from 1.5 million bags in 1990 (when export quotas were lifted) to 15 million in 2000. Brazil was another source of added supply, due to large investments in acreage and new technology. Meanwhile prices for the highest quality coffee, arabica, fell from a high of $2.00 a pound in 1980 to $1.30 in 1995 and just over $.50 in 2002 (all in 1990 dollars). The combination of modest production increases and drastic price decreases tells us what we most need to know about the causes of the coffee crisis. Figure 5.12 on the next page, which is only slightly different from Fig. 5.4, captures these numbers vividly.

With demand so inelastic, it takes only small increases in supply to result in large drops in the market price. Each producing country, by trying to increase its exports so as to make up in quantity what it is losing in value, makes the problem that much worse for all of them. The International Coffee Agreement, which kept the supply curve modestly to the left, was welcomed by consumers but sorely missed by producers.

What can we learn about the uses of supply and demand from this example? The most important lesson is that the supply and demand model of markets does not provide any answers in itself; it is a convenient framework for sorting out

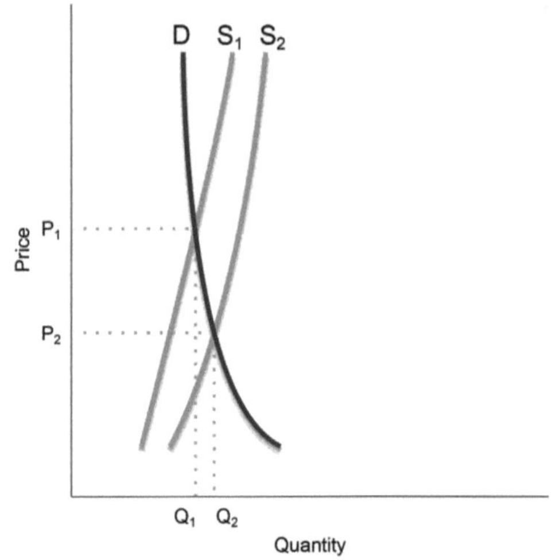

Fig. 5.12 Contours of the coffee crisis. With the ending of export quotas, supply of coffee rose from S_1 to S_2. This led to a decline in the equilibrium price from P_1 to P_2

information and organizing our thinking. In this respect it is like a language: it provides a syntax that makes it easier to produce certain complex ideas—at the cost (which is also true of language) of making it harder to produce other types of ideas. In this case, we saw that we were able to disentangle information about production and demand. Asking about elasticity drew our attention to certain features of the coffee market that are highly relevant to understanding the crisis, but which might have been overlooked otherwise. Above all, it gave us a simple way to imagine the relationship between relatively small quantity effects—a 7 year rise of 28 %—and very large price effects—a corresponding decline of 62 %.

This illustrates the general point about models. If we are willing to make a number of simplifying assumptions, we can construct potential scenarios for real-world events. The power of models lies in their ability to highlight logical interconnections that might be difficult to see without them. The weakness stems from all the assumptions we have to make, some of which might blind us to important aspects of the problems we care about. What were some of those assumptions in our coffee analysis? We assumed that nothing important happens between the sale of coffee by growers and its ultimate purchase by consumers; all the complications of middlemen, marketing arrangements and brand identity are simply ignored. Also, the international character of this market—its production and distribution across national boundaries, requiring the conversion of different national currencies—is put to the side. (The market is treated as if it all took place at a single location.) Finally, specific sub-markets, such as those for organic, fair-traded and "gourmet", are not taken into consideration. In other words, the coffee market is not nearly as homogeneous as the model implies. Some of these excluded complexities could be reintroduced through more detailed use of supply and demand analysis, but others are hard to squeeze into this model.

In addition, we should be clear about what we get from using economic models. These devices do not "prove" anything; they assist and illustrate. Moreover, useful models are flexible. They don't give predetermined answers to questions, but help us gather and organize information. It wasn't the supply and demand model that told us about the importance of the International Coffee Agreement, but instead the information we dug up, prompted by the needs of the model. In another market we might well come to a completely different understanding of the key forces at work; in fact, this will be the case when we revisit the coffee crisis in Chap. 14.

Models, because they purchase their insights at the price of their assumptions, should be used with care. This warning applies with special force to economic models, because the problems they are directed at are extremely complex, and because economics is just one of many perspectives that people have found to be helpful.

The Main Points

1. The following simplifying assumptions make it possible to employ the supply and demand analysis presented in this chapter: (a) each market corresponds to a single category of homogeneous goods, (b) producers and consumers adopt the roles of sellers and buyers, (c) all market participants are self-interested and (d) rational, (e) the law of one price holds, (f) each participant's desired choices are independent of everyone else's except through their effects on the market price, and (g) market "time" is instantaneous and not repeated.
2. The supply curve registers the amount producers of a good or service wish to offer to the market across a range of potential prices. Because it is about what they *want* to offer, it is a behavioral relationship: a given price induces a given desired supply. Of course, the amount offered will be a function of many factors, including the cost of inputs, the technology that transforms inputs into outputs that can be sold, the number and capacity of potential suppliers, expectations of future supply conditions, and the price buyers are willing to pay. To draw a supply curve, all of these factors must be held constant *except* the sale price, so that it is possible to determine the quantity offered at each price. If none of the factors being held constant (the *ceteris paribus* factors) change, there can be only movement *along* the supply curve as demand conditions change. If one or more of the *ceteris paribus* factors changes, there is movement *of* the supply curve: a different quantity will be offered to the market even at the original sale price. The supply curve is normally upward-sloping: an increase in the sale price will typically induce suppliers to offer more of their goods or services to the market.
3. The elasticity of supply tells us how responsive the quantity of market supply is to the price at which the supply can be sold. The formula is:

$$\text{elasticity of supply} = \frac{\%\ \text{change in quantity supplied}}{\%\ \text{change in price}}$$

If the elasticity of supply is greater than one, we say that supply is "elastic". If it is less than one, we say it is "inelastic". An elastic supply curve is relatively flat and points toward the vertical axis; an inelastic supply curve is relatively steep and points toward the horizontal axis.

4. The demand curve registers the amount consumers of a good or service wish to buy across a range of potential prices; it too is a behavioral relationship. The amount buyers desire to buy is a function of many factors, such as their personal preferences, their incomes, the price and availability of substitute goods, expectations of future conditions, and the purchase price. We draw the demand curve by holding all other factors constant (*ceteris paribus*) except for the price. If none of these other factors change, there can be only movement along the demand curve as the price changes. If one or more of them does change, we will see movement of the demand curve. The demand curve is normally downward-sloping: an increase in the purchase price will normally lead to a reduction in the amount buyers wish to buy.
5. The price elasticity of demand tells us how responsive the quantity of market demand is to the price buyers have to pay. The formula is:

$$\text{price elasticity of demand} = \frac{\%\text{ change in quantity demanded}}{\%\text{ change in price}}$$

   If the (absolute value of the) price elasticity is greater than one, we say that demand is price-elastic. If it is less than one we say it is price-inelastic. An elastic demand curve is relatively flat and situated more toward the NW (upper-left) portion of the price-quantity quadrant; the opposite is true for an inelastic demand curve.
6. Market equilibrium occurs when both behavioral conditions—the supply and demand curves—hold at the same price and quantity. That is, the equilibrium price is the one at which buyers and sellers both want to buy/sell the same quantities, and the equilibrium quantity is the one which would be purchased/sold at the same equilibrium price. In the simple models of this chapter, this is where the two curves intersect. Note, however, that equilibrium is a general concept in economics—a state in which all parties are acting simultaneously according to their preferences, such that their choices are mutually consistent—and it applies to "supply = demand" only under particular conditions. Later we will see examples where equilibrium occurs when supply does not equal demand.
7. A second aspect of equilibrium has to do with the tendency for a situation to return to equilibrium if it departs from it for some reason. In the case of a simple supply and demand model, this results from assumptions about excess demand and supply. We assume that, if there is excess demand, potential buyers who are unable to make purchases will offer to pay higher prices, and sellers will agree to do this: in this way, the price rises until excess demand is eliminated. If there is excess supply, some sellers are unable to find buyers, so we assume they offer to lower their sales price. This continues until the price falls to the point at which excess supply disappears.

8. Many goods that could be produced and sold do not actually exist. Supply and demand theory tells us that there is no price at which at least some producers wish to sell for which there are at least some buyers willing to buy.
9. There is no presumption in economics that equilibrium situations are "good". The concept of equilibrium is used for predictive and explanatory (positive) purposes only; it has no normative content. A situation could be horrendous for society, and even for most direct participants, and still be an equilibrium.

▶ Terms to Define

Ceteris paribus
Demand curve
Elastic vs inelastic supply/demand
Elasticity of supply
Excess demand
Excess supply
General equilibrium
Market disequilibrium
Market equilibrium
Movement of vs movement along a curve
Price elasticity of demand
Supply curve

Questions to Consider

1. Suppose you are given the job of estimating the global supply curve for coffee, so that your supply and demand curve can be based on real numbers. How would you go about doing this? First, clarify in your mind exactly the information you will need; then suggest a research strategy. (You can assume you have an unlimited budget at your disposal.)
2. Suggest a good whose supply curve, like coffee, is likely to be highly inelastic. Select another you think will be highly elastic. Explain your reasoning.
3. The amount of oil under the surface of the earth is fixed; no more can be created within a time scale meaningful to human beings. Does this mean that its supply is inelastic?
4. In recent years a vigorous international market has developed in kidneys. Impoverished but healthy people in developing countries are paid to undergo surgical removal of their kidneys, which are then sold to wealthier kidney patients who need a kidney transplant but can't get one through legitimate channels. What would it mean for this market to be in equilibrium? Do you think it should be in equilibrium? If not, what would you propose to do about this problem?
5. For hundreds of years there have been programs, and proposals for programs, to stabilize the supply of agricultural commodities like coffee, building up reserves

after abundant harvests and drawing them down after poor ones. How would you show this process using supply and demand curves? How does this differ from the quota system of the International Coffee Agreement? Which, if either, would you favor as a response to the coffee crisis? Why?

Markets and Human Well-Being 6

6.1 Introduction

The preceding chapter was almost entirely about positive economics: how markets work, and how the apparatus of supply and demand analysis can be used to explain economic outcomes or predict how future events may alter the fortunes of individuals and groups tied to the economic system. This is economics as plumbing or dentistry—no values to speak of, just technique. But the great interest most of us have in economic issues is not just technical. We care about meeting human needs, improving living standards and pursuing other goals like liberty, equality and sustainability. This means that we care deeply about the normative side of economics, what it can tell us about whether economic arrangements are *good*. So this chapter is an introduction to normative models in economics, the foundation for thinking analytically about the desirability of economic institutions and policies.

To see normative economics in action, just open a newspaper. Would people be better off if taxes were lower or if they were raised? And who are the "right" people to carry the lion's share of the tax burden? Should the minimum wage be raised? Do corporations use their power to exploit workers and the general public, or should we provide more public support for them so they will make more investments? Should people who download music or movies from the internet be tracked down and prosecuted? How serious are the economic consequences of global warming likely to be, and what is the most effective way to combat it? Should all national borders be open to free trade in agricultural goods, without tariffs or subsidies? What, if anything, should be done to reduce unemployment?

People have opinions on these things, but being opinionated is not enough. As we will see, it is possible to analyze such questions systematically, to use the tools of modeling and evidence-gathering to demonstrate that some opinions have more basis than others. The particularly economic approach is to try to forecast and evaluate the *consequences* of adopting one policy or another. The measuring stick is human well-being.

P. Dorman, *Microeconomics*, Springer Texts in Business and Economics,
DOI 10.1007/978-3-642-37434-0_6,

6.2 A Historical Detour

There are two ways we might think about economics and well-being. We could ask, how well do market systems respond to human interests? Does a "free" market, one left to function without political interference, do this well on its own, or does it need to be managed and directed? Under what conditions are the flaws of market systems more pronounced? What types of interventions can repair markets that malfunction? The other way is to ask, how can we use the market mechanism to promote the values we care about, both economic and noneconomic? Are there limits to the usefulness of this mechanism, and if so, what are they? The first approach begins with the reality of markets and asks how well they conform to our values. The second begins with the reality of our values and asks how well markets can be harnessed to them. Both converge in the same sort of analysis, as we will see, although they have somewhat different political and ideological histories.

The first question is associated with Adam Smith, perhaps the greatest of all economic thinkers (given the state of knowledge in his day). Smith was born in Scotland and lived from 1723 to 1790—as we have seen, a time of rapid social and economic change. The industrial revolution was in full swing, even as the traditional institutions that governed British life, the aristocracy and the church, were receding in influence. Huge fortunes were being made, new cities sprang up where there were once swamps and cottages, and age-old ways of life were disappearing with alarming speed. What terrified contemporary observers more than anything else was the sense that no one was in control. Society was being transformed, but no conscious body of thought or organization was setting a direction or guarding against potential disasters. It was Smith's great contribution to argue in his most famous book, *On the Wealth of Nations*, published in 1776, that the lack of control was a virtue, not a vice. He explained that self-interest could work to social advantage providing there was a system of general competition, pitting the ambitions of each citizen against the others. Such a system he dubbed an "invisible hand", and the term has stuck. The Invisible Hand argument holds that free, competitive markets, powered by the self interest of their individual participants, will guide society towards the attainment of social values more surely than any government's visible hand of regulation and control.

But Smith did not prove his Invisible Hand hypothesis; he only explained it in persuasive language. In fact, it was nearly a century before a new generation of economists would begin the systematic investigation of whether, and under what circumstances, the hypothesis really holds. Out of their labors came the set of economic models we will consider in this chapter. As we will see, the case for unregulated markets is not nearly as strong as Smith thought, and many flaws, which can be specified with great precision by modern economists, demand attention. From an original utopia of free markets, as envisioned by Adam Smith, we make our way toward a more complicated, mixed system to serve our individual and social interests.

The second question was posed by a near-contemporary of Smith, Jeremy Bentham (1748–1832), the founder of the philosophical school of

Utilitarianianism. This is a term that is often misunderstood, since its philosophical meaning is different from its everyday use. Usually, when we speak of a "utilitarian" attitude, we refer to an emphasis on usefulness. If you are more likely to spend a sudden infusion of money on a vacuum cleaner or a garden tool than a painting or a vacation, we would probably call you utilitarian. This is fine for ordinary usage, but in philosophy the word means something else altogether. To be a philosophical utilitarian is to hold that the rightness of any action can be determined by adding up the sum of its consequences for human happiness: add (in some fashion) all the additions to happiness it causes and subtract all the deductions from happiness that may also result. That act is best which produces the highest happiness total: "the greatest good for the greatest number". One way to think about this philosophy is to focus on what it *doesn't* say. It denies that there are any general rules for how people should act, nor that the concept of rights should play a role. For utilitarians, the ends—the calculable consequences of any act—justify the means. Further, it considers only human happiness worthy of promotion, not any other objective, and it treats this ineffable entity as something that can be manipulated with mathematical precision.

For our purposes, the radical stance taken by Benthamite philosophy is not relevant. What matters is that Bentham was the first political thinker to take seriously the notion that policies and institutions should be justified *instrumentally*, on the basis of the consequences they would likely lead to, rather than on first principles of one sort or another. (Of course, many great thinkers, from Mo-zu to Ibn Khaldun, had thought deeply about the effects they expected from their recommended policies, but mainly to substantiate the general principles they held, not as ends in themselves.) Bentham took as his starting point the emerging liberal (individualistic[1]) society in which he lived: most people undertook most acts on the basis of their perceived self-interest. They were not idealists, and it was impractical to base political decisions on the hope that they would transform themselves into idealists just because someone told them to. Rather, Bentham posed the problem, how can we make the self-interest of individuals conform to the interest of society? What changes can we make through laws and regulations that will lead each individual to act in such a way that it results in the attainment of the utilitarian ideal of maximum happiness? Because he was unencumbered by bonds of tradition or conceptions of inalienable rights (to use the term penned by Thomas Jefferson), Bentham was willing to manipulate political and economic conditions without limit—provided it "worked" according to his criteria. To put it differently, the only limit was the technical limit of the methods themselves.

[1] In this text we will use the world "liberal" in its original meaning: a policy or institution is liberal if it minimizes restrictions on free individual choice. Espousal of free markets is one of the clearest examples of liberalism in this sense; so is freedom of speech, freedom to travel etc. In contemporary US usage, a liberal is someone who favors more rather than less economic regulation, but also less political control over private behavior. This means that a liberal (in the everyday sense) is a liberal (in our sense) in social policy but not economic policy. Also, note that the word carries no moral weight for us; it is not necessarily good or bad to be a liberal in either sense.

(If Bentham in his day could have performed brain surgery on every British citizen to get them to want to promote the public good, he would have done so without hesitation.) Since most of his methods involved economics, increasing the cost of acts that foster unhappiness or the reward to acts that foster happiness, this comes down to the limits of the economic system itself. In the end, Benthamite tinkering converges, more or less, on Smithian fixes to the Invisible Hand

6.3 The Invisible Hand

Leaping forward to the present, we are ready to undertake the analysis of what markets actually do for (or to) us, and what they might be enlisted to do. Recall the concepts of cost and benefit that were introduced in Chap. 4. Keep in mind their specifically economic meaning: a benefit is measured by the amount a consumer would be willing to pay for some product of the economy, and a cost is the value of an input used to produce something, usually an opportunity cost but sometimes a disutility. Finally, remember that economic efficiency, the supreme normative value in conventional economics (but not in some of its older and newer variants), demands that we maximize the surplus of benefits over costs. Two more terms will need to be introduced, **marginal benefit** and **marginal cost**.

Marginal benefit is the additional benefit that results from some activity. Prior to the activity there was a certain amount of benefit available to the members of an economy; after there was a bit more. The difference is the marginal benefit. Here's an example. Suppose our economy has a certain number of bicycles in use. Those who ride them derive benefits, and we can say for the sake of analysis that each of these benefits can be measured by the maximum amount the individual involved would be willing to pay for the bicycle he or she owns and rides. If we add up all these quantities, the sum would be the monetary value of the total benefit derived from bicycles. Now suppose one additional bike is produced, and somewhere there is a person who wants it more than anyone else. If this potential buyer is willing to pay a maximum of $400 for that bike, we can say that the marginal benefit it generates is $400. (Perhaps with this added bike the total benefit derived from all bikes has increased from $4,691,818,253 to $4,691,818,653. I'm making this up.)

Similarly, we can talk about marginal costs. The marginal cost of something is the additional cost entailed by it. Suppose the cost of producing that one additional bike is $300; that would be its marginal cost. Perhaps before the bike was produced, a total of $4,113,738,701 was expended to compensate the opportunity costs and disutility involved in bike production, and afterward the number rose to $4,113,739,001. The difference is the marginal cost of the additional bike.

> Stop and think for a moment. Do you expect that economists would be likely to recommend that this extra bike be built? Why or why not? If you can see the argument that's beginning to emerge, much of the remainder of this section will strike you as obvious.

As already discussed in Chap. 4, the net benefit to society of some activity is the total benefit of that activity minus the total cost:

$$NET\ BENEFIT = TOTAL\ \ BENEFIT - TOTAL\ COST$$

The mathematical character of this definition—the sense that costs can be subtracted from benefits—depends on both being measured in the same unit, money. If they were not in the same units, and if there were no way of comparing the quantity of one to the other, the concept of net benefit would be obscure or even meaningless. Thus, it is a bit odd (robotic) to speak of the "net benefit" of a friendship; the costs of maintaining a friendship are difficult to compare to the benefits. But the scope of economics has widened in recent years to encompass many non-obvious applications, such as the decision to marry or to have children, based on ingenious methods for quantifying intangible costs and benefits. Most economists, to carry on their craft as they usually understand it, are dedicated to expressing as many things as possible in monetary units.

The concept of net benefit applies at any level, individual, community, national or worldwide. I can ask whether I get a positive net benefit from buying a gallon of milk, whether my community would get a net benefit from a new dairy being established in the region, or whether the world would be better off if there were an international agreement to limit government subsidies to dairy farmers. For economists, finding and taking advantage of opportunities to increase net benefits is the entire point of their profession. Recall the image of an economy as a machine, with costly inputs entering at one end and beneficial outputs emerging at the other; economic efficiency means maximizing the net benefits produced by this machine.

Now we arrive at the central question posed by Adam Smith: does an economic machine based on the framework of free markets tend to produce a maximum (or sufficiently close to maximum) amount of net benefits? This is equivalent to asking about the relationship between the individual choices made by the people who make up those markets and the (hypothetical) choice an entire society would make if it had all the relevant information about the potential costs and benefits of everything that might be done in production or consumption. If the two coincide—if the individual choices in a market economy add up to a corresponding social benefit—Smith's faith in the free market would be vindicated; if not, we would have to look elsewhere for economic guidance. This is why people have spent the past two centuries plus change debating the merits of Smith's Invisible Hand.

6.4 The Market Welfare Model at the Level of a Single Market

A simple way to formalize the Invisible Hand argument is to present it in the form of a logical deduction which we will call the **Market Welfare Model** (MWM). Note, incidentally, that the world "welfare" is used in the general sense of well-being rather than the narrow one of "payments to beneficiaries of public programs".

In this context, think of welfare as in the phrase "promoting the public welfare", not "being on welfare".

The Market Welfare Model has three premises and a conclusion.

Premises:

1. The demand curve for a good or service represents its marginal benefits to society.
2. The supply curve for this good or service represents its marginal cost to society.
3. There is a single, stable market equilibrium represented by the intersection of these two curves.

Conclusion: The market equilibrium represents the level of production of this good or service which maximizes its net benefit to society.

Stated this way, the MWM is an if–then proposition: *if* the following conditions hold, *then* a particular conclusion can be drawn. All three assumptions must obtain in any situation for the conclusion to be valid; violating any one of them calls the conclusion into question. To restate it slightly, the MWM stipulates the precise conditions that must be met at the level of a single market if the Invisible Hand proposition is to be accepted.

If you are familiar with calculus the proof of this proposition is almost trivial. Since the formula for net social benefit, NB, is

$$TB - TC = NB \tag{6.1}$$

where TB is total benefit and TC is total cost, simply take the derivative and set it equal to zero:

$$MB - MC = 0 \tag{6.2}$$

We can write Eq. 6.2 because MB is the derivative of TB, and MC is the derivative of TC. Since, by assumption, MB is the demand curve and MC is the supply curve, maximum net benefits occur where their magnitudes (i.e. heights) are equal—at market equilibrium. (The non-trivial part of the proof is what establishes that there is only one such point of equality; without going into detail, it is enough at this point to say that the third condition of the Market Welfare Model addresses this in a loose, descriptive manner.)

It is just as easy to show this proof graphically. To do this, we need to know how marginal costs and benefits would be depicted visually. For an answer, consider a possible demand curve for bicycles:

The curve tells us how many bicycles would sell at each possible price. If the price falls to $400, we can imagine that one more person, who was not willing to buy a bike at a higher price, is just barely convinced to put his money down. Let's call this person George. George is the buyer of this last bike, and his willingness to

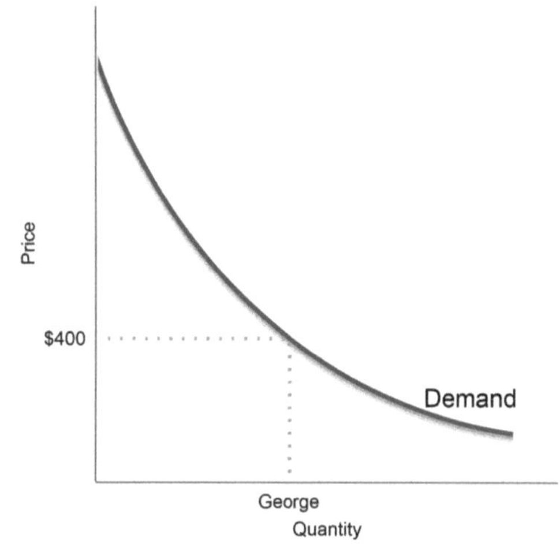

Fig. 6.1 A demand curve for bicycles, with particular attention to George. When the price falls to $400 one more bicycle is sold, to someone named George. George is exactly willing to pay $400 for it—not a penny more. This willingness to pay reflects the marginal benefit of the bike to George and to the society that includes him as a member

pay for it is exactly $400. If we accept the notion that the willingness to pay (WTP) represents the benefit that the individual gets for something, and that the benefit to society is nothing more than the sum of the benefits to the individuals that make it up, then the acquisition of this bike generates $400 more benefit to George *and* to his society. (George's own net benefit is zero, of course, because the amount he is paying is exactly equal to the value he receives.) This is nothing other than the marginal benefit of this last bicycle. We can represent it on the diagram as a vertical line going from the horizontal axis up to the demand curve—the dotted line in Fig. 6.1.

But this is just the marginal benefit of one bicycle. In addition to George, there are lots of other people who are also making purchases: everyone to the left of George, which is to say everyone whose willingness to pay exceeds $400. For each of these buyers there is a marginal benefit line, as there was for George, covering the vertical distance from the horizontal axis to the demand curve at the point on that curve represented by that person. For instance, if Louise has a very high willingness to pay for bikes, she will be on the left side of the diagram where the demand curve is higher. If we draw the vertical line corresponding to everyone of these buyers—all who buy a bike if the price is $400—and if we assume that the willingness to pay of each person represents their marginal benefit, we end up shading in the area depicted in Fig. 6.2 on the next page.

This shaded area can be thought of as the sum of all the individual vertical lines corresponding to each person's willingness to pay. If the social benefit is simply the sum of these individual benefits (as assumed in the MWM), this area is the total social benefit provided by bicycles. To sum up: the height of a line from the horizontal axis up to a point on the demand curve represents the willingness to pay (and therefore the potential marginal benefit) of the individual represented by that point who is just induced to buy when the price falls to the same level as WTP; the area under the curve up to that point represents the sum of the willingness to pay

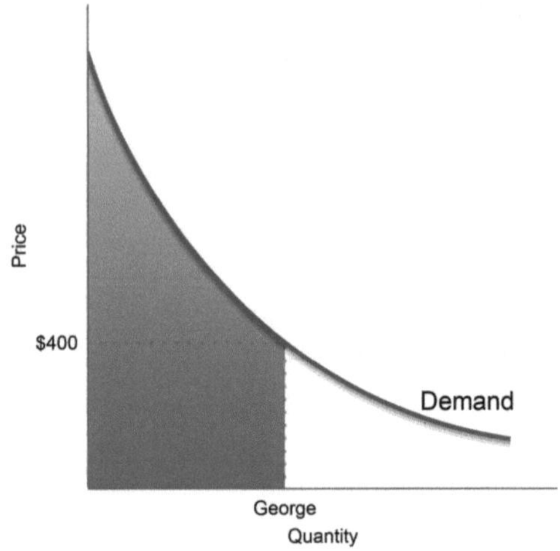

Fig. 6.2 Sum of the marginal benefits from buying bicycles. When the price falls to $400, all the bike buyers who value bikes more than George are still going to buy them. They are positioned to the left of him on the Q axis. If we draw a vertical line from the origin to the demand curve for each of them, the result will be the *shaded area* as shown to the right

(and therefore the potential marginal benefit) of all other buyers who will make purchases at that price.

We can do the same thing for the supply curve. The height of the supply curve at any point represents the minimum amount some seller must receive to supply that particular unit—again, say a bicycle. We might, in the spirit of the MWM, assume that this amount represents the economic cost of producing this bike—the opportunity and disutility costs that must be paid for by someone. (Remember that this is an assumption and is not necessarily true.) Then we can draw Fig. 6.3 (on the next page), the marginal cost of producing George's bike.

There is some bike company which is just barely willing to make and sell a bike for $300, and this is the particular bike that corresponds to the additional market supply necessary to satisfy George. That is, suppose that three million bikes were being produced and sold before George decided to buy. Then one additional bike would have to be made available. This bike would have to be produced by someone, and the curve in Fig. 6.3 says that this someone will make this bike available so long as the price is at least $300. According to our provisional assumption—which we will later feel free to drop—this is the same as saying that there is a marginal cost of $300 to produce this bike.

Already we know one thing: the marginal cost of producing George's bike is less than the marginal benefit he gets from it; to be exact, there is a net benefit of $100. What we don't know is who will get this net benefit. If the price is $400 all of it goes to the seller. If the price is $300 all of it goes to George. If the price is somewhere in between they will split it.

But what about all the other bikes already being produced and sold even before George walks into the bike shop? In Fig. 6.4 on the following page we can see all the other marginal costs for these other bikes.

Each of these bikes has its own vertical line going up to the S curve. Putting all of them together, we get the shaded area under the curve and up to the total level of

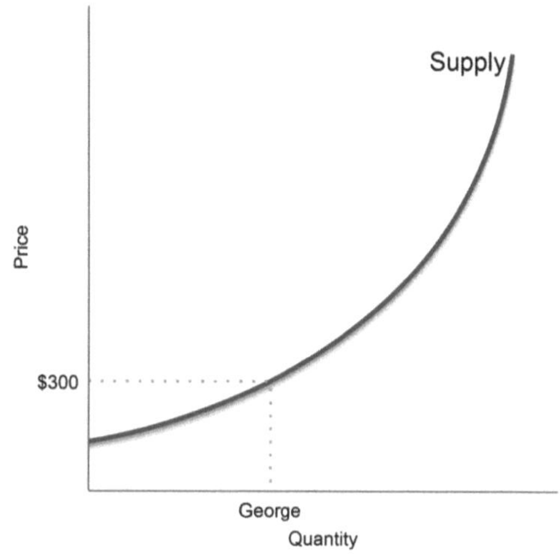

Fig. 6.3 A supply curve for bicycles, with particular attention to George's bike. If one more bike is sold (to George), there is a producer who is willing to sell for any price above $300. If the marginal cost of this bike is equally $300, it is represented by the vertical line going up from George's spot on the Q axis to the supply curve

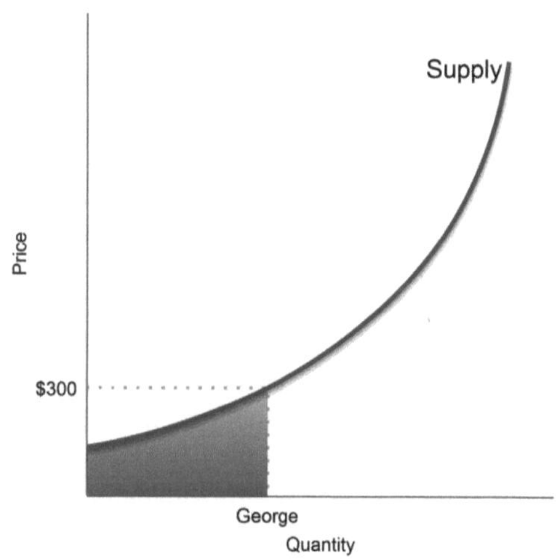

Fig. 6.4 Sum of the marginal costs of producing bicycles. In addition to George's bike, producers are making bikes for everyone to the left of him. If the *vertical line* from the Q axis to the supply curve continues to measure the marginal cost of each of these bikes, the *shaded area* represents their sum

production implied by the last bike, which is George's. If additional bikes were to be built and purchased, the area would expand to the right, still taking in all the space under the S curve and extending up to the quantity represented by the total number of bikes.

Since NB = TB–TC, we can represent the net benefits to society when all consumers whose WTP is greater than or equal to George's are buying bikes, and all such bikes are being produced; as Fig. 6.5 on the next page shows, it is the shaded area in Fig. 6.2 minus the shaded area in Fig. 6.4.

Each of these vertical lines represents the net benefit of that particular bicycle: the height of the demand curve minus the height of the supply curve for that bike. As drawn, the net benefit is highest for the first bike and then declines with each succeeding bike until we get to George. Overall, there are many net benefits

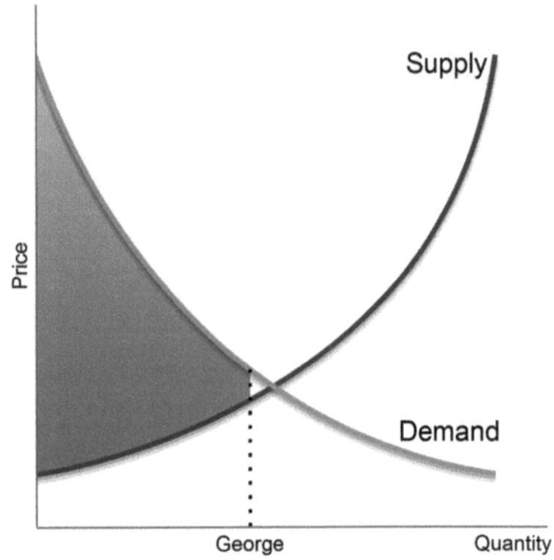

Fig. 6.5 Net benefits from bicycle production if George is the final consumer. The *shaded area* represents the net benefit—total benefit minus total cost—of all the bikes produced and sold when George's bike is the final one

depicted. Still, could we do better? The answer is clearly yes, since there are additional net benefits that could be created by producing and selling more bikes; at higher quantities the demand curve is still above the supply curve. In fact, to maximize the net benefits, we ought to produce up to the quantity Q* in Fig. 6.6, seen on the following page: this amount captures all potential net benefits, and it doesn't, like quantities to the right of Q*, involve the production of any bikes whose marginal costs exceed their benefits.

But—surprise—Q* turns out to be the quantity produced and sold at the market equilibrium price, P*. This demonstrates the equivalence of market equilibrium and maximum net social benefit *if (if if if if if)* (a) the supply curve represents true marginal social cost, (b) the demand curve represents true marginal social benefit, and (c) the curves are drawn with this approximate shape so that equilibrium occurs at their intersection. In other words, we have a geometric demonstration of the Market Welfare Model.

Note one more thing about Fig. 6.6. When the quantity is Q*, P* tells us the height of both the demand and supply curves for the last unit produced and purchased. That is, P* equals both the marginal cost and the marginal benefit of this last bicycle (or whatever the item is). Thus, if we believe that the world conforms to this model—if we believe that markets are usually in or very close to equilibrium, and that the conditions of the MWM usually hold—we can regard market prices as telling us what one more of something costs to produce or contributes to society. This is the basis for the tendency of economists to see market prices as telling us the "truth" about products, grounded in the deeper realities of production costs and consumer values, and not just signifying random, meaningless fluctuations. When asked to give advice, economists are likely to begin by saying, "Get the prices right." Seeing to it that prices reflect marginal costs and benefits is what they have in mind.

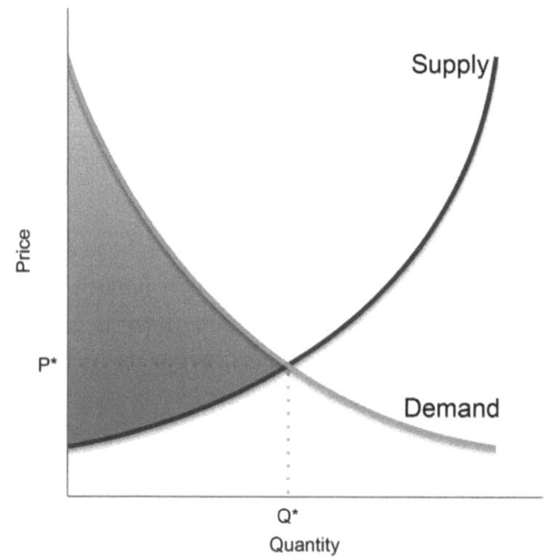

Fig. 6.6 Maximum net benefits obtainable from bicycle production. At Q* the net benefits from the production of bicycles are maximized, and P* tells us both the marginal cost and the marginal benefit of the last bike produced and sold. This is also a market equilibrium. This happy coincidence depends on the three assumptions of the Market Welfare Model: the supply curve represents marginal costs of production, the demand curve represents marginal benefits to consumers, and the curves have an intersection like that in the above diagram

Let's look at this from one more perspective. Normally, when people decide whether or not to buy or sell something, they perform an individual cost-benefit test. If they are producers, they consider the cost of making something and the benefit (revenue) they will receive by selling it, and they decide to follow through if the benefit exceeds or at least equals the cost. If they are consumers, they compare the benefit (the value of acquiring this item) with the cost (the price they must pay), and only if the benefit exceeds or at least equals the cost do they actually make the purchase. Thus, each market transaction represents a dual cost-benefit test: both parties must compare costs and benefits, and a completed transaction is possible only if both sides perceive net benefits or at least not net costs. (We are assuming in this context that all people act rationally when they make these decisions.)

It is normal for people to make these types of calculations, but do they add up to a corresponding social calculation? If each person buys or sells on their individual interest, is the result beneficial from a social perspective? If the conditions of the MWM hold, the answer has to be yes. The first condition says that the demand curve represents marginal social benefits (MSB). This means the MSB must equal or exceed the price that is being paid by all buyers, since people buy only if the price is at or below their willingness to pay. The second says that the supply curve represents marginal social costs (MSC). This means that the marginal cost must be equal to or less than the price for all sellers, since people sell only if they receive revenue equal to or greater than their cost. Since the price at which things are bought is equal to the price at which they are sold (two sides of the same transaction), it follows that MSB ≥ MSC for every good or service transacted in the market, again assuming that the MWM conditions are in effect. This is summarized in the following inequality:

$$\underset{\text{(buyer)}}{MSB} \geq P = P \geq \underset{\text{(seller)}}{MSC}; \therefore MSB \geq MSC$$

This says that every voluntary, rational transaction between two parties will be in the social interest by contributing more to society's benefit than it adds to society's cost. Whether *all* such potential transactions take place is determined, in the MWM utopia, by whether we are at a market equilibrium as in Fig. 6.5. By thinking in these terms, we can see why economics places so much stress on cost-benefit calculations. We can also see how markets, when the MWM conditions are in effect, fulfill Jeremy Bentham's dream of fusing individual incentives and the social interest.

6.5 Implications of the Market Welfare Model

It is difficult to exaggerate the tremendous sweep of the Market Welfare Model. Here is what it purports to show:

1. A market economy, if it operates according to the three assumptions of the model, produces exactly those goods that should be produced. Just because it is technically possible to produce something doesn't mean it should be produced. The world is not worse off because we lack personal helicopter chairs or solar-powered can-openers; such things could be built, but not at a price anyone would be willing to pay. In slightly more technical terms, we can say that non-produced goods are those for which the equilibrium quantity is zero, as in Fig. 5.6 from Chap. 5. Such goods *shouldn't* be produced, of course, since at any output level their marginal cost of production would exceed the corresponding marginal benefit. On the other hand, for typical produced goods, as in Fig. 6.6 above, it is in society's interest to have a positive level of production.
2. A market economy, if the assumptions hold, produces exactly the right number of goods. This follows directly from Fig. 6.6.
3. A market economy, under these assumptions, produces exactly the right *qualities* of goods. According to this principle, cars should have the right safety features, airlines the right schedules, and rock bands the right music and lyrics. Why? Each aspect of a good or service can be analyzed as though it were a commodity in itself. Consider our first example—the crashworthiness of cars. Manufacturers can make cars more crash resistant, but only at a cost, and that cost presumably rises as the car is made more invincible. Consumers want greater crashworthiness, but not at any price, and presumably their willingness to pay for the last iota of security is less than for previous improvements. Since each producer can offer a line of cars with different features, and since different companies can compete over safety, the consumer faces an *implicit market* in car safety. Where supply

and demand curves intersect determines the qualities that will be incorporated. The Market Welfare Model claims that, under the appropriate conditions, these will be the *right* qualities. The same approach can be applied to the qualitative aspects of any good or service.

4. A market economy, again under these assumptions, uses the best technologies available, combining factors of production in the most efficient ways. The imperative to use the best technology comes from the competitive process itself, while the optimal use of inputs is another application of the Market Welfare Model, in this case pertaining to the market for inputs. Since the MWM is conditioned on the assumption that the demand curve for an input by firms represents its marginal value to society, and its supply curve represents the marginal cost of provision by its owners, market equilibrium yields the socially optimal use. For instance, every year a certain number of students graduate from colleges and universities with a degree in economics and look for employment. These new economists represent the supply side of the market: they offer to supply their own labor. The market supply curve represents the true cost to these budding economists of offering their labor—assuming, of course, that the Market Welfare Model applies. The demand for economists comes from government, the educational system, and private businesses, and if the MWM conditions apply this curve represents the marginal value economists can add to these enterprises. Equilibrium in this labor market would then mean that resources are being deployed in the most efficient possible way, maximizing the benefit society acquires from its investment in economics training. Moreover, since supplying a factor in some sense means creating it (like getting an education to qualify for a certain type of job), the implication of the MWM is that society *develops* its resources in the best possible manner.

To summarize, neoclassical economics holds that, in the ideal world of perfect competition and no market failure, the *individual rationality* exercised by firms and households in the marketplace coincides in every respect with the *social rationality* that ought to guide the operation of our economy. To the extent that the social criterion is the maximization of society's net benefit from production and the conditions of the Market Welfare Model are fulfilled, there is no justification for external guidance or interference. Stripped to its essentials, the Market Welfare Model adopts one criterion, maximization of net benefits to society, and makes three assumptions: (1) the supply curve represents marginal social cost, (2) the demand curve represents marginal social benefit, and (3) the curves have the property that both market equilibrium and social optimality converge to a single point (as in Fig. 6.6). These assumptions are predicated, in turn, on a methodology or set of definitions, presented in Chap. 4, that assigns meaning to the terms "social cost" and "social benefit".

Box: Hurricane Charley Dumps High Prices on Florida

When Hurricane Charley blasted through Florida on Friday, August 13, 2004, it left thousands without homes and large parts of the state short on basic supplies. No sooner had the storm passed, however, than a small army of price gougers appeared, offering Floridians what they needed—at a substantial markup.

Motels tripled their rates for a night's stay. Construction materials went for as much as ten times their normal price. Generators were highly prized and made small fortunes for those who sold them. Even ice was at a premium; some paid $2 a scoop in a desperate effort to prevent their perishable foods from rotting in the post-storm heat. As of the following Tuesday, the state Attorney General's office reported 1,400 complaints of exorbitant prices. This is a crime under Florida law and risks a fine of $1,000 if it is determined there has been a violation.

But should it be a crime? The logic of the Market Welfare Model says no. Clearly, if a generator that normally sells for $250 now commands $2,000 (this actually happened), someone is believed to be willing to pay that amount, reflecting the greatly increased benefit they get from it. If there are two potential buyers at this price, $2,000 represents the opportunity cost of the generator as well. (To put it at the disposal of one individual is to make it unavailable to someone else.) Hence, if the price is to reflect both the marginal cost and marginal benefit of the item, it should be $2,000 and not $250.

A supporter of the Invisible Hand would also point to the longer-term consequences of letting prices rise. If there are huge profits to be made selling generators in Florida, dealers around the country will have a powerful incentive to ship them there. This will speed up the recovery process—exactly how an efficient economy should respond to such a disaster.

There are two counterarguments, however. First, permitting price gouging makes those who were hardest hit by Charley double victims, first of the storm, then of high prices. Wealth will be transferred from one segment of the population to another for no other reason than the bad luck of having been caught in the path of a hurricane.

Second, to allow or even encourage price gouging is to discourage voluntary assistance. Few would give of their time and resources to help those displaced by the storm if others were visibly profiting from it. This raises the practical question of whether the increased for-profit support would be enough to offset the loss of voluntary aid, as well as the deeper issue of the social and cultural character of the two types of responses.

Hurricane Charley was an extreme weather event, and the price gouging that followed it was a more extreme version of everyday market forces. Disadvantaged consumers, such as travelers stranded at airports or residents

(continued)

Box (continued)
of small towns with only one supplier of a particular good, can expect to pay more, and a heat wave that leads to heavier use of air conditioners normally drives up the price of energy. Where would you draw the line between regulating prices and letting markets have their way?

6.6 Market Failure

Up to this point we have been willing to live in (or at least temporarily visit) a mythical world of perfect markets in which the highly idealized assumptions of the MWM about costs and benefits have been permitted to guide the analysis. Few would expect that this world has much to do with our own. Rather, the norm can be assumed to be a state of **market failure**, understood as the failure of markets to conform to the MWM conditions. Nearly all economists regard such failures as ubiquitous, although they disagree over how consequential this is for practical questions of policy. (Many economists think that markets come "close enough" to meeting the MWM conditions, and many others are inclined to believe that most things we try to do to fix these markets will make matters worse, not better.) In this section we will very briefly review the main grounds for anticipating market failure; we will return to this issue in much greater detail in Chaps. 13, 14 and 15.

In general terms, there are four commonly recognized sources of market failure: **externalities**, **public goods, monopoly** and **asymmetric information**.

Externalities: Externalities arise when actions undertaken by individuals have impacts on others that are not transacted in markets. This drives a wedge between the supply and demand curves that depict what people pay or receive in markets and the actual social costs and benefits resulting from their choices. A negative externality is a cost imposed by an action that the one imposing it doesn't have to pay for; a familiar example is pollution. These are sometimes referred to as "hidden" costs, but what makes them hidden is not that they are difficult to see, but that there is no legal requirement for them to be compensated. Naturally there is a tendency for goods with negative externalities to be produced in excessive quantities or in excessively damaging ways. A positive externality is a benefit which is not paid for by its recipient. It is generally believed that education generates positive externalities, since its beneficiaries are partially the fellow citizens, neighbors and coworkers of those who have benefitted directly from education. These indirect beneficiaries do not pay for this privilege, at least not through markets, and so their interest would tend to be underrepresented. This is one reason why our society spends a lot of money subsidizing education at all levels. Economists, as we will see in more detail in Chap. 13, look for ways to make prices reflect significant negative or positive externalities; they refer to this as "internalizing the externality".

Public goods: Here again we confront a situation in which the everyday use of a word differs from its technical use. Most people use “public” to refer to the government: something is public property if it is owned by a government agency, and a public enterprise is a business owned and run by the government. Economists attach an entirely different meaning to the term, however: a public good is something that has at least one of two characteristics: it has a zero, or near zero, marginal cost of production, or it is not practical to try to prevent people from using it if they don’t pay for it. The first is referred to as the *nonrivalry principle*, the second as the *nonexclusion principle*. Radio stations provide examples of a public good in this sense: there is no cost to making its programming available to an additional listener (nonrivalry), and it is difficult to prevent someone from listening if they haven’t paid a membership fee (nonexclusion). This means that it is unlikely that normal market methods (self-interested buying and selling between listeners and broadcasters) will do a good job of meeting the social need for such radio stations. On the other hand, the post office, which certainly is a government enterprise, does not provide a public good. It costs extra money to mail each letter users of the service wish to send (positive marginal cost), and the Postal Service has no problem in refusing service to those who don’t pay, i.e. those who fail to put a stamp on their envelope. Economists look to government, or in some cases cooperative nongovernmental, solutions to public goods problems.

Monopoly: A monopolist is someone (usually some company) that has acquired a decisive degree of control over a particular market. This makes it possible to raise prices or cut corners on quality without worrying too much about consumers switching to substitutes. A well-known example is Microsoft, whose overwhelming shares of the computer operating system and productivity (word processing, spreadsheet, presentation) software markets give it the ability to charge prices well above its costs of production, and to take a lax attitude toward quality issues, like the stability and security of Windows and its other offerings. Because the value of software depends on how widely it is used (attracting more compatible programs from other companies and permitting more users to share their work with each other), there is a significant cost to leaving the Microsoft universe. By keeping its prices higher and its quality lower than would otherwise be the case, Microsoft has managed to become one of the most profitable companies in history. Most economists regard this as an economic problem to be solved, however, since monopoly has led to a gap between the supply curve (or at any rate the prices at which Microsoft makes its products available) and the marginal costs of computer software—including, as above, the implicit market for software quality.

Asymmetric information: The supply and demand curves can represent true costs and benefits to society only if the sellers and buyers they represent make decisions based on adequate information. A difficult problem arises, however, when one side of the market generally knows much more than the other about the likely effects of any transaction. Examples include highly trained professionals like doctors and attorneys who understand the quality of their services better than their customers and borrowers who know more about how likely they are to repay loans than the banks or other lenders they borrow from. This can result in deceptive practices, but economists have discovered that more is at stake. Those who have less information may look at prices not only as the amount they have to pay or be willing to accept, but also as signals of hard-to-observe quality. Is a doctor who charges less than the competition a bargain or a quack? Is the borrower willing to pay a higher interest rate a good investment or a riskier one? If prices are viewed as quality signals, buyers may choose to pay higher prices and sellers may offer lower ones, violating the logic of the previous chapter. We will study examples of this process in more detail later; for now the point is that asymmetric (unequal) information removes us from the world of the Market Welfare Hypothesis.

From this brief survey, we can see that market failure is widespread, so economists spend much of their time devising strategies to counteract it. Their usual approach is to try to calculate the "true" marginal cost or benefit curves—the ones that diverge from the actually existing supply and demand curves. Then they think of ways to alter the economy's rules so that the actual supply and demand curves shift in a way that approaches MC and MB. In this way, they set limits to their willingness to intervene in markets: their goal is not to reach any particular outcome they might favor, but to permit society to be guided by true production costs and consumer preferences. For instance, in setting forest policy, economists will look for ways in which the supply curve for forest products diverges from the marginal costs to society of making these products available, or divergences between the demand curve and the willingness to pay of all those who benefit directly or indirectly. Marginal benefits and costs are considered to be "objective" quantities, which researchers can estimate from surveys and other data sources. Economists are reluctant to make personal judgments about what the ideal policy should be. Noneconomic values are put aside, and the only goal is to maximize the surplus of total social benefit over total social cost, as these are defined and measured using economic techniques.

One final point needs to be made about normative economics: the entire field has recently been thrown into turmoil due to the more careful study of human psychology that has arisen under the banner of "behavioral economics". Fundamentally, contemporary research is demonstrating that choices made in the marketplace often have little if anything to do with "maximizing utility". As we will see in Chap. 11 and elsewhere in this book, people often make consumption and investment decisions that fail to improve their well-being. Indeed, the entire concept of utility may be groundless, since its mathematical properties are contradicted by psychological and neurological evidence regarding the determinants of human happiness. If the emerging message of behavioral economics proves to be correct, the entire field of normative analysis will have to be revised.

At the moment, however, it has to be said that these questions do not trouble most economists who evaluate policies or enlist normative methods for other purposes. They still calculate costs and benefits in terms of utility and assume that markets maximize utility in the absence of specific market failures. Their goal is to correct for these failures so that markets can be restored to a condition resembling the Market Welfare Model. Their techniques, such as cost-benefit analysis and the use of optimization models, still dominate the discipline, even though they rest on assumptions that are increasingly in doubt.

There is inertia built into any branch of knowledge, since practitioners want to stick with the tools they spent so much time and effort learning how to use. This is no less true for economics, and an additional factor is that behavioral economics has thus far been more successful at undermining conventional methods than in devising new ones. After all, it is better to have some sort of systematic thinking about complex issues like economic well-being than none at all, even if one's ideas are somewhat flawed.

Taking all of this into consideration, perhaps the best description of the current moment is to say that it is transitional. A gap has opened up between ordinary economic practice, based on utility theory and the framework of the Market Welfare Model, and a rapidly expanding body of research into the actual effects of economic choices on human welfare. What transpires in the future will depend on where the new research in behavioral economics takes us, and in particular whether it leads to a new framework for assessing policies and institutions that is well-grounded and practical. Events are moving quickly, and a textbook chapter such as this one may read very differently in just a few years. These are interesting times!

The Main Points

1. The question of whether markets alone ought to regulate economic life is centuries old. Adam Smith thought that the "natural liberty" of individuals in the marketplace could, if competition were sufficient, ensure a high level of social well-being. Jeremy Bentham, the founder of utilitarian philosophy, sought to create "the greatest good for the greatest number", and he expected that, in most cases, self-seeking in markets would result in this. Yet it has turned out that the analysis of markets as instruments of social well-being is extremely complex. Much of modern economics explores this topic.
2. Marginal benefits encompass additional benefits due to a small increase in some action, good or service. Marginal costs encompass additional costs due to the same small increase. Net benefit is total benefit minus total cost. "Benefits" and "costs" in this context are used as they were defined in Chap. 4.
3. The Market Welfare Model summarizes a relationship between market behavior and social well-being. It has three conditions: that the supply curve represents marginal social cost, the demand curve represents marginal social benefit, and there is a single market equilibrium where supply and demand curves intersect. If all three conditions are met, it can be concluded that the market equilibrium represents the combination of prices and quantities that maximizes net social benefits. If this is true throughout the economy, the Invisible Hand proposition of Smith holds.
4. The Market Welfare Model follows directly from the use of calculus on the net benefit formula. It can also be demonstrated graphically using supply and demand curves, recognizing that the total cost (benefit) generated by a good or service is represented by the area under the supply (demand) curve.

5. If the conditions of the Market Welfare Model hold, the equilibrium price conveys important information: the marginal benefit of one more unit of the good or service in question, and also its marginal cost of production.
6. One interpretation of the Market Welfare Model is that, if its conditions hold, it demonstrates the market is performing a cost-benefit test on behalf of society. Each seller considers whether the price is greater than or equal to the marginal cost of supply. Each buyer considers whether the price is less than or equal to the marginal benefit of purchase. If these individual valuations also correspond to social valuations (all costs and benefits to society are exactly as they are perceived by individuals in the marketplace), and if there is a single equilibrium where price = marginal cost = marginal benefit, every item sold has passed a social cost-benefit test (and every item not sold has failed this test).
7. If the conditions of the Market Welfare Model hold, four specific conclusions follow: (a) a market economy produces exactly the goods that should be produced, (b) it produces exactly the right number of goods, (c) it produces exactly the right quality of goods, and (d) it produces these goods in best possible way.
8. There are four commonly recognized forms of market failure that prevent the conditions of the Market Welfare Model from being met: externalities, public goods, monopoly and asymmetric information. At a deeper level, questions about human behavior and the nature of "well-being" have called into question the entire model.

Terms to Define

Externalities
Implicit market
Invisible Hand
Liberal
Marginal benefit
Marginal cost
Market failure
Market Welfare Model
Monopoly
Nonexclusion principle
Nonrivalry principle
Public goods
Utilitarianism

Questions to Consider

1. Recall the issue of the market in kidneys described in the previous chapter. Suppose the question is whether to legalize this market; how do you suppose a utilitarian would go about answering it? What data would she need? What questions would she *not* ask? How comfortable do you feel about settling this question on utilitarian grounds? Why?
2. Review the discussion of the coffee crisis in the previous chapter. Do you think the Market Welfare Model is likely to apply to global production and consumption of coffee? Does the declining price correspond to the declining marginal cost of production and benefit of consumption? Explain.
3. Some economists are in favor of breaking up the public school system and replacing it with private schools that would compete for students. Under this scheme, the government would give each student a voucher worth a certain amount of money which they could spend at any school they chose. The schools would be free to set their own academic policies, prices and admission criteria (perhaps under certain restrictions, depending on the details of the proposal). One of the chief arguments for this approach has to do with the possible emergence of an implicit market in educational quality. How might such a market arise? What incentives would this market have on private schools? Are there aspects of education that might be lost in this free-market approach? You will want to think about what "quality" means in an educational context—what it consists of and what its sources are.
4. As we have seen, the US Postal Service is not an example of a public good. If it were fully privatized (turned into a private, for profit company) would you anticipate any of the other three types of market failure to arise?

Appendix: Markets and Freedom

While we will be concerned primarily with the utilitarian case for markets (whether markets improve human well-being), we would be burying our heads in the sand if we didn't take note of the political value that many people put on free, unregulated markets. From their vantage point, freedom in the marketplace *is* freedom, and free markets would be justified even if the outcomes they produced were inferior in some respects. The most consistent version of this view is libertarianism, the belief that restrictions on individual freedom of choice should be minimized as much as possible.

Consider an example, the regulation of food additives. The US Food and Drug Administration is charged with determining which chemicals can be added to foods produced in the United States. It commissions laboratory tests and, based on the evidence (usually), decides whether restrictions ought to be placed on particular substances. For many years there was controversy over artificial sweeteners, for instance: some tests showed that laboratory animals (and therefore potentially humans) were placed at increased risk of disease when fed large doses of cyclamates and similar products. On the other hand, at least in the eyes of some people, these products promised to add sweetness to the diet without the empty calories of sugar. (There is also controversy over their dietary advantages.) In its decision-making, the FDA was supposed to be concerned only with the health and consumer satisfaction consequences of permitting or banning the additives, in the spirit of the outcome-oriented framework of this chapter.

But there is another way to approach the question: do consumers have a *right* to add artificial sweeteners to their diet if companies are willing to sell them? Doesn't the FDA violate the personal liberty of individuals and companies on both sides of this market? If consumers, on examining the scientific evidence, still decide that the gain is worth the risk, who are government officials to tell them otherwise?

This argument, in fact, can be applied to almost any aspect of economic life, particularly if we accept the metaphor of exchange as capturing what economic life is about. In free markets exchanges are voluntary and therefore reflect the decisions of both parties. Surely freedom must have *something* to do with being able to make such choices and not having them overruled by the force of the state.

Positive and Negative Liberty

A useful starting point for thinking about the political case for markets is the distinction between positive and negative liberty initially put forward by Thomas Hill Green, a British philosopher of the nineteenth century (who drew heavily on his predecessors). In modern usage, positive liberty is the freedom to do something, involving access to the resources needed to do it. The positive liberty to play the guitar means actually having the opportunity to play it: having the time, the agreement of others around you to let you play, and of course access to a guitar itself. It also assumes that one knows what a guitar is and has had an opportunity to consider the benefits of being a musician. For such freedoms to be universal, there is typically a need for public programs to guarantee access to all citizens so they can make use of them. For instance, if everyone is to have the positive freedom to play a guitar, society may have to subsidize them or provide low-cost studios where people can go and use a guitar for an hour or two. The mental preconditions (knowing about guitars, being introduced to music) suggest the need for universal education, so that the people who might want to become guitarists can find out who they are. Negative liberty is much simpler; it means simply that one is left alone, unimpeded by outside forces. The negative liberty to play the guitar means only that no one prohibits you from playing; you would have this freedom even if you are never able to actually touch an instrument, or even if you had never had any exposure to music of any kind. In shorthand, positive liberty is "freedom to", while negative liberty is "freedom from".

Using this framework, we can see that free markets promote negative rather than positive liberty. They give people the right to make choices free of outside interference, but they do not guarantee, or even necessarily facilitate, a distribution of resources and experiences that would make it possible for most people to discover and do what they would like. A philosophical attachment to free markets is equivalent to a belief in negative liberty and a rejection, or at least de-emphasis, of positive liberty.

The legal expression of free markets is freedom of contract. This means that two or more individuals are free to enter into any agreement they mutually choose, and no outside force—in particular, no government institution—is allowed to overrule them. I can agree with a landowner to buy a parcel of land, and no one can interfere. I can agree with a building contractor to have a building placed on the land, and no one can say otherwise. I can agree on any sort of building I have in mind, provided I get the consent of the builder. Once it is built I can rent it out to any tenant who agrees to occupy it. I can paint the building pink. I can place a radio transmitter on it. I can open a drug rehab center in it. And so on and on: freedom of contract means that I can enter into any business relationship I choose, provided it is agreed to by all parties to the transaction, and there can be no prohibition or regulation on the part of government or any other third party. No society has ever had pure freedom of contract, but libertarianism upholds it as an ideal.

To look at this distinction more closely, let us introduce some formal terminology. Suppose there are two individuals, A and B. (Either could be a collective entity, like a business or government, but we will stick with individuals for now.) We will define **coercion** as the imposition by B of a penalty on A for an action which A would otherwise, were it not for the penalty, prefer to take, under conditions in which A is not free to break off contact with B. There was a saying in Stalinist Russia that anyone can say anything they want about Comrade Stalin. . .once. The point is that coercion does not prevent a person from doing something (standing on the street corner and denouncing the dictator), but by exacting a price, changes the victim's calculation of costs and benefits. Moreover, there is no way for the victim to sidestep the penalty by refusing to accept it.

An other example may make this clearer. Suppose A is being robbed by B in a dark alley; B pulls out a gun and announces, "Your money or your life!" In the absence of coercion, A would prefer to break off contact with B and continue on his way, but that is not an option. Instead, A may have to accept a choice he would otherwise never make, to turn over his valuables to the robber. What this suggests is that the extent of the disagreeableness (disutility) of the choice A may be coerced into accepting is limited only by the intensity of the penalty B is able to impose. If the penalty is death, there is almost no limit to how grim A's choices may come to be. This is one reason why coercion can be bad: it has the potential to create a situation in which people can be made to accept terrible choices in all aspects of their lives. They have been deprived of the one choice they would most like to have: to say no and walk away.

Another reason is that B's influence over A can be turned to self-interest. Of course, this is exactly what robbery is, but the point is more general. Governments, democratic as well as dictatorial, have immense coercive power: they can issues fines, imprison and even employ deadly force. We like to think that this power will not be abused, but history and logic suggest otherwise: with so much potential for individuals or particular interests with sway over government to use this power for their own gain, the risk never disappears. In practice this abuse may occur only rarely, but certainly a high degree of vigilance is in order.

What makes libertarianism attractive is that it consists of a general opposition to all forms of coercion as defined above. It opposes robbery, war (except in self-defense) and nearly all exercise of government authority. The only legitimate roles for government, in the eyes of libertarians, have to do with suppressing other forms of coercion, employing limited military and police powers. In other words, in order to avoid the greater coercion of crime and invasion by foreign armies, libertarians accept the lesser coercion of government—but in these realms only.

Nevertheless, libertarianism has limits as a political philosophy. There is much to be said for Green's positive freedom too, freedom in the sense of "doing what you desire to do", or would desire if you had the chance. (This last phrase reminds us of the importance of exposure to music as a basis for the positive freedom to become a guitarist.) Freedom from coercion falls short of providing this; it only indicates that you will not have to make choices you despise, but it doesn't say that you will be able to make choices you like (or would like if you knew about them). To use our formal language, suppose coercion is not an issue, but the choice A would prefer to make depends on cooperation from B. This choice will be unavailable if B withholds this cooperation. How bad is this for A? It depends. At the worst, it could mean that A will not be able to improve his situation at all; every desirable choice that would make him better off has been rendered impossible.

Suppose what I really want to do is make movies. The type of movies I want to make (big budget disaster epics) are not possible as a solo venture; I need to work with hundred of technicians, actors and other professionals to get the results I want. Of course, I need someone to finance this dream, or it will never get off the ground. My (positive) freedom to make such a movie depends on being trained or apprenticed in a film academy or studio and then having access to the necessary resources (money, equipment, people); if these opportunities and resources don't exist or are withheld from me, I can't do what I would most like. This means I will have to do something else: make lower-budget movies (intimate family dramas), or no movies at all. At worst, I am back where I started, doing whatever I did before (waiting on tables), but, unlike coercion, being denied opportunities cannot make me worse off than I was originally.

This sounds like freedom from coercion is more salient than freedom to have opportunity, but it is not always so clear. What if A is not self-sufficient—what if he would starve to death or face a health crisis without access to resources controlled by others? This is clearly not an idle question; indeed a vast majority of the world's people are in exactly this situation. Without employment (which depends on the cooperation of others to hire and pay them) and without access to medical services they would be (and in many cases are) in dire trouble. If the initial condition, prior to cooperation, is not viable, then denial of opportunity may be just as crushing in its consequences as forcible coercion. Even short of these dire constraints, most of us would find life seriously impoverished if we were forced to live as isolated individuals, without access to the resources of society. Denial of positive freedom is not trivial for anyone.

So let us now briefly consider positive freedom as a value. We can define it as the ability to do what you most want, based on having had the opportunity to discover this want, and subject to these restrictions:

- What you want to do is reasonable in some broad sense. People who are mentally deranged or otherwise poor decision-makers are not served by being free to make highly self-destructive choices.
- What you want to do is feasible if other members of society provide you with the available resources, including their participation, to facilitate it. It makes sense to speak of a positive freedom to attend college; it does not make sense to speak of a positive freedom to learn all the subject matter of a college education in 1 month so you can spend the rest of your time partying. You simply do not have this ability, whatever the opportunities opened up to you.

Positive freedom is about opportunity in an interdependent world. It generally implies the need for collective action—the exercise of political will—to bring it about. Your ability to attend college quite likely depends on the availability of public and private funding, as well as the willingness of college admissions officials to allow you to attend. You need to be able to afford not only the immediate financial costs of going to school (tuition, room and board, other expenses), but also the opportunity cost of not doing something else instead (like holding down an additional job). This in turn depends on economic policies that put you in a position to make these choices.

Sometimes negative and positive freedom seem to complement one another. Consider the situation of someone who wants to play the guitar, as discussed earlier in this appendix. For one thing, she needs the negative freedom from coercion by those who might punish her for playing this instrument. In some societies, such as Afghanistan under the Taliban, who opposed the playing of music on religious principle, this is a real issue. But just being free from restrictions on playing will not be enough to make a musician out of her; she also needs to own or have access to a guitar to practice on, and perhaps also the opportunity to take lessons. Thus both negative and positive freedom have a role to play.

Quite often, however, these two types of freedom tend to come into conflict with each other. Let's return to the example of attending college. The positive freedom to be a college student requires financial support, typically through taxes—but tax collection occurs on the basis of government's power to punish (coerce) those who do not pay. Admissions offices must also not be able to discriminate against applicants based on considerations unrelated to qualifications; they cannot refuse whole categories of people based on ethnicity, gender, religion, etc. (A few colleges do this, but positive freedom would be infringed if the practice were widespread). The "cannot" in this last sentence is enforced by government anti-discrimination laws backed, as before, by the civil and criminal justice systems. Finally, most economic policies are more than friendly suggestions; they are administrative requirements whose force depends on the potential for coercion. In other words, almost everything governments do to provide positive freedom to attend college conflicts with someone's negative freedom to avoid coercion.

Inner Freedom

To make matters somewhat more complicated, there is a third notion of freedom, beyond negative and positive, that you may want to think about. As defined above, freedom is about freedom from constraint, whether coercive (negative) or lack of opportunity (positive); both threats to freedom are essentially external. Nevertheless, there may also be significant internal threats, barriers to freedom within our own minds. It is reasonable to speak of a free person as someone who is not a prisoner of social convention, ignorance, habit or addiction. This notion comes to us from an intellectual movement dating from the late eighteenth century that has gone under names like romanticism (England), idealism (Germany) and transcendentalism (the US). To some extent, it is an alternative framework that downplays the role of external inhibitions, as in the saying "stone walls do not a prison make". In this sense its scope is entirely personal; it calls neither for or against any particular laws, other than freedom of expression. Many political philosophers, however, have argued that the ability of individuals to pursue freedom of this sort depends greatly on public institutions and policies, including universal education (of a certain type) and alleviation of poverty. To the extent they are right, the claim of "inner" freedom coincides with that of positive freedom defined above.

Freedom and Obligation

To conclude this all-too-brief discussion, it is useful to consider the larger context. We have been examining different conceptions of freedom, but freedom, as precious as it is, is not the only thing of value. People also place value on a wide range of other qualities, such as health, general economic well-being, personal and social justice, and the quality of the culture and natural environment we pass on to future generations. For instance, consider the aggressive measures sometimes taken in a public health emergency, like the outbreak of an epidemic. Restrictions are placed on people's movements in order to prevent the spread of disease. You could try to make an elaborate argument about health and positive freedom, but in fact the justification is not about freedom at all; it's simply to safeguard our health. If the health benefits are large enough, it would be a good idea to ignore modest infringements on freedom, at least temporarily. It would not be difficult to come up with many other examples from other spheres of life, involving not only the avoidance of harm but also opportunities to achieve substantial gains.

A particularly important limitation to freedom is that, in order for human society to function acceptably, someone has to take responsibility for those unable to care for themselves. This includes children, the very old, and those restricted by illness or disability—in other words, all of us at some times during our life. It has been pointed out that, in the past, philosophers were nearly always men who could count on women, such as their wives, to see to these responsibilities, leaving them free to spend their days thinking about freedom. This freedom would have been imperiled if the women in their lives had claimed it too. Today we expect a political philosophy to encompass everyone, women as well as men, as we should. But if personal obligations to care for others are unavoidable, erasing the gender barrier means not only extending men's freedom to women, but also women's care obligations to men. It would be nice if everyone freely assumed these obligations, since that would allow us to reconcile freedom with social need, but if they don't some restriction on freedom is inevitable.

There are two further aspects of the need to provide care that ought to be considered. First, this responsibility can be shouldered either privately, by individuals and their families, or publicly, through government programs. Doing more of one releases obligations on the other. For instance, most societies today have, or are moving toward, a system of publicly financed education for all children, public pensions for the elderly, and access to health care and social services for the sick and disabled. The regulations and tax collections that make these programs possible certainly constitute a large deduction from negative freedom. On the other hand, these programs release us from many of the caring responsibilities we would otherwise have to assume in our private lives, allowing us to enjoy a much higher level of positive freedom: more opportunities to pursue the activities we find fulfilling. Of course, a freer lifestyle is not without costs as well; we lose something valuable when we face no responsibility at all for caring for others. All of these considerations speak to the complicated question of how far society should go in collectivizing obligations that were once private—and not always well met.

A second question has to do with boundaries: whose needs are we obligated to provide? Our own children and parents, of course. (But not always.) Other members of our family? What about people in need in our community or elsewhere in our country? We now expect the government to provide emergency assistance in the wake of natural disasters, but that means we allow ourselves to be taxed and regulated so that these programs can function. Is it a social obligation to ensure that all children have access to a good education, and that everyone, whatever their age, has food to eat and a roof over their head? And why stop at national borders? There are hundreds of millions of children around the world who lack the basic necessities of life. Millions of families live in refugee camps, and many more face intolerable poverty. Finally, does history confer responsibility? Do non-native Americans have a responsibility toward native peoples whose lands and livelihood were taken from them in the past? What about the descendants of slaves or other particularly exploited people? And how do we balance our obligations to care for others with a commitment to personal freedom? There is no easy answer to this last question, except to say that neither extreme—all obligation and no freedom, or all freedom and no obligation—is very appealing.

The Main Points

1. The libertarian case for free markets is that they maximize human freedom: no one, according to this view, should tell anyone else what they must do or what they cannot do. Any interference with market behavior, or a substitution of some other decision-making process for markets, could be seen as a violation of this freedom.
2. A relevant distinction in political theory is between "negative" and "positive" freedom. The first refers to the noncoercion principle: one is not forced to do or not do something. The second refers to having the actual option to engage in a desired activity. In an interdependent society, fulfillment of positive freedom normally requires some restriction of negative freedom.
3. The practical case for libertarianism is that there is no limit to the amount of harm individuals may be forced to accept under conditions of coercion. The practical case for interfering with markets is that our dependence on one another is often substantial, and many would suffer serious deterioration in the quality of their available options without institutions that organize (and compel) measures of social support.
4. There is an "internal" conception of freedom as well, concerned with freedom from mental and emotional shackles. To some extent, freedom of this sort does not depend on how much or little positive or negative freedom is available. It can be argued, however, that a society that wishes to promote "internal" freedom has to place greater weight on positive freedom as well.
5. However defined and understood, freedom is one of many political, social and economic values, and tradeoffs are unavoidable. A particular tradeoff of importance is between freedom and the obligation to care for those who need the help of others. Social programs that provide this care collectively release individuals from obligations that would otherwise fall on their shoulders, but at the cost of reducing negative freedom from taxation and regulation.

▶ Terms to Define

Coercion
Freedom of contract
"Internal" freedom
Libertarianism
Negative vs positive freedom

Question to Consider

Fifty years ago, in large parts of the United States stores, restaurants and other public facilities were segregated: many where "white-only", refusing to serve to black customers. On February 1, 1960 a group of black college students sat down at a segregated drug store lunch counter in Greensboro, North Carolina, refusing to leave unless they were waited on. The owner called the police, but the students' arrest only served to further inflame the civil rights movement in Greensboro and elsewhere. Eventually the Federal Government passed the 1964 Civil Rights Law prohibiting restaurants and other businesses from discriminating on the basis of race. What negative freedom was at stake in this controversy? What positive freedom? What lessons would you draw from this episode regarding the balancing of positive and negative freedom? Would your evaluation change if, instead of black college students, it was homeless families that were being denied lunch (assuming they had the money to pay for it)? What about people wearing Republican campaign buttons being told to leave a restaurant owned by an ardent Democrat? Finally, what effect, if any, do anti-discrimination laws covering business services (like restaurants) have on the "internal" freedom of the people in our story—the owner of the drug store, his or her employees, and white and black customers?

Part II

Institutions

Markets

7

There is a tendency among economists to refer to "the market" as if it were like a clock. You can find all sorts of clocks, running on different kinds of power, analog or digital, mounted on walls or on your wrist, with different numbering styles and decorations, but in the end they are all just clocks. They tell you what time it is on a 12 or 24 hour cycle. If you need this basic information, any clock will do.

Not so with markets, however. Markets do bring buyers and sellers together, but beyond that they differ not only in appearance but also in purpose and performance. Markets comprise a class of social institutions, like families and governments, and their characteristics have a profound effect on economic outcomes. This has become particularly apparent in the course of the transformation of the formerly Communist countries of Asia and eastern Europe to more capitalist principles. All are becoming "market economies" in some sense, but their success depends crucially on the *kinds* of markets they are developing. Fortunately, economics has some useful things to say about the different ways markets solve the problems put to them. Based on this, we can not only choose intelligently between markets and other systems of allocation, but also among different market types.

7.1 Markets in History

As far as we are able to know, there have been markets for as long as there has been organized human society. Archeological evidence from Europe, Asia and the Americas indicates that prehistoric humans used objects that were gathered or produced hundreds or even thousands of miles away, and presumably some form of exchange was the basis for transferring these goods from one location to another. With the dawn of civilization in China, India, Egypt and Mesopotamia we find coins and designated trading sites.

Markets in all such societies were *places*. They were central locations where goods were brought together for sale and where negotiations over transfers of ownership were carried on. Nevertheless, markets fulfilled other, less directly

P. Dorman, *Microeconomics*, Springer Texts in Business and Economics,
DOI 10.1007/978-3-642-37434-0_7, © Springer-Verlag Berlin Heidelberg 2014

economic functions. The Greek agora, for instance, was a marketplace, but it was also where political decisions were made and social relationships developed.

Only in the last few centuries have people begun to think of markets as pure, disembodied realms of exchange, placeless institutions with no other function than to facilitate trading and establish prices. Indeed, some markets appear to have those characteristics today. Think of financial markets, which take their ethereal existence across global computer networks. Trading in standardized assets like stocks and government bonds is entirely anonymous; no one knows or cares anything about the person whose trade shows up on the computer screen. All that matters is the price and quantity.

Actually, markets have never entirely separated themselves from their social context. As we will see, they still have to insert themselves into networks of information and expectation, and these are the products of complex social organization. Even the financial markets are less disembodied than they appear. (This becomes apparent during episodes of fraud, when the hidden role of those who make markets function rises to the surface.) All markets have to solve, or try to solve, certain problems, and all such solutions, as we will see, require active human intervention to produce results. The rest of this chapter will identify the most common problems and strategies for coping with them.

7.2 The Enforcement Problem

Consider this story: Fred and Ginger run into each other at the market. Fred looks at Ginger and says, "I like your backpack"; Ginger looks at Fred and says, "I like your watch." As it happens, Fred has a box full of watches back at home, and Ginger keeps a backpack collection in her closet, so Fred would rather have Ginger's backpack than the watch he is wearing, and Ginger would rather have Fred's watch than her backpack. A mutually profitable trade appears to be in the offing.

Now let's make two further assumptions. First, as is common in economics, we will assume for convenience that both individuals are purely self-interested. Fred gets no pleasure from Ginger's feelings, nor Ginger from Fred's. Second, we assume that each person's action is entirely independent of the other's. That is, both Fred and Ginger decide separately what to do with their possessions, and whether or not a trade occurs will only be known after the fact. Based on this, and with two goods and two individuals, we can envision four possibilities, each of which can be ranked by Fred and Ginger according to their desirability. The most desirable outcome for Fred, which we will designate as a 4, is that he keeps his watch and also acquires Ginger's backpack. The second most desirable is that he gives up his watch but gets her backpack. The third is that he keeps his watch and fails to get her backpack. The fourth, of course, is that he loses both. A similar ranking holds for Ginger, except that she prefers having a watch and no backpack to a backpack and no watch.

Each person has the option of taking one of two actions, supplying what they have to the other or keeping it for him or herself. Using the game theory notation of

		Ginger	
		D	C
Fred	D	(2, 2)	(4, 1)
	C	(1, 4)	(3, 3)

Fig. 7.1 Payoff matrix for a potential trade between Fred and Ginger. Fred and Ginger are the players; C (supplying the good already possessed) and D (not supplying it) are the choices. There are four possibilities depending on which choices are made, ranked from 1 (worst) to 4 (best). Within each set of parentheses, the payoff for Fred is given first, then the payoff for Ginger

Chap. 3, call the first option cooperation and the second defection. The result is the payoff matrix shown in Fig. 7.1.

As this diagram makes clear, Fred and Ginger face a Prisoner's Dilemma. Each has an incentive to try to acquire what the other has without giving up what they have. Whether or not Ginger gives Fred her backpack, Fred is better off by hanging onto his watch, and the reverse is true for Ginger. If each follows a purely individualist motivation, they will end up in the cell in the upper left-hand corner, keeping everything and exchanging nothing. Only through mutual cooperation can they make themselves both better off by each giving what they have to the other. **A market exchange is a solved Prisoner's Dilemma.**

This last statement may seem a little extreme. Surely, you would think, the billions of transactions that occur daily in a modern economy can't all be intricate negotiations of collective action problems. Above all, doesn't the assumption of independent choice (Fred's decision to part with his watch is completely independent of Ginger's decision to give Fred her Backack) contradict how markets usually work? When you buy a loaf of bread in a store, you do not give up your money independently of getting the bread, nor does the store hand you the bread until you pay for it at the cash register. If decisions are not independent, then the upper-right and lower left-hand cells (where one person gets everything and the other nothing) are not possible, and the only choice is whether to exchange (lower right) or stand pat (upper left).

These are valid criticisms, but experience indicates that it would be a mistake to reject the independence assumption altogether. Many market transactions involve promises which come due at different times. It is certainly possible for people to break their promises, either on purpose or because they are not as careful as they might be to avoid circumstances that will lead to the promises being broken. Loans provide obvious examples, but much the same could be said of other longer-term contracts, as when one company promises to make future shipments of supplies to another. Moreover, it is often possible for sellers to cut corners on quality, and this is comparable to a sort of withholding. Suppose you agree to buy two machines from me, each of which costs me $500 to make. If I quietly cut back on quality, lowering my cost to $250 apiece, what is the difference (for me) between this form of deceit and only shipping one rather than both at the original quality? As for you, it depends: maybe two lower-quality machines are better than one higher-quality one and maybe not.

The general point is that, for markets to succeed and exchanges benefitting both parties to take place, there has to be a reliable expectation that buyers and sellers will keep their promises. The expense of bringing about this expectation, and having it borne out in most cases, is one type of **transaction cost**. A transaction cost is the cost of using market exchange to achieve an economic objective. This category covers everything from searching for suppliers and consumers to comparing various offers to writing up contracts to enforcing them. It is perhaps the single most important concept for understanding markets as institutions. If it is too costly for people to use a market, they won't and the potential advantages of this system of allocation will be lost.

To return to our problem of promise-keeping, we can identify several approaches that have worked in different times and places to ensure that markets do not break apart in an epidemic of mutual defection.

Social norms. As we saw earlier, markets did not arise in isolation from other human activities, and they are not usually isolated today. People who take part in markets have social as well as economic lives. They are raised to internalize the values of their culture, and they respond to signals from those they interact with that tell them whether they are behaving appropriately or not. Recall the argument from Chap. 4, for example, that if most members of a society are calculating the costs and benefits of engaging in crime, the battle has already been lost; the first line of defense is always the inculcation of values that favor honesty and respect. Fred is not likely to try to cheat Ginger, partly because it is likely that he has been raised to feel uncomfortable about cheating (even if he gets away with it), and also because he would feel bad if Ginger found out about it and let him know. Multiplied by millions and billions of people and transactions, this is an irreplaceable foundation for successful markets.

Social scientists use the term **social norm** to refer to a rule for behavior that has the properties of being nearly universal within a society and binding on its members. Once such a rule gets established it can have considerable inertia behind it. If everyone else expects you to observe a particular custom, you pay a price for violating it—but if you go along, you become part of the "everyone else" for other members of your society. Healthy societies have rules for promise-keeping, among other behaviors, that facilitate the operation of markets. Much depends on the maintenance of these norms.

Unfortunately, it is also possible for the expectation of promise-keeping to unravel. If a few individuals violate this norm visibly and are seen to prosper from it, they will attract imitators. After all, in situations with characteristics approximating a Prisoner's Dilemma, there is a powerful material incentive to take advantage of the cooperation of others. Before long, as defection becomes the normal expectation, it simply becomes too costly for most of those clinging to the cooperative norm to hold out. Worse, a situation of generalized defection (a dog-eat-dog world) can also be self-reinforcing and therefore stable. The message here is that it is extremely important for societies to police the boundaries of social norms relating to honesty and mutual respect. Violators cannot act with impunity.

Reputation. Adam Smith was well aware of the problem posed by dishonesty in an incipient market economy like Britain's. He argued that most people would realize that it was in their interest to act fairly, since the short-term advantage of opportunistic behavior would be overshadowed by the long run cost to the scoundrel's reputation. In more modern terms, he recognized that the Prisoner's Dilemma game of the market, if that was indeed what it was, would be played repeatedly among a small enough group of players that each would be able to remember who had behaved honorably in the past. In this way the healthy virtues on which useful markets depend would be inculcated naturally. Indeed, Smith expected that individuals would come to see their own behavior through the eyes of those they dealt with, so that reputation would be truly internalized: people would experience the views of others as their own. In other words, if you have a positive reputation, this would be reflected in positive feelings you would have about yourself, and you would do the right thing in order to enjoy these good feelings.

Unfortunately, unless this internalization is permanent and very powerful, Smith's argument depends crucially on the assumption that the number of players is small enough that reputations will follow each of them around. This was plausible in the Britain of his day. Small-scale transactions, such as those between landlords and tenants or shop-keepers and customers, were largely confined to local markets based on face-to-face recognition. Larger financial deals were conducted among a small class of property-owners who knew of one another despite being relatively more dispersed. As markets grew larger and more anonymous, however, it became evident that neither the direct or indirect effects of social reputation would play a sufficient disciplinary role without some measure of conscious support.

Modern economies use a variety of means to reinforce the power of norms and reputation. Think of the role played by newspapers and television, which aggressively report on businesses accused of offending the public trust. Most of us are familiar with the mass media, but in some ways even more important work is done by the specialized business press, which digs up the dirt on culprits within its domain. Every major sector of a modern economy has such a publication, and readers pay close attention to reports of dishonesty or incompetence. Another example is the trade or professional association. In principle, doctors, attorneys, accountants and other professionals police their own ranks; if they find someone has stepped out of bounds, they revoke his or her license to practice. Trade associations also take complaints and may publicize or expel violators. Governments may also maintain lists of approved or licensed firms based at least in part on adherence to a minimal set of standards for lawfulness and honesty.

The importance of the roles played by such institutions is illuminated for us when they fail to do their job. During the US corporate scandals in the early part of the previous decade, for example, information emerged that major accounting firms were acquiescing in dishonest bookkeeping by the companies that hired them, hiding their expenses and reporting fictitious income. This harmed the interests of their legitimate business partners, investors and employees. What failed in this case was not just the integrity of individual accountants and their companies, but the oversight of the profession as a whole. Among insiders in the field there were certainly suspicions, and perhaps even hard evidence, that standards were being violated, but the information was not made public. Reputations that should have been tarnished at the first whiff of impropriety were allowed to remain intact.

Contract design. For interactions that take place over time, it is sometimes possible to introduce elements into a contract that provide an incentive for one party to perform to the satisfaction of the other. There are many familiar examples: a contractor engaged to build a house will be paid in stages or even in a lump sum at the end of the project rather than upfront, a worker may be hired at a lower pay scale with raises tied to performance, and a bank may charge borrowers a penalty if they are late in their payments. What all of these have in common is that one party to the contract, typically the one in a better bargaining position, gets the other to agree to an arrangement in which the stronger will be in a position to evaluate and reward the weaker at regular intervals. From the point of view of the side that is able to extract such concessions, the contract goes a long way toward solving the enforcement problem. The weaker side may not be as pleased, however. For instance, most employment contracts are written in such a way that firms have more leeway to alter wages in response to their evaluation of the work an employee is doing than the employee has to alter, say, effort in response to the firm's follow-through on matters like working conditions and training.

In recent years there has been a flurry of interest among economists in the study of contract mechanisms that can embody their own internal incentive systems. A poorly designed contract can be self-defeating, encouraging one side or the other to behave in a way that makes the relationship unproductive. Consider, for example, a contract in which a producer of upholstery agrees to supply an automobile manufacturer with seat covers over the course of a year. If the agreement provides for bonuses for on-time delivery but no penalties for defects, you can imagine what the supplier will try to do if production starts to fall behind schedule. Similarly, is it a good or a bad thing to reward someone for success over which they had only partial control? A company that rewards its workers when profits go up would seem to be on the right track, except that profits depend on a great many things in addition to workers' effort and skill. What effect would paying this reward have if profits rose as a result of the mistakes of the competition, and not for anything the company, including its workforce, did on its own? As we will see in the next chapter, there can be large costs from failing to think through all the consequences of contract design.

Contract law. The last line of defense against fraud and abuse in the market is the legal system. It can't be the first line, because it would be too expensive to litigate every possible violation, but no system of norms and reputation will deter all potential opportunists. The main branch of the law that adjudicates complaints arising from failure to keep promises is contracts. Attorneys for the plaintiff argue that the terms of a contract were violated, resulting in harm to their client. Defendants' attorneys dispute the interpretation of the contract or the facts of its performance. Judges, usually with extensive training in contract law, conduct the trial and render an opinion. The entire system is a backstop for the effective functioning of the market system.

There are many ways for such a system to malfunction. The law itself may be undeveloped, as has been the case in some countries emerging from Communism. (Hungary, for example, delayed its privatization of state enterprises until its entire body of property and contract law could be rewritten.) Attorneys may not adhere to high professional standards; they may fail to make effective arguments or may try to use political or other pressures rather than the force of legal evidence. Finally, and perhaps most important, the judiciary itself may not be independent or competent. Judges may have a personal stake in the disputes before them (a conflict of interest) or may be under the control of outside political or economic factions. Perhaps they just don't know how to sort through the complexities typical of modern contract law. All of these shortcomings have appeared in countries that have tried to rapidly introduce market systems during the past two decades, but they also appear from time to time in countries with longstanding market economies.

7.3 The Complexity Problem

Legally, market transactions normally take the form of either bills of sale (immediate exchanges of goods for money) or contracts (exchanges of promises). The first of these is simple and straightforward; take a look at your next cash register receipt. Contracts, however, can be complicated to draw up, and if they are they will also be costly to execute and enforce. The smooth functioning of a market economy depends on its ability to keep most contracts to a manageable level of complexity.

An example will reveal what is at stake. The real estate market is the venue for the buying and selling of land and buildings erected on it. Such transactions tend to be lengthy, complicated and expensive. Much may depend, for instance, on exactly where the boundaries of a property are located, so this must be ascertained as part of the agreement. Houses must be inspected for hidden as well as visible features, and detailed instructions must be drawn up for items that may or may not be conveyed, such as appliances, fixtures and even decorative elements (like stained-glass windows). There are many ways third parties can have a claim on real estate (as collateral, through easements, etc.), so all such claims must be researched. It usually takes many weeks from the initial sale agreement to the final closing, and, between them, the parties should expect to pay a few percent of the sale price to the small army of lawyers, accountants, appraisers, insurers and others who process the complexity of the transaction. If every market in the economy were as complex and costly to operate as real estate, the system would soon grind to a halt.

At its heart, what makes real estate such a complicated business is that its product is nonstandard. You can't just say "acre" (or "hectare"), "house" or even "three-storey Victorian" and leave it at that; every parcel and structure has to be scrutinized characteristic-by-characteristic. Think how different this is from "car". Buying a car is also complicated, but much less so. If it is a new car, you write up an agreement specifying make, model and any additional features desired. Also to be agreed on are the terms of payment—how much down, what interest rate and over what period of time. It is a bit inconvenient, but nowhere near as costly and cumbersome as real estate.

The difference can be summed up in a single word: standardization. A few specifications are sufficient to indicate everything that needs to be indicated about the car, because each is standardized. Every car with those specifications should be identical to every other. If cars were built by hand, one at a time, according to the passing whim of the builder, buying cars would be more like buying houses. (There is indeed a small market in custom-built cars, but even here there is more standardization than in real estate.) Standardization, which in some ways we lament as bleeding serendipity and richness from life, is essential to a modern economy.

How do economies achieve standardization of most goods and services traded in markets? Here are three broad approaches:

Private sector standardization. Standards are often set by the producers themselves, either separately or through associations. Since converging on a few standards can help expand the market for their products, firms are usually well aware of the issue. If a single firm (a monopoly) can command a decisive share of the market, it is in a position to make its own standards the ones all others must follow. (We will take a closer look at the advantages and disadvantages of this phenomenon in Chap. 13.) The most familiar contemporary example of monopoly standardization is the Microsoft Windows operating system (and related Microsoft software). For just over a decade, from around the time of World War I to the late 1920s, the Ford Motor Company had similar standardization influence in the US auto industry.

Trade associations have long sought to standardize the products of their members. This can be seen in the regulations promulgated by German producer guilds going back to the Middle Ages—consider the German Beer Purity Law, dating from 1487—but an interesting American example can be found in the grain trade. When white settlers moved to the middle west, such as Illinois and Iowa, they found some of the most fertile land for growing corn, wheat and similar crops in the entire world. They began to farm, and bags of grain were soon loaded onto ships and trains heading east to the large urban markets. Initially, each farmer's grain was bagged separately, with the grower's name attached. Since the commodity in question was "farmer X's grain", which would normally be different from farmer Y's (due to differences in seed, growing conditions and farming methods), each farmer had to negotiate separately for his price. The system was complicated and burdensome to both growers and buyers. A farmer had to consider whether the price he could get from a different buyer or in a different region might be better than the one offered him at the moment. There was no way to find out except to cart his bags somewhere else and negotiate all over again.

This logjam was broken by an association formed by the railroad companies. They had no interest in keeping track of which bag was grown by whom; they were building giant grain elevators and wanted to just dump the cargo en masse. Their solution was to devise a system of grading. Rather than being identified by its grower, each shipment would be classified by general variety (such as summer or winter wheat) and by rough standards of quality (number 1, number 2 and so on). This immediately had several effects. It removed the uncertainty over price, since all grain of a standardized type and quality would be paid the same. It made shipping far more efficient, since grain could be moved in common containers and mechanically dumped into elevators. And of course it also gave the railroad companies more leverage over the growers, since they were the ones who decided what the quality categories would be and did the actual judging. Beyond this, it stimulated the growth of secondary markets, such as trading in grain futures. (A futures contract is an agreement to buy or sell a specified quantity of a specified quality at a specified price at a specified time in the future.) With the standardization of grain it became possible to speak of, say, number 2 winter wheat as the "same" commodity now or in 90 days, even though the actual wheat might be grown by two different farmers a thousand miles apart. In reflecting on this system, we can recognize both gains and losses. The farmers lost a bit of clout, and subtle differences in the product itself were erased through the imposition of broad standards. On the other hand, the far greater efficiency attained by standardization ultimately benefitted most farmers, if not to the same degree as others in the industry (shippers, middlemen, speculators).

Without looking too far, you should be able to find many other trade groups that have succeeded in constructing standards to facilitate trade.

Public standardization. Government agencies sometimes play a lead role in standardizing products. Many states, for instance, regulate apprenticeship programs in the building trades for such skills as electrician, carpentry, masonry, etc. There are multiple reasons for doing this, but an important one is to standardize what it is to be, say, a mason and what skills a client can expect to be purchasing.

A controversial recent example at the Federal level is the "organic" designation for food products. After months of hearings, the Agriculture Department issued a set of standards that all growers would have to meet if their produce was to carry an organic label. These included the number of years of continuous organic practice and the specific types of fertilizers and pest control substances that could be used. Certification has proved expensive, discouraging many smaller growers from taking advantage of the system. In addition, it has turned out that there isn't a clear line separating organic from conventional; it is a matter of degree, and minimum standards fail to reward growers who go beyond the lowest common denominator. All the same, the standards appear to be facilitating the rapid expansion of this industry by removing confusion over which goods should be marketed under what set of guarantees.

Technological standardization. Quite often standardization is achieved not through any conscious intervention but through the technical dictates of the production process itself. Railroads have a common gage (distance between left and right wheels) because they have to in order to run on the same tracks. Air traffic control signals have to be standardized internationally because airplanes fly through multiple control regions. Above all, by its very nature, mass production standardizes products in order to achieve economies of scale. (This term will be defined and discussed in Chap. 12.) That is the underlying reason why buying a car is not like buying a house. The car you buy will be nearly identical to thousands of others, not so the house. If we ever transform housing construction into a mass production industry with cookie-cutter products, real estate transactions will become simpler (and perhaps houses will become less personal).

7.4 Markets and Information

In many ways, markets are remarkable instruments for discovering and bringing together information about the economy. Each participant is in a position to make decisions about what and how to produce or consume based on the information that, perhaps, only they know. Drawing on what they have learned they can make and accept offers, and the prices that result in the marketplace will reflect, in some sense, the accumulated knowledge of everyone who participates. As this is being written, for instance, there is uncertainty in the global petroleum market due to the unsettled prospects for the world economy. If the major industrial countries are able to recover and resume economic growth, their demand for petroleum will go up, adding to already increased demand from countries like Brazil, India and China. If there is a second global slump or a slowdown in China in particular, however, demand will fall. There is also much debate about future supply, for reasons of both geology and feasibility (especially in deep-water deposits). Further down the road, there is uncertainty over actions governments might take to curtail energy use as a means to limit climate change. Meanwhile, around the world there is a constant buying and selling of oil contracts, and the price of the precious fluid is in flux. When traders anticipate greater demand, the price goes up; when they anticipate less, the price falls. In this way day-to-day price movements track the perceptions of those who are following the situation closely. If someone has an informed hunch that suggests a large new oil deposit is going to be announced, she might put in an order to sell, speculating that when this news gets around the price will fall (increase in supply) and she will be able to re-buy the oil she has just sold at a lower price, and therefore a profit. Sitting in front of my computer screen several time zones away, I have no knowledge of who this trader is or what she thinks she knows, but if she and several others like her have an effect on the market, I will see the price dip. This tells me that there has been a change in the perceptions of traders: they think supply will rise, demand will fall or perhaps both.

This episode tells us four things:

1. Markets reward people for having information that is better or sooner. Those who speculate in oil, or even just those who think carefully about major purchases or employment decisions, will fare better if they are better informed. Just as you would have an incentive to research the repair record of a used car you are considering buying, an oil trader has an incentive to learn all she can about the industry and its prospects. Information is valuable.
2. Market prices reflect the perceptions of all the people who participate through buying and selling. This is true for better or worse; if traders are misinformed or if they misunderstand the signals they are getting the price will reflect this too.

Market failures can also disrupt the process, as we will see in more detail in the chapters to come. Nevertheless, because of the first point, markets are somewhat more likely to be right than wrong in their perceptions. There will always be a range of views, of course, but markets summarize them through aggregation—yielding a price that reflects the relative pressures of overall supply and demand.
3. All the information that flows through a market is condensed into a single number, the price buyers are willing to pay and sellers willing to accept. What gets lost is all the richness: where the tip about the discovery of new oil fields came from, how reliable it is, and even that the information pushing down the price of oil is about potential future increases in supply and not, say, a drop in expected demand from a major consumer like China or Brazil. Nevertheless, with millions of prices being set every day, it is a great convenience to have information in this simplest of forms.
4. People in other sectors of the economy have to take prices into account, and when they do this they are, in effect, incorporating the information on which the prices were based. If the price of oil goes up, for instance, a community group may have to reconsider its decision to send several of its members to a conference in another city; perhaps they can no longer afford the cost of transportation. This group knows nothing about oil exploration or controls on offshore drilling or other arcana of the oil industry, but they know a higher price when they see one. This price induces them to make decisions that are consistent with the new information, however: if, in this example, the supply is likely to be reduced, consumers should look for alternatives. The point is that the price system not only summarizes information, it invests information with economic force.

That is the good news. The bad news is that this machine does not run all by itself. There is still a need for people to actually ferret out the information that markets trade on, and how the market is organized can have an effect on the costs entailed. Also, the process by which information is brought together in markets is fraught with pitfalls. We will now look at these two problems more closely.

7.5 Search Costs

Much of the information that people need is about what is happening in the marketplace. Who are the other buyers and sellers? What goods are they offering or trying to buy? At what prices? What are their reputations? In order to make a wise choice, first you have to know what the choices are. Market decisions are complicated when goods are less standardized and when producers are smaller and more numerous. Sometimes the crucial information is virtually invisible, such as the true creditworthiness of a particular borrower or the skill and character of a worker.

As information becomes harder to get, some people specialize in digging it up. This leads to a *market for information*. A simple example is the newspaper want ads or Craigslist; the service being provided is little more than a bulletin board. More sophisticated are trade journals (take a look at *Advertising Age* or *InfoWorld*) and various firms that provide industry data for a price. These enterprises are business opportunities for those who own or work in them, but they are crucial elements of the market system as well. Market information services are to a market economy what political information—a free press—is to political democracy. If they are ineffective or simply underdeveloped, markets will do their job more poorly.

When information becomes costly, either in terms of your own time or someone else's (and therefore your own money), you will have to learn how to economize on it. Information that is essential will have to be acquired one way or another, but information of only moderate relevance or importance may not be worth the expense. If you consider the implications of this rather obvious point, you will see that it undermines the model of rational decision-making presented in Chap. 3. Recall that the decision-maker is viewed as maximizing her expected utility (EU), where

$$\mathrm{EU(B)} = \sum_i p_i v_{\mathrm{B}i} \quad i = 1, 2, \ldots., n \quad \sum_i p_i = 1$$

This formula says that the expected utility of an option B is the sum of all the values it might have, each multiplied by the probability that it will be the actual value. To perform this calculation, an individual would have to know and be able to evaluate all these values and also place a probability on each one. Then it would be necessary to do this for every available option, so that the one that maximizes expected utility is selected. If information is costly, however, there will be missing pieces in this formula. Some values and probabilities will simply not be identified or estimated. What then?

A plausible answer was given by Herbert Simon, an early winner of the Nobel Prize in economics. A decision-maker will first decide what outcome will be deemed good enough; this sets a benchmark. Then he will begin looking at options, not with the intention of calculating their exact expected value, but just to see whether it meets the good-enough standard or not. This usually requires less information. As soon as one option passes the test, the process stops. The decision-maker selects this one and declares himself satisfied—or, to use Simon's term, *satisficed*. **Satisficing** is a decision process whose goal is to identify at least one course of action that meets a sufficient level of adequacy. Imagine that you are buying a house in an urban area, for instance. There are a multitude of houses for sale, each unique in its location and features. You also have to consider future possibilities that might affect your choice, such as where new development will be located, transportation bottlenecks in the years ahead, and whether particular neighborhoods are likely to become more or less desirable. Since gathering the information to answer all these questions would either take you several years or require you to hire an army of real estate analysts, picking the single best house over the full range of scenarios is out of the question. Instead you should go into the process with a rough idea of what sort of house, at what price, you will accept and then start looking. When you find one that appears to meet your expectations, make an offer.

A good rule of thumb is this: the more complex the information for a given market and the less support one can get (or afford) from information services, the greater will be the difference between the satisficing standard and the maximum expected utility that could be had from a full-blown investigation. This is an important insight; it says that information burdens can reduce the value people can expect to get from participating in a market.

Thus far we have been treating information as a homogeneous good. You can have more or less of it, but there are no distinctions to be made between different sorts of information. Of course, in the real world it is exactly the opposite. It is always easier to get some types of information than others. Houses for sale in some neighborhoods are listed more prominently or are more convenient to visit. It takes less technical know-how to understand some differences between alternative computer configurations than others. It's easier to interview a job applicant who comes from a similar social background.

In this context it is important to bear in mind that markets do not exist in a vacuum. They are surrounded by a complex layering of social networks based on family relationships, ethnicity, friendship, shared activities, etc. Every social connection is a channel that transmits information, so the types of networks that market participants are involved in will determine to a considerable extent the types of information that will be abundant or scarce. Studies of geographically concentrated industries, such as Silicon Valley in California or high-end apparel in Italy, have shown that clubs, associations and other groupings play a key role in conveying information about job openings, potential markets, business opportunities, etc. Indeed, there is an interesting chicken-or-egg question here. Which comes first—do markets develop in a region and eventually lead to wider and deeper social ties, or do dense social networks provide the basis for markets to prosper? Many economists now think that the second possibility plays the greater role, and this is having an impact on policy research, particularly in developing countries.

7.6 Asymmetric Information

Every market transaction has two sides, and each requires information. Thus far we have looked at the information problem from just one person's point of view, but now we will consider the impact on markets if information is not just incomplete but *unequal*. There are many reasons why this might be the case, but one is especially important: people, typically sellers, often know something about themselves or their products that others, usually prospective buyers, don't. Job applicants, who want to sell their labor, normally know a lot more about their own abilities and intentions than someone who just reads their resumés would be able to figure out. Sellers of specialized equipment often know more about their specifications than buyers who have to make a wide range of purchases and don't have time to study each one in detail. Borrowers, who are effectively selling a loan to a bank or other lender, know more about their likelihood of repaying than outside credit analysts. This situation, in which one party to a transaction has private information unavailable to the other, is called **asymmetric information**, and it is widespread throughout the economy.

One solution to this sort of problem would be a rule requiring everyone offering to sell a good or service to disclose all their private information, even (and especially) if it contradicts the impression they wish to create. Such regulations have been imposed, for instance in the used car market: sellers are required to inform prospective buyers of all defects they are aware of. Such rules cannot completely do away with private information, of course, but they can greatly reduce its scope.

The opposite tradition, however, has been dominant in most capitalist countries over the past several centuries. At its most extreme it takes the form of **caveat emptor**, "let the buyer beware". It indicates that the seller is not obliged to disclose anything, and it is up to the buyer to find out the information on her own or to convince the seller to put guarantees of quality into the contract. To take one striking example, it is not against the law to lie on your resumé—for instance, to claim you have a college degree when you never attended college at all. It is up to employers, the potential buyers of your services, to find this out for themselves. If they do, they can refuse to hire (or can fire) you, but that is it. You are free to send your fraudulent resumé to the next job opening. (Do I have to say that I am not encouraging you to do this?) In the world of employment, it's caveat emptor in nearly every case.

There is a longstanding debate among legal theorists over the merits of this doctrine. It has the virtue of encouraging people to be responsible for their own choices—to do research, to demand guarantees if appropriate, to determine what risks are worth taking. It reduces the burden on the judicial system, which might be overloaded if every disappointed buyer thought he deserved a day in court. On the other hand, there is always a case to be made for combating dishonesty and guile. Current debate focuses on the role of contract clauses like warrantees that guarantee quality. If consumers are in a position to purchase them, they can decide whether such a guarantee is worth the price they have to pay to the seller. If not, they have no recourse, and strict caveat emptor may undermine the confidence on which markets rely. These comments are very general, however, and careful analysis of the issue usually turns on the particularities of different markets.

So let us assume that asymmetric information in much of the economy is unregulated; where can it lead? There are many possible outcomes, but we will focus on one that was first introduced by Joseph Stiglitz, a major figure in the economics of information (and other fields as well). To do this, we will construct a simple but telling model.

Here is the situation: an employer has a fixed sum of money M to spend on hiring workers to do a project. Each worker will be paid the same wage w, so M/w gives us the number of workers N the employer can afford:

$$N = M/w$$

The goal of the company is to produce a quantity of product designated as Q. The more workers, the more product, so it would appear that there is little to figure out:

the employer should pay the lowest possible wage that will attract enough workers. Let's say that there is a larger labor market that sets a standard wage w_m; at this wage a large number of workers will apply for a job, but not below it since they would find other work that pays w_m. If this were the entire story, the firm will pay w_m and hire M/w_m workers to produce as much Q as possible.

But now let's introduce a wrinkle: workers differ by quality, and quality affects output. Specifically, if we designate the average quality of the workforce as v, output is a function of this variable and the number of workers:

$$Q = \mathrm{f}(N, v)$$

To make matters a little more complicated, let's assume that, while each worker knows his own quality, this information is not available to the employer. Asking will not help, because workers will claim to be high quality whether or not they actually are. Fortunately for the employer, there is one clue available: no worker will work for less than what he knows he is worth. If he knows he is 10 % more productive than the average, he will hold out for a 10 % higher wage, thinking that his value will eventually be recognized somewhere. The employer's problem is to determine a wage w^* that results in the highest possible level of output P^*.

Variables in the Invisible Worker Quality Problem.
M = the fixed sum of money available to the employer for paying wages
w = the wage paid to all workers
w_m = the minimum wage that will draw applicants, set by the market
w^* = the wage the results in the highest production of output
N = the number of workers employed
Q = the quantity of output produced
Q^* = the maximum possible quantity of output
v = average quality of the workforce

For simplicity, we can divide this problem into two components. The first is establishing the size of the workforce. From this perspective, as we have seen, there is little to consider; lower wages mean more workers and more output. Figure 7.2 on the next page displays this relationship, assuming, for the moment, that v remains unchanged.

Now let's look at the impact of raising or lowering the wage on average worker quality, leaving aside its effect on the number of workers that can be hired. At any wage equal to or above $\mathrm{w_m}$ all workers of the lowest quality will apply, but better workers will apply only if the wage rises to meet their higher expectations. Thus a worker who is 10 % more productive than the average $\mathrm{w_m}$ worker will demand a wage that is 10 % higher. In this way, the further the wage rises above $\mathrm{w_m}$ the more and better workers will apply. This means that the average quality of the applicant pool also rises, so that, even if the employer doesn't know which individual workers are the best, over a large number of randomly selected hires she will find the average quality going up. This is reflected in Fig. 7.3.

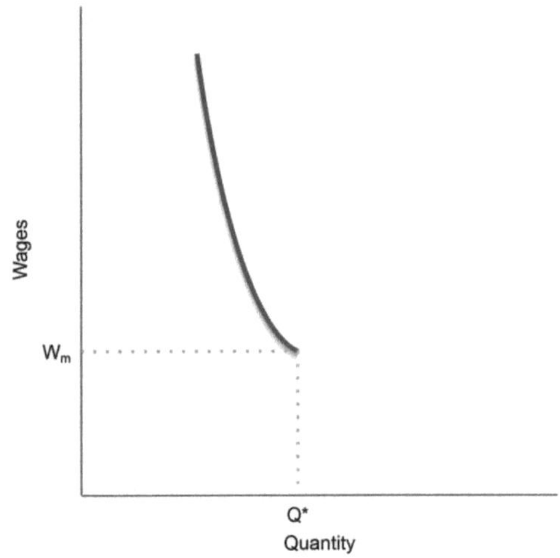

Fig. 7.2 Wages and output in the invisible quality problem, holding worker quality constant. w_m is the lowest wage the employer can pay and attract a labor force. Given a fixed amount of money to spend, this wage leads to the highest number of workers and, holding worker quality constant, the highest level of output Q^*

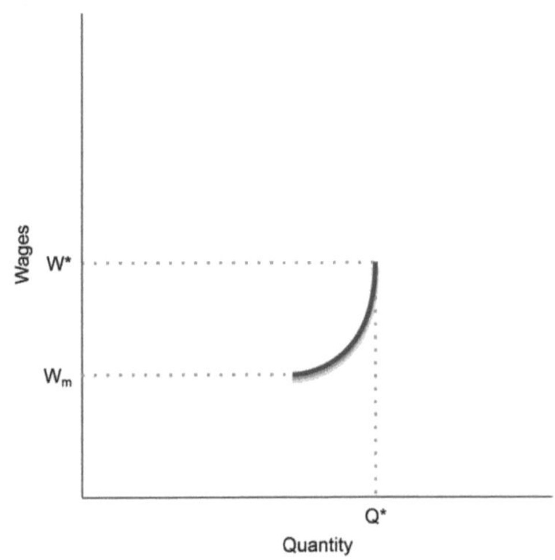

Fig. 7.3 Wages and output in the invisible quality problem, holding the number of workers constant. Average worker quality rises as the wage rises and therefore so does output. This relationship tails off as fewer workers remain to be discovered with very high quality levels. At w^* the very highest quality worker joins the applicant pool, and there are no further advantages to raising wages

Now let's put both effects together in one diagram. Naturally, how they combine depends on their relative strength, and we have not provided any basis for determining this. One possibility is that, over an initial level of w above w_m the quality effect is stronger, but after that the numbers effect takes over. This would give us a combined wage-output relationship as in Fig. 7.4 on the following page:

As the wage rises above w_m output rises due to the predominance of the quality effect. Maximum output occurs when $w = w^*$. Above that level output declines. The employer in our story will therefore agree to pay a higher-than-market wage out of self interest.

Our story is completely hypothetical, of course, and it was tailor-made to yield its interesting outcome. It is fair to ask whether it has any real world counterparts. Many economists are inclined to say that it does. It is common for firms to pay

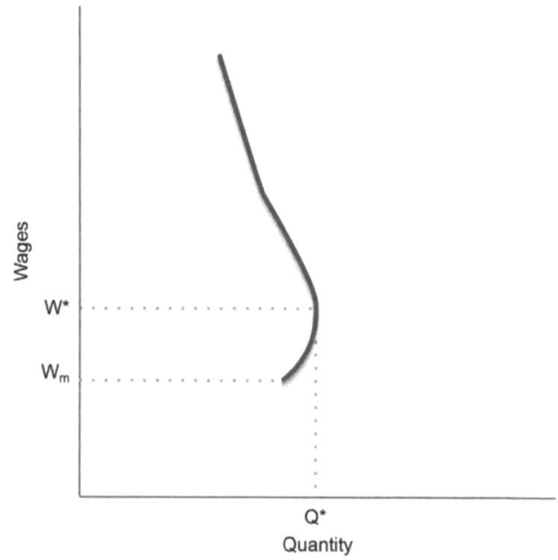

Fig. 7.4 Wages and output in the invisible quality problem, all effects included. Because of the quality effect, the wage that produces the most output, w^*, is higher than the lowest wage that attracts enough applicants, w_m

wages above the lowest level they would need to attract a workforce and, while other motives might account for this, there is some evidence that asymmetric information is a factor. Similarly, many firms are reluctant to lower their pay scales even during times of general wage slippage. Again, there are other explanations, but students of personnel practices think that maintaining applicant quality is a consideration. And the phenomenon extends beyond employment. A similar story can be told for lending: a bank that charges the highest possible interest rate is likely to attract borrowers who are, on average, less creditworthy than the lender might like. After all, if you think you have a high probability of defaulting on a loan, you may not care at all what the interest rate is; whereas if you expect to pay faithfully the interest rate is much more important. Since creditworthiness is, to a great extent, private information—something borrowers know a lot better than lenders—interest rates may influence the quality of borrowers in a manner similar to the effect of wages on the quality of workers. The lesson economists draw is that asymmetric information can fundamentally alter the way markets work, diminishing the role prices play in equilibrating supply and demand.

7.7 Market Efficiency

In recent years there has been increased attention given to exactly how markets work on a transaction-by-transaction level. This is because some markets hum along like well-oiled machines, while others operate slowly and clumsily, but it is also because economic policies often call upon us to *create* markets from scratch, where they have not existed before. Proposals to auction the public airwaves or allow trading in pollution permits, to mention two examples, depend for their success on whether the markets they require can be crafted to work efficiently and well.

What does "efficient" mean in this context? How would we determine whether a market was efficient or not? First, we should be clear that an efficient market is not the same as an efficient economy. Economic efficiency is about the relationship between outputs and inputs, whereas market efficiency is about one piece of this, the extent to which markets expedite transactions, process information and achieve equilibrium. It is a more narrowly technical conception than economic efficiency, but not without significance.

Unfortunately, although the term "efficient markets" is used in many branches of economics, there is no consensus on the exact criteria that should be used to determine whether any given market should be deemed efficient or not. This means I am free to offer my own:

1. Cost. An efficient market has low overhead costs. In particular, search and enforcement costs should be minimal relative to the economic advantages available to those who participate in the market. The advent of computers, for instance, has greatly reduced the cost of operating financial markets, thereby increasing their efficiency. (What their effect on *stability* has been, however, is another story, as we will see in the book on macroeconomics.)
2. Speed of equilibration. An efficient market reaches equilibrium (as defined in Chap. 5) quickly, especially in comparison to the speed of events that dislodge it from equilibrium. In this respect as well, financial markets score highly. Even though the stream of news that upsets supply and demand is almost continuous, the adjustment is virtually instantaneous, again thanks to the computer. Labor markets are the opposite, slow and usually caught in disequilibrium. Excess supply or demand for labor can last for years, and the wage for identical jobs can vary from one employer to the next.

   When markets are in disequilibrium, or divided into regions or other fragments with little cross-communication, it is common for multiple prices to appear for the same good. This creates an opportunity for **arbitrage**, which is buying a good in a market in which its price is low in order to resell it in a higher-priced market. Arbitrage is a consequence of disequilibrium, but it is also a force that tends to restore equilibrium, since any additional buying in the low-price market drives up the price to some extent, and selling in the high-price market drives it down. Antique dealers who go to estate sales in order to buy items that they resell in their shops to tourists at a large markup are engaging in arbitrage.
3. False trades. This concept is a bit more complicated. The basic idea is this: some buyers want an item (are willing to pay) more than others, and some sellers are willing to sell for less than others, but these inclinations are not visible. When trading begins, and before an equilibrium has had a chance to establish itself, transactions are more or less random: some buyers find sellers and vice versa, but others don't. There is only a weak relationship between having a greater desire to trade (high willingness to pay, willingness to accept a low price) and success at finding a suitable trading partner. Meanwhile, each transaction has its own price. Eventually the market comes to an equilibrium, with a price that registers the willingness to pay of the marginal buyer and willingness to accept of the

marginal seller. We can use this price as the benchmark, in the spirit of the Market Welfare Model.

Now ask the question, during the chaotic period during which the market equilibrium was being established, were any trades made that involved buyers whose willingness to pay was below the (future) equilibrium price or sellers whose minimum acceptable price was above it? This could happen. Suppose the eventual equilibrium price for a new strain of rice proves to be $.20 a pound. Before this become clear, there may be trades above and below that price. In itself this is not a problem; If my willingness to pay is $.70 and your marginal cost (and minimum acceptable price) is $.15, even though we may exchange at $.40 a pound, the trade itself is beneficial. Your marginal cost is less than the equilibrium price and my benefit is greater. But if we trade at $.40 and your marginal cost is $.25, then we have exactly the sort of exchange that an efficient market ought to prevent: once the price settles at $.20, it will be below your marginal cost.

The underlying point, then, is straightforward: markets should encourage sales by those whose costs are less than the equilibrium price and discourage sales by those whose costs are greater; and they should encourage purchases by buyers whose willingness to pay is above the equilibrium price and discourage purchases by those whose willingness to pay is less. Since it takes time for the equilibrium to assert itself, perfect success is not at all guaranteed. Transactions that violate this stricture are referred to as **false trades**. To minimize them, markets should not only reach equilibrium sooner, they should also not depart too far from equilibrium during transition periods. To a considerable extent this is a function of the effectiveness of information flows between market participants. An example of a market that generates plenty of false trades is real estate: when buyers and sellers have spotty information about the other sales taking place within a large urban market, for instance, they are prone to make transactions they may later come to regret.

4. Utilization of information. Since markets are, among other things, information processing mechanisms, their efficiency depends on the extent to which they actually do incorporate all available information. This really has two levels, individual and collective. At the individual level, participants in an efficient market will acquire all the information that bears upon the goods being traded. As we have seen, this is called into question by the likely presence of search costs. In addition, at the collective level there should be incentives that lead better informed choices to replace poorer ones. For instance, suppose the market under examination is for next year's rice. At the individual level, if the market is to be efficient individuals must be motivated to dig up information pertinent to next year's supply and demand. But this is not all: some people will do this better than others. The ones who get the most, best and soonest information should be rewarded by the market; their expectations, rather than those of more poorly informed traders, should be the ones that set prices in the future. Suppose I am the first to observe a clue that indicates that next year's rice harvest will be below average. If the current price is $.20 a pound, I will be happy to make a

commitment to buy at that rate next year, thinking that scarcity will make rice more expensive. If a further clue develops, more traders should come to the same conclusion. This will increase the future price to, say, $.25 and reward my earlier instinct, for now I can already sell next year's rice that I bought for $.20 and make an immediate profit of $.05 a pound, even without waiting for next year to come around. That's how an efficient market *should* work: prescient expectations should drive out mistaken ones.

How can we tell, in fact, whether markets utilize information in this way? Consider a market whose participants are in the process of gathering information. At any moment their information is incomplete, but new information appears regularly. Sometimes current prices will prove to be too low, since the next batch of information shows that demand is (or will be) greater than thought, or supply less. Sometimes it's the opposite and prices are too high. Economic theory tells us that, in an efficient market, there will be no systematic bias; no one will be able to predict whether today's price is too high or low based on the previous record. If they could that would be information that someone should have utilized, and it should already be factored into the price. To put it differently, new information, if it is truly new, comes as a surprise, and we should not be able to predict it before it occurs. Since we can't predict what the information will be, we can't predict how it will affect prices.

This may seem like an arcane point, but we will see that it has important implications for the analysis of financial markets in particular. If the price of a bond or a share of stock incorporates all available information, then no one should be in a position to regularly outguess the market. Future price movements are simply unpredictable, and there is no point to paying someone for her investment advice. Is this actually true? We will look at this question in more detail in Chap. 18.

With these four efficiency criteria under our belt, we can turn to features of markets that promote or interfere with their efficiency. This is an enormous topic, and to give you a feel for it I will look at just one issue, how prices are determined for individual transactions. What follows is a small taste of the fast-growing field of **market microstructure**, the study of the rules that different markets follow in their detailed operations.

The most natural pricing rule, the one that is honored in markets and bazaars around the world, goes like this: the buyer makes an initial price offer, the seller counteroffers, and they go back and forth until they agree somewhere in the middle—or not. The technical name for this procedure is a **double auction market**; parties on both sides of the market are free to bid their offers up or down. Research has shown something useful: double auction markets are highly efficient in their speed of equilibration. If there are many buyers and sellers all bidding with each other on the same item, the market as a whole will tend to arrive at an equilibrium price quickly with few false trades. If you want a picture of this to place in your mind, think of a farmers market. Dozens of farmers arrive early in the morning, each with the morning's harvest of lettuce. For simplicity, assume that every head of lettuce is identical. No price is posted at any stall, because the farmers expect to negotiate. Next a swarm of consumers descends on them, and individual consumers begin to haggle with individual farmers. Exchanges begin to be made, and both farmers and consumers begin to notice the emerging price patterns. Before long they are using this information to guide their own bargaining, and before the morning has barely begun all are agreeing on a common price. This is what we would expect, given the results of experiments conducted by economists.

Unfortunately, there is a downside to double auction markets: what works for individual products and face-to-face relationships can be inapplicable to transactions at a distance or over a large, diversified range of products. In fact, markets of this sort play a limited role in allocating most consumer goods in industrialized economies. Far more common is another approach, in which the seller puts a price tag on the item and leaves it to the consumer to decide whether to buy or not. This is referred to as a **posted offer market**. Such markets require much less engagement on the part of those that participate in them. The negotiating over a bag of rice may be fun (or at least bearable) in a farmers market, but it is hard to imagine how one could bargain over every item in a large store. The downside of posted offer markets, on the other hand, is that they equilibrate very poorly. Excess supply and demand are fixtures in our economy largely because we rely, as we probably must, on market mechanisms that stumble slowly towards equilibrium.

The Main Points

1. Markets are less place-based and more abstract in modern times than they were long ago. Even so, there are important social and institutional differences between different kinds of markets.
2. When the goods that trade in markets have an element of promise—commitments to do something in the future—enforcement becomes important. An exchange under these circumstances is a solved prisoner's dilemma: individuals have succeeded in cooperating, making a mutually beneficial exchange, instead of taking advantage of the other party. Bringing about this sort of cooperation can be expensive, involving writing complex contracts, monitoring and enforcing them—what economists refer to as transaction costs. Fortunately, social norms and reputation effects often facilitate exchanges of promises so that cumbersome enforcement measures aren't necessary.
3. If goods are not standardized, market transactions become costly in other ways. Effort has to go into determining and communicating the unique characteristics of each item, special forms of protection against risk may be needed, and mass production technologies are difficult to implement. An important example in modern economies is the real estate sector. For these reasons, standardization plays an important role in the development of markets. Goods can be standardized by private agreement among producers or consumers, by monopoly control, government regulation or technological change.
4. Market prices reflect the information that participants have, or think they have, about the goods being traded. We often use expressions like "the markets think...." to express this. Summarizing all the information individuals possess

in a single number, the price, had advantages and disadvantages. We lose the richness of this information—what is consists of specifically, how credible it is, etc.—but it is easier to act on. In fact, since the price has real effects on producers and consumers, it invests the information flowing through markets with economic force.

5. Information is often costly to acquire, which makes it expensive for market participants to try to maximize their gains according to the expected utility formula. Instead, they are likely to satisfice, setting a benchmark level of value or benefit and accepting the first option they come across that meets this standard.
6. A widespread, complicated problem is asymmetric information, which occurs when one party has access to information that the other doesn't. The most common case is when the seller has private information about him or herself or about complex products that could vary a lot in quality. In situations like this, buyers will interpret the seller's offer price as a signal of hidden quality. The result is that prices will not be set simply by supply and demand, but may result in excess demand or (more likely) supply.
7. Markets differ tremendously in how efficient they are, where efficiency refers to (a) low transaction costs, (b) a high speed of reaching equilibrium, (c) little initial deviation from the ultimate equilibrium (reducing false trades), and (d) maximum use of all available information (and therefore unpredictability). Efficiency is strongly influenced by the rules that govern how markets work at the level of individual transactions—market microstructure. As an example, a double auction market tends to be extremely efficient, but most consumer markets follow the posted offer model.

Terms to Define

Arbitrage
Asymmetric information
Caveat emptor
Efficient markets
False trades
Market microstructure
Satisficing
Social norm
Transaction cost

Questions to Consider

1. One reason we don't perceive most market exchanges as solutions to Prisoner's Dilemmas is that we take the legal guarantees for contract enforcement for granted. It is instructive to consider the pressures placed on markets that are not backed by law. One example is the trade in illicit drugs such as cocaine. A buyer who received inferior or insufficient product, or a seller who is not paid promptly and in full, cannot file a claim in court. Can you create a payoff matrix for a drug deal that conforms to the structure of a Prisoner's Dilemma? How well do you think this model applies? In the absence of legal recourse, what other factors make it possible for drug dealers to conduct their business?
2. When a company adopts a policy of branding, it is making its ownership of its various products more visible to consumers. Such a company wants you to know that everything it sells is a part of its enterprise, and it wants you to be more likely to buy because you know this. In a sense, the advertising campaigns to build up brands are creating a general corporate reputation that can be applied to all the products sharing the brand logo. Does this mean that branded products are more likely to fulfill the promises made for them because of the need to preserve this reputation, or is this function undermined by the advertising strategy on which branding is based? In answering this question, it may help to think of particular branded products, comparing them to similar products sold by companies, perhaps smaller, that do not engage in branding.
3. Can you think of another good or service in our economy, besides real estate, that is highly nonstandardized? Describe the process by which purchases are made. Is it as costly and time consuming as real estate?
4. Most countries evaluate their hotels, assigning them between one and four or five stars based on facilities, service etc. A tourist can then book a hotel without knowing anything else about it, just on the basis of how many stars it has been given. What are the advantages and disadvantages of such a system?
5. Does the asymmetric information problem apply to auto repair services? If so, what is the private knowledge? Do people who need their cars repaired sometimes pay extra for reasons analogous to the "invisible worker quality" story? Explain.
6. What experiences have you had with double auction markets? Do you think the transactions you were able to make were better (fairer, more likely to produce benefits for both you and your trading partner) as a result of the opportunity for both sides to negotiate? (Try to imagine how the same transaction would transpire under a posted offer system.)

8 Firms

The United States, Europe and Japan are often said to possess market economies, implying that the role played by markets is the most important characteristic they have in common. This may be true, yet one could just as well call them corporate economies, for their large-scale business organization is arguably no less important. These are the engines of productivity, and they also define the landscapes of wealth and economic power.

It is interesting that the private business enterprise, conceived as an entity separate from those who work in it or own it, is a relatively modern invention. The first instances occurred during the sixteenth century, when joint-stock companies (businesses whose shares of ownership could trade hands among investors) were first chartered by European monarchs. Nevertheless, it was not until late in the nineteenth century that this form of business organization began to play a predominant role in economic life. Moreover, as we will see, important aspects of their structure and operations have continued to change right up to the present. It is probably not a bold prediction to say that the corporation of the future will look quite different from we take for granted today, but who will shape this evolution and for what purposes?

8.1 A Taxonomy of Business Organizations

A firm is, for our purposes, any organization that produces goods or services and has an identity distinct from any particular individual affiliated with it. I can start a business called "Economic Answers", and it can consist of just me and my strange ideas, but simply by giving it a name of its own I have established it as a firm.

Perhaps the most common basis for differentiating different types of firms is ownership. A firm can be privately or publicly owned, or some combination of the two. Public ownership means ownership by some governmental entity. The US Postal Service is an example on the federal level; municipally owned electrical companies are publicly owned as well. Public colleges and universities are enterprises owned by state governments, and if a university owns its own radio or

P. Dorman, *Microeconomics*, Springer Texts in Business and Economics,
DOI 10.1007/978-3-642-37434-0_8,

TV station, this too is publicly owned. Private ownership, on the other hand, means any ownership that isn't public. IBM is a privately owned firm, but so is a local nature sanctuary that might be the property of the Sierra Club. Private colleges and universities are privately owned in this same sense, as are churches, synagogues and mosques. Actually, many businesses that are mostly privately owned have some element of public ownership, as when a government agency or, more likely, public pension fund purchases shares of ownership. Calpers, for instance, is the state agency that invests money on behalf of the pension fund for California state employees; when this chapter was first being written it had a portfolio of $166 billion, about two-thirds of it invested in the stocks of otherwise private firms.

Within the world of privately owned business there is a distinction to be made between for-profit and not-for-profit enterprises. IBM is operated for profit; Harvard University is not. This doesn't mean that it is impossible for IBM to lose money or, for that matter, for Harvard to turn a profit from time to time. (Harvard has a profitable sideline in royalties stemming from research by its faculty.) Rather, the distinction comes from law and tax policy: for-profit enterprises are assumed to have no purpose other than to generate income for their owners, and so they are treated differently from organizations that operate according to other motives.

Narrowing our universe further, within the category of private, for-profit enterprises are three different ownership forms:

Proprietorships. These are firms owned by a single individual. This person has full authority over its operations and can dissolve it at will. If its owner dies, the proprietorship dies too. This is a common ownership structure for small businesses, but there are large proprietorships as well.

Partnerships. These are firms owned by a designated group of individuals. Law firms normally take this form, and the goal of junior employees is to some day "make partner"—be selected to join the partnership, taking one's place as one of the owners. Partners have authority over the enterprise as a group; they must all agree in order make a decision. If anything happens to one or more of the partners, the entire ownership structure must be reconstituted.

Corporations. A corporation is owned by its shareholders, but these people are not specified, so they can buy into and out of the business without changing its ownership form. In this sense, the corporation is a fully independent entity, not tied to any particular individual or group. The principle of authority is one share, one vote. At meetings to decide company policy, shareholders are given votes based on how many shares they own. Thus there may be many shareholders at the moment a meeting takes place, but only a few may hold enough shares to have a real say in the outcome. Shareholders can dissolve a corporation or merge it with another, but otherwise, so long as it remains solvent (avoids bankruptcy) the corporation continues indefinitely. Its owners come and go, but the corporation is granted immortality.

The numbers and economic heft of these three ownership forms in the US is given in Table 8.1. As we can see, proprietorships make up by far the largest number, but corporations vastly outweigh them in sales.

Table 8.1 Population and revenues of US private, for-profit firms, by ownership type, 2003

ownership type	Population (millions)	Revenue (trillions of dollars)
Nonfarm proprietorships	22.6	1.3
Partnerships	3.1	5
Corporations	5.8	27.3

Source: Statistical Abstract of the United States (2012)

Within the even narrower world of private, for-profit corporations there is one more distinction, between publicly and privately traded. This is somewhat confusing, because we have already encountered the public/private dichotomy at the level of ownership. A privately traded corporation is one whose shares circulate privately between individuals entitled to buy and sell them. The Cargill Corporation, for example, is one of America's largest. Its assets are reported at over $72 billion and its sales at nearly $120 billion. Nevertheless, all its ownership shares are owned by members of the Cargill family. They are free to buy and sell them to one another, but they cannot sell them to outsiders. A publicly traded corporation, on the other, has exactly this license. Its shareholders are unrestricted in whom they can sell to. When a privately traded corporation "goes public", it gains the legal right to issue shares to the general population. This makes it possible for its small number of private owners to cash out a portion of their shares; rather than having all their wealth tied up in this one company (which is risky), they can sell as many shares as they wish to the public and use the money to diversify their holdings. Being able to do this is clearly a big advantage, but it comes at a cost: the Securities and Exchange Commission requires all publicly traded corporations to file financial reports disclosing their current health and future prospects. Privately traded firms like Cargill have no such requirements, which is why we know a lot less about them.

An important variant of the private corporation is the **cooperative**. A cooperative is based on the principle of one member, one vote rather than one share, one vote. The people who are given this voting power differ depending on what kind of cooperative is being considered.

- Worker cooperatives. These are run by their workforce on a democratic basis. Workers normally provide the startup capital, and new employees are asked to make an investment as part of taking the job, but differences in the amount of individual ownership, if any, are not taken into account in governance. The largest and best-known system of worker cooperatives in the world is the Mondragón Cooperative Corporation in the Basque region of Spain.
- Supplier cooperatives. These are run by those who sell to the cooperative, typically on the basis of one supplier firm, one vote. This type of business is most often found in agriculture, where it is also known as a marketing cooperative. Sunkist oranges, Ocean Spray cranberries and Land O' Lakes butter are all products of such enterprises.
- Consumer cooperatives. These are governed by boards of directors elected by consumers and arise most frequently in retailing. Cooperative grocery and

department stores are common in most industrialized countries; one well-known consumer coop in the US is Recreation Equipment, Incorporated (REI), which specializes in outdoor goods.

8.2 Aspects of the Modern Corporation

What accounts for the size and productivity of today's corporate behemoths? To examine these questions we have to take a closer look at how they are organized, who runs them and how.

The place to start is with their defining characteristic, their independence from those who own or are otherwise affiliated with them. In recent years there has been renewed controversy over the "personhood" of corporations. Why should it be, it is asked, that a business, particularly one whose only purpose is to make a profit, should be accorded the rights of persons under the US constitution? Certainly a corporation, whatever it is, is *not* a person, and so the case for granting it the same rights as real living, breathing human beings cannot be assumed. Nevertheless, the separateness of the corporation from its owners, and therefore its status as an independent entity, is the foundation upon which industrialized economies depend.

To understand this, consider what happens if you start your own company, borrowing money in the hope of making a profit. Even if your business is based on sound ideas, luck may turn against you, and you may have to shut it down. If you do, and if your business is a proprietorship, you personally are liable to repay your business loans in full. Even though your business had its own name, it was not independent of you. It was not a separate person, so to speak, and so, when it collapsed, its debts became yours. This is the risk you take when, as a business proprietor, you incur liabilities.

It is obvious that, under such a system, few really large investments will be made. The bigger the investment, the bigger the risk, and no one wants to be saddled with a debt that may take a lifetime or more to pay off. Who would borrow the millions or billions of dollars necessary to build railroad lines, steel mills or electrical power plants? In addition, if ownership of even a single share of a company's stock were sufficient to expose you to the risk of being personally responsible for its debts, there would be a powerful disincentive to spreading your income across a large number of such investments—exactly the opposite of the diversification strategy that reduces individual risk. (We will study this in more detail in Chap. 18.)

The solution is **limited liability**. This concept means what it says: if a business is operated under limited liability, its owners are not fully liable if it fails. Normally, liability is limited to the firm's **equity**, the ownership stake held by its investors. If the firm goes under, the investors lose the value of this ownership, but beyond this they have no obligations to anyone. The firm may owe its creditors hundreds of millions of dollars, but shareholders are not responsible for it. Limited liability is a legal creation. Governments must create a form of corporate ownership that embodies it, laying out the rules that have to be followed to enjoy its benefits.

As it happens, the United States led the world in the creation of limited liability enterprise. The first law making it an accessible and predictable opportunity was passed by the state of New York in 1811, and within a generation it had become the norm in many other economically important states. Similar statutes were not enacted elsewhere for many decades: Sweden in 1844, followed by England (1856), Portugal (1863) and Belgium and France (1867). Thus, by the time the US Supreme Court endowed the corporation with the legal standing of a "person" in 1886 the important economic safeguards were already well in place. (The main effect of the Court's action was to restrict the ability of governments to pass laws regulating corporate activity.) Taking the broad view, it is not surprising that this international wave of limited liability laws coincided with the development of large-scale industrial technology; the possibility of the second necessitated the adoption of the first.

Limited liability cements the separation between the enterprise and its owners, but this is a two-way street. To the extent that the corporation really is an independent entity, it also has the potential to be independent of the owners' control. This separation of ownership and control has been a gradually evolving phenomenon, the subject of intense scrutiny by economists, managers and others. At first, in the nineteenth and early twentieth centuries, it was normal for owners to keep a close eye on day-to-day business operations. Such legendary figures as John D. Rockefeller and Henry Ford wanted to be on top at all times and distrusted professional managers. Over time, however, the advantages of trained managerial expertise became evident and owners receded into the background. While there are still some large corporations whose owners remain dominant, most are now firmly in the hands of full-time managers.

To the extent that owners have ceded power, questions are raised about **corporate governance**. This term refers to the structure of decision-making that determines what corporations do, from detailed production and marketing questions to broad matters of strategy. Figure 8.1 on the following page provides a rough sense of the relationship between the different players.

At the top are the shareholders; collectively they are the ultimate authority. Nevertheless, in practice their power is highly attenuated. For one thing, there are usually a great many of them, and they are likely to be widely dispersed with few lines of communication for discussing their common interests. Moreover, if the corporation is publicly traded the faces of the shareholders are constantly changing. Many hold stock for short periods of time and have little incentive to get involved in company policy. If they don't like how things are being done, the simplest course of action is to sell their shares and buy stock in some other company.

One step below is the board of directors. This group is elected by the shareholders at regular intervals, serving as their eyes and ears. They attend meetings several times a year and have access to all important company documents. The directors have the power to approve major decisions and to hire and fire all managers up to and including the CEO (chief executive officer). How much influence they have in practice depends on how much they take. Some boards are notoriously lax; their members draw comfortable incomes but pay little attention to

Fig. 8.1 A general model of corporate governance. Corporate governance is usually portrayed as a *top-to-bottom* hierarchy starting with the shareholders and ending with the non-managerial workforce

the company they are supposed to oversee. (When scandals erupt in high corporate offices, directors usually plead that they had no idea what was going on, as if it were not their job to know.) If you follow the business pages of a major newspaper, however, you will see many examples of highly interventionist boards that keep close tabs on the managers who serve under them.

Who serves on the board of directors? It varies from company to company, but some typical backgrounds are these:

- Representatives of major creditors. If a corporation has borrowed extensively from a bank or other financial institution, it is likely that an officer of this institution will serve on the board.
- Representatives of major suppliers or customers. A company that generates electricity might have a director hailing from an industry that is a major energy consumer in the region, or vice versa.
- Experts in the corporation's line of business. Corporations with major investments in chemicals will have chemists; banks will have economists; aerospace companies will have engineers.
- Directors and managers of other corporations. It is assumed that broad experience in overseeing and managing other companies will introduce a valuable perspective. When two or more firms share the same director it also shores up information-sharing, joint projects, etc.
- Prominent citizens. Often a board will have a member with high name recognition but no evident connection to the company's line of work. University presidents, Nobel prize winners, star journalists and similar luminaries add glamour to the roster.

When election time comes around, a board of directors will nominate a slate of candidates, consisting primarily of themselves. Election of these slates is usually pro forma, because most shareholders don't vote. Any vote not cast is transferred to a designated board member, called a **proxy**, which increases that person's voting power by that one share. If a large percentage of shares is not voted by its owners, the proxy can have a controlling influence all by himself. On occasion a dissident slate will emerge, unhappy with the performance of the current board. They will publish notices in *The Wall Street Journal* and similar outlets, trying to convince shareholders to transfer voting rights to them instead of to the board. This battle is called a **proxy war**; the cards are stacked in favor of the incumbents, but sometimes the challengers prevail.

Below the board of directors, but holding the day-to-day reins of power, is the top management team, the CEO and his or her immediate appointees. They are responsible for the strategic direction of the company and for establishing its procedures and operating culture. At one time these high-level managers rose through the ranks, but now it is more common for them to move laterally from one company to another. In other words, it is thought that strategic management in any given corporation has more in common with this role at other corporations than it does with more operational tasks further down the ladder in the same firm.

With so much mobility on the part of CEOs, corporate analysts began to worry that their loyalties might not be centered enough on their current job. Boards of directors could seek out and hire the managers with the best resumés, but how could they be sure that, once on board, they would serve the company and not their own wider career goals? Two general answers emerged during the 1970s and '80s. First, it was argued, financial institutions should aggressively lend money to strong corporations seeking to buy out weak ones. A corporation is weak if the price of its shares is low, because this makes it less expensive for outsiders, wealthy individuals or other corporations, to buy up a controlling interest. When a corporation is bought out, typically its top managers are released. The upshot is that, fearing for their jobs, managers will do all they can to boost the price of their company's shares. It is the availability of buyout funds, provided by banks and other financial institutions, that keeps the process going. The general name for this arrangement is the **market for corporate control**.

The second proposal was to pay managers less in straight salary and more in bonuses, options and other instruments tied to share prices. An example is the **stock option**: this is a piece of paper that entitles the holder to buy a certain number of shares at a stated price. If the stock rises above that price, the holder can make money by "exercising the option"—buying the shares at the lower option price and immediately reselling them at the actual market price. This is a particularly lucrative opportunity if the option price is set low, if the number of shares that can be optioned is large, or if the market as a whole is moving upward, as it was during the 1980s and 1990s. In a few cases, fortunate CEO's made hundreds of millions of dollars this way in a single year. Promoters of the stock option concept argued that it would encourage CEO's to run their companies in a manner that would be reflected in higher stock prices, and that this would be good for the economy as a whole. They showered Congress with arguments, and campaign contributions, and were rewarded with a law that specified that the value of stock options did not have to be considered a business expense for the purpose of calculating profits.

What both of these approaches have in common is the belief that stock prices are a reliable indicator of the dexterity with which corporations are being managed: if prices go up, this must mean that the enterprise is more profitable, which in turn reflects successful management. Moreover, proponents also argue that corporate profitability is also a measure of the return to society on its members' investment:

more profits mean greater efficiency and social well-being. These are strong claims about the functioning of the stock market, of course, and there is certainly less optimism about them today than when they were first made. If the economic plunge of the late 2000s was related to the profit surge in the years immediately preceding it, for example, that surge did not reflect the long-term consequences of decisions made by corporate managers. We will explore this issue in greater detail in Chap. 18.

There are also important issues of corporate management and organization below the top tiers. Among these is the rise of the **M-form** enterprise. In Fig. 8.1 we pictured a simple top-to-bottom flow of authority, and this would make sense if the firm were engaged in a single line of work. Modern corporations, however, are usually more diversified, making and selling different products, or pursuing activities that are qualitatively quite different, such as, in the case of automobile companies, producing cars and also operating lending operations to finance consumer purchases. A modification of the basic organizational form is presented in Fig. 8.2 on the following page.

Governance at the top is the same, but each qualitatively different activity has its own parallel hierarchy. In effect, each line of operations is organized as if it were an independent company, but instead of its own board of directors it answers to the top management team. It is a simple departure but has two important repercussions.

First, it permits corporations to grow as large as they wish without overtaxing their operational management. Consider an automobile company. For each new line of cars it introduces, it can create a new hierarchy with its own specialists in finance, accounting, personnel, etc. Similarly with extending the business to foreign countries or even to goods or services that aren't automobiles—adding new activities does not complicate managing old ones. This would not be the case if, for instance, there was one personnel office for the entire corporation; then each new operation would make the personnel function larger and more cumbersome.

To understand the second implication, it will help to pause for a moment and consider the difference between what I have been calling "top" and "line" or "operational" management. The term "line" comes from military organization. Imagine an army lined up before its top officers. The commanding general and his immediate team are called the "staff"; officers who have more direct contact with the troops are distributed through the line, and that's why they are called "line". This distinction has been carried over to the corporate world; now the CEO and other top managers are staff and those who supervise specific operations—who have direct contact with the work and those who perform it—are line.

M-form organization does not change line functions, except to make them slightly more independent. Its big impact is on staff. What does the top management team do, in fact, in such a system of organization? The answer is that they make strategic decisions involving the transfer or resources between different units and the phasing out of old units or the creation of new ones. In other words, they are allocating resources across divisions that resemble independent firms; they are economic planners. They leave it to their subordinates to worry about how the work gets done within each division. (This exaggerates a bit, but only a bit.) From

Fig. 8.2 The M-form model of corporate organization. The M-form system of organization is characterized by parallel hierarchies below the level of top management

this point of view, the introduction of M-form organization replaces a portion of the invisible hand of the market with the visible hand of strategic high-level managers. (This term, the "visible hand", comes from Alfred Chandler, a hugely influential business historian who first called attention to these issues.)

Even at the base of the hierarchy, at the level of operating and maintaining equipment, personal contact with customers, transporting supplies, etc., there are significant organizational questions. The traditional model assumes a top-down hierarchy in all activities, since only in that way can the intentions of higher-level management (and ultimately the owners) be fulfilled. It is only at the top, the theory goes, that the work of large numbers of people can be coordinated, and so a regimented workplace is the price we pay for efficiency.

There are four general problems with this claim.

First, it is far too sweeping. In many work situations horizontal communication between workers offers a degree of coordination superior to hierarchical control by supervisors. This depends on the location and flow of information through the enterprise, which is partly a function of technology but also depends on the system of organization itself.

Second, it conflates two issues that ought to be kept separate, authority and coordination. The claim of authority is not just that it is a better vehicle for coordination (which it may or may not be), but that it reflects the priority that some interests have over others. This is a difficult matter, but for now the point that needs to be made is that, in a sense, the fundamental question of economics is whether, and under what circumstances, the market-influenced interests of firms actually coincide with more general social interests. In instances in which they diverge, it may well be the case that owners' interests should *not* be given automatic priority. We recognize this, for example, in whistleblower laws that protect workers who reveal information about corporate malfeasance, even if in doing so they violate company policy.

Third, a manager's possession of authority can be thought of as a type of competence. That is, her accountability to the chain of command puts her in a better position to make certain types of decisions. But putting it this way makes it less absolute, for there are many other competencies that may be pertinent. Knowing how to keep a machine running with minimum downtime for repairs, or knowing what the most common customer complaints have been during the past week, are also competencies. In workplaces where many types of knowledge and skill are germane to the success of the enterprise, it makes sense to create work teams that have decision-making authority corresponding to the practical abilities people bring to them, even though such teams may cut across formal layers of authority.

Finally, workplaces are never just locations of production; they are also social settings. People form bonds and animosities; they communicate or fail to connect. If the requirements of the workplace as a social setting are ignored in the name of a rigid adherence to hierarchy, performance is likely to suffer.

The role of authority in the workplace has been one of the most contentious issues throughout the history of capitalism, and it remains in dispute today. Economics has something to offer to this question: an analysis of production that points to the efficiency benefits and costs of hierarchical systems of organization. We have barely skimmed the surface of this topic.

8.3 The Need for a Theory

As odd as it may seem, to an economist the first question to be asked about firms is why they exist in the first place. The main focus of modern economics is on markets: how they function, how well they perform as allocative institutions and how they can be improved. The bias of most economists is on the side of using markets to get things done. Firms operate within markets, but on the inside they are predicated on the notion that, for some tasks, markets are the wrong tool.

At the core of market organization is voluntary exchange. Buyers and sellers come together, establishing prices and quantities traded. In this way goods are brought together so that they can be used for new purposes. A firm also moves goods and services between people and locations, as when a legal opinion prepared by a staff lawyer is sent to a manager in the same company to help her decide whether to take a certain action. The difference is that, inside firms, these transactions are not made on the basis of exchange or prices, but administrative decision. The staff lawyer does not sell a legal brief to management; she is paid a salary to provide general legal advice, and a manager decides which briefs are to be written by which lawyers. (This echos the discussion of markets and administration as allocative devices in Chap. 3.) But if markets are so effective in coordinating complex economic activities, why do we see administrative decision-making in firms?

At the operational level, this question takes the form of the "make or buy" problem. Suppose you operate an ice cream stand. You are renowned for your ice cream and draw on a loyal clientele. One day it occurs to you, why buy your cones from some other producer; why not develop your own recipe and produce exactly the sort of cones you think will complement your ice cream? In speculating on this, you are deciding whether to make or buy. *A firm is an economic entity that makes at least some, or some part, of the goods and services it sells.* If absolutely everything were purchased there would be no firm, only exchanges taking place in a market. If your ice cream company buys all its food items, contracts with another company to scoop and serve, another to publicize the product, and so on, then there would be nothing for you to do but make purchases in the market, just as consumers do. Your company wouldn't be a company at all.

When a business chooses to make something itself, it is effectively committing itself to "buying" that item only from its own internal producers. If you decide to make your own ice cream cones, you are foregoing the opportunity of shopping for a better deal from an outside supplier. This has an obvious cost attached to it: if someone else can make cones better and cheaper than you can, you are passing on the opportunity to buy from them instead. (True, you could always reject your own products and buy them from other suppliers, but then you would lose the value of your investment in in-house production.) If markets are *thick*—that is, if they have many buyers and sellers—by producing yourself you are taking an especially brave stand, for you are implying that none of the other firms can match your own work. In our ice cream example, to invest in your own production of cones is to determine that no cones purchased from any other producer can surpass yours, at least in the context of your own stand. If you don't believe this, you should buy, not make.

Consider in more detail the example of a company with a legal department that gives it advice and handles routine litigation. A firm with such a department has chosen not to *outsource*, not to buy its legal services from an outside law firm. This means that, all other things being equal, it will be bigger; it will have more employees and undertake more activities. If it changes its mind, it will lay off its lawyers and get smaller. Looked at this way, you can see that if a firm outsourced absolutely everything, it would have no employees at all, do nothing, and exist in name only. (It could even outsource its outsourcing operation, paying someone to buy all the goods and services it gets from suppliers.)

In this way, how the firm resolves the make or buy decision determines the boundaries of the firm. This is pictured in Fig. 8.3 on the next page. Each star represents an activity; the lines between them represent the process of bringing activities together. If the arrow is contained within the boundaries of the firm it represents an administrative operation; if it crosses a pair of boundaries it represents a market exchange. Some firms are smaller, choosing to combine activities by buying part of what they need from other firms; some are larger because they choose to do more themselves. Economists are interested in where these boundaries are drawn, and why.

Stepping back from this analysis, we can see why it matters. Some firms in our economy are extremely large, encompassing a vast number of related, or even largely unrelated, activities. Others are small, doing just a few things. What accounts for this? Does this size distribution benefit our economy, or would we be better off with fewer, larger corporations or more, smaller ones? This is one of the two fundamental questions economists try to answer when they develop theories about the role of firms in organizing economic activity.

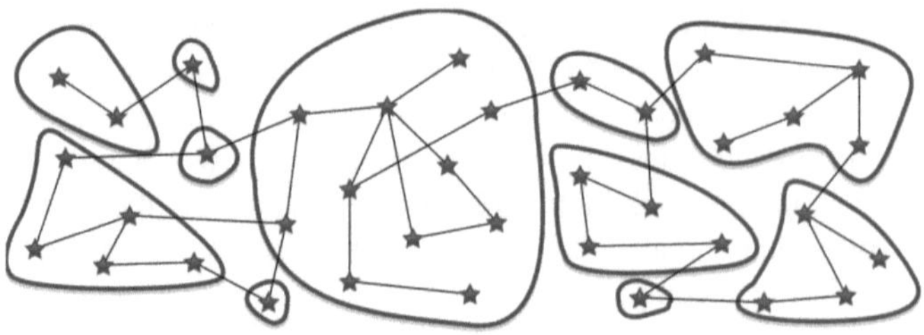

Fig. 8.3 The make or buy decision and the boundary of the firm. Each *star* represents an activity; the *rounded shapes* are firms. *Lines* connecting activities show them being brought together. If this happens within a firm it is organized administratively; if it happens across their boundaries it is organized through a market

The second general question concerns the way they operate. In much economic writing we can see firms described as if they were individuals. "The firm", we are told, maximizes this thing or chooses that thing. Yet firms are not monolithic entities; they are comprised of a great many individuals and the complex work relationships between them. How then can we say anything precise about business decision-making? For instance, it is often assumed that the guiding objective of firms is to maximize their profits, but is this true? Some people within the firm may have this motive, and others may not. What determines whose views win out, and why?

This has much to do with the internal organization of enterprises, of course. Corporate governance and the decision-making structure at the level of operations will largely decide how different interests will be balanced. There is a purely descriptive aspect to this: we can observe how actual corporations are run and draw the appropriate conclusions. Economists are interested in explanation, however; they want to know *why* corporations are run the way they are and whether their methods are in the public interest. Is there a model of socially beneficial business organization that plays a role in answering these questions similar to that of the Market Welfare Model in assessing the performance of markets?

8.4 From Adam Smith to Alfred Marshall

Adam Smith had a lively interest in how labor could be made more productive. In a celebrated passage in *The Wealth of Nations*, he wrote about a pin factory:

> One man draws out the wire, another straights it, a third cuts it, a fourth points it, a fifth grinds it at the top for receiving the head; to make the head requires two or three distinct operations; to put it on is a peculiar business, to whiten the pins is another; it is even a trade by itself to put them into the paper; and the important business of making a pin is, in this manner, divided into about eighteen distinct operations, which, in some manufactories, are all performed by distinct hands, though in others the same man will sometimes perform two or three of them. I have seen a small manufactory of this kind where ten men only were employed, and where some of them consequently performed two or three distinct

> operations. But though they were very poor, and therefore but indifferently accommodated with the necessary machinery, they could, when they exerted themselves, make among them about twelve pounds of pins in a day. Each person....might be considered as making four thousand eight hundred pins a day. But if they had all wrought separately and independently, and without any of them having been educated to this peculiar business, they certainly could not each of them have made twenty, perhaps not one pin in a day....... The division of labour, however, so far as it can be introduced, occasions, in every art, a proportionable increase of the productive powers of labour.

There is a chain of logic at work. A larger demand (which Smith elsewhere referred to as the "extent of the market") leads to a larger scale of operations, which leads to more specialization in the work process, which leads to more output per worker. Much has been written about the exact form that specialization can take and the way it can contribute to productivity, but here our interest is in the middle link in this chain, the issue of scale. Smith is giving an example that illustrates **economies of scale**, where the greater size of the enterprise enables it to achieve a higher level of productivity. He was observant enough to recognize, at the dawn of the industrial age, that increases in scale would be central to future economic development.

This is a simple but powerful theory of the firm. It explains the existence of firms on the basis of their ability to capture economies of scale, and it predicts that firms will choose to make rather than buy if, by folding an additional operation into their production system, they can achieve a greater economy of scale than that of the firms they might buy from.

Smith's ideas were further developed a century later by the great English economist, Alfred Marshall. Marshall was perhaps the most influential economist of his era, and his economics textbook instructed every new English-speaking entrant into the field for several decades after its publication in 1890. (Chaps. 5, 11 and 12 in this text, which are similar to chapters you will find in any other contemporary introductory textbook, are based on material first introduced by Marshall.) Marshall was, like Smith, a close student of the way businesses organized production, and he agreed strongly that economies of scale were a critical aspect of success.

In Marshall's view, every firm wishing to increase its productivity will try to grow larger, but its ability to do this is limited by competition. He saw firms as somewhat analogous to trees in a forest. Each tree tries to grow to its maximum height, but its ultimate size will be determined by competition for nutrients, water and sunlight. There is, in this vision, a potentially self-reinforcing process by which the most successful firms, to continue the tree metaphor, rise above the canopy and spread their roots further and deeper than the others, thereby giving them an even better environment to extend their domination. In other words, competitive success leads to greater growth, which leads to greater economies of scale, which leads to further success and growth. For the firms that surpass all competitors, this process comes to an end only when the technical limits to economies of scale are reached. This will vary from one industry to the next. It may be at a relatively small size for a restaurant, but a much larger size for a computer manufacturer.

An interesting implication of the Marshallian view of the firm is that it may reasonably choose to maximize growth rather than profits, at least over short-to-medium time horizons. It may be worth suffering through a period of lower returns, or even losses, in order to gain a decisive size advantage that can later be turned to underselling the competition; in this way profits are enhanced over the long run. There is plenty of evidence that ambitious firms follow exactly this strategy, particularly in new industries in which no market leaders have yet emerged.

Marshall saw another route to increased specialization and greater productivity. Firms within the same industry might remain smaller, he thought, but congregate in a specific geographic location, called an **industrial district**. A well-known example is Silicon Valley, the region just south of San Francisco, in which a great many small hardware and software firms sprouted up during the 1980s to accelerate the development of computers and information systems. When this happens specialization can occur between firms rather than within them, so that economies of scale can be realized despite smaller individual firm size. For instance, many firms focused on writing software for medical computer systems might be in close proximity to each other. This would permit one of them to specialize in writing just a particular piece of code, say for a network connecting heart monitors, since they could combine it with other pieces through direct contact with other firms. A different way of saying this is that industrial districts achieve through shared location what large firms achieve through common administration—the ability to attain economies of scale in detailed operations.

There is nothing fundamentally wrong with Marshall's analysis, but economists have found it to be too narrow. Economies of scale provide only one of many routes to efficiency, and the theory says little about what other factors might determine who the winners will be in the competitive struggle. Also, as we will see at the end of this chapter and later in Chap. 12, there are indications that the computer revolution is having a profound effect on the role that scale plays in productivity and economic success.

8.5 Transaction Cost Theory

Suppose there were no economies of scale at all, and it would be just as efficient for ten people to produce something in ten different places as for them to gather together under one roof and produce as a team. Would we still see firms?

An influential point of view among economists says that we would. It was first put forward by the Nobel laureate Ronald Coase in 1936, but not for another forty years or so was its force appreciated. Unlike Marshall, Coase begins with the premise that markets are *nearly always* a more efficient system of organization than the administrative hierarchies of firms. From the vantage point of the make or buy decision, there will generally be a producer somewhere else in the economy who can sell at least as good a product for at least as good a price. Productive efficiency, in his view, is the wrong way to think about it.

The right way, according to Coase, is to focus on the costs of using the market, which he dubbed **transaction costs**. The firm that chooses to buy rather than make must invest time and effort in finding out who the other producers are, what their products are like and how much must be paid for them. It may have to negotiate a contract, especially if the transaction is not standardized. This contract may need to be enforced in the courts if a dispute arises. All these costs, when added up, may more than outweigh the purely efficiency-related advantages of using the market and suggest that the better choice is to make, not buy. Multiply this reasoning over millions of make or buy moments, and the result is the pattern of firms, large and small, that we see in the economy today.

In his writing on this topic, Coase attributed a rationality to firms that resembles the conventional (among economists) view of individual rationality. Firms were assumed to calculate all the benefits and costs of using the market versus producing in-house, and they always selected the option most favorable to them. This suggests that the existing boundaries of firms are optimal. Large firms are large because they face greater transaction costs relative to the efficiencies of the market, and small firms are small because their transaction costs are less. It would be a mistake for outsiders, such as government policy-makers, to try to impose any other pattern. Of course, there is a role for sound policies to reduce transaction costs; this would benefit everyone by enabling them to make better use of markets, and, all other things being equal, it would lead to an economy populated by smaller enterprises.

The second great theorist of transaction costs is Oliver Williamson, another winner of the Nobel prize who has devoted his life to identifying the types of costs most troublesome to firms. He argues that the complexity of many economic transactions exceeds the capacity of written contracts. There are too many contingencies and too many adjustments that might be required. Consider the problem of an auto company trying to decide whether to make or buy seat cushions. The cushions have to be built to match the seats, which may vary from one model to another. It is difficult to predict in advance how well each model will sell and therefore what its production schedule will be in the months to come. The maker of the cushion also depends on shipments of supplies, like foam and fabric, and these may change in price or availability. It would be difficult to encompass every future possibility in a contract, short of one that would be a playground for lawyers. Inevitably there is a need for trust in such a relationship.

This is where a fork in the road emerges. How essential, and how precarious, is this trust? For some relationships it is not a crucial issue, and market transactions will usually be sufficient. If there are many potential suppliers of seat cushions, and if small differences in the quality or price of cushions don't have much effect on the overall prospects of the auto company, transaction costs, in Williamson's sense, are low and the likely decision will be to buy rather than make.

Now suppose that, instead of seat cushions, the company is considering whether to outsource production of its engines. As before, there are many contingencies that can't be put in writing, and a measure of trust is necessary between the auto company and its suppliers. Insofar as the engine is a crucial component of the finished car, the auto company's calculations may change. Very small changes in engine construction may have drastic impacts on the quality of the car that houses it. Worse, by designing its other components to fit precisely with the specifications of its engine, the auto company has made itself a virtual hostage of the engine supplier. If the supplier, halfway through the duration of the contract, suddenly announces that increased costs on its end require it to raise prices or cut corners in some respect, there is little the auto company can do. The engine is such a specialized part that no other producer can be found on short notice, and it would be far too costly to let its semi-finished assemblies pile up on the factory floor for lack of an engine.

In a case like this, the firm is well advised to make the component itself and use its powers of administrative control to prevent opportunistic behavior by the engine-makers it employs. In fact, the critical word is *control*. For transaction cost theorists, the single most important characteristic of a firm is that, internally, it is an authoritarian entity, with managers in the higher echelons giving orders to those beneath them. If the market depends on trust, and if trust is expensive, the better alternative is to bring the necessary activities into the enterprise and exercise direct control.

At this point it should be clear that, unlike the Smith-Marshall theory of economies of scale, the Coase-Williamson theory of transaction costs predicts not only where firms will draw their boundaries, but also how they will conduct their internal affairs. The transaction cost world is one of universal suspicion—*noir* economics. Businesses distrust suppliers and may, if the benefits of doing so exceed the costs, convert them into workers, but they also distrust their workers, and this accounts for the hierarchical character of their social organization. If the hierarchy is effective, and if workers really do the bidding of their overseers, the firm will remain the instrument of its owners, but that is always an "if" for transaction cost theory.

The normative message of this theory depends on whether you think the owners of businesses are serving the public interest by pursuing their own profits, in the spirit of the Invisible Hand. If you believe this to be generally true, and most proponents of the transaction cost view have taken this position, both the size distribution of firms and their top-down character are socially desirable. Businesses, by balancing the advantages of using the market against the disadvantages of incurring the cost of being rendered vulnerable to self-interested outsiders, are following the path of greatest social benefit in an imperfect world. Of course, there is nothing in the theory that requires belief in the Invisible Hand, and it may just as well be the case that the control exercised through managerial hierarchies creates more problems than it solves. We will return to this question shortly.

8.6 Entrepreneurial Theory

A very different approach to the theory of the firm is taken by economists who emphasize **entrepreneurship**. This is not an easy term to define, because it can mean different things. In its popular use, it refers to owner-management, especially in new or expanding enterprises. Used this way, it draws attention to the role of innovation: someone comes up with a new idea and starts or reinvigorates a business. Entrepreneurship of this sort is contrasted with bureaucracy, management-by-committee, etc. A second meaning refers to the qualities of the individual entrepreneurs themselves. Here entrepreneurship is a state of mind, emphasizing self-confidence and a willingness to take risks. The third meaning, more familiar to readers of the business and economics literatures than the general public, focuses on innovative activities themselves. To be entrepreneurial in this sense is to bring resources or ideas together in new ways; it can be done by owners, managers or even rank-and-file workers. (Sometimes entrepreneurial activity below the top rank of an organization is called *intrapreneurship*.) There is an overlap to these three meanings—some owner-managers are risk-takers and act entrepreneurially—but it is also possible to have entrepreneurship in one sense without the other two.

For our purposes the third meaning is the most relevant, which is to say that business owners and their psychology are important only insofar as they are vehicles for creating innovation. This raises two broad issues for economics.

1. To innovate is to enter territory that is at least somewhat unknown, and the greater the degree of innovation also the greater the uncertainty. For this reason, while many aspects of innovation can be planned systematically according to the model of rational decision-making presented in Chap. 3, this can never be the whole story.

   The aspect of innovation that defies calculation fascinated Joseph Schumpeter, perhaps the greatest name associated with the study of entrepreneurship. Schumpeter was born in Austria and served as that country's central banker (we will study central banking in conjunction with macroeconomics) before emigrating to the United States, where he finished his career at Harvard University. Schumpeter emphasized that, while formal economic theory focused on the decision rules that would maximize profits in a given market, the purpose of entrepreneurship was to alter or even invent markets. Many innovative firms will fail, but the ones that succeed will earn profits far beyond the ordinary. Thus the pursuit of the "next big thing" is like a contest, but one in which the losers will eventually be crushed by the winners.
2. An innovative enterprise produces something different from the rest, or at a different time or place, or in a different way. For this reason alone, it cannot choose to buy rather than make everything it does; if every aspect of the product were available to be bought it wouldn't be new or different. (Bringing an old product to a new market is also an element of the production process, one that could, in principle, be outsourced.) On the other hand, a firm that wants to focus its energies on innovation should try to buy most of the goods or services it needs *except* for those on which its new ideas are based. For instance, until recently there were several small startups in the United States trying to develop electric automobiles. The strategy of most of them was to purchase vehicles or vehicle parts from large established firms, which they retrofitted with electric motors and other components tied to the power source.

Innovation also works at a deeper level, however. Markets, as we saw, are based on the principle of bilateral exchange; everything that occurs in them boils down to two-way exchanges between a buyer and a seller. Two activities, performed by individuals or teams of individuals, are brought together in the market if at least one party sees an advantage to their being together instead of separate. A supply of ice cream cones is of greater value when brought together with a supply of ice cream. In a healthy market, participants are actively scouting out new opportunities for value-enhancing exchanges; if they exist there is a strong likelihood they will be found by someone.

Significant innovation, on the other hand, often entails new *configurations* of activities. That is, rather than just bringing together one useful piece at a time, as markets do, entrepreneurs combine many elements, some pre-existing, some new, into a pattern whose overall logic is different. Consider again the problem of building an electric car. This vehicle, if it is to compete successfully against its gasoline-powered rivals, needs many new components simultaneously: a new engine, but also a device for storing power, new, lighter-weight construction materials, and new technologies for quickly charging batteries. It is inconceivable that market exchanges, all by themselves, could result in a new vehicle whose elements fit together harmoniously. It may be, for instance, that the materials won't work without a new body design, but that the design also requires a new battery technology, and so forth. Instead, we see teams of designers who conceive an overall plan for such a car and bring together the pieces that will make it work. Some of these pieces may even be technologies rejected by other companies because they were inefficient in the traditional car designs they were familiar with.

This point gets to the heart of how firms differ from markets and deserves to be emphasized. A market creates something new one piece at a time, through the accumulation of exchanges between individual buyers and sellers. An exchange takes place only if it is advantageous in the context of everything already taking place around it. Think of a shopping district in which one store opens, then another, then a third. Each is the product of an exchange between a business owner and a building owner, and each is independent of the other. No store will open unless someone thinks that, taken as an independent business venture, it has a prospect of being profitable.

Now thing of a shopping mall, a large structure with pre-designed retail spaces, enclosed walkways and central delivery bays. This is not the result of many small-scale market decisions, but of a plan that encompasses a large number of simultaneous elements. It creates, for better or worse, a shopping district that would not emerge from separate exchanges between individual retailers and land owners. This points to the characteristic feature of innovation: it brings together many elements simultaneously and therefore requires both a plan and the means to carry it out. The plan is in the mind of the entrepreneur or entrepreneurs; the means is the business firm or other organization. (All kinds of organizations can be entrepreneurial in this sense, not just those that produce goods and services for profit.)

This perspective on entrepreneurship foregrounds the connection between innovation and planning. A firm is an organization that implements economic plans, and this capacity enables it to create new products and methods that far exceed what markets alone would accomplish. This claim can be translated into the language of information: when goods are exchanged in the market, normally only the product changes hands, and the knowledge that went into its production stays in the hands of its producer. When firms organize multiple activities inside their walls and oversee the process of bringing them together, they have access to both the goods *and* the knowledge. Such an information advantage can be the basis for innovative planning, since new ideas are normally based on seeing new patterns in existing knowledge. Business analysts sometimes use a phrase like "the learning enterprise" to encapsulate the dynamic advantages of bringing together a wide range of competencies, with the goal of generating new concepts and skills.

One of the tensions at the heart of innovative organizations concerns the role of hierarchy in administration. To speak of planning is usually to have in mind a top-down flow of authority, since the plan is commonly lodged in the top level of management, and only if the workforce follows a common set of dictates will the plan be carried out. (Cooperative allocation can also be based on planning, but this is seldom seen in large organizations. Computerization may change this.) Nevertheless, there is no law of nature that says only high-level managers can produce innovative plans. On the contrary, to the extent that organizations create rich information flows between their diverse units, every worker who is positioned at the intersection of one of these flows is potentially able to make new and valuable connections. Sometimes a greater degree of closeness to the operational level can reveal innovative opportunities more readily than the wider, but less detailed, purview of the top echelons. This issue, and others like it, have become more visible as the role of entrepreneurship and innovation has been elevated in importance in the contemporary economy.

8.7 Current Debates

Corporations—their ongoing metamorphoses and the new demands being made on them—are at the heart of current economic debate. Two issues will be discussed here

1. The virtual corporation. For most of the twentieth century, the tendency was for corporations to grow larger and larger, encompassing ever greater numbers and types of activities. Whether because there were greater economies of scale to capture, increasing costs of using the market or bigger plans to be envisioned and implemented, corporations everywhere sought to expand.

The corporate sector as a whole continues to add assets and market share at the expense of other business forms, but the drive for individual firms to expand seems to have abated. Increasingly managers are admonished to focus on the "core competencies" of their enterprise and outsource everything else. Computerization has made it possible to separate the planning and implementation functions to a greater extent than in the past, as laboratories and offices can transmit detailed instructions to producers half a world away and receive feedback in real time.

An exemplar of the new approach is Nike, the seller of running shoes and other sportswear. Nike does not make its shoes; it outsources this function to a global network of suppliers. What it does do is design, marketing and finance. Its laboratories produce plans and prototypes, which are then sent to other companies for actual manufacturing. Its marketing office sets an overall strategic plan for appealing to consumers, and then the scripting and production of specific advertisements are outsourced to agencies specializing in that kind of work. More than anything else, Nike is an enterprise devoted to moving money around—concentrating it from the earnings of retailers and allocating it to production, design and marketing functions. Design, coordination and financial management are its core competencies.

The extent to which this model is being adopted by other corporations is not fully known; a debate has emerged among economists and business analysts over whether the productive behemoth of old is mutating into the virtual enterprise of the future. Certainly some firms are moving in this direction, and the vision is attractive to many more.

The transformation of the corporation, if that is what we are seeing, is bound up with the debate over globalization, since much of the outsourcing being pursued by corporations in the industrialized countries is to manufacturers based in low-wage exporting regions. As corporations become more virtual, the jobs they shed are those that used to be performed by industrial and clerical workers in the North. Between automation and outsourcing, these jobs are vanishing, probably forever.

At the same time, the tendency towards virtualization has transformed the culture and internal operations of corporations. Increasingly they are discarding large administrative apparatuses for more market-like arrangements. This is intrinsic to outsourcing, of course, but it also makes its appearance even when activities occur in-house. It has become common among automobile companies, for instance, to treat their internal units as if they were outside suppliers. Each unit keeps its own separate financial records, recording sales and purchases from other units, and each is expected to show a profit. If a unit cannot offer to "sell" its output to other units at a price competitive with outside suppliers, the company will shut it down and shift to outsourcing. Sometimes companies deliberately underproduce parts internally so they will be forced to outsource *and* purchase in-house; this is thought to keep the competitive fires burning.

These new strategies have had a large impact on workers. Once there was an implicit promise that employment would be for life, and new hires would expect to slowly rise up the corporate ladder, depending on where they came in. They regarded other workers as colleagues, all engaged in the same general enterprise. Wages were set to balance different interest groups within the firm, such as older versus younger workers or individuals with similar job assignments but in different units. Day-to-day routine involved carrying out instructions from above and sometimes politicking for a change in policy.

Today all that is changing. Few workers today are under the illusion that anything is promised; work will be available as long as it is convenient and not a day longer. Career paths are more likely to move across firms than just within them, and other workers are often competitors, particularly if management is pitting units against one another. Wages are now set in light of outside market forces; if a particular service can be acquired more cheaply through outsourcing, workers producing the same service in-house may have to choose between wage cuts and being let go. Meanwhile, units are increasingly managed as if they were separate companies on contract: they are given detailed specifications to meet, but how they go about meeting them is left up to their own determination. This means they have more control over their day-to-day operations but less over the larger purpose of their work.

Proponents of virtualization claim that this form of organization takes full advantage of the new potential opened up by computers. Older systems of management, they say, were always clumsy and slow to adapt, and people put up with them because there was no alternative. Now it is possible to do more work and less managing, leaving coordination up to the computer. Such a system will be more decentralized, just as markets are. At the same time, it is now possible for a small team, with access to more information than could have been imagined in the past, to make the key decisions for large networks of production. Such an arrangement might give us the advantages of both markets and planning, but tilted more toward the market than previously.

The dark sides to this transformation are emphasized by its critics. They see less scope for real input on the part of most workers, more uncertainty and, for most, lower pay. The virtual corporation, they say, concentrates strategic power but outsources responsibility. Another complaint is that, when the "soft" operations (finance, marketing, research) are separated from the "hard" ones (production, point of sale), innovation is restricted to the "glitz", leaving work and technology largely untouched. Thus, the sophistication of Nike's marketing and some of its design concepts ("air" sneakers) coexists with sometimes primitive production methods among its subcontractors. This points to a cultural criticism, that the virtual corporation is the product of a society that values style over substance.

This is not an either/or debate. (Most debates aren't.) A wealth of research demonstrates that new, more decentralized forms of organization are required if the advantages of computer technology are to be translated into economic gains. It is also true that the organizational inclusiveness of the traditional corporation played many positive roles, and thought has to be given to how they are to be preserved or compensated for in the future. It will be interesting to see, in the years ahead, whether the current retreat from bigness proves to be a fad or a new framework for economic life.

2. Corporate responsibility. Firms respond to markets. They produce what they think consumers will buy, and they choose their production methods in light of the cost of labor and materials, as well as the technologies available to them. The principal yardstick for measuring what they contribute to society is the Market Welfare Model: if the market is providing signals that reflect the real benefits and costs to society, then corporations will produce the right items in the right way. If not, conventional economic wisdom would advise us to adjust how markets work (we will see this in more detail in later chapters), not to have corporations ignore or overrule them.

Nevertheless it is not quite this simple. Even the most ardent believer in the Invisible Hand should admit that markets will always fall short of perfection, and there are many criteria for what is desirable or harmful in this world besides economic ones. We live with these shortcomings and have to consider how to cope with them.

Vivid examples can be found in news reports about sweatshop conditions in firms that supply to multinational marketing firms like Nike and Wal-Mart, environmental destruction stemming from mining operations, the violation of the rights of indigenous people as a result of deforestation or oil drilling. These stories are embarrassing to the companies involved, but, rhetoric aside, what ought to be their responsibility to prevent or fix them?

The case against corporate responsibility is that solving larger economic and social problems is not what these firms know how to do very well. They have no particular wisdom regarding what policies are correct, and their personnel are not hired for their expertise in social amelioration. To the extent that their attention is diverted by these new considerations, they will be less productive in what they do better, produce to market demand and make profits. It might be argued by some that making corporations responsible for social objectives as well as their continuing private ones would only enhance their power and the extent to which the rest of us rely on them, both of which may already be greater than they should be.

Nevertheless, demands on corporations to behave according to higher principles are not likely to go away. There are two general reasons for this:

1. To the extent that corporations profit from activities that are burdensome to other members of society, they have an obligation to bear their share of the responsibilities as well. Most corporate managers understand this.

2. I have argued in this chapter that corporations are perhaps the foremost modern institutional repository of economic power and competence. They have proved remarkably adaptable, responding to technological and political change with a steady stream of innovations. Those concerned about the human and environmental costs of doing business will turn to them because they are the organizations with the greatest capacity to effect change. This remains the case even though their core competencies lie elsewhere. Also, corporations can, if they need to, outsource the operational details of their social responsibility initiatives. (Companies trying to improve working conditions among their subcontractors have hired accounting firms, NGO's and academic researchers to do the job.) Yesterday's corporation may have had no particular talent for addressing social concerns, but this does not have to be true of tomorrow's.

Before leaving this question, it is appropriate to remind ourselves once again that the issue of corporate responsibility arises only because markets do not succeed in meeting our needs. If the markets themselves can be fixed—and in subsequent chapters we will look at ways to do this—the burden on corporations to act as reformers can be lifted. It would be a mistake to assume that corporations, for all their power, are the only vehicles for creating a better world.

The Main Points

1. Firms can be publicly or privately owned, for profit or not-for-profit. Within the universe of private, for profit firms, there are proprietorships, partnerships and corporations. Corporate shares can either be privately held or publicly traded. An interesting type of corporation is the cooperative, based on the principle of one member, one vote. The three types of cooperatives are differentiated by who constitutes its membership—workers, suppliers or consumers.
2. A critical aspect of the modern corporation is limited liability. Owners are at risk of losing their equity, but the rest of their assets cannot be seized in order to meet financial obligations incurred by the firm.
3. Corporate governance in the US usually takes the form of a top-down system, with power flowing from shareholders to the board of directors to the CEO (chief executive officer) and down through the administrative ranks. One characteristic problem is how upper levels (shareholders and boards) influence managers to act in the interest of the owners; pay incentives and the threat of buyouts are methods used to achieve this. A governance wrinkle of some interest is the M-form, in which parallel administrative pyramids are established, with a team of strategic managers coordinating all of them at the highest level. This can overcome diseconomies of scale in management, while emphasizing the role of enterprise-wide planning.
4. Theories of the firm attempt to answer questions like "Why do firms have the boundaries they have?", "Why are they organized as they are?", "What policies do they tend to pursue?", and "To what extent do they act in the social interest?"
5. Alfred Marshall, building on the ideas of Adam Smith, proposed a theory emphasizing the role of economies of scale. Firms are expected to grow until these economies are exhausted.
6. Transaction cost theory, pioneered by Ronald Coase and elaborated by Oliver Williamson, argues that markets are always more efficient that administrative methods, but sometimes the costs of using the market can outweigh the benefits. Important transaction costs include information-gathering, contract-writing and enforcement, and the risk of being taken advantage of by opportunistic counterparties. Firms exist to impose administrative procedures when these costs become too onerous.
7. Entrepreneurial theory, associated with Joseph Schumpeter, views firms as existing in order to implement innovative plans that markets cannot otherwise arrive at. This often involves a coordinating function, when many elements have to be brought together simultaneously in order for innovation to be successful.
8. The structure of firms appears to be undergoing a radical change under the influence of computerization. Firms are becoming more decentralized, with fewer layers of managerial authority. As more function are outsourced, the firm may earn the designation "virtual".
9. There is increasing pressure on firms to uphold standards of social responsibility, in addition to their usual goals of profitability.

▶ Terms to Define

Balance sheet
Cooperatives (worker, supplier, consumer)
Corporate governance
Corporation
Economies of scale
Entrepreneurship
Equity
Firm
Income statement
Industrial district
Limited liability
Market for corporate control
Outsourcing
Partnership
Proprietorship
Proxy
Public vs private ownership
Publicly vs privately traded corporations
Transaction costs

Questions to Consider

1. What are the advantages of one share, one vote as a governance principle, compared to the cooperative system of one person, one vote? What are the disadvantages? Do you think that people who pay more taxes should have more votes in electing governments? Are the problems of political and corporate governance fundamentally similar or different (or both)? Explain.
2. What risks accompany the advantages of limited liability for corporations? Do you think the owners of corporations should ever be fully liable for their liabilities? Does it matter what the cause of the liability is—whether it is due to poor business judgment, bad luck, or court judgments stemming from harm imposed on third parties (like pollution)? In your answers, think carefully about the incentive effects of different liability rules.
3. How would each of the three major theories of the firm we surveyed analyze the rise of the M-form corporation? Which, if any, do you find most convincing?
4. What make or buy decisions are faced by your college or university? What have they decided to produce themselves, what do they outsource, and why? Are there any decisions you would consider reversing?
5. How would each of the three major theories approach the issue of the virtual corporation? In particular, how would they explain the timing—why this trend has emerged over the past decade and not in earlier periods?
6. What, if anything, do the three theories tell us that would be relevant to the corporate responsibility debate?

9 Government

Government is a referee who also plays the game. It is government courts, agencies and legislatures that set the rules by which the economy operates, but governments are also major economic players in their own right. They own and operate businesses and generate and spend vast amounts of income; in fact, in every economy the government (pulling together all its levels and branches) is by far the largest single economic entity.

Figure 9.1 on the next page, which tells us what portion of the economy's output of goods and services was purchased by government in several countries, is clear on this point. It is never less than 10 % and may approach a fourth. In this chapter we will not come to any conclusion about whether any of these numbers are too small or too large, but we will look closely at how governments go about their business and what problems their activities pose for economic analysis.

9.1 State Capacity

At the time Adam Smith wrote *The Wealth of Nations*, governments had few of the resources we take for granted today. The annual revenue of the British crown, for instance, was just 10.7 million pounds in an economy estimated at 125 million pounds. There were no government agencies to regulate finance, shipping or other commercial activities, beyond keeping an official set of weights and measures. There were no departments of public health, no government-financed or -operated schools, and no income tax either. There were courts to interpret the laws and constables to enforce them. Above all, the government of Smith's day was optimized for war and conquest: His Majesty King George III kept about 50,000 men under arms during peacetime (many more in periods of combat) and maintained a navy of about 500 vessels. (He also outsourced some of his military needs to foreign mercenaries, such as the soldiers from the German principality of Hesse who were surprised by George Washington's men on the day after Christmas in 1776.)

P. Dorman, *Microeconomics*, Springer Texts in Business and Economics,
DOI 10.1007/978-3-642-37434-0_9,

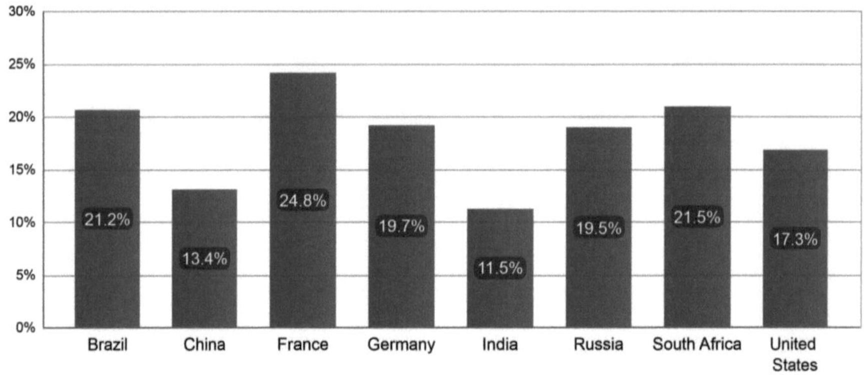

Fig. 9.1 Government consumption as percent of GDP, selected countries, 2010. (*Source*: World Bank World Development Indicators)

Thus far we have looked at the emergence of modern capitalism as encompassing the rise of markets and ever-larger business organizations, but the gradual development of modern forms of government is equally a part of the story. The concept that sums up this aspect of government is **state capacity**; it refers to three factors that determine how much government can accomplish alongside, and often explicitly against, markets and firms: its autonomy, its revenue base and the competence of its workforce.

1. Autonomy. King George could not do exactly as he pleased. There was a long tradition in England of constraints on the monarch, punctuated by the Magna Carta in 1215 and the compromise known as the Glorious Revolution of 1688; both established rights of the lesser nobility that the king was obligated to respect. Indeed, by 1776 the Parliament, which was elected by men of landed property, was the more powerful force. This changed what government was—it was now Parliament and its ministers and commissions and not just the monarch—but it also changed which social groups had influence over policy. Landowners could use the government as an instrument to promote their interests, even if the king was opposed. Given the rules under which the system operated, as well as the nature of the British economy of the time and its main sources of wealth, there could be no other force as great. The landowning class could, and did, disagree amongst itself, of course, and this led to competition between political parties.

As the British and other economies grew and diversified, and as the right to participate in governance was extended to new social classes, there was no longer a simple relationship between social class and government power. Soon industrialists, financiers and merchants, and after a while ordinary urban workers and farmers, began to have a voice. Government was no longer the direct instrument of any one group, and by playing them off against one another (appealing to shifting coalitions on different issues) it could attain a high degree of independence. In this way, the British government evolved to be an autonomous force in society.

Autonomy is easier to see when it isn't there. In many Latin American countries the landowning class remained preponderant well into the twentieth century, and government never established its independence. Policies, whether they involved education, urban services or international trade, were not adopted unless the landowners approved. Governments in such societies had great power over other social classes, of course, but they were powerless to take any action that landowners perceived as against their interests. This greatly reduced the scope of potential government activity and warrants the judgment that such states lacked an essential aspect of capacity.

2. Revenue. Governments must purchase the services they require, and so, like the rest of us, they depend on their sources of income. Early governments often depended on **tax farming**, a system in which officials were granted a territory and could retain a portion of any taxes they raised there, using almost any means they might impose. This not only created injustices for the local people, it also limited the control of the king over his own income: it was the tax farmer, not the king, who decided in practice how much would be extracted from the population and what the method would be. (The Roman Empire, incidentally, was stronger because its revenues did *not* arise from tax farming; there were fixed percentages of produce or revenues that subjects were required to pay.)

A major advance occurred with the growth of international trade. Governments began to impose **tariffs**, which are taxes on the value of imports into the country. These have the convenient property that they are paid by foreigners, at least directly; hence all governments came to rely on them. The biggest breakthrough, however, was the invention of the income tax in the nineteenth century. (Nearly 20 years elapsed between the first federal income tax law in the US, which was struck down by the Supreme Court in 1894, and the passage of the Sixteenth Amendment to the constitution, which overturned the Court and authorized income taxes, in 1913.) Even so, there is a great variation in the ability of governments to actually collect such taxes. Tax avoidance is a problem everywhere; in some countries this is a nuisance, in others a serious limit to state revenues.

There is an important linkage between the taxation system and state autonomy. Governments have more freedom of action if their revenue does not tie them too closely to any single social group. A country with a single major industry, for instance, will have a single revenue source for government, which means that those who control that industry have control over state finances. This gives them influence which can weaken the independence of government authority.

When their spending needs outgrow their tax revenue, governments borrow money. This can have contradictory effects on their autonomy. To the extent that borrowing frees them from the grips of any particular economic interest it promotes autonomy, but debt gives rise to a new class of creditors who can take this autonomy away. We see this now in an extreme form in Europe, where indebted

Eurozone countries are being pressured by creditors to take measures that are sometimes highly unpopular. There is no general rule about deficit spending and state capacity, then; it depends on the circumstances.

3. Competence. Governments didn't emerge into this world with innate abilities to regulate and manage; these skills had to be acquired slowly, often through trial and error, and this process continues to the present. An example of a current search for competence is the regulation of the internet. No one quite knows how to do this, and governments are experimenting with different approaches. It will be several years before effective means of regulation are found, or until the limits of regulation become clear.

The single most important element in the development of government competence is the creation of an independent, professional civil service. The hallmarks of such a force are formal qualifications and a high level of job security. Without them, there is no accumulation of know-how, nor will government functions be carried out according to professional rather than political criteria. In every society there is a tug of war between the immediate political interests of those in temporary control of government and the permanent employees who staff the apparatus. The political motive seeks to remove as many posts as possible from civil service jurisdiction and to exercise as much control as possible over the work of the bureaucracy. The maintenance of state capacity depends on institutions that safeguard civil service prerogatives and keep political forces at bay.

9.2 Powers of Government

Very generally, we can speak of three types of government involvement in the economy: its judicial function, public enterprise and regulation of the private economy.

1. The judicial system. Courts have the function of applying laws to cases. Many of the laws they deal with are passed by legislatures, but, in the Anglo-American tradition a majority are not. They are descended instead from the **common law** tradition, so named because it was carried on by magistrates in England whose job it was to make the administration of law common throughout the country. Three branches of this law are particularly relevant to economic questions:

- Property law. This governs who owns what, and what rights ownership entails. Some economists argue that a system of secure property rights is the single *sine qua non* of successful economic growth and point to the early emergence of this law in England as an example. Hernando de Soto, a Peruvian economist, thinks that the lack of such rights for poor people's property in much of the developing world is responsible for economic stagnation. On the other hand, China is at the forefront of current economic growth, and it has one the world's least defined systems of property. Another paradox is that it was not until the turn of the twentieth century that property in ideas (intellectual property), such as copyrights and patents, received general support from industrialized countries, yet there is no evidence that economic growth before that time was impeded on this account.

- Contract law. This is the realm of law that governs agreements between consenting parties; like property it is essential to the development of a market economy. Specifically, the law of contracts addresses such matters as when a contract comes into force, what performance each party can demand of the other, what obligations, if any, parties have to one another outside the explicit terms of the contract, and in what manner contracts can be dissolved. Why do the parties to a contract expect the backing of the courts for what is essentially a private agreement? One reason, as we saw in Chap. 7, is that legal enforcement greatly reduces the costs of using markets, with large returns to society as well as to the private parties themselves. Another is that a contract, once it is guaranteed enforcement, enables each party to make secure plans based on the presumption that the other will come through as promised. A world of such planning will be more secure and more productive than one of uncertainty and shorter time horizons.
- Tort law. Property rights can be infringed not only by outright seizure but through actions that damage individuals and their assets. I can violate your right to land that you own by taking control of it to plant my own herb garden, but also by dumping toxic chemicals on it or even setting up a bee-keeping business next door, if my bees take to stinging you. The law of torts governs damages of this sort; its remedy is generally to require the individual causing the damage to compensate the victim in proportion to the harm. This has traditionally been the least settled and most controversial aspect of the common law as it relates to the economy, because most tort situations describe a conflict *between* property rights. That is, the damage to one person or her property is the result of the free exercise of someone else's property rights. Pollution, for instance, destroys property, but it also results from the use of property. For this reason, property-oriented legal systems are always somewhat ambivalent about the extent to which torts should be pursued. We will take up this issue in more detail in Chap. 15.

2. Public enterprise. In a sense, all government employees are engaged in the production of goods and services. Factory inspectors provide factory inspection services, teachers provide teaching, soldiers provide fighting, and so on. In practice, two distinctions are important. First, some services are provided from the government to the government and are not experienced as benefits to the public. Federal marshals, for instance, protect government officials and installations, generally remaining out of sight. Services like these are *intermediate goods*, deriving their value from other goods to which they contribute. If a service is a *final good*, however, the public benefits from it directly in some way. As an example, consider the pollution monitors who test lakes and rivers for the presence of contaminants. If they do their job properly they make most of us better off by giving us useful information about our water supply and by discouraging those who would pollute it. We normally don't think of these sorts of services as having economic value, because we don't purchase them; nevertheless they *are* valuable in the same way

that things we buy are. (People sometimes buy filters for their own private water supply.)

This suggests a second distinction, between the government services we pay for and those we receive "for free" (putting aside our tax payments). If end users pay for what they get, the government activity that produces it has all the trappings of a business, and the term used to describe it is **public enterprise**. The Postal Service is such a business, as we have seen, and so are public colleges and universities, at least in part—the part they sell to students and other users.

In principle, any business can take the form of a public enterprise. Communism as practiced in the Soviet Union, China and eastern Europe prior to the 1990s placed nearly all businesses in public hands. Until recently many developing countries, like India and Brazil, had public enterprises in most important sectors of the economy. Even in the private enterprise-oriented US there is a long history of publicly owned and operated businesses. Railroads, insurance companies, mining and many more—all have been run as public enterprise.

3. Regulation and policy. The final general function of government is to tell others what to do. (Most government activities do this, of course, but now we are interested in pure rule-setting.) The principle vehicle for this is the regulatory agency. Generally speaking, legislatures pass broad, goal-setting laws and administrative agencies interpret and implement them. The Clean Air Act, for instance, mandates certain general health standards that should be met throughout the country, and the Environmental Protection Agency translates this into specific maximum allowable concentrations for a precise list of pollutants. The EPA also establishes a monitoring and enforcement apparatus, making case-by-case judgments concerning how to respond to violations.

Economists have become deeply involved in debates over regulation. Their favored instrument is **cost-benefit analysis**, a procedure that identifies all the social costs and benefits of a proposal, estimates a monetary value of each, and then compares the sum of the costs to the sum of the benefits. The procedure itself is controversial, both in its core assumptions and its operational methods. There is still plenty of uncertainty how, or even whether, to attach monetary values to outcomes like changes in public health and environmental quality, but the last six presidents have all mandated cost-benefit tests for major public regulations, and so the studies pile up.

The other large area of government intervention concerns economic policy-making in all its dimensions. Here the list is long, but anti-trust (competition) policy, trade policy, industrial policy, monetary and fiscal policy are the main spheres of activity. In Box 9.1 there is discussion of risk management, an area of government activity that overlaps many of these. We will discuss government programs in greater detail as they arise in the course of this text. For now it is enough to say that the public has come to hold governments accountable for their success or failure in meeting economic objectives—this in spite of the fact that the weight of a capitalist economy falls predominantly on the private sector, and it is not clear that governments always have the capacity to play a determining role.

Box 9.1: Government as Risk Manager

All life, and certainly all economic life, is inherently risky, but government is uniquely positioned to reduce the burden of risk on members of society, either by addressing the sources of risk or by reallocating it.

Governments can do this through regulation. We saw in the previous chapter, for instance, how limited liability for corporations shields shareholders from the risk of losing more than the amount of their investment, thereby encouraging larger-scale and more ambitious projects. Of course, by granting limited liability, governments are not reducing the risk of financial losses by corporations; they are shifting part of the cost from owners to other parties, such as workers and suppliers, who can no longer demand that investors fulfill all the obligations of a corporation in bankruptcy proceedings.

Many government agencies set performance and safety standards for products. This imposes a greater burden on producers, but it reduces the need for consumers to do extensive research to find out whether certain minimal criteria are met. The Food and Drug Administration, for instance, requires drug companies to show that their products are effective for the purposes they are supposed to serve. The tests demanded by the FDA have been criticized for slowing the introduction of potentially beneficial new drugs, but they reduce the risk that doctors will prescribe ineffective drugs without knowing it.

Perhaps the largest risk management program of government, however, is **social insurance**. Its purpose is to remedy some of the limitations of private insurance by using the power of government to place everyone in the same system. Here's how it works:

The purpose of insurance is to reduce the element of risk in life by pooling together the fortunes of large numbers of people who don't know in advance who will incur an expense and who won't. Health insurance is a familiar example. Getting sick can be very expensive, beyond the means of most people if the problem is serious enough. Few would want to take the chance that they will be the unlucky ones who will need kidney dialysis or an extended hospital stay to battle lymphoma. Instead they will want to pool their risk with a large population, each paying a modest amount into a fund that is then used to pay the extraordinary expenses of a few. Rather than have a small risk of financial catastrophe, most of us find it is better to have the certainty of a smaller payment we know we can afford. (Economists refer to this preference as risk aversion.) One problem with private insurance, however, is that insurers competing with each other to offer lower premiums are in a position to select only those customers in the safest risk categories. Thus, it makes financial sense for a private health insurance company to allow young healthy people to place themselves into a separate insurance pool and be offered lower rates. As more companies get better at doing this they will

(continued)

Box 9.1 (continued)

succeed in dividing the population into many separate groups, each with its own risk level and financial cost. *This violates the original purpose of insurance, which was to spread individual risk across a diverse population.* Rather than everyone making the same payment, the situation reverts in the direction of few costs for some and high costs for others. (As soon as someone is diagnosed with kidney disease, they will be taken out of the lower-cost pool and be forced to pay very high insurance premiums—if they can find insurance at all.)

Social insurance can solve this problem by putting the program in the hands of government and applying a common set of rules to everyone. With no competition, there is no need to offer anyone lower premiums than anyone else. True, some social insurance systems do set different rates, but in situations in which people have the power to *change* their risk. For instance, workers compensation, which insures workers for some of the costs of occupational accidents, charges higher premiums for roofers than for bookkeepers. That's because these risks are chosen by workers and employers, and reducing all premiums to the same level would eliminate the incentive for dangerous jobs to become safer. Catastrophic health insurance provided to the elderly by the government, on the other hand, does not distinguish between individuals at lower and higher risk of cancer due to their family history; there isn't much chance that charging people more for health insurance will lead to better histories!

In general, industrialized countries have more extensive social insurance programs, but the United Nations and the international financial institutions—the World Bank and the IMF—have signed on to a Social Protection Floor initiative, one of whose main elements is the extension of basic insurance to all people, even the poorest people in the poorest countries.

9.3 Democracy

To what extent are governments the instruments of the people governed by them? In fact, by what criteria would we answer such a question? Who are "the people" and what does it mean for them to exercise control over government?

These are questions posed by *democratic theory*, the branch of political theory devoted to explaining what democracy is or could be and how it does or could work. Economists have long been interested in these questions, since a core issue for them is how individual preferences are combined to yield social outcomes. It is not an accident that several of the prominent contributors to democratic theory, such as John Stuart Mill and Kenneth Arrow, have been economists.

Actually, there are two general types of democratic theory. One we can call *constitutive*: how can a people constitute itself as a democratic polity, with democratic government included among its attributes? This view, adumbrated by a tradition extending from Jean-Jacques Rousseau to John Dewey and Jurgen Habermas, examines modes of interaction between people that can give rise to jointness of purpose. Popular control over government in such an approach is a byproduct of popular self-determination more generally.

We will not pursue this direction but instead survey some of the ideas in *procedural* democratic theory: given a society with a range of political preferences and a set of social groupings (classes and interests), what is the likely effect of different rules for voting, financing, constraining or otherwise shaping government affairs? Once a particular set of rules is in place, how responsive can we expect government to be to the preferences of citizens? To be even more specific, we will take majority voting rules as a point of departure and consider a series of problems that will affect the ability of government to achieve popularly desired economic goals.

9.4 Majority Rule

The most common procedural definition of democracy is majority rule: to be adopted, a proposal must garner at least 50 % plus one of all the votes cast. There are many potential methods for electing candidates, however, such as majority, plurality and proportional representation. In what follows we will assume, unless stated otherwise, that elections are contested between two candidates, with the one getting the most votes being declared the winner. This is not an accurate description of most electoral systems, but it is simpler and corresponds to the majority voting rule for proposals. (Keep this excuse in mind when sweeping generalizations are later made on the basis of winner-take-all majority voting.)

Economists are very interested in the similarities and differences between political and market mechanisms for aggregating (combining) the preferences of large numbers of individuals. There is a sense in which every purchase made in a market is a ballot, adding to demand and altering society's mix of what is produced for whom. Of course, market choices are made on the basis of one dollar (or other currency unit), one vote, since the more income a consumer has, the more votes he can cast. The differences between political and economic regimes are still greater than this, however.

When citizens vote in a two-way contest, they have only two options, or at most three if we include abstention. There is no way to apportion a part of one's voting power to one proposal or candidate; each vote goes all one way or the other. (Some proportional representation schemes do permit this, however.) In a market, by contrast, people can decide to pay more or less money for something, thereby registering the intensity of their preferences. A good will be produced if a small number of consumers is willing to pay a high price for it.

This difference between political and market mechanisms is thought to encourage stronger representation of minorities in the economic sphere. If 60 % of the public wants to spend money on more roads for cars but none for railroads, and the other 40 % wants to spend it all on railroads and none for cars, the political process is likely to produce an outcome approaching 100 % spending on roads. If these options were presented to people in a market, however, the result would be split, since each group can spend independently of the other, and differences in willingness to pay would also have an effect. For instance, if the railroad-lovers are willing to pay more on average than the road-lovers, more total money might well be spent on trains. To the extent that differences in willingness to pay depend on differences in income, a democrat might recoil, but if they reflect different levels of interest and commitment their impact is consistent with democratic principles.

Yet there is another argument that suggests that political systems will reflect highly concerned minorities even better than markets will. Suppose there is a cost to political participation. This could be measured in time spent volunteering, money spent to promote candidates or policies, or simply the cost of paying attention. A self-interested individual in the economics mold will get involved only if the potential benefits outweigh these costs. Now imagine a proposed policy that will have a large positive impact on a few people but a very small negative impact on everyone else. This might be a tax loophole that saves a few businesses billions of dollars but increases the tax burden on the rest of the population by just a small amount. According to our assumptions, few if any of the lightly-affected taxpayers will bestir themselves to actively oppose this measure; its impact is too limited to overcome the cost barrier. Each of the business owners, however, will be putting as much energy as possible into lobbying for the loophole. In this way, the ultimate decision may well go in favor of the highly interested minority. In fact, there is plenty of evidence that this is the way most political systems operate. The difference between the political and the market systems, from this perspective, is that the all-or-nothing character of political decision-making can be harnessed (or even hijacked) by a strongly motivated minority.

These two effects do not cancel each other out. Rather, they coexist, leading to the tendency of political systems to both over- and under-represent minorities. The question that has to be answered in any actual situation is, which minorities will benefit from the biases of the process, and which will be suppressed?

Now consider the forces at work in a two-candidate election for office. Suppose voters are lined up along a single ideological continuum; for convenience we can call this left-to-right (following a convention first established during the French Revolution), but it could just as easily be hawk-to-dove, secular-to-religious or some other range of views. Suppose there is an odd number of voters, say 91. Somewhere in the middle of the pack is a voter who exactly holds the balance. To her left are 45 voters, and to her right are 45 more. By joining one side or the other, she determines where the majority lies. The term used to describe her is the **median voter**, and both candidates will pursue her; this prediction is called the **median voter rule**. After all, if it takes only 46 votes to get elected, it doesn't matter how many additional votes a candidate can get; he or she still wins. It is the 46th vote that really matters.

If this analysis is correct, candidates will have a powerful incentive to pitch their appeal to this voter. If a candidate comes from the right, for instance, if voter #46 can be wooed, presumably those to her right will be even more supportive. The same logic, but from the opposite direction, holds for the candidate from the left. The result will be a centrist political campaign, with arguments tailored to the median voter. Stronger views on the fringes of the spectrum will be ignored.

The calculation changes somewhat when the role of money is taken into account. Modern political campaigns are expensive; to reach voters, candidates need to draw on the contributions of wealthy supporters. If the political spectrum of the wealthy coincides with that of the general public, the median voter rule still holds. If the wealth spectrum is skewed one way or the other, however, so will be the political stance of the strategically-minded candidate. The degree of skew (left or right of the median voter) will depend not only the political views of potential campaign contributors, but also the effectiveness of money in influencing votes.

Adding money to the analysis also changes what we might say about the representation of minorities. Recall the argument about highly-interested minorities versus slightly-interested majorities; the claim was that the former will be disproportionately represented in political, compared to market, systems. That conclusion is reinforced if money influences votes, since a minority with a high willingness to pay for a policy change can, in effect, purchase other votes as well as cast its own. This state of affairs is sometimes defended on the ground that, in practice, there are a great many well-heeled, concentrated interests, and competition among them produces a political balance not too far from the democratic ideal. (This position is called interest group pluralism.) Whether this is true or not depends on whether the diversity of special interests is reflective of the larger social diversity, and also whether the process of competition itself permits a consideration of each claim on its merits.

Thus far we have been considering two-way choices, but there is a world of difference between two options and three. This was proved over 200 years ago by French thinker the Marquis de Condorcet (1745–1794), in his celebrated voting paradox. Suppose there are three voters, 1, 2, and 3, and three ballot options, A, B, C. Individual 1 prefers A to B and B to C; individual 2 ranks B over C and C over A; individual 3 agrees that C is better than A but likes A better than B. This state of affairs is summed up in Fig. 9.2 on the following page. If A and B are put to a vote, 1 and 3 will vote for A and only 2 will support B. By majority rule, then, A > B. Similarly, if B and C are put on the ballot, B wins by a vote of two to one. But if the choice is between A and C, the tables are turned; C wins two to one. This is clearly an inconsistent set of results: if A > B and B > C, how can C > A? What we might expect is an unstable succession of coalitions, now proposing one course of action, now another, paralyzing the political process. Writing his PhD. thesis in 1951, later published as the book *Social Choice and Individual Values*, Nobel laureate Kenneth Arrow demonstrated that this is not a figment of a specially cooked example; it is impossible for a political process that obeys democratic

	INDIVIDUAL		
	1	2	3
	A	B	C
RANK ORDER	B	C	A
	C	A	B

Fig. 9.2 The Condorcet voting paradox. Individuals 1, 2 and 3 are choosing among proposals *A*, *B* and *C*. *A* is preferred to *B* by 1 and 3, so it would win a two-way vote. *B* is preferred to *C* by 1 and 2, so it would also win. But *C* is preferred to *A* by 2 and 3. This third result is inconsistent with the combination of the first two

norms to guarantee a rational, consistent set of social preferences; this is called the Arrow Possibility Theorem, although it actually establishes the *im*possibility of finding a perfectly satisfying set of voting rules (Fig. 9.2).

While Arrow's analysis is striking (and has spawned a large literature exploring the consistency of slightly different voting rules), it has had a limited role in explaining real-life political events. What we would expect to see, if the paradox holds, is a form of **political cycling** in which first one proposal, then another, then a third, and so on are successively adopted; there would be no stable majority preferences. In fact, such instability does occur, but it may well be due to fluctuations in political influence rather than inconsistent preferences.

9.5 Government and Society

In democratic rhetoric we often describe government as the servant of the people, but in practice the relationship may be reversed. Government has powers of coercion and may use them to extract economic resources or political submission from those it governs. Economists are particularly concerned about the first possibility, **government predation**.

If the incomes or prestige of government officials are tied to the size of the assets or income of the agencies to which they are attached, they will have an interest in using their political power for institutional aggrandizement. There has been much concern, for instance, about laws that permit police departments to seize the property of individuals accused of selling illegal drugs. Police officers benefit when these items are auctioned off; the proceeds are used for better equipment and more personnel, which in turn provide better working conditions for police department employees. The problem is not that working conditions improve, of course, but that the rules in place create an incentive for exercising more rather than less power over the public. Similar concerns are raised when the salaries of officials employed by regulatory agencies are tied to the numbers of citations they issue, or by the possibility that some in government may have an interest in increasing tax revenues.

The difference between the public and private sectors in this context is worth considering. Many workers in the private sector are paid partially or entirely on commission. No one worries too much about this, since market exchanges are voluntary; to sell more to the public is normally to do a better job in finding out what the public wants and getting it to them. Government, however, wields the power of coercion. More "business" for government agencies does not necessarily reflect more social demand; it can be the result of a more determined exercise of power.

A related issue is bribery. This is a two-way connection between government officials who are using their influence for personal gain and private interests who purchase government favors. The likelihood that bribery will be a significant problem depends on several factors: the presence of self-interested minorities with enough money to spend (already a problem for democracy, even under an honest regime), enough scope for discretionary action on the part of government employees or politicians for them to have something of value to offer, insufficient monitoring by parties with an interest in suppressing corruption, and the weakness of social norms that would otherwise restrain public officials and private interests alike.

A fascinating example of these factors at work is what observers have called the "natural resources curse". There is some evidence that, other things being equal, countries with endowments of highly valuable natural resources, particularly petroleum, suffer from slower economic growth—just the opposite of what might be expected. Indeed, a recent report to the World Bank found that investments in energy development often actually made developing countries worse off. (See Box 9.2) It should be added, however, that the overall evidence is mixed, and that it may be a mistake to leap to generalities.

Box 9.2: The Extractive Industries Review

In 2001 the World Bank, responding to criticism of its loans for energy resource development, created an Extractive Industries Review panel to examine the evidence and report its findings. The report, *Striking a Better Balance*, was completed at the end of 2003. They concluded that further loans in this sector should not be extended until reforms were made in governance, environmental protection and human rights. Here are some selections that exemplify the natural resources curse:

> In a number of countries, extractive industries have been linked to human rights abuses and civil conflict. Such abuses have been documented, for example, in cases where the army has been called in to guard extractive industries projects. Indigenous peoples and local communities may be forced off their lands to make way for projects, and those protesting the development may be locked up or physically harmed. The large economic rents generated by extractive industries may help provoke or prolong civil conflict. Indigenous peoples are particularly vulnerable. They have a strong connection to their land, and their unique way of life can be

(continued)

Box 9.2 (continued)

destroyed if they are displaced by a project. While indigenous peoples' rights are recognized in international law, they are often in a weak position in negotiations with governments and industry over proposed extractive industries projects—assuming they even get the chance to participate in negotiations at all. (p. 6)

Data on real per capita gross domestic product (GDP) reveal that developing countries with few natural resources grew two to three times faster than resource-rich countries over the period 1960–2000. Of 45 countries that did not manage to sustain economic growth during this time, all but six were heavily dependent on extractive industries, and a majority of them also experienced violent conflict and civil strife in the 1990s. (p. 12)

Twelve of the most mineral-dependent nations and six of the world's most oil-dependent states are classified as Highly Indebted Poor Countries, with some of the worst rankings on the Human Development Index prepared by the U.N. Development Programme. The *Human Development Report 2002* shows the highest levels of mismanagement and failed development in many of these countries, as indicated by the discrepancy between a country's place in the Human Development Index and its GDP ranking. Many of these same countries also show a high level of misappropriation and diversion of resource revenues. (pp. 12–13)

Why might there be a resource curse, at least in some cases? One possible explanation is that the wealth generated by oil and similar resources goes primarily to those who control them, not to those who provide productive services. Competition quickly develops between groups with insider influence for access to the wealth stream, and this typically involves payoffs of various sorts. Before long, government has become steeped in corruption and is unable to fulfill its positive role in the economy. Meanwhile, those who capture the resource wealth have little incentive to "reinvest" it, since it was not the result of productive investment in the first place. This income is likely to leave the country for other, more honest economic environments where it can earn a higher rate of return.

Even when governments are immune to corrupt practices, competition for their favors can be economically wasteful. Every regulation issued by a public agency creates winners and losers, which means that all those potentially affected have an interest in trying to influence the agency. They will hire lawyers and lobbyists, finance advertising campaigns, perhaps even pay economists or other policy professionals to construct more sophisticated arguments supporting their cause. Each private interest is hoping to capture the benefit of the regulation and shift the cost to someone else. Insofar as the resources they devote to this are rendered unavailable for more truly useful activities, they create an opportunity cost with no corresponding social benefit. Economists call this **rent-seeking**, and it is seen as one of the chief drawbacks of any regulatory program, no matter how much it is otherwise justified.

It is difficult to determine just how much is lost to rent-seeking. The visible expenses on lobbying and issue advertising are very small relative to the size of the overall economy and also relative to commercial advertising in general, which may be a more significant source of economic cost, as we will explore in Chap. 11. Nonetheless it has loomed large in recent economic debate, perhaps reflecting the antipathy felt by some economists toward most forms of state intervention in the economy.

Thus far we have been treating society and the state as if they were two entirely separate, independent entities. This is, in principle at least, the Anglo-American tradition. It is an expression of liberalism, defined as before to emphasize the maximum possible independence of the individual from government authority. There is another tradition, however, that is arguably more important worldwide, and which focuses on the interconnection between government and social institutions at all levels, from overall policy formation to the daily interactions people have with public employees. A full treatment of this perspective is beyond the scope of this text, but one particular version of the "embedded state" has special relevance to political economy; so we will discuss it here: **corporatism**.

Corporatism is an approach to government which is premised on the existence of social organizations representing all or most citizens. These can be labor unions, business associations, ethnic groups, religious bodies or clubs promoting particular philosophies, like environmentalism, or activities, like sports or playing music. Each group selects its own representatives, and these representatives meet in larger councils to advise government policy-makers. An example that is important in many countries is having an economic council composed of union and business leaders. They meet in three-way negotiation with government economists to set policies on matters of common interest, such as wage rages. In return for its seat at the table, each side is expected to sign onto the compromise that ultimately ensues. This is quite different from the liberal approach in which the independence of each group is treasured, and conflict and litigation replace negotiation and compromise. Most continental European countries have a system of interest group representation, as well as some in Latin America and Africa. The situation in Japan, China and elsewhere in east Asia is less clear, but many would say that their systems, which of course differ greatly between countries, share some of the features of corporatism.

The corporatist approach also operates at lower levels of government activity. Social groups expect to be consulted in the implementation of laws and regulations; here too there is less reliance on the courts and more on negotiated cooperation. When Denmark, for example, wanted to extend its occupational safety and health system to the newly-recognized problem of ergonomics (the effect on the human body of postures, movements and strains), rather than issuing new requirements, it called on business managers, workers and public health officials to meet at both the national and local levels and formulate mutually acceptable action plans. These plans were to be revisited on a regular basis by the same groups that devised them, to see if they needed updating.

Corporatism, by reducing the friction surrounding economic policy, promises gains in efficiency. Rent-seeking is minimized, and the specific knowledge of groups in society most affected is incorporated into decision-making. Cooperation is enhanced, as is the recognition that groups with contrary interests can learn from one another. There are also costs to bear in mind, however. Individual points of view are sacrificed in order to promote the collective views of organized groups. Each group gives up the freedom that comes with *not* being represented in the final decision; in this way corporatism enforces moderation and dampens dissent, which often serves a vital, creative role.

Evaluations of the pluses and minuses of corporatism may soon be moot, however, since it is becoming increasingly difficult for corporatist structures to survive under the impact of globalization. The necessary precondition for bargaining and compromise between competing groups is the belief that they will face each other again and again. Crushing or humiliating the other side is a less attractive option if you can expect to sometimes be on the receiving end in the future. At the heart of the globalization process, however, is the ability of at least some interests, those representing internationally mobile capital, to opt out of any national system viewed as too hostile or restrictive. If the Danish employers, for instance, tell the workers and health officials that there is nothing to negotiate because they can move to another country that doesn't demand ergonomic concessions, the system collapses. Thus far this hasn't happened in Denmark on the issue of working conditions, but the potential is there. The viability of corporatist arrangements in the face of globalization is a much-debated question; observers agree that there is pressure to weaken them, but there is also resistance to this pressure, and the situation remains in flux.

The uncertain fate of corporatism typifies a distinction first introduced by Albert Hirschman and subsequently embraced by many economists and political scientists, between **exit** and **voice**. Each is a way of influencing a situation, but largely at the expense of the other. To threaten to leave (exit) a relationship is to gain a measure of power over it. This is the power that consumers have over the sellers of goods and services, for instance; by threatening to take their business elsewhere they induce companies to pay attention to their preferences. The alternative approach is to maintain a relationship but try to use one's powers of persuasion (voice) to make the other party more responsive. Students do this, for instance, when they urge a professor to change the due date of an assignment or substitute one reading for another on the syllabus. To threaten to leave (exit) is to reduce one's commitment to the relationship and therefore one's standing in it, and this reduces the effect of voice. To become more engaged in a relationship by exercising one's voice is to take credibility away from the threat to exit.

The liberal model of governance is predicated above all the role of exit. Candidates are made accountable by the threat of voting for someone else. If a government official is seen as too aggressive in enforcing a regulation, the party being regulated will threaten court action or some other form of obstruction. Markets, which are largely based on the power of exit—taking business elsewhere—are held up as the ideal mechanism for allocating resources. Corporatism is based on the primacy of voice. Social groups are expected to maintain cooperative relations with one another and with the state; rather than threaten to drop out of the system, they try to make it enough to their liking that they can remain within it. Who wins an election does not necessarily determine what policies will be adopted, because intergroup negotiation also plays a key role. Obstruction and litigation are strongly discouraged.

These are ideal types; the real world is much more ambiguous. Most systems have some elements of both voice and exit. Nevertheless the differences between liberal and corporatist approaches to government are apparent to anyone who has lived in both types of societies, and the general drift toward exit-based strategies, under the influence of globalization, is widely recognized. This is a point we will return to often in the chapters to come.

The Main Points

1. Governments play a large role in every modern economy. They consume at least a tenth of total output even in countries with relatively "small" governments, and their share is as large as a fourth in some cases.
2. The ability of government to manage and control—state capacity—cannot be assumed; it takes time to develop this capacity, and its level can go down as well as up. State capacity has three main components, the autonomy of the state from any single interest group, the ability of the state to raise large amounts of revenue, and the competence of its officials. The last of these depends on the maintenance of an independent civil service.
3. Governments perform three main functions in an economy: they provide a judicial system that defines and regulates property, contract and damage (tort) obligations; they provide goods and services to the public, often in the form of public enterprises; and they create and enforce regulations limiting the freedom of private participants in the economy in various ways.
4. Government plays an important role in risk management. Its regulations often have the effect of reallocating risk from some individuals and businesses to others, and it is in a unique position to provide social insurance, under which everyone pays a modest contribution to reduce the risk of an extreme loss due to an unpredictable event.
5. A major concern of economists is the difference between majority-rule voting and market "voting" in the extent to which outcomes reflect the preferences of the people who make up the system. Markets allow minorities to have a greater voice insofar as they permit split decisions (changing the shares of production and consumption rather than setting an all-or-nothing outcome) and provide opportunities for those with more intense preferences to have a greater voice (through greater willingness to pay). Majority rule, on the other hand, may give the most influence to the median voter, or it may empower small minorities who have concentrated interests in a particular issue or more money to invest in political clout, or all of the above.
6. The Arrow Possibility Theorem demonstrates that, once there are at least three voters and three options, majority rule voting can lead to collectively inconsistent preferences, raising the possibility of political cycling through unstable coalitions. This has not been seen so often in practice, however.

7. Government involvement in the economy carries with it several risks that may flare up into significant problems. If those who set government policy benefit personally from the income that can be extracted from the private economy, government can become predatory. A dramatic case of this is the "resource curse". In addition, the resources devoted to influencing government policy by potential winners or losers—the cost of rent-seeking—can be a drain on society. Corporatism, a system of institutionalized compromise based on participation by private interest groups, can reduce these costs, but pressuring all sides to comprise has its own set of costs and benefits.
8. A useful dichotomy in thinking about individuals and organizations is the choice between exit and voice. One gains influence by threatening to leave—stop buying a product, voting for a different candidate—or by participating more actively in order to have one's views heard. Each impinges on the other to some extent. Liberalism relies primarily on the threat of exit, corporatism on the role of voice and persuasion.

▶ Terms to Define

Constitutive vs procedural theories of democracy
Contract law
Corporatism
Cost-benefit analysis
Exit vs voice
Government predation
Insurance principle
Median voter rule
Moral hazard
Political cycling
Property law
Public enterprise
Rent-seeking
Risk pooling
Social insurance
State capacity
Tariffs
Tax farming
Tort law

Questions to Consider

1. The United States has a lower profile for government than many other industrialized countries, as indicated in Fig. 9.1. What might account for this?
2. Which aspects of state capacity are likely to be promoted under a liberal regime, and which under a corporatist one? Can you think of examples from countries you are familiar with?

3. One of the abiding political questions in the United States concerns how much policy-making and enforcement should occur at the Federal level, and how much should be left to the states. In general, which level of government has the greater capacity as defined in this chapter? Does this differ by type of policy—for instance, economic versus social regulation? Should authority normally be delegated to the level of government that has the greatest capacity?
4. Federal judges are appointed for life, which insulates them from popular sentiment, whereas state and local judges must often stand for election. Given the economic role of property, contract and tort law, do you think they are best interpreted by judges who are more responsive or less responsive to outside pressure? Why?
5. The Iraq and Afghanistan Wars have drawn attention to the greatly-increased role of private, for-profit security forces in American military policy. The armed forces contract out much of the work formally performed by soldiers, such as guarding public officials and staffing military prisons, to these businesses. What are the advantages and disadvantages of shifting this work from the public to the private sector? Overall, is it a wise or an unwise policy?
6. Most schools in the United States are owned and operated by the public sector. At the high school level and below they are largely in the hands of locally elected school boards. What are the advantages of maintaining this system of widespread public enterprise? What are the disadvantages?
7. One of the problems with any insurance system is that it reduces the incentives for those covered by a policy to reduce the risk being insured against; economists call this **moral hazard**. Insuring individuals against the risk of poverty in old age, as public pension systems like Social Security do, poses the moral hazard that individuals will reduce their savings. How strong an argument is this against retirement insurance? What have governments done, or what could they do, to retain the advantages of social insurance without the costs of moral hazard?
8. Make a list of policy areas in which, in your opinion, self-interested minorities in the US have too much power. What changes in the procedures by which our democracy operates would counteract this power? Can you think of examples in which similar minorities have too *little* power?
9. Would you expect corruption to be a greater or lesser problem in corporatist, rather than liberal, political systems? Why?
10. If you haven't already done this, use the exit versus voice framework in your analysis of question 6, on the pluses and minuses of a mostly-public school system.

Civil Society

10

"There is no such thing as societies, only individuals and their families," said former British Prime Minister Margaret Thatcher. Most social scientists would disagree; for them the importance of the myriad ways people come together in society is obvious. (One type of way, of course, is through families.) In any practical discussion of economic policy, social institutions are likely to play a significant role. Whether the groups in question are religious denominations, unions, human rights or environmental advocacy organizations or some other group of people with a purpose, their impact has to be taken into account.

This chapter will appear to be more of a grab bag than the others, since the concept of civil society is essentially a residual; a group or interest belongs to civil society if it is not governmental and not in business to make money for itself in the marketplace. This includes a lot of things which have relatively little in common, except for the social space they share and the many effects, small and large, they have on each other. We will begin by exploring the relationship between civil society and the economy in general terms, but the centerpiece of the chapter will be a detailed look at the problem of organizing voluntary collective action. We will conclude with briefer considerations of the role of family structure, kinship and the overall density of networks connecting people unrelated by birth ("social capital").

10.1 Why Civil Society Matters

Let's make a list of organizations and other social elements that would be included in a civil society roll-call:

There are not-for-profit groups that play an important role in many aspects of the economy, such as private schools, foundations that make grants to support research and social action, publications that are produced to promote ideas rather than make money, groups that promote the causes of consumers, animal rights, hunters, retired people, and many more.

P. Dorman, *Microeconomics*, Springer Texts in Business and Economics,
DOI 10.1007/978-3-642-37434-0_10, © Springer-Verlag Berlin Heidelberg 2014

There are religious institutions at all levels, as well as the social service organizations that religions often set up. There may be competing denominations or spiritual views within a religion, and these too may be organized.

There are unions, professional associations and trade groups. These are closely tied to the economy, but they are not economic organizations in the same sense that businesses are. They sell services to their members, but, unless they have succumbed to corruption, they aim to make their members wealthier, not themselves.

There are self-help groups and the not-for-profit businesses that have sometimes evolved out of them. Organizations for recovering alcoholics or cancer survivors fit this mold, and in a sense so do automobile clubs.

There are social clubs for sports, music or other activities that not only promote their common interests, but also provide opportunities for networking. The social connections they establish can play a role in economic life. Nearly every large city, for instance, has a social club (or several) that have as their members the leading local business owners and managers. Their conversations can be expected to extend beyond how to play a particular hole on the golf course or what to order for dinner.

Families themselves are social groups, of course, especially if we take into consideration the tendrils of kinship that spread out from them. Kinship networks, as we will see, play a crucial role in some economic contexts. Families also organize most of the unpaid labor which, while largely unmeasured, plays an indispensable role in every economy.

Finally, there are valuable resources that societies hold in common, some the product of nature and others of human culture and custom. These are essential to the functioning of the economy, but it is also possible for the economy to put them at risk.

How can we sum up this kaleidoscope of social groupings, relationships and possessions? I would propose three general functions the elements of civil society perform in relation to the economy:

- They produce and distribute valuable goods and services. Unpaid production in the household will be one of focuses later in this chapter, as will the contribution of resources held in common. We will have less to say about not-for-profit and self-help organizations, but this should not be taken as a sign that they are less important. As for distribution, the connections people establish to both formal (organized) and informal networks play an important role in what they can expect to gain from the economy, a topic we will return to when we consider social capital.
- They help shape the other institutions in society, including markets themselves. In Chap. 7 there were references to the "embeddedness" of markets in social networks; in this chapter we will see some of those networks in action.
- They perform a regulatory role alongside or in place of the state. During the past few decades in particular, non-governmental advocacy groups have arisen to pressure corporations and markets to change their products, methods and social practices. These may prove to be a permanent fixture in modern industrial economies.

Our survey will begin with a detailed consideration of the problems of organizing and sustaining social action; then we will look at recent economic research into one specific type of social institutions, the family. We will end with a brief look at an emerging area of economic debate, the role of social connectedness—"social capital"—in economic outcomes.

10.2 Collective Action

We will begin with an example which, while not earth-shaking, may be familiar to many readers. Suppose a neighborhood wants to revitalize itself, beginning with a clean-up campaign—a community event to pick up and dispose of waste and litter. A day is set aside for this event, which is announced in flyers, local publications, perhaps on a billboard. Who will show up?

Start with the assumption that every individual in the neighborhood is rational and self-interested in the conventional economic sense discussed in Chap. 3. They value two things, clean streets and yards but also their own free time; in other words, they want the neighborhood to be clean but they don't feel like doing it themselves. This assumption is not too farfetched, is it? Another will be that each resident has just two choices, to participate in the cleanup or not. To keep matters as simple as possible, we will not worry about how many minutes they spend participating or how hard they work; it will be just a yes-or-no decision. Finally, we will assume that what others do (whether they participate or not) will be unaffected by each individual's choice, that there are enough of these others that the effort of each individual alone has a minuscule effect on the cleanup, and that they will either mostly take part in the cleanup or mostly sit it out, in which case the neighborhood will stay messy.

Given this set of assumptions, there are four possibilities that can arise for each person:

(a) They participate and others do too.
(b) They participate and others don't.
(c) They don't participate but others do.
(d) They don't participate, nor do others.

Based on their preference for not working, we know that each individual prefers c to a and d to b, and their preference for a clean neighborhood means they value a over b and c over d. To put it bluntly, they would like to do something else that day, but they want their neighbors to pitch in. What we don't know at this point is how they would compare a and d. If the benefits of a clean neighborhood weigh more in their estimation than the cost of spending a day cleaning, then a is preferred to d and we have once again our old friend, the Prisoner's Dilemma. This is apparent from the payoff matrix in Fig. 10.1, which uses the familiar device of treating "everyone else" as a single, composite player.

As before, we designate the action that benefits the other player as C; so participating in the clean-up is cooperating and not participating is defecting. From the standpoint of a single, self-interested individual making an independent

		Everyone Else	
		D	C
One Person	D	(d, d)	(c, b)
	C	(b, c)	(a, a)

Fig. 10.1 Payoff matrix for a two-player prisoner's dilemma. One person and everyone else are the players; *C* (cooperation) and *D* (defection) are the choices. Of the four possible outcomes, d > b, c > a, a > b, c > d, and a > d

decision, it is always preferable to defect. Each "one person" is better off defecting if "everyone else" defects because d > b, and better off defecting if everyone else cooperates because c > a. Since everyone feels the same way, no one would show up and the result is d—no participation, no clean-up—for all. What makes this a dilemma is that each person would prefer result a—universal participation—instead. It is a case of individual rationality standing in the way of collective rationality.

To prepare ourselves for a closer examination of this problem, let's represent it algebraically. Let P_C be the expected payoff to cooperation for a given individual, P_D be the expected payoff to defection, π be the probability that the other player (or "everyone else") will choose C, and $(1-\pi)$ be the probability that the other player will choose D. (Recall that probability is a number lying between 0 and 1, such as 20 %—0.2.) Then we can say that

$$P_C = \pi a + (1 - \pi)b \tag{10.1a}$$

$$P_D = \pi c + (1 - \pi)d \tag{10.1b}$$

Combining the two, we get:

$$P_D - P_C = \pi(c - a) + (1 - \pi)(d - b) \tag{10.2}$$

Since

$$c - a > 0 \text{ (the advantage of unilateral defection)} \tag{10.3a}$$

$$d - b > 0 \text{ (avoiding the disadvantage of unilateral cooperation)} \tag{10.3b}$$

it doesn't matter what the probability π of B's cooperation is; the right-hand side of Eq. 10.2 has to be positive. Thus the individual's expected payoff from defection always exceeds the payoff from cooperation. Since the payoffs are symmetrical, the same logic applies to every individual involved in the dilemma. Note that the algebra embodied in Eq. 10.3 is exactly the same as the technique of reading the columns in the payoff matrix. (Since c > a and d > b, it doesn't matter for A's choice what B is expected to do.) It presents another view of what social theorists have come to call the **collective action problem**: the difficulty in getting people to cooperate for mutual benefit when it is in their individual interest to abstain from cooperation.

10.3 Cooperation in the Repeated Prisoner's Dilemma

This algebraic version of the story, simple as it is, gives us a tool to approach one of the most important complications of the Prisoner's Dilemma model, the possibility that the game might be played repeatedly. If you think about the logic of the model, the assumption of a one-time-only game is highly unrealistic; in most real-world situations people interact with one another over a period of time. In our neighborhood clean-up story, for instance, it is unlikely that the only contact neighbors will ever have with each other is the one-day work party. The neighborhood action group will probably plan more events, and neighbors might connect through other networks as well. To take the simplest case, suppose that the clean-up event will be repeated once a month. In this case people have to consider not only what the consequences of their actions will be for the current clean-up, but also the future ones. If they don't participate, this may make it less likely that others will participate in the future, and that effect ought to be taken into account in their calculations.

We can express this additional time dimension algebraically, using the convenient device of collapsing a long string of interactions into two periods, "now" and "the future".[1] For the first period the payoffs to cooperation and defection will be exactly as they are in Eq. 10.1a–b, but the second period raises additional complications. When each player must choose C or D without knowing what the other player will do, he or she faces a fixed (but unknown) probability π that the other player will cooperate. In the two-period game, players are in a position during the second round to respond to the choices made in the first round. Suppose one player cooperates in round 1. It is possible that the other, seeing this, will be more likely to cooperate in round 2, as a way of rewarding "good behavior". By the same token, if the first defects, the second may be more likely to defect one round later. Moreover, knowing this, each individual is in a position to anticipate that cooperation today will increase the likelihood of return cooperation tomorrow, and similarly for defection. This fundamentally changes the nature of the problem. For the first time, each player may have a purely selfish interest in cooperating, since that behavior now may elicit favorable behavior from others: "Do unto others and others will do unto you."

[1] Strictly speaking, there should be more than two time periods, and players should not be certain which one will be the last. If they were sure that period t was the end of the sequence, they would choose to defect then for the reasons laid out in the analysis of the one-period game. Expecting certain defection in the last round, they would also defect in the next-to-last round, and so on right back to the beginning. This type of logic is called "backward induction"; it is common in the mathematical analysis of sequences and chains. Fortunately, most real-world repeated games are of uncertain duration, so backward induction does not apply in this strict manner.

The challenge is representing this algebraically, so that we can see *exactly* what is needed for this new-found altruism to become dominant. There are different ways to do this; the simplest relies on another convenient assumption: suppose there are only two possible strategies *over time* available to both players. One is the familiar D strategy: defect in both time periods. The other, C, involves cooperating in the first period, and then cooperating in the second only if the other player also cooperated in the first; otherwise defect. In other words, begin with cooperation, and then cooperate only if the other side cooperates. The name given to this strategy by game theorists is **tit for tat.**[2] Finally, let's suppose that both players are fully aware that these are the only two strategies but don't know at the outset which of these the other player has selected. Thus each is in the position of having to guess what the other will do; as before, we can use π to represent the probability of cooperation and $(1-\pi)$ to represent the probability of defection in the first period. In the second period, however, there are no doubts: the first player knows that if the second has defected in the first period, then she must defect in the second, while if the second player cooperated in the first period then she will continue to cooperate if the first player began with cooperation; otherwise she will switch to defection. This is all we need to express the situation algebraically. An individual's expected payoffs are

$$P_C = [\pi a + (1-\pi)b] + \frac{1}{1+r}[\pi a + (1-\pi)d] \tag{10.4a}$$

$$P_D = [\pi c + (1-\pi)d] + \frac{d}{1+r} \tag{10.4b}$$

These are only slightly more complex than Eqs. 10.2a and 10.2b. Consider Eq. 10.4a. The right-hand side has two terms. The first of these, enclosed in brackets, is the same as the right-hand side of Eq. 10.1a; this represents the payoff to cooperation in the first period. The second term represents the second-period payoff. It is discounted by $1/(1 + r)$, where r is the individual's **discount rate**. This is the rate at which he scales back the importance of the future. (Recall that the equation describes the payoff he *expects* to receive before choosing either C or D in the first round.) For instance, suppose that $r = 0.10$. This means that this player would require an extra 10 % utility in period two to offset its being in the future—110 utility units in period two mean the same in the present as 100 units in period one. Equivalently, if $r = 0.10$, $1/(1 + r) \approx 0.91$. The second term is worth about 91 % of its future value in the present. Of course, r may be greater or less than 0.10, and this variability will prove to play an important role later in the analysis.

[2] Identifying cooperation with tit for tat has become standard among game theorists, since it greatly simplifies the analysis of cooperation problems. This is also the reason I am adopting it here. In the example we are looking at, little is lost and much is gained by assuming that responses of cooperators to the other player's C and D are so cut-and-dried. Nevertheless, some care should be taken. There do exist problems for which the results obtained by analyzing tit for tat cannot be generalized to other cooperative strategies.

The expression inside the bracket in the second term represents additional consequences of a player's original choice to cooperate. If the other player is also cooperative (with probability π) then both will continue to cooperate in the second round, with a continued payoff of a. If the second player is a defector, however, the first will also defect in the second round (tit-for-tat) and receive d. Thus, if the first chooses C in the first period, he will receive a in both periods if the second is cooperative, and b in the first and d in the second if she is "defective".

Now look at Eq. 10.4b. The first term, representing the first-period consequences remain identical to Eq. 10.1b, while the second term is very simple. If the first player defects at the outset it doesn't matter whether the second is inclined to cooperate or defect; either way she will choose D in the second round and both players will receive d, which is discounted to its present value by $1/(1 + r)$.

The key question is whether the new features found on the right-hand sides of Eqs. 10.4a and 10.4b change the overall incentive for a player to defect. For this we turn to Eq. 10.5.

$$\begin{aligned} P_D - P_C &= [\pi(c-a) + (1-\pi)(d-b)] + \frac{1}{1+r}[d-\pi a-(1-\pi)d] \\ &= [\pi(c-a) + (1-\pi)(d-b)] + \frac{\pi}{1+r}(d-a) \end{aligned} \tag{10.5}$$

Once more, the first bracketed term on the right-hand side is the same as that found in Eq. 10.2. The second term, after the now-familiar discount factor, is also not very complicated. It says that if a player chooses to defect rather than cooperate, he runs the risk (π) that the other player will turn out to be cooperative, in which case he loses the benefit of mutual cooperation over mutual defection (d−a), discounted by its being in the future. Thus, the anticipated payoff in the second round depends on whether the "standard" incentive to defect, captured in the first right-hand term of Eq. 10.5 and which is characteristic of a one-period prisoner's dilemma, is offset by the interest each player has in trying to encourage future cooperation on the part of the other. We don't know in any general way which force will be stronger, but at least it is a possibility that cooperation-seeking may prevail.

One reason for thinking it might is that, lurking behind this equation, is the notion that period two really represents not just one period, but all future periods rolled into one. If the first player cooperates in round one and the second reciprocates, the first can enjoy the benefit of this reciprocation and continue it in round three, round four, etc. The advantages of cooperation can persist for a very long time. By the same logic, if the two players find themselves locked into a spiral of mutual defection, that can go on for a long time as well—a fact that ought to make each think very carefully before defecting in the first place. On the other hand, the future is the future and now is now; that's what the discount factor represents. If r is large enough, the long-term disadvantages of defection may not carry enough weight to override the short-term advantages.

What can we conclude? It is clear that the repeated prisoner's dilemma is not loaded in favor of defection the way a one-period prisoner's dilemma is. While the

Table 10.1 Factors that make cooperation more likely in repeated prisoner's dilemmas

Factor	Effect
1. High payoff to cooperation	Makes players more willing to bear the risks of cooperation
2. Likelihood of retaliation in response to defection	Increases the future cost of defecting in the present
3. Few gains to players who defect while others cooperate	Reduces incentive to "cash in" on defection in the present at the cost of less cooperation in the future
4. Few losses to players who cooperate while others defect	Reduces the risk of cooperating in the present
5. Low discount rate	Increases the value in the present of cooperation in the future

complexity entailed in analyzing variations of the repeated prisoner's dilemma is beyond the scope of this discussion, you should be aware that it has been studied very closely, and the conclusion that has been reached is that, while no guarantees can be offered, general cooperation can emerge as a stable outcome. (This result is known in the game theory literature as the "Folk Theorem".) While the analysis does not provide the basis for firm predictions, it does highlight the factors that play a role in determining whether collective action can succeed: there must be sufficient rewards to each player from the cooperation of other players, sufficient punishments to each player from the defection of other players, relatively modest incentives to unilaterally defect or avoid unilateral cooperation, and a sufficiently low discount rate r for most players. If all these elements are in place, bringing about cooperation is not too difficult to envision (Table 10.1).

10.4 Cooperation in the Many-Player Prisoner's Dilemma

Now let's turn to a different complication, the reality that "everyone else", a device I have used to simplify games between many players, is not really a single person at all, but a representation of a large, diverse group. If you think about the neighborhood cleanup example, lumping all the neighbors together except a single individual in one group and postulating that they all make the same choices, as I did above, is rather sneaky. It tries to get around aspects of multi-player games that might make the prisoner's dilemma less harsh. After all, maybe only some players will shirk their cleanup obligations and others won't. One possibility, for instance, is that if a few neighbors show up for work, each's contribution will be more noticeable than if the event drew either everyone or no one. Or it might be that the work will be unpleasant if just a few neighbors participate, but more enjoyable if it is a true community-wide endeavor. In other words, the fraction of "everyone else" who participates can alter each individual's payoff, potentially in a manner that might reduce the dilemma aspect of the Prisoner's Dilemma.

These questions can be addressed using a geometric device, providing we specify a few additional aspects of the game. Up to now, we have referred to the outcome for each player, determined by his or her choice in conjunction with the other player's choice, as a single payoff that sums up all the effects in one number or letter. In multiple-person games, however, it is useful to distinguish between the costs and benefits that go into this payoff, since they may respond differently to changes in the overall level of cooperation.

The potential benefit to cooperation is whatever good it brings about. In the original prisoner's dilemma story it was the withholding of evidence from the prosecution (a good for the prisoners if not for the rest of society); in the neighborhood cleanup example it is the improved environment for all residents. Generally speaking, the benefits can have one of two characteristics: either they are constant no matter how many or few players cooperate, or they change (usually increase) with the number of players who choose cooperation. Both can occur in many contexts, but we will explore only the second, since it is most clearly relevant to the problems facing social action groups. In nearly every circumstance, more participation creates more benefits. An additional wrinkle we will add, however, is this: the benefits from collective action usually take the form of a **public good** in the sense that they cannot be withheld from those who don't contribute to them. (Public goods will be one of the topics of Chap. 15.) The benefit of a clean neighborhood is an advantage for me if I live there, whether or not I take part in the effort to clean it. Because this seems to be a general pattern, we can usually assume it, but we should be aware that there are other possibilities.

The potential cost of cooperation is the harm individuals may expose themselves to by choosing to cooperate. In the prisoner fable, the cost of not talking to the police is that sentencing may be more harsh. The cost of participating in the cleanup is the sheer unpleasantness of it. Once more, this cost can either be constant or it can depend on how many of the players choose to cooperate. Most social action situations are of the second type; whatever demands an organization makes of its members, they are more easily borne if they are more widely shared. A vivid example is a labor union; if just a few workers join they are at risk of getting fired, but as the membership expands they are more able to protect one another. We will expect, then, that the cost of cooperation depends on the extent of cooperation, once again being aware that this may not be true in particular contexts.

Assuming then that both the costs and benefits of cooperation are variable as more cooperators take part, we can depict the relationship between the payoff to cooperation and how widespread it is in Fig. 10.2 on the following page.

It illustrates the interactions between cost, benefit, and the extent of cooperation along the lines we have been discussing. The vertical axis measures utility (understood in the usual, if somewhat implausible, economic sense), while the horizontal axis measures the extent (spell that x-tent) of cooperation. The intersection of the utility axis by the X axis at 0 indicates that utility can be negative as well as positive. K, L, M and N are points, the line B represents benefits, and the line C represents costs. Benefits are zero when no one cooperates; this point is marked 0. They rise continuously as X increases. The costs of cooperating are very great at zero cooperation; this is given by the line segment from 0 to L (the measure of L's negative utility). The C curve rises as cooperation becomes more widespread,

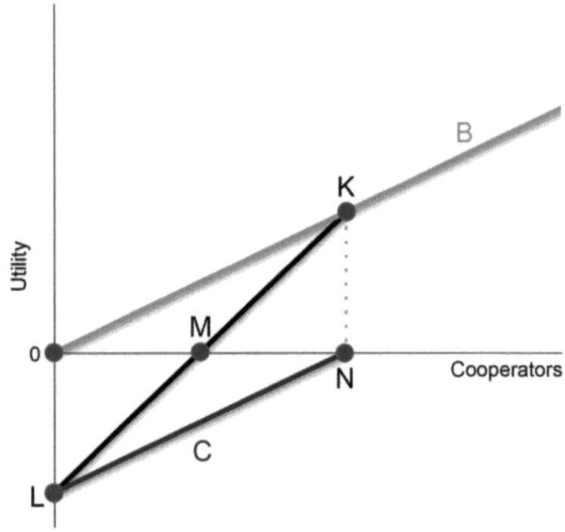

Fig. 10.2 Many-person prisoner's dilemma with variable benefits and costs. The utility (U) of an individual adopting cooperation is portrayed as a function of how many cooperators (X) there are. *B* is the benefit from cooperation; *C* is the cost. At the number of cooperators indicated by *M*, the individual breaks even; after *N* there are no more costs, only benefits

which is to say that the costs fall. At a sufficient level of cooperation, N, the costs disappear altogether. From this information we can determine the utility levels of cooperators and defectors, each represented as a function of X, the number of cooperators. The utility of defectors is straightforward; it is simply equal to the B curve, since defectors receive the benefits of cooperation (they are assumed to be public goods) but incur none of the costs. They begin at 0, rise through K, and keep on going as X increases. The cooperator story is more complicated. They receive the utility denoted by the B curve minus the cost represented by the C curve. At zero cooperation there are no benefits and L costs, so L is their (negative) utility. As cooperation increases, cooperators benefit in two ways, from the increase in cooperation benefits and the decrease in its costs. This puts them on the line segment LMK, with a steeper slope than either B or C. At M cooperators pass from the position of being net losers of utility to net gainers. At levels of X greater than N costs remain zero, so the utility function for cooperators mergers with that of defectors and follows B.

This diagram makes it possible for us to see that this many-person game has the same essential features as the two-person prisoner's dilemma: (1) There is still an incentive to defect when others cooperate, at least at any level of cooperation below N. (2) There is still a cost to cooperating when others defect, again at $X < N$. (3) General cooperation is better than general defection; all players are better off on the right side of the diagram than on the left side. As a result, a large group of individuals, such as our neighbors contemplating a cleanup, may be unable to achieve collective action despite an overwhelming common interest in it. That's the bad news. The goods news is that this simple diagram is powerful enough to provide insights that those promoting cooperation may find useful.

First, while cooperators are disadvantaged relative to defectors at lower initial levels of cooperation (below N), they are *absolutely* disadvantaged only over a lower range, below M. If it is possible for organizers to shift the attention of the players away from comparisons with defectors and toward the extent to which cooperation is personally sustainable (not causing them net harm), the threshold level of cooperation needed to make the strategy work can fall significantly. We will return to this insight shortly.

Second, even after cooperation succeeds, we ought to be worried that it might unravel. If there are benefits to unilateral defection, no cooperative outcome is safe. First one individual, then another, and finally the entire group may try to gain an advantage by free-riding on the cooperation of the others. In the language of game theory, we are asking whether general cooperation is a **stable** equilibrium. It is clear that in Fig. 10.2 cooperation **is** stable, since, at $X > N$ the cost of cooperation is zero, and cooperators and defectors enjoy exactly the same level of utility. It is not in anyone's personal interest to switch from cooperating to defecting. In practical terms, this means that the organizer's problem (in this model) is to bring about collective action; once it is established it should maintain itself on its own.

10.5 Cooperation in More Realistic Models of Social Behavior

We have gingerly relaxed two restrictions on the original Prisoner's Dilemma model, permitting the game to be replayed many times over and allowing for large numbers of diverse players. This has brought a slight whiff of realism to the analysis, but most readers will, rightly, be unpersuaded. The fundamental simplification in the model surely has to be the presumed psychology of the players, rigidly self-interested and calculating. These do not look like the people we know (and are), and dire predictions of the failure of cooperation are hardly credible if they depend on the assumption that people are entirely asocial to begin with.

Fortunately, the recent turn towards behavioral sophistication in economic research makes it possible to discuss collective action problems more constructively. What follows is a brief survey of some of the relevant themes emerging from theoretical reflection and laboratory experiments.

1. Altruism. Recall from Chap. 3 that the common view of human motivation advanced by economists has been that people are entirely self-interested, in the sense that they consider only the consequences of an action that fall on them and ignore all the rest. This is related to the notion that markets are anonymous: no one knows who they are buying and selling from, and no one cares.

   We know from laboratory evidence, as well as common sense, that **altruism**, concern for the well-being of others apart from its effect on ourselves, is widespread but unevenly distributed. Nearly everyone is somewhat altruistic, and some people are deeply so. We would expect altruists to be more likely to choose cooperative strategies in Prisoner's Dilemma situations, and this is in fact what happens. At the same time, altruism is not a complete solution; even die-hard altruists are likely to switch to defection if their cooperative offerings to other players are not reciprocated. Part of the problem is that not everyone is an altruist; another part is that it is often difficult to tell at a distance who is an altruist, so it is not usually possible to arrange your interactions only with those likely to cooperate with you. As we saw in Chap. 3, personal contact makes cooperation feel good to people with an altruistic streak, but much of the economy is fundamentally impersonal.

To summarize a vast outpouring of research during the last several years, it is fair to say that levels of trust and cooperation in laboratory versions of the Prisoner's Dilemma fluctuate in an intermediate range between the extremes of universal defection, as predicted in the classical two-person, one-time Prisoner's Dilemma, and no defection at all.

A reasonable question to ask is, what promotes or inhibits altruism in collective action situations? One important insight that has emerged is that there seems to be a tradeoff between appealing to self-interested and altruistic motives. An examples concerns **side payments**, which are additional benefits made available to players on the condition that they cooperate. For instance, our neighborhood cleanup group might offer participants a free raffle ticket or some other inducement. This is a common strategy, in fact, and it appears in a wide variety of contexts. If the payment is great enough that it plays a major role in attracting self-interested participants, however, it appears to crowd out the altruism motive among those who might otherwise feel it. (Unsurprisingly, this is referred to as the "crowding out effect.") In other words, the strategy of buying the loyalty of some people comes at the cost of discouraging those who would contribute for free. (We raised this possibility in the discussion of price gouging following Hurricane Charley.) Thus altruism, which is a resource at the disposal of those trying to organize collective action, presents its own dilemma: does a group tailor its appeal to altruists or the self-interested when forced to choose?

2. Social norms. People do not come to collective action situations as blank slates; they are shaped by their history and culture to respond to situations in fairly predictable ways. Indeed, current research in anthropology demonstrates conclusively that the propensity to cooperate under various conditions (as modeled by different sorts of games) differs dramatically across cultures. A Prisoner's Dilemma game played in Boston will not have the same level of cooperation as one played in a village in Kenya or Papua New Guinea. There are even large differences within cultures based on regional, ethnic and other differences.

   One approach that has proved useful is to identify particular **heuristics** that are shared by most members of a culture. A heuristic is a rule or procedure that simplifies the task of making a decision; an example is "never accept gifts from strangers". (This may or may not be your own rule of thumb, depending on your background.) Some heuristics specify circumstances under which people ought to act cooperatively, and these can be exploited by organizers. It may matter, for instance, whether people are asked to contribute in a public or private setting, or by members of the same or opposite sex, or by someone older or younger than they are. Sometimes new groups piggyback on the success of older groups in mobilizing cooperation, as when a political action group uses pre-existing religious networks; in effect, they are trying to borrow the heuristics that have arisen as a result of the social acceptance of prior forms of cooperation.

One norm in particular deserves a paragraph of its own: **fairness**. There is a large literature in economics that analyzes exactly what might be meant by this term, but we will use it more loosely. A social situation is viewed by an individual as fair if it distributes costs and benefits to those who take part in it in a manner consistent with that individual's norms. What these norms will be depends on who the individual is—her personal history, her group identifications, her time and place. For us the important issue is not the details of any particular fairness norm, but simply the fact that such norms exist and have force. There is a wealth of experimental evidence that fairness (as understood by those being studied) plays a powerful role in determining how much cooperation people will offer to others. From the standpoint of eliciting support for collective action, however, perceptions of fairness are double-edged. On the one hand, they often lead people to cooperate under conditions in which the traditional Prisoner's Dilemma analysis would predict defection, and they also encourage punishment of others when they defect. This, as we have seen, increases the costs to defection among the self-interested. On the other hand, however, they emphasize the payoffs an individual gets from cooperation *relative* to the payoffs received by others. The analysis of Fig. 10.2 makes clear, however, that such comparisons are an impediment to cooperation in a many-sided game. Organizers will want to distract people from such thoughts and get them to focus instead on what cooperation can do for *them*.

3. Prospect theory. Economics sometimes has the tendency to treat human beings as utility thermometers: given the possibility of obtaining one bundle of goods, utility rises into the hot zone, but given another it slides back down toward lukewarm. The thermometer could be dipped into any economic "payoff", and a number read off the scale. This is certainly the implication of expected utility theory as described in Chap. 3.

This is not at all how most of us react to the world most of the time. Instead, we usually make comparisons: how well am I doing compared to how well I might be doing? And, rather than putting ourselves on a continuum of utility and disutility, we respond very differently depending on whether we are doing better or worse than the alternative we focus on. This model of human behavior has two elements, then, the notion of comparison and its effects.

The alternative we compare ourselves to is called the **reference point**, and it has obvious parallels to the concept of a reference group studied in sociology. Like reference groups, reference points are not ordained by fate; there are many potential points of comparison available to us, and much depends on which one we gravitate toward. How healthy do I feel? Compared to what? To how healthy I felt a year ago? Or to how healthy most people in my age group that I see at work seem to feel? Or to the apparent health of the actors I see on TV? Or my older relative in a nursing home? How I see myself will depend enormously on who I compare myself to.

The second aspect is the role played by reference points. Considerable evidence indicates that people respond quite differently depending on whether they think they are above or below this point. Above the point of comparison, most of us feel we are OK; we may invest some energy in further improvement, but not usually very much. Below, we feel that we are doing badly and will feel a greater motivation to change our situation. In other words, the reference point is a point of discontinuity in our evaluation, marking the change from one sort of response (complacent well-being) to another (intense concern). Putting the two together—the establishment of reference points and their effects—we have the model known as **prospect theory**. (This theory gets its name from the assumption of its authors that the reference point is generally the status quo, so that the analysis applies to the process of looking forward, but it lends itself to a more general interpretation, as I have done here.)

To see the power of this theory, it is enough to consider almost any collective action situation. Return, for instance, to the problem of organizing a labor union. Will the workers in a particular company or occupation be willing to accept the risk of getting fired and the other costs of joining the effort? It depends in part on how they view the potential benefits of unionization. And this in turn depends on their sense of whether their current situation—pay, benefits, working conditions, etc.—is seen as "good enough". But what is good enough? If these workers compare themselves to workers at a different company across town they might have one standard for comparison; if they think about how well off they would be without their job they would have another; and if they think about how well off they would be if they had a larger share of influence within the company an even higher standard might emerge. From the point of view of the union organizer, the goal is to have workers judge their situation on the basis of a higher standard rather than a lower one. Thus, even if workers in other companies are doing just as badly, attention should be refocused on the potential for gains if the union is successful. There is no guarantee, however, that this refocusing will actually occur. Rather, we could say that it is the organizer's job to bring about this change in reference points: that is a large part of what the activity of "organizing" is really about. Of course, those who might oppose the union, such as the company's owners or managers, will try to have the workers think in terms of how much better off they are with the job than without it. This conflict would make no sense in the world of continuous utility adjustment postulated by conventional economics, but it is central from the vantage point of prospect theory. To repeat: in this example, the willingness of workers to engage in collective action depends crucially on what reference point they compare their situation to, and one of the chief tasks of the organizer is to encourage them to select a more demanding reference point—to set their standards as high as possible.

What makes prospect theory particularly relevant to the Prisoner's Dilemma model is the claim that people who think their well-being is below their reference point will be strongly motivated to alter that situation. It is exactly such feelings of intense need that have the potential to break through the dismal calculations of the standard one-period game. This dynamic is often observed in social movements: a moment arrives when individuals are willing to take significant risks, such as the risk of unreciprocated cooperation (taking a stand when others back down), in response to a sense of deprivation. It is exactly this push that can propel a group past the "hump" represented by points to the left of M in Fig. 10.2 and lead to a new, stable equilibrium of cooperation.

It is important to bear in mind, however, causation runs not only from psychology to action, but also from action to psychology. Collective action plays a role in the determination of reference points by enlarging the field through a redefinition of what is possible. In the absence of collective action, when each individual acts alone, possibilities are limited, and this is likely to be reflected in the standards of comparisons people establish for themselves. Good enough is what you can do by your own efforts if you are reasonably successful. When they act together, however, people can potentially accomplish more, so it is reasonable for them to set higher standards. In this way individual perceptions and attitudes and the extent of collective action are mutually reinforcing; either low reference points and widespread defection or high reference points and widespread cooperation can be stable equilibria.

4. Social networks. One of the most interesting aspects to the study of collective action, and one of the most difficult to model, arises from the fact that most people find themselves incorporated into overlapping layers of social networks. People who might take part in a neighborhood cleanup event or join a protest group may know each other from going to school together, belonging to the same church or bird-watching club. Some of these ties may have themselves been forged in previous collective action projects, giving those who took part some experience in developing cooperation and trust. Even if they weren't, however, they provide possible channels for conveying intentions to reciprocate, and they provide additional situations in which defection can be punished.

   The density of social networks in a community is sometimes referred to as its level of "social capital". (This is just one use of the term, however; we will soon see it in a different context.) Communities with plentiful social capital are thought of as having a greater capacity to self-organize in order to meet their needs. They are more likely to have their collective voices heard and to provide the sort of services that voluntary social action is best equipped to offer.

10.6 Families as Economic Units

Before there were markets, corporations or even governments as we know them today, there were families: although they were not primarily economic institutions as we defined them in Chap. 1, they performed essential economic functions that sustained untold generations of our ancestors. Even now they are responsible for a large share of the economic production that occurs in every country, and they play an important role in determining how goods and services are distributed.

Let's begin with distribution, since it is somewhat simpler to describe. The conventional view of economics, at least for the past 200 years, has been that households receive income from labor or the ownership of property and then either save it or spend it on the output of businesses. (This will be developed more fully in the macroeconomics portion of the text.) From this perspective, the main issue in determining how much people will be able to consume is the distribution of income across households, and this is what we will investigate in detail in Chap. 19. Nevertheless, once income enters the household the actual decisions about who consumes what are made, in most cases, by families. Depending on social customs and the relative influence of different family members, resources may be divided equally or they may go largely to just one person, the "head" of the family.

One example will illustrate the importance of this process. Children rarely earn enough money from paid work outside the home to support themselves. Child labor is widespread, and children contribute income to their families, but usually their pay is far lower than that of adults, and they tend to work fewer hours as well. Thus they are dependent on the willingness of adults to share income or other resources with them. This dependence becomes a critical variable during times of famine, when families may have to make difficult choices about how to apportion too little food among too many mouths. During particularly severe episodes, relief agencies will set up programs to distribute emergency food supplies to families, hoping to sustain them until normal economic conditions return.

In the past, relief workers would give food packages to the individual designated as the head of the household, usually an elder male, but they often found that this made little difference in the incidence of malnutrition among children. This is because it is the custom in some societies for adult men to feed themselves until they are satisfied, and only then to share food with women and children; because of this, unequal distribution within the family was perpetuating starvation. Based on research conducted by economists and anthropologists in household food distribution patterns, relief agencies began to make it a policy to give the food to women rather than men in such cases, and they found that child malnutrition declined.

Even during less desperate times, distributional inequalities within the family can have a large impact on economic life. They often determine, for instance, which children will have access to education, costly health care and other goods and services. There has been renewed interest in these issues in recent years, and economists have developed more precise models to explain differences in distribution rules between families or in response to changed circumstances, particularly as they affect the access of women to family resources compared to men.

Families also retain a large and underappreciated role in the production of goods and services. This role has diminished somewhat in the industrialized countries as commercial products replace those formerly produced at home, such as restaurant meals and child care programs. Nevertheless much remains: most house-cleaning, a large percentage of food preparation, and above all a significant share of what feminist economists have come to call **caring labor**. By this they mean the expenditure of time and effort (often emotionally demanding) to minister to family members in periods of need. This includes nursing the sick and elderly, child-rearing and responding to emergencies of various sorts as they arise.

By most calculations, these activities have enormous economic value, in the sense that it would cost quite a lot to produce them as services for sale in the market. They also have great human value, of course. Survey research, as well as common sense, shows that if people are cut off from the care of others, even high levels of money income are not enough to restore their feeling of well-being. The point would seem to be so obvious that it could be taken for granted, but it shouldn't be.

Caring labor is labor. It absorbs time and energy that might otherwise be available for other purposes, and so it has an opportunity cost. Since it is performed disproportionately by women, it shows up as a level of stress that is often difficult to sustain, particularly if those expected to provide such services for free are also employed outside the household—the infamous "double day". The demands of caring have been shown to diminish women's opportunities to advance in paid work, or even in some cases to keep a job at all. This has led to demands for a more equitable sharing of caring and other household work, as well as for greater accommodation on the part of employers.

One important implication of this topic concerns the economics of health. There has been a steady stream of studies showing how expensive ill-health is in industrialized economies: diseases, many of them preventable, occupational and traffic accidents and other risks we face are responsible for hundreds of billions of dollars in economic costs annually. Until recently, however, the same recognition has not been given to health risks in developing countries. With fewer hospitals and health practitioners relative to the size of its population, a typical developing country is likely to show far fewer economic costs of poor health. What we have learned in the last few years, however, is that this difference is illusory: the economic value of health is just as important in the developing world, perhaps more so. One reason is that ill-health causes a great expansion of caring labor at the expense of other uses of people's time. The lesson is that, just because the costs do not show up in paid services, like hospital stays and increased workload for doctors and nurses, doesn't mean that they don't exist. Unpaid caring labor is real labor with real economic consequences.

A final point to make about families is that they constitute one of the most important social networks affecting the way markets and other economic institutions operate. One example may illustrate how this can work. Throughout the world there are enclaves of ethnic Chinese settlements, and in many countries, particularly in the Pacific basin, these communities have played a leading role in establishing local businesses. Why? A large part of the story is that in Chinese culture family connections extend widely, including distant cousins and others who might not be recognized in other societies, and there are strong bonds of obligation between family members. These extended family networks have been used to provide the start-up support for new enterprises, such as loans, advice, tips on potential suppliers and customers and initial orders. As more family members become established in business, this increases the resources available to new start-ups, and so on from one generation to the next.

Family-based business development is not restricted to the Chinese, of course; it is seen across the world in almost every society. It is so commonplace we may not notice it, but its role should not be overlooked in economic policy. One of the challenges facing highly mobile societies with increasingly fragmented family structures is finding new networks that can offer similar economic advantages.

10.7 Social Capital

In Chap. 3 it was argued that all human knowledge relies on metaphor, and that economics is no exception. The concept of social capital exemplifies this, for it is a metaphor built on other metaphors. First comes the notion of capital itself, which we will see later in this text is already somewhat metaphorical. It refers to assets that have the property of being productive and therefore enabling a return to their owner(s). Normally we think of capital as taking the form of either goods used in production or the money invested in such goods. (These, as we will see, are not the same thing.) From an economic standpoint, however, it could be imagined that anything which is productive, whether or not it is an asset in the conventional sense, could be regarded as capital, and this is the kernel that gives us social networks as a form of capital.

One type of social capital has already been encountered, the role of social networks in facilitating collective action. Since, in a wide range of situations, collective action is more productive than the independent efforts of separate individuals (cooperation is superior to defection), anything that makes collective action easier to attain is itself productive. The implication, of course, is that the community whose social capital is being assessed actually faces Prisoner's Dilemmas and has a stake in overcoming them. Among those who have taken up the study of social capital, this view is widely held.

A second type of social capital is closely related to the first. Many researchers, following the lead of political scientist Robert Putnam (and before him Alexis de Tocqueville), contend that government is more effective in societies that have a large number of voluntary organizations embracing most of the population. Such organizations promote trust and cooperative behavior, on which governments can draw to provide services more consensually and efficiently. This is of interest to economists, of course, since government services are themselves economic goods, and also because of the role, positive or negative, that government plays in setting the rules that other institutions, such as markets and firms, are obliged to follow. In addition, businesses themselves benefit directly from greater trust between workers and employers, suppliers and purchasers, and firms and their regulators.

The third type operates at the individual level. We have already considered some of the evidence that indicates that social networks, such as family ties, can channel resources to individuals for purposes like starting a business; the same logic applies to other opportunities like getting an education or finding a job. This implies that the lack of such networks may be partly responsible for people ending up in poverty, and that building up networks in low-income communities may serve as an anti-poverty strategy. Attaching the term social capital to this perception essentially re-lables an insight that derives from sociological research dating back to the early years of the twentieth century.

Table 10.2 Varieties of social capital

Type	Effect
I	Promotes further collective action in civil society
II	Improves the efficiency of government and business through cooperation and trust
III	Increases resources individuals can draw on for education, employment and business formation

To sum up, the three forms of social capital all have the same basis but transmit their effects through different channels. All look to social networks as the essential raw material: richer, more encompassing networks mean more social capital. Where they differ is in the realm of society where the effects show up. In the first type, it is the facilitation of collective action, in the second improvement of government, and in the third individual opportunity. These are summarized in Table 10.2.

The Main Points

1. The realm of civil society includes many types of social organizations and groups that have a large impact on the economy, such as unions and professional associations, clubs, and families. They produce goods and services directly, facilitate the development of markets, and play a role in regulating them.
2. Voluntary collective action is a prisoner's dilemma. Fortunately, the pessimistic prediction of the one-time prisoner's dilemma (the logic of joint defection) can be mitigated in real-world situations. Often the interactions are repeated, and participants have a greater incentive to cooperate in order to induce more cooperation from other players in the future. Factors that favor cooperative outcomes in the repeated prisoner's dilemma include high payoffs to cooperation, the likelihood of retaliation against defectors, low payoffs to those who defect when others cooperate, fewer losses to those who cooperate when others defect, and a low discount rate (less devaluation of the future) by participants.
3. If there are a large number of individuals playing a prisoner's dilemma, the tipping point for cooperation (the level of cooperation at which collective action is a stabile outcome) is usually less than 100 %; a dedicated minority can often keep voluntary organization in healthy shape. This depends on the extent to which the costs and benefits of individual cooperation vary with the number of cooperators.
4. Other real-world factors may promote voluntary cooperation. These include the possibility for organizations to provide extra benefits to those who cooperate, the presence of social norms that lead individuals to cooperate even when it is not in their immediate personal interest, the creation of reference points (in prospect theory) that increase the perceived benefits of collective action, and the piggybacking of collective action organizations on pre-existing social networks.
5. Families are productive units within society: their members engage in caring labor, which is responsible for many of the essential services all of us depend on, like child-rearing, household maintenance and food preparation. This labor may

be invisible to many of the statistics by which we measure our economy, but it is no less significant for the economy than work performed for wages. In addition, family networks often facilitate job search, entrepreneurship and credit provision.

6. Social capital has become a major frontier of economic research during recent years. Three types of social capital have been identified: social and culture resources that favor collective action, the foundation of trust on which political and business organizations depend, and the social and cultural support that give individuals more skill and self-confidence in their various economic roles.

Terms to Define

Altruism
Caring labor
Civil society
Collective action problem
Discount rate
Heuristic
Prospect theory
Reference point
Side payments
Social capital (types I, II and III)
Tit for tat

Questions to Consider

1. Create a list of five voluntary organizations you are familiar with whose purpose is to promote a particular cause or point of view. What effects, if any, do they have on how the economy operates? Do any of them also provide goods or services, either to their members or society at large, as well?
2. Take another look at the list you created for Question 1. How significant, in your opinion, is the collective action problem for these five groups? Do you know any of the strategies they have adopted to encourage cooperation?
3. Do you practice tit for tat in some aspects of your life? Does it "work" to evoke the cooperation in others you would like to receive?
4. It is sometimes said that people in a collective action situation have an *obligation* to perform the punishment part of the tit for tat strategy; that is, if they see others failing to cooperate, they should punish them in some way. That will benefit the whole group, it is claimed, by increasing the likelihood that cooperation will become more widespread in the future. Do you agree? For instance, do you think that someone who observes an act of littering (failure to cooperate in keeping the environment clean) has an obligation to confront them or report them to the police or other authorities?
5. Can you explain in your own words why, in a many-sided Prisoner's Dilemma situation, cooperation will be more widespread if people who are considering it

refrain from comparing themselves to non-cooperators? Can you give an example of this principle in practice?

6. Consider a voluntary collective action group that you belong to or participate in. Is this group's appeal to you and others based primarily on altruism or self-interest? Do you think there is a tradeoff between these two types of appeals in this case?
7. When you think about whether you are satisfied attending your current college or university, what is your reference point? When you talk to other students, do you find that differences in reference points explain some of the differences in your levels of satisfaction?
8. How equally were (are) resources and opportunities distributed in your family? How was this distribution determined? Did your share depend on whether you were earning an outside income? If so, why?
9. Based on the experience you have had in your own family (or families), how prevalent is the "double day" problem for women today? What, if anything, should be done to alleviate it?
10. For many people, according to current sociological research, work provides most of the social contact outside of family life. Does this mean that there is less scope for social capital? Or can social networks in the workplace fulfill the same functions as those created by truly voluntary organizations? In answering this question, you may find it helpful to think about your own social experiences at work and the extent to which they promoted cooperation and trust, or better access to non-work opportunities.

Part III

A Closer Look at Markets

11 The Theory of Demand

In Chap. 4 we saw that, according to the usual economic worldview, the sole purpose of economic life is to produce goods for purchase by consumers. Producing the right goods in the right amounts, with the characteristics consumers desire, is what an efficient economy should be doing as much of the time as possible. Clearly, in order to translate this broad objective into specific policies we require a theory of the consumers themselves: what governs the choices they make and how their individual decisions in the marketplace affect their ultimate well-being.

As we will see, however, economics has developed a theory of consumer choice that is nearly useless for these purposes. (This is not a controversial statement.) It is very elaborate and contains more than a few valuable insights, but it falls far short of what policy-makers, or marketers for that matter, are looking for. Yet this is not entirely fair, since the purpose of the conventional economic theory of consumer choice is not to answer substantive questions about the impact of consumption on well-being or to predict future consumption patterns, but simply to identify the conditions on the demand side of the market that must be met for the Market Welfare Model to hold. In other words, its purposes are internal to economic theory itself, rather than outward-looking or pragmatic.

This is an important function, one we will take seriously in the pages to come. Nevertheless, if we were to end the story at that point many readers would feel frustrated. They may be interested in the logical nuances of normative economic modeling, but they also want to know whether the economy they are living in is truly delivering the goods, as measured by the well-being of the population. An economics text is not the place for detailed examination of such questions, or even of the theoretical tools such an examination might employ, but we will survey briefly some of the main ideas that have emerged in two alternative approaches to consumption. The purpose is to set in relief what is truly unique about standard economic theory in this field.

P. Dorman, *Microeconomics*, Springer Texts in Business and Economics,
DOI 10.1007/978-3-642-37434-0_11,

11.1 Utility and Utilitarianism

The place to begin is language, specifically the central term in economic discourse about consumption, **utility**. We have been using this word loosely up to this point, but it is easily misunderstood and deserves further clarification. As mentioned previously, what utility does *not* mean in economics is usefulness. A completely useless item can still give people utility if they desire it for some reason. Sometimes a hot fudge sundae can offer more utility than a healthy, nourishing salad.

What utility does mean is difficult to say precisely. We imagine that people could sum up their happiness in a given situation with a single evaluation and then say whether, on balance, they were better off than they would be in another situation. If the difference between the two situations is that in one an individual has less money but a hot fudge sundae, and in another she has more money but no sundae, the comparison tells us whether the extra money is worth the gooey pleasures of the sundae. Economists would say that the utility of one is greater or less than the utility of the other. In other words, utility is the measurement of desire corresponding to the preference of one thing, or group of things, over another. If I want ice cream rather than salad, and I am willing to actually make this choice if given the opportunity, this means that, in this situation, I get more utility from ice cream than from salad.

We can imagine that people might make every possible comparison between different assortments of goods, with and without different amounts of money, and at the end of the process produce a complete set of rankings. For each comparison they are prepared to say which they would prefer, or whether they evaluate both exactly equally. From this we would be able to rank all the possible choices from highest to lowest, and this would also tell us which choices were above the others in terms of utility. Economists call such a ranking a "preference map" and they see it as the best guide to the study of consumer satisfaction.

In this book we are going to cut a few corners. Rather than make the minimal assumption that individuals do no more than compare sets of options (but this is already a lot, since they have to compare *all* such sets), we will go further and assume that they can actually put a numerical measure on each choice. Like Olympic judges, they give this sundae an 8.7 and that salad an 8.3. Doing this for every possible good produces a complete numeric scale, with a utility score for each. Since this entails more demanding assumptions, economists will be a bit uncomfortable with it, but nothing of importance for our survey will be lost; nearly everything we will be doing with this numerical conception of utility also works, but in a more complicated way, with the just-make-comparisons approach.[1]

It will be useful to step back for a moment and consider the implications of the analysis we are about to embark on. People are making choices in the market; they are paying money and buying goods and services. This is observable and even measurable: willingness-to-pay, after all, can actually be computed from economic

[1] In the language of economics, we will use a cardinal rather than ordinal approach to utility.

data. What we would like to know is how all this buying affects people's true well-being. This is invisible and possibly unmeasurable. The problem is to infer the second from the first, if possible. Economists typically make the assumption that at the individual level the two correspond to one another perfectly, that if any good is chosen over any other it makes the individual better off as well, and that willingness to pay is a satisfactory numerical measure of how much additional well-being a consumer can expect to get from an item he purchases.

All of this is incorporated into the concept of utility. Utility is the element of well-being corresponding to the units of money people spend on things. In such a scheme people are never disappointed; the goods they buy deliver exactly the payoffs they anticipate, which in turn are encoded in the prices they are willing to pay. As a theory it is difficult to justify, but it has the convenience of enabling economists to discuss well-being (normative economics) with exactly the same tools they use to analyze observable consumption behavior (positive economics).

Before we dismiss the whole enterprise as improbable, we should consider the case in its favor. It rests primarily on the question, if you don't trust an individual to make the choice that will turn out best for her, who do you trust? If the expectations of utility people have in their minds when they make their purchases differ in some way from the well-being they actually receive, does it matter if this is still the best guess anyone can make about what the effects will be? In that case we could say that utility theory is approximately correct, and that following its guidelines is the best course of action. It's a bit like saying you have a thermometer that sometimes gives too high a temperature and sometimes too low. You can acknowledge this, but if this is the only or best instrument you have, and if you are unable to tell what the error is for any particular reading, all you can do is record the temperature it gives you and hope for the best. This argument, however, depends on the strong claim that there is, in fact, no better guide to human well-being than consumer willingness-to-pay, and, as we will see, there are many who would disagree.

There is also a political aspect to the question posed in the previous paragraph. Surely individuals deserve a benefit of the doubt in their choices on the grounds that this safeguards their autonomy to choose as they please. The danger in having some other theory of well-being is that it can justify intrusions by well-meaning authorities that put individual freedom at risk, the problem of **paternalism**. Logically, there is no requirement that an objective theory of well-being (one that can be determined by "outsiders" like academic researchers rather than the individual whose well-being is at stake) must necessarily lead to infringement of freedom, but there will typically be a temptation. Take the case of smoking cigarettes. This has severe health consequences but also provides at least some pleasure for smokers. We could let smokers decide for themselves whether the health cost is worth it. On the other hand, public health experts might conclude that, no matter what smokers may think, smoking makes them worse off. They could issue this opinion and leave it at that, but some would see it as a basis for laws restricting the freedom to smoke. (Taxes on cigarettes, which exist nearly everywhere, do this, for instance.) Is this a bad thing? Without passing judgment, it should be clear that, if nothing else, the lost freedom of smokers ought to be a consideration—it is not without some value. For many economists and others who subscribe to the tenets of political liberalism (as understood in the context of this book), utility theory ("the smoker always makes the choice that maximizes his utility") is a bulwark against those who would give individual freedom too little weight.

One final point: utility theory performs the magic of making possible a reconciliation between liberalism and utilitarianism. Liberalism says that people should be free to make their own choices over how to conduct their lives, including what to buy in the market. Utilitarianism says that the goal of policy should be to maximize the total well-being of the individuals who make up society. They can coexist, even potentially, only if individual choice always serves to maximize individual well-being. If this were not the case, we would have to choose between choices that are free and choices that make people better off. Economists want to preserve both of these, and the simplest way to do it is to simply assume that they are compatible. Even so, however, we will see that the conditions under which free individual choice maximizes well-being are quite limited. (We should be prepared for this result after our repeated encounters with the Prisoner's Dilemma.) Thus there is something important to be learned from standard utility theory: we can make the most favorable possible assumptions about the relationship between free markets and human happiness, and even then we may find that the two diverge. That is why the subject is interesting and important.

11.2 Utility and Individual Choice

So now let us suppose that an individual whose utility broadly conforms to the description we've just considered is buying shoes. If he has no shoes at all, he probably has a strong need for a pair; that is, this first pair of shoes will give him a lot of utility. Perhaps he think he needs to stock up, however, and buy different shoes for different occasions. In what follows, to make things as simple as possible, we will assume that all shoes, whatever their make or purpose, cost exactly the same. If the first pair is for work, maybe he needs another pair for dancing. This second pair also provides plenty of utility, although not as quite as much as the first. (If it had provided more, it would have been the first pair he bought.) Still, there are other reasons to buy shoes: for walking in town, for walking in the mountains, for wearing to formal occasions and so on. Our shopper goes from one part of the shoe store to another, buying pair after pair. We can assume that each successive pair gives him a bit less utility. Finally he gets to the point at which he would not accept another pair of shoes even if it were given to him.

The situation is illustrated in Fig. 11.1, where the utility received from each pair of shoes is measured on the vertical axis and the number of pairs is measured on the horizontal axis.

Recall from Chap. 4 the concept of "marginal"; it refers to the additional amount of some quality. There we introduced marginal cost and marginal benefit, and here we will use the term **marginal utility**. Marginal utility is the additional utility someone gets from acquiring or consuming one more unit of a particular good.

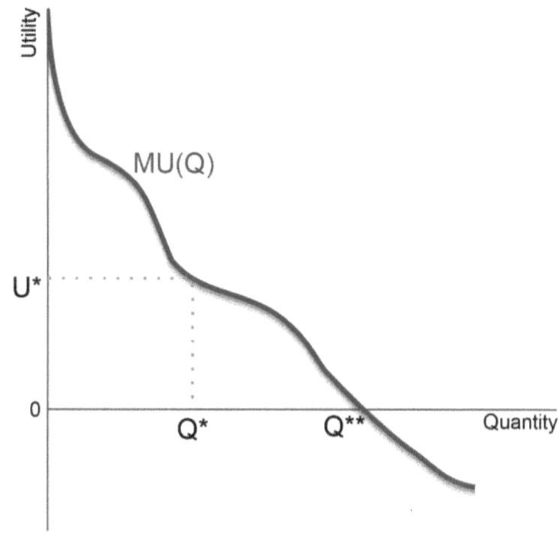

Fig. 11.1 Diminishing marginal utility from buying shoes. The U axis measures the marginal utility an individual receives from buying a pair of shoes; it is negative below 0. The Q axis measures the number of shoes purchased. Marginal utility declines until it reaches 0 at Q** pairs. If U* is the utility corresponding to the price of shoes (assumed constant), Q* is the number that will be bought

In this example it is the extra utility that comes from buying an additional pair of shoes. I have drawn the marginal utility curve MU(Q), which represents marginal utility as a function of the number of shoes being purchased, as downward-sloping. What this says is that, the more shoes a person buys, the less additional utility he will get from each additional pair. Why assume this? Economists suspect that this pattern holds for the vast majority of goods and services people acquire and call it the "law" of diminishing marginal utility.

(When Ferdinand Marcos, president of the Philippines, was forced to leave office after popular demonstrations in 1986, it was discovered that his wife Imelda had amassed a collection of 3,000 shoes. What surprised the public was not her wealth, which was well-known, but the implication that the law of diminishing marginal utility did not seem to apply to her, at least in the realm of footwear.)

To read Fig. 11.1, begin at the left of the diagram, at the very first pair of shoes bought. Here the MU curve is at its highest, indicating that this first pair is strongly desired. As we move to the right along the Q axis, we are observing the second pair purchased, then the third and so on. The downward slope of MU indicates that the marginal utility of each subsequent pair is declining. At Q** (greater than 3,000 for Imelda) the curve enters negative utility territory, signifying that, even if money were no object, the individual would stop acquiring shoes; they are more trouble than they are worth.

Of course, money *is* an object. We will continue to suppose that all the shoes sell for the same price, and that there is a utility corresponding to that price that we can designate as U*. For example, if a pair costs $40 U* represents the utility of having an extra $40 in your pocket. As long as the utility acquired from an additional pair of shoes exceeds U*, it makes sense to buy it. In our diagram this is true for several pairs. If the utility of the money is greater than that of the shoes, however, no further purchases will be made. Thus the utility-maximizing shopper will stop at Q* pairs. This last pair just barely justifies itself, and any more would not be worth the price.

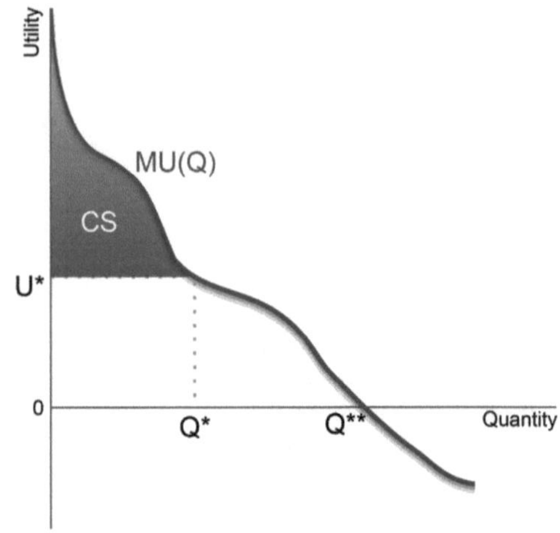

Fig. 11.2 Consumer surplus, measured in utility, gained from buying shoes. This diagram is identical to Fig. 11.1, but with the addition of consumer surplus, the difference between the utility gained from a pair of shoes and given up due to the money paid for it, summed over all the pairs purchased

We can imagine what the impact would be of a change in prices. If the price of shoes goes up, for instance, so will U*: more money translates into more utility. The horizontal line at U* will intersect the MU curve at a lower number of shoes; Q* will go down. This is exactly what we would expect, of course, and it shows that the utility story we are telling is consistent, at least in this respect, with common sense.

What is happening to the well-being of the person buying all these shoes? If the utility equivalent of the price is U* and the quantity he is purchasing is Q*, the last pair leaves him no better or worse off, but every other pair gives him a net addition to his "store of utility". If Q* is five pairs, for example, then the marginal utility of each of the first four pairs exceeds the utility given up to buy them, U*. Figure 11.2 illustrates this. It is identical to Fig. 11.1, with the addition of a shaded area representing the net increase in our hero's welfare—the sum of the net utility gains resulting from all pairs up to Q*. This is referred to as the consumer surplus, here measured in units of utility. What determines its size are three factors, the slope of the MU curve, the level of Q* and the level of U*. A steeper slope, more Q* and less U* all contribute to greater consumer surplus.

If we think back to Chap. 4 and the claim that the sole purpose of having an economy is to increase consumer welfare, consumer surplus is the key to it all. It is not the utility given up by spending money that measures economic success, nor the total utility gained from the goods purchased, but the second minus the first, at least for this one person and this one commodity. More consumer surplus signifies greater economic gain.

This is all well and good but, unfortunately, utility, as we have seen, is invisible and unmeasurable (if indeed it is a meaningful concept at all). What can be observed is not utility but money. So let us look at the same situation in money terms, as in Fig. 11.3. It is identical to Fig. 11.2, except that, instead of utility being measured on the vertical axis, it is money. Instead of a marginal utility curve, we picture a demand curve whose height at any particular Q is the consumer's **willingness to pay**. We can directly observe the price actually paid, P*, and we

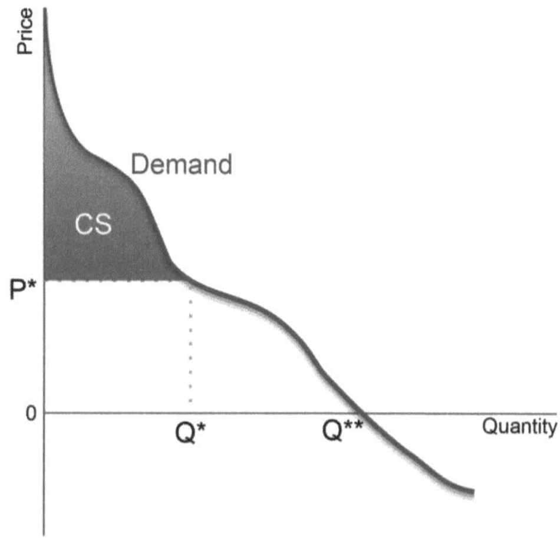

Fig. 11.3 An individual demand curve and consumer surplus for buying shoes. This diagram is identical to Fig. 11.2, but expressed in terms of money rather than utility. D is the demand curve for an individual, P* is the price charged, and Q* is the amount purchased at that price. Consumer surplus is represented by difference between willingness to pay (the height of the demand curve) and the price, summed over all the goods purchased

can, in principle, ask the consumer how much he would be willing to pay for every pair of shoes, from the first one he buys to those he would not buy at the current price. (Some of the readers of this book may have been asked exactly this sort of question by market researchers at shopping centers or other public places.)

Figure 11.3 is real in a sense that Fig. 11.2 is not. Prices are real, and so is willingness to pay. Utility is imaginary, an idea conceived by economists and philosophers but not directly measurable in the way that prices are. Nevertheless, from the standpoint of normative economics (how to make people better off), it is utility—Fig. 11.2—that matters, not money. The question naturally arises, what exactly do we need to infer Figs. 11.2 from 11.3? The answer, aside from the whole apparatus of utility itself (which we discussed at the beginning of this chapter), is what we might call the "exchange rate" between money and utility. That is, for any given amount of money in Fig. 11.3, what is the corresponding amount of utility in Fig. 11.2? The exchange rate analogy is helpful; you could think of these two diagrams as representing the same thing but in different currencies, like euros and yen. So many euros are worth so many yen, and similarly for money (in any currency) and utility. The name given to this exchange rate by economists is the **marginal utility of money**. Like a currency converter, it tells you how many units of utility an individual gets per additional unit of money and vice versa. If we can believe that something like this exists in the mind of our hypothetical shoe-buyer, we can go back and forth between diagrams 2 and 3 without great difficulty.

11.3 Market Demand, Consumer Surplus and Utility

The next step is to bring all the consumers together and examine the demand for shoes throughout a given market. (This market might be local, national or global depending on the purposes behind our analysis.) To see the relationship between

Table 11.1 Number of shoes purchased by three consumers at various prices

Price per pair	Huey	Dewey	Louie	Total
$20	8	5	3	16
$30	8	4	1	13
$40	8	4	0	12
$50	6	2	0	8
$60	5	1	0	6

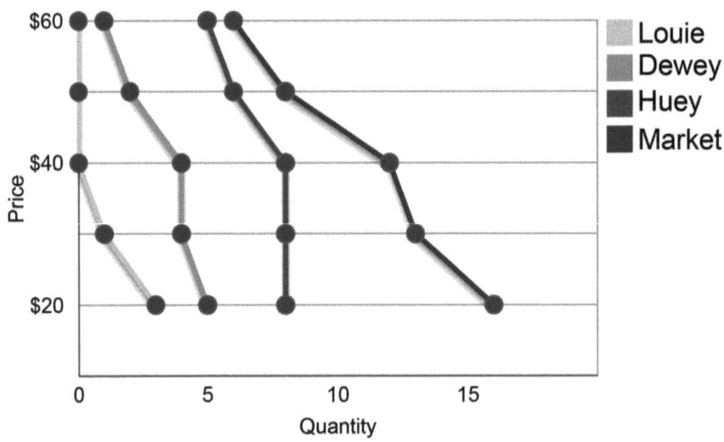

Fig. 11.4 Individual and market demand for shoes. Individual demand curves are given for three consumers and for the market consisting of all three. The market demand curve is the horizontal sum of the three individual demand curves

individual and market demand, consider the hypothetical **demand schedules** of three consumers, Huey, Dewey and Louie.

Table 11.1 tells how many pairs of shoes each is willing to buy as the price rises from a low of $20 to a high of $60 per pair. These data are plotted in Fig. 11.4.

This diagram demonstrates the relationship between the individual demand curves and the market demand, when the market consists of just these three. At $60, for instance, Huey buys 5 pairs, Dewey 1 and Louie none, so the total is 6. Tracing this for each of the possible prices constructs the market demand curve as the horizontal sum of the individual curves. As long as no individual will buy *more* at a higher price (as long as individual demand curves are either vertical or downward-sloping), the market demand curve will never be upward-sloping. The negative relationship between the market price and the amount consumers want to buy is called the **law of demand**. Like all laws it is sometimes broken, but it holds in the vast majority of cases.

The second implication is that each point on the market demand curve represents someone's willingness to pay for that item. When the price falls from $40 to $30, for instance, the market demand goes up by one. That "one" is Louie, who buys his first pair of shoes at that point. He is willing to pay $30 but not $40, so his willingness to pay is represented by the market price. (Because of the large price intervals, he may be willing to pay more, but let us assume this represents the most he would pay. If space were not a constraint in this book, we could watch the price fall penny by penny.) We can call Louie the **marginal consumer**, the individual whose preferences are represented by the point on the demand curve corresponding to $30. Thus, every point on the demand curve "belongs" to a marginal consumer somewhere and represents his or her willingness to pay.

A third implication is that we can sum the consumer surpluses of the individual consumers in order to calculate consumer surplus for the market as a whole. Suppose the actual price charged turns out to be $40 per pair. Total demand will be 12 pairs, of which Huey will buy 8 and Dewey 4. (Louie has been completely priced out.) Of the 8 pairs purchased by Huey, he would have bought 5 at $60 and a sixth if the price were to fall to $50. The final two he buys only when the price falls further to $40. This means that five pairs give him a consumer surplus of at least $20 each and one pair at least $10. How large the surplus is we cannot say, since we don't have information on intermediate price levels, only on ten-dollar increments. For instance, perhaps one of the final two would have been purchased at $45 dollars rather than $40; this mean it would add another $5 to his consumer surplus. We do know the minimum, however: it is $110. For Dewey this same amount comes to at least $30. Now turn to the market demand, which is 12 pairs when the price is $40. Of these, six are worth at least $20 more than that to their buyers, because they would be bought at $60, and another two are worth $10 more. Thus the market consumer surplus is at least $140, which is the sum of the two individual surpluses.

From this simple exercise we can see how individual demands sum up to the market demand, but what about utility? We were able to go from Figs. 11.3 to 11.2 with a few handy assumptions; is there any way to translate Fig. 11.4 from money into utility units?

Recall that the key to translating money into utility at the individual level is the marginal utility of money. The problem at the social (market) level is that each person is likely to have a different exchange rate. There are two general reasons for this. First, some people are more materialistic than others. Henry David Thoreau and Mohandas K. Gandhi were both famous for placing other values above material ones; they could be said to have had low marginal utilities of money. Others have an insatiable craving for things that money can buy; their marginal utilities will be higher. The second reason is that money is likely to obey the law of diminishing marginal utility in the same way most other goods do. The more money you have, the less additional utility you get from an additional dollar. Equal dollar amounts have very different utility significance for rich and poor (See Box).

Box 11.1: Traffic Fines in Finland

In most countries fines for violating the law are set in monetary terms. A parking ticket is a certain sum of money no matter who has to pay it. This is fair in some respects, but it puts a greater burden on low-income groups.

(continued)

Box 11.1 (continued)
Wealthy people can ignore fines that would create a small crisis for someone living on a tight budget. Finland is different, however. Finland sets fines as a percentage of the violator's income in order to equalize the utility cost paid by offenders. Other European countries do this too, although Finland is unique in having no ceiling on the amount that can be assessed.

On a June day in 2000, police in Helsinki pulled over Anssi Vanjoki for doing 45 miles per hour on his motorcycle in a 30 mile-an-hour zone. Because Vanjoki was a senior vice president for the cell phone company Nokia and had earned over $5 million the previous year, his ticket came to $103,000. Vanjoki appealed, arguing that his income had suffered a nosedive in 2000 and that police should have taken it into account. He won, and the fine was reduce to "only" $5,245. Other wealthy Finns have been fined in the tens of thousands of dollars for comparable offenses.

The Vanjoki case set off a debate in parliament. Some legislators argued for scrapping the system and setting fixed monetary amounts for small offenses, but not all. Parliamentarian Annika Lapintie was quoted as saying, "The law is a deterrent. It would be totally unjust if the poor and wealthy pay the same because the wealthy wouldn't feel it." In between were lawmakers searching for a compromise, keeping the percentage of income formula, but putting a cap on it to avoid potentially embarrassing outcomes.

What this means is that, in general, it is not possible to infer utility amounts from dollar amounts at the market level. For instance, suppose that consumer surplus in one market is $10,000 and in another it is $15,000. We can't conclude that the surplus in utility terms is greater in the second than the first, because it is possible that the average marginal utility of money in the second market is substantially less.

Naturally, economists find this state of affairs frustrating. They want to be able to make judgments about which policies will make people better off, but they are lacking a crucial piece of information they would need to convert monetary measurements into assessments of human welfare, since marginal utilities of money are unobservable and nearly impossible to estimate. In the end, they have these options:

- They can assume that the average marginal utility of money in a group is a function of its average income (which can be measured). One way to do this would be to express monetary values as a percentage of income rather than an absolute amount; this is a strategy similar to that used in Finland in Box 11.1. This approach assumes that differences in income are primarily responsible for different utility values of money, or at least that the differences due to personal values will mostly cancel out at the group level.
- They can assume that all marginal utilities of money are the same. If the groups are relatively similar in composition this may not be too much of a stretch. In fact, often the comparison is between different consumer surpluses for the same

market, when different policies are being considered. The specific people whose surpluses are being summed may change somewhat from one policy to another, but often not greatly. Another argument is that, if we have to make many decisions that will affect consumer surplus in a wide variety of markets, differences in the marginal utility of money will largely cancel out. For instance, it is not likely that the groups that benefit from a particular bridge being built, or from lower postal rates for certain types of magazines, or from publicly financed research into specific diseases will all be disproportionately rich or poor, even though any one such group might be. Thus, over the course of a large number of economic policy decisions, the goal of maximizing consumer surplus may yield results that are in the interest of all social groups. On the other hand, it might also be the case that, for many such decisions, the richest and poorest citizens may indeed find themselves lined up largely on opposite sides.

- They can refrain from making utility comparisons at all. This approach is theoretically unimpeachable; if you would need to know everyone's marginal utility of money in order to say which consumer surplus corresponds to the most utility, and if there is no way to get this information, why not just give up? The problem (or challenge) with this choice is that it greatly limits the number of decisions that can be justified with economic analysis. (We will look at the consequences of this approach more closely in Chap. 21.) Yet it is not always possible to pick and choose between decisions; often they simply have to be made on *some* basis. If not judgments of utility, what? We will return to this question later in the chapter.

We are now in a position to sum up the significance of the utility-based theory of demand for the Market Welfare Model. Recall that the model puts forward three premises and draws one conclusion:

Market Welfare Model

Conditions

1. The demand curve represents the marginal benefit to society from the consumption of some good.
2. The supply curve represents the marginal cost to society from the production of this good.
3. The supply and demand curves have a single, stable equilibrium.

Conclusion

The market equilibrium maximizes the net benefits to society of the production and consumption of this good.

The utility theory of consumption puts the first premise under a microscope. It identifies the underlying conditions which, if all met, would enable the premise to be accepted. For convenience, they are listed in Table 11.2.

If all of these things are true, logically the first premise of the Market Welfare Model follows as well. In our brief survey of utility theory, we assumed the first item in this table for the sake of discussion. The second and third were results of the analysis and, at least for now, appear plausible. The fourth point is dubious but not impossible (and there is always the hypothetical transfer of money to set things

Table 11.2 Sufficient conditions for the demand curve to represent the marginal benefits to society

1. Benefit to society can be represented as the sum of individual utilities
2. Each point on the market demand curve represents the willingness to pay of the consumer who is just induced to buy this one item
3. That willingness to pay reflects the amount of utility of this marginal consumer
4. The ratio of marginal utility to willingness to pay, i.e. the marginal utility of money, is equal across consumers
5. There are no other impacts of the consumption of this good other than what is represented by consumer willingness to pay

straight). The final point will be discussed in Chap. 15; for now, let's also assume that it holds. The result is that much depends on the fourth point.

One interpretation of this discussion is that the Market Welfare Model is more plausible in societies with more equal income distributions, or with more active income redistribution programs. Free market allocation of a scarce but crucial good, like potable drinking water in some countries, has greater justification when there aren't large differences in income and wealth. To say that you would distribute water according to market principles is to say that those who are willing to pay the market price would get water and those who aren't won't. If these differences in willingness to pay reflect true differences in the need people have for water, there may not be a problem. If they reflect mainly differences in income, a too-rigid adherence to market principles may result in disease and death as the poor are cut off from their water supply. The preceding analysis of marginal utility of money is not academic hair-splitting; it is the basis for many present-day controversies in economic policy.

A second way to make this point is to recall the geometric argument for the Market Welfare Model, Fig. 6.6 from Chap. 6. This is reproduced below with one additional element as Fig. 11.5 on the following page.

Here we add consumer surplus to the picture. It comprises one portion of net benefits, the part acquired by consumers when the value of what they buy, measured by their willingness to pay, exceeds the price they have to pay for it. The marginal consumer at Q* gets no surplus, but all those to the left of her, who would be willing to buy at prices higher than P*, do receive a surplus. The area marked CS is the sum of all these individual surpluses. From this diagram it is clear that consumer surplus represents the consumer side of net benefits (as the area below P* represents the producer side). Unfortunately, we also recall that there is no necessary relationship between the size of consumer surplus in monetary and utility terms. Thus, insofar as the amount of net benefit depends on the amount of consumer surplus, the Market Welfare Model, if it is to be a model of welfare and not just money, requires some solution to the problem posed by different marginal utilities of money. Since we live in an imperfect world, we might say that the problem is not too great and get on with other tasks, but how great is it? The take-home message from this analysis is that the answer depends on the circumstances, so it pays to be informed.

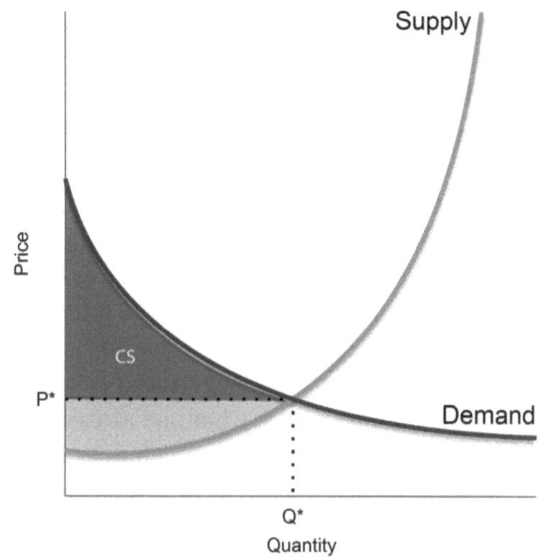

Fig. 11.5 Maximum net benefit and consumer surplus in the Market Welfare Model. The total *shaded area* represents total net benefit according to the Market Welfare Model, assuming the necessary conditions are met. The more heavily shaded area below the demand curve but above the price is that portion of the net benefit captured by consumers, the consumer surplus

11.4 Do Consumers Maximize Utility?

Let's continue to adopt the utility model, at least provisionally, but put aside the assumption that people are always rational—that they choose the option that maximizes their expected utility. If that is the case, there may be a gap between willingness to pay and utility due to systematic bias. In other words, people may regularly overestimate or underestimate how much utility they will get as a result of a purchase. Regular errors are those which are describable and predictable; is this true of consumer choice?

A very large body of research says it is. One of the main currents in behavioral economics is the study of consumer choice; it joins a more venerable effort by marketing specialists to figure out what makes consumers tick. Some of the biases that have been discovered are these:

- Faulty self-perception. People systemically overrate themselves in most respects: they think they are better drivers than they are, they plan to exercise more regularly than they actually will, and they buy ingredients for elaborate meals they will never make. While this affects many aspects of life, it has a definite bearing on consumption choices. They buy products for the person they think they are, not the one they actually are.
- Mental accounting. People divide choices into different categories and then make decisions separately for each category. If a restaurant meal is eaten on vacation, it may be assigned to the "vacation" category, and spending decisions will be made that would never occur at a similar restaurant under ordinary circumstances. Here's another example. Suppose you get money from a relative for your birthday; you might save part or all of it. On the other hand, what if you get a camera as a gift, but you already own one? You take it to a store and get money back for it; will you spend this money the same way you would spend the

money you are given directly? Laboratory evidence suggests you wouldn't: having already had a consumption good in the form of a camera, you place the money in a (mental) "consumption" account and spend it. The gift money, which goes into a different mental account, is more likely to be saved. Accounting heuristics like this lead to inconsistent behavior by consumers.

- Status quo bias. People are more reluctant to part with something they have than they are eager to acquire the same thing if they don't have it. In other words, exactly the same item will have two different prices for the same person, the price they would sell it at and the price they would pay. If the good in question is a small part of the person's overall wealth (and therefore has little effect on the marginal utility of money), there is no evident reason for this discrepancy other than a preference for what one already has.
- Misperception of risk. Many choices in life involve risks. We can buy a new car at a higher cost but a lower risk of repairs over the first few years or a cheaper used car that might turn out to be a money sink. The decision to borrow money, or to lend it, is risky, and so is choosing a specialized major in college that may not lead to a job. If people are to make such choices effectively, and not squander utility in a predictable way, they need to estimate risks accurately. Much research has shown, however, that this is frequently not the case. People place too much importance on very small risks of catastrophe and not enough on much more likely risks of moderate loss. They are unduly swayed by vivid examples rather than evidence of riskiness drawn from extensive experience. Partly because they overestimate their own abilities, they also give insufficient weight to risks that they think they may be able to influence, compared to those over which they have no control at all. These and other biases interfere with choices that will actually make people better off rather than play to their insecurities or, paradoxically, their sense of invulnerability.
- Poor forecasting of feelings. When considering a purchase, a consumer is often confronted by a strong anticipation of pleasure. If the item is something she wants, she will feel a surge of excitement at the thought of buying it. Research, however, suggests she is likely to attribute too much importance to these passing emotions. The long-term effects of positive economic events (like a purchase or an increase in income) on well-being are usually less than we anticipate, while this is less likely to be the case for noneconomic events (like a change in health or marriage). Especially for the consumption decisions economists are most interested in, then, people have a tendency to confuse the immediate emotional impact with the long-term effect on well-being, if any, that will remain after the initial jolt has worn off. The problem is made worse by the tendency, substantiated by psychological research, that the emotional state of the consumer at the moment a decision is being made has a significant impact on choice. (Don't go shopping for food when you're hungry.) If people were truly rational they would look past their transitory mood and consider their feelings down the road.

These and other traits represent systematic, rather than random, deviations from the postulates of rationality that economists have historically applied to consumers and other decision-makers. Taken together, they indicate that the choices people make give them less utility than they might otherwise be able to get. Thus, if utility remains the guiding framework, we must make a choice between deferring to consumer behavior in the marketplace or devising policies to offset the loss of utility from faulty decision-making. But utility is not the only framework.

11.5 The Pursuit of Happiness

If it is really well-being we are interested in, why don't we just ask people how well off they are? This may seem too direct an approach to work; perhaps people wouldn't know, or maybe their answers would mean different things to different respondents. As it happens, however, researchers have been using survey methods to find out how happy or satisfied individuals say they are, and their results have been repeatedly validated. Thus, those who say they are happy with their lives are more likely to be described by others who know them as happy; they are more likely to smile and initiate social contact; they tend to live longer; they put in more effort and take fewer absences at work. Recently neurophysiologists have begun to compare the brain activity of happy and unhappy people, and they are discovering the patterns their training has led them to expect: neurotransmitters in the appropriate regions of the brain are fired in ways that correspond to subjective reports of happiness or well-being. All evidence suggests that we should believe the answers people give to questions about their emotional state.

The direct measurement of happiness promises to rectify two problems with the utility theory of consumption we have just reviewed. First, utility theory rests on a set of assumptions that may simply be wrong, particularly in believing that consumers are rational, reliable utility maximizers. Second, utility theory, based as it is on inferences from consumption behavior in the marketplace, applies only to goods that are traded in markets. Shoes can be assessed for the utility they offer but not the pleasure of seeing a rare bird in your backyard. Economists have proved clever at using market transactions to infer nonmarket prices, as we will see in Chap. 15, but there are limits to such ingenuity. Using survey methods to assess happiness has the potential to measure *any* factor that the researcher wants to find out about.

This second point is particularly important, since one of the large questions before industrialized societies is where to draw the line between economic and noneconomic activities. Should we spend less time working, even if this means producing and consuming fewer goods? Should we sacrifice economic growth to other considerations, like a greater emphasis on family life or a healthier environment? Utility theory can tell us something (maybe) about how economic goods should be traded off against one another, but not about the tradeoff between things we acquire through the economy and the aspects of life that are crowded out by working and spending.

How do economists and others do happiness research? An example is presented in Box 11.2, which explains how two economists put a value on being sexually active.

Box 11.2: Money Can't Buy Me Love

What is the contribution of sex to happiness compared to that of money? While it surely varies from one individual to another, an average relationship was worked out by two economists, David Blanchflower and Andrew Oswald, drawing on the data in a survey of 16,000 US adults.

To do this, they constructed a formula for predicting the answer people would give to a question about their overall well-being. If H is the number people report on a happiness scale, where a higher value of H signifies greater happiness, the formula would look like this:

$$a + b_1{}^{*}\text{age} + b_2{}^{*}\text{gender} + \ldots + b_{n-1}{}^{*}\text{income} + b_n{}^{*}\text{frequency of sex} + e = H \quad (11.1)$$

Here a is referred to as a **constant** (I will explain it shortly), and the various b's are **coefficients**. The formula says that an individual's happiness score is approximately equal to a fixed number (the same for everyone) plus their age multiplied by its weight in the formula (the coefficient b_1) plus a number representing gender (say, 1 if male, 0 if female) times its weight b_2 + many more factors times their weights (signified by the "...") plus income multiplied by its weight b_{n-1} plus the frequency of sex times its weight b_n. If we plug in the values for any given individual for all n factors and apply the right values for a and all n weights (coefficients), the formula will tell us what his or her happiness score is likely to be. The formula won't be perfect, however. There will be error in its prediction, which is what e signifies. Finally, we can understand the meaning of the constant a by supposing that the value of every factor included in the formula is zero; then H would approximately equal a.

So where do all these numbers come from? The values for all the individual characteristics and the happiness score come from the survey. The values for a and the various b's come from statistical techniques designed to select them in such a way that this formula, applied to everyone in the survey, produces as little error as possible.

The weights are the whole point of the exercise. The sign of a given weight tells us whether the variable it is attached to makes a positive or negative contribution to H. For instance, suppose in the gender variable that 1 = male and 0 = female. If b_2, the coefficient (weight) attached to gender is negative, it indicates that, considered independently of all the other factors being studied, being male lowers the predicted value on a respondent's H score. In addition to the direction—positive or negative—of the weight, its size and significance matter too. The size tells us how big the effect is: if $b_2 = -0.1$, it says that being male, considered separately from everything else, lowers a person's predicted happiness score by a tenth of a point relative to females.

(continued)

Box 11.2 (continued)
Finally, there are statistical measurements that suggest how likely it is that the coefficient is truly different from zero and not just a random fluke. If that likelihood is high enough (if such a fluke would happen only about once out of twenty studies with similar data) the coefficient is called **statistically significant**.

This has been a technical detour, but a useful one, since a large percentage of economic research follows an approach along these lines. The real reason you are still reading this, however, is because the topic is sex, and you want to hear what they found. Now you will find out:

As you would expect, the coefficients for income and sex were both positive and significant. Once Blanchflower and Oswald had determined their size, they could ask, how much of a reduction in yearly income would it take in this equation to exactly offset a particular increase in the frequency of sex—say from an average of once a month to once a week? The answer was approximately $50,000: on average, people will report themselves as equally happy if they have either the extra sex or the extra money.

They also found other results of interest. Marriage, which increases the average frequency of sex (they asked) is worth $100,000, while divorce deducts $60,000. (Better to have loved and lost…) Holding the frequency of sex constant, having fewer sexual partners produces more happiness, and being gay (again holding all else equal) has no impact one way or the other. The researchers caution us, however, that they were unable to determine that it is sex that makes for happiness, rather than a pattern in which people who are already happy find sexual partners more easily.

For the full story, read "Money, Sex, and Happiness: An Empirical Study" by David G. Blanchflower and Andrew J. Oswald, National Bureau of Economic Research Working Paper No. W10499 (May, 2004).

Now on to an important consumption-related issue to test whether happiness has something to offer that utility doesn't. One of the pressing economic questions facing the United States is whether the spectacular increase in suburban and exurban development in recent years is desirable or not. (An exurb is an area beyond the suburban fringe populated primarily by residents who commute to the suburbs or cities.) More than half of all Americans now live in suburbs, displacing large tracts of what was once farmland. Highways leading into and out of the major cities are choked with traffic during rush hour, and the daily commute can take as much as two hours in each direction. Is this a problem?

If consumers are rational utility-maximizers, perhaps not. The main cost faced by someone who chooses to live far from where she works is the time and expense of commuting; the benefits are having a pleasant neighborhood with good schools, a desirable house and lot, etc. When choosing where to live and where to work, our hypothetically rational individual will factor in all these considerations. She would not choose to live in a distant suburb, for instance, unless she calculated that the extra commuting burden would be at least made up by all the other advantages. Thus, if utility theory is our guide there is no case for public intervention—at least, not to rescue her from her rush hour misery. (There may be environmental or other considerations, of course.)

The utility maximization argument is based on the *assumption* that people maximize utility. Since there is no way to measure it directly, there is no way to test this assumption. On the other hand, happiness, at least as reported in surveys, is measurable. A recent study found that, even after taking into account all other factors, such as those the rational person would consider, longer daily commutes are associated with lower happiness scores. It appears as though, when choosing jobs, houses and apartments, people systematically underestimate how miserable their commutes will make them.

Does this mean that a government agency should take this decision out of the hands of private citizens? Not necessarily, but there are other possibilities. The happiness finding, if it holds up in other studies, might provide a justification for taxes, such as on gasoline, that favor people who live closer to their jobs. This would give people an extra incentive to make the choices that will, on average, increase their happiness anyway. At the very least, happiness research in this case neutralizes the argument that public policies on land use should not be adopted because they interfere with the choices people have made in a rational, fully informed way.

We will encounter happiness research again in the volume on macroeconomics, when we ask whether per capita Gross Domestic Product can serve as an indicator of general well-being. For now, its main purpose is to demonstrate that practical alternatives to utility theory exist and are being employed by economists. The field is still new, however, so it will probably not send quite the same set of messages several years from now when more results are in.

11.6 Capabilities

Happiness and utility are both essentially subjective concepts; they ask and try to find out about the feelings people have in their mind. It is also possible, however, to approach well-being from the more objective standpoint of evaluating the goods, resources and opportunities people actually have, whether or not they say they value or are even aware of them. The problem is to define what these valuable things might be in a way that is specific enough to be measurable, but also general enough to apply across individual and cultural differences.

Nobel laureate Amartya Sen has attempted to do this in his theory of **capabilities**, which he developed in conjunction with the philosopher Martha Nussbaum. Their idea can be traced back to Aristotle, who argued that, through observation of a number of communities, some of them successful and some not, it would be possible to determine objectively what conditions would have to be met for human beings to "flourish". When Aristotle wrote this he had in mind a smattering of small Greek city-states; today we have the experience of the entire world to draw on. Is it possible to draw up a list that will work in Los Angeles, Hong Kong and Johannesburg?

The trick, according to Sen, is to put aside specific goods and concentrate on fundamental human functionings. To have the ability to carry out those functions is to have, in Sen's terms, the capabilities they require. An obvious choice would be nutrition: without specifying exactly what people should eat, it is clear that they need a sufficient nutritional intake to function without hunger or health impediments. Other basic needs enter in a similar way. But Sen goes further and argues that essential capabilities also include the social and cultural aspects of life. He points, for instance, to Adam Smith's observation that all people need the wherewithal to "appear in public without shame". This may mean one type of clothing in Bengal and another in Italy, but the same fundamental capability is at stake. Comparable arguments can be made about types of education, access to transportation and other resources: what is being measured, in principle, is not any particular set of goods and services but the capabilities of individuals to participate in various ways in the life of their communities. In fact, some of the capabilities on Sen's list are not economic in the conventional sense, but political and cultural, such as freedom of expression and the democratic accountability of government.

The capabilities approach was originally developed under the auspices of the World Institute for Development and Economic Research, WIDER, an affiliate of the United Nations, and during the past two decades an effort has been made by several international agencies to translate the theory into quantitative indices. Its greatest impact has been at the level of society-wide evaluation: what overall effect does a national policy strategy have on the capabilities of its citizens? How can we rank different countries according to their success in meeting economic and social goals? At this point it is not refined enough to apply to the narrower questions that are asked of particular industries and products. It does serve to remind us, however, that there is a case to be made for evaluations of well-being that take into account how people actually live, and not just their self-perceptions. Indirectly, it endorses the position of specialists in fields outside of economics, such as public health and education; the goals they pursue can be justified normatively on their own terms, now understood as capabilities, without being translated into the synthetic amalgams of utility and happiness.

The Main Points

1. The main purpose of demand theory is to support normative economic analysis; it proposes a relationship between market demand and the well-being of people who purchase goods and services. It has little to offer for positive analysis since it takes preferences as given: it doesn't examine why people have the preferences they have, or what factors might cause them to change their preferences.
2. Utility is proposed as the "substance" of well-being. It is something of a black box, being whatever it is that people hope to acquire by purchasing items for sale. It does **not** signify usefulness in particular, however.

3. The "law of diminishing marginal utility" states that, as one buys more and more units of a particular good, the additional utility acquired from one more unit declines. This is seen as the psychological basis for the "law of demand", which is that a lower price normally results in a higher quantity being demanded in the market.
4. The world of market demand—prices offered and quantities purchased—is visible; the world of utility, to the extent that it exists, is invisible. The "exchange rate" that converts the first into the second is the marginal utility of money. Individuals differ in their marginal utilities of money for two general reasons: the more money one has, the less additional utility one is likely to get from having a little bit more, and people differ in how much they value the things money can buy compared to the things it can't.
5. Consumer surplus is the difference between what individuals would be willing to pay for an item and what they actually have to pay—the market price. It is common to measure this in monetary terms, although, strictly speaking, consumer surplus in utility cannot be inferred from market demand because of differences in the marginal utility of money.
6. The analysis of market demand based on utility theory permits a formal statement of the conditions that must hold if one is to accept the Market Welfare Model interpretation that the demand curve represents the marginal benefits to society: (1) the utility theory of benefit is accepted as correct, (2) the demand curve is derived from willingness to pay, (3) willingness to pay is an accurate measure of marginal utility, (4) the marginal utility of money is equal across consumers, and (5) there are no impacts of consumption other than those measured by willingness to pay.
7. Research in behavioral economics casts doubt on the utility theory developed in this chapter. Findings include faulty self-perception on the part of consumers, the existence of multiple "mental accounts" that lead to inconsistent behavior, status quo bias, misperception of risk, and poor forecasts of the benefits derived from the goods people purchase.
8. Because of this there has been an upsurge of interest in an alternative measure of well-being, self-reported happiness or satisfaction. Evidence supports the notion that answers given by individuals to questions about well-being in surveys is consistent with objective indicators, like displays of emotion and neurological response. Research finds, however, that people do not maximize self-reported happiness corresponding to the way they are supposed to maximize utility.
9. An alternative approach to well-being is the theory of capabilities, which proposes that there are universal human needs and activities which economies can support to a greater or lesser extent.

▶ Terms to Define

Capabilities
Coefficient
Consumer surplus
Demand schedule
Law of demand
Marginal consumer
Marginal utility
Marginal utility of money
Paternalism
Statistical significance

Questions to Consider

1. Does a consistent liberal (in the sense we are using in this book) have to be opposed to laws banning drugs like marijuana, cocaine and ecstasy? Are the laws we currently have paternalistic? Do you get the same answers to these two questions if they asked about regulations taking ineffective medications off the market?
2. Does the concept of consumer surplus describe the benefits you get from what you buy? Think of a recent purchase: how would you compare the marginal utility of the good you bought with the utility value of the money you paid for it? Are there aspects of this purchase that don't fit comfortably with the consumer surplus model?
3. What do you think about the issue raised in Box 11.1? Should fines be set to equalize the monetary cost or the utility cost? In your answer, do the incentive effects of the fines play a significant role?
4. Discuss with a friend your relative marginal utilities of money. If it is greater for one of you, why?
5. A parcel of land adjoining a river is coveted by two groups. One consists of fishermen; they want the river to remain in a healthy condition so it can support fish, which they can then try to catch. The other is a mining operation that would dump tailings into the river, killing the fish. The market solution is to let them both bid on the land and have it sold to whoever expresses the highest willingness to pay. Can you extend this story in a way that brings differences in the average marginal utility of money between the two groups into the picture? In practice, how significant a factor is this issue likely to be in disputes between preservationists (like the fishermen) and developers (like the mining company)? Why?
6. Scan the list of consumer biases on pp. 229–239. How many apply to you? Have any of them had serious consequences?
7. Revisit the answers you gave to question 1. Do you think happiness research could have a role to play in these issues? In the first, the question is whether drug users are more or less happy because of their drug use; in the second, it's whether

pharmaceuticals that are deemed ineffective in laboratory experiments nevertheless contribute to greater happiness on the part of those who take them.

8. Sen says that, among the capabilities that all should have, an important one is access to education sufficient to permit everyone to participate effectively in political debate. What level of education is that in the US? How close are we to meeting that goal?

Appendix: Indifference Curves

The relationship between the price world and the utility world in this chapter is explained by juxtaposing two diagrams, Figs. 11.2 and 11.3. I appealed to your intuition to establish the logical connection between them. If you are still skeptical and want a more worked-out proof of the relationship, this appendix may provide it. It assumes somewhat more familiarity with analytical geometry than does the main body of the text.

The entire analysis is conducted at the level of a single individual. For simplicity, we will assume that only two goods, bread and cheese, are available for consumption, although nothing we say would have to be altered in a many-product world. Let's also assume that, for each possible combination of particular quantities of bread and cheese, the consumer is able to attach a utility value. Thus, five loaves of bread and two pounds of cheese have one value; three loaves of bread and four pounds of cheese have another, which may be less, more or equal.

Each of these combinations can be depicted as a point in plane defined by two (orthogonal) axes, one for bread, the other for cheese. Figure 11.6 on the following page locates two such points, (five loaves, two pounds) and (three loaves, three pounds).

Each point in Fig. 11.6 exists in two dimensions, bread and cheese. What we are interested in is utility, however, and that constitutes a third dimension. You could say that every point ought to transmit three pieces of information: the amount of bread, the amount of cheese and the amount of utility. From this perspective, utility constitutes a third dimension, rising up out Fig. 11.6; we show this in Fig. 11.7 as an optical illusion:

At point D the consumer has a bit more bread but a lot less cheese than at point E. The difference in utility is represented by showing E at a higher elevation on the vertical utility axis. If every possible combination of bread and cheese were given its corresponding utility value and plotted in three dimensions in Fig. 11.7, the result would look like the **utility surface** loosely pictured by the shaded area above. Any point along this surface would be traceable in three dimensions: bread, cheese and utility.

The utility surface can be compared to any surface in three dimensions. Consider a landscape, for instance. Suppose it encompasses a mountain rising out of a surrounding plain; this too is a surface in three dimensions, west to east, south to

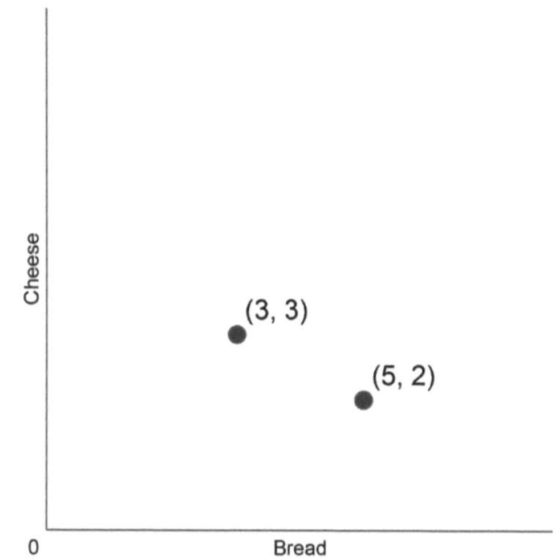

Fig. 11.6 Two combinations of bread and cheese. Loaves of bread are measured along the horizontal axis, pounds of cheese along the vertical axis. Two points are represented, with the quantity of bread given first in parentheses

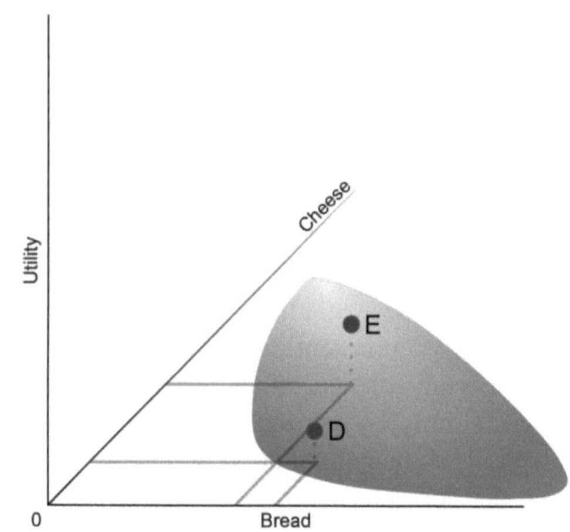

Fig. 11.7 Combinations of bread, cheese and utility. Two points, D and E, represent different combinations of bread and cheese. E is at a higher elevation on the utility axis than D, meaning that it provides more utility

north, and down to up. We could pick any two points and, if we knew their exact location and place on the mountain slope, we could say which one was higher.

Three-dimensional landscapes can be depicted in two dimensions with the aid of **contour lines**, which connect points of equal elevation. This gives us a contour or **topographical** map, familiar to hikers and other outdoors people. In Fig. 11.8 I have reproduced part of the contour map for Mt. Ranier, a large volcanic peak near my home in Washington State. (Yes, it's an active volcano.) The contour lines tell us how we would have to walk if we were following the exact contour of the slope, neither gaining nor losing elevation. By looking at how they are placed, we can determine which way the slope is facing, which way is up and even how steep it is (by the distance between contours). This is very useful for those traveling in this region.

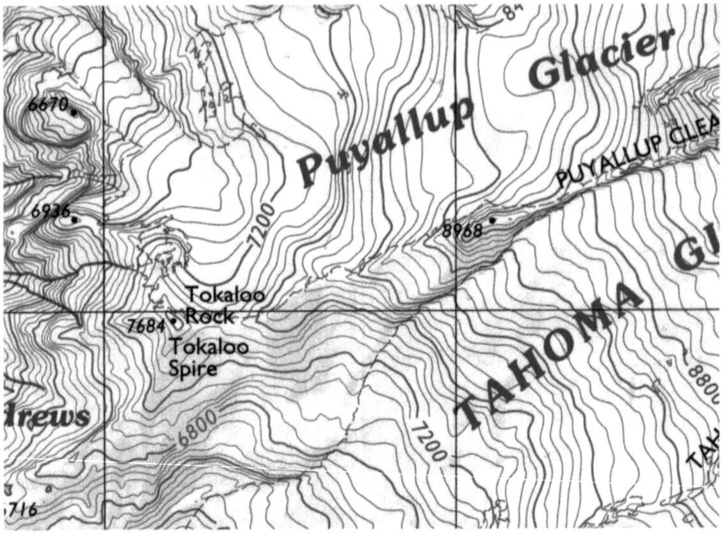

Fig. 11.8 A contour map representing a portion of Mt. Ranier

The consumer's utility surface can also be mapped in two dimensions by using **indifference curves**, lines connecting combinations of bread and cheese with equal levels of utility. The analogy is precise: indifference curves are to three-dimensional utility surfaces as contour lines are to three-dimensional mountain slopes. They are called indifference curves because the consumer is said to be indifferent between alternative combinations of goods along the same curve. Incidentally, representing utility surfaces in this way has an advantage beyond graphic convenience, since individuals could construct their own indifference curves simply by asking themselves, "Do I prefer the combination of goods in this point to the combination in that one, or vice versa, or am I indifferent?" Every time they decided they were indifferent, they would put those two points on the same indifference curve. Eventually, after asking this of every possible pair of points, they would be able to construct a complete **indifference map**, the utility equivalent of the outdoor lover's topographical map. This sounds like a lot of comparison (and it is), but it is less fanciful than supposing that people good assign actual utility numbers to each point. ("I like this combination of bread and cheese; I think I'll give it a 91.") In other words, using the language introduced earlier in this chapter, the indifference map can be constructed ordinally and not just cardinally.

Figure 11.9 shows a portion of such a map, picturing three different indifference curves for a consumer. Which do you suppose represents the lowest utility and which the highest? (You should stop and think about this for a moment.) The only way to know for sure is to introduce another assumption, that the individual always prefers more to less of every good. (The technical name for this is the *nonsatiation principle*.) As a universal statement it is not very appealing, and in fact puts us dangerously close to Imelda Marcos territory, but it is probably true for a majority

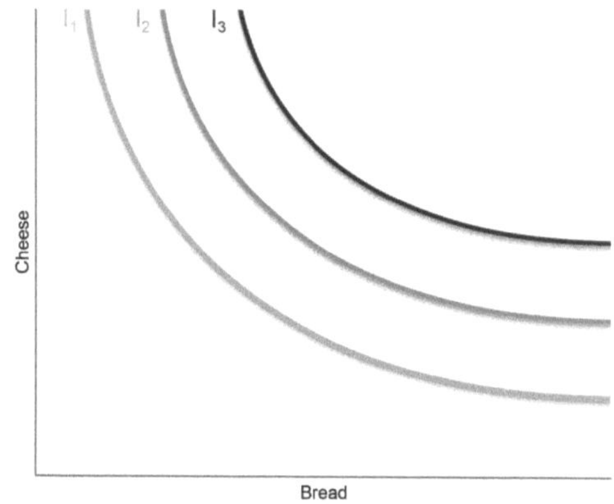

Fig. 11.9 Three indifference curves for an individual consumer acquiring bread and cheese. I_1, I_2 and I_3 are three indifference curves in order of lowest to highest utility. Each represents combinations of bread and cheese giving equal utility to some consumer

of goods the majority of the time (at least for those of us whose limited incomes regularly force us to buy less than we might otherwise). Once we accept this principle, however, we know that the indifference curves to the northeast must be at a higher utility level than those to the southwest. The reason is that, for every point on a lower curve, such as I_1, there is another point on another curve further from the origin, like I_2, that has at least as much of one good and more of the other, or indeed more of both. According to the nonsatiation assumption, the second point must be preferred to the first, and therefore all the points of equal utility to the second are preferred to those equal to the first.

If preferences are consistent, the indifference curves can't cross. If this were to happen, then one point would be on two different indifference curves, meaning that the combination of goods it represents would be equal to two other combinations which were not equal to each other. This would be a logical inconsistency—as it would be if two contour lines crossed on a topographical map.

Note that the indifference curves drawn in Fig. 11.9 are convex to the origin—why? To answer this, we need to understand more precisely what the slope of the curve signifies. The slope of an indifference curve at any point equals the slope of a straight line tangent to the curve at that point. This is depicted in Fig. 11.10 on the next page.

The tangent has the property in the vicinity of D that utility is not changed for small movements to or from D. This is because, as the movement along the line approaches D, it approximates movement on the indifference curve around D. (As you learn in the calculus, this is exactly true as the movement along the tangent from D approaches zero if the curve is smooth and continuous, which we assume it is.) Moreover, movements along the indifference curve do not alter utility, as we know from the definition of indifference. Put these two considerations together, and you can specify the equation for the tangent:

$$\mathrm{MU(B)}^{*}\Delta B + \mathrm{MU(C)}^{*}\Delta C = 0 \tag{11.2}$$

This equation reads "the marginal utility from bread times the change in the bread consumed, plus the marginal utility of cheese times the change in the cheese

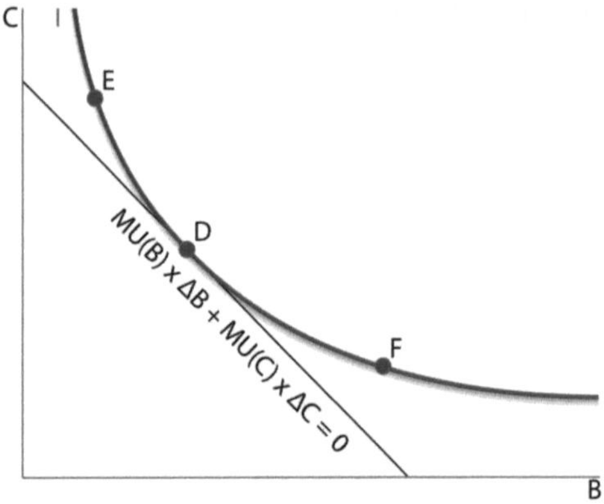

Fig. 11.10 The slope of an indifference curve taken at a single point. The slope of the indifference curve at point D is given by the slope of the line tangent to it, whose equation signifies that utility is unchanged. This slope would be different at points E and F

consumed, equal zero." Movement up and down this line increases the amount of one good at the expense of the other; this leaves utility unchanged only if the additional utility gained by increasing one exactly offsets the additional utility lost by decreasing the other, and marginal utility means simply the additional utility plus or minus with the change in a single unit (loaf of bread, pound of cheese).

The slope of this line is the change in its vertical component divided by the change in its horizontal component, or, in this case, ΔC/ΔB. We can calculate this from Eq. 11.2 with a little algebra:

$$-\mathrm{MU(B)}^{*}\Delta B = \mathrm{MU(C)}^{*}\Delta C \tag{11.3}$$

Divide both sides by MU(C) * ΔB:

$$-\mathrm{MU(B)}/\mathrm{MU(C)} = \Delta C/\Delta B = \text{slope of indifference curve at D} \tag{11.4}$$

Let's explore the meaning of this result. The slope is negative, because it takes more of some good to make up for less of the other if utility is to remain constant. This negative amount is *the inverse ratio of marginal utilities*; that is, if ΔC/ΔB = x, then –MU(C)/MU(B) = 1/x. If, for instance, the marginal utility of bread is twice that of cheese, utility will remain constant if the reduction is bread is half the increase in the amount of cheese. This is not very profound, and it follows directly from Eq. 11.2, but what is interesting is that it enables us to infer the ratio of marginal utilities from the changing slope of the indifference curve, if we know what to look for.

Consider another point, E. As drawn, the slope of the indifference curve is steeper here than at D; it takes a bigger increase in the amount of cheese to make up for a smaller decrease in the amount of bread. From Eq. 11.4 this means that the ratio of the marginal utility of cheese to that of bread has gone down. Conversely, at point F it takes a smaller increase in cheese to make up for the loss of bread, and the marginal utility of cheese must therefore have risen relative to that of bread. Put it all together and what you see is that, as the consumer specializes in cheese relative to bread (in the northwest portion of the diagram), the marginal utility of cheese relative to bread is falling, and similarly if the consumer specializes in bread relative to cheese (in the southeast portion). *The more the consumer specializes in the consumption of a particular good, the less relative marginal utility he or she gets from it.* This is nothing other than the law of diminishing marginal utility, applied to a situation in which two goods are being considered in relation to each other.

We can now answer the question we asked ourselves about a page and a half ago: the reason the indifference curve was drawn convex to the origin was to have this property of diminishing marginal utility. If I had drawn it concave to the origin (imagine the indifference curve in Fig. 11.9 attached to the tangent at D by a ring, and flip it over to the other side of the line), we would have depicted increasing marginal utility—the more I have, the more I want it—instead.

Now we will add one more wrinkle, a fixed amount of money and prices for the two goods. The consumer cannot buy an unlimited amount, but must now figure out how to apportion the money between bread and cheese in order to maximize utility. How much of each item to buy will depend on both factors—how much money is available to spend and how much each costs.

The limitation on how much the consumer can buy is called the **budget constraint**, and it is portrayed in Fig. 11.11 on the following page. If all the money is spent on bread, B_{max} is the amount of bread that can be bought; if all of it is spent on cheese the amount is C_{max}. Intermediate amounts can be purchased by buying more of one and less of the other; these are on the straight line connecting B_{max} and C_{max} because the tradeoff (and therefore the slope) is unchanged due to the prices remaining unchanged. The consumer can buy any combination of bread and cheese, provided it is to the southwest of the line or just on it. Anything to the northeast is unaffordable. The equation for this line simply says that the consumer spends all available money:

$$B^{*}P_B + C^{*}P_C = Y \tag{11.5}$$

where B and C are the amounts of bread and cheese purchased, P_B and P_C are their prices and Y is the amount of money to be spent.

Visualizing the best option for the consumer will be easier if we return to the example of a topographical map. Suppose some of the land in Fig. 11.8 is on private land and some in the Mt. Ranier National Park, with the dividing line as shown in Fig. 11.12; what is the highest point on private land in the region depicted in the map? The answer is, where the boundary line just barely grazes a contour line, in this case at 7,200 ft: that will be the highest contour attainable if you have to stay out of the park. This is given by point A in the map.

The same logic holds for our indifference map. If we superimpose our budget constraint on the original indifference map in Fig. 11.9, we arrive at Fig. 11.13:

The highest indifference curve that can be attained is I_2. Points along I_3 would be preferred, but they are out of reach. The budget constraint barely permits the consumer to select point A, representing B* loaves of bread and C* pounds of cheese.

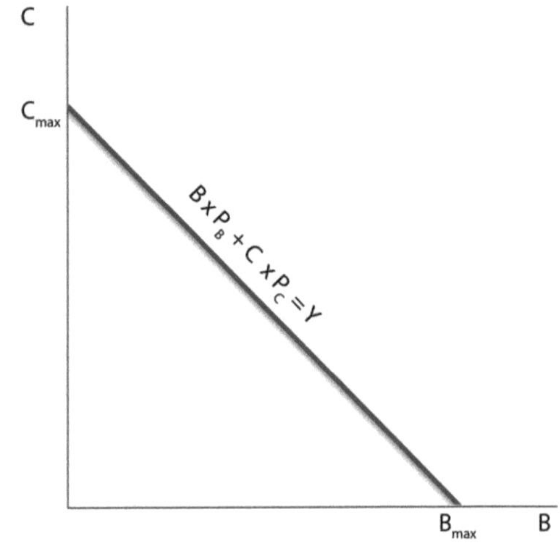

Fig. 11.11 A budget constraint for bread and cheese. Given an amount of money Y and prices P_B and P_C for bread and cheese respectively, the consumer cannot purchase combinations of bread and cheese beyond the budget constraint drawn above

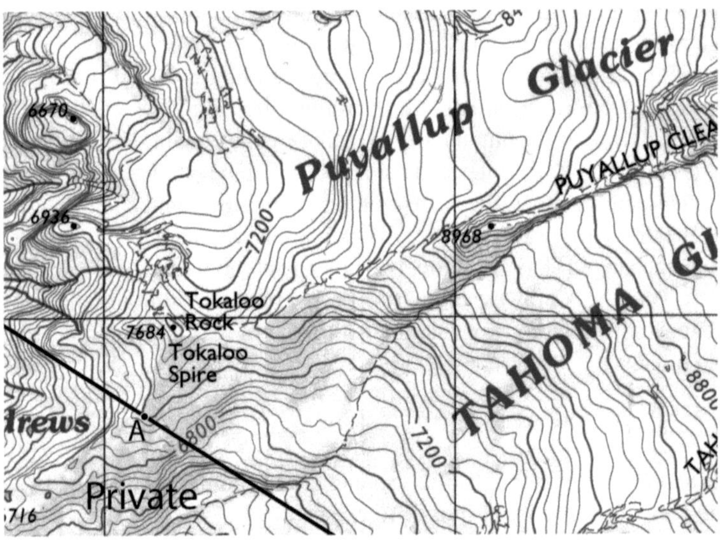

Fig. 11.12 Mt. Ranier topographical map with hypothetical line separating private from public land. Land to the SW of the boundary is private land; land to the NE is public. The highest point that can be reached without entering the park is *A*, where the boundary is tangent to the contour line

Of course, we have already worked out what it means for a straight line to be tangent to a point along the indifference curve; its slope tells us the inverse of the ratio of marginal utilities. Now, however, we have a new piece to add, because the budget constraint given in Eq. 11.6 must obey the condition

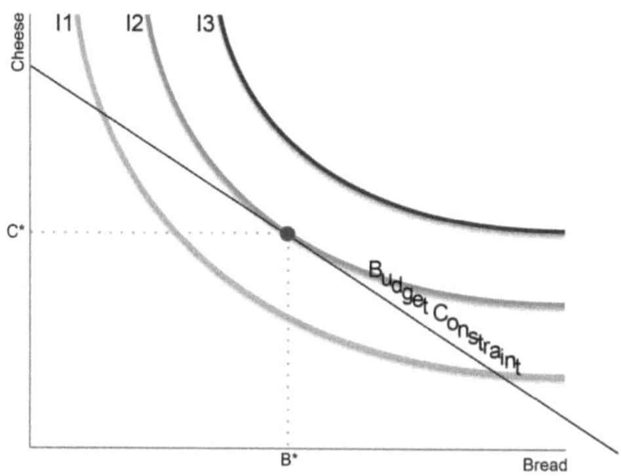

Fig. 11.13 Three indifference curves for an individual consumer acquiring bread and cheese, plus a Budget Constraint. When the consumer faces a budget constraint as above, the highest indifference curve that can be reached is I_2, where the budget constraint is tangent at point A. The consumer will buy B* loaves of bread and C* pounds of cheese

$$\Delta B^* \mathrm{P_B} + \Delta C^* \mathrm{P_C} = 0 \tag{11.6}$$

That is, if you increase the amount of bread purchased, that will deduct $\Delta B * P_B$ from your budget, which can only be made up by saving $\Delta C * P_C$ on less purchases of cheese. But, as before, $\Delta C/\Delta B$ is the slope of the line, so we need to rearrange Eq. 11.6:

$$-\Delta B^* \mathrm{P_B} = \Delta C^* \mathrm{P_C} \tag{11.7}$$

Now divide both sides by $\Delta B * P_C$:

$$-\mathrm{P_B}/\mathrm{P_C} = \Delta C/\Delta B = \text{slope of budget constraint} \tag{11.8}$$

The slope of the budget constraint will be negative (the line is downward-sloping), so it will equal the inverse ratio of the prices. The steeper the slope, the greater the shift in cheese needed to offset a shift in bread, and the lower the price of cheese relative to bread.

Since the slope of the budget constraint is also the slope of the indifference curve at A, we can bring Eqs. 11.4 and 11.8 together:

$$\begin{aligned} -\mathrm{MU(B)}/\mathrm{MU(C)} &= -\mathrm{P_B}/\mathrm{P_C} = \Delta C/\Delta B = \text{slope of budget constraint} \\ &= \text{slope of indifference curve} \end{aligned} \tag{11.9}$$

The ratio of marginal utilities will be equal to the ratio of prices when the consumer maximizes utility subject to a budget constraint. Logically, we can imagine the prices being imposed from the outside (from the market) and the consumer adjusting purchases so that the equality in Eq. 11.9 is established. For instance if the price of cheese rises relative to that of bread, the slope of the budget constraint will become flatter. This will lead to a new optimum purchase combination somewhere to the right of point A, presumably on a different indifference curve. Since the new purchase decision will involve increasing the amount of bread (which is what it means to be to the right of A), the marginal utility of bread will diminish relative to that of cheese. This process is complete when those two ratios (prices and marginal utilities) are once again equal. Incidentally, notice that the law of demand works in this model: increasing the price of one good leads to a shift in purchases to the other.

The equality of the price and marginal utility ratios is exactly the result in the two-good case that corresponds to the relationship between marginal utility and willingness to pay in the one-good case. Note that Eq. 11.9 does not say that the marginal utility from either good equals its price. This would be meaningless, since the two are measured in entirely different units. It does say that, whatever the ratio between the price and marginal utility of a good, that same ratio applies to the other good. This is because, by dividing both sides of Eq. 11.9 by $-P_B/MU(C)$ we get

$$MU(B)/P_B = MU(C)/P_C \tag{11.10}$$

Consider this: we have developed the model using two goods, bread and cheese, but we could have done it for any two goods, or any larger number of goods, for that matter (although we would not be able to use two-dimensional diagrams for more than two goods). What if one of the goods were money itself? Then the price of money would, of course, be exactly one. (It costs exactly one dollar to buy a dollar if you're paying attention.) This means that the left side of Eq. 11.10 becomes simply the marginal utility of money. Since this equals the ratio of the marginal utility of some, or any, other good to its price, we are directly back in the world we created in the first half of this chapter.

Equation 11.10 can be given a somewhat different interpretation as well. You can read it as saying that, if you divide the marginal utility you get from any good by the price you pay for it, the result will equal the same operation for any other good. More bluntly, the marginal utility you get per dollar will be equalized across all goods when you maximize your utility while remaining within your budget constraint. There is an intuitive logic to this. If it were not the case, you could take a dollar out of a good whose marginal utility per dollar was low and reallocate it to something else where it was higher. By doing this, however, you are increasing your purchase of the higher marginal utility good which means, according to the law of diminishing marginal utility, that it will go down. The process continues until it has dropped to the level of the good you are buying less of—which of course, because you are buying less of it, will give you greater marginal utility. This notion is a bit idealized, because it assumes that you can make dollar-by-dollar reallocations, whereas real-world goods often have to be purchased in lump sums of many dollars. With "lumpy" purchases of this sort, you would never attain the perfection of Eq. 11.10, but you would come as close as you could.

The interesting thing about Eq. 11.10 is that it ought to hold for *every* individual in the market, since all face the same set of prices. Thus we come to the same point as in this chapter: if we could just say that the marginal utility of money were equal for all individuals, or even if we knew the ratio of each individual's marginal utility of money to the average, we could derive utility information for the entire population just by observing market prices. It is difficult to justify this step, however, so we are pushing the outer limits of what the theory has to say to us beyond the level of a single individual.

12 Production Costs and the Theory of Supply

At the beginning of Chap. 11 it was noted that the utility-based theory of demand is not really a theory that tells us much about consumer choice; its real function is to disentangle the assumptions necessary to support the first condition of the Market Welfare Model, that the demand curve represents the marginal benefits to society. The situation on the supply side is a bit different, however. While the main function of the analysis of production costs is to do for the supply curve what utility theory does for the demand curve, the cost theory we will look at in this chapter is a genuinely useful tool for studying issues of technology and the organization of production.

The payoff is not immediate, unfortunately. We will have to wade through a long discussion of different approaches to the measurement of cost and their algebraic and geometric properties before we can take up interesting questions about the impact of technology on the size and structure of firms. Don't give up hope, though: we will spend a few pages at the end of the chapter on the nature of mass production and the impact of computerization, one of the most significant economic issues of our time.

12.1 The Meaning of Cost

Before launching into the analysis itself, it is important to review the concept of cost, so that we know what we are actually talking about. Recall that, for economics, there are only two types of costs, opportunity costs and disutility. The vast majority fall under the heading of opportunity costs, meaning that the main cost of using resources for one purpose is that they become unavailable for other purposes. A less common cost is disutility, the intrinsic disagreeableness of certain activities. Both costs are measured by the amount of money that must be paid to get others to bear them, but the money itself is not the cost. This is a crucial point to keep in mind, since sometimes, as we will see, the money paid for something can be greater or less than its true cost. When that happens, it is the measuring stick, money, that is

P. Dorman, *Microeconomics*, Springer Texts in Business and Economics,
DOI 10.1007/978-3-642-37434-0_12, © Springer-Verlag Berlin Heidelberg 2014

not doing its job; there has been no change in the substance being measured, opportunity cost or disutility.

When you think of the costs incurred by operating a business, it is not difficult to trace most of them to their underlying economic requirements. Often the largest single cost is labor. Wages, salaries and fringe benefits are financial costs that firms must pay in order to compensate workers for their opportunity costs—the value that their time could have if put to other uses—and, occasionally, the disutility of the work itself. In Chap. 17 we will ask whether the money paid to workers is a good measure of these costs, but for now let's assume it is. (We will have enough complexity as it is.) Another type of cost consists of payments to other businesses for raw materials, services and other inputs. These can include items like wooden 2×4's, paper and ink, legal assistance, electricity and so on. In each case, we can assume that the money paid for such things compensates the sellers for the money *they* had to pay to those who provided the inputs needed to produce these goods. In other words, these are ultimately reflections of opportunity and disutility costs in the same way that payments to labor are. The same can also be said for capital investments, such as buildings and machines. These are simply inputs like any other, except that their productive effects continue over long periods of time rather than being used up all at once. Natural resources, like land and minerals, are slightly different to the extent that they were not produced by human activity, but the principle of opportunity cost applies to them as well; a parcel of land used for an office development cannot be used simultaneously as a farm. If these are the two best uses, the value of one use is the opportunity cost of the other.

One business cost is a little more difficult to identify, however: the cost of capital. Some companies have a high cost of capital, in the sense that they must borrow at high interest rates to acquire the money they need to meet their other expenses. Others can borrow on more favorable terms. Some companies don't borrow any money at all; they are completely self-financed. If money is the measuring device but not the true cost itself, what are these different expenses measuring?

The answer economists give is that, in any economy at a specific moment in time, one can speak of a social **opportunity cost of capital**—the rate of return for money in its best but least risky alternative investment. Imagine that there are a certain number of "sure things"—investments that are more or less guaranteed to earn a certain rate of return. In Fig. 12.1 we see them lined up, with the most profitable ones to the left and the least profitable to the right. (This lineup is referred to as the **marginal efficiency of investment** schedule.) Perhaps the one at the farthest left, for instance, offers a guaranteed return of 50 % per year, but to the right they approach the point at which they are just barely positive. Clearly investors will, if they are able to evaluate these potential returns accurately, choose the investments beginning at the left and moving to the right. At some point they will stop, since there are always more potential investment projects than there is money to finance them. This is marked in the diagram as I*. At this point all projects up to this one are being funded, and the one immediate to the right is next in line. Assuming a very gradual tapering off of rates of return, without much inaccuracy

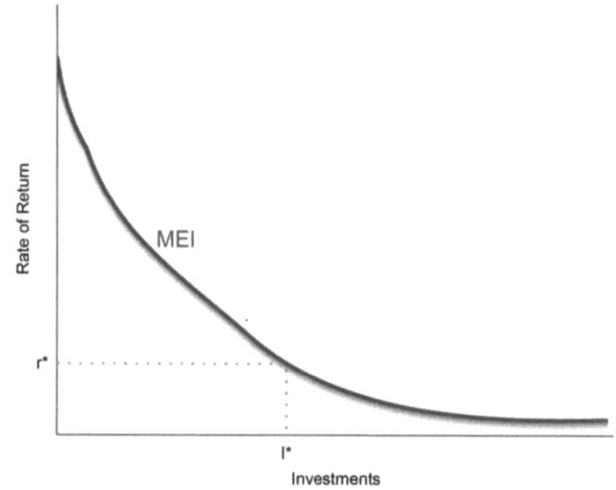

Fig. 12.1 Rates of return to investments with the lowest risk. The marginal efficiency of investment (*MEI*) schedule shows the rate of return on investment projects, ranked from highest to lowest. In this case, only the lowest-risk investments are pictured. When I* investments are funded the marginal return is r*

we could say that r* represents the return on both the last project financed and the next one investors will turn to.

By our definition of opportunity cost, this investment, which is the most attractive alternative to any other use of money at the moment, represents the opportunity cost of capital. (We are restricting ourselves to the least risky set of investments not because they are always the best, but because, according to an argument we will explore in Chap. 18, once we make adjustments for risk we would get the same result—the same opportunity cost of capital—for investments of any risk level. This means the least-risk investments provide a simpler basis for discussion: no adjustments to make.)

The one remaining problem is measurement: where should we look to find r*, since there are a great many rates of return on money in the economy at any point in time? The answer most economists would give is the market for government bonds. These are unlikely to be defaulted on, and they guarantee a fixed payment of interest to those who hold them. There are risks associated with inflation, as we will see in later chapters, but overall these investments are probably as low-risk as one could hope for. As such, they compete for the funds of investors looking for low-risk opportunities. Thus, if r* is the marginal return in low-risk investment projects, government bonds should also pay r*. If they paid more, people would shift their money out of other low-risk options and into bonds, driving down their return. If they paid less no one would buy them. The market for government bonds is in equilibrium, then, when its yields (interest rates) correspond to those of other investments of comparable risk.

All of this is a roundabout way of saying that the capital invested in *any* activity should be assigned an opportunity cost (net of compensation for risk) equal to the return it could earn on government bonds. If a company is borrowing at higher interest rates, it is paying a premium above the opportunity cost of capital; unless it shows some other offsetting advantage, it should not be borrowing the money. If a company is self-financed it should still be thought of as incurring a cost for the money tied up in it.

An example should make this clear. Suppose a business has invested $100,000 and each year pays out costs of $50,000 to employees and suppliers and takes in revenues of $55,000 from customers. In simple accounting terms, it might be regarded as having a profit of $5,000 a year, but we should also take into consideration the opportunity cost of its invested capital. If government bonds pay an interest rate of 4 % per year, profit is reduced to just $1,000; if $r = 6$ % the business is actually *losing* $1,000. In theory, it could shut down, put its money into bonds and come out $1,000 ahead. This numerical example illustrates the difference between **accounting profits** and **economic profits**. The former does not include the opportunity cost of capital, while the latter does. Throughout the rest of this chapter we will adopt the assumption that economic profits are being measured; so production costs always include the opportunity cost of capital as well as other inputs.

Before leaving this topic, it should be noted that the logic underlying the opportunity cost of capital is not air-tight. Within any economy at any moment in time it is true that the next best available investment determines the implicit cost of every other, but this argument is less certain across economies and over time. At the time this is written, interest rates are a bit higher in Europe than they are in the US and higher in the US than in Japan. Much of this may reflect factors that change the relationship between rates of return on assets and the productive contribution of the investments they finance, such as differences in the division of firms' profits between outside investors and other claimants. If only half of such profits go to investors in Europe, for instance, but three-quarters do in the US, the measured opportunity cost of capital, as set by rates of return in investment markets, may understate the true European return. This is hypothetical, but the underlying issue is real. There are loose ends in the theory of capital, and these show up in the greater unreliability of the opportunity cost of capital concept in large-scale (geographical, historical) comparisons.

12.2 The Structure of Short Run Production Costs

The starting point in our more detailed analysis of costs will be the **production function**. This is an algebraic expression that relates the amount of a good or service produced to the inputs of various productive resources. The generic formula looks like this:

$$Q = f(x_1, x_2, \ldots, x_n) \tag{12.1}$$

where Q is the quantity of output, the x's (from 1 to n) are different inputs (or **factors of production**) and f is a function that describes how the inputs are translated into outputs. This could be a recipe for cookies, for instance. Q could be the number of cookies, x_1 could be the amount of flour, x_2 could be the amount of sugar and so on up to, say, x_9 (if there are nine ingredients in the recipe), which might be the amount of cinnamon. The contribution of f is to tell us how much of each we need to bake one batch. But it could equally be a recipe for bicycles, restaurant meals or music CD's. It is an all-purpose language for describing the relationship between inputs and outputs that depends on just a few assumptions:

that the units of input and output are all homogeneous (one cup of flour is the same as any other in our recipe), that other determinants of productivity are held constant (such as organizational efficiency), and that the quantities of inputs are indeed the limiting factors governing how much output is produced.

This is not enough to tell us how much it will cost to produce a given quantity of output, however; we also need to know the prices of all the factors of production. Once we have that information and can use f to tell us how much of each we need, the production function can be turned into a **cost function**:

$$C = c(Q, f, p_1, p_2, \ldots, p_n) \tag{12.2}$$

The total cost absorbed in production will be determined by the amount produced, the production function f, and the prices of all the inputs. (We take a moment to recall that the opportunity cost of capital is one of these prices.) These are combined according to the cost function c, which is normally simply a matter of adding up the price times the quantity of all the inputs needed to produce Q. Sometimes we refer to f as representing the technology of the production process, with the understanding that improvements in technology usually show up in the form of needing fewer inputs to produce the same amount of output.

Equation 12.2 tells us the total cost of producing a quantity of some good, but we can also speak of the **average cost** (AC) and the **marginal cost** (MC). The average cost is simply the total cost divided by the number of units produced, or

$$AC = C/Q \tag{12.3}$$

The marginal cost is the change in total cost resulting from a change in output levels, or

$$MC = \Delta C/\Delta Q \tag{12.4}$$

For instance, if a company spends $500 to produce two additional bicycles, the marginal cost of each is $250.

Another important distinction is between **fixed and variable costs**. In almost any production process, certain expenditures have to be made before any production can take place at all, and this initial investment remains constant over an extended period of time. Examples include building or purchasing a warehouse, buying a truck, hiring an accountant or taking out a loan. These are the fixed costs of doing business. Variable costs arise from purchases of materials and labor tied to the amount of production taking place. These could take the form of call center workers employed, components purchased from other companies or electricity purchased from a power provider.

The line between these two types of cost is clear in principle but sometimes fuzzy in practice. The critical variable is *time*. Over a given time period certain expenditures are difficult or impossible to adjust. It takes time to buy a building or recruit a highly specialized worker. Within that time horizon, any factor of production that can't be altered is fixed, and any that can is variable. This leads in turn to the distinction between **long run** and **short run**. The short run is a period of time during which some factors of production are fixed; in the long run all are variable, since with enough time any factor can be increased or decreased. The long run may be only a few months for a law office—just enough time to acquire more facilities if it wants to expand (or sell if it wants to downsize) or find specialized employees to permit it to branch out into new fields. In the electric power business the long run is measured in years, the amount of time that must transpire between first planning a new power station and actually putting it on line. These two distinctions, fixed versus variable costs and short versus long run, effectively define each other.

Algebraically, since all costs are either fixed or variable, but not both, total cost is the sum of each, and so is average total cost:

$$C = FC + VC \text{ (the cost equals the sum of fixed cost and variable cost)} \quad (12.5)$$

$$\begin{aligned} AC = AFC + AVC \text{ (the average cost equals} \\ \text{the sum of average fixed cost and average variable cost)} \end{aligned} \quad (12.6)$$

Equation 12.6 follows from Eq. 12.5 because it is simply Eq. 12.5 with each term divided by Q, as in Eq. 12.3.

Now that we have all the pieces spread out in front of us, we can begin to assemble the puzzle. We will begin with the short run, classifying different types of costs, seeing how they can be graphed and what relationship they should be to one another. Then we will do the same for the long run.

12.3 The Individual Firm's Cost of Production in the Short Run

Since this is the short run there are fixed and variable costs. Let's look at fixed costs first. Their most important characteristic is that they are, well, fixed and therefore neither increase nor decrease in the short run. That leads immediately to an interesting observation: average fixed cost, total fixed cost divided by output, is a decreasing function of output, as shown in Fig. 12.2 on the next page. It is not hard to understand why: producing at a higher volume spreads the fixed costs over more units.

It is a bit more difficult to specify what form average variable costs will take. The usual assumption made by economists is that they will be governed by **the law of diminishing marginal returns against a fixed factor**. This is a mouthful. What it says is that, if some factors of production are in fixed supply (as they are in the short run), the others will become less productive as the amount employed goes up. Imagine a restaurant with a fixed investment in dining room and kitchen space. If it expects a sudden surge of demand it can hire more cooks and waiters, and it can also try to squeeze in more tables. Nevertheless, we would expect that this strategy will become increasingly expensive the further it is pursued. The next cook hired will certainly be able to turn out an additional quantity of food, and so also

Fig. 12.2 Average fixed cost for a single firm in the short run. The average fixed cost declines as more units (Q) are produced

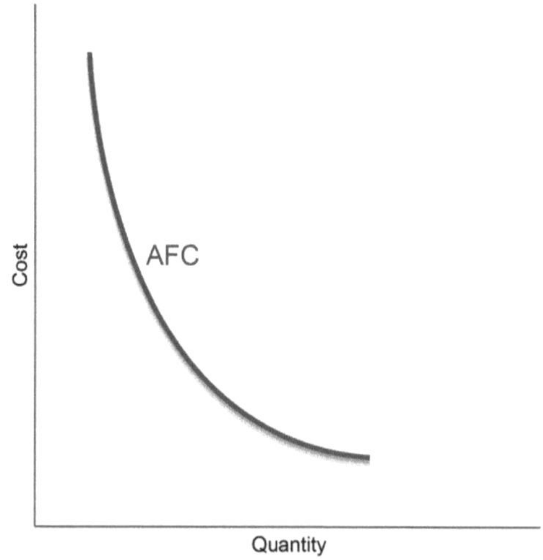

the cook after that, but with limited kitchen space they will soon find themselves waiting for others to finish their tasks. Thus there is some marginal (additional) return to hiring cook after cook, but it goes down with each new hire. The same could be said for dining room staff. Note that this argument does not apply in the long run; if the restaurant can expand its kitchen there is no reason another newly hired cook should contribute less than the others already behind the stove. Of course, if there are diminishing marginal returns to additional workers or other productive inputs in the short run, this will translate into rising costs. In particular, we can say that the marginal cost, according to the above-mentioned law, should be upward-sloping, as in Fig. 12.3. (We don't have to say "marginal variable cost, since there is no marginal fixed cost; the fixed cost doesn't change as more or fewer units are produced.)

The average variable cost is also depicted in Fig. 12.3. The relationship between the two curves can be explained logically (and also mathematically with the calculus). The marginal cost is the cost of the latest unit produced, while the average variable cost averages the marginal cost of all the units up to and including this last one. This means that, if the marginal cost is going up throughout the diagram, so is the average variable cost, and the marginal cost is above it, "pulling" it up. This will become more apparent when we look at a numerical example in a few moments.

Now that we can surmise something about the shapes of the AFC and AVC curves, we can construct a likely candidate for the AC curve itself. From Eq. 12.6 we know that AC is simply the sum of the other two; since we are adding up costs, and since the C axis is vertical, this means adding vertically the two average cost curves from Figs. 12.2 and 12.3. This is shown in Fig. 12.4, which reproduces AFC, AVC, and MC for convenience.

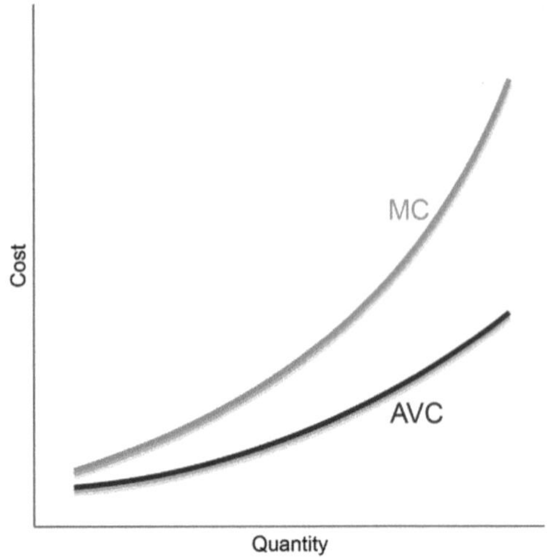

Fig. 12.3 Marginal cost for a single firm in the short run, assuming diminishing marginal returns. Assuming the law of diminishing marginal returns against a fixed factor, the marginal cost of production rises in the short run as more units are produced. The average variable cost rises with it at a slower rate

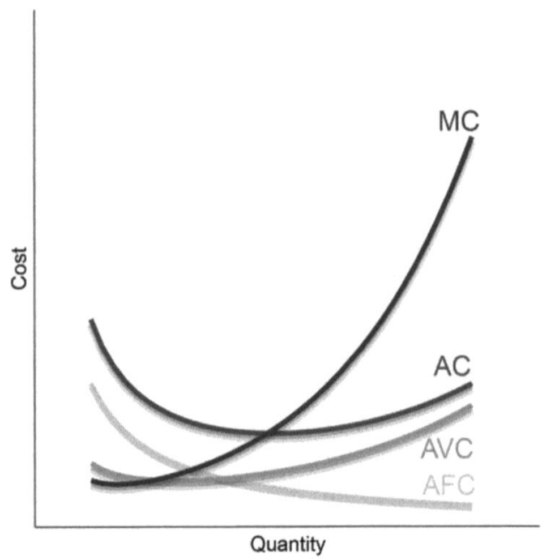

Fig. 12.4 Marginal cost and average fixed, variable and total costs for a single firm in the short run. Marginal, average fixed and average variable costs are carried over from Figs. 12.1 and 12.2. Average total cost AC is the vertical sum of AFC and AVC

It is not an accident that the average total cost curve intersects the marginal cost curve at its (the AC's) lowest point. As long as the additional cost of one more unit is below the average cost, this will reduce the average, and as long as the additional cost is above the average, this will increase it. Thus, if the marginal cost is exactly equal to the average (which is where the two curves intersect), the average is unchanging, which is to say flat. That is the point at which AC bottoms out, before it begins its rise.

Many of these logical relationships are easier to see in a numerical example, so let's consider Table 12.1, which represents the production costs faced by a hypothetical company.

Table 12.1 Production costs at a single company

Q	FC	VC
5	30	25
6	30	32
7	30	40
8	30	49
9	30	59
10	30	70

Table 12.2 More production costs

Q	FC	VC	TC	AFC	AVC	ATC
5	30	25	55	6	5	11
6	30	32	62	5	5.33	10.33
7	30	40	70	4.29	5.71	10
8	30	49	79	3.75	6.13	9.88
9	30	59	89	3.33	6.56	9.89
10	30	70	100	3	7	10

In this example Q is the quantity produced, FC is the fixed cost of production, and VC is the variable cost.

It can be expanded to include total cost, average fixed cost, average variable cost and average total cost from the formulas on the previous page.

Take the first row, where Q = 5, for instance. Total cost (55) is the sum of fixed cost (30) and variable cost (25). Average fixed cost (6) is total fixed cost (30) divided by quantity (5), and a similar calculation gives us average variable and average total costs.

Marginal cost is a little trickier, since it pertains to the changes *between* different quantities. Thus, going from the fifth to the sixth unit entails going from a total cost of 55 to 62; hence the marginal cost is 7. The full schedule is given in Table 12.3 on the next page.

The average and marginal costs are graphed in Fig. 12.5, with the points representing marginal cost being placed between the quantities whose change is being registered. Note that, as promised, the average cost curve intersects the marginal cost curve at the lowest level of average cost.

Now we have introduced our cast of characters, the various cost curves; the next step is to see how firms can use them to make production decisions.

Box 12.1: A Useful (and Largely Realistic) Simplification of Cost Analysis

The derivation of total, average and marginal cost curves we have just surveyed is based on the assumption that the law of diminishing marginal returns against a fixed factor holds at all levels of production. In other words, each new worker hired or new batch of materials purchased contributes less to output than each previous one. This overstates the role of diminishing returns in most production processes and needlessly complicates analysis. We can

(continued)

Table 12.3 Calculating marginal cost

Q	TC	MC
5 → 6	55 → 62	7
6 → 6	62 → 70	8
7 → 6	70 → 79	9
8 → 6	79 → 89	10
9 → 6	89 → 100	11

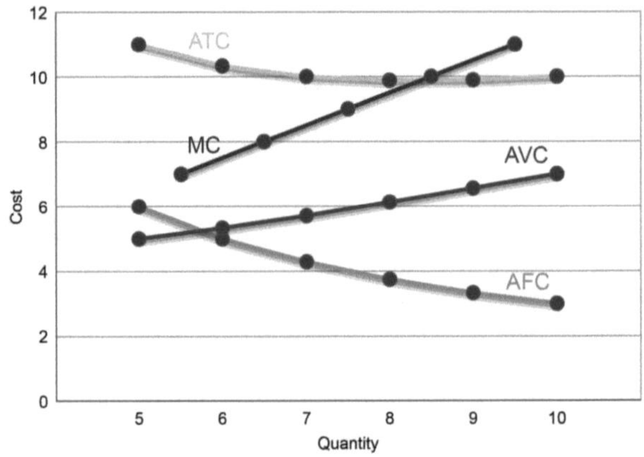

Fig. 12.5 Graphing the average and marginal costs. Average fixed, variable and total costs are graphed along with marginal cost

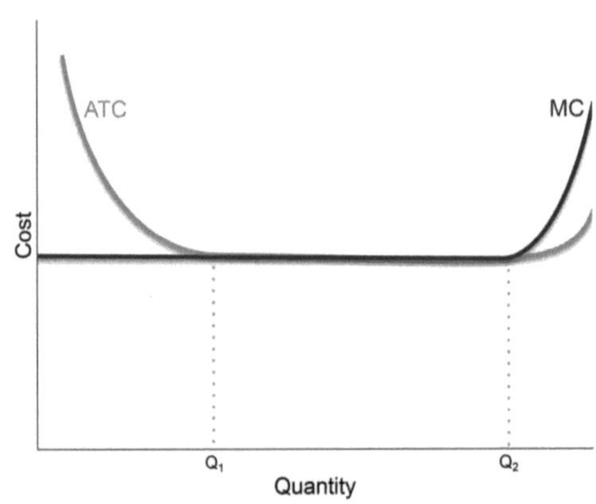

Fig. 12.6 Average and marginal cost, with diminishing returns only at near-capacity. The decline in average costs due to spreading fixed costs out over more units is largely exhausted at Q_1; the increase in marginal costs due to diminishing marginal returns doesn't set in until Q_2. Between Q_1 and Q_2, then, average and fixed costs are constant and equal to each other. These are the cost conditions commonly faced by many producers

Box 12.1 (continued)
make our life easier and our economic insights more relevant by assuming that, in most production processes, there is a range of output over which returns to variable factors are constant.

Consider a hospital. Fixed costs include buildings, the legal and financial setup, and essential services like heat and energy. Variable costs are items like employees (doctors, nurses, orderlies and clerical staff), equipment (beds, monitors, scanners, lab items) and supplies (medicines, syringes, IV fluids). The size of the fixed investment—particularly the buildings—determines the ultimate capacity in the short run (before new buildings can be built or purchased). As this capacity approaches the law of diminishing returns almost certainly takes effect, but at most levels of operation it may be in abeyance. As long as there is extra space (office, bed, lab etc.) available, hiring an extra nurse should not entail any loss in extra potential output. If most hospitals are operating far enough below their absolute capacity most of the time, it would be reasonable to picture them as facing flat (neither increasing nor decreasing) average and marginal cost curves.

It is common in practical, applied economics to make the assumption that relevant costs (those likely to be encountered) are not subject to diminishing returns, as in Fig. 12.6 on the previous page. At very low levels of production average costs will still be falling, due to the effect of spreading out fixed costs over a lower number of units. At very high levels average costs rise as diminishing returns take over. Between these two extremes average cost is constant at the level set by marginal cost. (Once fixed cost per unit is negligible, the average cost is equal to the additional cost of increasing output by one.) Many, if not most, producers find themselves operating in this constant average cost zone most of the time, so we can often simply assume that ATC and MC are fixed. In the remainder of this chapter we will not make this assumption, since we want the analysis to stick close to the more elaborate version that has become standard in the textbooks. (Drawing a horizontal MC curve would also complicate the presentation of the firm's decision over how much to produce.) In later chapters, however, we will find the constant-cost simplification too useful to set aside.

12.4 Production Costs and the Supply Curve in the Short Run

In what follows we will make three enormous simplifying assumptions, that the firm in the short run has no objective other than the maximization of profits (or the minimization of losses), that all units produced can be sold at a price set by the market, and that the only decision over which the firm has control is the level of production—all other matters of technology, product design, internal organization,

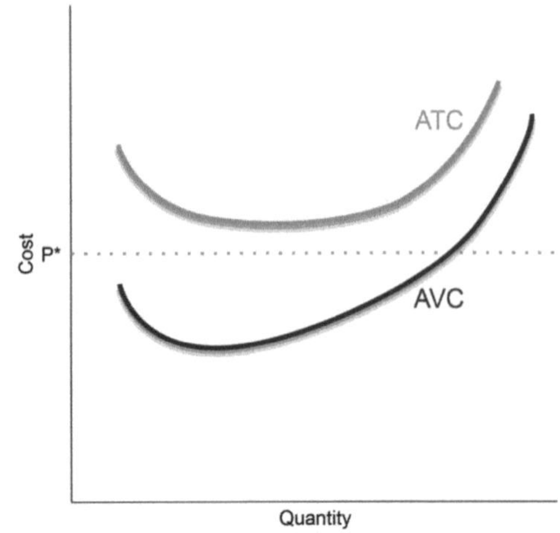

Fig. 12.7 A firm should produce if P > AVC, even if this means it loses money. When the market price is above the lowest point on the average variable cost *(AVC)* curve, the firm's best choice is to continue producing. This is true even when there is no output level at which the price can cover average total cost (*ATC*), as above. By producing, the firm will lose money, but not as much as it would lose if it didn't produce at all

marketing, etc. have already been determined or are not capable of being altered. These are obviously unrealistic, yet, as we will see, some interesting conclusions can still be drawn from the simplified world that remains.

The first decision facing the firm is whether to produce at all. Since it is operating in the short run it faces fixed costs that it cannot eliminate, but there are sometimes circumstances in which it is better to simply swallow these costs: pay them but don't incur any additional costs of production. This arises when the revenue that can be gained from production doesn't even cover the variable costs. To determine whether this is the case, the firm should look at the AVC curve, noting its lowest point; in Table 12.2 on p. 257, for instance, the lowest AVC is no greater than $5. It may be lower, but we don't know have the information for quantities between 1 and 5. Suppose it exactly $5: in that case price the good can be sold for should be no less than $5, otherwise it would be better to produce nothing. Note that this decision rule could still lead to the firm earning losses. Consider Fig. 12.7 at the top of this page, for instance. Here the price lies between the low point on the AVC and ATC curves. Since P > AVC at its nadir, less money is lost by producing than not producing. On the other hand, the price is not high enough to cover all the average costs of production, fixed and variable, so the firm will lose money on each unit produced and sold.

The price P* is above the lowest average variable cost but below the lowest average total cost. The first means it should remain in production, the second that it will lose money nevertheless. Costs and prices are positioned on the same axis, because they are both measured in money.

The second decision is exactly how much to produce. Here you might be tempted to say, produce at the lowest cost of production—where the ATC curve is at its lowest point. True, this would maximize profit per unit produced (profit margin), but is this the same as maximizing profits, period? Not quite. Consider the following thought experiment: suppose you are running the firm, producing a quantity of goods and selling them at the going price. You are minimizing your

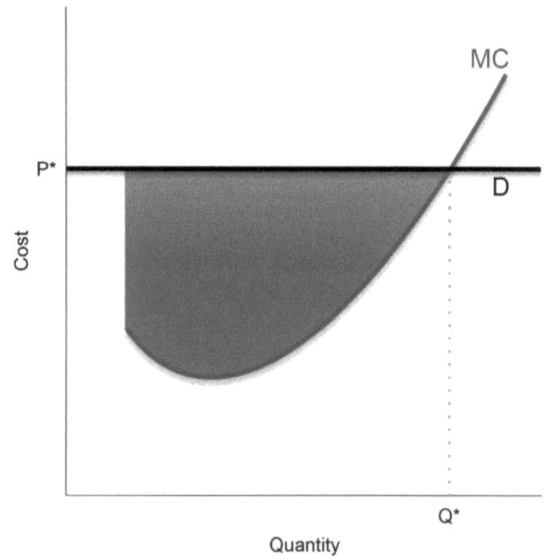

Fig. 12.8 A single firm facing a horizontal demand curve maximizes Profit where P = MC. The *shaded area* represents total profits, which are maximized at Q* where P = MC. Shading is not applied to the left of the MC curve as drawn, since we don't know the relevant cost information

average costs, and these are below the price, so you are making money. You could ask yourself whether it would make sense to produce just one more unit. If you do you can sell it and your additional revenue will be the market price. The additional cost would be the marginal cost of that one unit. Whether it makes sense to produce it depends on the relationship between price and *marginal cost*, not price and average cost. In fact you should conduct this analysis one unit at a time, extending your production run until you finally reach the unit whose marginal cost is no longer below the price. At this point you stop, satisfied that you have squeezed the last ounce of profit from your situation.

This process is portrayed in Fig. 12.8 above, which shows how following the rule that price should equal marginal cost does in fact maximize profits. Here we introduce the convention of calling a horizontal line at P* the firm's demand curve; it indicates that the firm can sell as little or as much as it wants at that price. It can't charge more because no one would buy (they would go somewhere else), and it won't charge less because there's unlimited demand at P*. This situation might exist for a very small seller in a very large market. For every unit along the Q axis, the height of the D curve indicates the revenue that can be obtained by producing and selling it, the height of the MC curve indicates the additional cost of producing that one unit, and the difference is the profit on that marginal unit. The shaded area sums up all the profits from units produced up to Q*. At any production level to the left of Q* there are potential profits not being made; at any level to the right there are units whose additional cost does not cover their revenue and which are therefore drawing down the amount of profit. At Q* profits are maximized.

Now imagine that the price P* begins to fluctuate. First it moves down. As it does it intersects the MC curve at lower levels of Q*, and so the firm, to continue its mission of maximizing profits, must reduce output. Then it begins rising again, and the firm expands output to keep abreast of the rightward movement of Q*. What this is telling us, in fact, is that *the marginal cost curve is the supply curve for the*

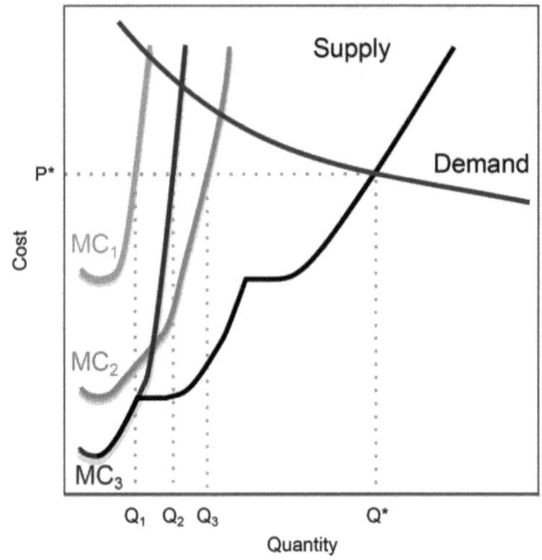

Fig. 12.9 Individual and market supply curves. The market supply curve S is the horizontal sum of the individual supply curves for the three firms shown, each of which is also the marginal cost curve. Q_1, Q_3 and Q_2 are the amounts produced by firms 1, 3 and 2 when $P = P^*$, as given by the intersection of the market supply and demand curves

individual firm. It indicates the amount that the profit-maximizing firm will want to produce given any potential price. This conclusion only holds, of course, when our assumptions do. In this case a particularly important assumption is that the demand curve is perfectly horizontal at whatever price is being set by the market. As we will see in the following chapter, even the slightest tilt to this curve changes the analysis. For now, however, we will stick with the horizontal demand curve.

With the supply curve for the individual curve under our belt, we are now prepared to tackle the market supply curve. The main thing to see is this: if the horizontal demand curve rule applies to all firms (yes, it is a big if, but we will have plenty of opportunity to examine it later), then the rule $P = MC$ applies to all of them, and since all face the same market price, all will produce at the same marginal cost.

In some ways this is a stunning conclusion. Imagine an industry with many firms that conforms to the assumptions we've just made. Some firms are large, some are small. Some are modern and use the latest methods; some are using practices that were outmoded a generation ago. Each is different in a variety of ways, but all choose their output in such a way that the marginal cost of production is everywhere the same. This situation is illustrated in Fig. 12.9 above, which for simplicity assumes there are only three firms in the market (much as we assumed only three consumers in the previous chapter). The market supply curve is the horizontal sum of the individual supply curves; it is the amount they all produce together at the going price. Note, however, that the demand curve is no longer horizontal *at the market level*. It is a "normal" downward-sloping demand curve. Where it intersects the market supply curve determines, as before, the equilibrium price, and it is this price which appears in the form of a horizontal demand curve to *individual* firms.

Suddenly we are face to face with the second condition of the Market Welfare Model, that the supply curve represents the marginal costs to society of producing

Table 12.4 Sufficient conditions for the supply curve to represent marginal costs to society

1. Every cost, including the cost of capital, incurred by every firm is an opportunity or disutility cost to society
2. Every such opportunity or disutility cost is paid for by firms
3. Firms seek systematically to maximize profits
4. Firms have only one decision to make, how much to produce
5. Each individual firm faces a perfectly horizontal demand curve

the good or service. If all the assumptions we have made in this chapter are accepted, this second condition is satisfied, since every point on the market supply curve is simply the sum of the points on individual firms' marginal cost curves. For convenience, these assumptions are assembled in Table 12.4 above.

If all of these conditions hold, so also does the second condition of the Market Welfare Model. As I argued in the previous chapter, there is no point in being a perfectionist. If a market comes reasonably close to fulfilling these five demands, we may suppose that, on the supply side at least, it is functioning in the neighborhood of the welfare ideal. On the other hand, if one or more of these demands is significantly unmet, that can tell us something about the nature of the problem and what to do about it. We will pursue this line of inquiry further in the chapters to come.

12.5 Production Costs and Market Supply in the Long Run: The Adjustment Process

So let us now shift to the long run, the time horizon over which all factors of production can be adjusted and all costs are variable. We will approach it in two ways, first as a dynamic process of adjustment through time and then as a planning problem—how firms make long run decisions in the present on the basis of forecasts of future cost and demand possibilities.

From an adjustment perspective, the big difference between the long and short run is that, in the long run, a firm can alter its scale of operations. If it wants to increase its capacity it can do that. If it wants to shrink it, that's an option too. It can even quit a line of business entirely or enter a new one. For simplicity we will restrict ourselves to these last two options, exit and entry. The first occurs when an old firm leaves the market, the second when a new firm joins it.

We begin our story where we left it. Every firm is maximizing its profits as in Fig. 12.9 on p. 262, and together they comprise the market supply which, in conjunction with the market demand, sets the price. We ascertained that they were maximizing profits from Fig. 12.8, which shows that P = MC is the rule to follow for that purpose. What we don't know yet, however, is whether they are actually *making* profits, rather than simply minimizing their losses. This is the question first raised in the discussion of Fig. 12.7: it is entirely possible that firms

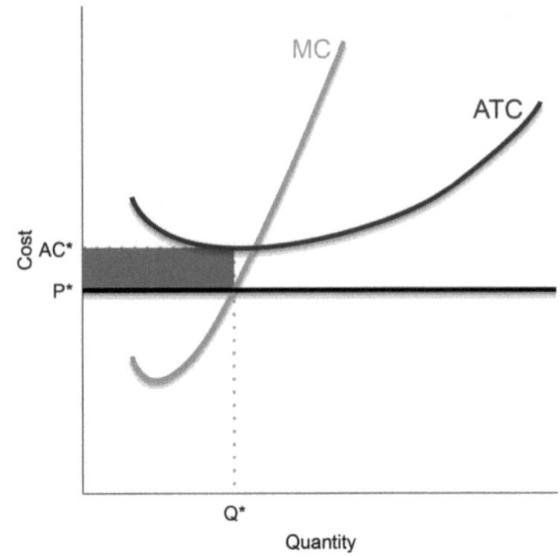

Fig. 12.10 A firm that is unable to make economic profits in the short run. The firm selects output at Q*, where P* = MC. At this quantity the average cost AC* is greater than the price. The *shaded area* represents the firm's total economic losses

are doing the best they can, producing in the short run, but still losing money. Or it may be the case that profits are rolling in because P* is far in excess of their average total costs. Let's consider each possibility in turn.

1. Firms are making economic losses. Consider the case of a representative firm in Fig. 12.10: market demand is so low, or costs of production are so high, that when this firm sets its production level to equalize price and marginal cost, its average costs are still well above the revenue it receives per unit. With each unit it produces it is losing money (although not as much as it would if it didn't produce at all). Recall, incidentally, that this calculation of loss is based on all the costs of production, including the opportunity cost of capital. Thus the firm whose fate we are lamenting may be earning operating profits in an accounting sense, but it is not covering the opportunity cost of the money tied up in its investment. If the low-risk rate of return is 5 %, for instance, a firm that earns only 3 % is actually losing 2 % in economic terms.

When the firm chooses its output at Q*, its average total cost of production is AC*, the height of the ATC curve at Q*. (This is not the lowest point on the ATC curve, which would be where the MC curve intersects it.) The difference between AC* and P* represents the money lost for each unit sold. Multiply this by the number of units, and the result is the total losses of operation. This total loss appears in the form of the shaded rectangle, whose area is its length (number of units produced) times its width (difference between cost and price per unit).

Figure 12.10 captures a firm in a single short run period, but it is not likely its owners or managers will want to repeat it. Unless they expect the market demand (and therefore P*) to rise, they will cut back on their operations, either reducing their productive capacity or exiting the market altogether. The calendar time it takes for them to do this depends on the nature of the business, but in economic terms this is simply the long run, as we've defined it. If many firms are in the same boat, the

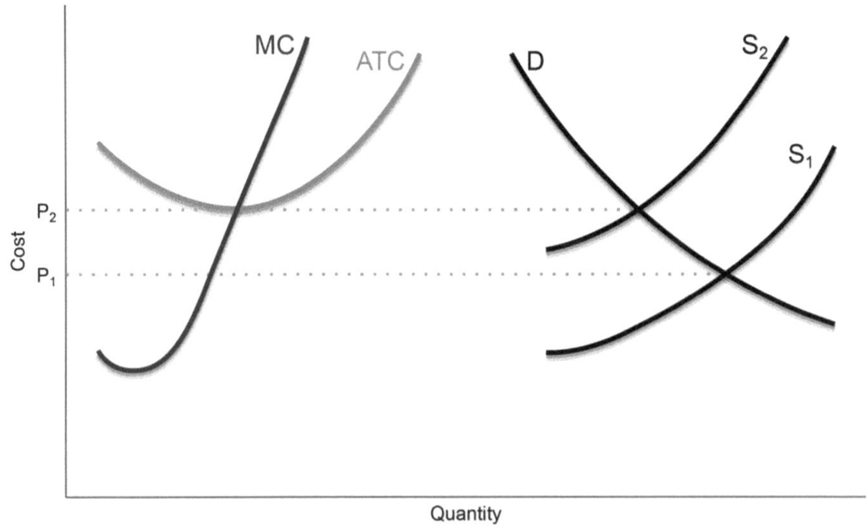

Fig. 12.11 The exit of other firms makes it possible for one that remains to cover its costs. At the original market supply curve S_1, the price P_1 is too low for the firm whose MC and ATC are given to break even. As other firms leave, the market supply curve shifts to S_2. A price increase to P_2 is just sufficient to end the firm's economic losses

long run will see a significant decline in the overall industry capacity and therefore a leftward shift in the industry supply curve. That in turn will raise P*, and the process will continue either until all producers decide to quit, or until P* rises high enough so that the remaining producers are covering their full cost. This last possible is depicted in Fig. 12.11, which shows the result for a single firm.

2. Firms are making economic profits. If the market price is high enough, firms will earn beyond their cost of capital. This will lead to a situation for some representative firm like the one depicted in Fig. 12.12 on the following page.

Once again the firm selects output where P* = MC; at this level it finds that its unit cost, given by the height of the ATC curve at Q*, is less than the revenue it receives for each unit produced. The net profit per unit is given by the difference between P* and AC*; multiply this by the number of units, and the result is the shaded rectangular area.

The prospect of profits greater than the opportunity cost of capital will attract additional investment, either in the form of new entrants into the market or the expansion of existing firms. Either way, the market supply curve will shift to the right, as shown in Fig. 12.13, thereby lowering P*. Eventually the price falls to the point at which this industry is no more attractive than any other, and a new long run equilibrium is reached. This is shown by the situation of the firm on left of the diagram which is now just able to earn the opportunity cost of its investment.

In short, these diagrams are telling a story in which the absence of any barriers to the entrance or exit, expansion or retrenchment, of firms creates a tendency in the

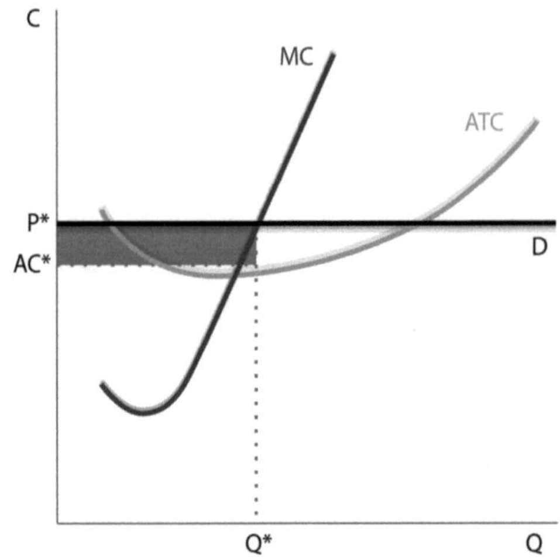

Fig. 12.12 A firm that makes economic profits in the short run. The firm selects output at Q*, where P* = MC. At this quantity the average cost AC* is less than the price. The *shaded area* represents the firm's total economic profits

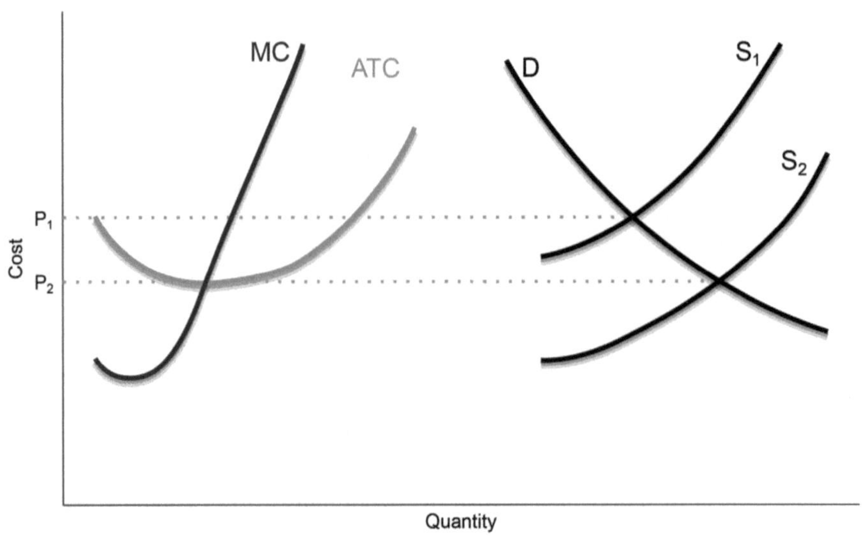

Fig. 12.13 The entrance of new firms eliminates the economic profits of an existing one. At the original market supply curve S_1, the price P_1 was high enough for the firm whose MC and ATC are given to earn economic profits. As new firms enter, the market supply curve shifts to S_2. The price falls to P_2, at which the firm just recovers the opportunity cost of its investment

long run for economic profits to fall to zero. As Adam Smith would have hoped, generalized competition is leading to a situation in which investment in this industry—and in every other subject to the same competitive conditions—is tending toward an equal rate of return. There are no pockets of extra-high profit being cornered by some lucky investors, nor is there low-return capital hanging on year after year, waiting for the profits that never come. The allocation of capital across industries is as efficient as anyone might want, and there are no persistent unfair advantages to particular segments of the investment community. This further underlines the claims of the Market Welfare Model, since it demonstrates a type of efficiency that applies across markets as well as within them.

Of course, like all stories told by economists, the credibility of the long run adjustment tale we have just spun depends on its underlying assumptions. In addition to those listed in Table 12.4, we have added a new one: there are no barriers to the free entry and exit of investment in this industry. As we will see in the next chapter, investment barriers can take many forms, and not just, say, legal prohibition, so this stipulation is not easily met. On the other hand (as we will also see), many economists draw from this story the lesson that it should be a goal of economic policy to hunt down all such barriers and try to eliminate them.

12.6 Production Costs and Market Supply in the Long Run: The Planning Process

We now move to the second form of long run analysis, which looks at the planning horizon of firms in a position to make decisions about the future. Figure 12.14 on the following page might be drawn up by an engineer submitting a report about possible investments available to company officials. Each investment creates a production capacity as indicated by an ATC curve. The firm could select investment #1 and, when it comes on line, face a cost structure like ATC_1, or it could choose investment #2 and find itself with ATC_2, etc. The decision has to be made in the present which cost structure will prove most profitable over the course of its usable life. That clearly depends on how much the firm expects to sell. If the market will absorb only Q_1 in output from the firm, for instance, it is well advised to go with the first investment, since at that quantity average costs will be much higher from any other. Similarly, if Q_2 is anticipated, the investment that gives ATC_1 would be a mistake, for now its costs would be higher. We can imagine that this is a forecasting problem that companies have to solve all the time. (It should be noted that the attention given to Q* rather than P* in the previous story suggests that demand may not be unlimited for firms in the long run. We will see why shortly.)

For the sake of discussion, suppose foresight is perfect, and the firm will always make the investment that gives it the lowest cost of production for any output level it forecasts. Thus, if it expects Q_1 it will invest so that its average cost is C_1, and if it expects Q_2 it will invest to produce at cost C_2. In fact, every possible level of Q could be matched with its appropriate ATC curve, making possible its lowest possible average cost. If we did this for every level of output, the relationship between output and cost would be given by the **long run average cost curve** LRAC depicted in Fig. 12.15.

The LRAC is an odd curve. A firm cannot move up or down this curve over time because it does not exist in time. It brings together pieces of potential short-run

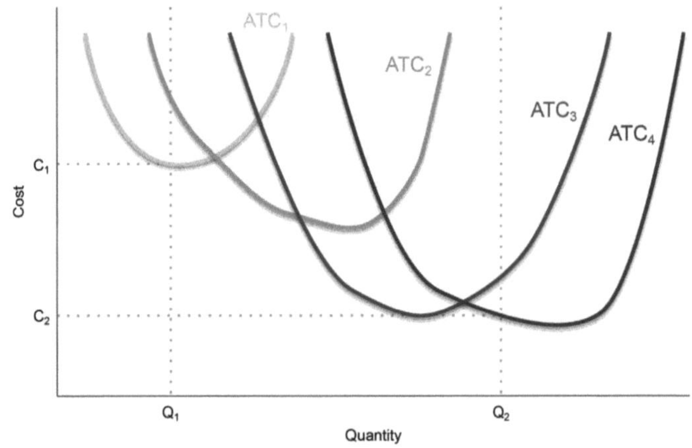

Fig. 12.14 Multiple investments available to a firm within its planning horizon. Each investment generates a different short run average total cost curve. Which will prove to be lowest-cost depends on the projected level of output. At Q_1 ATC_1 is the lowest-cost investment; at Q_2 it is ATC_4

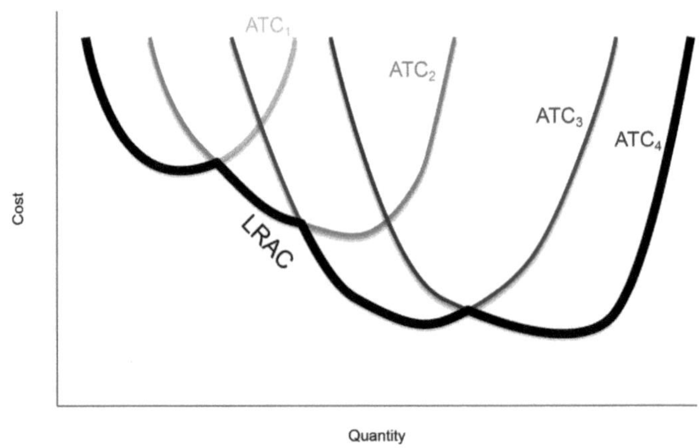

Fig. 12.15 The long run average cost curve. The long run average cost curve LRAC consists of the lowest costs for which any level of output Q can be produced

curves, each of which is an alternative to the others. Its existence is as an aid to planning; it lets analysts forecast potential costs and outputs over multiple scenarios which could arise in the future. Economists refer to curves like this as **envelope curves**; they mark the outer extent of many smaller curves taken together, in this case the low-cost boundary.

If we were to put every possible scale and type of investment together into one diagram and construct its LRAC envelope, what in general would it look like? We expect that bigger investments, ones with more fixed costs, will be able to produce at higher volumes than smaller ones, but also that they will need to. This is because, if the fixed costs are not spread out over a large enough volume, the average cost of production will be too great. On the other hand, the virtue of high-fixed investment methods is that they usually make possible lower cost production at high levels of output. Think of two investments in automobile production, one taking place in a small shed with workers using hand tools, the other in giant factories with assembly lines and robots. The first is a lot cheaper to get up and running, and it is the most efficient way to produce one or two custom-made cars. The large-scale factory needs a huge production run to justify its fixed costs, but when it is running full tilt its unit costs are far below the hand-made alternative. The sequence of ATC's in Fig. 12.15 was intended to capture this effect.

The possibility of producing at lower costs when production volume increases is called an **economy of scale**. This recalls the discussion of Adam Smith's pin factory in Chap. 8, where a larger scale of production enabled greater specialization and increased efficiency. Smith himself pointed to the possibility of mechanization as one of the reasons a more finely-tuned division of labor could reduce costs, and the downward-sloping portion of the LRAC curve reflects this reasoning. Some types of work have more scope for these economies than others, but all exhibit at least some range of output over which costs tend to fall.

Economies of scale don't last forever; eventually production reaches a point at which all opportunities for augmenting efficiency have been exhausted. Here there is a fork in the road, and there are two hypotheses about how costs will trend at very high levels of output, reflected in Fig. 12.16a, b on the following page. Both are identical up to Q*, but Fig. 12.16a bottoms out and turns upward, while Fig. 12.16b remains at its lowest cost indefinitely. Figure 12.16a is U-shaped, Fig. 12.16b L-shaped (sort of).

The upward-sloping portion of LRAC to the right of Q* in Fig. 12.16a represents **diseconomies of scale**, factors that make production more costly as the scale of operations expands. This could occur if it is simply too difficult to coordinate very large-scale activities, or if some crucial inputs into production are in fixed supply, thereby invoking the law of diminishing marginal returns against a fixed factor. This was how Alfred Marshall expected long run costs to look, and from it he drew the implication that firms would generally not be larger than necessary. They might be smaller if competition prevented them from growing large enough to produce at Q*, but they would discover that it was in their interests to stop at that point and not try to operate at an even larger scale.

In a famous article written in the 1920s, Italian economist Piero Sraffa challenged this view, arguing that it contradicts the logic of the long run in which all costs are variable. Indeed, a firm could simply replicate its most efficient scale of operations and avoid diseconomies of scale altogether. This is in fact how automobile companies function: they don't build mammoth factories to produce everything at one site, but many smaller factories that are optimized for an efficient scale of production. (Henry Ford experimented with the one-big-production-site model but eventually gave up on it.) Even management attention is not a limiting factor, since the M-form structure we considered in Chap. 8 replicates operational management as well. As Sraffa pointed out, if the LRAC looks like 16b the size of the firm remains unknown. It can get larger and larger and still continue to produce as

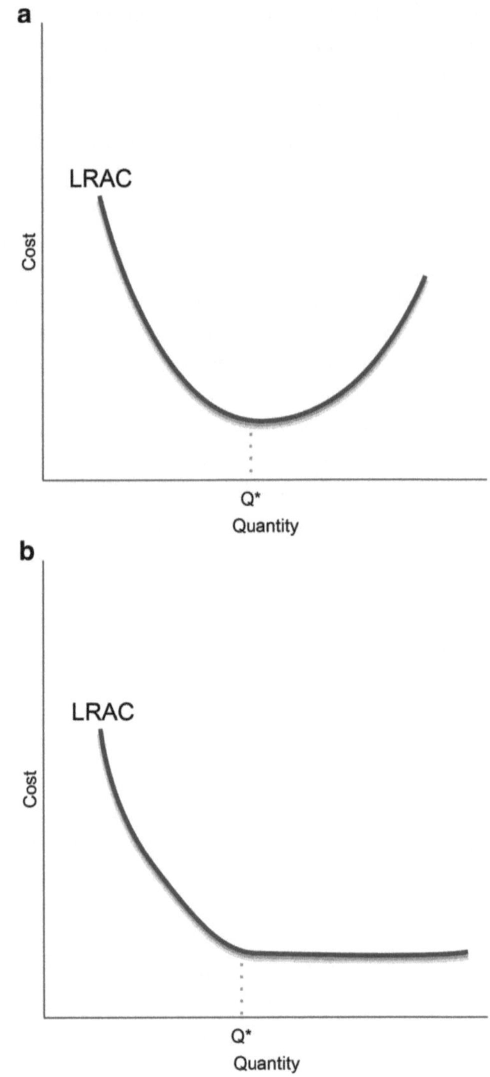

Fig. 12.16 Two possible shapes of LRAC. (**a**) *Above*, displays economies of scale up to Q*, then diseconomies of scale. (**b**) *Below*, displays economies of scale up to Q* but constant costs past that point

efficiently as before. If bigness is regarded as a potential social problem for some other reason, as it often is, it would be a mistake to rely on the market to keep firms at their optimal size without additional oversight.

So which is it, U-shaped or L-shaped LRAC? In most industries the empirical evidence points to L-shaped long run costs, and the main focus of research is on the location of Q* the **minimum efficient scale**. In some natural resource-based activities, however, costs really are U-shaped, since certain resources cannot be replicated at will the way other factors of production can.

12.7 Mass Production, Computers and the LRAC Curves of the Future

Perhaps no other revolution has played as large a role in modern economic growth as the emergence of **mass production** in the late nineteenth and early twentieth centuries. In industry after industry, costs were driven down to a fraction of their earlier levels through highly mechanized production of standardized goods in large production runs. This is true for steel beams, automobiles, electrical power, consumer appliances and, more recently, retailing, containerized shipping, agribusiness and many other sectors. The power of mass production over the imagination of our age is reflected in the never-ending attempts to apply it to activities where it encounters resistance, like construction, health care. . ..and education.

Society has always been of two minds about mass production, however. We appreciate the abundance that these methods have made possible, but the costs are also apparent. Standardized goods make life less interesting and sometimes fail to meet our needs as we would like. (This is a common complaint about fast food.) Routinized production methods are often mind-deadening and alienating. Mass production systems are unstable, since they require continuously high demand to justify their large fixed costs; when consumers fail to purchase in sufficient quantities, businesses are awash in red ink and have to slash their investments. Also, the enormous scale of production required for a business to compete effectively is a considerable barrier to competition in much of the economy, leading to domination by a few. The cornucopia is also an octopus.

In the last decade or two, however, there have been signs of change, mostly due to the rapid development of computer and communication technology. Because their operations are so easily reprogrammed, computerized equipment can produce efficiently over a wider range of tasks. Goods do not need to be as standardized, because computers are smart enough to adjust their operations to take account of differences. The advantages of large-scale coordination can be achieved by linking small teams together through high-speed networks. In short, there is reason to suspect that at least some of the LRAC curves on the left side of diagrams like Fig. 12.14 are shifting downward: they can produce at efficiency levels rivaling the largest operations, even though they remain small and keep fixed costs to a minimum. If this becomes a general phenomenon, we will begin to see wholesale shifts of LRAC's as in Fig. 12.17.

This would enable us (maybe!) to have the best of both worlds: efficient low-cost production without standardization and economic concentration, cornucopia without the octopus. What we observe, however, is a paradox: a trend toward smaller units of production more scattered across distant locations *and* ever-larger corporate entities, linking more closely with one another and increasingly planning their operations on a global scale. Organizations have flatter hierarchies (fewer layers) but more effective control from the top, as it becomes possible to manage the work of more people more closely. Thus improved computing and communication have given us half a revolution. What the other half will look like is impossible to tell at this point. Perhaps there is room for a measure of choice, so that the full effect of

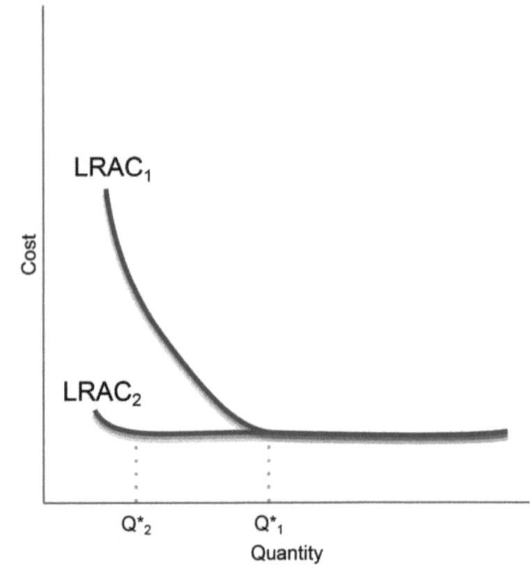

Fig. 12.17 A shift in long run average costs due to computerization? It is possible that computers and improved communications will dramatically reduce the role of size and fixed costs in achieving productive efficiencies, depicted as the shift from $LRAC_1$ to $LRAC_2$ and from Q^*_1 to Q^*_2

these new technologies will depend on the policies and institutions we craft for them. If so, this will probably not happen in a single act, like a sweeping law or institutional reform, but as the accumulated result of many smaller-scale decisions at locations throughout the economy—in the spirit of the technologies themselves.

The Main Points

1. All production costs take the form of either opportunity costs or disutility. These are measured by the monetary payments that those who bear these costs demand as compensation. Usually, but not always, this can be observed in the markets for inputs into production, like labor and materials. A special case is the opportunity cost of capital. Economists estimate this by using the interest rate on government bonds, since this is a nearly risk-free investment; it reflects a "sure" return that a business could make on its funds, whether borrowed or internally generated, if they were not allocated to investment.
2. By representing production costs in the form of a cost function, it is possible to construct measures for the total, average and marginal cost of production. Moreover, costs can be divided into fixed (those that do not change in the short run) and variable.
3. Fixed costs decline over output as they are spread out over more units. Marginal costs are often assumed to rise as output increases, although in many practical cases it is reasonable to represent them as constant. Average cost curves would be U-shaped if diminishing fixed costs dominate at low production levels, while rising marginal costs dominate at higher levels.
4. Firms maximize profits when they produce and sell a level of output where the price equals the marginal cost. This means that a firm in a competitive market, which can't influence the market price, has a supply curve identical to its marginal cost curve. The market supply curve is the sum of these individual

curves, so it reflects the marginal cost for every producer. This provides partial support for the Market Welfare Model.

5. In the short run, a firm should continue producing as long as the market price covers its average variable cost. In the long run, however, firms have the option of entering or leaving the market. If the market is fully competitive, firms will be expected to enter, or existing firms will increase their capacity, if the price exceeds average cost. If the price is below average cost, this will lead some firms to exit, or reduce capacity. These adjustments will tend to bring about a long-run equilibrium in which price and cost are the same: zero economic profits.
6. A firm, as it creates its plans to increase or decrease production capacity in the long run, can forecast its long run average cost curve; this curve combines the minimum average costs of all the short run cost curves it could bring about depending on its choice of investments. In general this curve is L-shaped. Costs decline as economies of scale are realized at higher levels of investment until all such economies are exhausted. The minimum output level that permits the firm to achieve all possible economies of scale is the minimum efficient scale. A firm can maintain this level of cost by investing in a way that duplicates its most efficient production system at any higher level of demand it might forecast.
7. It is expected that computerization will reduce the minimum efficient scale in most industries. This will make it possible for smaller firms to compete effectively with larger ones, at least on the basis of production costs.

▶ Terms to Define

Accounting versus economic profits
Average cost
Cost function
Diseconomies of scale
Economies of scale
Envelope curve
Factors of production
Fixed vs variable costs
Law of diminishing marginal returns against a fixed factor
Long run average cost curve
Long vs short run
Marginal cost
Marginal efficiency of investment
Mass production
Opportunity cost of capital
Production function

Questions to Consider

1. According to the discussion of the opportunity cost of capital, a firm that earns a rate of return below the interest rate on government bonds and has no prospect of ever earning a higher rate, should be shut down—even if it is making accounting profits. Do you agree?
2. The production function approach isolates the choice of how much to produce as the main determinant of average costs; it assumes that questions of scale in the short and long run can be separated from the other problems facing enterprises. How realistic is this? Is it more realistic in some settings than others? Be specific.
3. Consider a local bakery in your community. Is its marginal cost curve likely to be flat or increasing at output levels typical of normal operation? How does it determine how much bread to bake each day? (You could interview the owner to find out for sure.)
4. The auto repair industry is generally considered to be highly competitive, with few barriers to the entry of new firms or the departure of old ones. How well do you think it corresponds to the Market Welfare Model stipulation that the supply curve for services equals the marginal cost to society of providing them? In your answer, considered the assumptions that need to be made in order for this conclusion to follow.
5. Suggest one industry that probably has a U-shaped LRAC curve and another that has an L-shaped curve. Justify your choices.
6. Do you think the computer revolution will eventually result in fewer economies of scale in higher education? Will there be less need for colleges and universities of the size we see today? Why or why not?

Monopoly Power

13

Up to now, the dimension of power has been missing from our analysis. We have imagined an economic world in which individuals and organizations compete for their advantage, but their choices have all been about themselves—how to produce more efficiently, what to purchase, and so on. Now we take the next step and consider situations in which competitors act strategically to dominate or exploit others. We will do this using two models, one portraying the power to control prices in order to gain higher profits, the other the power that results from having a superior bargaining position. The first will be taken up in this chapter, and bargaining will be examined in Chap. 14. Taken together, they provide the beginning of an explanation of how a system based on free choice in the marketplace can result in concentrations of wealth and power.

13.1 Perfect Competition: A World Without Power

In the previous chapter we painted a picture of perfect competition in the market for any good or service. In the short run no seller or buyer has any control over the market price; there are simply too many of them for any individual to make a difference. Prices are set by the intersection of supply and demand over the entire range of the market, and each participant adapts as best they can. The story is told in Fig. 13.1a–c:

No individual buyer or seller can have any influence over the price at which goods exchange. All they can hope to do is make the best of this situation by choosing the right amounts to purchase or produce. Note that sellers will try to hold down their own costs, but they are buyers in other markets for the goods and services they need to produce. If these markets are perfectly competitive as well, their cost-reduction strategies cannot include lowering the price they have to pay for labor, materials or other inputs. The logic of perfect competition applies to any market with these characteristics, whether the goods being exchanged are in finished form, like consumer items, or whether they are the things businesses purchase in order to make things to sell to consumers.

P. Dorman, *Microeconomics*, Springer Texts in Business and Economics,
DOI 10.1007/978-3-642-37434-0_13, © Springer-Verlag Berlin Heidelberg 2014

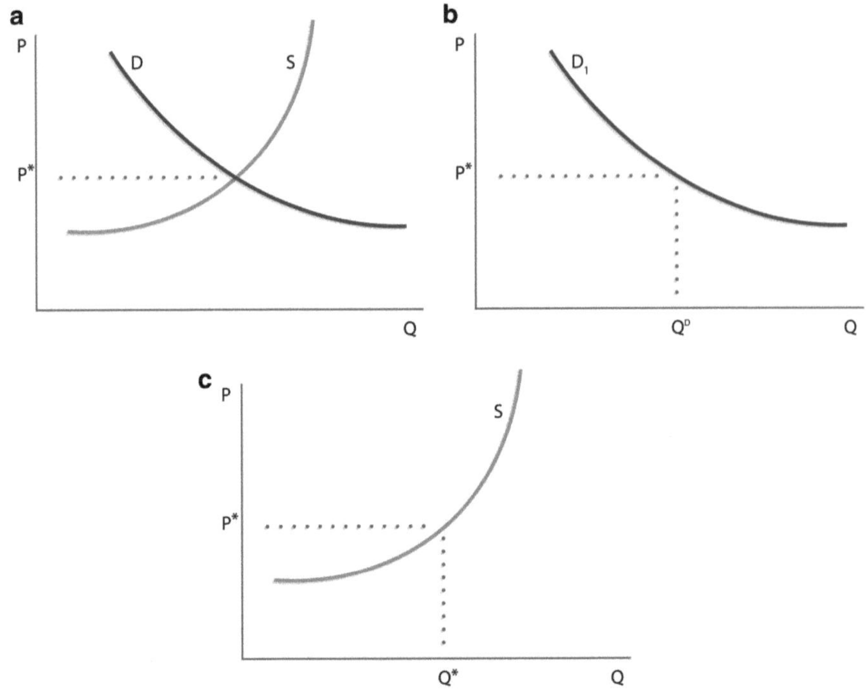

Fig. 13.1 Buyers and sellers are price-takers under perfect competition. (**a**) The equilibrium price P* is set by the equilibrium between market supply S and market demand D. (**b**) The individual buyer takes P* as given and chooses to buy Q^D based on the individual demand curve D_i. (**c**) The individual seller takes P* as given and chooses to offer Q^S based on the individual supply curve S_i

The second feature of perfect competition arises in the long run: there are no economic profits to be made by any producers. Firms can cover their costs, including the cost of capital, but they cannot make more than this. The zero-economic-profit condition is enforced by freedom of entry and exit, a crucial aspect of perfect competition. If extra profits are temporarily available in such a market, new producers will enter or existing producers will expand production. This will shift the market supply curve to the right, lowering the equilibrium price. If prices are too low to cover the opportunity cost of capital, on the other hand, some production capacity will be withdrawn and redirected to other sectors of the economy. This will shift the market supply curve to the left, raising the equilibrium price. In either case, the process will come to a halt only when the rate of profit in this one market is equal to the average throughout the economy; in other words, when price conditions permit firms to recoup the opportunity cost of capital but no more. This is depicted in Fig. 13.2.

Consider for a moment the meaning of a world in which there are no extra profits to be had, in which each producer is equally well off producing for this market or another one, or not at all for that matter. (They could sell off all their equipment and

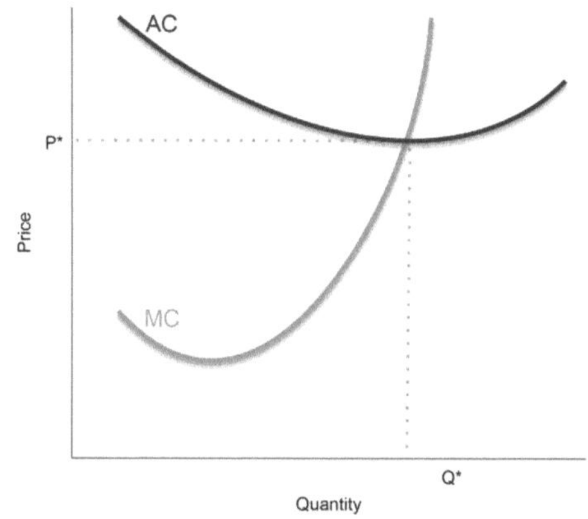

Fig. 13.2 There are no economic profits in the long run under perfect competition. When the long run equilibrium is reached, each producer finds that, when they maximize profits by producing where p = MC (at Q*), the price is just sufficient to cover the average cost of production, including the opportunity cost of capital. There is now no incentive for new firms to enter or existing firms to leave the market

materials and get the same return on their investment by buying government bonds.) What would relationships between such firms look like? They would no doubt compete furiously, since there is no margin of safety separating them from suffering economic losses. (If their average cost curve rises just a hair they are no longer covering their costs at P*.) At the same time, however, they would never be in a position to make any threats against one another, since there is no cost to leaving this market and setting up shop somewhere else. If one company tried to drive a harder bargain with another, the second can always say goodbye with no regrets. Since everyone knows this, no one will ever try, *and therefore relations of power and exploitation will never arise.*

The same analysis can be used for any kind of market in such an economy. If labor markets, for instance, are perfectly competitive, both workers and employers will find themselves in the same situation as zero-economic-profit firms. (We will explore labor markets in greater detail in Chap. 16.) Wages would be just high enough to cover workers' opportunity (and perhaps disutility) costs—no more. If an employer made any attempt to pressure such a worker, such as making her work harder or threatening her with being fired, she would just quit and switch to another job or some other activity whose value is just as great; this is what is meant by saying that wages exactly equal opportunity costs. Similarly, suppose that the benefit employers get is exactly equal to the wages they pay for their workers—how could workers apply any pressure to the companies they work for? If they demanded a raise, employers would just replace them with other, equally profitable applicants.

The general point is this: in a world of perfect competition, no one has the ability to alter the prices or wages they face, and no one has any leverage over anyone else, since no one can be threatened with the loss of some advantage not available in other jobs or markets. This is a world without power in any meaningful sense. To say this, however, is to realize that perfect competition must be a rare exception in the world we actually live in, since power relationships are commonplace. There are powerful companies, powerful economic interests, and sometimes powerful employees, and so there must be advantageous opportunities to be fought over—advantages that are not simply washed away by the tides of competition.

13.2 Barriers to Competition

What prevents competition from being the universal, equalizing force it seemed to be in the previous chapter? Elsewhere we will consider limits to competition in labor markets; here we focus on competition between businesses. Our topic is **barriers to competition**, features of the economy or its legal environment that make it difficult for new businesses to break into markets with above-average profits. Here is a partial list:

1. Legal restrictions. Sometimes the government prevents competition by decree. This was the case in the chartered monopolies of Adam Smith's day. The crown would specify that only a particular corporation would have the right to enter a line of business, such as the East India Company, a private, for-profit enterprise that was actually given the right to rule—and exploit—India after its conquest by England. Putting a company in charge of an entire country would be considered excessive today, but it is still commonplace for competition to be denied in such fields as water, electricity, railroads and other utilities.

   Sometime legal restrictions are indirect: instead of specifying that only one company has the right to do business in a particular market, governments may create conditions that have this effect. The most important example, which we will return to later in this chapter, is patent and copyright law. These permit businesses to gain exclusive control over techniques or commercial identities that may be indispensable to effective competition. A drug patent, for instance, gives a single company the right to produce that drug; any competitor must try to buy the right to copy it, and they can be turned down for any reason or no reason. From the world of copyright, consider the "Mickey Mouse Law". Mickey's copyright was set to expire in 2003, meaning that after that date anyone, and not just his Disney creators, would be able to make a movie or a comic book featuring the legendary rodent. The Disney Corporation lobbied Congress, and the result was a new law that extended control over Mickey's character for an additional 20 years. This means that only Disney will be able to use Mickey in its entertainments, a barrier to competition, given his enduring popularity.
2. Intimidation. In some cases businesses will use illegal methods to suppress competition, including the threat or use of force. This is particularly common in markets that are illegal to begin with, such as those for drugs, gambling and prostitution, but organized crime has sometimes muscled out competition even in such "legit" activities as trash hauling.

3. Economies of scale. As we will see later in this chapter, large economies of scale relative to the size of the market can make competition all but impossible. Even more moderate economies of this sort, however, can make competition difficult. As a practical matter, the size compulsion applies to marketing and finance as much as, or even more than, manufacturing. Big companies can spread advertising costs over a greater volume of sales, and they are often able to diversify risk (Chap. 18) more effectively. When successful participation in the market requires a vast scale of operations, drawing on large investments of money and time, potential competitors may be discouraged. The result is that companies already operating on the necessary scale will have a relatively free hand.
4. Product differentiation. Competition between companies is effective only if buyers believe that their goods are more or less substitutable for one another. To the extent that a producer can convince the public that their product is distinctive, it is released from competitive pressure. Once a restaurant, for instance, establishes a reputation of serving higher quality meals than any of its competitors, it is in a position to raise its prices and take in economic profits. It may not help at all for other establishments to cut their prices in retaliation; on the contrary, consumers might take this as further evidence that they are unable to compete on quality. New entrants into the restaurant market must somehow establish an aura of high quality if they are to take on the dominant players, and this may be difficult to do.

   A particularly important form of product differentiation is **branding.** This is a strategy in which companies try to get consumers to form a positive image of the company name or logo, which is then used to sell an entire line of products. Typically it begins with consumer acceptance of one or more items the company already markets. Perhaps these were truly superior, or perhaps they benefitted from clever marketing in the past; it doesn't matter for brand development. The goal is to have consumers transfer these positive feelings to the overall company identity, so that any additional products it introduces can enjoy a marketing edge. If the strategy is successful, the company insulates itself from a degree of competition, since no one else offers quite the same brand. The most powerful evidence for the ability of brand identity to capture economic profits is the value successful brands capture in the marketplace when established firms (and their brands) are bought out through mergers or acquisitions. (We will look at this process in more detail in Chap. 18.)
5. Scarcity of key inputs. Sometimes the biggest barrier to new competition is simply the inability to acquire the skills or materials needed to market a competitive product. This is especially evident in two sectors of the economy, natural resources and professional services. In the first, it is nature that limits the potential supply; in the second it is the variability of human talent and effort.
   - A vivid example of scarce natural resources is given by premium wine grapes. Many regions have the combination of soils and climate to grow grapes, but few can produce the highest quality varietals that go into the best wine. One such area in the US is the Napa Valley in California, where land prices have gone into the stratosphere: an acre of prime vineyard land now goes for as

much as $300,000. As you might expect, this is a an enormous barrier to competition; few investors can afford the risk involved in entering Napa's wine industry, particularly since the ability to convert this land into cases of highly sought-after wine is far from a sure thing. What if you paid all that money but couldn't quite master the obscure art of winemaking?

- The limited availability of skilled labor is primarily important in services. If there are only three chefs with a background in Italian food in a given city, there can be at most only three (good!) Italian restaurants. The same logic holds for accountants, hydrologists and neurologists. At the international level, there are just a few premier leagues in the major sports (basketball, football/soccer, tennis) because there is a limited number of professional athletes the public is willing to pay to see.

6. Network effects. In recent years economists have begun paying attention to the role played by connections between users in markets for information and communication. Computer users, for instance, often need to exchange files with one another, and this is easier to do if the files were created with the same software. The more users there are of any one software program, then, the more advantageous it is for others to switch over to it as well. The same argument goes for a format in which movies or music can be encoded, although here the edge comes from the interest that content providers (film and music companies) have in making their wares available in the most popular formats. If the formats are proprietary—if they are owned by a single company rather than being in the public domain—this advantage can lead to a virtual monopoly. The same result arises in computer software and is responsible for the near-monopoly position of Microsoft in certain categories.

These, then, are the primary barriers to competition that can result in a few firms having power over the market. When you look at the entire list it becomes obvious that less-than-complete competition is not the exception, but the rule, in modern economies.

13.3 Pure Monopoly

A useful way to approach the problem of incomplete competition is to look at the most extreme case, in which a single firm's sales account for the entire output of the market. Formally, such a firm is called a **pure monopoly**; it is the single seller to which all buyers must come. Though it is extreme, pure monopoly is not uncommon. Such firms can be found in many parts of the economy, sometimes for natural reasons, but often because they are protected by laws and regulations.

Where do we see them? Sometimes at the local level, because the market isn't large enough to support more than one seller of a particular good. This is especially a problem in small towns and rural areas. Wal-Mart, a company we will return to in the next chapter, got its start setting up its large retail outlets in exactly these types of locations. They were the only source within an hour's travel for a wide array of goods, and this gave them an initial advantage. Similarly, sometimes there is only one restaurant open after 9 p.m. or on Sunday morning in a particular region, and diners have no choice if they want to eat out.

Often monopolies are protected by the rules established by government. A **patent monopoly** is an example of this, as we saw above; only one company, the one that holds the patent, has the right to produce and market the product. Governments often assign monopoly rights to utilities, such as power and cable companies, in return for a fee. Public schools increasingly lease food services to private providers, giving them a monopoly over a particular group of students for part of the day.

So with these examples in mind, let's consider the case of a market with just one seller. Our starting point will be the geometry of production costs explored in the previous chapter. Here will take advantage of the simplification suggested in Box 12.1 and assume that, for all relevant levels of output and sales, average and marginal costs are constant and equal to one another. Leaving aside quantities below (declining ATC) and above (increasing ATC) this range, the result is a picture like Fig. 13.3 on the following page.

In Chap. 12 we brought in the demand side (the firm's sales) by assuming that a price was set in the market that no individual producer is able to change. A firm can decide to produce and sell more or less, but it must accept the going price as the one it must charge. This was represented by a demand curve in the form of a horizontal line across the diagram. (This was also the reason that we didn't use the constant-cost simplification above: our parallel lines would never meet.)

How would we portray the demand conditions facing a monopolist—a firm that *is* the market? The simplest answer is this: the demand for their products is the market demand curve itself, which, as we saw in Chap. 11, will generally be downward-sloping. But this in turn means that the price can change—or more precisely, that the price can *be* changed by the profit-hungry monopolist. It is possible to charge more and not fear that a competitor will steal away all the sales. And that, of course, is exactly what most monopolists will do most of the time.

But how much more does it make sense to charge? Let's assume that the monopolist has only one interest, making as much profit as possible, and is unconcerned by any future consequences from consumers, government or potential competitors. To help think this through, we will create a simple numerical example. Suppose that the demand curve is represented by Table 13.1. The units may be measured in the millions (copies of software) or they may actually be ten or under (custom-built furniture). We don't have to worry too much about realism at this point, because the important thing is to understand the logic.

Let's further suppose that the marginal and average cost are constant at \$8. (Recall from the previous chapter why these must be equal when average cost is constant.) It is obvious that the firm could afford to maximize its sales by charging \$8 per unit, but this would result in no profits at all. If profit is truly the goal, the price should be higher.

Raising the price to \$15 is one possibility. It appeals to a certain narrow-minded greed, but it is not very smart, because it leads to such a sharp drop in sales.

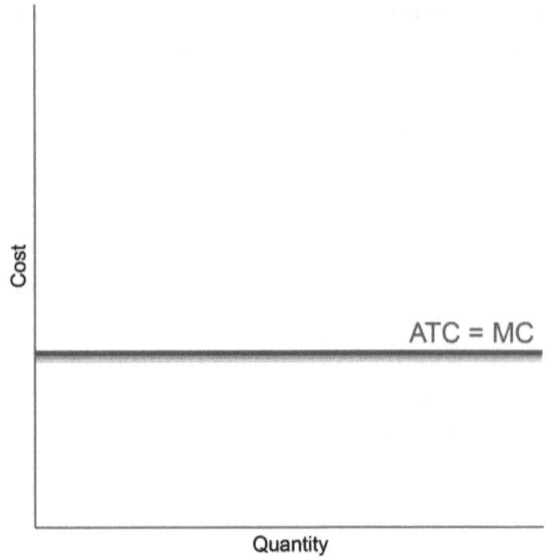

Fig. 13.3 Constant costs of production in the short run. It simplifies the analysis to assume that average and marginal costs are constant at some fixed level. This is unlikely to be true at very low and high levels of Q, but it is often true at intermediate levels relevant to real-world production choices

Table 13.1 Hypothetical demand schedule facing a monopolist

Price	Quantity demanded
15	3
14	4
13	5
12	6
11	7
10	8
9	9
8	10

The profit per unit, $7, is handsome, but only three units are sold, resulting in a total profit of $21. As we will see, it is possible to do better.

Try setting the price at $14 instead: now the profit margin is down to $6, but sales are 4; so total profit is $24. If the price is set at $13, total profit is slightly higher yet at $25. And this turns out to be the best choice, as any lower price will not quite match the profits raked in at $13. (Check to see if this is right.)

We can get to the logic of this process by looking at it algebraically. Consider any two adjacent prices, P_1 and P_2, and the associated levels of demand, Q_1 and Q_2. Total revenue is therefore either P_1*Q_1 or P_2*Q_2. Total cost is either $C*Q_1$ or $C*Q_2$, since average cost C is the same at both quantities. The firm's choice, then is between two levels of profit (Pr):

$$Pr_1 = P_1 * Q_1 - C * Q_1 \text{ or}$$
$$Pr_2 = P_2 * Q_2 - C * Q_2$$

The comparison is

$$Pr_1 - Pr_2 = (P_1 * Q_1 - C * Q_1) - (P_2 * Q_2 - C * Q_2)$$

In each parenthesis on the right-hand side is a revenue term (with P) and a cost term (with C). Grouping them together, we get

$$Pr_1 - Pr_2 = (P_1 * Q_1 - P_2 * Q_2) - (C * Q_1 - C * Q_2)$$

Algebraically, this just says that the first price yields a higher profit than the second if there is an increase in total revenue that exceeds the increase in total costs. But recall that we have shorthand expressions for these two things, **marginal revenue** and **marginal cost**. Marginal revenue is the change in total revenue between one output level and a slightly different one; marginal cost is the corresponding change in total cost. (If Q_1 and Q_2 are exactly one unit apart, marginal cost is simply C.) We can then simply say that

$$Pr_1 > Pr_2 \text{ if } MR > MC, \quad \text{where MR and MC are calculated going from } Q_1 \text{ to } Q_2.$$

This is the rule our profit-seeking monopolist is looking for. Always increase price if the marginal revenue from doing so exceeds the marginal cost of production. Adding MR to Table 13.1 gives us Table 13.2 on the next page.

Since marginal cost is $8, it is profitable to raise the price until somewhere between $12 and $13, where marginal revenue is also $8. Graphically, the procedure is illustrated by Fig. 13.4.

There is a lot going on in this diagram, so let's examine it one element at a time:

- For simplicity, we are assuming that average cost ATC is constant. (The analysis would work just as well if ATC were U-shaped, as in the previous chapter.)
- The demand curve D is the average revenue curve faced by the firm. It displays the amount of output that can be sold at any chosen price level. Since the price will be the same for every unit sold, it is also the average revenue—total revenue divided by the quantity sold.
- Since AR is downward-sloping, MR is below it. This follows the same logic regarding the relationship between an average and a marginal curve as we uncovered in the previous chapter's discussion of average and marginal cost. If an average result is going down, the marginal result is below, "pulling" it down. This relationship is illustrated in Table 13.2.
- Profits will be greatest if the firm produces at the quantity Q* where MR = MC. If it produces less than this amount, the additional revenue it could get will be greater than the additional cost it would take on by expanding production. If it produces more, the additional cost exceeds the additional revenue.
- By producing at Q*, the monopolist is able to raise the price to P* and still sell all its output. This is worth spending an extra moment to consider. The firm could, if it were in a generous mood, charge only C, its cost of production. This would mean that profits would be zero, since there would be no surplus of price over cost. Since we are assuming that the monopolist wants to maximize its profits,

Table 13.2 Calculating marginal revenue for the monopolist's hypothetical demand schedule

Price	Quantity demanded	Marginal revenue
15	3	
14	4	11
13	5	9
12	6	7
11	7	5
10	8	3
9	9	2
8	10	−1

Marginal revenue is calculated in this table by going from a higher price to the one just below it. Thus MR is 11 as the monopolist goes from P = $15 to P = $14.

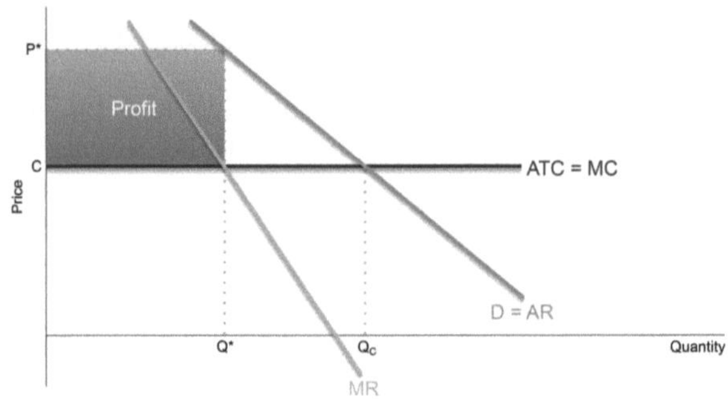

Fig. 13.4 Profit maximization for a hypothetical monopolist. The monopolist achieves the greatest profit by producing a quantity Q at the level where marginal revenue equals marginal cost. At this quantity a price of P* can be charged, yielding a profit per unit of P* − C and total profit (unit profit times quantity) equal to the *shaded area*

however, it makes sense to raise the price to the highest level possible at which Q* units will be purchased. In our numerical example this was $13.

- The profit per unit is (P* − C), the price minus the cost. This is commonly referred to as the firm's **profit margin** on sales. It is represented by the vertical distance between P* and C on the horizontal axis.
- Total profit is calculated by multiplying the profit margin times the number of units sold. This is seen in the shaded area, since the height of the rectangle is (P* − C) and its length is Q*.

Thinking back to the Market Welfare Model, it is clear that monopoly production and pricing, as depicted in Fig. 13.4, poses several problems. First and most important, the price is not equal to the marginal cost. There are people who would purchase the product we are considering if its price were lower than P* but above C. These people put more value on the product than it would cost to produce it, yet nothing is produced for them. This is economically inefficient. A different way to frame this would be to notice that the quantity produced by the monopolist, Q*, is less than the amount that would be produced in a competitive market, where the demand curve D intersects the supply curve—which would then be the marginal cost curve. This higher quantity is labeled Q_C in the diagram.

Second, we can no longer say that the supply curve equals the marginal cost curve because. . . .with a monopoly there is no supply curve! What does this mean? We defined the supply curve in Chap. 5 as the amount suppliers wish to produce and make available to the market at various potential prices. It was based entirely on their costs and was unaffected by shifts in the demand curve. This is the logical basis for the main use to which we put supply and demand analysis: looking at what would happen if one curve shifted while the other remained fixed. But in the current example of a monopoly, there is no supply curve to remain fixed as demand changes; price and production decisions of the monopolist will depend in a complicated way on both the position (to the left or right) and slope (flatness or steepness) of the demand curve. In other words, there is no such thing as supply and demand analysis if the supplier has a monopoly.

Third, there has been a large transfer of wealth from consumers to the monopolist. Recall that we have defined the cost of production C to include the opportunity cost of capital, the rate of return available on alternative investment opportunities. This means that the profit margin represents "super profits" beyond those normally earned. These extra earnings come directly out of consumers, who pay the higher price P* instead of the competitive price C. This transfer contributes to overall economic inequality to the extent that the owners of the monopoly are, as is usually the case, wealthier than its consumers. Whether it is a further source of economic inefficiency is a question we will put off until later in the discussion.

These three problems can be found wherever there is monopoly, but their severity depends on how captive consumers are in the market that has been monopolized. Consider the two possibilities depicted in Fig. 13.5 on the next page.

This demonstrates vividly the crucial role played by the price elasticity of demand, the percent change in quantity demand corresponding to a percent change in the price. In Fig. 13.5a, demand is highly elastic: MR is only slightly below the demand curve, and P* is just a shade above MC.[1] Monopoly has a limited effect. In Fig. 13.5b, on the other hand, demand is inelastic, and the difference between competitive and monopoly outcomes is striking: a big drop in output, a big increase in price, and a wide gap between price and marginal cost.

Now we can see one more reason for developing the elasticity apparatus in Chap. 5. Recall the argument presented there for the underpinnings of elasticity: it depends on the possibilities open to consumers for substitution. Where substitutes are plentiful, demand is elastic and consumers are free to seek alternatives to higher monopoly prices. Where they are scarce, consumers must dance to the monopolist's tune.

[1] To see for yourself the relationship between the slope of the demand curve and the slope of MR, substitute different quantity figures in Table 13.2 and see how they affect your calculation of MR. For instance, instead of letting the quantity sold rise by 1 unit with each $1 reduction in price, let it rise by 2 units, then calculate total revenue and the change in total revenue from one price to the next. Graph the old and new pair of AR and MR curves.

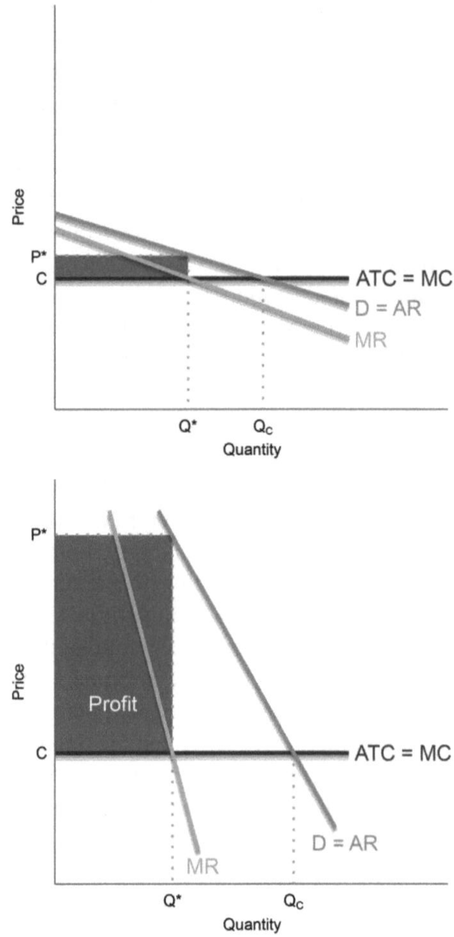

Fig. 13.5 The effect of price elasticity of demand on the extent of monopoly distortion. (a) demand is price elastic, which minimizes the difference between competitive and monopoly production ($Q_C - Q^*$) and the amount of extra profits in the *shaded area*. (**b**) demand is price inelastic; so the reduction in output and the transfer of income from consumer to monopolist is greater

Consider two examples. First, should consumers fear a monopoly in red onions? Probably not. If the supplier raises prices by a significant amount, buyers can switch to onions of a different color—yellow or white. The diagram representing this situation would look like Fig. 13.5a, where monopoly is a modest inconvenience. But now consider the problem posed by a monopoly in water supplies. The privatization of water utilities, selling public water systems to private companies, is highly controversial, above all because many consumers use water primarily for essential purposes like drinking and hygiene. If a private supplier gains a monopoly, there may be little alternative to paying whatever price is charged. (Such systems are usually regulated, but regulation may not be enough protection.) Thus, where water plays a subsistence role demand may well take the form of Fig. 13.5b, and monopoly is a serious concern. (The situation may be different where water is used in a discretionary manner, such as landscaping. There the alternative to high prices may be switching to more drought-tolerant plant species.)

13.4 Between Pure Monopoly and Perfect Competition

Few real-world markets are either completely competitive or completely monopolistic. Usually there is some rivalry between producers seeking the consumer's loyalty, but not to the extent that producers have no leeway at all over prices. Thus we are in an intermediate situation, with some of the characteristics of competition and some of monopoly. How far markets veer in one direction or another depends on many factors, which will look at in a moment. First, however, we should try to clarify what we might mean by "in between monopoly and competition".

Up to this point we have sketched the competitive and monopolistic worlds as extreme cases. In competition firms have no control at all over the price they charge; it is dictated to them by the market. The market supply curve, which is the sum of all the individual supply curves, represents the marginal cost at each level of production, and prices equal this cost in equilibrium. Firms tend to receive an average rate of profit, just covering their opportunity cost of capital. Those that are less profitable eventually shut down; those that are more profitable attract new competition. In either case, prices in the long run will adjust to guarantee that profits revert to the average. In such a world the consumer is king; firms knock themselves out to meet demand in the most cost-efficient way.

Monopoly is a reverse-image of this situation. The monopolist can raise the price to whatever level promises the greatest profit; supply is determined by calculating how much consumers can be squeezed. Price is above marginal cost, often by a large margin. There are severe barriers to competition, so even in the long run consumers get no relief. Here the supplier is king, dictating terms to buyers and reaping the rewards.

What would it mean to speak of an intermediate situation between these two extremes? Economists have developed a variety of models to answer this question. If you continue to more advanced courses you will have a chance to study them; here it is enough just to say that the key results can be placed along a spectrum that stretches from very competitive to very monopolistic. In more competitive situations there is less monopoly distortion in most respects; in more monopolistic situations the distortion approaches the form it takes in pure monopoly. In this sense the "degree of monopoly" functions somewhat like the price elasticity of demand in Fig. 13.5: it determines how significant the departure from competitive pricing and production is likely to be. Two practical ways to measure this departure using real-world information are the average spread between price and marginal cost and extent of above-average rates of profit.

Limitations to monopoly can be either actual or potential. The most important actual limitation, of course, is the presence of other firms. As soon as the monopolist has less than 100 % of the market we have to take into account the role that other firms may play in introducing a competitive dynamic. A market with more than one producer but less than many is called an **oligopoly**; here a few firms, and not just one, sell to consumers. A market with even just two firms could be intensely competitive if each one fought for as much market share as possible by cutting prices down to marginal costs. By the same token, a group of firms can suppress competition by forming a **cartel**, an arrangement to jointly control prices and quantities. Cartels are illegal in many instances, but this doesn't prevent them from emerging. If a market is fully controlled by a cartel, it functions exactly as if it were purely monopolistic.

There are many factors that affect how competitively an oligopolistic market will tend to function. Some of the most important are:

- The degree of concentration. The greater the percentage of sales in a market that is concentrated in just a few producers, the more concentrated it is. One common measure is the four-firm concentration ratio, the percentage of the market that is accounted for by the four largest sellers. Generally speaking, the less concentrated a market is, the more competitive it is.
- The presence of a dominant firm. If one firm towers above the rest in a particular market, it is often in a position to maneuver the others into a less competitive orientation. The smaller sellers may fear the dominant player, or they may look up to it for leadership in setting prices.
- Conditions favoring collusion. Whether oligopolistic firms will choose to compete with one another or collude to control the market depends on the incentives they face and the conditions that make it easier or harder to act in concert. Inelastic consumer demand makes collusion more attractive, but aggressive surveillance by public regulators can be a strong disincentive. Barriers to entry and networks connecting the owners or managers of the firms can facilitate collusion. Adam Smith feared such relationships, saying, "People of the same trade seldom meet together, even for merriment and diversion, but the conversation ends in a conspiracy against the public, or in some contrivance to raise prices." (*The Wealth of Nations*)

Even pure monopolists, however, face limits to their ability to raise prices, even in the absence of competitors nipping at their market share; there is always the specter of *potential* competition. A firm that tries to take full advantage of inelastic demand, as in Fig. 13.5b, runs the risk that its riches will attract new competitors who will dissipate the advantages of monopoly. In practice, firms with overwhelming dominance usually choose to raise their prices less than immediate profit maximization would require.

Box 13.1: A Cruising Altitude for Airline Prices

Most collusion occurs behind closed doors, and we get only the most general account of it, if any. But one attempt at fixing prices was caught on tape, when Howard Putnam of Braniff Ailines secretly recorded a phone call he received from American Airlines CEO Robert Crandall on February 21, 1982. The transcript, cleaned up to meet refined textbook standards, went like this:

Crandall: I think it's dumb as hell for Christ's sake, all right, to sit here and pound the <bleep> out of each other and neither one of use making a <bleep>ing dime.

(continued)

Box 13.1 (continued)
Putnam: Well...
Crandall: I mean, you know, goddam, what the hell is the point of it?
Putnam: But if you're going to overlay every route of American's on top of every route that Braniff has— I just can't sit here and allow you to bury us without giving our best effort. (Pause.) Do you have a suggestion for me?
Crandall: Yes, I have a suggestion for you. Raise your goddam fares 20 %. I'll raise mine the next morning.
Putnam: Robert, we...
Crandall: You'll make more money and I will, too.
Putnam: We can't talk about pricing!
Crandall: Oh <bleep>, Howard. We can talk about any goddam thing we want to talk about.

Although Crandall's own words appeared to convict him of the federal crime of attempted price-fixing, he was able to get off because secretly taping a phone call is also illegal! The evidence could not be introduced into a court of law.

13.5 Is Concentration a Problem?

It depends! First of all, it depends on *why* concentration has come about. Adam Smith, as we saw, feared collusion; he thought that business owners might try to band together to limit competition. Karl Marx, writing 80 years later, expected big firms to swallow up their smaller competitors until there were just a few behemoths left in the marketplace. Neither prospect is particularly appealing, since in either case it would be the potential for monopoly pricing power that would guide business decisions.

A different perspective was suggested by Joseph Schumpeter, the Austrian economist we encountered earlier. He felt that monopoly, as a temporary state of affairs, was normal—the product of all-out business competition. A firm that successfully innovated—that discovered a new way to make or market its products—would destroy its competitors. This would give it the opportunity to enjoy monopoly profits, at least until the next round of innovation reshuffled the deck. Such profits were the *reward* for risk-taking and creativity, and it would be a mistake to try to limit them. As long as the game remained open for new players, so that monopoly was not protected by law or other means unrelated to meeting consumer demand, high profits perform a useful social role.

So how would we know who is right, critics of monopoly (like Smith and Marx) or its defenders (like Schumpeter)? When is monopoly a temporary prize earned for achievements in efficiency and innovation, and when is it a form of exploitation visited by the powerful against the weak or vulnerable?

In practice, economists have developed a number of tests to determine whether monopoly (or high levels of concentration) are against the public interest. The first is simply the history of the market itself: the sequence of events by which concentration came about. In particular, did monopolistic firms acquire their large market share through **anti-competitive behavior**? Did they owe their success not to their own higher level of performance, but to actions that interfered with the performance of competitors? An example would be exclusionary contracts, deals with suppliers or distributors that rule out business with other firms. The software giant Microsoft, for instance, was accused by the government of forcing computer manufacturers that wanted to install its Windows operating system to agree to not install any software by competitors. The point was that such a requirement enhances Microsoft's monopoly not because it has become a more effective producer of software, but because it has limited the business opportunities of competing producers.

Sometimes, however, it is clear that large market share is simply the result of consumer preferences. Coca-Cola, for instance, built its empire on the basis of a soft drink it created in the early twentieth century. It has kept its formula secret, and many consumers seem to prefer its flavor to that of the competition. Thus there is no reason to assume that, at least in the case of its flagship product, the Coca-Cola company has acted anti-competitively. This logic does not automatically extend, of course, to other products (such as bottled water) in which this company might also have a high market share.

Related to the question of possible anti-competitive activity is the scope for consumer choice. Do consumers have a wide array of alternatives available to them, or are they held captive by monopoly restrictions on choice? Variety is a good thing in itself (usually), and one of the potential drawbacks of monopoly is the possibility that consumers will be forced to settle for what is offered rather than what they want. The value of choice in itself was an important issue in the European and American court cases involving Microsoft and later Google.

Finally, does a high degree of concentration lead to less innovation or more? Do firms with a large market share become conservative, more concerned with protecting their existing assets than creating new ones? Or do they tend to spend more on investment and take more risks, drawing on the extra freedom of action that money and market share provide? The answer depends on the firm, its market and the strategy it adopts, and the study of these factors is of great interest to economists.

13.6 Natural Monopoly

One particular barrier to competition is so important that it deserves a discussion of its own, **natural monopoly**. This arises whenever economies of scale are so great compared to the size of the market that there is room for only one low-cost producer. Recall from the previous chapter the portrayal of average costs in the long run: it generally takes the form of a curve that initially slopes downward and

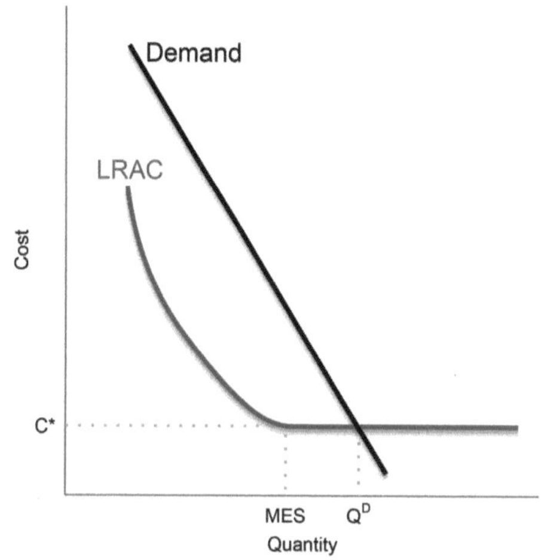

Fig. 13.6 Natural monopoly. If the size of the market, the quantity demanded at the lowest feasible price (Q^D) is less than twice the minimum efficient scale (where the average cost of production equals C*), there isn't enough room for two producers to compete at an efficient level of production

then levels off after **minimum efficient scale** (MES) has been reached. The downward-sloping part reflects **economies of scale**, but after MES there are no more such economies to be had, and average cost is unaffected by further increases in the level of output.

Figure 13.6 reproduces such a long run average cost curve, and adds to it an expected demand curve which predicts how much will be purchased at various potential prices. The lowest possible average cost is C*. The intersection between the long run average cost curve and the demand curve is given by Q*, which is the size of the market if a price equal to the minimum possible average cost is charged. (Recall once more that this cost includes the opportunity cost of capital.) The other critical quantity level is given by Q_{MES}, the level of output needed to achieve the lowest average cost. Natural monopoly is said to arise if $Q_{MES} > ½\, Q^*$.

What does this mean exactly? To compete on equal terms, a firm must have an average cost of production no greater than C*. This means it must produce at least Q_{MES}. For there to be more than one such firm able to sell all it produces, Q* must be at least twice Q_{MES}. Under a condition of natural monopoly, however, this is not the case; the market is big enough to accommodate only one lowest-cost producer.

Now we can see why such a monopoly is considered "natural": it is the result of technological and consumer demand factors and not the actions of government or the strategies of the firms themselves. If costs are to be kept low and consumers satisfied, there is no avoiding it.

The advantage of this analysis is that it gives us specific questions to ask if we want to know whether it makes sense to try to prevent a particular market from being monopolized. It comes down to the relationship between technology (economies of scale) and consumer demand (size of the market). These may be difficult to measure precisely, but it is not difficult to classify most cases one way or the other. For instance, the theory of natural monopoly was originally developed in the context of electrical utilities. (One private producer of electricity in particular helped subsidize the research on which the theory was based.) At that time, in the early twentieth century, it is quite possible that there was space for only one efficient electricity provider in most markets. (With only local transmission networks, these markets were small, and economies of scale were substantial.) On the other hand, one study has found that economies of scale in the retail grocery industry requires no more than four stores, so (if this is true) any region with enough demand to support at least eight has the potential for competition.

Reflecting on the underlying factors behind Fig. 13.6 makes it clear that natural monopoly should be a diminishing aspect of the world economy. We have already seen in the previous chapter that there are technological reasons, especially computerization, for suspecting that economies of scale are capable of being realized at lower levels of production. At the same time, globalization is increasingly fashioning the world into a single integrated marketplace. Thus, for most products, the size of the market is expanding while MES is drifting downward. For this reason, more than any other, most economists believe that the force of competition is greater now than in the past, and that this trend will continue into the future.

13.7 Competition Policy

Because monopolistic practices can sometimes have a harmful effect on an economy, governments have developed policies for monitoring market conditions and sometimes intervening to prevent the exercise of pricing power. Collectively these measures are known as **competition policy**; they constitute one of the most important roles played by governments in a market economy.

The first element of any such policy is surveillance: there must be a regular flow of information to alert authorities to the possibility that competition is endangered. For this reason, most developed countries have reporting requirements: firms must file documents indicating what markets they operate in, the value of their purchases and sales, etc. In particular, when companies consider merging with or acquiring their competitors they must submit a detailed proposal with enough information for regulators to evaluate the potential effect on competition.

Logically, a second element is the right of authorities to deny permission for mergers and acquisitions. Here regulators must balance the potential positive aspects of consolidation, such as economies of scale, against the negative potential for undesirable pricing power. Since the scope of such companies is often international, permission may be required from multiple regulatory agencies; most often, this means the United States and the European Union.

The third element is legal action to limit monopoly power after it has been established. All modern nations (and the multinational entity that is the EU) have laws prohibiting anti-competitive behavior. If a company is found to have violated such a law, either by unfairly inhibiting competitors or by engaging in practices harmful to consumers or other sectors of the economy, remedies can be sought. The most dramatic is breaking up the monopolist into smaller competing firms, as happened in the landmark case brought against John D. Rockefeller's Standard Oil monopoly in the United States. The dispute went to the Supreme Court, which ruled in 1911 that the company had to divest itself of some of its holdings and then split into 34 separate entities, each with an independent board of directors. A lower court order in 2000 similarly required Microsoft to separate into two competing companies (one for operating systems like Windows, the other for other types of software), but that ruling was overturned on appeal.

Short of breaking up the monopolist, regulators can demand that specific policies be implemented to reduce the threat to competition. In the case of Microsoft, for instance, the company was made to agree that it would discontinue the practice under which it charged computer manufacturers a lump-sum price no matter how many copies of Windows were installed on their machines. Instead, Windows would be made available on a per-copy basis. This made it possible for producers of alternative operating systems to compete, since the cost of an additional copy (the marginal cost) of Windows was no longer zero. By taking actions such as this, regulators are reconciling themselves to the dominant market position of a single firm, but trying to limit the potential negative impact.

Related to this is action against collusion by oligopolists seeking combined monopoly power. (We saw a case of attempted collusion in the Braniff–United Airline conversation above.) Setting up a cartel, for instance by setting quotas limiting how much each company can sell or by agreeing not to charge less than a certain price, is price-fixing, and it is against the law everywhere. Violators, if convicted, can be fined up to and beyond the extent of their illicit earnings, and other measures can be taken to prevent them from colluding again in the future.

Sometimes governments intervene proactively to set up a regulatory framework intended to maintain the advantages of monopoly while limiting its disadvantages. This is particularly common in the context of natural monopoly, as seen in such services as telecommunications and energy transmission. Thus, a monopoly will be granted to a private company, but its pricing, investment and other activities will be monitored by a special board empowered to overrule practices that take excessive advantage of this situation. For instance, an electrical company may have to petition for every rate increase, where it has the burden of demonstrating that the higher price is justified by higher costs. This type of arrangement is known as a **regulated monopoly**.

Finally, the government may decide that, if monopoly is unavoidable, it should be the one to occupy that position. Thus, many services thought to have characteristics of a natural monopoly, like local water and power systems, are owned by units of government. The expectation is that, operating without private investors, managers of public enterprises will be less tempted to raise prices or restrict output. Of course, a substitute must then be found for the positive effect of the profit motive—the incentive to cut costs or provide more highly valued services.

Competition policy is a fine art. No matter how carefully the laws are crafted, implementing them requires plenty of analysis and judgment. Is the monopoly of the natural variety, and therefore unavoidable? Was it the result of anti-competitive behavior or just competitive success? Do its potential advantages for the public outweigh the disadvantages? In the end each case must be decided on its own merits. Unfortunately, large sums of money are often at stake on all sides, and the risk of policy being determined by private rather than public interests is ever-present.

The Main Points

1. In a perfectly competitive market neither buyers nor sellers can individually alter the equilibrium price, and no economic profits are earned either. Thus, no one has the ability to alter the prices or wages they face, and no one has any leverage over anyone else, since no one can be threatened with the loss of some advantage not available in other jobs or markets. This is a world without power in any meaningful sense. To say this, however, is to realize that perfect competition must be a rare exception in the world we actually live in, since power relationships are commonplace.
2. Monopolistic conditions are the result of barriers to competition. These can take many forms, such as legal restrictions, intimidation, economies of scale, product differentiation, the scarcity of key inputs and network effects.
3. The impact of barriers to competition can be seen most clearly in the analysis of pure monopoly, where a single seller commands the entire market. The profit-maximizing monopolist will withhold supply to the level at which the marginal cost of production is equal to the marginal revenue from sales, taking into account the higher prices that can be extracted from consumers as supply is reduced. The monopolist will charge the highest price at which this quantity can be sold. This is advantageous for the firm in a position to do this, but it has several negative effects: it restricts output below the efficient level, it forces consumers to pay a higher price than they would otherwise, it reduces consumer surplus and correspondingly increases profits, and it interferes with the role that prices should play in conveying information about production costs.
4. The extent of monopoly output restriction and price increase depends on the consumers' price elasticity of demand: the distortion is greater the more inelastic this demand. The elasticity of demand depends on the opportunities for substitution available to consumers: how easily can they switch to different products when a monopolist raises the price of one particular product?
5. Most markets lie between the extremes of perfect competition and pure monopoly. They will have some characteristics of each. Factors which lead them to resemble monopoly include high levels of concentration, the presence of a dominant firm, the likelihood of collusion, and the height of entry barriers. In practice, economists look at the extent of anti-competitive behavior on the part of firms and the degree to which prices depart from marginal costs to assess the damage caused by monopolistic conditions.
6. Sometimes we face a natural monopoly; this occurs when the most of efficient scale of production is more than half the size of the market. This means that there isn't room for more than one efficient (low-cost) firm. Such monopolies may need to be regulated rather than prevented.
7. All modern economies engage in competition policy—government interventions to limit the costs monopolistic conditions and behavior impose on society.

They may try to limit the size of firms, control their anti-competitive practices, reduce entry barriers, or create public enterprises to compete with or supplant private monopolies.

▶ Terms to Define

Anti-competitive behavior
Barriers to competition
Branding
Cartel
Competition policy
Natural monopoly
Oligopoly
Patent monopoly
Profit margin
Pure monopoly
Regulated monopoly

Questions to Consider

1. Can you think of any portions of the economy in which competition is near-complete and power does not exist? Are all the participants able to go somewhere else and get the same economic return? Does anyone have leverage over anyone else?
2. What barriers to competition exist in the film industry? In what ways does it perform more like a monopoly? More like a competitive industry?
3. Pick an industry you are familiar with and discuss which barriers to competition, if any, apply. What are the consequences for where the industry stands on the monopoly–competition spectrum?
4. In general, do you think that the elasticity of demand is the same for most movies shown by a local movie theater? Why or why not? If not, why do theaters charge the same prices for all movies at a given time? Does your answer support or contradict the theory of monopoly (or monopolistic) pricing presented in this chapter?
5. One of the most celebrated anti-monopoly cases in recent years has involved Microsoft, which had to defend itself in US, European and other courts. Microsoft's computer operating system Windows still commands a near-monopoly share of the global market for personal computers. Based on the theory in this chapter, how serious a problem does this pose for the public? On what arguments do you base your conclusion?
6. Can you think of an example of a natural monopoly? Is it regulated? Is it a problem?

14 The Economics of Bargaining Power

In Chap. 5 we visited the troubled world of coffee, where growers suffered from declining incomes and the economies of whole countries were at risk. We saw that prices fell after a supply management system was ended in 1989, and that subsequent increases in production capacity, combined with inelastic demand, caused the bottom to fall out of the market. This gave us an example of the power of supply and demand analysis to explain important developments in economic and social life.

But there is more to the story than this. Look at Fig. 14.1 on the next page, which shows the percentage of the coffee dollar going to each of four groups:

- the growers in coffee countries who actually produce the coffee beans
- other groups, particularly government agencies, in the coffee-producing countries
- exporters and shippers, in the form of fees, transportation costs and shrinkage
- companies in the coffee-consuming countries, especially the well-known coffee importing and retailing corporations

Several facts stand out. First, growers get a small share of the money generated in the coffee industry. It was never much above 20 %, and it has fallen much lower at times. It would be fair to say that the desperation among these coffee farmers in the first years of the new century was a product of both the declining price of the bean *and* their declining share of that price. The bulk of the proceeds, on the other hand, go to a small number of multinational coffee corporations, who account for most of the blue area in the graph. Shipping costs, which include the reduction in the measured quantity of coffee as the beans "settle" in transit, has been a constant factor over the years. The biggest reduction has been experienced by the governments in the coffee-growing countries. During the heyday of the Coffee Agreement, they levied export taxes to support marketing boards, technical services and other programs for the coffee industry. (Some of this money was no doubt siphoned off by well-placed officials, although this varied according to how well-governed the country was.) With the advent of a competitive free-for-all in coffee production, the ability of governments to dip into the revenue stream has been sharply limited, since high taxes would price their growers' goods out of the market.

P. Dorman, *Microeconomics*, Springer Texts in Business and Economics,
DOI 10.1007/978-3-642-37434-0_14, © Springer-Verlag Berlin Heidelberg 2014

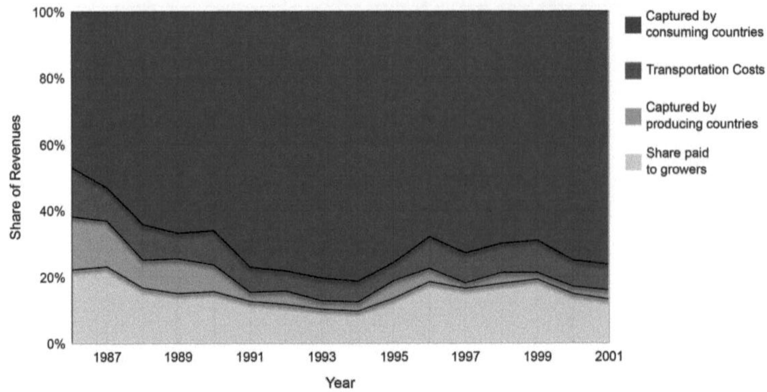

Fig. 14.1 The division of coffee revenues among major players. The share of coffee revenues, adding up to 100 %, taken at each of four stages: coffee growers, governments of coffee-producing countries, shipping and roasting/wholesaling/retailing in the consuming countries

Figure 14.1 clearly shows that it would be naive to try to help farmers just by raising prices on the retail end. If the shares remain unchanged, little of this extra money would make its way to the growers themselves. One response by some consumers in Europe and the United States has been to purchase "Fair Trade" coffee. This is coffee which has been purchased directly from growers (usually organized cooperatively) at a price premium by certified Fair Trade companies. Because the price is higher *and* the growers get a larger share, this is a beneficial arrangement for them. On the other hand, the demand for this more expensive coffee has not been able to keep pace with the number of growers who would like to supply it. The system depends on consumers being willing to pay more for their cup out of solidarity with distant farmers, but most still search out the lowest prices. Unfortunately, some growers who would otherwise switch to other crops have tried to stay with coffee, hoping to break into the Fair Trade market, and this may have kept supply a little higher than it would have been otherwise. (Go back to the analysis in Chap. 5 to see what effect this may have on the coffee market.) The result is that, while the Fair Trade system has helped some farmers, many more are still on the brink.

What can economics offer in this situation? It can provide tools to help analyze *why* the coffee dollar is divided the way it is—what underlying forces are responsible for a world in which those who grow the coffee receive perhaps a fourth of the revenue captured by the companies that market it to consumers. Our approach will be to examine the nature of **bargaining power** in economic life.

Box 14.1: Five Kinds of Power

People often use the term "power" loosely, but those who have studied it have generally come to the conclusion that there are several different kinds of

(continued)

Box 14.1 (continued)
power, and that the distinctions between them are important. In this book we have already introduced two such categories, market power and bargaining power. What is meant by power in general, and what other kinds of power are there?

These questions will not find a consensus answer among social scientists and philosophers. What is offered here is one possible mainstream approach, not too far from what most students of this subject would say.

In general, power is the ability to get someone else to do something you want them to do, which they wouldn't do otherwise. Thus the concept of power is inseparable from that of interest—what people want. It is only because there are conflicts of interest that power is a meaningful notion. If everyone's interest were always in harmony with everyone else's, no one would have any use for power over others.

We can identify at least five forms that power can take:

1. Power to withhold. This is what monopoly power, the topic of the previous chapter, is all about. If I have something you want or need, and there is no one else you can get it from, you are in my power. By withholding, or threatening to withhold, this good I can compel you to do what I want. As we saw, there are two dimensions to this power, the degree of monopoly (how much do you depend on me alone?) and the elasticity of demand (how inflexible is your need for what I have?). What the monopolist compels the consumer to do is pay a higher price than would otherwise be set in a competitive market.
2. Bargaining power. This is the subject of the current chapter, so it is not a good idea to give away all the key points just yet. But we can say this: bargaining power is a function of the degree to which the parties need an agreement; the party with the least need has the most power.
3. Coercive power. This was discussed in the appendix to Chap. 6. Coercion arises when one side is in a position to make threats against the other, and the threatened side is unable to escape the interaction.
4. Institutional power. The societies we all live in are organized through institutions, such as governments, corporations and other well-established structures. The educational institution you are (probably) ensconced in is a good example: it has decision-making hierarchies, and it puts teachers in a position of authority over students. (They give grades and assign credit.) In normal times these institutions are largely beyond challenge; we must live within their rules whether or not we like them. These rules give power to some over others. Teachers, for instance, have the power to make students do assignments they might not choose to do if there were no inequalities of power at work.
5. Cultural power. The deepest source of power is located in the systems of thought and language that govern how we view the world. To be able to

(continued)

Box 14.1 (continued)

persuade others to do what you want, especially if they are unaware that this is taking place, is the ideal solution. This is the power of propagandists and advertisers, but even more it is a power that permeates a culture, often behind the backs of both those who are manipulated and those who benefit from it. Indeed, sometimes the resort to more visible forms of power, such as coercion, is an indication that cultural structures are no longer doing their job. Teachers, for instance, often have a fair amount of cultural power that comes from the prestige of their position and the expectations that society has built up around their role in the educational process. Students may be following their lead without even being aware of it. If teachers use this influence to advance their own interests (psychological, economic, political or otherwise), the outcome is an exercise of power.

14.1 Where Does Bargaining Power Appear?

When we introduced the supply and demand apparatus in Chap. 5, we were careful to note that it depends on a large number of assumptions—simplifications that might be good enough in some situations but would probably never be entirely correct. Now we are in a position to see what will happen when some of them are changed.

Perhaps the most important of them was the assumption of anonymity. In the supply and demand world, nobody knows who anyone else is. Each buyer and seller confronts a faceless market, where there is nothing to be done but to accept or reject the going price. In the real world, however, participants in the economy often know the identities of the people they are dealing with. In that case, they do not have to take an offer as given; they can *negotiate*.

This type of recognition can arise when markets are "thin": when there are relatively few buyers or sellers, as in a small town with just a few auto repair shops and perhaps a few hundred cars. Specialty markets often have this characteristic too. Often there are just a few suppliers of a highly specialized input into a finished product, like certain types of computer chips or high-performance industrial ceramics. The companies on both ends of these supply relationships are likely to be aware of one another.

A second crucial assumption of the standard supply and demand approach is that each transaction is a one-time-only affair. Prices are quoted, an exchange takes place, and that's the end of the story. There is no sequel, at least none that any parties to the transaction need to take into consideration when they decide what to buy or sell today. In the real world, however, many economic relationships occur over and over, and this leads to knowledge of who's who in the business, and also to more strategic attitudes about what offers to make or accept.

As in most aspects of life that repeat themselves (and this includes political life, spiritual life, romance, etc.), structures emerge. Rather than reinvent the wheel every day, people fall into routines which may be informal or may take the form of organizations with explicit rules and expectations. So we have internet dating systems, churches and other religious institutions, political parties, and so on. In the realm of the economy we have relatively stable networks that make it easier for people to take care of their ongoing needs. These include business associations, labor unions and **supply chains**. This last is somewhat unfamiliar but important: it is the name given to the linkages that connect businesses engaged in different stages in the production of some good or service. A contractor overseeing the building of a house might need the services of an electrician or a mason, and all of them may be working under a builder or real estate developer. This describes a supply chain in the construction sector. Making a computer requires purchasing a large number of components, such as motherboards and computer screens, and the final product may then be delivered to a retailer who markets it to the ultimate consumer. This too is a supply chain.

The general point is this: wherever economic actors have repeated relationships with one another, formal or informal institutions are likely to arise. The economy can be viewed as crisscrossed by supply chains and other structures that break down the abstract, anonymous universe of supply and demand. When this happens, the result is likely to be bargaining, where each side tries to reach an agreement that satisfies not only its current needs, but also strengthens its ability to safeguard its future interests.

To investigate economic transactions between parties who know who each other are and who are thinking strategically, and not just reacting to current conditions, we obviously need a different type of model. Ideally, it would tell us how economic outcomes reflect what each side brings to the table, and it would give us a language to analyze strategic decision-making. What we are looking for can be found, in an imperfect but still evolving form, in game theory—in the branch of game theory that studies the bargaining process. We will begin with an extremely simple version of such a model and then consider how it could be elaborated to make it more applicable to real-world questions.

14.2 An Elementary Model of Bargaining

Just as we did with supply and demand, we will make several assumptions that, despite their unreality, serve to isolate an important aspect of the economy, as a starting point for more complex applications. In this case we will begin with two individuals who can either come to an agreement with one another or else go their separate ways. Agreeing results in the creation of something of economic value which is divided up between the two bargainers in the agreed-upon way. In the event of disagreement they each have another outside option to fall back on. These options also can be measured in economic terms and compared to the returns each side would get from a particular agreement. Finally, as is often the case when simple economic models are being constructed, we assume that they each have only one interest, acquiring as much benefit for themselves as possible. (All of these assumptions will be lifted shortly.)

In addition, in order to make the model as simple as possible, we temporarily make one further assumption: the effect of the agreement, if they can reach it, is to divide a fixed sum of money. This sometimes occurs in the real world—for example, in bargaining over wages or prices. A simple case occurs when one person offers to sell a possession like a used car, and another person offers to buy. Any additional money paid by the buyer is received by the seller. Economists call such a situation a **zero-sum game**, since the gains and losses from bargaining exactly cancel each other out. For now, let's assume that this is the case.

We can see this in Fig. 14.2 on the following page, which identifies the two bargainers as A and B. Let's call them Abe and Bev. The line going from the upper left of the diagram to the lower right is an **agreement curve**; it indicates the benefits for both Abe and Bev of each possible agreement. Since a fixed sum of money is at stake, the line has a slope of -1: any vertical change (for Abe) results in the exact opposite horizontal change (for Bev).

Identifying the disagreement option—the possibility that results from not agreeing—sheds further light on the situation. In Fig. 14.2 this is represented by the point D. By not agreeing, Abe would be settling for the benefit D_A; similarly, Bev would be settling for D_B. Immediately we can see that this rules out at least some of the potential bargaining outcomes. Abe would never willingly agree to any bargain to the southeast of S_2, since that would result in even less utility than opting out of any agreement at all. By the same token, Bev would not accept a deal to the northwest of S_1. Thus, only these two points and the line segment between them constitute a potential zone of agreement.

So far, so good—but what would determine where in this zone the two bargainers would end up? There is no conclusive way to answer this question, but the famed mathematician/economist John Nash proposed one solution that has been influential ever since. Nash enumerated a set of restrictions on what ought to constitute a solution and then proved that there would be a single outcome that could meet all of them simultaneously. For our purposes, one important restriction is that the solution be symmetrical, in the sense that the identities of the bargainers shouldn't matter; any two individuals placed in the role of Abe or Bev, with the same disagreement options, should arrive at the same results. When you think about it, this could be controversial, since one side might have many social or personal advantages, such as prestige or skill, compared to the other; we will show later how Nash acknowledged this possibility.

Without going into the full proof, it is enough for now to say that Nash's solution turns out to be simple and elegant: it is the point on the agreement curve which maximizes the product of each side's net benefit. What does this mean? The net benefit is the value of an agreement over and above the value of disagreeing; the product is what results from multiplying one net benefit by the other. This may still sound mysterious, but in our simple zero-sum case it has an obvious implication: the parties will agree to split the difference. Figure 14.3 tells the story.

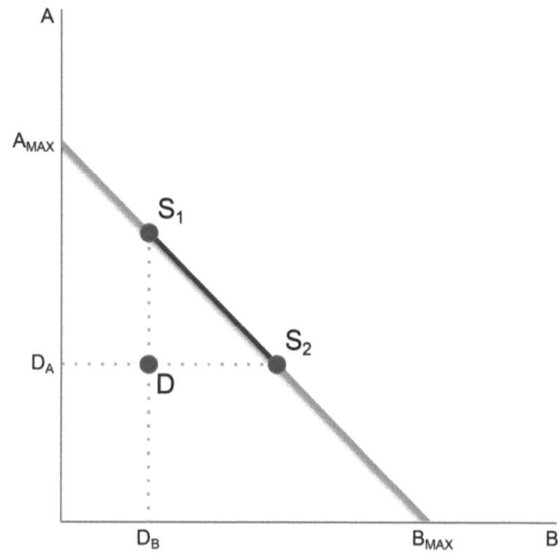

Fig. 14.2 Negotiating possibilities with default options in a zero-sum bargaining game. A and B can agree to create an economic value and divide it up. If A gets the entire benefit he receives A_{MAX}; if B gets it all she gets B_{MAX}. If they fail to agree they fall back on the disagreement option D, leaving D_A for A and D_B for B. A would not accept any offer worse for him than S_2 while B would not accept any worse for her than S_1

Consider any possible solution point S. Abe's net benefit is given by the vertical distance from D_A to height of S, and Bev's by the distance from D_B to the horizontal value of S. These two form the length and width of a rectangle whose area is the product of the net benefits. It should be clear that the sum of these two net benefits must be equal, since if, for example, S slides down to the right in Bev's direction, any increase in Bev's net benefit is exactly offset by a decrease in Abe's. So what S gives us the rectangle with the largest area? We know from elementary geometry that this has to be a square, with equal length and width. In other words, the agreement that satisfy's Nash's criteria is S*, halfway between S_1 and S_2.

This seems to be a wonderful outcome, as fair as anyone could want. Indeed, it harkens back to an ancient debate in economics over the meaning of a **just price**. Back in the European Middle Ages, philosophers and theologians argued over how prices ought to be set in negotiations: what approach to economics would be regarded as "spiritually correct"? The most influential answer was provided by Thomas Aquinas, who was canonized (made a saint) by the Roman Catholic church. He said that the just price would be the one that equalized the benefits of an exchange between the parties to it, measured as the gain from having the exchange as against not having it. St. Thomas would no doubt be pleased by Fig. 14.3 and would see it as a vindication of his argument.

Nevertheless, it is a fair outcome only to the extent that the disagreement options are fair. To see this, look at Fig. 14.4, which shows the effect of a change in disagreement options on Nash's solution. The first disagreement point, D_1, favors Abe and results in an agreement tilted in his direction. The second, D_2, favors Bev and has the opposite effect. The implication is that, while net benefits remain equal, this only means that those who start out from the best position end up in the best position.

In the simplest possible way, this diagram captures the essence of any bargaining theory useful to economists: it shows that agreements will tend to favor the parties

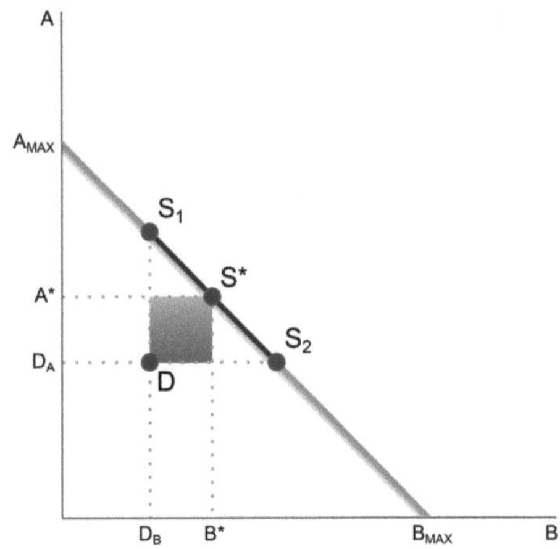

Fig. 14.3 Nash's bargaining solution in a zero-sum bargaining game. The solution point is S*, where the product of Abe's net benefit ($A^* - D_A$) and Bev's net benefit ($B^* - D_B$) is maximized. This is the area of the shaded square

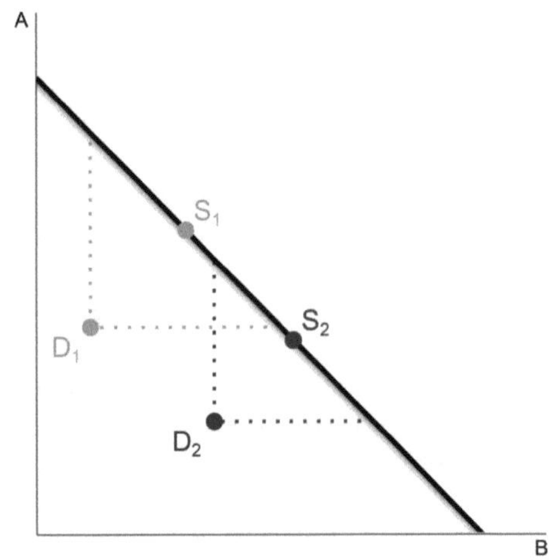

Fig. 14.4 The effect of a change in the disagreement point on Nash's solution. When the disagreement point favors Abe, as does D_1, so does solution S_1. When the disagreement point D_2 favors Bev, so does the corresponding solution S_2

who are best off *without* them. Having a better outside option is the soul of bargaining power.

Nash's analysis applies in similar fashion to bargaining situations in which tradeoffs are more complicated. In many contexts it is reasonable to suppose that, the more the parties share with one another, the greater their combined benefits will be—a **positive sum game**. This is reflected in Fig. 14.5, where the agreement curve bulges out in the middle and flattens at either end:

In this particular case the agreement curve is flatter for some distance to the right of S_1, indicating that over this range small concessions by Abe yield larger returns to Bev. This has the effect of pushing the solution further toward Bev's side; at S*, rather than at some point equidistant between S_1 and S_2, the area of the shaded rectangle is maximized. A different way of saying this is that bargains that favor

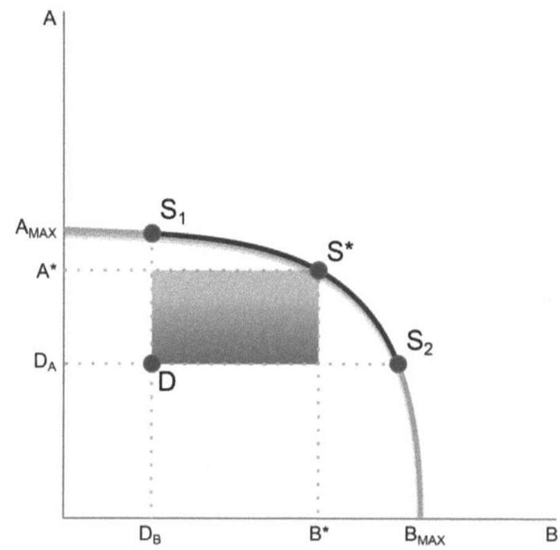

Fig. 14.5 Nash's bargaining solution when the bargaining is positive-sum. When the agreement curve allows for less than a one-to-one tradeoff between benefits to A and B, the Nash solution still calls for the rectangle of net benefits whose area is the largest

Bev offer greater gains to cooperation, and this is reflected in Bev being able to command a larger share of the enlarged pie.

One crucial assumption underlying Nash's solution is symmetry, that it doesn't matter what Abe and Bev bring to the table other than the simple facts resulting from the disagreement point and the shape of the agreement curve. Everything else—their histories, psychology, bargaining skills, etc.—is irrelevant. This is why there is a tendency toward outcomes that equalize net benefits or respect differences in tradeoffs. Nash had a simple suggestion, however, for incorporating personal differences: if one side is stronger in some sense than the other, we should convert this into a pair of weights and adjust the solution accordingly. For instance, if Bev is stronger than Abe, her weight might be 1 and Abe's only ½. Then, instead of an equal division of net benefits in the zero-sum game, Bev would get 2/3 and Abe just 1/3. A weighted solution could also be applied to the positive-sum case of Fig. 14.5.

The account of Nash's bargaining solution provided above may seem a bit arbitrary. This is because the amount of space required to present all of his mathematical reasoning would be too great in an introductory textbook—but also because it *is* somewhat arbitrary. Many game theorists have criticized it for making too many assumptions that have little empirical basis. Other solution concepts have been put forward and criticized as well. The reason we have focused on Nash is that his is the most popular approach; if you read articles in economic or business journals about bargaining, it is likely that they will refer to the Nash solution at some point. Nevertheless, it doesn't matter too much for our purposes what solution process we endorse. Any set of rules for predicting the result of a bargaining situation, as long as they are applied consistently, will give us the relationship between the disagreement point and the final outcome that we saw in Fig. 14.4, and *that* is the most important thing game theory has to offer: bargaining power is based on having favorable outside options.

Box 14.2: John Forbes Nash

John Nash was born in Bluefield, West Virginia in 1928. By the time he was in high school he showed signs of an extraordinary aptitude for math and science. He received a scholarship to attend the Carnegie Institute of Technology (now called Carnegie Mellon University) in Pittsburgh and then went to Princeton University for graduate study in mathematics.

As is often the case with mathematicians, his first work was his most influential. His Ph.D dissertation was published in the form of three articles in the early 1950s, establishing an equilibrium outcome for positive-sum non-cooperative games and proposing his solution for a two-person bargaining game (which we use in this chapter). He also published important papers in the theory of algebra, and within a few years he had been awarded tenure at the Massachusetts Institute of Technology.

It was at this moment of maximum success that Nash developed the symptoms of severe mental illness that would plague him thereafter. In 1959 he was placed in a mental hospital with a diagnosis of schizophrenia, and he lost his job at MIT. For more than a decade he wandered Europe and North America, in and out of mental institutions. Eventually he settled at Princeton University, where he earned enough money to live on, and where he would spend his days alone, filling notebooks and blackboards with equations.

Eventually his skills began to come back to him, and he was able to do more advanced theoretical work in game theory and other branches of mathematics. In 1994 he was awarded a Nobel Prize in economics in conjunction with two other game theorists, John Harsanyi and Reinhard Selten. The Nobel committee singled out for recognition the path-breaking papers Nash had published from his student work at Princeton.

Nash's life was the subject of a best-selling book, *A Beautiful Mind*, by Sylvia Nasar and a film, (very) loosely based on his biography, directed by Ron Howard.

A little reflection should lead to the realization that bargaining power of the sort we have analyzed can be found almost everywhere in the economy. It explains why, in most cases, employers have more bargaining power than employees: there are usually more workers seeking jobs in our economy than jobs seeking workers. The consequences of a failure to agree (on employment) usually leaves the worker in a worse situation than the employer. (But we will also see exceptions to this rule in Chap. 16.) A large manufacturer usually has bargaining power relative to a small supplier, particularly when many suppliers are available to fill an order. Men often have more bargaining power than women in family situations, since the result of splitting up would typically be that the woman would bear the greater burden of caring for children. (This would be intensified if the couple were currently sharing their income, but if the man's job pays more than the woman's.)

As we will see, bargaining power is not everything, but it is an important factor in many economic contexts. To apply it, however, we will need a more elaborate theory than the bare-bones model we have just outlined.

14.3 Extensions to the Basic Bargaining Model

Here we will take up, one at a time, complications that students of bargaining have examined in great detail.

1. The role of time. One of the least satisfactory aspects of the simple theory is that there is no bargaining process to speak of. That is, Abe and Bev are not doing the sorts of things bargainers do (making offers and counteroffers), nor is the passage of time, an important aspect of any economic relationship, represented in any way. Indeed, the notion that the outcome that results will be the one that two people would agree on if they had an infinite amount of time and could try out any proposal, not stopping until they had found the very best, is far removed from reality.

In the last 20 years an alternative approach to the study of bargaining has been developed that has time at its core. The basic idea is this: Abe and Bev would once again negotiate, but using a procedure that describes how they make offers to each other. Specifically, one side (say Bev) begins by proposing the terms of an agreement. The others side, Abe, can either accept or propose an alternative. This round of bargaining is thought of as taking a certain amount of time, which we could measure in minutes, days, or months. Now it is Bev's turn again: she can either accept Abe's counteroffer or make one of her own. And so it goes, back and forth, until a final agreement is reached or the two parties simply give up.

The first thing to notice about this new wrinkle is that it adds a second cost to delaying agreement or failing to agree. In the simple model we began with, the cost was that the parties would be brought back to their disagreement options, assumed to be less desirable than the potential agreements available to them. Now, in addition, by rejecting offers and extending the process, they put off enjoying these benefits, and postponing a benefit is a type of cost. (Hunger due to a meal that has been put off for too many hours is a clear example.) Thus there is an interest on both sides in speeding up the negotiation. This takes the form not only of a greater willingness to accept a less-than-perfect proposal, but also (and symmetrically) a greater willingness to make proposals that will be seen as attractive by the other side. In the simplest case, when both parties have complete information about all the costs and benefits of each possible proposal, as well as the desires of both themselves and their negotiating partner, and if each puts the same value on coming to an agreement quickly, the forces cancel out, and the result is the same division of benefits that Nash predicts.

Of course, for every assumption there is another possibility. In particular, one important difference between the instantaneous process we began with and the time-consuming process we are considering now is that differences in the value of time can lead to changes in the distribution of bargaining power. If Abe is in a hurry and needs an agreement *now*, while Bev is willing to wait a bit longer, this shifts power from Abe to Bev. This distinction has obvious economic significance. Individuals, companies and others with secure sources of income and assets to fall back on can afford to take a more relaxed attitude toward time. Those facing a lack of funds to provide for essential needs, or who are barely one step ahead of their creditors, or who live from paycheck to paycheck with little in the way of safety net—they are the ones whose bargaining power is likely to fall.

2. Long-term relationships. The simple approaches we have considered assume that each episode of bargaining is free-standing: the two parties come into it without any history (or at least none that's relevant), and they do not expect to meet again in the future. All that matters is what they can get out of the process *now*. Sometimes this is a reasonably accurate description of what happens. For instance, in many countries it is expected that buyers and sellers will haggle at the open-air markets that are common places for trade. If you are not a regular customer—if you are a tourist, for example—you will find yourself in a negotiating situation not all that different from the simple Nash model of Fig. 14.4. But in all likelihood this is the exception and not the rule. In most real-world contexts we bargain over and over with the same people: landlords, suppliers, workers or employers, etc. What difference does this make?

The answer is, quite a lot, but it is difficult to generalize. One way to think about the problem is that, in a long-term context, each bargaining proposal (or response to someone else's proposal) serves two purposes at once: it has an effect on the current negotiation, and it also sends a signal about one's intentions in future negotiations. We could imagine two different signals parties might want to send:

- Where there are large gains to cooperation, it may pay to moderate one's bargaining in the present in order to signal greater willingness to cooperate in the future. A familiar example is a close relationship between two people, such as a marriage. Each partner's well-being depends greatly on the ability of both to work together with as little friction as possible. Of course, from time to time issues come up over which there is a strong difference of opinion or interest. When deciding how forcefully to make its case, each partner, if it is acting rationally, should consider the message their behavior sends about how cooperative they intend to be in the future. The result will normally be less aggressive bargaining than would be expected between two strangers.
- Where differences in fundamental interests are likely to continue into the future, parties will be tempted to bargain even more aggressively than otherwise, in order to send the message that they are strong and determined and should not be challenged. This can sometimes be seen in negotiations between unions and managers. Each side knows there will be future negotiations, and they see an interest not only in getting a favorable agreement in the present, but also presenting a general image of toughness. This attitude, when adopted on both sides, can sometimes lead to escalating displays of aggression and ultimately conflicts that would otherwise not be in anyone's interest.

3. Behavioral complications. The bargaining models we have examined are all based on the assumption of pure self-interest: each bargainer has no objective other than getting as much benefit for him- or herself as possible, whether this is a one-time benefit (as in Nash) or a flow of benefits over time from an ongoing relationship. Assuming pure self-interest makes it easier to analyze the bargaining process (and most other aspects of economics as well), but it is not an accurate representation of how real human beings think and act.

Research into real-world bargaining behavior has grown by leaps and bounds during the past two decades, and it is hardly possible to summarize all the interesting findings. Here are just a few:

(a) Perceptions of *fairness* play a crucial role. In many situations people will not press a bargaining advantage because the result would appear unfair. They would feel ashamed to be benefitting from the weakness of others, or from advantages they do not feel they deserve. Laboratory evidence conclusively demonstrates this in the context of the "ultimatum game", for example. In this game, two players get to split a given amount of money if they can agree on how to divide it, but they get nothing if they can't. The bargaining process is simple and dramatic: player 1 gets to propose a split, and player 2 can either accept or reject it. That's all: no discussion or counter-offers. This gives player 1 a huge advantage, since he or she can propose a highly favorable split knowing that, as long as some tiny amount is left over for #2, accepting is more beneficial than rejecting. Yet this is rarely what happens, and a large percentage of offers are for an even division of the money—the triumph of pure fairness over pure self-interest.

(b) People often act on the basis of *reciprocity* even when it does not appear to be in their direct self-interest. Reciprocity can take two forms, making gifts (in the form of favorable offers) to those who have previously given to you, and imposing punishments (such as a refusal to agree) to those seen as having violated the rules of proper behavior. Both can be costly, since they both forego potential gains that a strictly self-interested negotiator might capture.

(c) People often adhere to *social norms* rather than push their own advantage as far as it will go. Over time, communities evolve agreed-upon solutions to many bargaining situations. Consider restaurant tipping, for instance. From a pure bargaining point of view, nearly all the advantage lies with the customer, particularly if this is not an encounter likely to be repeated. In fact, it is so one-sided that it is hard to call it bargaining at all. As a matter of self-interest, the diner, particularly one from another city, should get up from the table and leave nothing; there would be little the server could do about this. Nevertheless, each culture has a tipping norm, and most people obey it. (One of the first questions a traveler is likely to ask is, how much do people tip around here?)

(d) There are large differences in behavior across individuals. Some people appear to place a high value on fairness, others less. Some are far more reciprocal than others, or more reciprocal in one direction (such as giving) than another (punishing). There are also gender differences that have been identified in some cultures: women on average appear to be less aggressive in pursuing self-interest in bargaining situations and are more prone to reciprocating gifts than men. Why these differences exist—between individuals and across social groups—and how particular behaviors can be nurtured or discouraged is largely beyond our current knowledge, but despite (or because of) this it is one of the hottest areas for debate.

The field of behavioral economics, particularly as it illuminates bargaining, is in the midst of a revolution, and it is likely that a chapter on this topic written 5 years from now will look quite different from this one.

14.4 Bargaining Power in Action

The theories described in this chapter do not provide a magic decoding device for figuring out how bargaining works in real life, but they can be helpful in suggesting where to look for patterns. To illustrate, here are two important instances where bargaining power has changed in broad daylight, with consequences for large numbers of people.

1. Wal-Mart and its suppliers. Once upon a time in countries like the United States, manufacturers were large and retail stores were small. A few giant firms accounted for most of the production of consumer items, and many individual stores or small chains relied on them for merchandise. This gave the producers plenty of bargaining power: if one store wouldn't accept their terms, another would, but stores had few options for stocking their shelves. The result was much higher profits for the concentrated manufacturing sectors, and a scramble for much smaller profits in retail.

Not any more. Stores have gotten bigger and the chains more extensive, and no one illustrates this trend more than Wal-Mart in the US. Wal-Mart actually takes in more than 50 % of all retail dollars spent by US consumers; it is the indispensable connection between any manufacturer that wants to reach a mass market and the consumers themselves. For most manufacturers Wal-Mart accounts for such a large percentage of their sales that they simply *have* to agree to supply it. For their part, however, Wal-Mart has several manufacturers it can turn to, and it can also create its own house brand if that promises greater profits. In other words, the disagreement option for most manufacturers is much worse than it is for Wal-Mart. This gives the retail chain an enormous advantage in negotiating supply contracts.

The results are dramatic. Wal-Mart forces its suppliers to sell at lower prices and accept lower profit margins. It often withholds payment until *after* consumers have rung up their purchases. It can dictate packaging and shipping methods according to its own convenience. It can even pressure a producer to change its product line, for instance by introducing a stripped-down version of its flagship products even when this has the potential to undermine the supplier's brand strategy. Some of the outsourcing of production to lower-cost regions like China that has characterized the US economy is the result of price pressure exerted by Wal-Mart on its supply chain.

This is not to say that the shift in bargaining power between supplier and retailer is the only source of Wal-Mart's success, but it has been one factor.

2. The global coffee market. We began this chapter with some information about the changing share of the coffee dollar going to producers, governments, exporters, and sellers. The multinational companies that brand and distribute the coffee have largely gained at the expense of the others, especially the farmers and government agencies, and this was an important aspect of the Coffee Crisis.

Simple bargaining theory has something to say about this. Two trends have altered the disagreement options facing different levels of the supply chain. First, the farmers are less organized than in the past. Before, they often sold their coffee through government-mandated marketing arrangements. In fact, it was often a marketing board representing thousands of producers, rather than each individual producer, that negotiated a price. Second, there has been increasing concentration on the part of the coffee multinationals. Over half the market in the US is accounted for by just four firms; in England the percentage is even higher, perhaps more than 90 %. These numbers alone suggest that there is an imbalance between a handful of corporations bargaining with thousands of small producers. The corporations can play one off against another, but any individual farmer has few options if no supply agreement is reached. In fact, the situation on the ground is often even more unequal, since farmers are often isolated, with little reliable information about global price trends and poor infrastructure for moving their goods to locations where they might command a higher price. There is nothing surprising, then, about the weakening position of small farmers in the coffee world; it is what we would expect given the changes that have been taking place. As this is being written, NGOs and the World Bank are promoting cooperative marketing arrangements between coffee growers to return to them some of the bargaining clout they lost when the national marketing boards were dismantled 20 years ago.

The Main Points

1. There are five kinds of power: the power to withhold, bargaining power, coercive power, institutional power and cultural power. They are not mutually exclusive.
2. Bargaining relationships are likely to arise when there are few participants to a market, when the identities of participants are known to each other, and when interaction is repeated.
3. The agreement curve is a technique for portraying the options open to two agents bargaining over the division of a good or resource. Each participant has a disagreement point, the fallback value that results from failing to agree with the other; no one would voluntarily agree to a bargain that leave him or her

worse off than the disagreement point. Any potential agreement that meets this constraint is a possible solution.

4. The Nash bargaining solution is the agreement that maximizes the product of its net benefit to the two parties, where the net benefit is the value of the agreement minus the value of the disagreement point. If the agreement curve is linear, this solution lies midway between the two disagreement values: each party gets the same net benefit. For any consistent solution process, however, it will be the case that the agreement will be more in favor of the party that has the least need for it. In other words, if someone's disagreement point falls, their bargaining power falls and they can expect a less favorable bargain.
5. A popular alternative model of the bargaining process presents it as a sequence of offers and counteroffers taking place through time. In this model, the party least able to wait (for whom the cost of delaying the agreement is greatest) has less bargaining power.
6. Repeated bargaining between the same parties is complicated; no general rule can be formulated to predict what will happen.
7. The purely rational, self-interested bargainer of standard game theory is not representative of real human beings. Most individuals are motivated by perceptions of fairness, demand reciprocity, and adhere to social norms governing bargaining situations. Moreover, there is wide variation across individuals: some attach more importance to fairness than others, are more reciprocating, etc.

Terms to Define

Agreement curve
Bargaining power
Default option
Just price
Nash bargaining solution
Reciprocity (in bargaining)
Supply chain
Thin vs thick markets
Ultimatum game

Questions to Consider

1. What bargaining situations have you been in during the past month? Were these one-time situations, or were they repeating (part of a longer-term relationship)?
2. It is common for consumers and auto dealers to bargain over the price of new cars. It is not common for consumers and electronics retailers to bargain over the price of new computers. Why?
3. In one of the situations you listed in your answer to question 1, describe the disagreement options that you and your bargaining partner(s) faced. On whom did this confer the most bargaining power?

4. In the former Soviet Union there were often shortages of many consumer goods. In capitalist countries it is usually the other way around: firms produce a surplus of goods and have to convince consumers to buy them. Using the basic principles of bargaining theory, discuss who might gain and lose from each system.
5. For hundreds of years there have been regulations prohibiting grain merchants from driving up prices during times of famine. In many countries today there are still controls on the price of bread and other staples. What is the justification for this from the standpoint of bargaining theory? What disadvantages might there be with such a policy? Are there other ways to achieve the same objectives?
6. It has been said that wars could never arise unless at least one side miscalculates. Is this consistent with the bargaining theory presented in this chapter?
7. The example of Hurricane Charlie was brought up in Chap. 6. Reconsider it in light of the tension between self-interested and "fair" bargaining. Does this change your opinion? Explain.

Market Failure

15

There's a joke that goes something like this: how many economists does it take to screw in a light bulb? Answer: none, the invisible hand will take care of it.

Well, not exactly. It is true that economists tend to view the world through the prism of markets. The majority of them probably think the Market Welfare Model, the claim that market equilibrium is also the best outcome for society, is *mostly* correct, and they tend to have an above-average inclination to let markets run without interference. Nevertheless, economists do not go so far as to think themselves out of a job, for if markets could always be relied on to run smoothly on autopilot there would be no need for the services of economists.

It would be more accurate to say that most economists give markets the benefit of the doubt, but they are always scanning the horizon for exceptions, for situations in which markets either don't work properly or otherwise fail to meet the needs of society. (Note: this discussion applies only to microeconomics, the subject of this book. In the realm of macroeconomics most economist recognize the need for some sort of permanent economic management.) The core of this enterprise is the theory of **market failure**, a systematic analysis of why markets sometimes come up short and how they can be fixed.

In this chapter we will examine two of the main forms of market failure, public goods and externalities. Pay attention: nearly all microeconomic policy draws on one or the other of these concepts.

15.1 Public Goods

The theory of **public goods** is a bit of a composite, since it began imprecisely and only gained careful definition after many years of use. When the ideas got sorted out it became clear that there were two *different* criteria, and a good could meet one standard and not the other.

The first criterion is usually called **nonexclusion**; it describes goods for which it is impractical to deny use or access to those who do not pay for them. To understand the importance of this point, consider a typical item you might buy at a store, such

P. Dorman, *Microeconomics*, Springer Texts in Business and Economics,
DOI 10.1007/978-3-642-37434-0_15, © Springer-Verlag Berlin Heidelberg 2014

as a loaf of bread. The bread has a price; it is expected that you will stop at the checkout counter before you leave and pay this money to a store employee. If you don't you will be committing an offense, shoplifting, for which you could be arrested. The store stocks bread because it anticipates that those who want it enough will pay for it. Suppose, however, that for some reason it is not possible to prevent the shoplifting of bread or even discourage it: customers can take the bread home with them without giving it a thought and never pay a cent. Stores will discontinue carrying bread altogether, because they would suffer a loss with each loaf they "sell". Yet people may still desire bread and might even be willing to pay for it, if it were required of them.

The example is absurd, of course, because stores *can* make people pay for bread and similar items. (During natural disasters, riots and other disruptions, when stores have been abandoned by their employees, this ability to require payment vanishes, and the result is often looting.) But there are other goods that are very difficult to charge for. A classic example is national defense, the "good" that consists of defending a country against external attack. Could this be sold the way bread is? You could try: imagine a defense "company" which sells certificates entitling the bearer to freedom from attack by a foreign power. What would you do if someone chooses not to pay? Could you organize a defense of the entire country except this one non-buyer? ("We will defend our country, except that you can bomb this one house over here.") It's just not practical, and this is why it is difficult to organize national defense along the lines of a consumer market.

The same logic applies to clean air. Most countries now have agencies whose job is to regulate air pollution; could this be "sold" to customers on a cash basis? If someone decides not to pay their clean air bill could you cut them off—give everyone else clean air but make their air dirty? It turns out that there are a number of important goods in our society that resist the market approach of denying access to those who don't pay.

There are two subtleties to be aware of, however. First, goods are sometimes given away as if the nonexclusion property were applicable, when in fact it is simply a choice of the provider. A band might offer a free concert to its fans, for instance, but this doesn't mean that their music is nonexcludable. They can make the decision to do this, but it would also be practical to sell tickets and exclude those who don't buy them; bands do this all the time. So: just because users are not excluded doesn't mean that the good they are using is nonexcludable.

Second, there is a spectrum of nonexcludability in the real world. Take the case of police services. You might think this should be nonexcludable: can the police deny protection to individuals who haven't purchased a protection "ticket"? Well, no and yes. If an officer sees a crime being committed on the street, there will usually not be an opportunity to see who has paid what; protection must be automatic. But the payment of police for particular protection services (including from the police) is a common form of corruption, and, in addition, it is entirely possible for individuals or businesses to purchase "extra" protection from private police forces. (There are now more privately employed police in the United States than police working for all levels of government combined.) So police services are in a grey zone, partially falling under the nonexcludability criterion, partially not.

The second criterion is **nonrivalry**, but a more precise description would be that the good or service can be provided at (or near) zero marginal cost. Again, consider national defense. If the population of a country expands by one (a birth or the arrival of an immigrant), does defending the country become more expensive? Presumably the answer is no, so there is no marginal cost to defending the additional resident. The same goes for clean air: more breathers does not entail more cost. (More potential polluters does, but they are not *users* of the clean air regulations.) An early example in the economics literature was lighthouses: it doesn't cost more to maintain them if additional boats are guided by them through shallow or rocky passages.

As with nonexclusion, nonrivalry presents a large grey zone, since many goods have a low, but not zero, marginal cost of provision. A national park which is mainly used by hikers has some additional cost per user, because more hikers require more labor to keep the trails and campsites from being degraded. Nevertheless, the largest cost (by far) is the provision of the land itself, and this does not vary with use. For instance, a scenic mountain which has been preserved in its original state (more or less) for the satisfaction of hikers could otherwise have been developed into a ski resort. This might constitute the **opportunity cost** of using the resource for a park, and this cost is unrelated to the number of hikers who take advantage of the park. But perhaps the land has little use other than hiking (low opportunity cost) and maintenance is the main expense; in that case, on balance, the nonrivalry property may not apply. There is a lot of room for careful analysis and judgment.

These two properties, nonexclusion and nonrivalry, together define what it means for a good to be public in the way this term is used by economic theorists. If both properties hold it is said that we have a **pure public good**. But this is quite different from the way the word "public" is used in everyday contexts. Normally, "public" refers to the public sector; that is, government. A public agency is a branch of the government, unlike, say, the "private sector", which includes businesses but excludes the government. We are not going to rewrite the dictionaries, but it is important to clear up this source of confusion. Note well: *public goods in the economic sense are not necessarily provided by the public sector, and goods provided by the government are not necessarily public goods as economics defines them.* It may be helpful to reread this sentence and give it some extra thought; perhaps no misunderstanding in introductory economics is as widespread as the confusion between these two uses of "public".

Examples are not difficult to come by. Radio broadcasts (but not radios) are pure public goods. Nonexcludability applies, because it would be difficult to prevent someone with a radio from picking up a signal because they haven't paid for it. Nonrivalry applies because it is no more expensive to provide a broadcast to more people (within a given geographic area) than fewer. Yet most radio stations are private, for-profit enterprises. The trick is that they sell their audiences to advertisers, so that, from a business standpoint, the advertisers and not the listeners are the true users. When you look at it that way both criteria no longer apply: advertisements can be taken off the air if they are not paid for, and it is costly to provide airtime for each additional ad. Does this mean that the broadcasts were not public goods in the first place? To listeners they still are. Moreover, some radio stations are listener-sponsored: rather than selling ads, they plead with their listeners to contribute money during periodic pledge drives. And in most cases enough listeners send in money even though their listening privileges would not be revoked if they didn't.

Meanwhile, postal services are provided by public agencies in most countries. (In the US this is the job of the US Postal Service.) According to everyday usage, this would make their services "public". Yet neither criterion of economic publicness applies: the post office certainly has the ability to deny services to those who don't purchase stamps, and the delivery of each additional letter or package is costly. So this public outfit is *not* in the business of providing a public good.

So, if the theory of public goods does not predict which goods will be provided by the public sector, what's the point? The answer is that each criterion is associated with a particular sort of market failure. Either the failure is fixed, or there is a cost in terms of economic efficiency.

First consider nonexclusion. The problem that arises is that some people, maybe most, will use the good without paying; economists call this the **free rider problem**. That's fine for the happy freeloaders, but how will the good in question be financed? It costs money to provide, and if not enough can be raised by selling access, there may be no provision at all. If the clean air agency tries to fund itself by selling people the right to breathe clean air, each person may think, "Why should I pay when I can get the same air by paying nothing?" And if enough people think this way (which they will if they have the self-interested values economists ascribe to them), the agency will run short of money and have to shut down (or regulate less effectively). Free ridership can also lead to overuse of services that have significant marginal costs. As we will see in a later chapter, this has been the story of the world's fisheries. For each fisher, the population of fish has been a free good; no one has made them pay the true cost of depleting it. The result has been catastrophic overuse, to the point where it has become necessary to shut down entire marine regions so that the fish can repopulate.

The problem with nonrivalry, on the other hand, is the possibility that there will be *too little* use of the good. If the marginal cost is zero, then any price that may be charged will discourage some users whose personal benefit does not justify paying for it. Yet, as long as they derive any benefit, it is economically inefficient to exclude them. This point is illustrated in Fig. 15.1, where marginal cost is zero for all users and the marginal benefit is given by the demand curve.

The economically efficient level of supply is Q^*, since up to this point the marginal benefit exceeds the marginal cost for all consumers. Of course, that means that there is no revenue to defray any of the *fixed* costs the supplier incurs. So suppose a price P_1 is charged to cover these costs. Now only Q_1 units are sold to consumers. Yet consider a consumer who falls between these two points, to the right of Q_1 but the left of Q^*. This person would receive positive benefit, as

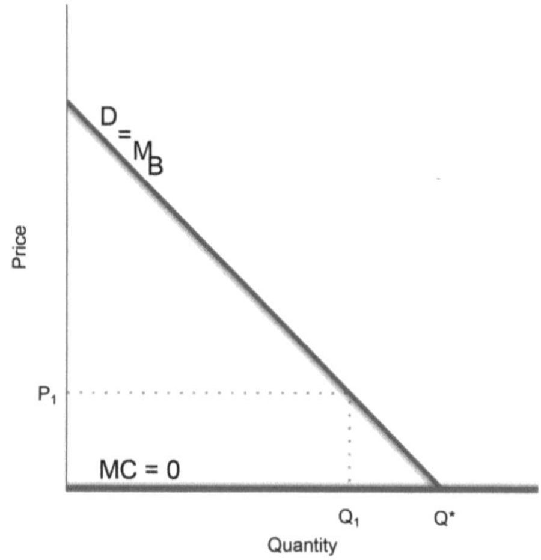

Fig. 15.1 Marginal cost and benefit for a perfectly nonrival good. When the MC = 0, the principle of MB = MC means that the optimal quantity is Q*. By charging price P_1, however, the seller excludes individuals (Q^*–Q_1) from the market

indicated by the demand curve, and she would not impose any additional cost. It would therefore be economically rational to enable her to acquire the good (MB > MC), but she has been shut out by the price. So Fig. 15.1 portrays a dilemma: either no money is raised to cover fixed costs, or a price is set which dissuades consumers who would be more than willing to pay their marginal cost (0). That's the problem.

The dilemma of nonrivalry is at the center of one of today's most hotly-debated economic questions, what to do about the explosion of digital reproduction over the internet. With each revolution in technology the relationship between the fixed and marginal costs of providing products like recorded music has shifted. Thirty years ago the fixed cost of paying musicians and studio engineers were matched by the expense of producing and packaging bulky LP's. Then came CDs, which were cheaper to produce and distribute. Now, with digital compression, inexpensive data storage and distribution through the internet, there is nearly no marginal cost of making an additional reproduction of music, movies or other information products. The situation closely resembles Fig. 15.1; users would like to download for free, bringing the quantity of files close to Q*. Companies holding copyrights in music, film and literature want to charge for each access, imposing a price like P_1. This is a true dilemma: if the downloaders get their way, there is a risk that artists, for example, will not be paid for their work. If the copyright holders win, many people who would receive a personal benefit from downloading these files, and who would not add costs to any member of society, would be priced out.

This just scratches the surface of the issue; there are many more complications, so I will leave it to you to think about possible solutions. In general, however, economists tend to favor one particular approach to public goods: tax the community of potential users and provide the good free of charge (at marginal cost). This is what we do for national defense; we levy a tax on the entire country and ask for no other form of payment. (Some—perhaps a lot of—military spending is not for defense per se; if it serves special interests, in principle it may be possible to ask those who benefit to pay for it. But waging war for the private benefit of a few also raises serious ethical issues!) This addresses both problems we described earlier. It overcomes the free-rider problem by requiring everyone to pay. It overcomes the nonrivalry problem by not charging for use.

This sounds like just the ticket, but it is not so easy in practice. First, there is the question of just how much of the public good to provide. With goods sold in the market the question is answered by supply and demand, but who decides how much is enough of any public good? Second, there are usually qualitative aspects of these goods that have to be determined. There are many ways to provide national defense; a clean air agency has to prioritize some health risks over others. Once again, there is no market guidance available, and choices have to be made. Third, it is rarely the case that public goods benefit everyone equally; there are usually some who have a stronger interest than others. For instance, while all of us presumably value clean air, people with asthma or other respiratory disorders have an even greater interest. Should those who benefit more pay more? How would you know who they are and how much greater their benefit is? Finally, all of the preceding questions take for granted the desire of the government to do the right thing, but as we saw in Chap. 9, it is not so simple. Governments may lack the capacity to do the job properly, or they may be captured by special interests with their own agenda. To remove public goods from the market and place them in the hands of government is not to solve the problem, but to replace one set of problems with another—which *might* be the right thing to do anyway. (Economists have given a lot of attention to the questions raised in this paragraph, and you will discover some of their answers if you take a course in Public Finance or Public Policy Analysis.)

15.2 Externalities

A market is essentially just the sum of lots of bilateral (two-party) transactions. Individual buyers and sellers find agreement and exchange money and goods. Each participant presumably acts in what he or she (or it, such as a company) believes is his or her best interest. All actions are voluntary in the narrow sense that if a transaction does not offer at least as much as the status quo it will not be accepted. So, putting it all together, it is plausible that market exchanges should never make anyone worse off than they were before, and that if every agreement that is potentially beneficial to two parties is agreed to, markets should work optimally to promote economic well-being.

This is the intuition behind the Invisible Hand hypothesis. Early economists like Adam Smith thought it was so self-evidently true that there needed to be little analysis of or argument for it. Nevertheless, it ignores a crucial possibility: what if an agreement between two people, say A and B, has significant effects on a third party, C, who is not part of the deal? Now the Invisible Hand falters. If these third-party, or **spillover**, effects are undesirable, then transactions could be made that lower the well-being of the community. And if the spillover effects are positive, then perhaps too few such transactions will be made, since A and B are not taking into account the benefits received by C.

In a nutshell, this is the insight that underlies the theory of **externalities**. Of course, there is much more to say than this, and we will discuss some of the wrinkles in the paragraphs to come.

For many years the topic of externalities was confusing even for high-level economists. After all, *every* market transaction affects third parties in some way. For instance, if you fill up your car with gas, the effects go beyond you and the gas station (or oil company). By adding to demand, you help increase the price (or slow down its decline), and this effects not only everyone else who might buy or sell gas, but also those in related markets, like autos, air travel, etc. In a well-developed market economy, just about everything is connected to everything else, so how can there not be third-party effects? Does this mean that all market transactions entail externalities? But the whole point to markets is that prices *should* reflect the decisions of buyers and sellers; that's what makes them tick. So what is the difference between an "externality" that reflects the proper operation of markets and one that undermines them?

All confusion was swept aside when Ronald Coase (who we met in the chapter on businesses) published a remarkable article in 1961, "The Problem of Social Cost". In it he not only defined an externality in a way that was both extremely simple and perfectly precise, but also placed it in a rich context of law, social institutions and individual interests. First the definition: an externality is an effect, positive or negative, of a missing market on those who would otherwise have been parties to it.

Suppose, for example, that you and I are neighbors. You have grass in front of your house, and I have a sheep. You might come to me and ask, "Would you be willing to have your sheep graze on my grass once a week? It gets too long, and I don't want to have to cut it myself. I'll pay you if you want." Then we could discuss how much you should pay, and the result would be that you get the benefit of having your grass cut, and I get some money to help maintain the sheep. This is a "normal" market transaction: there is a buyer, a seller, a service, a cost, a quantity, a time frame, a price. I might even take the prospect of a deal like this (or many of them, if I have many neighbors) into consideration if I am thinking about getting a sheep in the first place. The more you (and others) benefit and are willing to pay, the more it makes financial sense to acquire a sheep.

What if, however, you and I never made an agreement, but the sheep likes to wander around (or jump its fence) and graze on your grass anyway. You still receive the same benefit, but now you are not paying for it. This benefit is now an externality. There is no market (buying, selling) between us, but a benefit has been delivered nevertheless. It is a potential economic issue because I may be less likely to buy the sheep initially if I don't anticipate being paid for the good it does for others. In Market Welfare Model terms, there is a difference between the marginal benefits generated by the sheep and the marginal benefits *I* receive from it, so my calculation of personal cost vs benefit does not reflect the wider neighborhood interest.

Of course, having a sheep graze randomly wherever it wants can be a problem as well. Perhaps you have planted vegetables by your house, and now the sheep is nibbling on them too. If I insist on letting the sheep roam freely (or not fixing my fence), you could come to me and say, "You have no right to ruin my vegetable garden with your sheep. If you want to continue this, I think you need to compensate me." And we could discuss just how much compensation you would need. Such a transaction would convert your personal cost, vegetables, into my cost, money. I would have to take it into consideration in all sheep-related decisions: whether to buy a sheep at all, whether to fix the fence, etc. The marginal costs and benefits of each decision would each play their proper role.

The other possibility, however, is that my sheep ruins your vegetables, but you are not in a position to make me pay for this infringement. Perhaps we live in a society whose laws do not give you any right to take action against me and my sheep. In that case there would be a missing market, and you suffer a negative externality. Then, if I am self-interested (as always, the default assumption in economics), your cost no longer enters my calculations. I will buy and raise sheep without any consideration of the impact it has on you. I will be too willing to purchase sheep and not willing enough to confine them.

In both instances, the critical feature that separates a "normal" market outcome from an externality is the presence of a market at all. If someone gains a benefit or bears a cost, and if there is no market to purchase the first or sell the second, then we have an externality—and therefore a market failure. Figure 15.2 on the next page depicts these two cases, where the cost of sheep is the cost the owner pays to acquire them, while the benefit is the sum of all the benefits me and my neighbors get from the sheep *minus* any costs they impose on us. For simplicity it is assumed that the marginal cost of buying sheep is constant; each animal costs the same.

In the first diagram we assume there are **positive externalities**. This means that for any given sheep, the marginal (additional) benefit to society (MSB) will be greater than the marginal private benefit (MPB). The vertical distance between these two curves, for instance the height of the triangle at Q_1, reflects this difference. (As drawn the size of the externality does not change from one sheep to the next—the curves are parallel—but this does not have to be the case.) The sheep owner, being self-interested (assumption), considers only his or her private benefits. This leads to Q_1 sheep being purchased: every sheep to the left of this provides a private benefit greater than the cost; every sheep to the right a cost greater than the private benefit. Nevertheless, if one were to add in the external benefits and use the MSB curve, it is clear that the desirable number of sheep is larger, at Q_2. Each individual sheep between Q_1 and Q_2 generates a marginal social benefit above the cost; adding these surpluses of benefit over cost all together gives us the area of the shaded triangle, the net benefits society would have had at Q_2 and foregoes at Q_1.

The situation is slightly different in the diagram on the bottom. Now the externality is assumed to be **negative**, so the marginal social benefit curve is below the private benefit curve. Failure to take externalities into account (because they don't have to be paid for) leads the sheep owner to buy Q_2 sheep when the social optimum would have been Q_1. Now the shaded triangle represents the net costs to society of having too many sheep.

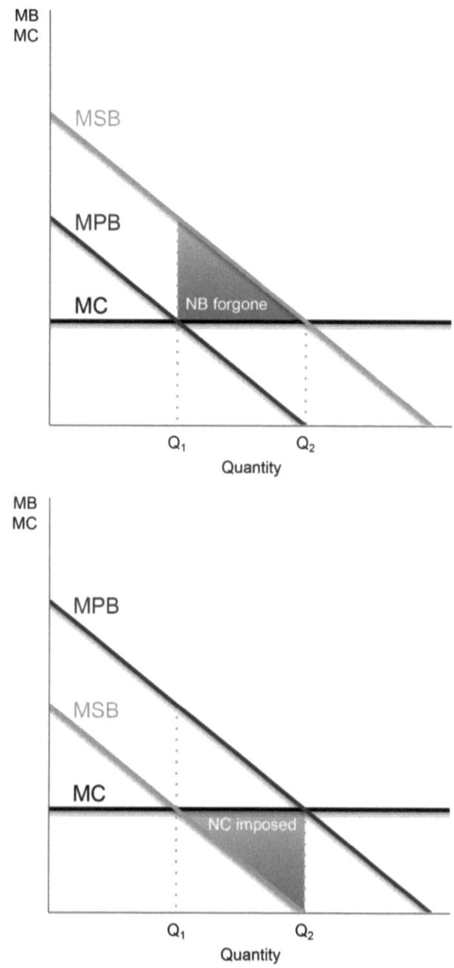

Fig. 15.2 Private vs social benefits of owning sheep. (**a**) Due to a positive externality, the marginal social benefit (*MSB*) of sheep ownership is greater than the marginal private benefit (*MPB*). Self-interest leads to Q_1 sheep being acquired, rather than the social optimum, Q_2. The shaded triangle shows the amount of net social benefits (total benefit minus total cost) forgone at Q_1. (**b**) Due to a negative externality, the marginal social benefit (*MSB*) of sheep ownership is less than the marginal private benefit (*MPB*). Self-interest leads to Q_2 sheep being acquired, rather than the social optimum, Q_1. The shaded triangle shows the amount of net social cost (total cost minus total benefit) being imposed at Q_2

To summarize the argument so far, the logic of a market economy is that, if decisions about what and how to produce and consume are made by individuals acting separately in the market based on their personal benefits and costs, then there needs to be a market for every one of these impacts. If there are beneficial effects that no one has to pay for (due to a missing market), there will be an undersupply of them. If there are harmful effects that no one has to be paid for accepting, there will be an oversupply. It's a problem to have "holes" in the market system.

To illustrate the logic of externalities it was useful to have a purely hypothetical example that comes to us without all the usual real-world complications, but to see the theory in action, let's switch back to reality.

The most important negative externality in the real world is pollution. Many production processes, and many consumption processes as well, generate harmful byproducts that foul the environment and threaten our health. This represents a market failure insofar as these harmful effects do not have to be paid for by those who produce them. That is, a factory has to pay workers for giving up other uses for their time and accepting the authority of the employer. It has to pay the local electricity company for using electricity. It has to pay a bank for any loans it may have taken out—the use of the bank's money. But, in general, it does not have to pay for the use of the air, water and other natural resources it may damage through pollution. When it issues its quarterly report it has to calculate its profits, and these include the revenues it gets from sales and the costs it has to pay to operate. Costs *not* paid for, like pollution externalities, are not part of this calculation. If the business is guided by the profit motive it will choose production methods that minimize the costs that have to be paid and shift more of the impact to those that don't. If a factory has to pay more for materials and labor to cut down on pollution, in the absence of any force outside the market, it will pollute more and keep a lid on its monetary costs.

Looking at the situation from the perspective of an economist, we can recognize quantity effects and price effects. The quantity effect is that there is too much pollution. If firms had to pay the true cost of pollution to society there would be a lot less. (If firms could employ labor for free they would use too many workers as well.) The price effect is that the cost of the goods we buy often does not reflect the true marginal cost to society—the resources that are actually used in production. Burning petroleum products produces air pollution and contributes to global warming, but these costs are not included in the price. This means that gas oline, diesel and similar fuels are priced below the true cost to society of burning them. Insofar as the cost of fuel enters into the pricing of many other goods, the entire system of prices is divorced from the costs and benefits they are supposed to reflect. Thus, key externalities ripple outward through the economy, causing distortions in the pattern of what we produce and consume.

Box 15.1: A Humourous Look at Pollution Externalities

A Cuban animation released in the 1970s begins with a man working in a factory. He has a bad cough, and it just gets worse. Finally he puts his tools down, clocks out, and leaves. You watch him walking down the street, which is enveloped in clouds of soot and smoke coming from his factory. He coughs all the way to a drug store, where he buys some cough medicine. Glug, glug: he drinks it down, and his throat is soothed. Now he can go back to work. You see him walk past the factory again, belching its pollution. Then the camera pulls back, and you see what the factory produces: cough medicine!

But not all externalities are negative. Education produces enormous positive externalities, benefits to society for which students, whose choices make this possible, are not paid. Very loosely, every time a student increases her education level there are private benefits and external ones. Private benefits include better job prospects, the satisfaction from learning more about the world, and greater self-knowledge.

External benefits include the improved functioning of democracy (which thrives in an educated citizenry) and additions to the fund of knowledge available to everyone, such as in the sciences and arts. But the decision to acquire more education is made at the individual level on the basis of private costs and benefits—the financial cost to the student, the opportunity costs, the effort required to succeed in class, the personal gains expected to result. Since no one pays the students for the services they also provide to society this doesn't enter the calculation. Presumably there are some students who, on the basis of their own costs and benefits, would choose to pass up school, but who, if one considers the social as well as the personal aspects, *should* go to school. The result would be an under-educated society. (Note: this analysis applies even if each student has perfect foresight about the future benefits of education, which is hardly the case.)

15.3 Remedies for Externalities

Since externalities are extremely common (some would say ubiquitous), and since many of them have important consequences, economists have given lots of attention to the search for solutions. Very generally, we can speak of four types of responses:

1. Moral suasion. In many cases individuals can be urged to consider the impacts their actions have on others; in other words, they can be asked to be less self-interested. Since such appeals normally coincide with social norms in most societies, they can be effective. For instance, studies have shown that one of the most powerful anti-pollution policies instituted by the US government was the Environmental Protection Adminstration's Toxic Release Inventory. This program named names: it listed all the major manufacturers and provided a record of how much (and what kind of) toxic chemicals they emitted into the environment, even if perfectly legal. This exposed the companies to public pressure, and the evidence is that they took extra steps to lower their profile as polluters. To at least some extent this represented a retreat from raw self-interest, although it is possible that a bad environmental reputation might also hurt sales, employee recruitment and other bottom-line factors. Much of the corporate social responsibility movement, which we surveyed in the chapter on firms, is predicated on the belief that moral suasion can work.

2. Direct regulation. Often we turn to the government to issue directives telling those who create externalities how to modify their behavior. There are laws limiting the amount and type of pollution firms can emit into the air, water and soil. Neighborhood associations lobby for regulations that discourage some land uses and encourage others, since development can have either positive or negative external effects on those living next door. There are other regulations on the content of radio and TV broadcasting, based on the belief that externalities arise here too. Many economists are skeptical of the value of these regulations, believing that they tend to be cumbersome and inefficient, and that they create opportunities for special interests to gain unfair advantages. Changing a few words in a regulation can

provide a bonanza for some producers and an insuperable handicap for others. Economists who feel this way tend to support market approaches (see below), but the general public tends to be more inclined toward regulation because of the ethical message it sends: "it is right to do it this way, so we will make you do it".

3. Taxes and subsidies. These are also sometimes called "Pigovian" taxes and subsidies after their renowned advocate, A. C. Pigou, a professor of economics at Cambridge University (England) during the first decades of the twentieth century. To see the logic, look again at Fig. 15.2a, b. In the first case, for instance, too little is produced or purchased because of positive externalities. The marginal private benefit curve functions as a demand curve, representing the benefit perceived by the decision-maker(s). Pigou's solution is to *subsidize* such a good by an amount equal to the vertical distance between the two curves. By doing this, the decision-maker would now face the direct gains from sheep-buying (or whatever), as well as the financial benefits of the subsidy. The combination of the two would add up to the MSB curve, which would now be the new demand curve. Thus Q_2 rather than Q_1 would be the amount produced.

Alternatively, look at the bottom figure. Here the externality is detrimental, and the demand curve, the private benefits on which the decision-maker bases his or her decision, is above the true marginal social benefit curve. In this case the idea is to *tax* the good by this same vertical difference, pulling the demand curve down to the level of MSB. Facing such a tax, the decision-maker would now select the appropriate quantity Q_1 rather than the excessive quantity Q_2.

In either case, the job of the public authority is to estimate the size of the externality and impose a tax or subsidy equal to it. There is no need to precisely specify what decisions ought to be made: if the prices once again reflect the true costs and benefits of each action, it can safely be left to each decision-maker to choose the option that seems best. Indeed, under Pigou's approach, there is no need for the government to know what the best corrective actions are; they need to know only the size of the externalities. Individuals looking out for their own interests may well come up with innovations—new ways of producing or consuming—that the government could not have predicted. On the other hand, switching from direct regulation to taxes and subsidies mutes the ethical message the public may wish to send, and it also requires that a monitoring apparatus be put into place to accurately determine who should be taxed or subsidized and how much.

A hybrid of direct regulation and the Pigovian approach that has proved popular in pollution control is **cap-and-trade**: regulators establish a maximum allowable quantity of pollution and allow those who pollute less than their share to sell their surplus to those pollute more. Like taxes and subsidies, these markets in pollution permits (the right to emit a certain quantity of pollution) create incentives for companies to find less-polluting techniques and products (so they can sell more permits or buy less of them). One disadvantage is that, whereas a traditional regulation will typically result in less pollution than allowed, because some companies will "underpollute", cap-and-trade virtually guarantees that the full allotment will be utilized, since for each "underpolluter" there will now be a corresponding "overpolluter". Of course, regulators can anticipate this and set the allowable pollution level lower under cap-and-trade. One practical question with potentially large financial implications is how the permits will be allocated initially—whether they will be handed out for free or sold in an auction. On this choice may ride billions of dollars in such economically crucial pollution markets as sulfur and carbon dioxide.

4. Assigning property rights. Now we move into Coase's own territory, as set out in his 1961 article. Let's go back to the negative externality version of the sheep story, the one with the sheep gnawing on your lettuce, since it is similar to one told by Coase. We can imagine that there is a law in the community we live in that says each person has the right to grow vegetables without interference from their neighbors or their neighbors' sheep. The law is enforced with great severity, and I would never think of violating it. Of course, if I could get you to *agree* to have my sheep eat your vegetables, I wouldn't be a criminal, and I could save myself the expense of building higher, stronger fences. So I might enter into a negotiation with you: how much, I ask, would you be willing to accept as compensation for the damage caused by my sheep? You might propose a figure, I would counteroffer, and perhaps we could arrive at an agreement. Whether an agreement is possible depends above all on whether the damage caused by the sheep (the least you will accept) is less than the cost of enhancing the fence (the most I am willing to pay). If this is the case there is a potential zone of agreement, and we are in something like the bargaining world explored in the previous chapter. If not, all deals are off—and they *should* be off, since the cost of restraining the sheep is less than the damage they do if they run free.

As Coase pointed out, the above story does *not* describe an externality, because the requisite market, rather than going missing, is there is broad daylight. You are indeed in a position of selling, and I in a position of buying, the right to impose harm. The market exists for two reasons. First, property rights have been unambiguously assigned to you. You "own" your land in the sense that you have the right to deny me and my sheep the use of it. This gives you something to sell and me something to buy. Second, it is not difficult for the two of us to enter into a negotiation over the price of this transaction. In Coase's terminology, which we encountered in an earlier chapter, there are low **transaction costs** to this process. We are able to communicate easily enough, and it would not be too difficult to draft and enforce a potential agreement.

But Coase noticed something else. Suppose the legal context is different; now there is a presumption that sheep have the right to roam freely, despite their bad habits. The shoe would then be on the other foot: it would be up to you to ask me to confine my sheep, and to make it worth my while you would propose a payment. Would I agree? It turns out that the decisive criterion is the same, whether the cost of building up my fence is less than the damage done by the sheep. If so, we can bargain; if not, bargaining will get us nowhere. Note again: *the potential for an agreement depends on the cost of the negative impact and the cost of preventing it; it is the same irrespective of whether rights are assigned to the one who suffers the impact (and who must be paid to accept it) or the one who imposes it (and must be paid to prevent it).* This is a striking insight, one that is obvious when you think about it, but which might easily be overlooked. (In fact, Coase went one step further and tried to show that the actual agreement—the price paid, the amount of damage agreed to—would be the same under either system of rights. This turns out to be false for reasons we will return to shortly.) In addition, of course, an agreement in which you pay me to confine my sheep also requires the same two premises as before, that my right to let my sheep run free is unambiguous (and can therefore be bought or sold), and that there are few transaction costs to the process of bargaining.

So Coase recognizes that any clear assignment of property rights can be the basis for a bargaining process—that is, a market—that eliminates the problem of externalities. But Coase is a realist. He knows perfectly well that externalities occur quite commonly, which means that the sort of bargaining mechanism we have been talking about often fails to occur in the real world. Why is this? Sometimes it is due to a poor definition of property rights. We may not know who actually has the right to permit or restrict, and this makes it difficult to set up markets for buying and selling these permits or restrictions. But the main culprit tends to be transaction costs.

We set up an apocryphal situation with sheep and vegetables, but most real-world spillover problems are more convoluted. Take the case of air pollution. Here it is often difficult to identify both the perpetrators and the victims. Many pollute the air simultaneously, each in different ways. Many breathe the air, and each has somewhat different interests and preferences. Assembling both groups into single entities that can bargain as a collective is extremely difficult and expensive. Moreover, as we saw above clean air is a public good, so a bargaining process would have to overcome the free rider problem as well as the zero marginal cost problem. The fact that we seldom see such negotiations taking place is a sign that the costs of surmounting all these difficulties is simply too great.

But once we see the issue through the lens provided by Coase, it becomes possible to envision another approach to remedying externalities: with a big assist from government we might indeed set up a bargaining arrangement that, by constituting a market, eliminates the externality. Japan, for instance, has used this approach in its policies to limit the pollution of its coastal waters. Coasts are important to Japan: as an island nation it has lots of coastline, and it depends on fish and seaweed from these regions for a significant part of its diet. At the same time, a large percentage of the population lives in coastal cities, and the combination of industrial, residential and agricultural runoff has caused severe pollution episodes in the past. As one part of its policy system, the Japanese government assisted the formation of fishing cooperatives, with one coop representing each of the major estuaries. These coops were assigned rights to water quality within their jurisdiction; so anyone who want to dump waste into a river or stream (which will eventually flow to an estuary) has to pay the cooperative for permission. It is not a perfect system, but it helped reverse a serious threat to the country's natural resources.

Coase originally presented his approach as an alternative to the system of Pigovian taxes and subsidies we considered above, but most economists today see them as two sides of the same question. Suppose we find a town situated on a river that also serves as a waste receptacle for a paper mill. It is more profitable for the mill to emit a higher level of pollution, but residents of the town prefer a lower level. If the town passes a law requiring the mill to pay a pollution tax, what it has done is to effectively claim property rights to the water quality of the river. It is as if the people of this town said, "This is our river, and we are going to charge you to use it." It is not difficult to imagine a period of de facto bargaining, which could take the form of the mill threatening to shut down unless the tax is reduced, and some compromise tax finally being agreed to.

The interpretation of a Pigovian subsidy is exactly the reverse. If the town passes a law offering payments to the mill in return for its adoption of a less-polluting production process, they are in effect saying, "We recognize that you have the right to continue polluting if you wish, but we want to pay you so that you will pollute less anyway." Again, this could be the opening salvo in a bargaining process, paving the way for ultimate agreement.

The point is that there is a correspondence between the type of financial mechanism used to reduce an externality problem and the implicit property rights on which they are based. If the public pays the polluter, the polluter has the implicit right to pollute; if the polluter is compelled to pay the public, it is the public that is acting on its ownership rights. The right policy depends to some extent on what you think ought to be the assignment of rights between the polluters and those who have to cope with the pollution.

One final note: would the agreement between the town and the mill turn out to be the same in either case, as Coase originally thought? Almost certainly not: (1) The assignment of rights affects the disagreement position of the two parties. If the mill has the right to pollute, the default position (if an agreement is not reached) is that the pollution continues. This is better for the mill and worse for the town. If the town has the right to be free of pollution, the default is worse for the mill and better for the town. As we saw in the previous chapter, such a large change in the disagreement position would almost certainly lead to a change in the final bargaining outcome. (2) There are dynamic effects to the assignment of rights. If the town has the right to prohibit pollution and imposes a tax, it will be less profitable to produce paper there. In the long run there will be less investment in paper-making than would otherwise occur. If the mill has the right to pollute and becomes the recipient of subsidies, this will attract new investment to the region—why not open a new mill and apply for these subsidies too? So in the long run there will be more mills and therefore more pollution at any given level of subsidy. (3) There is plenty of evidence that people tend to demand more to give up something they have than they will offer to get something they don't. That is, they are likely to demand more in taxes than they would offer in subsidies. The reasons for this are still under active debate, but the pattern itself is not doubted.

Bottom line: policies to limit detrimental externalities through financial incentives are also expressions of property rights. The choice of whose right should prevail has large economic consequences. These are summarized in Table 15.1.

Table 15.1 The assignment of property rights and economic outcomes

Property rights	Assigned to polluters	Assigned to those affected by pollution
Financial instrument	Subsidies to polluters	Taxes on polluters
Size of financial incentive	Generally smaller	Generally larger
Resulting level of pollution	Generally higher	Generally lower

15.4 New Types of Externalities

Actually, the externalities are old, but the thinking about them is new! Much recent research has gone into **network externalities** and **positional externalities**. These concepts offer new ways to think about longstanding social issues.

Network externalities refer to the spillover effects of individual consumption decisions when the value of a good or service depends on how many users it has. A familiar example is the telephone. If you were the only person in the whole world who had one, it would have little value except perhaps as an art object. It takes two to have a conversation, and the more people who have their own phones, the more benefit this device will give you. To take the opposite extreme, if you were the only person who did *not* have a phone, you would probably feel you were missing something important. In societies where telephone access is nearly universal, all sorts of activities require phone contact.

The same goes for computer software. The value of a program increases as more people use it. With the vast majority of computer users adopting Microsoft word-processing and other programs, for example, those who prefer to use competing programs have to worry about the compatibility of their files: will they be able to exchange files with friends and coworkers? Also, as the number of Microsoft users increases, so does the availability of other programs that add to or take advantage of the features in Microsoft products. (There is a bigger market, which attracts more businesses.) The same issue has appeared in cellphones and tablets with the availability of apps.

It is reasonable to call this effect an externality, because it results from the lack of a market in spillovers. My choice of software (or in the case of the telephone, hardware) changes the benefit you get from your choices, but you cannot negotiate with me to offer incentives so I will make the choice you prefer. True, the spillover for any individual choice is small, but over millions of users the cumulative effect can be enormous. Obviously, the transaction costs required to set up spillover markets on the scale necessary would be beyond calculation—the whole idea seems bizarre.

And why would anyone care about such externalities? One reason is that network effects can lead to the adoption of inefficient technologies. Once a product with network externalities is in wide use, it will be more advantageous for new consumers to adopt it, even though another product might be even better if it were adopted as widely. Without a market in externalities, there is no way to coordinate a mass migration from the lesser to the better product. The product that arrives first on the market and has an opportunity to build up its network can lock out a later, better alternative.

Positional externalities arise in situations where what matters is not how much you have or how well you do, but how much or how well in comparison to others. Suppose, for example, that the best students in a particular country all want to be admitted to Elite University, which is known for its unsurpassed resources, the brilliance of its teachers, and the top jobs awarded to its graduates. Suppose also that admission to Elite depends almost entirely on a student's performance in a standardized test. Since there are a limited number of openings at Elite, what counts is not the score a student gets, but how well that score ranks in comparison to all the other scores. Getting 90 % of the answers right is no consolation if so many students do better than this that all the available slots at Elite will be taken by them.

Aware of the situation, you might hire a professional coach to help improve your score. If you are the only student who does this, your chances for admission will go up (if the coaching works). But others may have the same idea. If everyone hires a coach, and if everyone's score goes up by 5 %, this makes everyone look smarter, but the same people end up getting into Elite as before. The problem is that, since it is one's *position* in the rank-order of test-takers, and not the score itself, that matters for admission, each person's improvement comes at the expense of everyone else. If all improve, these effects cancel out, and no one has gained. The effects are externalities of particular sort—positional externalities.

This also explains the inefficiency, and in most cases the impossibility, of replacing the administrative organization of firms with lots of individual contracts between workers and owners. Each worker would try to bargain for what he or she wants: better working conditions, lighter or more interesting work assignments, a higher status within the enterprise. Many of these interests, however, come at the expense of other workers. If there is a limited number of good job assignments available, for instance, my getting one comes at the expense of you or someone else. These positional externalities would overwhelm any attempt at organizing production via one-on-one negotiations. Instead, firms have administrative structures that attempt, for better or worse, to take all these interconnections into consideration and allocate tasks and other job-related matters in a systematic manner.

When positional externalities are allowed to proliferate without restraint, the result is often an *arms race*. All participants invest more resources in getting ahead, but the outcome is only that the total amount of investment has gone up. What is rational from each individual's perspective is socially wasteful, much as universal defection (which it resembles) was seen to be an irrational outcome in the Prisoner's Dilemma.

15.5 Taking Stock

From the beginning, this book has argued that it is a misunderstanding to see economics only as a hymn of praise to the wonders of free markets. There is a whiff of that in some economic writings, since economists often feel that the general public fails to see the positive aspects of a well-functioning market system. Yet one could also say that economics is centrally focused on the *failure* of real-world markets, the defects that prevent them from achieving the nirvana promised by the Market Welfare Model. This provides the justification for most of the policies that economists analyze and debate.

But just as a scrupulous economist should not accept market outcomes without carefully inspecting the process for public goods, externalities and other distortions, neither should she throw up her hands if she finds that market failure has occurred. Economic theory has classified and dissected these failures, and it has much to say about how, and even whether, to remedy them.

Defining a problem as precisely as possible is the biggest step toward identifying a solution. The theories outlined in this chapter provide a starting point for much of the work applied economists do in the policy arena. They estimate the value of public goods that fail to be produced due to free-rider problems and the difference between private and social benefits or costs in the presence of externalities. *Economics does its best work when markets need a helping hand.* The deep understanding of market failures offered by economics would not have been possible without a vision of ideal markets to compare them to. Logically, this chapter should be seen as a culmination, not a revision, of Chap. 6 on the Market Welfare Model.

At the same time, however, the problems that now shadow the Market Welfare Model should also be seen as casting doubt on the market failure framework. As we have learned in earlier chapters, the traditional theories of utility and rational choice which underpin the Market Welfare Model have been buffeted by new findings in the field of economic psychology. Individuals do not always make the choices that maximize their well-being, and happiness, as measured in surveys and physiological responses, does not correspond very well to utility as this has been defined by economists. This means that we do not necessarily need a theory of market failure to identify shortcomings in the way markets work: misguided decision-makers or simply the biases of market incentives that may impinge on happiness could lead to the same conclusion. Even more disturbing, it is entirely possible that correcting a market failure could lead to even *worse* outcomes as measured by happiness or capabilities. For instance, a negative externality in production like pollution could lead to less food crops being harvested, But what if our food consumption choices do not improve our health or happiness? Counteracting the externality, and thereby increasing the supply and reducing the price of "junk food" ingredients, for instance, might actually make us worse off.

Taken on their own terms, the criticisms emanating from economic psychology and happiness studies are deeply at odds with the perspective of both the Market Welfare Model *and* the market failure theory sketched in this chapter. Some economists would argue that utility theory should be rejected as faulty and anachronistic. The majority, however, continue to use utility theory and base much of their policy advice on market failure reasoning, even though they are aware that the basis for this approach has been called into question. They are guided by the faith that traditional economic ideas remain approximately right, in spite of their demonstrated shortcomings. At the same time it would not be an exaggeration to say that the current situation remains fluid, and that economics is in the midst of some sort of transition on these issues. Where this transition will take us, and how much weight will be given to notions like market failure in the years to come, it is too soon to tell.

The Main Points

1. Public goods are those which have one of two characteristics: either there is a zero or near-zero marginal cost of provision (nonrivalry) or it is impractical to prevent access to them if no payment is made (nonexclusion). Some public goods are provided by the public sector, but not all. Many goods provided by the public sector are *not* public goods in the economic sense.
2. The problem with nonexclusion is that there is an incentive for users to not pay; this is referred to as the free-rider problem. The problem with nonrivalry, on the other hand, is the possibility that there will be too little use of the good. If the marginal cost is zero, any price that may be charged will discourage some users whose personal benefit does not justify paying for it. Yet, as long as they derive any benefit, it is economically inefficient to exclude them.
3. Externalities arise as a result of missing markets. If an activity produces beneficial goods or services that users need not pay for (due to a missing market), there is a positive externality and a tendency for underprovision of that benefit. If an activity produces harmful outcomes that suppliers do not need to pay for (due to a missing market), there is a negative externality and a tendency for overprovision of that harm.
4. There are several potential remedies for externalities. One is moral suasion—persuading individuals to produce more goods with positive externalities or fewer with negative. Another is direct regulation by the government, such as laws prohibiting or limiting certain forms of pollution. A third is the use of monetary incentives—taxes and subsidies—to induce more provision of goods with positive externalities and less of goods with negative externalities. Finally, it may be possible to create the missing market by establishing new property rights or otherwise encouraging bargaining between creators and recipients of externalities.
5. The so-called Coase Theorem (which Ronald Coase himself did not propose) states that the assignment of property rights, whether rights belong to the creator or the recipient of an externality, does not alter the amount the externality that will be arrived at through bargaining. This hypothesis is false, however, due to the impact of the assignment of rights on bargaining power, its effect on entry or exit of those who create the goods being bargained over, and the psychological tendency referred to as status quo bias.
6. New types of externalities are attracting the interest of economists. One is network externalities, the effect that one person's choice of a good has on others whose benefit from that good depends on how many people use it. Another is positional externalities, where individuals invest in goods that increase their rank or place in a queue at the expense of others in the same ranking or queuing order.

Terms to Define

Cap-and-trade
Externalities
Free-rider problem

Market failure
Negative externalities
Network externalities
Nonexclusion
Nonrivalry
Pigovian taxes and subsidies
Positional externalities
Positive externalities
Public goods
Pure public good
Social vs private costs (or benefits)
Spillovers
Zero marginal cost problem

Questions to Consider

1. Older economics textbooks sometimes mentioned streets and roads as examples of nonexcludable goods: while a few toll roads might charge for access, most didn't, and it did not seem remotely practical to set up toll booths at every intersection. This meant that road-building and maintenance would have to be financed out of taxes rather than user payments. Now, however, the technology exists to charge drivers for every stretch of road they drive on, even tailored to the time of day or season of the year. Each license plate can have a transmitter that sends signals to receptors placed by the side of the road, so that the number of times the vehicle passed (and when it passed) can be saved and stored. Periodically the driver can be charged for the roads he or she used. What do you think of this system? Would you be in favor of dropping tax support for roads and replacing it with user fees along these lines? Should the government subsidize research in new technologies that have the potential to keep track of each person's use of other goods, like parks, pedestrian walkways, etc.?
2. As we saw in this chapter, the potential problem of zero marginal cost has been solved by broadcasting companies that sell advertising based on the number of viewers or listeners. This same approach now shows up on the internet, where free content, like on-line newspapers or search results, is financed by ads. Is this a satisfactory solution to the nonrivalry characteristic of digital information? What are the advantages and disadvantages of relying on ad revenue? Can you think of any alternatives?
3. Airplanes produce a lot of noise when they take off and land, and this is a problem for people who live near airports. Is it an externality? Explain, using the definition provided in this chapter. Should there be financial incentives to reduce this noise? If so, should they be based on an assignment of "quiet rights" to nearby residents or "noise rights" to airports and airplanes? What difference would the choice of rights make for the amount of the incentive, the level of noise, the location of airports and the location of residential communities? If you don't favor taxes or subsidies, what do you propose—some other policy to control noise or no policy at all?

4. It could be argued that one of the most important examples of a network externality is the adoption of a language. Explain why the number of people who learn and speak various languages is influenced by network externalities. Is this a problem or a solution to a problem or both? Should something be done for languages that might decline as global communications become more integrated?
5. Some consumption items are regarded as "status goods": their main value is to confer social status on those who own or use them. Can you think of any examples that fit this description? If so, does the problem of positional externalities apply? Is there an "arms race"? Should some corrective action be taken?

Part IV

Microeconomic Challenges

Labor and Employment 16

For most of us, there is no aspect of economics more important than the study of employment, wages and the conditions of work—for the simple reason that most of us participate in the economy as workers or plan to participate that way in the future. As we saw in Chap. 4, the perspective of economics puts consumption at the center, but for almost everyone work is what makes consumption possible, and useful and interesting work is valuable in its own right. In this chapter we will survey the concepts economists employ when they try to explain or predict wages and job opportunities.

Before going forward, however, two points are worth noting. First, as we also saw in Chap. 4, employment is viewed as a *cost* in economic theory, not a *benefit*. The creation of jobs per se is not seen as desirable; rather, having more people at work is good if and only if the value of the goods and services they produce exceeds their cost of employment. Similarly, higher wages are not necessarily beneficial. A country would not make itself richer by passing a law requiring everyone's wages to be doubled. The goal is to generate jobs that are productive, so that high wages can be justified by high productivity. Second, when we study the market for employment, the roles we were accustomed to earlier in this book have to be switched. Firms, which were the suppliers of goods to consumer markets, are now on the demand side: they are the ones that buy labor. Households, which were consumers of goods and services, are now represented as suppliers of labor.

As a warm-up for the main theme of this chapter, we will begin with a general discussion of **factor markets**—the supply and demand for factors of production, which include not only labor but the other resources on which our economy depends. This will give us a framework for analyzing labor markets in particular, which can be complicated since human beings are neither standardized nor passive the way other items traded in markets tend to be.

P. Dorman, *Microeconomics*, Springer Texts in Business and Economics,
DOI 10.1007/978-3-642-37434-0_16, © Springer-Verlag Berlin Heidelberg 2014

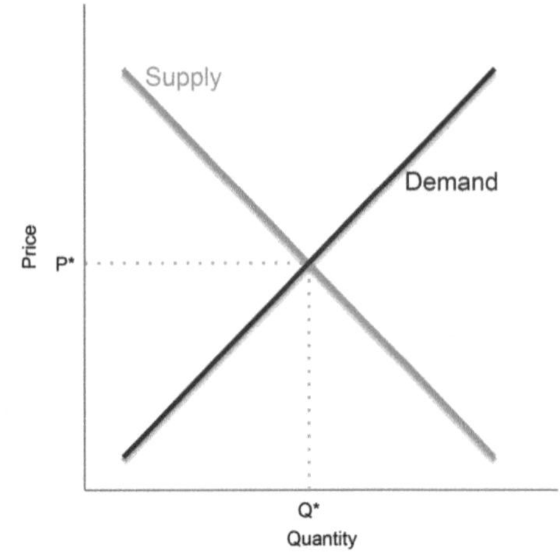

Fig. 16.1 Supply and demand for a factor of production. A factor market can be depicted in the same way as any other market, with supply and demand curves. If equilibrium requires that S = D, P* will be the equilibrium price of the factor and Q* its equilibrium quantity

16.1 The Theory of Factor Markets

At a *very* high level of abstraction, factor markets are just markets. There is a demand for a factor of production, like land or labor, a supply of it, and a resulting price and quantity traded. Thus the familiar apparatus of a supply and demand diagram is the logical starting point, as in Fig. 16.1.

The differences between factor and other markets appear when we look more closely at what determines supply and demand, and also at the conditions for equilibrium.

Supply: The resources needed for production are assumed to be privately owned. These include the human capacity for work (measured in units of time), natural resources, and **capital goods**, items like machines and buildings that are produced by the economy but also serve as long-lived inputs to future production. Of course, some of these—especially natural resources—are not always privately owned, and we will have to adjust the theory to account for that. (This will be taken up in the chapter on economics and ecology.) But where private ownership occurs, we can assume that the motive for supplying factors of production is essentially the same as for any other good, to get the best possible economic return.

The owner of a factor is assumed to have many possible uses to choose from, and this means that the decision to supply the factor to any particular use will entail an **opportunity cost**. You could imagine that each factor owner has a different opportunity cost, some higher and some lower. At very high prices in a particular market most of them would find that the price covers this cost, and so they would supply the resource. At a lower price fewer would supply. The result is that the market factor supply curve, which combines all these individual factor owners, would be upward-sloping, just like the supply curves for other goods.

Demand: The story behind the factor demand curve is more complicated. The entities on the demand side of the factor market are firms; they look to purchase factors of production in order to be able to produce goods and services for sale on other markets. To make things simple, let's assume they can sell as much as they can produce at a fixed price, so that the only issue is productivity. (This is a highly unrealistic assumption, of course, and you will see what happens when it is dropped when you study *macro*economics.) Another assumption that plays a crucial role was introduced in Chap. 12, that there are diminishing marginal returns to any factor of production when the supply of other factors is held constant. Recall the logic at work: if a firm increases the amount of all the resources it uses in production, it can increase its output at least proportionately, for instance by replicating its most efficient operations. In the short run, however, at least some factors are in fixed supply; this is in fact the meaning of "short run" in economics. In this case, adding more of the variable factors (the ones that can be increased) will result in less-than-proportional increases in productivity. (For the full story, you may want to revisit Chap. 12.) This can be depicted graphically, as in Fig. 16.2a on the following page.

In Fig. 16.2a the MP_F curve, which reflects the **marginal productivity** of some factor of production F, is downward-sloping but still above zero. This means that additional inputs of F into production continue to increase final output, but by smaller amounts as more F is added. Imagine, for example, that F represents computers in an office. The first computer installed could have a very large effect on production, and this might be true for the next dozen or even hundred, depending on the size of the office. But at some point adding more computers, while still of some value, will produce less effect, and eventually their marginal productivity will fall to zero. (It could even become negative if computer boxes take up so much room that it is difficult to carry on normal business.) Notice that this example holds only in the short run, when the size of the office is fixed. If you could increase the number of workers, the amount of building space and all the other factors of production at the same time, there is no reason why the marginal product of computers should fall.

Figure 16.2b is the same as Fig. 16.2a, but with one important difference: now, instead of measuring the productivity of F in terms of the amount of output it creates, we are measuring it in terms of the *value* of this output. This explains why the terminology is changed to the ***value* of the marginal product**, VMP. Recall that we assumed that all output could be sold at a given price; if this is true, the only difference between Figs. 16.2a and 16.2b is that the vertical axis in Fig. 16.2b represents the physical output of F (as in Fig. 16.2a) times the price per unit of output. To return to our office example, suppose that what is being produced is insurance contracts. The Q_O axis in Fig. 16.2a represents the number of such contracts; the R axis in Fig. 16.2b represents their economic value, measured as the number of contracts times the money earned by the office for each contract it produces (revenue). The marginal product curve remains the same in either case; only the units on the vertical axis change when we transform the MP_F curve on the top into the VMP_F curve on the bottom.

To transform Fig. 16.2b into a demand curve, all we need to do is consider the effect that factor prices have on the purchasing decisions of firms. This is pictured in Fig. 16.3 on p. 343.

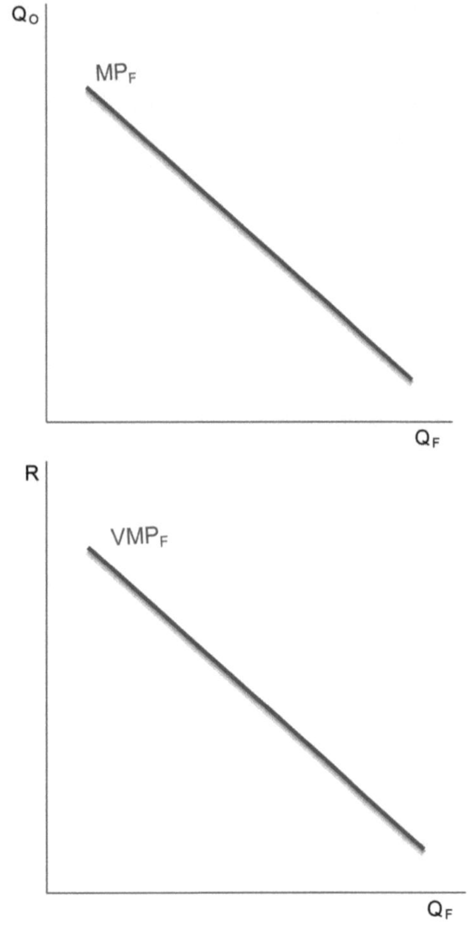

Fig. 16.2 Marginal factor productivity in the short run measured as output and value. (**a**) Each additional input of the factor, measured on the Q_F axis, produces a smaller additional quantity of output, Q_O, when the supply of some other factor is fixed in the short run. The height of the MP_F curve measures the marginal product of the factor F in units of output. (**b**) This depicts the same marginal productivity relationship between the factor F and the output it is producing, except that the vertical axis is measured in terms of monetary value, calculated as the quantity of output times its price

Here we have drawn a horizontal line at P_1, indicating that the firm can purchase as much of the factor as it wants, but always at the price P_1. This is equivalent to saying that the factor market is perfectly competitive: the firm has no control over the price of the factor, perhaps because there are very many such firms all bidding for the same resource. This would be true when the factor is a computer, for instance, for all but the largest companies. Computer manufacturers quote a price, and most offices are not in a position to try to lower it. To continue the example, imagine that the office purchases its first computer. Its productivity rises dramatically, so that its additional revenues, given by the height of the VMP_F curve, greatly exceed the computer's price. It keeps buying more computers, but when it purchases the last computer that brings it to a level of Q_1 in stock it will discover that the financial benefit is exactly equal to the cost. Any additional computer beyond that point will cost more than it produces. So the firm maximizes its profit (revenue minus cost) by purchasing exactly Q_1 computers when the price is P_1.

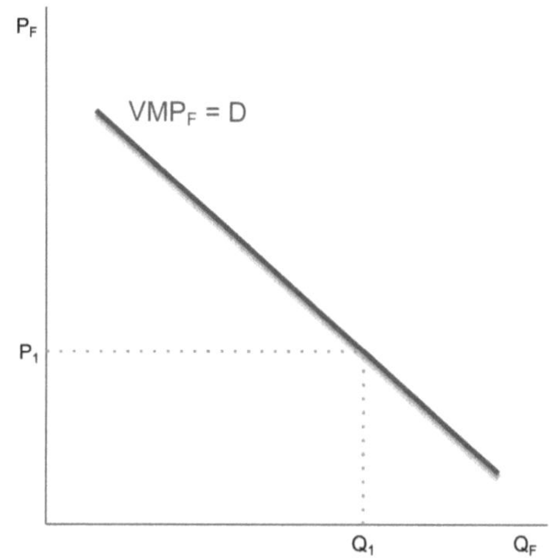

Fig. 16.3 The demand for a factor of production by a single firm. P_1 is the price of the factor and VMP_F is its marginal product measured in value (revenue) terms. At low levels of factor use, the value created by additional factor purchases exceeds the cost. This is no longer true at Q_1; here the additional purchase of F exactly pays for itself in increased revenues. Beyond Q_1 the marginal product of F is below its price, so purchasing these units would lose money. A profit-maximizing firm will therefore acquire this factor up to the level Q_1 but not beyond it. Since this logic holds for any potential price above or below P_1, the VMP_F curve is also the firm's demand curve for factor F

If the price were higher than this, the firm would buy less—again given by where the height of VMP_F equals the new price. If the price were lower, more would be bought. In this way it is clear that the VMP_F curve is also the demand curve for the factor.

If this accurately describes the behavior of a single factor-purchasing firm, the market demand curve would be simply the horizontal sum of all such firms. In our computer example, if there are 50,000 offices all in the market for computers, we would construct the market demand for computers by adding up all the purchases at P_1, another price P_2 and so on until we could associate every potential price with a combined demand. (You may recall that this was exactly the technique we used in Chap. 11 to go from individual to market demand for consumer products.)

What does this analysis tell us? Very generally, it explains the basis for factor demand: for any given factor price, the amount that will be demanded depends on the marginal productivity of that factor—what it contributes to production when the supply of other factors is held constant—and the value of the output produced. The first of these can be thought of as "technological", the result of the way production is organized. This, of course, is influenced by the availability of other factors of production, since the productivity of any particular factor (such as computers) depends on the other resources (such as labor) it is paired with. It is also influenced by the quality of the factor itself, since a higher-quality factor (e.g. a better computer) would generate a higher MP_F curve. The second depends on the demand for the things the factor produces, which is why factor demand is often described as "derived". In our computer example, the demand for computers is derived from the demand for the many services that computer-using offices produce and sell. So the full list of conditions that determine the demand for a factor would include:

- the technologies used by firms that use the factor,
- the quality of the factor as it influences its use in production,
- the price, quality and other supply characteristics of other factors,
- the demand for the goods and services the factor is purchased to produce.

Equilibrium: Our general definition of equilibrium incorporates two conditions, that there be no impetus for change, and that there be a process that leads to equilibrium if we are out of it. In most supply and demand situations we have accepted the intersection of supply and demand curves (if they do in fact intersect) as equivalent to equilibrium. This is because, at the equilibrium price, the amount sellers want to supply and the amount consumers want to buy is equal—neither wants to change—and either excess supply or excess demand will set in motion a process that moves the price back in the direction of equilibrium. Based on this, we would expect that equilibrium in factor markets would also occur at a price where supply equals demand.

In many cases this is true, but we have to be careful, since it often happens in factor markets that excess supply is the norm. We can see this in the form of unemployed workers or land that sits idle for years on end. These would not occur if the markets for these factors performed the way typical consumer markets do.

Economists do not yet agree on the reasons for persistent excess factor supply. This is a topic that receives more treatment in macroeconomics; for now a simple observation will have to do. Many factors are highly specialized in the sense that they are more productive in a few production processes than they are in most others. This is true of land in particular locations, machines built to particular specifications or workers with particular skills. Owners of these factors will not want to sell to the first buyer who comes along; instead they will take their time, looking for the most productive match. Many of the unsold factors, then, are in the process of being shopped around; as they eventually find the right buyers, new ones enter the hunt, giving the impression of permanent excess supply.

To sum up, factor markets *may* have equilibria similar to other markets, where supply equals demand at a common price. It is also possible, however, that there could be persistent excess demand, particularly for factors that have highly specialized uses.

16.2 Labor as a Factor of Production

Now that we have surveyed the general theory of factor markets, let's move to our main interest in this chapter, the peculiar factor of production that takes the form of human labor. Our starting point will be a single moment in the complex world of work and employment: the filling of a few vacancies at a single firm. Our perspective will be that of a personnel manager who must recruit enough applicants to meet the firm's needs while keeping wage costs as low as possible. This person must be aware of both the demand side of the market, representing the employer's interests, as well as the supply side, the prospective workers' willingness to apply. We will start once again with supply.

16.2.1 Supply and Demand at the Level of a Single Firm

In all but the most isolated regions, workers have many potential employment opportunities. They can consider different employers, different occupations, and even the option of moving to another city or country to find a better job. For the personnel manager in our story, this makes the recruitment task extremely clear: a wage must be offered that will attract a sufficient number of workers, where these workers take into account their own opportunity cost, set by the offers being made by *other* employers. In the language of economics, the firm must match the **reservation wage**, the opportunity cost of employment, of at least as many workers as it hopes to hire. For the personnel manager, this means keeping a close watch on the wages and hiring rates of other firms in the community. Unless there is a large reserve of unemployed workers, it is unlikely that many recruits will show up unless these wages are matched. In fact, in a perfectly competitive world, with many workers, many firms, perfect information, and no differences between workers, all firms would pay exactly the same wage. They could pay no less, because then workers' reservation wages would exceed the firm's offer, and no workers would apply. They would pay no more, since there is no gain from paying extra. Thus the individual firm's labor supply curve would be perfectly elastic as in Fig. 16.4 on the next page.

Beginning with this diagram, we will adopt the convention of labeling the axes W (for wages) and N (for the number of workers). This corresponds to the P and Q on other supply and demand diagrams, since W is the price and N the supply of or demand for labor. In this case, W* is the market wage which any individual firm is constrained to match. It is also the reservation wage for workers; they will be indifferent between working at any firm offering that wage.

From our earlier analysis we now know that the VMP_L curve will be the demand curve for labor, based on the market value of the additional production each individual worker could make possible. If the initial employment level is N_1 hiring is increased; if it is N_2 dismissals occur. In either case the process stops once N* is reached. To say this is not to answer all the questions we might be interested in. After all, *how* does the firm adjust employment? Does it simply hire new workers or dismiss old ones, leaving all other aspects of its production process the same? Does it change its technology, replacing workers by machines, for instance? Does it change its product mix, producing fewer products that require lots of labor input and more of others requiring less? We are not in a position to explore these issues in our simple example, since we would need to know much more about the firm's technological opportunities and market position. These points are brought up to remind us that we are just scratching the surface of a *real* analysis of employment policy.

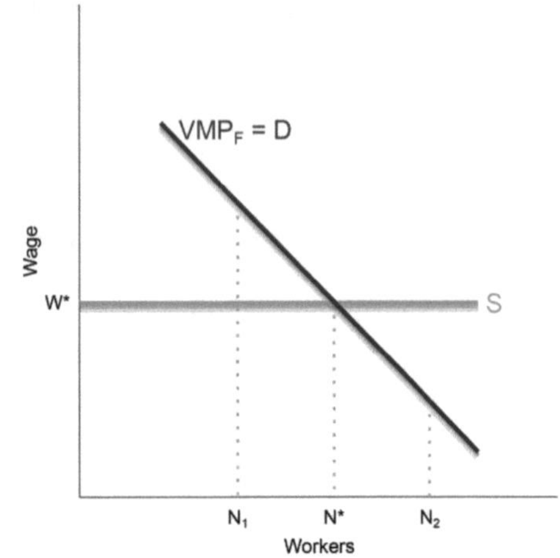

Fig. 16.4 The demand for labor in a single, perfectly competitive firm. A perfectly competitive firm can hire as many workers as it wishes so long as it pays a wage at least equal to W*. If it has a labor force of N_1 employees it hires more. If it has N_2 workers it dismisses some of them. Either process continues until the firm has exactly N* workers, the profit-maximizing number

Another aspect of this supply-and-demand story that deserves attention is the *elasticity of demand.* Recall from Chap. 5 that the price elasticity of demand is defined as the percentage change in quantity demanded divided by the percentage change in price:

$$elasticity\ of\ demand = \%\Delta\ in\ Q^D/\%\Delta\ in\ P$$

If demand for labor is highly inelastic the demand curve will be steeper and located further to the southeast of the diagram; if it is highly elastic it will be flatter and located further to the northwest. The elasticity of the demand curve is a crucial piece of information for workers who might want to ask for a raise. If the demand for labor is inelastic, workers can try to win large percentage pay increases without worrying much about losing their jobs. If demand is more elastic, a fairly small pay increase can lead to large layoffs. For the record, a firm's elasticity of demand for labor depends primarily on these factors:

1. The elasticity of demand for the product being produced: if consumers are highly sensitive to price increases, firms are more likely to be sensitive to wage increases.
2. The elasticity of substitution between labor and other factors: if it is easier to replace workers with machines, greater use of raw materials, or some other productive input, firms will respond to wage increases by making these substitutions.
3. The elasticity of total cost with respect to labor cost: if wages paid to workers constitute most of a firm's total cost of production, the firm will be more likely to respond to wage increases by using less labor.

As elsewhere, the key word to remember when thinking about elasticity is *substitution.* In the case of the demand for labor, the substitutions that matter are the consumer's (of one product for another) and the employer's (of one factor of production for another). On one extreme, consider the current debate over sweatshops in developing countries that produce clothing for sale in Europe and North America. Workers in these sweatshops have little bargaining power: small increases in wages will lead to a great loss of employment. This is due to the ease of substitution on all sides: labor costs are an important part of the total cost of production in garments, and consumers are very sensitive to price. At the same time, firms are able to close down production in one country and open in another if wages go up even a little. Hence the demand for garment workers in the developing world is highly elastic. An opposite case would be the situation of a star athlete. Sports fans are attached to particular teams and pay somewhat less attention to ticket prices; if they follow the game on television there is no monetary price to be paid at all. The teams themselves are in a poor position to resist pay increases, since there are few really skilled athletes; hence there is no alternative "factor of production" to shift to if pay goes up. Finally, while athletes' pay is an important part of a team's total cost, it is a smaller part of the total cost of the sports enterprise, including TV coverage. As a result, the demand for professional athlete's labor is highly inelastic, and this gives athletes more bargaining power.

In the world of perfect competition we have been considering, of course, there is no need for bargaining power, since neither side has anything to bargain over. Look once more at the equilibrium (W*, N*) in Diagram 4. Workers are receiving the same wage at this firm that they could get at any other, not more or less. In other words, they are paid exactly their reservation wage. They might want to make more, but, given that the firm can obtain a virtually endless supply of labor at this wage, there is no chance that the wage will go up. By the same token, firms are maximizing profits subject to the limitation that they are forced to pay W*. By setting employment at N* they have done the best they can under the circumstances. They might want to reduce the wage, but, since there are many other firms offering W*, this is out of the question. To speak of bargaining, then, is to imply that labor markets are not perfectly competitive. We will return to this issue later in the chapter, as we try to make our theory of employment and wages more realistic.

16.2.2 Supply and Demand for Labor Across an Entire Economy

Once we move from the level of an individual firm to that of an entire economy (or an entire region if labor mobility is restricted within a smaller geographic area), things become somewhat more complicated. In the case of a single firm, by assuming perfect competition, we took it as given that the size of the firm was small relative to the economy as a whole, and this meant that there would surely be enough available labor if the price was right. At the level of a whole economy, the total amount of labor available cannot be taken for granted. If the supply of potential workers falls short, this could have an enormous impact on wages and employment. At the same time, once we look at all workers and firms simultaneously, the reservation wage is no longer a given. Rather, it is determined as part of the overall market equilibrium and is therefore something we need to explain.

Similarly, on the firm's side the prices that can be charged for the goods labor produces cannot be determined separately from the wages that workers, who are also consumers, will receive. While we cannot address all of these questions in this chapter, we will begin by sketching a picture of economy-wide labor market equilibrium—one that would arise under perfect competition and without any of the complicating factors that make their appearance later in the chapter.

16.2.2.1 Labor Supply

Once again we can divide our analysis of labor supply into two portions, as we did earlier with factors of production in general: total availability and willingness to sell. The total availability of labor refers to the number of able-bodied individuals in an economy of employment age—roughly from their late teens through their 60s. This brings us first of all into the world of **demography**, the study of population patterns and population growth. The size and age structure of a population is the consequence of many factors:

- the previous size of the population, since, all else being equal, more people produce more people
- the age and gender structure of the population, in particular the proportion who are or will be women of child-bearing age, since this governs the potential reproduction rate
- the average number of children borne by these women
- the public health conditions that determine infant mortality, longevity, and the rate of disabling disease

In general, economic development is associated with a pattern called the **demographic transition**. In the early stages of development both birth rates and death rates are very high. As development proceeds, the death rate falls, but the birth rate doesn't, since the cultural factors associated with high birth rates, such as the use of children as "social security" in parents' old age and the lack of alternative opportunities for women, persist. This means that population growth is dramatic. Eventually, however, economic and social development alter a nation's culture and birth rates come down. At the end of the process is a stable, low- or even negative-growth population based on long lifespans and small families. This sequence is depicted in Fig. 16.5, in which population growth rates are plotted on the vertical axis against time on the horizontal axis.

Economists are interested in plotting the course of the demographic transition for many reasons, but for our purposes the most important implication concerns the changing availability of labor over the course of the development process. In the earlier stages of development, as a country's population is rising rapidly, labor is abundant, and the most difficult economic challenge is that of creating enough jobs. At a later stage of development, however, population grows little if at all. This means that rapid rates of economic growth cannot be sustained without tapping a new source of labor: either increasing the percentage of the adult population employed in paid labor (at best a temporary expedient) or bringing in new workers as immigrants or on a short-term basis. With some countries at an advanced state of development while others are just beginning, a dynamic is created that leads to

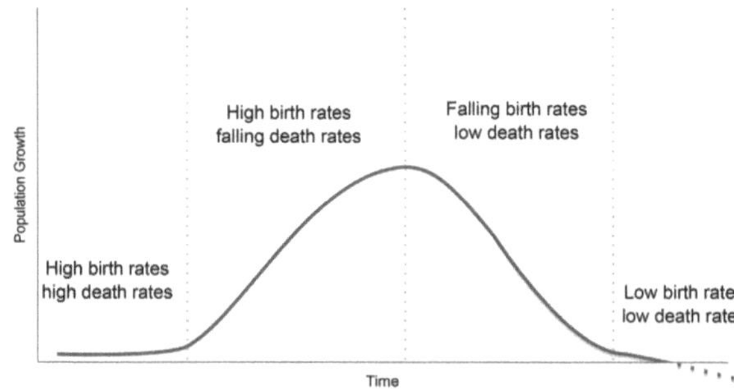

Fig. 16.5 Demographic transition. A typical pattern is for countries to emerge from a long history of high birth and death rates. At first death rates fall which birth rates remain high, resulting in rapid population growth. After a delay (which can be measured in decades) birth rates begin to fall as well, slowing population growth. Eventually a new balance between birth and death is reached; at this point population may be stable or even, as in many European countries, declining

sustained, large-scale international movements of people. The huge migration from the less to the more developed countries is one of the major phenomena of recent decades.

Given a total supply of potential labor, the next question is, how many of these people will make their services available to the labor market? Some can't because they are confined in prison or health care institutions. This institutionalized portion of the population is small in most developed countries, but higher in a few, such as the United States. For the noninstitutionalized majority, however, the critical issue is the **labor force participation rate**, the percentage who either are working, actively looking for a job, or who indicate that they would accept a job if one were offered. Time trends in labor force participation for several countries appear in Fig. 16.6 on the next page, ending before the disruptive effects of the financial crisis of 2008. Clearly, the long-term trend in most cases is up. Why?

To answer this question, we need to consider the factors behind the decision to seek employment. Recall from earlier in the chapter that economic theory identifies opportunity costs as the crucial variable: what are the alternative uses of time that would be unavailable if people work for pay? In modern societies there are as many alternatives as there are individuals, but we can group them this way:

- household production: time not spent on the job could be spent at home, raising children, keeping house, gardening, etc.
- self-employment: people could work for themselves in household enterprises, making crafts, providing personal services (like daycare or yardwork) to neighbors, or starting a larger business
- leisure: work cuts into the time available for playing music, camping, reading novels, talking with friends in cafes, and the other good things of life

To some extent this list helps explain the time trends we see above. Less household work may be necessary as technology improves in the home and more services, like childcare and food preparation, are offered in the market. Self-employment becomes a less viable option as an economy develops, since many

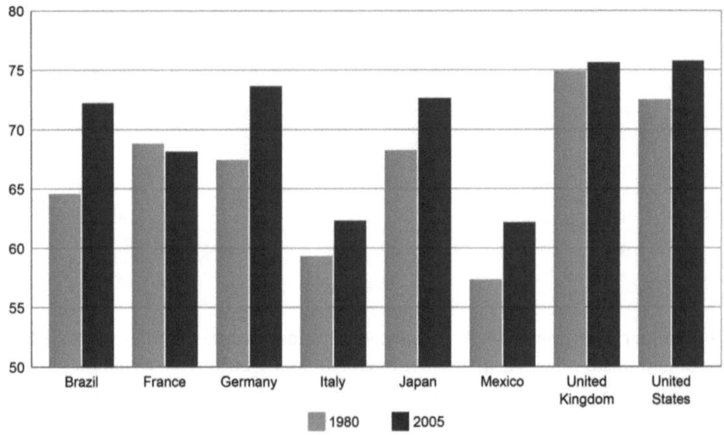

Fig. 16.6 Labor force participation rate, 1980 and 2005, for selected countries, in percent

modern technologies are efficient only if they are used on a large scale. (Of course, there are still a large number of goods and services that can be provided very effectively by individuals.) On the other hand, the loss of time available for leisure is a bit of a paradox, since modern consumer societies enhance the potential for fun and fulfillment outside work.

A closer look at the data, however, opens up another avenue of investigation. When we separate the trends in labor force participation for men and women, we find no trend for greater participation by men; all the growth is among women. Most would agree that this reflects a social and cultural change: the increased demand on the part of women to participate equally in all aspects of life. In most industrialized countries women expect to be part of the labor force, whether married or unmarried, with children or without. They are also entering occupations formerly closed to them, and laws have been passed in Europe and North America to break down the barriers of discrimination. From an economic viewpoint, the increasing labor force participation of women provides a new source of labor supply to economies that have undergone the demographic transition. Of course, as women's participation comes to equal that of men, the potential for labor supply growth will be exhausted.

Putting all of these factors together—the demography of the adult population, the degree of institutionalization, the opportunity costs and the value systems motivating women—we can propose an upward-sloping labor supply curve (S_L), as in Fig. 16.7a. The position of this curve and its slope depend on the specifics of each of these factors; a useful exercise would be to ask what impact a change in any of them might have on the S_L curve. But there is still another aspect to the willingness of households to supply any factor of production: the income effect. If workers become less interested in money, and more interested in other uses of their time as their income rises, greater pay could be associated with *less* labor supply, as in Fig. 16.7b. For instance, as wage rates rise, some households might prefer to have only one member work for income. From a theoretical standpoint,

Fig. 16.7 Two scenarios for the economy-wide labor market. (**a**) As the wage rises, more workers find that the value of supplying their labor exceeds the opportunity cost of their time. (**b**) As the wage rises, workers place greater value on non-work activities, reducing their labor supply

there is no basis for predicting which way the labor supply curve bends; either could be true. Indeed, it is possible that one effect might predominate at one income level, and the other at a different level. For instance, it may be that, at low wage rates, wage increases will draw more individuals into the paid labor force, whereas at higher wage levels the income effect will prove more powerful. In real world labor markets, the answer is probably "all of the above", with the shape of the S_L curve changing from region to region and pay level to pay level.

In both cases the labor demand curve, D_L, is unchanged: it is the horizontal sum of the demand curves emanating from individual employers, in just the way any economy-wide factor demand curve would be derived. Note, incidentally, that this demand is implicitly for labor of a particular country: one reason it is downward-sloping is that, if labor costs (the result of wages and worker productivity) are higher in one country, employers can shift production abroad or import products made by foreign workers. This is particularly the case if the goods being produced are inexpensive to trade.

What about labor market equilibrium? We know that it is typical that, at any given moment, many workers are unemployed, and this may suggest that excess supply of labor is the normal state of affairs. Actually, as we will see, it is not so simple. Nevertheless, there are many reasons given by economists for why there *might* be excess supply. For instance, it is difficult for firms to reduce wages when the labor demand curve shifts to the left, as it does when there is less demand in the economy for the things labor produces. This is because wage-cutting can have negative effects on worker morale, and the result can be even lower profits than when wages are kept at a higher level. Another consideration is that the employment relationship usually involves mutual expectations, sometimes in writing, other times informally. Workers may have been promised a degree of security in wages, or even opportunities to receive raises, and wage-cutting would constitute a violation of this pledge. Whatever the reason, there is plenty of evidence to suggest that wages are more readily raised than lowered in the developed economies.

As with factor markets in general, however, there is also a matching problem in the world of employment. The problem may be even more severe with labor, since not only is there the issue of specialized skills to consider, but also the preferences workers have for location, the social environment of work and other factors. Normally we would expect job searching, for both workers and employers, to be costly and time-consuming. Indeed, economists suspect that, for many workers, rejecting job offers and remaining unemployed may be a price that has to be paid to locate a *better* job. If this is true, we would expect to see a certain amount of unemployment based on search considerations alone.

So let us assume that the labor market is constantly in motion, with some workers working, others between jobs and still others unable to find work at all. One simple interpretation of labor market equilibrium under these circumstances is that it occurs when the number of workers searching for jobs equals the number of jobs searching for workers. That is, if we could freeze the economy in place until each worker had located his or her job opening, there would be no unemployment—but the economy never stops, and search takes too long for all workers and jobs to find one another. A graphic representation of this sort of "full employment" appears in Fig. 16.8 on the next page. The vertical axis measures the number of jobs looking for workers; the horizontal axis measures the number of workers looking for jobs. If the economy is in a recession we would expect there to be more workers looking for jobs than jobs looking for workers; this would occur at a point like A. When the economy is booming at an unsustainable rate there may be more unfilled jobs than unemployed workers; this would occur at B. A curved line has been drawn connecting all the possible combinations of available jobs/available workers that are feasible in a given economy at a given time; it is referred to as a **Beveridge Curve**, named for a prominent British policy analyst of the mid-twentieth century, William (Lord) Beveridge.

Any point along the Beveridge Curve is possible, but which one corresponds to labor market equilibrium? Let us suppose for a moment that equilibrium means that

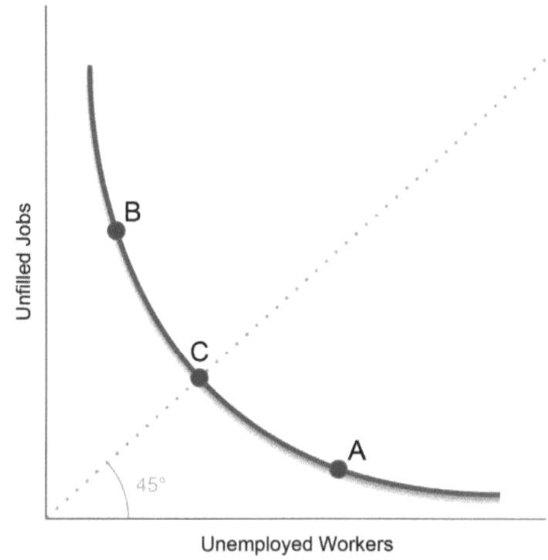

Fig. 16.8 The Beveridge Curve. At *point A* there are more workers looking for jobs than there are jobs to be filled; the opposite is the case at *point B*. *Point C*, where there would be just enough jobs for all workers if they could be matched, represents a possible labor market equilibrium. The *dotted line* represents all such potential points at which the supply and demand for labor would be equal (along different potential Beveridge Curves)

the supply and demand for labor are equal at a common price. In this case the point on the Beveridge Curve representing labor market equilibrium would be C, which lies at the intersection of the curve and a line going out from the origin at a 45° angle. All points along the 45° line represent equal numbers of unemployed workers and unfilled jobs. Since the number of *filled* jobs equals the number of employed workers by definition, this second equality is necessary to achieve S = D in the labor market. (Labor supply is the total number of workers working or looking for work; labor demand is the total number of jobs filled or looking for workers.) At C, the economy is simultaneously at its tradeoff between unemployed workers and unfilled jobs (reflecting the search efficiency of its labor market) and meets the condition that supply equals demand. The rate of unemployment at C depends on the position of the curve: the closer it is to the origin the lower the unemployment rate. It is obviously beneficial to have an efficient matching process, so that a point like C entails less unemployment.

The matter is a bit more complicated, however. At point C it is true that S = D, but it is not clear that this is in fact an equilibrium. On what basis could it be argued that only C represents a point at which there is no impetus to change, and what is the process that brings us there? *If* the labor market worked the way consumer markets do, we could say that wage adjustment would do the trick. At point A, where so many workers are chasing so few jobs, wages should fall, bringing more demand into play. At point B, where employers are on the short end, wages should rise, with the opposite effect. Only at point C would there be no reason for wages to adjust. This is the story that corresponds to market equilibrium as we considered it in Chap. 5. But we have already seen that the labor market is different. Wages do not necessarily adjust to equalize supply and demand, and we know from experience that a point like A can characterize the economy for a long time. Further analysis is the domain of macroeconomics; for now all we can say is that point C appears to be a desirable position for the economy to be at, with neither excess demand for or supply of labor, but we can't trust that the labor market will actually bring us there.

Even this may be a bit simplistic, however, since the economy consists of many types of labor and job requirements, and it might not be the case that a given number of workers could be matched to the same number of jobs even if all search information could be acquired instantaneously. At best, point C provides an initial benchmark for evaluating the efficiency of the market in bringing workers and jobs together.

16.3 Labor Markets When Jobs and Workers Are Not the Same

In the simple models above we have made the sweeping assumption that all workers and all jobs are essentially the same. There is one market wage that every employer pays and every worker receives. This is acceptable for an initial introduction to the study of labor markets, but it exhausts its usefulness rather quickly. One of the distinguishing features of the labor market is exactly how *different* workers and jobs really are. The main concern most of us have as workers is finding a "good" job, and the main concern of most employers is finding "good" workers. In this section we will explore some of the ramifications of *heterogeneity* on both the supply and demand sides of the labor market.

16.3.1 Differences in Jobs

What makes for a good job, other than higher wages? A short list would probably include these characteristics:

- Good fringe benefits. These might include health insurance or the provision of pensions, where these are not provided by government. Some firms provide other nonwage benefits like more vacation time, educational benefits for the worker's children, meals at company cafeterias, housing, etc.
- Good working conditions. A good job would be comfortable to perform and would not expose the worker to significant risks of injury or illness. It would be high in interest and low in stress. The worker would be treated with consideration and would have substantial autonomy in designing and carrying out his or her work.
- Good opportunities for advancement. A good job would help workers advance in their careers either within the firm or by moving to a new firm. In the first case this would mean plenty of opportunities to move into higher-echelon jobs, with no limit to how high one can rise. In the second it would mean lots of training and experience that other employers will value. The very best jobs would supply both of these, of course!
- Good job security. A worker may not want to spend the rest of her life with her current employer, but she wants this to be *her* choice. A good job is one that is stable and dependable.

In the real world there are few jobs that score high in every respect. Workers must trade off the attractive aspects of each job against its drawbacks. If a job is not

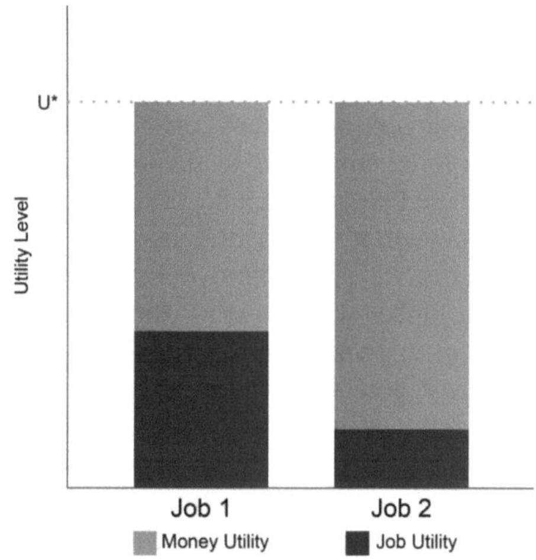

Fig. 16.9 A compensating wage differential for unequal utility from work. Employers must match the utility level U* in a competitive labor market. Some of this utility comes from the money wage, some from the work itself. Differences in the direct utility from the job must be offset by differences in wages

particularly attractive in *any* of these respects, however, employers may find it necessary to pay higher wages to attract the applicants they need. These pay increments for substandard work are called **compensating wage differentials** and they show up periodically in labor markets in which supply has a hard time keeping up with demand.

Figure 16.9 illustrates the logic. Suppose employers face a competitive labor market and must pay the same market-determined wage to all workers they hire. (The market could be for workers with particular qualifications or skills; obviously, there will be different markets for workers with different attributes, as we will see shortly.) The twist this time is that we will envision this wage in utility, not monetary terms: competition forces employers to offer the same utility payoff to any worker who will agree to accept a job with them. There are two sources of utility depicted, job-utility, the direct satisfaction workers receive as a result of spending their days doing this work, and money-utility, the utility equivalent of the wage they receive (the wage multiplied by workers' marginal utility of money). In Fig. 16.9, we compare two different jobs, one that offers more job-utility and less money-utility, the other more money-utility and less job utility. Both sum to the same amount.

As depicted, Job 1 is more satisfying to work at than Job 2, so Job 2 must pay a higher wage to attract its workforce. The difference is the compensating wage differential, measured here in utility terms. Workers in the two jobs are equally well-off, but in different ways. (What would Fig. 16.9 look like if job-utility in Job 2 were negative? This question appears at the end of the chapter.)

This is a highly simplified model, but it allows us to see the most important features of a world in which compensating differentials are paid. (1) Workers in unpleasant or dangerous jobs are no worse off than those in easier, safer or more interesting jobs. Differences in pay put everyone on the same level. (2) Workers can sort themselves into the jobs that match their preferences. Those who place a higher value on the satisfactions of work itself can gravitate toward Job 1; those for whom income is a priority can search for Job 2. (In this case, while most workers would get more utility from one job than another, it would be the *marginal* worker, one who is largely indifferent between the two jobs in equilibrium, whose job choice would force employers to set U*, and it would be this worker's utility which is represented in the diagram.) (3) Employers can choose to specialize in the kinds of jobs they offer. If a particular type of work is difficult or expensive to make interesting or safe, employers can give up on trying to improve it and simply offer a higher wage instead. But this also means that undesirable work is costly for them to provide, since it *must* be compensated with higher wages. This extra monetary cost to the employer provides an incentive to make work more satisfying—an incentive based on workers' own preferences between job- and money-utility. (4) Outside observers, including economists, can measure the amount of money it takes to exactly offset differences in job quality. This would tell us the price that workers and employers place on these job characteristics—information that would be useful to know in some circumstances. For instance, if workers who have more dangerous jobs make more money, how much money is the equivalent of, say, one extra chance in a thousand per year of having a serious accident or coming down with a case of occupationally-induced cancer? This would tell us a lot about how people value their life and health.

Above all, if the disutility of work is fully compensated by higher wages, an important element of the Market Welfare Model would be set in place. Recall from Chap. 4 that there are two fundamental types of economic cost, opportunity costs and disutility. If they are to be represented by the supply curve, it is essential that the money paid by producers compensate workers, resource suppliers and others whose goods and services they utilize for these two costs. The great majority of economic costs are opportunity costs, and the presumption is that owners of goods and services demand payment to cover them wherever there are markets for them to participate in. (This is why the missing market aspect of externalities is a problem.) Nevertheless, disutility is also a real burden that people bear in order for economies to be productive. Many jobs are difficult, dangerous or simply boring. If these human costs are to be reflected in market prices, compensating wage differentials need to be paid to reimburse them. Imagine, for instance, that there are two chemicals that can be used for metal polishing in industry, one that causes cancer in workers and one that doesn't. If employers who use the carcinogenic chemical have to pay higher wages to their workers, this will reduce the demand for the chemical or raise the cost of goods these firms produce if the chemical continues to be used. If compensating wage differentials are not paid, however, the hazardous chemical will be overused, and products will be purchased whose true economic costs (including the health risks to workers) exceed their benefits. To be clear: compensating wage differentials provide the most important potential channel for incorporating disutility into market prices.

So what do we find in the real world? Does it look like Fig. 16.9, or is there a lack of compensation for poor work or working conditions? The answer (as nearly always) is mixed. In occupations in which workers have scarce skills, are organized into unions or otherwise enjoy substantial bargaining power, compensating wage differentials, explicit or de facto, are common. It is common for corporations to pay managers higher salaries for posting in unpleasant locations. Unionized workers generally make more if they have to work night shifts. Welders working on the top floors of skyscrapers will generally earn more than those working near the bottom, since skilled welders are in short supply and must be paid extra to induce them to accept highly dangerous jobs. We can't know for sure whether the extra payments to workers in these cases are *fully* compensating, but we can see that they exist. On the other hand, there is an enormous body of research on the role of occupational health and safety in wage patterns, and the evidence for the US indicates that few workers whose skills are less in demand and who are exposed to the greatest risks at work are paid a wage premium, with many even earning less for bearing this cost. Those at the bottom are victims of bad luck: the good jobs were taken by others and they got stuck with ones that both pay less and endanger them more. From the standpoint of fairness, most would agree that, in an ideal world, workers in the riskiest jobs, or those exposed to the greatest threat of sudden unemployment or other hazards, *should* earn a compensating differential. Moreover, the spotty record of wage compensation for risk and other undesirable aspects of work indicates that, in this respect, the Market Welfare Model is largely unfulfilled. Financial compensation for disutility is still a goal to be fully realized.

16.3.2 Differences in Workers

In simple models like the ones illustrated in Fig. 16.7, workers are represented as perfectly interchangeable. On the horizontal axis is the number of workers (N), based on the assumption that any worker may substitute for any other. This is obviously false. People bring a wide range of skills and abilities to the labor market, and this is why the matching process is so arduous.

Some differences are the result of who we are—our different abilities to do certain types of physical and mental work, or the strengths and weaknesses of our personalities. An important aspect of skill, however, is acquired through education and experience. By investing time and effort in acquiring new skills, an individual can hope to enjoy many years of future benefits, measured not only by extra income, but also by the satisfaction that comes from meaningful, interesting work. Skills that are acquired in this way are called **human capital** by economists, since, like other types of capital, they are the result of investment for the purpose of earning future returns. Once again we encounter the power of metaphor in economics: the terminology used to describe education and other forms of skill-enhancement calls attention to an aspect of the process that is shared by other activities that promote long-run economic growth. Of course, there are ways in which human capital is not at all like other types of capital. A firm can more easily borrow money to finance the purchase of a new building because the building, a form of physical capital, can serve as collateral for the loan. If the firm's revenue falters and it is unable to pay off its loan, the lender can take possession of the building. This is not true for human

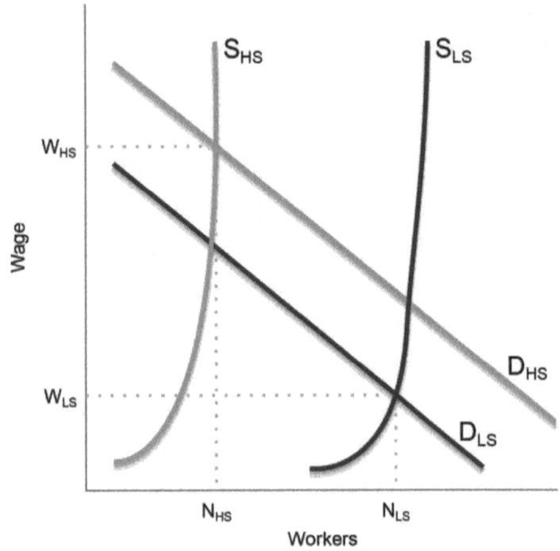

Fig. 16.10 High skilled and low skilled labor markets. Two labor markets are placed on the same diagram for comparison. High skilled (*HS*) work is more productive, so its demand curve is higher. There are fewer HS workers, so their supply curve is to the left. The result, assuming full employment in both markets, is that fewer HS workers are employed than LS workers, and the HS wage is above the LS wage

beings: if I borrow money to finance an education, and if I default on the loan, unless I have other assets the lender is simply out of luck. As we will see, this difference between "human" and "physical" capital has important implications.

A simple illustration of the economics of skill is presented in Fig. 16.10. Here we see two different labor markets in one diagram; for simplicity, we refer to them as high skilled (HS) and low skilled (LS). The value of the marginal product of HS labor is assumed to be higher, so the demand curve is higher as well. It is also assumed that fewer HS workers are available to be employed, so their supply curve is further to the left. For simplicity, we further assume full employment, so that $S = D$ in both markets. The result is that more LS workers are employed, but at a lower wage.

From this simple exercise we can see something very important: the return to skill in the labor market depends above all on two factors—how productive the skill is and how scarce it is. The productivity difference pushes the demand curve up, raising the expected wage. Scarcity pushes the supply curve to the left, also raising the wage. A skill must be both productive and scarce to earn a premium in the marketplace.

This explains, for example, why well-trained tax lawyers earn high incomes. A shrewd specialist can save a company or wealthy household many millions of dollars on its tax liabilities; from the standpoint of those who hire such specialists, this represents a high level of productivity. At the same time, it takes many years of education and experience to learn the loopholes in the tax laws, and few are truly qualified. Thus high returns to this profession are a simple matter of supply and demand.

It is important to recognize, however, that the economic definition of skill is not the same as the everyday use of this word. Normally, we refer to someone as skilled if they have a well-developed ability to do something, whether or not this skill is economically productive or scarce. Thus we speak of good social skills or driving skills. Let's consider each of these.

Good social skills can make a big impression, but they are not always economically valuable. Someone who handles customer complaints for a large store may have a very demanding job, requiring the ability to interact calmly with people who are angry or frustrated, but how well they do this may have little effect on the store's profits. In this case, a worker can be very skilled in the everyday sense and yet be seen as essentially unskilled by his or her employer.

A different case is represented by driving. A delivery company depends on the safe driving skills of its employees; an accident can be extremely costly. And driving is a real skill: after decades of development we are just beginning to see high-tech driverless vehicles. But skillful drivers are not likely to earn high salaries because this skill is widely distributed in society. Thus both a skill's productivity and its scarcity play key roles in determining how it will be valued in the labor market.

Even if skills are amply rewarded, however, there remains the problem of acquiring them. Who will pay the cost of the many years of education or practice required to attain mastery of the advanced skills on which our economies now depend? To illuminate this issue, economists have found it useful to distinguish between what they call **general and firm-specific human capital**.

General skills (comprising general human capital) are those that are productive in a wide variety of work situations; knowing how to use commercial computer software would be an example. Individual businesses are not likely to pay for their acquisition precisely because these skills are portable: a worker could acquire them in one job and then quit, taking their greater productivity somewhere else. This puts the burden on the worker, but as we have already seen, it can be difficult to borrow money to invest in education or apprenticeships because human capital cannot be collateralized. Unequal access to schools and internships is a problem in many countries, and this is one reason why such programs are often subsidized by the government.

Firm-specific skills represent a better investment for the firm. These are of much greater value in one particular workplace than in any other, for example knowing how to use a computer program that was developed in-house for a single enterprise. Such skills are imparted mostly through **on-the-job training**, where work and education are combined. Providing this training can be costly, since it may require that workers take time off from their normal assignments or take on new tasks even though their productivity is temporarily lower. Nevertheless it often pays for itself through longer-term increases in productivity that workers cannot take with them to a competing firm.

From a social standpoint, the single most important institution that upgrades the skill of the labor force is the educational system. This is not by any means the only, or even perhaps the most important, function of education, but it is essential to economic performance. Because of this dominant role, we are accustomed to think of skill in terms of educational attainment, so that more years of education translates into higher skill. As a rough approximation this is not too far off the mark, and decades of economic research have shown that higher levels of education *are* highly productive, whether measured at the individual level through higher wages, or socially through higher rates of economic growth. On average, for instance, each additional year of schooling in developing countries is associated with about 10 % higher wages each year throughout a worker's career. This is an investment in human potential that needs to be made.

On the other hand, we should be careful not to identify education and skill too closely. Skills are valuable to the extent that they are productive and scarce, but not everything a student learns is, or should be, productive, nor are the educationally important types of knowledge necessarily those that are most scarce. Sometimes the most economically valuable skills are those that are learned outside of school by actually doing what needs to be learned—"learning by doing". Finally, education serves not only to impart skills but also to publicize them by issuing grades and diplomas. Economists refer to this as their **signaling** function. But the signal is not the skill. In some cases students who have more education may earn more not because they are more skilled but because their credentials have given them an extra advantage in the labor market. One piece of evidence that supports this hypothesis is that, if we separate out the wage effects of each year of higher education, the most "productive" year is the final one before receiving a diploma. Is this because students really learn more in this year, or because the diploma itself is the source of advantage? If it is the diploma, we have to take account of the potential **positional externality** resulting from the competition for credentials.

16.3.3 Differences in Performance

In the end, the most important difference between labor and other factors of production is that workers are people and can *choose* how much, and what type of, effort to put into their work. A machine that fails to live up to its specifications is defective; a worker that puts in less than 100 % at every moment is human. But how workers are hired and paid can affect the kind of job they do, so differences in performance are an important part of the labor market story.

Consider once again a labor market like Fig. 16.7a. If wages are set so that labor supplied equals labor demanded, workers would be paid just enough to cover their opportunity costs. That is, since the wage at one job is the opportunity cost at another, if they all pay the same, work is equally rewarding everywhere. What would such a world look like? From a management point of view it would be impossible, because there would be no basis for power or authority on the job. Ultimately the only source of power is the firm's threat to fire the worker, but this would carry little weight if all jobs were equally attractive. The worker could disobey any order whenever she might feel like it, since it would not be a problem to find another job at the same level of pay.

Of course, this possibility depends on a highly simplified view of the labor market. In the real world there would be at least some costs to the worker if she walks out the door. As we have seen, the matching process takes time, so there would probably be a spell of unemployment. Perhaps there has been an acquisition of firm-specific human capital, so that the worker would be less productive, and would earn a lower wage, at other jobs. Or maybe she has made friends at her current workplace and doesn't want to have to start over again fitting into a new environment. For any of these reasons there may be real force to the employer's potential threat to dismiss the worker, which is the foundation of workplace hierarchy and control.

On the other hand, for some firms these attachments may not provide enough leverage by themselves, and further actions may be taken to exert more control. There are two main options available to employers to increase the power that comes from the threat of dismissal, paying higher wages or deferring a portion of the wage to the future. The second plays an important role in most economies, but it is complex, so in this chapter we will look only at the first.

It seems paradoxical that a firm could bolster its profits by paying workers more, but sometimes this is the case. Of course, all else being equal, the higher the wage set by the firm the lower its profits; we will call this the "wage effect". It is because of the wage effect that we have assumed up to now that firms would not pay more than the reservation wage needed to attract enough applicants. But all else is not equal: when workers are paid higher wages they become more attached to their work, and this could make them more willing to follow the employer's instructions so that they can continue to hold this job. (Higher wages could also make workers feel grateful and inspire them to make corresponding "gifts" to the firm in the form of greater effort.) We can call the extra effort or obedience of the workforce due to receiving higher wages the "performance effect". Assuming that the firm's demands on its workers are always correctly designed to maximize profits (not always true!), the performance effect enhances the bottom line—again, all else being equal. Figure 16.11 on the following page depicts these two effects for a hypothetical firm.

On the horizontal axis ΔW represents the additional wage the firm might offer beyond the minimum necessary to attract enough job applicants; at the far left where it intersects the vertical axis, $\Delta W = 0$, and the firm offers no more than the workers' reservation wage. ΔP represents the change in profits resulting from changes in wages. The performance effect shows the positive impact higher wages can make on profits, due to the greater desire of workers to keep their jobs. The wage effect has a negative impact on profits, because it is expensive to pay higher wages.

If the firm begins by offering the lowest possible wage, it finds (according to this diagram) that small wage increases provide more in productivity benefits than they cost; that is, the performance effect is greater than the wage effect. This difference increases up to a point but then begins to shrink, and eventually much higher wages do more harm than good to the bottom line. The profit-maximizing wage increment, ΔW^*, occurs where the difference between positive and negative effects is at its greatest. The firm will therefore choose to offer a total wage of $W_R + \Delta W^*$, where W_R is the reservation wage. This combined offer is called the **efficiency wage** in the economics literature.

The efficiency wage is a theoretical possibility; does it occur in practice? Economists think it does, but they disagree about how common it is. For instance, when Henry Ford announced in 1914 that he would pay all his workers at least five

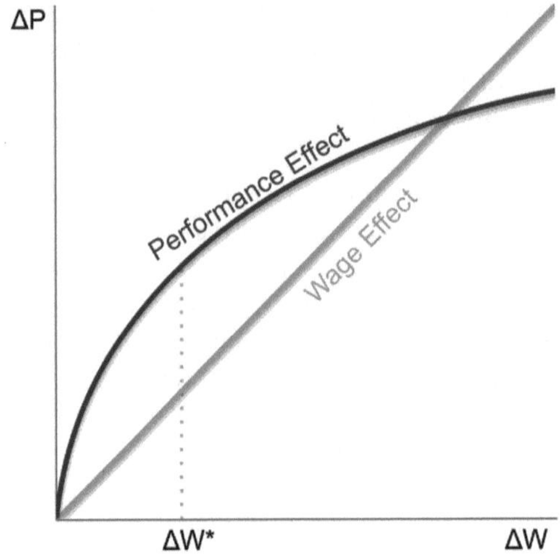

Fig. 16.11 Efficiency wages at a hypothetical firm. A firm considers how much extra wage (ΔW) to offer above the worker's reservation wage, where the vertical axis measures the effect on profit (ΔP). The wage effect has a negative impact on profit: higher wages increase the firm's costs. The performance effect has a positive impact on profit through higher worker productivity. Profits are maximized where the vertical distance between the two effects is the greatest, at ΔW*. This wage premium, when added to the reservation wage, is called the efficiency wage

dollars a day, he was offering a little, but not a lot, more than other manufacturers. Researchers who have pored through the records of the Ford Motor Company have found that the higher wage more than paid for itself in reduced turnover and greater worker willingness to cope with the company's innovative but taxing assembly line. Yet this is just one case out of many, and it is difficult to generalize.

At this point you might be thinking something like this: Yes, it is possible for any one firm to pay more than the worker's opportunity cost and gain greater commitment as a benefit. But the opportunity cost for a worker at one firm is what he or she might make at another, so if all the companies decide to follow this policy the opportunity cost would go up and there would be no extra wage for anyone. If you were aware of this possibility, congratulations—that's a real insight! And it is correct as far as it goes: if all companies follow an efficiency wage approach, then the efficiency wage will become the new reservation wage. Nevertheless, the *effect* of this higher wage may remain. The reason is that, at this new market wage, there is likely to be more unemployment, since higher labor costs will induce some firms to substitute other factors of production for labor. If this happens, workers may still be concerned to avoid dismissal, not because they earn more than they could anywhere else, but because they would face a longer period of unemployment before finding a new job. In fact, some economists think that the need to pay efficiency wages is responsible for much of the unemployment we see in modern economies—but this hypothesis is controversial.

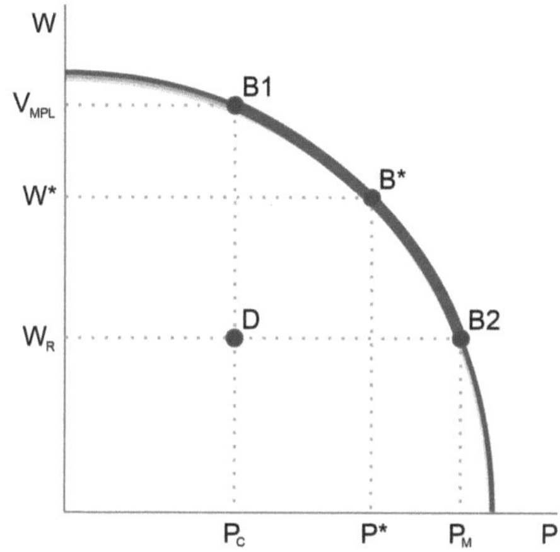

Fig. 16.12 Bargaining between a single worker and a single employer. The *curved line* represents potential wage-profit bargains between an employer and a worker. The worker will not accept a wage below W_R, the reservation wage, which means that the maximum profit P_M is the most the employer could get. The employer will not accept a profit below the competitive level P_C, where the wage is equal to the value of the worker's marginal product, VMP_L. Therefore the agreement must lie on the thick portion of the line from B_1 to B_2, representing the bargaining curve. A typical outcome would be B*, where the worker and the firm benefit equally relative to where they stand at the disagreement *point D*

16.4 Bargaining Power at Work

We have been talking rather loosely about how workers might bargain for a higher wage and why employers might give in a bit, but we can do better by applying the theory of bargaining power we developed in Chap. 13. Let's be more specific about the bargaining curve and the potential costs to each side of a failure to come to agreement.

Figure 16.12 depicts a bargaining situation between a single worker and the firm he or she works for. The horizontal axis measures potential profit to the firm, the vertical axis potential wages for the worker. The first point to be made is that *both* sides can expect to benefit from an agreement: wages can be higher than the worker's opportunity cost *and* profits higher than the competitive situation where the wage equals the value of labor's marginal product. How can this be?

The answer is based on two related factors. First, workers and job demands tend to be specialized; there are better and worse matches between worker and task. A good match creates a surplus above the other available options—alternative jobs from the worker's point of view and alternative workers from the employer's. Specifically, this means that the worker in such a match can expect to earn more than what most other employers are willing to pay, while the employer can get a bigger productivity boost than what would result from employing the "standard" worker (as in the VMP_L curve).

Second, precisely because such matches are worth making, both workers and employers are willing to take the time to search for them. This time is costly, however: potential periods of unemployment for workers and understaffing for firms. Thus, when considering the cost of failing to come to agreement, both sides must take into consideration the likely future search costs. This means that the worker's reservation wage is lower than it otherwise would be, and so is the profit the firm can expect if it has to search for a replacement.

There is now a large body of economic research that shows that a gap between the potential gains from a good match and the costs from dissolving a match and starting over is the normal state of affairs. This is why we can speak of a bargaining process, which distributes the benefits of a stable match, rather than a simple equilibrium as in Fig. 16.4.

Analytically, Fig. 16.12 should be read in this way: The worker is unwilling to agree to any wage less than W_R, her reservation wage. The firm is unwilling to accept any profit less than P_C, the competitive rate of profit where the wage equals the value of the worker's marginal product. This means that a bargaining curve is available, represented by the thick portion of the line running from B_1 to B_2. A bargaining theory like Nash's would predict an outcome such as B*, where the worker receives W* and the firm P*. In this case the wage is above W_R and the profit above P_C (but below P_M, the maximum profit that would arise if the wage could be driven to its minimum). The sum of these two differences represents the surplus available from the searching-matching process.

This apparatus can be used to predict the effect of potential changes in the labor market or the firm's production environment. For instance, suppose the rate of unemployment goes up. This increases the worker's search cost, reducing W_R, but it *decreases* the firm's search cost, so P_C shifts to the right. (Roughly speaking, you could say that the firm achieves the competitive rate of profit in future periods at less temporary cost due to searching for a new worker.) The result is that the disagreement point D shifts to the southeast (lower wages, higher profits) and B* moves down the contract curve toward the P axis. To see if you understand this, try drawing the new diagram on your own.

16.5 Unions and Worker Bargaining Power

Thus far the bargaining power analysis has considered the case of a single worker and a single firm. Introducing a labor union into the equation changes it dramatically. In principle, a bargaining relationship between a union and an employer is different in two major respects.

1. Unions diminish to some extent the matching effect resulting from finding the most appropriate worker for the job. Each worker is a better or worse match and could therefore expect a somewhat better or worse individual agreement; unions negotiate a common agreement for all workers. This means that the surplus which would otherwise be available to the potentially best-matched workers will no longer be offered to them.

Fig. 16.13 Payoff matrix for the union collective action problem

		2: D	2: C
1	D	∘ Both 1 and 2 have individual bargaining power	∘ Both 1 and 2 have union bargaining power ∘ 1 does not pay the cost of supporting the union but 2 does
	C	∘ Both 1 and 2 have individual bargaining power ∘ 1 pays the cost of supporting the union but 2 does not	∘ Both 1 and 2 have union bargaining power ∘ Both pay the cost of supporting the union

2. Unions add a new cost that employers must take into consideration in the event of a failure to agree, the possibility of a strike that would disable the enterprise or some part of it for a period of time—a shutdown cost. This means that the disagreement point D shifts to the left: if negotiations break down and there is a strike, the result could be profits well below the competitive level, or even losses. This increases the bargaining power of the workers as a group. The strength of the shutdown threat depends on a variety of factors, such as the replaceability of the workforce, the cohesiveness of the union, and the legal environment, to mention just a few.

Organizing a union and maintaining a common front during negotiations and a possible strike present **collective action problems** to the workers. These should be understood in terms of the framework of the Prisoner's Dilemma developed in earlier chapters. Using the simplifying device of labeling one worker as "1" and all the others as "2", the basic payoff matrix looks like Fig. 16.13 on the following page.

We will look at this from the point of view of worker 1, since any individual could be in this position. There are two strategies, cooperation (C), supporting the union, or defection (D), not supporting it. Worker 1 must consider the costs and benefits of each choice, whether or not the others cooperate or defect. Suppose first that the other workers defect; now we are in the first column of the matrix. In this case the union will not succeed, and workers will have only the bargaining power they can obtain as individuals. The difference for worker 1 is that if he cooperates he will have to bear this extra cost, which could simply be paying membership dues, but could also take the form of being singled out as a "troublemaker", which in turn could lead to being fired or perhaps worse.

Now suppose the other workers cooperate, giving us column 2. Whatever 1 does he will receive the extra bargaining power that comes from having a union. The difference, of course, is that if he cooperates he pays his share, whereas he can save this expense by defecting.

In either case it is individually rational for 1 to choose defection. As we already know, however, if each worker thinks this way the result will be that all defect, resulting in the upper left-hand cell instead of the lower right-hand one. If union bargaining power is worth its cost—if it has the potential to win wage and other benefits that outweigh the financial and other costs of organizing and supporting it—this is an inferior outcome from the workers' point of view.

As we saw in Chap. 7, the barriers to achieving mutual cooperation are not insuperable. Not every worker has to jump in right away; it is enough to attract a critical mass. If the union is seen as ongoing—which is to say, if the jobs are seen as stable and the workers intend to hold them for a long enough time—the benefits of future cooperation can outweigh the short-term costs. In the real world unions are an often-seen aspect of the labor market.

One difficult issue arises in occupations where there are different levels of skill involved and where the matching effect is expected to be stronger for some workers than others. There may be some workers for whom the net effect of having a union—the difference between the bargain they can get as part of a group and what they could get as individuals—is small or even negative, because their skills are well-matched to the employer's needs. They may be less willing to put up with the costs of collective action. Others, those who do not expect to benefit so much from matching, have a stronger need for collective representation. This is one reason it is more difficult to organize unions in fields that have high professional qualifications or other characteristics of individual skill differences. On the other hand, as the work process in such fields is made more routine (less dependent on the qualities of the individual worker), unionization becomes more attractive.

The extent of union membership has declined in some countries, such as the United States, but the economic and legal issues surrounding unions remain important. Some countries, like Germany, have a legal system that strongly encourages unionization, while others, such as the US, make it much more difficult. Canada, whose economy is similar to that of the US in some respects, has a much larger and more stable union sector. The future of unions and other forms of worker organization is an important topic, especially as issues of inequality move up on the political agenda.

▶ Terms to Define

Beveridge Curve
Capital goods
Compensating wage differentials
Demographic transition
Demography
Efficiency wage
Factor markets
General vs firm-specific human capital
Human capital
Labor force participation rate
Marginal product
On-the-job training
Reservation wage

Signaling (in labor markets)
Value of the marginal product

Questions to Consider

1. Are you planning on entering a line of work for which the demand is inelastic? If so, did this play a role in your choice? If not, do you see this as a potential problem in the future? What can you do to make this demand more inelastic for you individually?
2. Is your own personal labor supply curve forward- or backward-sloping or both? Try to draw it in a diagram, with the number of hours per week on the horizontal axis and the hourly wage (or its salary equivalent) on the vertical axis. Do you think your demand curve is typical or atypical?
3. Consider your own experience and the experience of your friends with the problem of finding out which jobs are available and would constitute the best match. How efficient do you think labor markets are at solving this problem? Can you come up with any ideas for improving this aspect of labor market performance?
4. Returning to Fig. 16.9, suppose that Job 2 actually provides negative job-utility: the danger or disagreeableness of the work outweighs any positive psychological benefit it provides. Draw the column representing money-utility and job-utility for Job 2 in this case.
5. Make up a list a five occupations that, in your opinion, expose workers to particularly dangerous or unpleasant conditions. Do any of these jobs tend to pay compensating wage differentials? If your answer is yes, what factors explain why some receive this compensation and others do not?
6. As a general rule, the older the children a teacher works with the more he or she is paid: teachers who work with infants make less than primary school teachers, primary school teachers make less than secondary school teachers, and all of these make less than university professors. Does this reflect differences in the skills required for these jobs? Do the two economic criteria for "skill" apply here?
7. Have you ever held a job that paid an efficiency wage? Did it have the intended effect on you and your coworkers?
8. How much bargaining power do you think you have in your current job? Are you a member of a union? If so, how much additional bargaining power do you think this gives you? If not, would you have more bargaining power if you were represented by a union?
9. Suppose a union is trying to represent employees of grocery stores in a particular region. It has a limited budget to spend on organizing and wants to focus its efforts in the cities where it expects to get the most support. What factors should it look at in the local labor market situation to determine whether a particular city should be given higher or lower priority?

17 Financial Markets

For many people, the financial markets, where stocks and bonds are traded, are the most visible aspects of the economy. When you hear the phrase "economic news" on TV or read it in a newspaper, there is a good chance that you are about to find out about the latest gyrations in stock prices and interest rates.

At the very beginning of this book we confronted the myth that economics is a primarily a guide to making money, and in subsequent chapters we have been able to go into some detail about the workings of the modern economy without ever mentioning the role of finance. This tells us that money isn't everything, but it should also be a warning sign—that unless we bring the role of financial investment into the picture, something important will be missing.

In this chapter we look at the markets in which financial assets, valuable pieces of paper like stocks and bonds, are bought and sold. We will have two main purposes, to simply describe what these markets are and how they operate and to examine the effects they have on the allocation of resources in society. As we will see, the rise and fall of prices in these markets can have far-reaching effects on what gets produced, by whom and how. What we will *not* consider in this chapter is the role of financial markets in economic growth, employment and inflation, since this is the domain of macroeconomics. But there is more than enough microeconomic significance in finance to keep us busy.

First, however, we need to take a short detour and explore the meaning of "capital" in economic theory. This will tell us something about what financial markets represent and also about the dangers of ascribing too much importance to them.

17.1 The Mystery of Capital

It is common to refer to the modern profit-driven economy as capitalist, so we should know what we mean by "capital", right? Well, it's not so easy. There are two very different meanings to this word, and although economists have struggled since

P. Dorman, *Microeconomics*, Springer Texts in Business and Economics,
DOI 10.1007/978-3-642-37434-0_17, © Springer-Verlag Berlin Heidelberg 2014

the time of Adam Smith to bring them together into one consistent theory, it has not yet happened and may prove to be an impossible dream.

Very generally, by **capital** we refer to resources that have three characteristics:

- They are created by an initial process of investment.
- They are used to produce further goods and services, including, perhaps, more capital.
- They are not immediately used up in production.

The first of these points to a typical time pattern of costs and benefits: there is a beginning phase in which expenses are incurred to create capital, followed by a second phase in which capital is employed productively, yielding a return. Two types of measurement are often used to describe how much benefit a capital investment creates compared to its cost, the payback period (how many time periods of productive use will be needed to recoup the initial cost of investment) and the rate of return (the ratio of the value of revenue it generates over its lifespan to the value of its costs). As we saw in the previous chapter, any activity that has this time structure of costs followed by benefits is likely to be designated a form of a capital by economists, including the human capital of investments in education.

The third characteristic is what distinguishes capital from raw materials or semi-finished goods like fabrics or auto parts. A bit of fabric that goes into the making of a shirt is used up simply by being used. A piece of capital equipment, like a truck, contributes value to production but normally survives to be used in future periods. True, a portion of its value is lost, which is referred to as **depreciation**, but the ability of capital to be used over and over is the basis for its time structure of costs and benefits.

"Real" capital, the kind that is actually used in production, consists of **capital goods**, specific pieces of equipment, buildings and other items that possess the three characteristics of capital. The stock of these goods comprises the major part of what we might think of as "the wealth of nations", to use Adam Smith's phrase. If we want to convey to someone exactly how much capital a particular country possesses at a moment in time, we would have to draw up a very long itemized list, indicating each particular type of capital good and how much of it is available.

Of course, no one does this for a country, and even most businesses, once they get to a sufficient level of size and complexity, give up the task of enumerating each capital item on hand. Instead, people measure the value of these goods, and the total monetary value of all of them combined is accepted as an answer to the question, "How much capital is there?" In this way, individuals, businesses and governments have come to see capital as a sum of money, referred to as **financial capital**.

Let's suppose for a moment that these are essentially the same—that financial capital is simply the monetary equivalent of a stock of capital goods. In that case, we could analyze the market for capital by considering the factors underlying its supply and demand. First, consider supply, which in this case means the amount of money made available for financial investments. Money used in this way is unavailable for other purposes; instead of purchasing goods that can be consumed in the present, for example, the investor is opting for the prospect of earning even more money in the future. Different people, of course, will require different incentives for making this choice. Some, who have little desire for more spending power in the current period, will invest their money at a relatively low rate of return. Others, for whom immediate financial needs are more pressing, will require a higher rate of return to supply their money to financial markets. And even the same individual might supply some money at a lower rate and more at a higher one. The overall effect would be an upward-sloping supply curve: more money is made available for purposes of investment as higher returns are offered. In this way the supply side of the market would draw on the observation that there is a general rate of return on money in the marketplace, the rate of interest.

The demand curve, on the other hand, would reflect the productivity of this money when it is invested in capital goods by those who borrow it. In this case, we can imagine that there are many such productive investments available to those with the funding to make them. We could line them up from most profitable to least, as in Fig. 17.1 on the following page, which is a repeat of Fig. 12.1. In a different approach to make the underlying logic clear, we use columns to indicate profitability, designated by the rate of return r, as if there are just a few specific investments to display, along with a curve that shows the profitability relationship if there are so many investments that it becomes continuous.

At any actual interest rate, say r*, there is one particular investment, or group of investments, designated by I*, whose expected rate of return is exactly equal to it. This would just cover the cost of the money used to finance it, since the interest rate is the cost of money and the rate of return is what it earns. Any investment to the left of I* would more than justify the cost of funds; any investment to the right would not. This means that, as r falls, more investments are desired, and more money would be used to finance them. In other words, our investment ranking curve is also the demand curve for financial capital.

Putting supply and demand together would yield a typical diagram like Fig. 17.2, which superimposes a supply curve onto the demand curve of Fig. 17.1. Now r* is an equilibrium rate of return on money. If the interest rate rises above this, there will be an excess supply of funds on the market looking for takers, and this would be expected to result in lending offers that would bring the rate back down, and vice versa for interest rates below r*.

What is particularly interesting to us is the interpretation of r*. It represents the interest rate that is just sufficient to convince the marginal lender (the one who provides the last dollop of money) to make it available to the capital market. It must therefore just equal this person's perceived cost of postponing access to this money's spending power until the future. This is referred to as the **marginal time preference** of the community, the rate at which the present is preferred to the future. For instance, if I think, all else being equal, that having a sum of money a year from now is 10 % less desirable than having it today—my degree of time preference—it will take a 10 % return on my money to just induce me to lend it out anyway. To speak of the marginal time preference in the market as a whole is to indicate that the last infusion of money has exactly that psychological barrier to overcome.

Meanwhile, on the supply side, r* represents exactly what it did before: the rate of return on the last investment made at this interest rate. In other words, r*

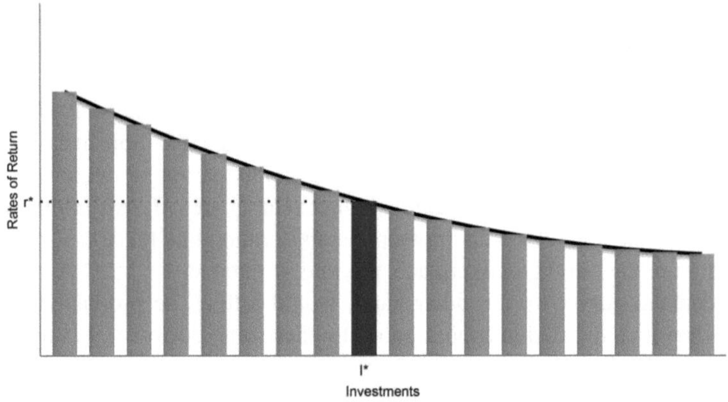

Fig. 17.1 Potential investments ranked by their prospective rates of return. Investments are ranked by their rates of return (r), from greatest to least. The bars represents specific investments when there are relatively few; the curve represents a continuous ranking when there are a great many investments. At r* investment I* exactly covers its financial cost, and all investments to its left would more than cover it

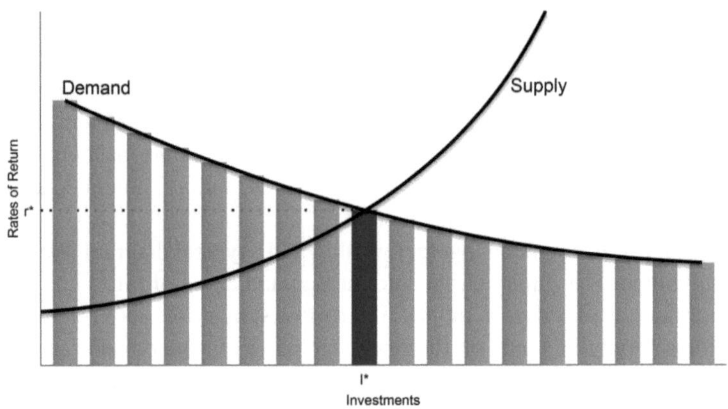

Fig. 17.2 The supply and demand for capital (financial and physical). When an upward-sloping supply curve is added to the demand curve, we have an account of the market for "capital" which is simultaneously financial capital (money) and capital goods (physical assets). The equilibrium return, r*, represents both the marginal time preference for money and the marginal return on investment

represents the **marginal return on capital**. If you want to have more investment by bringing online investments to the right of I*, you would have to lower the interest rate paid by investors.

This seems like an appealing result: the marginal cost of supplying an extra bit of money to the capital market is exactly equal to the marginal benefit this money provides in the form of enhanced future productivity. It reminds us of the Market Welfare Model, since the supply curve represents the marginal cost of supplying funds, the demand curve the marginal benefit of using them, and there is a single, market-clearing equilibrium. All investments whose productivity justifies the cost of financing them take place, and none of the rest. What's not to like?

There is just one small problem. The supply curve is based on people's preference to have money today rather than in the future—that is, on financial capital—while the demand curve is based on the productive potential of capital in its physical state, capital goods. If these were just two ways of describing the same thing, all would be well, but they aren't. It is entirely possible—normal, in fact—for the amount of financial capital to rise while the stock of capital goods is constant or falling, or vice versa. We will discuss this point in more detail shortly, when we delve into the operations of the stock market. Even in the ideal world of economic models, where messy complications are dispelled under the **ceteris paribus** assumption, there is no predictable correspondence between the two types of capital. (This was established in economic theory as the result of a bitter controversy that erupted during the 1960s.)

The result is that the analysis incorporated in Fig. 17.2 is not valid. As in so much of economics, the operative question has become, *how* not valid? Many economists like to think that the difficulties caused by combining two inconsistent definitions of capital are small enough to be ignored. They prefer to accept the interpretation of capital markets as adhering to the Market Welfare Model, with its implications for the interpretation of equilibrium interest rates. Some are more cautious and regard the normative evaluation of capital markets as beyond our current understanding.

This fissure also creates a problem for writers of economics textbooks. Capital is important because it is productive, but the markets (like stock exchanges) on which capital is traded deal in financial capital, not capital goods. It would be convenient to ignore this distinction, but in what follows we will take financial capital on its own terms, as simply a vehicle for the movement of money, and make limited inferences about what the stock markets tell us about society's capacity for production. Actually, as we will see, keeping the two forms of capital distinct in our minds will prove to be an advantage when we examine the forces that drive financial markets.

17.2 Equity Markets

In Chap. 8 we considered the nineteenth century innovation of the public joint-stock company, one of the fundamental building blocks of a modern economy. In that chapter we looked at this structure from the viewpoint of the company, with a focus on the greater size and security that distinguishes corporations from other business forms. Here we will look at this same development from the perspective of investors, those who possess or manage enough financial wealth to buy and sell stakes in corporate enterprises. These stakes are also called **equity** and their value is measured by the price they command in the marketplace. In other words, if you multiply the number of shares of a corporation held by its shareholders times the price per share, you get the total equity of that corporation, its market valuation.

Recall that two developments are necessary for a corporation to be traded on a stock market. First, the ownership of the corporation has to be subdivided into shares, pieces of paper that represent fractions of the firm's net worth. Typically a large corporation has millions or even billions of such shares available for ownership, so that each represents a tiny portion of the total value of the company. Second, the firm must be "public" in the sense that it allows any member of the public to buy or sell these shares. (Some corporations are private; they restrict ownership to particular individuals rather than putting it up for general trading.) Corporations that choose to be public must list themselves on one or more stock exchanges. A stock exchange is an organization dedicated to facilitating markets in corporate equity; examples include the London, Frankfurt, Hong Kong and New York exchanges.

Stock markets, like all financial markets, are purely creatures of supply and demand. At any point in time some people wish to purchase the stock of a given company and some wish to sell it. Transactions can take place only if there is an agreed-upon price, so the price rises and falls as buying or selling pressure becomes more predominant. It is not too far from the truth to regard most of these buying and selling decisions as bets, placing money on the belief that future events will yield a profit rather than a loss. Clearly, if A sells a share of stock to B at a given price, A is betting that the price is more likely to fall and B that it is more likely to rise. Differences of opinion are the fuel on which financial markets run.

Very generally, we can recognize two different approaches to analyzing such bets. The first is referred to as relying on the **fundamentals**, the underlying economic prospects of the firms whose equity is being traded. Owning a share of a company means having a claim on the profits this company will make. Such profits can either be returned to owners directly in the form of **dividends**, periodic distributions to shareholders on the basis of how many shares they own, or indirectly through reinvestment, which should increase the value of the firm in the future. So, according to this line of thinking, the price of a company's share should reflect the best possible estimate of that company's future earnings. Many private analysts are employed by investment houses and other organizations to scrutinize the future business prospects of companies listed on the stock exchanges, providing information and analysis to guide trading strategies.

A different approach focuses on the market itself, and for this reason has been called **technical**. "Winning" in the stock market means placing bets that are ultimately vindicated by the market in the future, which is to say thinking like everyone else, but just a little sooner. From this perspective, the strategy is to examine the market as carefully as possible, looking for patterns in its recent history and divining the psychology of its most influential participants. The goal is not to predict the future performance of firms over some long period of time, but to anticipate the moves the market will make in the next few days, hours or moments. With the advent of computerized trading, it has become possible to incorporate complex technical algorithms in software, so that the speed of response can become nearly instantaneous. As a larger percentage of all trading is triggered by programs of this sort, the potential for sudden, extreme market events could be increasing, although no one knows for sure. (This has emerged in recent years as the problem of “flash crashes”.)

Do these two methods converge? That is, are the share prices predicted by the best fundamental analysis more or less the same as those predicted by state of the art technical analysis? Sometimes yes, sometimes no. The real-world meaning of convergence between fundamental and technical outlooks can be seen by comparing two dramatic sell-offs in the recent history of New York equity markets. The first was in 1987: in less than a day the Dow Jones Industrial Average, an index composed of 30 leading stocks, fell by 22.5 %, the worst such decline ever. Nothing had changed in the real economy or the profit potential of the firms being traded, however, to justify this panic. The second began in 2000 and continued for over a year, when the so-called “dotcom” bubble burst, and hundreds of companies that had staked their business strategies on the internet saw their share prices collapse. It is estimated that the total equity of these firms fell by about eight trillion dollars during this time. It was a severe sell-off, but probably justified, at least in part, on fundamental grounds, since the share prices had previously risen to astronomic heights based on unrealistic expectations of future earnings growth. Very roughly, we could say that the two approaches diverged in 1987 but mostly converged at the beginning of the new century.

A second way to distinguish between traders is by whether they are on the buying or selling side of the market. Those who want to buy, who are optimistic about future trends in share prices, are called **bulls**; those who want to sell are the **bears**. A market whose share values are rising over time is called a **bull market**, since the bulls outnumber (or are more enthusiastic than) bears; the opposite is called a **bear market**. It has been noted for a long time that bullishness and bearishness have a strong psychological component; some prominent market players are congenitally one or the other irrespective of the course of economics events. When then-Chairman of the Federal Reserve Alan Greenspan famously warned against “irrational exuberance” on Wall Street in 1996, he no doubt believed that psychology had run away from careful, objective analysis.

Whether driven by views about business fundamentals, market patterns or gut psychology, share prices have a life of their own. The economic value of a company, as measured by share prices, tends to fluctuate substantially and is difficult to predict in the short run. At the same time, however, the stock of productive assets the company owns, things like land, buildings, patents and so on, changes more slowly. In the end, you might ask, what is a company really worth—its valuation on the stock exchange or the amount of money it would cost to buy all its assets, one by one? It is worth looking at this question in more detail.

It turns out that there are two different ways to measure the value of an asset like a piece of equipment. You could find out how much had been spent to purchase it in the past, its **purchase value**, or how much it would cost to replace it today, its **replacement value**. Because prices are always changing, these are rarely the same. It is easiest for firms to record purchase value, since all they have to do is keep track of past transactions, but the better measurement is replacement value, since it is today's price that should determine today's value.

Public corporations have to file financial information on a regular basis, and one of the types of information they must disclose is the replacement value of the physical assets they own. This is sometimes referred to as the corporation's **book value**. It is believed that publicizing this number, broken down into its major categories, helps make stock markets more fair and efficient.

But as we have already seen, stock markets provide us with a different way to place a value on firms, their total equity (also called capitalization) based on the market value of all the shares they have issued. When a company's stock price rises, its total market value goes up irrespective of whether its book value has risen, fallen or remained the same. This divergence between the money tied up in a firm's stock and the calculated replacement value of its capital goods mirrors the distinction between financial and physical capital introduced earlier in this chapter.

A handy way to summarize these two types of value is **Tobin's *q***, defined as the ratio of market valuation to total replacement value, and named for Nobelist James Tobin, who introduced the idea in 1969. This ratio should always be equal to or greater than one; otherwise shareholders could increase their wealth by ordering the firm to be liquidated, selling off all the assets and distributing the proceeds. (Sometimes q does fall below one temporarily, but this is an unstable situation.) In the normal state of affairs, q is more than one, and this indicates that the company is viewed as adding value to its stock of assets: if the stock price is in line with fundamentals, these assets are more valuable used in combination by the company than they would be if sold off one-by-one.

Another useful statistic is the **price-earnings ratio** of a particular firm or an entire market. As we saw above, from a fundamental perspective a share of stock is simply a claim on the future profits of a firm. No one knows what they will be, but one possible indicator is the firm's current profits. The price-earnings (P-E) ratio relates the total market value of the firm to its profits during the most recent period. If the P-E ratio is high, it presumably indicates that investors expect future profitability to rise. In some cases, like the internet retailer Amazon, investors paid substantial share prices even though earnings were negative for many years, because they believed in the company's long run business plan. It should be noted, however, that the variability of earnings for an entire market is a lot less than the variability of any particular firm. Firms fluctuate between years of spectacular profits and painful losses, but most of this cancels out at the level of the whole market, where P-E ratios should normally be more stable.

The stock market plays an important role in allocating society's resources. An economy has only a limited capacity to make investments, and somehow decisions must be made to invest in one industry or technology rather than another. Many of these decisions are made within firms according to motivations discussed in Chap. 8, but the resources available to the firms themselves must be divvied up as well. The stock market helps perform this function, but not always in the most visible ways.

A direct connection can be seen in the procedure known as an **initial public offering** (IPO). This occurs when a new corporation forms or when a private corporation goes public. New shares of stock are offered to investors, and the higher their initial price, the more money flows to the enterprise. Some of this may go to its former private owners, who can now cash out, leaving less of their wealth tied up in one asset, but the rest goes to the firm itself. These funds are available for making new investments, and gaining this access to financial capital is one of the main spurs to making an IPO. Firms that are already publicly traded sometimes offer new shares for the same reason.

All the same, the vast majority of stock that trades on the world's financial markets was issued in the past, and the money paid for it just flows from one group of investors to another. This money is *not* channeled into the purchases of new capital goods, at least not in this way. Nevertheless, fluctuations in share prices have profound indirect effects on business decisions, a topic we will return to in greater detail toward the end of this chapter. For now, it is enough to say that managers keep a close eye on the stock market, and if share prices fall they are likely to worry for their own livelihoods. Thus, high prices are seen as ratifying current investment decisions and encouraging more; low prices have the opposite effect. In the extreme case, which is becoming less extreme in recent years, a low enough price can lead the firm to liquidate its assets, effectively un-making all its investments.

An interesting use of financial market data, particularly information from the world's stock exchanges (which are all publicly available) is **event analysis.** This involves looking at changes in share prices that correspond to events that might alter the underlying profitability of the companies involved. For instance, suppose the government passes a law regulating a particular industry. This could affect profits in that industry either positively or negatively depending on what the law specifies (and which interests promoted it). To do an event analysis, you would look for the moment when the regulation becomes "news" to people who trade on financial markets—either the day new information comes out that makes it likely the law will pass, or when the contents of the law are clarified, or some other decisive point. Recall that players in the stock market will trade on their expectations, so "news" is whatever changes their expectations. (Usually by the time a regulation is signed into law it is no longer news in this sense.)

When you have pinpointed the moment of news you look for signs of a response in the stock market: did the company's share price go up or down? By how much? If you believe in the fundamentalist approach to stock price evaluation, this price bump, if it occurs, should reflect changes in the expected profitability of the company. In fact, by multiplying the bump times the number of shares of stock outstanding, you can get an idea of how large a profit gain or loss is expected to result from the news.

But be careful. Event analysis is based on the notion that a change in a company's stock price is related to an unexpected event that financial market participants find out about at a certain point in time—but stock prices fluctuate for all kinds of reasons. In doing this analysis, look at the longer term price trend of the stock to separate out a one-time bump from longer-term tendencies. Pay attention to the size of the bump in relation to the typical gyrations of the share price: how likely is it that such a bump could occur by chance? (This is an example of separating the "signal" from the "noise" in data analysis.) Finally, look at what was happening to other, unrelated companies over the same time period, for instance by tracking an index of the entire market. If all companies were experiencing approximately the same bump, it would probably not be due to an event that affected only one of them.

Event analysis is relatively easy to do, the data are readily available, and the results can be fascinating.

17.3 Credit Markets

In stock markets investors put up money to take an equity stake in a firm; in credit markets they make loans. A loan is embodied in a piece of paper called a **bond**. The creditor provides money to the lender; the lender provides a bond entitling its owner to a series of future payments. Like all financial assets, bonds can then be traded to new investors, so that their owners at any point in time are not the same people as those who originally lent the money. To put it differently, in a sufficiently liquid market (one with enough participants and low transaction costs), it is possible to become a creditor and then, if desired, quickly become an ex-creditor by selling the bond to a third party.

Some bonds are originally issued by private companies, others by government agencies. Some have only a general legal obligation to repay—a topic we will return to when we discuss defaults—while others are tied to particular items of collateral. All are traded in credit markets, but their different characteristics are reflected in the range of prices they command, as we will see shortly.

Before we look at the two sides of the credit market, we need to take care of a technical matter concerning bond prices and interest rates. Sometimes one hears a news report like, "There was a rally on the bond market today, with prices rising..." or "There was a rally on the bond market with interest rates falling..." These are two ways of saying exactly the same thing. Here's why.

Suppose two pieces of information are given to us, the future payments specified on a particular bond and the market interest rate; our goal is to figure out what the price of the bond should be. To make things simple, let's assume that the bond pays $100 every year forever. (Some bonds actually do this.) If we use r for the interest rate and P_B for the price of the bond, we can write the formula in Eq. 17.1:

$$r = \frac{\$100}{P_B} \tag{17.1}$$

This is simply a definition of what r stands for. The interest rate is the rate of return on money, and the bond, measured by its price P_B, is a repository of money, so the yearly income as a percentage of the money invested to obtain it *is* the interest rate. If we assume that competition in the marketplace will lead to a single interest rate on all equivalent investments, then the price of the bond must be such as to produce the economy-wide r.

By multiplying both sides by P_B and dividing by r, we can rewrite this as Eq. 17.2:

$$P_B = \frac{\$100}{r} \tag{17.2}$$

Now it is easy to calculate P_B for any r that might prevail. If $r = 5\ \%$, for instance, $P_B = \$2{,}000$. If $r = 10\ \%$ $P_B = \$1{,}000$. Notice that, if r rises, P_B falls, and vice versa. Investors make this happen by pricing bonds so that their return is equal to the interest rate. If they didn't, someone could make money by either borrowing at r to buy P_B or selling P_B to invest in some other asset at r. It is unlikely that such easy profit opportunities would persist for very long.

Now that we have this relationship clearly in mind, we can analyze credit markets as the supply and demand for either money or bonds. If we choose money, lenders are the suppliers, borrowers provide the demand, and the price is the interest rate. If we choose bonds, issuers of bonds are the suppliers, buyers of bonds provide the demand, and the bond price is set in the market. Once again, these are two ways of analyzing exactly the same thing: the buyers of bonds are the lenders of money, and the issuers of bonds are the borrowers of money. Figure 17.3 on the next page illustrates this by looking at the effect of an issuance of new bonds that increases the volume of lending in the credit market.

In Fig. 17.3a we see the market for money; by issuing new bonds, borrowers are expressing an increased demand for loans. Given a fixed supply curve, this will lead to a higher equilibrium interest rate. In Fig. 17.3b we see the market for bonds. Now borrowers are on the supply side, offering bonds to investors. By issuing new bonds, they increase their supply from S_1 to S_2, which will have the effect of reducing the equilibrium bond price. Since money trades for bonds in the credit market, these two diagrams are different ways of depicting exactly the same event.

While the identities of the credit market participants are easy enough to identify in most cases, their motives are complex. Some who supply credit are saving for the future; some are speculating (gambling) on the future prices of bonds. Still others may need to park their money for a period of time; for them a bond is a convenient store of value. Borrowers may also have different motives. Some are companies raising money for investments or to survive a downturn in earnings. Some are consumers, taking out mortgages to finance a house or other types of loans for education or travel. The largest supply of bonds comes from government, which must borrow whenever its spending exceeds its tax revenues. All of these play a role in determining the level of borrowing in the economy and the interest rate borrowers must pay.

Thus far we have been treating bonds as if they were identical, but they aren't. They come in different sizes (amounts of money being borrowed) and repayment terms, but for our purposes the most important difference is the risk of default. By

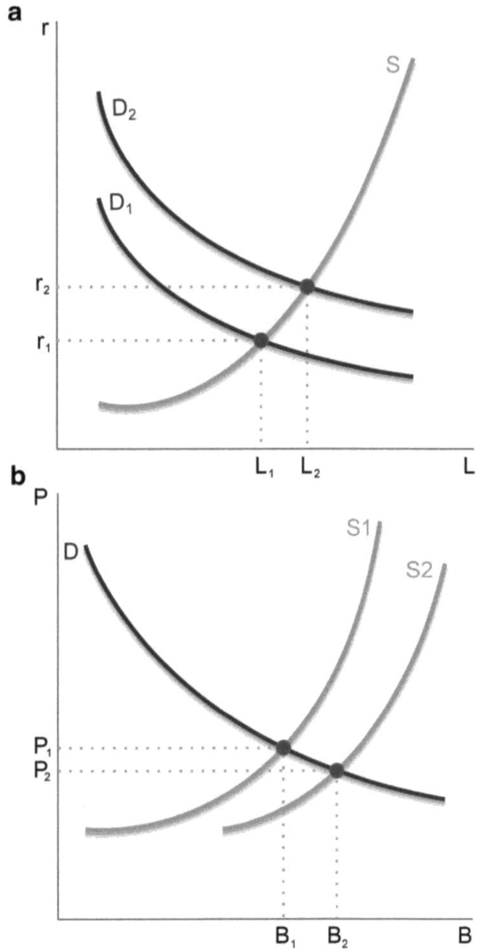

Fig. 17.3 The effect of a new bond issue. (**a**) In the market for money, *L* is the amount of money loaned and *r* the interest rate. A new bond issue increases loan demand from D_1 to D_2, raising the equilibrium interest rate from r_1 to r_2. (**b**) In the market for bonds, *B* is the amount of bonds purchased and *P* is the price of a bond. A new bond issue is shown as an increase in supply from S_1 to S_2, lowering the equilibrium price from P_1 to P_2

default we mean the possibility that the issuer of the bond will not make the payments the bond specifies. For a bond that requires an annual payment, like our hypothetical asset in Fig. 17.3, this could mean postponing a payment, reducing the amount of payment or stopping payment altogether. Of course, the borrower is legally obligated to follow through on the terms of the bond, but that may be little consolation to bondholders if the borrower is simply short of funds.

Several factors govern the risk of default. Public borrowers, governments, are usually considered more reliable than private bond issuers, like corporations. Governments can raise taxes more easily than companies can raise revenues, and the debts of particular government agencies are usually backed by the "full faith and credit" of the government as a whole. Bonds are also considered more secure if they are backed by collateral. Mortgages, for example, are secured by the possibility that the mortgage-holder can repossess the land and buildings in the event that the borrower defaults. As long as the market value of these hard assets exceeds the value of the bond, the mortgage-holder is not at risk. (In a declining housing market, where market values fall below the loans taken out in earlier periods, this risk re-emerges, as we have seen on a dramatic scale in recent years.) Finally, the financial prospects of borrowers provide a crucial indicator of their repayment capacity. Companies like Moody's and Standard & Poor's research the financial health of borrowers and rate their bonds on a scale that ranges from "prime" (virtually secure) to "junk" (purchase at your own risk). The failure of these rating outfits to properly identify the risk in mortgages, and the complex securities based on them, was one of the causes of the recent financial crisis.

The differentiation of bonds according to their security gives rise to a **risk premium** in the marketplace. Less secure bonds must pay this premium, measured as an increment above the interest rates paid by the most secure borrowers, for instance government agencies—at least, in the US and other countries where governments have high credibility. A poor bond rating can therefore make all the difference between having access to affordable credit and having this credit effectively shut off.

It is worth considering what credit rating and risk premiums mean for the allocation of society's resources. At any point in time there are many companies with potential business ideas. Many or most require loans to carry them out. There is not enough money to finance everyone, so choices must be made. Credit-rating companies, market analysts and others examine the companies proposing to issue bonds and the intended uses of the money they hope to borrow. Some borrowers are given a seal of approval and can sell bonds at the lowest interest rate available in the market, while others are seen as risky and must pay a higher price. In this way the financial resources of the economy are rationed.

One dramatic example of this process was the reversal of the nuclear power industry during the 1970s and 1980s. Nuclear power plants are extremely expensive to build, and revenues from their operation do not begin until the plants are completed, as many as 10 years after the investment process begins; for this reason their financing comes almost entirely from bond issues. During the '70s the market looked favorably on this technology and the companies that relied on it. Government regulation was friendly, there were handsome public subsidies, and most of the scientific experts seemed to have confidence in the future of the industry. Then a series of events altered this perception: a large protest movement arose in opposition to nuclear power, waste disposal became a contentious public problem, and high-profile accidents like Three Mile Island in Pennsylvania and Chernobyl near the Ukraine-Moldova border undermined the confidence of the general public and experts alike. Within the space of a few months bond ratings for utilities investing in nuclear power plummeted, and there was even a major default. The supply of new funding dried up. As a result, resources were pulled out of nuclear power in the US and many other countries and transferred to other uses. This decision was made not by governments or panels of scientists, but by investors acting within credit markets.

17.4 Commodity Markets

Our main interest in this chapter is stocks and bonds—equity and credit—but other financial markets exist and can sometimes play an important economic role. The biggest of these is the **commodities market**, in which claims to standardized agricultural and mineral products are traded. Examples of particular commodities include wheat, coffee, copper and gold.

The reason these can be considered financial markets is that there is so much trading taking place that participants never have to worry about actually having to take possession of these commodities; only paper and money circulate. If I buy the right to be delivered 10,000 tons of wheat in 3 months, I don't have to worry about buying a warehouse. Long before the delivery date arrives, I will be able to sell this claim to someone else. Eventually, just before delivery, the paper embodying this claim can be sold to an actual mill or other agricultural business, so that the wheat goes to someone who can use it. Even more conveniently, a claim to possess this wheat can be combined with another piece of paper that promises to supply it, so that the two claims cancel each other out. The same argument holds for other widely-traded commodities, including metals.

Much of the activity in commodity markets is of the purely speculative variety we encountered in the stock market. Participants are guessing which way they think prices will move, and they place their money accordingly. Commodity market instruments, the paper claims traders buy and sell, have become increasingly complex, taking the form of rights to execute contracts under a set of specified conditions—not before this date or after that one, if the price of one good is below or above a "trigger price", etc. Arcane mathematical models are required to price these contracts, and even the best minds are sometimes unable to sort out the difficulties.

For all the nerdy glamour of this trading arena, commodities markets do have real-world effects. As we have seen earlier in this book, the gyrations of the coffee market have life-or-death consequences for millions of coffee farmers around the world; the same could be demonstrated for wheat, rice and copper. For decades economists have argued about the merits of separating the speculative from the practical aspects of commodities markets through some sort of price stabilization scheme. Again, we saw the rise and fall of such an approach in the global coffee trade. Attempts to manage commodity prices are much more the exception than the rule, however, especially at the international level. One problem is that some speculative trading is essential, since one of the main purposes of a well-functioning market is to bring future conditions to bear on current prices. If there is good reason to expect a shortage of wheat a year from now, for instance, it makes sense for the current price to rise, thereby encouraging conservation on the part of buyers and more intensive planting on the part of producers. Commodities markets serve this role by enabling trades over future deliveries, so that current and future supplies can be exchanged for each other—as paper.

17.5 Default

The entire edifice of modern financial markets is built up on the premise that borrowers will be able to fulfill the terms of their loans. If they fail to make their payments creditors and stockholders alike can find themselves holding worthless pieces of paper. "Default" is normally the last word they want to hear, but it is always present in the background as a risk to be considered, and its occurrence is an unavoidable aspect of modern economic life.

At any moment in time a business or individual can be thought of as possessing both a stock of assets—things of value that it owns, like money or buildings—and liabilities like debts. The value of assets minus liabilities is its **net worth**; as long as this is a positive number the organization or person is described as **solvent**. Should this become a negative amount, however, we can speak of insolvency. Just because a borrower has become insolvent, it does not mean that loan payments must stop, because it is possible that there is enough cash on hand to keep the payments going for a while. In the long run, of course, insolvency, if it persists, must lead to default.

It is important to recognize that a business or individual can be entirely solvent, with assets well in excess of liabilities, and still be unable to make payments on a loan. This is because payments require money, and too large a percentage of assets may be tied up in items that cannot easily be converted to money. This is referred to as a liquidity problem: not enough **liquid assets**. This sometimes happens when borrowers become too optimistic, making long-term investments in capital goods without enough short-term cash flow to keep lenders happy.

When scheduled loan payments are not made the borrower is held to be in default. This triggers a series of economic and legal changes that can potentially be extremely important not only for those directly involved, but also the entire economy.

The first thing that happens, of course, is that the lender fails to receive expected income from the bond or other loan. This can cause hardship in itself, and it can sometimes lead to a chain reaction if the lender is also a borrower, one default leading to another.

Very quickly, financial markets will absorb the new information and reconsider the structure of risk premiums attached to other credit assets. If this borrower has unexpectedly defaulted today, how many others might do so tomorrow? In this way, it is likely that interest rates, incorporating the added risk of default, will increase, with the biggest rate hikes in sectors of the economy believed to be linked to the one currently experiencing default. (As we will see in the macroeconomics portion of the text, lending may be choked off by credit rationing—simply denying loans to prospective borrowers—as well as higher interest rates.)

As for the borrower who defaulted, new borrowing is out of the question, at least temporarily. If it is a corporation, and if the default is seen as signifying insolvency, share prices can fall to near zero. These developments make it that much harder to get back on track to repay existing loans.

Modern economies have also developed special legal procedures to handle default, the realm of bankruptcy law. They differ across jurisdictions, but all have the same general form. First, the defaulting borrower is placed under the protection of the court. This means that they are temporarily relieved of the legal obligation to repay creditors, but in return they must give up some or all control of their assets. If it is a corporation that is in default, the court is likely to appoint someone to take operational control. The purpose is to operate the company in a way that maximizes the likelihood that creditors will eventually be repaid. Under some systems the creditors themselves are represented in this control.

Bankruptcy, therefore, does not mean the immediate dissolution of a company. Some firms have been run for years under bankruptcy statutes, with their earnings earmarked for debt repayment. Of course, the original owners can only stand on the sidelines while this occurs. If a firm cannot even cover its operating costs, so that continued operation only increases the amount of debt needing to be serviced, a court can impose partial or full liquidation. This means that some or all of the company's assets will now be sold, with the proceeds to go to the creditors. If the company is insolvent, it is unlikely that creditors will recover the full amount of their investment. (Note: during the current financial crisis, governments in many countries have chosen to bail out firms in financial distress, meaning that the government itself assumes some of the debt obligations of particular insolvent borrowers. In that case, there are high-stakes political questions about how much of the debt the government will pay, whether the shareholders of the firms being bailed out will lose their equity, and whether the firms' managers will get to keep their jobs.)

In the case of individuals a similar procedure takes place. Courts can assume control over a borrower's assets and impose a repayment schedule that must be adhered to. Bankruptcy entails the liquidation of some or all of these assets, and the bankrupt individual may have to limit personal spending as well. These terms can be harsh, but they are not as onerous as the debtors prisoners of former times.

There is a lot of disagreement among economists over how strict bankruptcy laws, or how generous bailouts, ought to be. It is clear that there are risks to taking too harsh an approach, but too much leniency could be a problem too. If the laws are too lenient it could create a situation of **moral hazard**, where borrowers could be encouraged to take on too much debt or spend their borrowed money too recklessly, secure in the knowledge that failure to repay will not result in serious penalties. On the other hand, borrowers cannot always control the forces that determine their financial condition. Individuals, for example, can suffer an unexpected health problem that increases their expenses while reducing their income. Businesses, as we have seen, are often borrowers and lenders at the same time, so that failure to receive payment on loans in one context can lead to a failure to repay in another. Also, bankruptcy laws that impose high debt service costs can make it difficult for individuals and businesses to return to productive life.

Personal and business bankruptcy law is a hot topic in many countries, and, as we will see in the macro portion of this book, a debate has been taking place over whether some institution similar to a bankruptcy court is needed to stabilize the global financial system.

17.6 Two Models of Financing Business

As we saw earlier, financial markets play a major role in determining where and how society's resources are put to work—who gets the money to produce what and where. This is not equally true in all countries, however. In fact, the world is divided between countries where financial markets are paramount and others where they play a lesser role. The first of these we will call **market-centered financial systems** and the second **institution-centered financial systems**. In Chap. 8 we introduced this distinction in terms of corporate governance, the organizational basis for the control of business firms; here we will briefly describe each from a financial perspective and highlight their main strengths and weaknesses.

A. Market-centered systems are based on the principle that control of the firm should rest in the hands of its shareholders. This means that the interests of those who purchase stock, higher profits and share prices, should determine the firm's business decisions. As we saw in Chap. 8, this can be achieved directly, through shareholder election of the company's board of directors, or indirectly via the pressure that the stock market puts on corporate managers. The main exemplars of market-centered finance are the United States and Great Britain.

There are two arguments in favor of this approach. First, if market prices truly reflect the social costs and benefits of the productive activities of businesses, then the goal of maximizing net benefits (total benefit minus total cost) is identical to that of maximizing profits, since profit is simply revenue (what consumers are willing to pay for products) minus cost. Second, those who purchase a share of the firm's capital are putting their money at risk. They will be more willing to do this if they have control over how the money is used; others, like corporate managers, might regard this money as "free" and spend it less carefully.

The main ingredients of a market-centered financial system are these: First, most large firms must be organized as joint-stock companies (companies whose capital is divided up into many shares), and members of the public must be able to buy and sell these shares without limit. Second, there should be a system of stock-trading (such as stock exchanges) that make it possible for large numbers of people to take part in the process. This means that stock markets will be **liquid**; it will not be difficult to find buyers and sellers at the going price. Third, there needs to be a system of reporting on the financial condition of businesses so that a few insiders (such as company managers) are not in a privileged position; otherwise investors who are not in the know will feel cheated, and participation in the market will diminish over time.

An example of the creation of a new market-centered system in the current period can be found in the regulations promulgated by the European Union. Its goal is the creation of a single financial market for the ownership and control of corporations across its member states. To achieve this it has promoted privatization (to put ownership on a joint-stock basis), rules that prohibit restrictions on who can own shares (such as citizens of the country in which the corporation is situated, or its workers), and European-wide regulations to govern financial market operations.

B. Institution-centered systems rely primarily on financial institutions, such as banks, to play the dominant role in the ownership and control of businesses. Firms may issue stock, but a substantial portion is held by banks with close ties to the company and its management. These banks hold shares not primarily as a way to make money, but to fulfill their role as overseers of the companies they have a stake in. For this to be true, of course, the banks themselves cannot simply be profit-making enterprises; they have to reflect other economic and social interests. For this reason, institution-centered systems generally adhere to the stakeholder approach discussed in Chap. 8.

One well-known example of a bank-centric financial system is Germany. Several large private banks have longstanding ownership connections to the leading multinational firms in sectors like auto-making and chemicals. At the same time, more than half the assets of the German banking system reside in public and cooperative banks whose primary mission is local economic development. These banks are more likely to build relationships with mid-sized German enterprises. As you might expect, the German system has come under pressure from the EU, which would like to steer it toward a market-based model.

Another prominent example is Japan. Japan's innovation is to center several otherwise unrelated firms around the same "main bank", their provider of finance and source of oversight and guidance. Each bank, then, manages what might be thought of as a mini-economy, a diversified set of businesses whose prospects are only loosely correlated. The banks, in turn, take guidance from the Ministry of Finance, the branch of the Japanese government charged with overall financial policy. This system, which allocates capital in a more planned, systematic fashion than one would find even in countries like Germany, has been replicated in several other east Asian economies.

C. Comparisons

To those who may not have thought about the role of finance in modern economies, this discussion of different national styles of financial organization may seem arcane, but it could be argued that it constitutes the biggest source of economic differentiation in the post-1989 world. With the collapse of Communism, differences in the way capitalism is constructed are more sharply etched. Consider Box 17.1, for example, which reports some of the results of a survey of executives and managers of large corporations in several countries.

Box 17.1: Whose Company Is It?

Employees were asked the question, "Under which of the following assumptions is a large company in your country managed?" The average answers for four countries are:

	United states (%)	Britain (%)	Germany (%)	Japan (%)
Shareholder interest should be given the first priority	76	70	17	3
A firm exists for the interest of all stakeholders	24	30	82	97

Source: Yoshimori (1995)

The results could not be further apart. In the US and Britain, which adhere to market-centered models of business finance, companies put profits first. In Germany and Japan, where banks rather than private investors, play the central role, a variety of stakeholders, including employees, the local community and the general public have to be taken into account.

Here we can see how different financial systems translate into different policies for firms. Of course, the stakeholder/stockholder divide is not absolute. Companies in Germany and Japan are expected to make profits; if they don't their future is dim. Companies in the US and Britain are held to at least some standards of responsible conduct by governments, consumers and in some cases unions; gross illegality or other ethical violations can lead to financial ruin just as surely as poor earnings. Nevertheless, the difference in emphasis is clear and significant.

Supporters of the Anglo-American approach regard the bank-centered model as rigid and prone to corruption. Banks are conservative, they argue, oriented toward the successes of the past and overly cautious about the future. It is harder for an entrepreneur with a new idea to get financing from a bank's investment board than from the market, where one like-minded venture capitalist might be found who can put up the money. Worse, by dealing with the same companies and their managers over and over, year after year, banks become insular and even potentially corrupt. Funds are made available not on the basis of where they will do the most good, but who has the best connections. The charge of "crony capitalism" has been made against such arrangements, particularly in east Asia.

From a theoretical standpoint, defenders of market-centered finance are likely also to believe that the Market Welfare Model generally characterizes most aspects of the economy. As we saw earlier, if consumer demand truly reflects the benefit to society and if the cost of production equally reflects the opportunity and disutility costs of making goods available, then profit represents net benefit, a surplus of benefits over costs. A system that puts profit in the driver's seat, such as that employed by the US and Britain, would then operate in the interest of economic efficiency. An example of this way of thinking is provided by the experience of Wal-Mart, the retailing giant discussed in earlier chapters. Wal-Mart gains its profits by having a high level of sales at its stores while holding down every sort of cost: the prices of the goods it buys from manufacturers, the cost of holding inventories, and the wages and benefits of its employees. If its success in sales shows that it is genuinely benefitting consumers, and if its reduced costs are a sign of its greater efficiency of operation, Wal-Mart's profits truly reflect its positive social role.

Supporters of bank-centered finance, however, have their own points to make. In their view, the Market Welfare Model is often a poor guide to true social costs and benefits. Wal-Mart's sales do not reflect the interests of consumers if the goods are poorly made or if the company's advertising is misleading. Holding down wages and other benefits to workers may simply be a means of transferring income from one segment of society (low-wage workers) to others (shareholders), rather than a reduction in the underlying (opportunity cost and disutility) basis for true social cost. Guiding the company by other signals than simply profit can help correct these possible flaws. (It is interesting that Wal-Mart was unable to compete even on low prices in Germany and was forced to abandon the market to local retailers: stakeholder-oriented firms are not necessarily inefficient.)

Another argument is that there is a large public interest in the opportunities for employment and economic development that business investment offers. It may be in the public interest, for example, for businesses to operate with somewhat lower rates of profit if this is the result of greater investment in regions that especially need it. We have seen that German public banks make loans for this purpose to smaller firms that, while not profit powerhouses, export their wares successfully and boost local employment. Japanese banks put a premium on investments that build capacity in the "hot" technologies and stimulate entry into foreign markets. They think that a coordinated investment strategy makes it more likely for this ambitious approach to succeed.

Related to this is the claim that bank-centered systems promote superior decision-making. This could be because of the detailed knowledge of the strengths and weaknesses of businesses that banks can acquire through long-term relationships—a better basis for evaluating investment prospects, perhaps, than would emerge from markets whose participants are far removed from the scene. Also, it is often said that markets put a premium on short-run profits, whereas banks can afford to be more patient, since they hold their shares for years or even decades. Japanese banks in particular have a reputation for making investments whose returns are likely to be far into the future.

So it is clear that there is a case to be made on both sides of this debate. It is probable that one system works better for some parts of the economy or for some purposes, and the other works better for others. For example, market failures, such as public goods and externalities, play a more significant role in some industries than others, and even when they are acute it may not be the case that the stakeholders who matter in an institution-centered system are the ones who have an interest in correcting these failures. For instance, if the market failure is that the firm's products pollute the environment, and if employees or government officials are put in charge of economic development, are they the proper stakeholders to set matters right?

The problem of "insider" versus "outside" control is also difficult to evaluate in any general way. Sometimes insiders, like bank loan officers, have a more detailed knowledge of a company's future prospects, but sometimes their objectivity can be undermined and cronyism can set in. Patience is a virtue, but not obstinacy in the face of facts; in the name of long-term vision investment planners can sometimes go for years down a road to nowhere. (This criticism has been made of the Japanese main bank system in particular.) Market-based finance, on balance, probably does favor more innovation, but successful innovation sometimes requires coordination.

Even the evidence is moot, because there is no agreement on what the indicators should be. Is economic growth the best measure of success? If so, it is difficult to pass judgment, since market-based economies have grown faster in some periods but slower in others. Should the measure be high rates of employment? In the years leading up to the financial crisis this would favor the US and Britain, but since then several institution-based systems, in particular Germany, have turned the tables. Another indicator might be a country's trade balance—whether its exports are greater or less than its imports—since this shows which producers, as a group, do better in competition. Here the nod goes to the institution-based economies, which tend to have substantial trade surpluses. (The US, as we will see in the next volume, has the largest trade deficit in history.) All of these measures, however, by lumping entire economies together, may mask the more detailed strengths and weaknesses that can show up only at the level of particular sectors. A Germany versus US comparison, for example, may give different results depending on whether we look at auto production or computers, agriculture or retailing.

17.7 Are Financial Markets Efficient?

Since the markets for stocks and bonds play such central roles in modern economies, much research has gone into assessing how well they work. The central concept used by economists is that of market efficiency, but it has a specific meaning in the context of financial markets. Here efficiency means two things:

- Market participants have access to all economically useful information. This refers to all information whose value in the marketplace exceeds its cost of discovery, and it rules out the possibility that there is crucial inside information that only a few participants may have access to.
- Market participants use this information rationally in their buying and selling decisions. That is, they make the best possible decisions on the basis of the information they have access to.

These are difficult standards to meet, but modern financial markets are highly sophisticated, so it is possible that they might actually measure up. To see why we would care whether they do or not, let's assume for the moment that both criteria are met and that markets are efficient in this sense.

The first conclusion we could draw is that no particular participant has any reason to do better (make more money through clever trades) than the market as a whole. This is a powerful claim, one that would put many a stockbroker or financial analyst out of business if it is believed to be true. It also says that *you* should not expect to outperform the market either. Your return on your investments might be higher than the average return for a while, but it would fall below at other times, and over a long enough period of comparison it should come out about the same (if your investment strategy is rational, like everyone else's). Why should this be so?

One way of looking at it is this: if the rest of the market has access to the same information you do, and if their trading strategies are as rational as yours, why should you expect to do any better? Another way, which really gets to the heart of the matter, builds on the insight that, if markets are efficient in the above sense, the prices they set (for stocks, bonds and other assets) reflect all the available information. They will change only if there is new information—but truly new information cannot be predicted in advance, since otherwise it would not be new. Therefore the change in prices—whether a particular stock, for instance, will rise or fall in value—must also be unpredictable. In other words, an efficient market is one that fluctuates randomly with each new input of information, leaving participants in a permanent state of surprise. If this were not true, if future information and future prices *could* be predicted more often than not by certain clever traders, then this would mean that some either know more than others or can use information more effectively, in which case one or both of the two criteria for efficiency would be violated.

A second conclusion is that an efficient financial market, as we have characterized it, would provide society with the most accurate possible set of measurements for the value of its various financial assets. We could look to market prices to tell us how much each company is worth, what the true rate of return will be on bonds of different payment lengths (which implies a prediction of future rates of inflation, as we will see in the next volume), what risks of default need to be considered for different public and private bonds, etc. No individual, no matter how much research they do (and how many economics courses they take), can expect to provide a better set of assessments than the market as a whole. This is the social science side to financial market efficiency, just as the previous paragraph presented the personal investment side.

All well and good, you might say, but how realistic is this claim that markets could ever be completely efficient? This might be asking for too much, since, as with other aspects of economics, it is enough for practical purposes that markets be "sufficiently" or "mostly" efficient—efficient enough that individual participants would not outperform the market by more than a little, and that very high investments of economic research would be required to put only slightly more accurate values on bonds, stocks and other assets. So the bar is set at a level of reasonable rather than maximum efficiency. Still, how would we know?

There are two tests for financial market efficiency, one weak, the other strong. The weak test is that the movement of asset prices over time should be unpredictable, which is to say that they do not reveal a pattern that could be used to predict future movements. This is a purely mathematical test, and it is weak because, while an efficient market must meet this test, it could meet it for reasons that have nothing to do with efficiency. After all, if buying and selling decisions were based on the chirping of parakeets rather than the thinking of people, they would be random and unpredictable but without much rationality either. (My apologies to any parakeets who happen to be reading this.)

In fact, however, there is some evidence that even this weak test is not met. Financial markets have a tendency to move in certain directions on particular days of the week or seasons of the year. It ought to be possible for some participants to make extra money by anticipating these movements, which would then eliminate them. (If enough people know a stock will rise tomorrow, they will buy it at a higher price today—but then tomorrow's price becomes today's.) This does not happen, however, indicating that perfect rationality does not prevail in the market as a whole.

The stronger test is to look for a reasonable relationship between the market prices of financial assets and the "fundamentals", the information about likely future risks and returns, that ought to set them. Here it is agreed that market prices tend to rise and fall to a greater extent than the true value of the underlying assets. A little bit of good news often leads to a disproportionately large price increase, and a little bad news often has the opposite effect; economists call this process "overshooting". In the aggregate we sometimes see this in market frenzies, when prices rise to an unsustainable level (a bubble) or fall in a panic. Usually the underlying value of stocks and bonds do not fluctuate so wildly.

Consider Fig. 17.4 on the following page, for instance. This shows the daily closing prices of the Standard & Poor's 500 over the period from April 1997 to April 2007. The S&P 500 is an index representing a basket of 500 stocks traded on the New York Stock Exchange. The value of the index is proportional to what one would have to pay to buy one share each from these 500 companies. The story goes like this: when the period begins the index is below 800. It mostly rises until it breaks 1,500 in the year 2000. For the next 2 years it falls again, dipping once more below the 800 mark. After pausing at the bottom for the better part of a year it starts to climb again and nearly reaches 1,500 in April 2007. To summarize: this index, which represents the market value of 500 leading American companies, nearly doubles in the 3 years beginning in 1997, then falls to where it started from, then nearly doubles again. Did the actual value, the true long-term earning potential, of these companies rise and fall to a comparable extent? Hardly. The stock prices incorporated in the S&P 500 rose too much in the upswing and fell too much in the downswing. (We end this chart before the onset of the most recent crisis, since big shifts in profit expectations would be more justifiable post-2008.)

One reason for this tendency on the part of markets to exaggerate real economic factors has to do with the nature of the speculative process. Market participants make money by anticipating where the market will go next; in other words, the goal is to think like everyone else one day (or hour or nanosecond) sooner. The economist John Maynard Keynes, who will play a prominent role in the next volume, compared the situation to a beauty contest in which the judges are given a prize for choosing the entry that *other* judges have chosen as most beautiful. This creates a herd dynamic, where the crowd moves strongly in one direction, then races off in another. One implication is that financial markets provide better price signals when averaged over a longer run, compared with the prices that appear on any given day. They are efficient in the way that a mythical statistician was when he

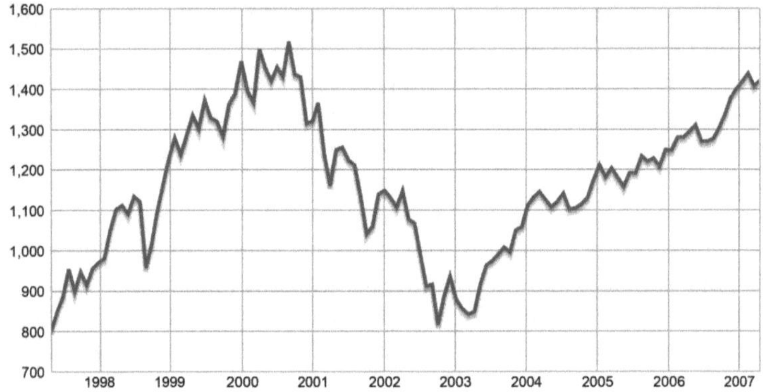

Fig. 17.4 Daily closing values of the S&P 500 index, April 1997 to April 2007. (Source: New York Stock Exchange)

took up hunting. He aimed at a deer, missing to the left. Then he aimed again, missing to the right. "A perfect shot!" he said, "—on average."

The Main Points

1. There are two meanings to "capital". It can either be a collection of goods, like buildings and equipment, that are used to produce other goods and are not immediately used up in the process, or a sum of money used to purchase financial assets that have a rate of return. Physical capital has an objective productivity in production, while financial capital reflects the willingness of wealth-holders to invest their funds. These don't have to equal each other because the two types of capital are different. The ratio of the financial valuation of a firm to its market (financial) capitalization is Tobin's q.
2. Equity markets are where shares of stock, which represent shares of ownership of firms, are traded. From a "fundamental" perspective, equity prices should be determined by the present value of firms' future expected profits. Many traders adopt a "technical" approach, basing their offer decisions on patterns they believe they can identify in the movement of share prices. Sometimes these two approaches yield similar prices, and sometimes not. Firms raise investment funds when they sell equity in an initial public offering, and they sometimes issue additional shares for the same purpose when they think the market can absorb them. The vast majority of stock trading, however, involves existing shares and has no direct effect on the availability of investment funds. To the extent that share prices convey market expectations of the future profitability of firms, we can use event analysis to try to link equity price movements to unanticipated events in the world occurring simultaneously; this provides an estimate of the expected effect of these events on firms' profitability.
3. Credit markets are where bonds, public and private, are traded. Since the rate of return on a bond is equal to its income flow divided by its price, there is an inverse relationship between bond prices and market interest rates. This permits us to analyze credit markets in two ways, as a market in bonds (borrowers supply

bonds, investors demand them, and the price goes up or down) or a market in funds (borrowers demand funds by selling bonds, investors supply them by buying bonds, and the interest rate goes down or up). The extra perceived risk of a borrower's default, relative to the least risky bond (such as a US Treasury bond), is compensated by a risk premium that raises the bond's interest rate. Credit markets play an important role in the allocation of capital, reducing borrowing costs for projects seen as most likely to be profitable and raising them for those seen as riskier or less promising.

4. Commodity markets are where standardized agricultural products, natural resources and their byproducts are traded. Few traders are interested in the products themselves, and it is mainly electronic claims to commodities that are bought and sold. These claims can be packaged in complex ways, as in future and option contracts. Futures markets in particular can serve a socially useful function by helping us anticipate and counteract potential surpluses and shortages.
5. Default is an ever-present possibility in the financial world. It sometimes arises because the borrower is insolvent, but it can also occur because the borrower is insufficiently liquid. When an individual or firm enters a bankruptcy process, it is typical for a court to protect them against the full set of creditor demands in return for supervisory powers designed to guarantee that debt repayment is a priority. Equity investors in firms that default normally lose their entire investment.
6. There are two main forms of financing firms in modern capitalist countries. In some countries, like the US and Great Britain, shares are held by a wide variety of investors who trade them in equity markets; this is a market-centered financial system. In others, like Germany and Japan, a large proportion of equity is held by banks and are not actively traded; this is an institution-centered system. The first approach is closely linked to the principle of shareholder primacy, according to which the primary or even sole purpose of the firm is to boost its share prices. The second is linked to a stakeholder framework in which firms exist to serve the interests of multiple groups including not only shareholders but also workers, business partners and public agencies. Both have performed well and poorly in different circumstances and according to different measures.
7. A financial market is considered efficient if market participants utilize all available information and base their decisions on the best possible concepts and models. A weak test of market efficiency is that price movement should be unpredictable, since at each moment the price should incorporate all predictable knowledge. A stronger test is that price movements are consistent with an objectively rational interpretation of existing information. Financial markets pass the first test most, but not all, of the time. They frequently fail the second test, however, as demonstrated by their tendency to overshoot the likely impact of new events. One reason for this is that the incentives in these markets promote herd behavior: each participant tries to trade like the others are expected to trade, but just a little bit sooner.

Terms to Define

Bear market
Bears
Book value
Bull market
Bulls
Capital goods
Capital
Commodities market
Default
Depreciation
Dividends
Equity
Event analysis
Financial capital
Fundamentals approach to financial markets
Initial public offering
Institution-centered financial systems
Liquid assets
Marginal time preference
Marginal return on capital
Market-centered financial systems
Moral hazard
Net worth
Price-earnings ratio
Purchase value versus replacement value
Risk premium
Solvent/insolvent
Technical approach to financial markets
Tobin's *q*

Questions to Consider

1. If financial capital simply measured the value of capital goods, a higher rate of return on money would imply a higher marginal productivity of capital. Check the newspaper or the web to see what are the current market interest rates on long-term government bonds (the baseline rate on which others depend) in different economies, such as the US, Britain, Germany and Japan. Do these rates signify that an additional investment would be more productive if made in the high interest-rate country? Do individuals in that country have a higher rate of time preference?
2. If Tobin's *q* falls below one for a particular company, should it be liquidated—should its assets be sold off separately to the highest bidders? Are there potential

mitigating circumstances? You might want to think about particular companies you are familiar with.

3. Until a few years ago it was common to have laws against usury, the practice of charging very high rates of interest on loans. These restrictions were removed, in part because it was argued that high interest rates are necessary if credit is to be made available to the riskiest borrowers, such as those with very low incomes. Let these borrowers, it was argued, decide whether the cost of money is too high. Do you agree?
4. In general, do you think bankruptcy laws should be more severe than they are now, or less? You might want to read up a bit on the current legal situation before passing judgment!
5. Based on what you have learned so far, do you tend to favor a market- or an institution-based financial system? Why? Does it matter whether you adopt the point of view of a potential investor, a potential employee or a citizen in the country businesses will be located in?
6. In an institution-centered system, what characteristics would be best for banks to do their job effectively? Should the banks themselves be in a competitive market, competing for deposits? Should they be public or private? What stakeholders in the banks should have the most influence?
7. Financial markets pick investments by putting prices on stocks and interest rates (including risk premiums) on bonds in accordance with the supply and demand decisions of traders. Governments pick investments by conducting their own research and making choices through agencies and commissions. Do you think governments can do this job as well as or better than markets? Does your answer to this question depend on how efficient you think financial markets are?

Reference

Yoshimori, M. (1995). Whose company is it? The concept of the corporation in Japan and the West. *Long Range Planning, 28*(4), 33–44.

Inequality 18

In the museum of the Louvre, in Paris, sits "The Raft of the Medusa", one of the most celebrated paintings of the nineteenth century, the work of Theodore Gericault. Here it is, in reproduction (Fig. 18.1).

Obviously the scene on board this raft is catastrophic. Bodies writhe in anguish, and a piece of cloth is raised in a desperate effort to get help. If you look very closely, you can see that there is a ship far in the distance. Will it see the raft and come to its rescue?

The story behind this painting is worth retelling. In June of 1816, a flotilla of four ships departed France carrying soldiers to Africa. One of them, the Medusa, struck a reef in the Atlantic Ocean and suffered serious damage. For 3 days its crew struggled to free the ship, but eventually the Medusa began to break apart and sink. The leaders of the expedition—the officers of the ship, the military commanders from France and a high-level government official—took control of the lifeboats, with the intention of saving only themselves. In response, the common soldiers and crew members lashed together a raft from the timbers of the failing ship and convinced their superiors to tie this raft to the lifeboats. It soon became clear that the boats could not make much progress if they had to tow the raft, so the rope connection was cut by one of the officers. The boats rowed to safety while the raft drifted helplessly in the middle of the ocean.

There were 154 people aboard the raft. They had little food or water and hardly any space to move. They were adrift for 11 days before finally being seen by a passing ship. By that time all but 13 had died horribly, including the cloth-waver depicted by Gericault. When the news traveled back to France, it was regarded as a scandal: how could some of the most privileged men in the country turn their backs on those whose work made their riches and power possible in the first place? It led to an upheaval in the government, and the appearance of Gericault's painting 3 years later was electrifying in an age before photography or rapid communication.

For many at this time, the terrible fate of these crewmen served as a metaphor for the development of the modern economy. With the explosion of new technologies and the rise of new business empires, some were becoming very rich, but most of

P. Dorman, *Microeconomics*, Springer Texts in Business and Economics,
DOI 10.1007/978-3-642-37434-0_18,

Fig. 18.1 The Raft of the Medusa (Gericault) (*Source*: Wikimedia Commons, available at http://upload.wikimedia.org/wikipedia/commons/1/12/Raft_of_the_Medusa.jpg)

the others, it seemed, were being left behind. Progress for the few was based on cutting the rope.

Modern historical research has shown that, in most of western Europe, improvement in living standards for the majority of the population lagged behind economic growth during much of this period. In England, for example, whose propulsive economy was already apparent by the middle of the eighteenth century, it was not until about the middle of the nineteenth that the benefits began to "trickle down" to most of the working class. One reason that so many farmers and artisans left Europe for the New World in this period is that their lives were not getting better at home.

But historians have also shown that, for the most part, the lives of the common people were not getting *worse*. (There are obvious exceptions, of course, such as the famine that struck Ireland during the 1840s.) In this sense, the Medusa parable is misleading. Most workers and farmers in Europe were not aboard a death raft but simply living as they had for generations. Yet it seemed far worse than this because some were doing so much better. In other words, it was not absolute deprivation that had exploded but *inequality*.

Societies have always been unequal to some extent, and certainly those built on slavery or aristocracy are the most unequal of all. Still, the emergence of capitalism has put the issue of inequality in a new light, since wealth is now being created at an unprecedented rate, but not for all. It is the promise of general abundance instead of general scarcity that makes inequality such an important topic today. For the first time, we can imagine that all human beings could live fairly comfortably, even though they currently don't.

This concern shows up in two ways. First, there is an interest in what we might call **general inequality**, the differences between income, wealth and living

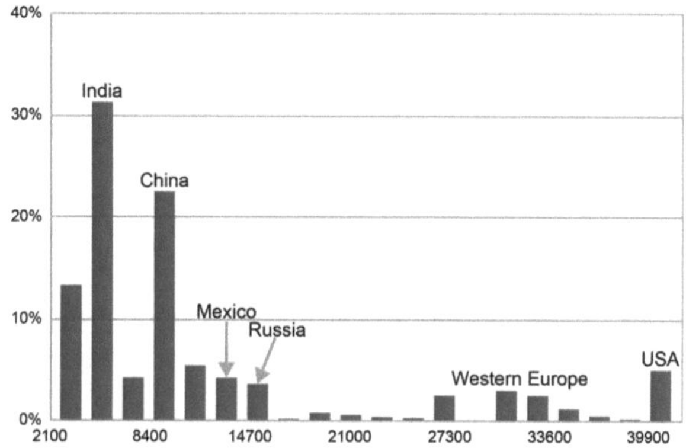

Fig. 18.2 Percentages of the global population by gross domestic product per capita, 2010 (Constant 2005 PPP). (*Source*: World Bank World Development Indicators)

standards across the population. Here the question is, how concentrated is the distribution of these things? Are they enjoyed primarily by just a few, or are they spread out more evenly among everyone? Second, we have become interested in comparisons between certain groups: racial and ethnic groups, men and women and higher and lower castes, for instance. Are some groups more advantaged than others? If so why, and what can be done about it?

Let's begin by surveying economic inequality in the world we live in.

18.1 Some Initial Evidence

It will come as a surprise to no one that this is a highly unequal world, with people in some countries having much higher incomes than others. Figure 18.2 shows the average income per capita for different fractions of the global population, based on the country they live in.

A few clarifications are in order. GDP, gross domestic product, is a measure of the value of everything a country produces during a year, which is also a measure of the income people receive from this production. GDP per capita is therefore approximately the average income in a country, which is not necessarily similar to the median, or typical, income. (A few very high-earners can pull the average up.) PPP is "purchasing power parity", a basis for converting income in one currency to a world standard; we will discuss its measurement in the volume on macroeconomics. Some countries did not report GDP data for 2010; the chart reflects only those that did. (They account for 97.7 % of the world's population.) Finally, the chart does not identify most of the countries, so the ones it does mention "stand in" for the others. For instance, neither India nor China has more than 20 % of the world's population alone; they are joined in their bars by other, smaller countries with approximately the same GDP per capita.

We can see that a large majority of the planet's people live in poorer countries, with average incomes well below $15,000 (PPP). Surprisingly few live in what might be termed the world's middle class of countries, with averages in the $15,000–$25,000 range. This is a Medusa-like picture.

Seeing the world's income in terms of country averages is incomplete, however. Within every country there are large differences among citizens; some fortunate residents of the poor countries are quite rich, while some in the rich countries are relatively poor. What would we find if we ignored national differences and looked at the world as a single population, with each individual holding his or her own place in line? Branko Milanovic, a World Bank economist, has spent many years trying to calculate this, and he finds that world inequality in this sense is equal to or greater than inequality in any single nation that has ever been measured. The world Gini coefficient, which we will define later in this chapter, is approximately 0.650, meaning that the world is roughly two-thirds of the way from perfect equality to the perfectly unequal situation in which one person would get 100 % of all income. To illustrate this, he writes:

> the top 5 percent of individuals in the world receive about 1/3 of total world (PPP-valued) income, and the top 10 percent one-half. If we take the bottom 5 and 10 percent, they receive respectively 0.2 and 0.7 percent of world total income. This means that the ratio between the average income received by the richest 5 percent and the poorest 5 percent of people in the world is 165 to 1. (Milanovic, 2006, p. 16)

If everyone worked an average of 2,000 hours per year (50 weeks times 40 hours per week), the richest 5 % would make more in about a day and a half (12 h) than the poorest 5 % would make all year.

As much as we might think of ourselves as citizens of the world, however, most of us spend most of our time among others of our own nationality, and this is the source for the usual comparisons we make when we think about how well-off we are. Also, the political institutions under which we live cannot currently control global inequality, but they have many policies that make income within our countries more or less equally distributed. So what is the level of income inequality at the national level?

Table 18.1 summarizes this for a sampling of countries, poor, rich and in-between. The measure is once again the temporarily mysterious Gini coefficient. For now, the only important feature of this statistic is that a higher value signifies greater inequality; it ranges between 0 and 1 (Table 18.1).

When reading this table, bear in mind that more equality alone does not mean "better"; there are also large differences in average income to consider. Income in Indonesia is distributed more equally than in Britain, but most residents of Britain have much higher incomes than most Indonesians. If you want to make comparisons, the logical ones would be between countries at approximately the same levels of average income—Indonesia and Cote d'Ivoire, for example, or the United Kingdom and Sweden. Certain generalizations seem to hold:

- Poorer countries tend to have more inequality than richer ones, but there are also many exceptions.
- Inequality is high in Latin America and the Caribbean.

Table 18.1 Gini coefficients for selected counties

Country	Year	Gini coefficient
Algeria	1995	0.353
Indonesia	2002	0.343
Argentina	2003	0.528
Iran	1998	0.441
Bangladesh	2000	0.318
Ireland	200	0.343
Bolivia	2002	0.601
Israel	2001	0.392
Brazil	2003	0.58
Kenya	1997	0.449
Canada	2000	0.326
Korea (South)	1998	0.16
Chile	2000	0.576
Mexico	2002	0.495
China	2001	0.447
Nigeria	2003	0.436
Cote d' Ivoire	2002	0.446
Russia	2000	0.456
Denmark	1997	0.247
South Africa	2000	0.578
Egypt	2000	0.344
Sweden	2000	0.25
France	1995	0.327
Tanzania	2001	0.346
Germany	2000	0.283
Thailand	2002	0.42
Guatemala	2002	0.551
Turkey	2003	0.436
Haiti	2001	0.592
United Kingdom	1999	0.36
Hungary	2002	0.269
United States	2000	0.408

Source: World Bank, World Development Indicators

- English-speaking countries tend to have relatively high levels of inequality compared to others at their income levels, and the United States has the highest of any of these.

In any case, it is clear that inequality varies enormously across countries, measured, as in this case by Gini coefficients, by a factor of more than two to one. The level of inequality in the United States is more than half again as high as in Sweden; the level in Brazil more than twice.

These simple national comparisons leave out a lot of detail. They don't tell us which social groups tend to benefit the most, or where in the distribution (the top or

Fig. 18.3 Income inequality among US families, 1947–2010, measured by Gini coefficients. (*Source*: Federal Reserve Bank of St. Louis)

the bottom) inequalities tend to be the strongest, or what changes are taking place over time. To get a closer reading we have to focus on just one country at a time. Here we will look at the United States, whose government and private research institutions collect excellent economic and social data.

The long-term trend in the US has been toward greater inequality. Figure 18.3 shows changes in the Gini coefficient for family income, which is somewhat greater than individual income, due to the tendency for higher income-earners to live in the same families.

There was a long post-WWII downward trend that reversed itself in the 1970s; since that time inequality has risen in most years. This pattern, particularly the accelerated movement toward inequality since around 1980, can be found in many other countries as well.

Even to those who are familiar with them, Gini coefficients can be a bit opaque, so on the following page are the same data grouped into quintiles (fifths), with the top 5 % broken out of the top quintile (Table 18.2).

The bottom 80 % of the family income distribution all had reduced shares of the total income between 1973 and 2000; the difference went to the top 20 %. Most of the gains of the top quintile were concentrated, in fact, in the top quarter of this group, those who made up the highest 5 % of all families. There has been some stabilization since 2000, although the share of the bottom 40 % continues to fall, and the share received by the top 1 % (not depicted) has risen substantially.

18.2 What About Mobility?

Inequality at any point in time would be more acceptable if there were few barriers in the way of moving up or down the economic ladder. If you were poor and were reading about someone who was fabulously rich, you might think, "I know there's a big gap between us, but maybe tomorrow I will be the one who's on top, and others will be looking up at me." The patron saint of this way of looking at temporary

Table 18.2 Percent of US family income received by quintiles and the top 5 %, 1947–2010

Year	Lowest fifth	Second fifth	Middle fifth	Fouth fifth	Top fifth	Top 5 %
1947	5	11.9	17	23.1	43	17.5
1973	5.5	11.9	17.5	24	41.1	15.5
1979	5.4	11.6	17.5	24.1	41.4	15.3
1989	4.6	10.6	16.5	23.7	44.6	17.9
2000	4.3	9.8	15.4	22.7	47.7	21.1
2007	4.1	9.7	15.6	23.3	47.3	20.1
2010	3.8	9.5	15.4	23.5	47.8	20

Source: Economic Policy Institute

inequality was Horatio Alger, a popular nineteenth century author in the US, who wrote stirring novels like *Struggling Upward, Sink or Swim* and *Bound to Rise*. In each of his creations, Alger presented a young, poor-but-plucky boy (always a boy) who seized opportunity and rose to the ranks of the elite. No doubt his story came true for many young people then as it does today. Of course, there are also those who try with all their might and are unable to overcome the obstacles in their path. The question is not whether there is mobility from bottom to top (and vice versa) in society, but how much.

A modern and more factual depiction of income mobility is given by Fig. 18.4 on the next page. It has been dubbed the "Great Gatsby Curve" in honor of the fictional hero (sort of) of another American novelist, F. Scott Fitzgerald. (*The Great Gatsby* is a penetrating look at the economic elite at the time of its writing in 1925.) As it makes clear, mobility across generations, rather than compensating for an increase in inequality within any single generation, has a tendency to make matters worse.

On the horizontal axis we see our familiar friend, the Gini Coefficient; remember that a higher Gini signifies greater inequality across individuals at a moment in time. On the vertical axis is intergenerational earnings elasticity. What this measures is the percentage change in your expected income today given a percentage change in (in this case) your father's income a generation ago. For instance, if this elasticity is .3, as it is, approximately, for Germany and New Zealand, if your father's income was 10 % higher than mine was 20 years ago, on average your income will be 3 % higher than mine today. Not surprisingly, every country in this sample has a positive elasticity of this sort: the advantages of one generation are always handed off, more or less, to the next. But the amount differs enormously. For the countries with the most intergenerational mobility—Denmark, Norway and Finland, 10 % more for the father translates, again on average, to only 2 % more for the child. In the US and the UK, on the other hand, 10 % more in the first generation implies 5 % more in the second: there is still some mobility but far less. What is especially interesting about this curve is that it is a *curve*. The straight line shows the overall trend, which is for countries that are more equal at a given year (in this case 1985) to also have more mobility across generations. The trend has a strong upward slope, and the actual points are not too far from the trend.

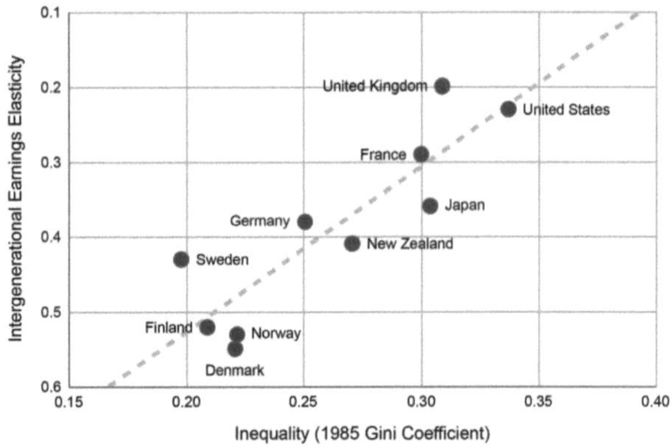

Fig. 18.4 Intragenerational inequality and intergenerational mobility. (The Great Gatsby Curve) (*Source*: Krueger (2012))

(The Gatsby relationship embodied in the trend line explains, on its own, three-fourths of the mobility differences between countries.)

As we think about inequality at one moment in time and across generations, the logic should not be surprising. The wider the difference between income groups, the harder it will be to make the trek from one group to the next. In general, the sort of policies that promote more inequality among the current population will also tend to promote more mobility up and down the ladder for the next generation.

18.3 Inequality by Gender and Race

One of the great revolutions of the twentieth century (it's too soon to say much about the twenty-first) has been the push for greater equality—economic, social and political—between men and women. Figure 18.5 shows the progress, and limits, of this revolution in the ratio of women's to men's hourly earnings. (In making sense of this chart, note that many workers have more than a high school degree but less than a college BA.)

Racial and other barriers are also slowly coming down. You can see how much progress remains to be made by examining the wage ratios by race and ethnicity shown in Fig. 18.6.

Blacks and Hispanics, as groups, fare worse than whites, and the trend over the past three decades is down somewhat. The trend is worse for Hispanics, but it is important to bear in mind that their population has changed dramatically between 1979 and 2007; not only have their numbers increased, but many more are likely to be first-generation residents. Incidentally, when economists analyze data like these, they prefer to adjust the results to control for factors like different levels of education and work experience. For instance, Blacks in the US have somewhat less education on average than Whites. Since, as we have seen, education is linked to earnings, it makes sense to ask how much of the Black-White wage difference appears to come from pure discrimination in the labor market rather than differences in years of education. On the other hand, this approach can lead us to

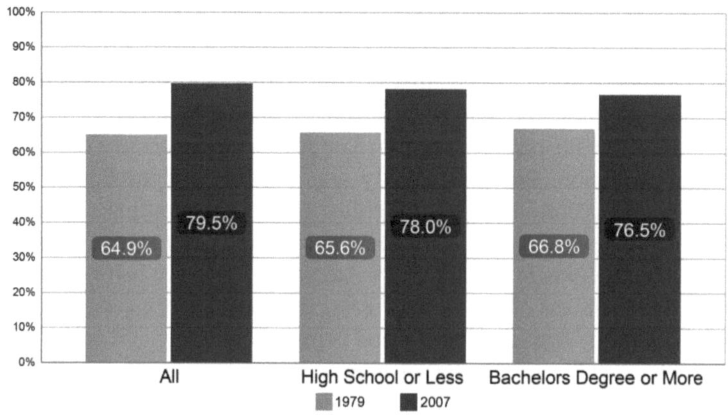

Fig. 18.5 Percent of women's to men's average hourly wage, US, 1979 and 2007. (*Source*: Holzer and Hlavac (2012))

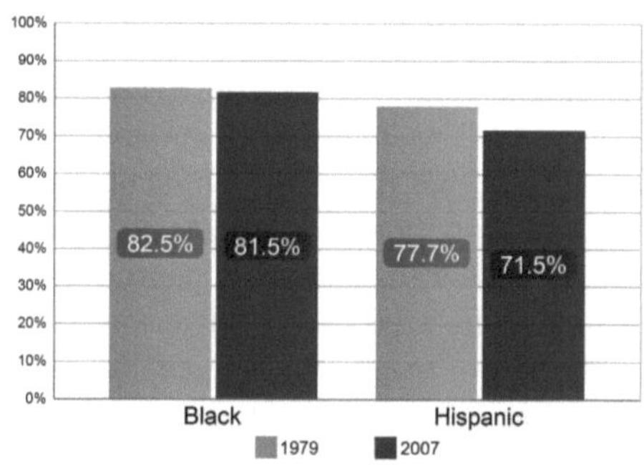

Fig. 18.6 Percent of median US white male hourly wage by race, ethnicity and gender, 2005. (*Source*: Holzer and Hlavac (2012))

underestimate the overall effect of discrimination on economic inequality. There is plenty of evidence of subtle and not-so-subtle prejudice in the schools, for instance, as well as differences in the quality of schools between inner cities and suburbs. Similarly, differences in overall work experience and the number of years at the current job between men and women are largely the result of different expectations women and men face concerning housework, childcare and taking care of the sick and elderly—themselves manifestations of a larger social inequality.

With these qualifications, and keeping this whirlwind tour of global and US income inequality in mind, let's take a look at some of the analytical tools economists and others have developed to examine and explain the numbers.

18.4 Measuring Inequality

The simplest approaches to quantifying the extent of income inequality in a population are to show the amount of income received by a particular portion of the population or by the person whose income places him or her at a particular point within the distribution. We have already seen examples of the first of these: the percent of income according to quintile (fifth), top 5 % and top 1 %. Very similar in spirit is to compare two people at different percentage point levels, for instance at the 90 % percentile (where exactly 90 % of the population lies below) and the 50 % percentile (the median). This is very easy to visualize because these are real incomes received by real, flesh-and-blood people.

The problem with comparisons of individuals and groups is that they capture only a part of the degree of inequality. For instance, in Table 18.2 we see that in 2005 the top fifth of US families received 48.1 % of the total income, but how equally distributed was the income within this fifth? We have one breakout, the upper 5 %, but this tells us nothing about the upper 1 %, 2 %, etc. Similar criticisms could be made about the data for the other fifths: they are quite broad and cancel out too much detail. In the end, the overall level of inequality is determined by the distribution at *every* point along the way from top to bottom. How can we quantify this?

There are several methods, but the most commonly encountered is the **Gini coefficient**. Before we can show how it is calculated, however, we have to first explore a related concept, the **Lorenz Curve**. Suppose we come upon a society in which income is distributed in a perfectly equal way, so that each individual (or family or some other unit of measurement) gets the same as every other. We could picture this in a chart like Fig. 18.7a. The horizontal axis measures the cumulative percentage of the population. To make things simple, consider two such percentages, 33 and 67 %. Since each has an income perfectly corresponding to its population size, 33 % of the people have 33 % of the income and 67 % have 67 %. This is shown on the vertical axis, which measures the cumulative percentage of income. In this way, by tracing combinations of population and income percentages we could draw a line from the lower left corner to the upper right. It emerges from the horizontal axis at a 45° angle and ends where 100 % of the population has 100 % of the income.

The other extreme is represented by Fig. 18.7b. In this case only one person has all the income. This means that the first third have nothing, the second third nothing, and cumulative income remains zero until the final individual is counted. The line running along the horizontal axis and then leaping up the vertical axis at the far end encompasses all the population/income points.

Both purple lines are examples of **Lorenz Curves**, but neither is very likely. A more typical case is given by Fig. 18.8, which is taken from the 2005 data for quintiles in Table 18.2.

We begin at 0 where there are no people and no income. Our first stopping point is at (20, 4.0), since the bottom 20 % of the population hold 4.0 % of the income. The next 20 % add an additional 9.6 %, so the *cumulative* income held by the

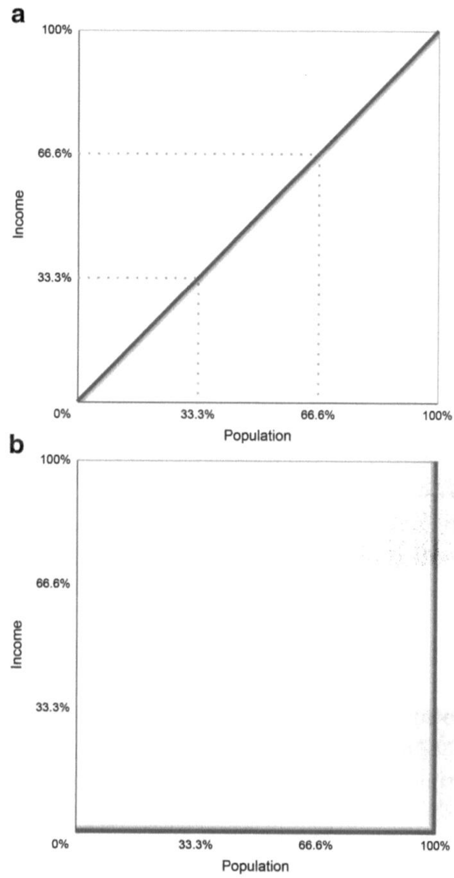

Fig. 18.7 Two extreme Lorenz Curves. (**a**) In a perfectly equal distribution, each percentage of the population (such as 33 or 67 %) receives exactly the same percentage of income. If the percent of population is measured along the horizontal axis and the percent of income along the vertical axis, a 45° angle line (in *purple*) includes all the population/income points. (**b**) In a perfectly unequal distribution, the percentage of income remains zero until we include the last individual, and then it goes directly to 100. Thus the line in *purple* includes all the population/income points

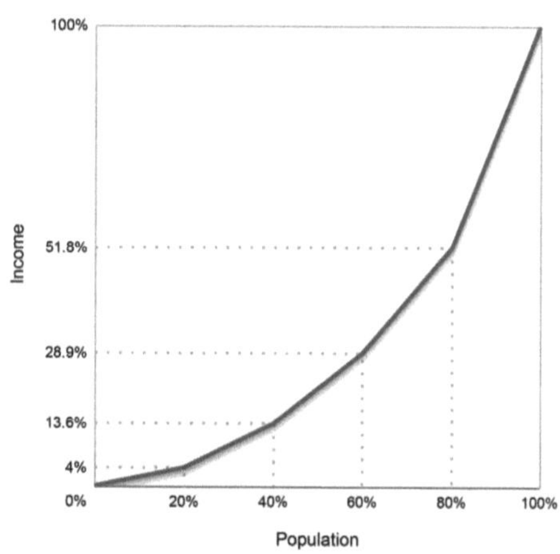

Fig. 18.8 A Lorenz Curve for US family income distribution, 2005. The *purple curve* is drawn from four points representing the cumulative income percentages received by the bottom 20, 40, 60 and 80 % groups, plus the zero-zero and 100–100 points, which always hold

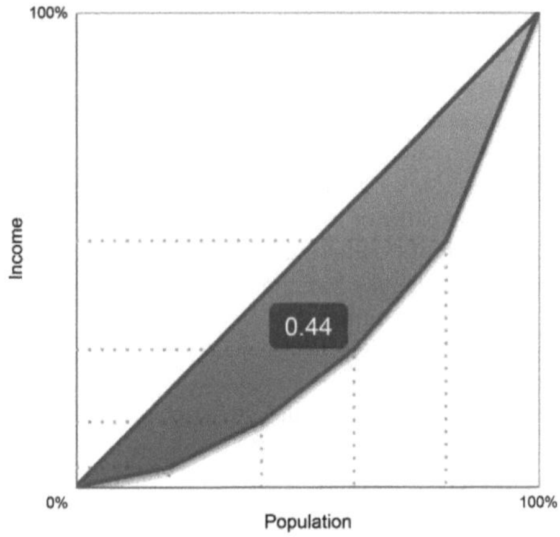

Fig. 18.9 Calculating the Gini coefficient for US family income distribution, 2005. The Gini coefficient expresses the area between the 45° line (perfect equality) and the Lorenz Curve (actual equality) as a fraction of the total area under the 45° line. This shaded area is a bit less than half the potential triangle

bottom 40 % is 13.6 %. This method continues for the next two quintiles, and we finally arrive at 100 % of the population receiving 100 % of the income. The reason the line looks a bit jagged is that it was drawn using only the five quintiles. Thanks to the size and accuracy of annual (and even monthly) census data, however, we could, without too much difficulty, fill in as many intermediate points as we might like, making the line smooth. In this way, our Lorenz curve would reflect the distribution of income across every household.

Now we are ready to consider a technique that reduces the Lorenz curve to a single number. How could we compare the distribution in Fig. 18.8 to a perfectly equal distribution, such as in Fig. 18.7a? Figure 18.9 shows both of them in one diagram, with the area between them shaded in. The more unequal the true distribution, the larger this area, as the Lorenz curve begins to look more like the extreme version in Fig. 18.7b. The Gini coefficient is simply the ratio of this shaded area to the entire area below the 45° line. Perfect equality would be zero (no shaded area), perfect inequality 1. In the US case, as we saw in Fig. 18.3, the Gini is about 0.44. This means that if we draw the Lorenz curve very accurately and base it on each potential data point (and not just the quintiles), the shaded area would be a little less than half the area of the entire triangle making up the bottom half of the box. This is why we can say that inequality in the US lies about halfway between complete equality and complete inequality.

What information do we lose when we reduce an entire diagram to a single number? The relative extent of inequality along different portions of the whole distribution. For instance, the Gini coefficient for the US does not tell us how much of the inequality is due to differences among low- and middle-income families, and how much because of inequality at the very top. In the US case, the top households have a big effect on the entire measurement; for instance, the top one-hundredth of one percent of individuals received about 8 % of all income in 2005. This would be reflected in extreme steepness of the Lorenz Curve as it approaches the upper right-hand corner.

Now that you have a better sense of how the Gini coefficient is calculated and what it means, look again at Table 18.1 and Fig. 18.3.

18.5 The Functional Distribution of Income

Thus far we have thought about the issue of inequality solely in terms of populations, but economists tend to approach the question in a rather different way. Beginning with the classical political economists of the eighteenth century, like Adam Smith, there has been a tendency to think about the sources of income, stemming from the roles different people play in the economy. For Smith and his contemporaries, the big question was, what determines the distribution of society's income into wages (to workers), profits (to owners of capital) and rents (to owners of land and natural resources). To this modern economists would add at least one other, returns to scarce human capital (highly valued skills and abilities), and sociologists would consider the reward to status, particularly to achieving a position high in corporate or similar hierarchies.

Profit has already made an appearance several times in this book. It first came to us in its average form, as the opportunity cost of capital—the return an investor could reasonably expect to get on a typical financial investment. Then we saw the role it plays in the theory of the firm, as the main goal of management (the sole goal in shareholder-driven financial systems). And it was seen to rise or fall based on the bargaining power of labor. We could say, then, that we already know quite a bit about profit, its origin and significance. Nevertheless, from the standpoint of income distribution there is something more to say.

The effect of profits on income distribution derive from two factors, the extent to which ownership of capital is concentrated in society, and the return on capital compared to the return on labor and other factors of production.

In all societies capital is very unequally owned. Once again, we can let the United States, with its rich sources of statistical data, stand in for other countries. If we take the broadest definition of wealth, the value of all household assets (stocks, bonds, pension accumulations, housing) minus all debts, we find that in 2004 the top 20 % of households held about 85 % of net worth, and the top 1 % just over a third. If we look only at net financial assets (stocks and bonds), the holdings of the top 1 % rise to over 42 %.

Returns on capital fluctuate greatly from year to year based on the performance of the financial markets. In good years, like the late 1990s in the US, profits shoot up. In bad years, like the early 2000s and the dismal year 2008, they are depressed. 2006, for instance, was between these two extremes. In that year a little more than half of all business and profit income went to the top 1 % of households, who received just over half their income from these sources. Overall, business and profit income together accounted for about 18 % of all income in society; about 65 % was a return to labor. (The remainder came from a variety of sources, including government transfers.) What this shows is that returns to investment (in one's own business and in financial assets generally) played a modest role in determining the overall level of income inequality in the US, but a very large role in determining the share taken at the very top.

Because of their interest in the role of human capital, economists have paid close attention to the tendency in the US and other countries toward a wider gap between the earnings of more- and less-educated workers. To take two groups in particular, in 1973, when there were almost four times as many workers whose education had stopped at high school compared to college graduates, the ratio of the average high school hourly wage to those of college grads was about 69 %; in 2005, when there were only half again as many high school-only workers as college grads, it had fallen to 57 %. Similar differences have expanded between other education groups, and not only in the US but in most other industrialized countries.

Organizational standing is most visible in the pay received by CEO's (chief executive officers) of corporations compared to the earnings of those who work under them. The average of this multiple in the US corporate sector has grown from 27 in 1973 to 262 in 2006, although this trend is not nearly as strong in most European countries and Japan. Similar, if not quite as dramatic, pay gaps have also widened further down the hierarchy, for example in the relationship between the earnings of managers and those they supervise.

Although the strengths of their effects vary, all the functional factors point in the same direction, toward a tendency to greater inequality in income across the population. This is one of the most important developments in the world economy during the past few decades, and it is even more striking when set against the long period of *declining* inequality that characterized the 20 years following the end of World War II. Why this has occurred and what, if anything, should be done about it are the questions we turn to next.

18.6 Income Inequality: Explanations and Policy Responses

Very broadly, four different theories have been put forward to explain the sort of evidence we have surveyed in this chapter: (1) "skill-biased technical change", (2) globalization, (3) deregulation and (4) "winner-take-all". Before we go into each one separately, it is important to bear in mind that they are not mutually exclusive; all may capture some part of the truth, and there may be other causes analysts have thus far failed to consider.

1. **Skill-biased technical change**. For anyone who has lived through the technological revolutions of the last 25 years or so, nothing has been as striking as the transformation of the digital computer from a costly behemoth sitting in the basement of large office buildings to the personal tool perched on the desktop, laptop or even in the shirt pocket. The proliferation of computers, along with email and the Internet, has changed how business is done and who does it. It would be surprising if it had no effect on the distribution of income among those with different computer skills or access to these technologies.

Many economists think that computerization is "skill-biased"; it increases the returns to those with greater education or other forms of human capital and decreases the opportunities for those who are less able to make use of them. Many studies have been done of the relationship between whether a computer is used at work and how much a worker earns; the results are suggestive but not yet conclusive. It is very likely, however, that the computer, by automating many routine tasks, both manual and mental, has changed the labor market in a way that is highly disadvantageous for those with less education.

2. Globalization. By reducing barriers to trade, particularly in manufacturing, but now also in many clerical and service occupations, globalization has intensified competition between the workers of different countries. Many in higher-income countries are seeing their wages decline as they and the companies they work for have to hold their own against increasingly productive workers in lower-wage regions.

At the same time, other workers have found their opportunities increased by globalization. Those with scarce skills are the beneficiaries of heightened competition, a phenomenon that can be seen in fields like finance and entertainment. As the world becomes more tightly integrated, the "world players" can operate on a larger stage. Also, the rules under which globalization is taking place have tended to protect some workers more than others. The result is a growing gap between globalization's winners and losers.

3. Deregulation. Behind this theory is the presumption that "raw", unregulated capitalism tends toward very high levels of inequality. If competition is the only force at work, some will succeed fabulously, others will fail dismally, and differences between the better- and worse-off will compound over time. This presumption may not be true, however, or it may be true only some of the time and for some portions of the population, but for now let us assume that it is mostly correct. What would this tell us about current trends toward inequality?

Throughout much of the twentieth century, in most regions of the world, there was a drift toward increasing economic regulation. This took many forms: direct government regulation of business, union involvement in wage-setting and work organization, restrictions on trade, minimum and maximum prices and wages, public enterprise, and many others. In general, they promoted greater equality of opportunity and outcomes across large sections of society, and they were often promoted with exactly this in mind.

Beginning in the early 1980s this trend was reversed in different ways and to different degrees in different countries. In some unions played a much reduced role; in others the economy was opened to greater international competition. Publicly owned firms were privatized, and market regulations were scaled back. Within firms as well, market-based competition began to replace more administrative systems of control, as we saw in Chap. 8. If it is true that competition is intrinsically inequality-producing, we would expect these political and economic changes to result in the sort of trends that have actually materialized.

It is probably too much to say that competition *always* has this effect, but economists have closely studied the effects of specific forms of deregulation, and there is general agreement that they explain at least some portion of the overall rise in inequality. When it comes to how much, the agreement breaks down.

4. Winner-take-all markets. Most competition occurs at the margin, as competitors try to acquire a little more or a little better. Companies seek to win market share from one another, and they measure success in percentage points. Workers compete for the best jobs, and success means getting a somewhat higher position, more money or other benefits than those who lose out. As we are used to thinking of it, the world is not divided between total winners and total losers, but between those who have gained a bit more and those who must settle for a bit less.

Some observers think that new forms of technology are changing this pattern. In many fields digital reproduction combined with faster and more thorough communication are creating conditions in which small advantages in productivity, quality or reputation can translate into enormous differences in outcomes. For instance, as financial deals between companies become larger and more complex, the impact of a slightly more skilled lawyer or analyst can amount to hundreds of millions of dollars, and this naturally shows up in the form of a very large income differential between the superstars and those in the middle of the pack.

Network externalities, which we surveyed in Chap. 15, also contribute to this effect. It is common for a particular software or internet-based service firm, for example, to capture nearly all of the available market by being the first to enter it or by having some small advantage over its competitors. This makes the managers and creative people who are little more effective in the speed and quality of their projects vastly more valuable to the companies that employ them.

Finally, digital reproduction and enhanced communication tends to concentrate market share for a wide variety of professionals. Top-level physicians now offer their diagnoses in difficult cases that arise halfway around the world; the designer of a new print font can have millions of users within the space of a few months. This is fine for those whose work is replicated or extended to faraway locations, but it diminishes the contribution of local, less exalted producers.

These are the main theories that purport to explain why this is an age of increasing inequality. Research on their relative importance is inconclusive, and it may well be that the actual processes at work are simply too complex to be described at this level of generality. Nevertheless, they provide the main basis for developing policies to limit or channel inequality in market economies.

Before sketching the most prominent policy alternatives, it should be mentioned that not everyone agrees that policies are needed in the first place. There is political debate over what criteria should be used to determine whether inequality has become too large, as we will see in the Appendix to this chapter. Also, many people benefit from this inequality, and it is in the nature of our political systems that those with the greatest economic resources also play a disproportionate role in setting the political agenda. So consider the list that follows as a guide to what can be done about inequality *if* there is public support for moving in this direction.

1. Enhancing human capital. If skill-biased technical change is the main reason for the upward trend in inequality, then spreading the necessary skills more evenly through the population is the logical antidote. Supporters of this approach would spend more money to improve public schools at all levels, paying particular attention to those who would otherwise fall behind or drop out. Early childhood programs are also favored, since there is evidence that learning skills are strongly affected by experiences children have before they enter school. Proponents of the human capital approach are confident that, if many more young people are given the skills to do intellectually demanding work, more jobs requiring those abilities will materialize; others are more skeptical.
2. Redirecting globalization. If intensified global competition is largely responsible for increased inequality, then the speed or direction of globalization may need to be altered. Here there is a wide variety of proposals: reduce the volume or velocity of capital investment flowing between countries, install financial mechanisms that would promote more stable and balanced trade, include labor standards in trade agreements. These ideas flare up each time a new trade agreement is drafted.
3. Reregulation. If deregulation is the culprit, then some of the mechanisms of regulation that have fallen into disuse could be resurrected, or new forms developed. Here too the specific ideas are varied: instituting or raising statutory minimum wages, changing the legal environment to make it easier to form labor unions, giving unions or other worker organizations more say in the running of enterprises, promoting other forms of stakeholder influence in business decision-making (as discussed in Chaps. 8 and 17), and using tax or subsidy incentives to encourage more egalitarian practices (or discourage very large privileges for those at the top). In practice, debate around these measures tends to center on whether they would impose an economic price in the form of less dynamism and slower growth.
4. Redistributive taxation. If the ultimate sources of the surge toward inequality lie in the nature of modern technology, and if the development of this technology is beyond political control (which may not be the case given the large role of publicly funded research), then great differences in the rewards dished out by the market will simply be a fact of life. The only way to offset this trend would then be to redistribute some portion of these unequal incomes through the tax system, by increasing the tax rate on the highest incomes or financial assets and transferring more of the revenues to the bottom. All industrialized countries already do this to some extent; the question is whether they should do so even more. Economists disagree on whether we should expect positive or negative growth effects from greater redistribution; in any case, the impact in isolation from other policies is not likely to be very large. The main question is whether such leveling is justifiable, an issue we will explore in more detail in the Appendix.

18.7 Discrimination

In every society there are groups which are at risk of being treated unfairly in the economy. In some places ethnic and racial minorities are in this position; in others the distinguishing factor may be religious or caste-based or the result of immigration or resettlement. Skin color often plays a role, and in most of the western hemisphere and parts of Asia indigenous people are singled out for inferior treatment. Moreover, in every country women struggle for economic equality vis-a-vis men. In speaking of **discrimination** in this section, we will refer to the unequal treatment of people who are equal in all relevant economic respects, and whose lesser outcomes are due to the social group they are part of. If two workers are of equal ability, but one is paid more than the other because of her race or national background, this would constitute discrimination—but so would paying them the same if the one from the disfavored background was significantly *more* able or productive, and if this group affiliation were the reason. Thus the definition of discrimination brings into play two elements, comparisons of treatment and the role of group membership. It is important to bear in mind that there is no agreement on which groups should be monitored for potential discrimination, so the definition will apply differently based on how it is interpreted. For instance, is it discriminatory to favor job applicants who are tall compared to those who are short, even if they are equally qualified for the work? There is some evidence that favoritism of this sort exists, but whether it is viewed as discrimination, and therefore a social problem, depends on whether we care about equal treatment among those of different heights.

To organize our thinking about discrimination, it will be helpful to do a simple algebraic exercise. Suppose there are two groups in society, the Uppers and the Lowers, or U and L for short. Suppose also that there are two types of jobs, Good and Bad or G and B. If the wage rate for good jobs is g and the wage rate for bad jobs is b, and if the percentage of Uppers in Good jobs is u and of Lowers in Good jobs is l, then the average wage gap can be written as:

$$[\mathrm{ug} + (1 - \mathrm{u})\mathrm{b}] - [\mathrm{lg} + (1 - \mathrm{l})\mathrm{b}] = \text{Average wage gap between U and L} \quad (18.1)$$

The first bracketed term on the left-hand side represents the average wage for the U group. A fraction u earns the Good wage g, while the rest $(1-\mathrm{u})$ earn only the Bad b. The second bracketed term represents the average wage for the L group, in which l earn g and $(1-\mathrm{l})$ earn b. Multiplying out the left-hand side and then simplifying gives:

$$\begin{aligned}\mathrm{ug} + \mathrm{b} - \mathrm{ub} - \mathrm{lg} - \mathrm{b} + \mathrm{lb} &= \mathrm{ug} - \mathrm{ub} - \mathrm{lg} + \mathrm{lb} \\ &= \text{Average wage gap between U and L} \quad (18.2)\end{aligned}$$

Now factor:

$$(u - l)\,(g - b) = \text{Average wage gap between U and L} \qquad (18.3)$$

(Multiply out Eq. 18.3 to make sure it's right.) What this final version of the equation tells us is that the average wage gap between the two groups—the degree of discrimination if the groups are equal in economically relevant respects—is the product of two factors, the difference in the percentages of each group who hold the Good jobs (u−l) and the difference in pay between Good and Bad jobs (g−b). To keep track of this, let's call the first factor the **selection effect** and the second the **reward effect**. Intergroup comparisons reflect both of them taken together.

What theories have economists developed to explain the sort of outcomes we saw in Figs. 18.4 and 18.5 above? Although there are many variations and wrinkles, we will summarize them as falling into three camps: taste for discrimination, statistical discrimination and differential bargaining power. As is often the case in the realm of economic theory, the arguments are not mutually exclusive; all may be true in some instances or even in most.

1. Taste for discrimination. This approach was pioneered by Gary Becker, who received a Nobel Prize for this and similar work. (We encountered him earlier when we explored the concept of human capital in Chap. 16.) He envisions a small business owner who hires a group of workers and supervises their work. This owner is not the single-minded profit-maximizer of traditional economic theory, however; he also derives personal satisfaction from enforcing discriminatory attitudes, such as hiring workers from a favored group even when they are less qualified or paying them more even when their performance is no better. In other words, in addition to having an appetite for profit, this business owner has a "taste for discrimination".

At its core, this is a rather minimalist analysis: it says that the owner discriminates because he wants to. What makes the theory interesting, however, are its predictions. Suppose this owner faces a perfectly competitive market, where the smallest difference in price can mean failure or survival. (This is what is signified by the perfectly elastic demand curve faced by the competitor in such a market.) By exercising his discriminatory taste, the owner runs the risk of being driven out of business. Hiring a less qualified worker, for example, will increase the cost of production. This would also be the result of paying some workers below and others above the value of their productivity: the first would be recruited away to other companies, while the second would earn more than they contribute. Ultimately, our discriminatory owner would face a choice: either accept a lower rate of profit, shut down the business (and lend out his money to others who earn the average rate of profit), or end his discriminatory ways. Over time, it is reasonable to expect that fewer and fewer would choose option 1, which means that discrimination would gradually disappear from the market.

There is some support for this prediction in real-world economies. Women, as we have seen, have seen their average earnings come closer to parity with men in the United States (and other countries); some countries with extremely rigid forms of job discrimination, such as South Africa under apartheid, have found them expensive to maintain in a globally competitive world. Of course, there are other reasons discrimination has diminished in these instances, above all the organized pressure brought by those being discriminated against.

Becker's theory becomes more open-ended when additional complications are introduced. For instance, markets are often less than perfectly competitive, and this creates space for discriminatory employers to continue to exercise their prejudices. Even if profits are somewhat lower they may remain above the opportunity cost of capital. Also, coworkers or customers may be prejudiced rather than, or in addition to, the owners. Bigoted coworkers, by withholding cooperation, can reduce the productivity of discriminated workers, "justifying" (in an economic but not ethical sense) their lower pay. Bigoted customers can have the same effect if they are less likely to buy from companies that have salespeople or other employees from disfavored groups. There is no reason to expect that these forms of discrimination will be competed away over time.

The prevalence of prejudiced attitudes over a wide portion of society can therefore lead to self-perpetuating discrimination in both the selection and reward effects described above. Groups suffering from discrimination will have less access to the better jobs, and the higher-level jobs that are open to them will tend to pay less than they otherwise would. There is substantial evidence that both effects operate in economies like the US.

2. Statistical discrimination. This theory was first proposed by another Nobel laureate, Kenneth Arrow. As formulated, it pertains mainly to the selection effect, assuming that differences in rewards are determined by other factors. Arrow begins with the observation that discriminatory individuals typically think on the basis of stereotypes: they attribute to all members of particular groups the characteristics that only some of them actually have. For instance, an owner of a trucking business might be less willing to hire female applicants, thinking that women, as a group, are worse drivers than men. Perhaps most of the stereotypes that fuel prejudice are wrong. In this case, it may well be the case that women drivers are no worse than men, or are even better on average. If so, over time we are back in Gary Becker's territory. If the assumption about women drivers is wrong, this will eventually show up in the form of lower profits for companies that discriminate against them and higher profits for those who don't. Market competition will weed out those who don't learn from experience. False stereotypes will be dispelled.

But Arrow recognized a second possibility: what if, in this case, the prejudice is true *on average*? That is, suppose (to continue our example) there is a great range in the quality of drivers among both men and women, but that somewhat more women are bad drivers than men? If the employer had full information about the aptitude of each applicant, it would be no problem to select only those with the highest skill, whether men or women. A somewhat higher proportion of those selected would be men, but by our definition there would be no discrimination, only rational employment practices.

In the usual case, however, the employer does *not* have this sort of information. Perhaps, for instance, it would be too expensive to give each applicant the sort of thorough driving test that could differentiate the skillful from the klutzy. In that case, it is entirely rational for the employer to discriminate on behalf of men: by doing this they would recruit a higher quality workforce, on average, than they would if they did not take gender into account. The result would be a male bias in the workforce out of all proportion to the true difference in average ability. This would be unfair to female applicants, but there would not be any economic cost to the employer—quite the contrary.

The statistical theory proposes a paradox. In the case of false stereotypes, there is no basis for discrimination and it can be eliminated without economic cost. But what if the stereotype is based on a true difference in the relevant group averages? What should be the tradeoff between fairness and efficient matching between jobs and workers?

3. Differential bargaining power. This theory is perhaps the oldest of all three; it is too ancient and widespread to ascribe to any particular thinker. Nevertheless, it has been given greater clarity with the emergence of game theory as a central analytical tool in economics.

Recall that in the model of bargaining power developed in Chap. 14, the critical variable is each party's outside option, what they would get if there is no agreement and they must go their separate ways. The one who needs the agreement most is at a comparative disadvantage. In simple terms, this model explains why members of groups subject to discrimination have worse outside options on average and must accept inferior bargaining outcomes. This is, as should be clear, primarily a theory of reward effects—why the jobs typically inhabited by members of some groups pay less than those inhabited by others.

One striking example of this form of discrimination is the situation faced by undocumented workers, who are subject to arrest and deportation if they are identified. Their outside option, if they fail to accept an employer's wage offer, may be exactly that, arrest and deportation. This means they have no bargaining power at all and must accept virtually any offer they get.

The more common state of affairs, however, is that the vulnerability of those subject to discrimination results primarily from the fact that this discrimination is widespread. If other employers pay you less, then this means your outside option is worse for the one employer you are bargaining with. This can be a self-reproducing situation, with each inferior outcome making the others "rational". It doesn't embody the optimistic prediction of Becker's main model of the discriminating employer because wages are assumed to be set at least in part by bargaining and not perfect competition.

One interesting implication of the bargaining model is that it gives a potentially important role to wealth inequality as a determinant of income inequality. Normally, if a worker refuses to come to agreement with an employer, this will entail a spell of unemployment while he or she looks for another job. (You may want to reread the section on searching and matching in labor markets from Chap. 16.) The cushion that makes such a spell bearable is the worker's savings. In fact, savings serve two functions: they make it possible to maintain approximately the same level of consumption during interruptions in income, and they give the worker more time to find a better job, rather than having to settle for the first one that comes along. In both ways they diminish the cost of failing to agree with any particular employer. It is often the case that, behind large differences in average group income, lie even larger differences in average group wealth. This is true, for example, for comparisons between Blacks and Whites in the United States.

Policy remedies for discrimination reflect the different viewpoints we have described, as well as the different interests that result from being on one side of the inequality or another. Here we will briefly look at anti-discrimination laws, affirmative action laws and policies to reduce reward effects in general.

1. Anti-discrimination laws. In many cases it is possible to see discrimination as it occurs. Job announcements may be written in a discriminatory way, pay policies may explicitly favor members of one social group, and prospective workers may be directly told that their applications have been rejected for discriminatory reasons. Such practices can be outlawed for specified aspects of the economy (hiring, pay, promotion, lending, etc.) and specified groups who are to be free of discrimination. These types of laws are common in the industrialized countries and are becoming more common in the developing world. They are particularly effective at addressing discriminatory tastes by employers, retailers, lenders and others. Usually they are written in such as a way as to permit at least some forms of statistical discrimination, but exactly how much to permit or prohibit is typically a contentious question.
2. Affirmative action laws. These regulations use statistical indicators as signs of potential discrimination. In some cases this is necessary because it is not possible to see prejudice in action. For instance, employers may not state directly that their reason for hiring only workers of one ethnic group for a particular position is due to discrimination, but if the numerical imbalance is so great that it could not be the result of chance, this could be taken as sufficient evidence of discriminatory intent. In this way, affirmative action laws often have the same purpose as anti-discrimination laws, but with a lower barrier of proof.

   A second use of these laws is to push employers (and others in a position of power) toward more equal selection choices, irrespective of motive. For instance, even if there is evidence of "rational" statistical discrimination, it may be felt that the social cost of unfairness outweighs the gains from discriminating. If this is the case, affirmative action is the most direct form of remedy. This could also be a response to discrimination due to the tastes of coworkers or customers, where employers would transmit this discrimination to hiring, pay and promotion even in the absence of any prejudice on their own part. Finally, affirmative action can play a significant role in equalizing bargaining power by providing better outside options for members of groups identified and helped by numerical indicators. The debate over whether such indicators should be seen as "hard" (mandatory) or "soft" (indicative, considered in conjunction with other factors) is about the relative weight of the costs and benefits of affirmative action in light of other social goals.

3. Reduction in reward effects. Much of the debate over reducing discrimination tends to center on selection effects: how can we fairly allocate the better and worse jobs generated by our economies? It is important to remember, however, that group differences depend on both the selection and reward effects, as modeled earlier in this chapter. Even if there is no change in discriminatory selection, group inequalities can be reduced by making the overall distribution of economic rewards more equal in society. To put it in the opposite way, even though many countries are moving strenuously in the direction of equalizing selection through anti-discrimination and affirmative action laws, they may be failing in their larger purpose of reducing discrimination due to the underlying trend toward greater income inequality overall. This means that the policies considered above pertaining to general inequality should also be considered as antidotes to discrimination.

The Main Points

1. If the world were a single country, the gini coefficient of its income distribution would be about 65, where zero is complete equality and one is complete inequality. This is approximately the upper limit for inequality measures within individual countries. More developed countries generally have lower gini coefficients, but English-speaking countries, other things being equal, tend to have higher ones. Latin America tends to have greater inequality. The United States has seen rising inequality over recent decades.
2. There is a broad tendency for countries that have more equal income distributions to also have greater mobility between income classes across generations.
3. Women in the United States have made slow progress toward wage equality with men in the United States since 1979; movement toward equality for Blacks and Hispanics has stalled.
4. There are several ways to measure inequality, including ratios between the income shares going to upper and lower groups. One of the most comprehensive is the gini coefficient. It measures the ratio of the area between the perfect equality (45-degree) line and the Lorenz curve to the total area beneath the perfect equality line, where the Lorenz curve depicts the increase in the share of total income accounted for as the share of the population is increased.
5. A different way to approach distribution is through the functional distribution of income—the shares received in the forms of wages, interest, profits and rents. Income from assets, which include the last three of these, is concentrated in a minority of the population, since asset ownership is concentrated. Human capital, as measured by education, is more evenly distributed than financial capital, and it also receives a return, which economists have been interested to measure.
6. Four general explanations have been given for the trend over recent decades for inequality to rise: skill-biased technical change (the tendency for new

technologies to increase the productivity of more educated workers compared to those with less education), globalization (which puts many categories of workers in competition with one another), deregulation (intensifying market pressure on both workers and employers), and the rise of winner-take-all markets (where slightly more productive workers capture a large proportion of market earnings).

7. Depending on the importance they attach to these different explanations, economists have looked to various policies to moderate or reverse the trend toward inequality: greater investments in education to reduce gaps in human capital, changes in the rules governing international trade to reduce its destabilizing effects, introducing new forms of regulation into labor and other markets that facilitate gain-sharing, and, if none of these are sufficient, redistributive taxation.
8. Discrimination is the unequal treatment of individuals who are, for economic purposes, equal. The difference between the average outcomes to two different social groups, which often provides the measurement for discrimination, can be broken down into a selection effect and a reward effect. The first represents the difference in the access members of these groups have to desirable economic positions, such as better-paying jobs. The second measures the economic gap between more and less desirable positions. In recent US experience, the economic gap between whites and blacks has widened even though economic barriers to blacks have been slowly falling; the remaining gap in opportunities has become bigger in economic terms due to rising inequality in general.
9. Economists have offered three theories to explain how discrimination arises and is affected by other economic forces: the "taste" theory (employers, consumers or coworkers have a psychological preference for discriminating), statistically-based judgments (employers, consumers or coworkers, lacking knowledge of the individuals they interact with, fall back on what they perceive to be the average characteristics of the groups these individuals belong to), and differential bargaining power (according to which discrimination can persist because those in disfavored groups have inferior default options). These are not mutually exclusive.
10. Policies to counter discrimination include anti-discrimination laws (prohibiting discriminatory behavior), affirmative action laws (setting quantitative targets for the allocation of jobs, student admissions or other sought-after opportunities across different social groups), and policies to reduce economic inequalities in general (to diminish the reward effect).

▶ Terms to Define

Discrimination
Functional distribution of income
General inequality
Gini coefficient
Lorenz Curve

Reward effects
Selection effects
Skill-biased technical change

Questions to Consider

1. Was it wrong for the officers to cut the rope to the Medusa's raft even if, by staying connected, they were completely unable to paddle? If not, would it be wrong if there were *some* difference in the ability to paddle? How much difference would separate right from wrong? Was the unequal access to lifeboats the "original sin" in this story? Would a more equal access to the lifeboats change how you think about cutting the rope?
2. Based on the data in this chapter, do you view global inequality as a serious problem, separate from average living standards? That is, does it matter how large the *differences* are between incomes around the world separate from the *levels* of income themselves? Does your answer to this question have any implications for the types of policies you would support at the national or international level?
3. Based on the data in this chapter, do you think inequality in the US is too high? On what basis? Does the trend toward greater inequality disturb you? Is your opinion affected by the international comparisons offered in Table 18.1?
4. Much of the political turmoil of the last 100 years or so in the industrialized countries has been centered on the conflict between "labor" and "capital". To what extent do the data in this chapter support the view that this is a central conflict of interest in society? What other actual or potential conflicts do they point to?
5. Have you experienced any of the four forces identified as possible causes of rising inequality in your personal experience at work? Do you know of any examples in the experiences of friends or family members? Which seem the most plausible to you based on what you have seen? Why?
6. Give examples of each of the four policy strategies to reduce general inequality. Which do you support or oppose? Why?
7. Are there any groups in society who are not currently protected (at least in law) from discrimination, but who should be? Which ones? Why?
8. Have you seen any of the three theories of discrimination in action in your own experience, or are you aware of them in the experiences of people you know? Explain.
9. Based again on the actual experiences of discrimination you have witnessed or heard about, what types of policies would be effective against them? Which, in your view, would be unjustified? Why?

Appendix: Theories of Distributive Justice

This chapter is about the positive analysis of inequality; this appendix addresses the normative side. In the end, most debates about inequality—whether it is a problem and what to do about it—center not on disagreements over the facts or how they are explained, but on the principles that ought to govern a "fair" distribution. In philosophy, this is the realm of distributive justice. Here our purpose is not to develop complete theories of fair distribution, weighing the arguments pro and con, but simply to present the core principles and the motivations behind them. The point is to be explicit about the criteria we are using when we pass judgment on economic inequality and to avoid fruitless disputes based on unexamined normative assumptions.

Before continuing, we should be clear that the theories we are about to look at all have one element in common, an attempt to apply logical analysis to the problem of inequality. This is not how many people think about it, however. For most of human history, and into the present as well, it has been more common to see the world as made up of "natural" hierarchies: some groups are viewed as above others by virtue of their parentage, gender, physical appearance, cultural aura or social or religious standing. This is the view that has given us kings, castes, the veneration of elders, racial and religious classifications, rigid gender roles, and tight networks of loyalty and patronage. From this angle, an economic distribution would be regarded as just if it corresponds to whichever hierarchies are seen as natural and proper. Even though this is a common perspective—especially if you acknowledge its subconscious force—here we will put aside all appeals to traditional authority and consider only the rationalist arguments associated with philosophy.

Keeping this commitment in mind, we will take up six general approaches to justice: that any outcome that results from neutral rules is just, that rewards should be in proportion to contribution or to effort, that fairness should depend only on initial equality of opportunity, that outcomes should be as equal as possible, and that the primary restriction on inequality should be that an acceptable minimum be guaranteed to all.

1. Neutrality of rules. For many centuries, the Chinese empire was administered by a corps of mandarins, highly educated scholars and officials. These were the highest positions one could aspire to if one was not born to a noble family. To become a mandarin you had to pass a difficult test; only those who had spent many years in study would be able to do this. Admission to the schools was based on achieving an initial level of skill at reading and writing. Of course, for most of Chinese history, only a small portion of the population ever attained literacy, and this meant that most households—mainly peasants and artisans—had no real chance to place a son (this was an all-male institution) in the mandarin corps. Would people of today accept this system as just?

It was extraordinarily unequal; mandarins lived a life that most of the population could only dream of. There wasn't anything approaching equal access to the schools that funneled children into the mandarin class. If you were poor you were mostly out of luck, although, on occasion, a poor child did manage to ascend through the system. Nevertheless, one argument in favor of this custom is that the rules were the same for everyone, at least everyone who was male. Nothing in the procedures prohibited poor families from trying to get a child admitted to a school, nor was there any penalty to children from poor families if they made it as far as the final exam. The rules were perfectly neutral.

Even today there are some who argue that, as long as the rules that govern who gets ahead are neutral, making no distinctions between anyone, whatever outcomes result should be accepted as fair. Admission to universities and hiring decisions should be "blind", taking no account of any information about the candidates other than requirements that apply equally to all. What would be unfair, from this point of view, would be any rule that *did* make distinctions, that applied one set of criteria to this person and another set to someone else.

The great advantage of neutrality as a principle of justice is that it minimizes the opportunity for elites to rig the game in their own favor. As soon as you allow procedures that deliberately give an advantage to some over others, you create incentives for insiders to use them to make sure that the advantage is theirs. In the Chinese example, suppose, instead of having a single exam and scoring system for everyone who wanted to become a mandarin, officials were able to choose which applicant would get which exam or could give extra credit to some, but only some, of the exam-takers. In all probability, the children of those who already had the most wealth and power would be given special advantages, and those who came from poor backgrounds would find their way blocked by barriers they might never see.

The disadvantage of neutrality is that the societies we live in are not neutral. As in China during the empire, today we have wealth and poverty, children with every advantage money can buy and others who are up against enormous odds. If the rules are neutral, nothing will intervene to reduce the inequality we have inherited from the past. In the words of Anatole France, "The law, in its majestic equality, forbids the rich as well as the poor to sleep under bridges, to beg in the streets, and to steal bread." Do we want the laws to make distinctions—to have one set of laws for the rich and another for the poor? Maybe not, but then we might want something else, other programs, policies or institutions that do more than simply determine what is legal or illegal, but intervene in other ways to limit economic inequalities. What these measures should be is the question the other criteria below try to address.

2. Reward according to contribution. A plausible approach would be to say that what individuals get out of a social or economic system should depend on what they put into it. The main virtue is pragmatic: it provides a strong incentive for each person to make as great a contribution as possible. The result will be more to share for everyone, at least if this theory holds true. Indeed, one of the attractive features of the Market Welfare Model is that, if its conditions are met, individuals and organizations (like firms) will earn from the market exactly what each puts in. Thus, each worker would receive the economic value of his or her marginal product, and if that value is correctly measured by prices—as it would be in a Market Welfare Model world—then the worker's earnings equal the consumer's benefit from this

work. If the assumptions of the Market Welfare Model are not fulfilled but we continue to accept reward according to contribution as our guiding principle, we should try to fix the market failures or other impediments responsible for supply curves not representing social costs or demand curves not representing social benefits. And failing that, we should use the benchmarks of an idealized perfect market to help us set prices and regulations that will approximate those of a Market Welfare Model world as closely as possible. This, as you should know by now, is the program laid out by conventional welfare economics; see, for instance, the discussion in Chap. 6. The normative underpinning of this project is the belief that rewards in the economy should be governed by contribution.

The ethical basis for this approach is reciprocity, that each should give and get in equal measure. Nevertheless, there are ethical dilemmas that have weakened the appeal of contribution as the main criterion. One is that the contribution one ends up making to society is strongly influenced by pure chance. A worker who works for a particularly innovative or well-run company contributes more than one who works for an average or less effective outfit. According to the principle of reward for contribution, it is appropriate that the first worker should earn more than the second. Nevertheless, it is often a matter of luck which type of job one ends up getting. Perhaps Worker 1, who is employed by the high-powered company and gets a fatter paycheck, has connections that helped her get through the door, or perhaps she was just at the right place at the right time. Is it fair that she should get the greater reward?

Another issue has to do with native human talent. Some simply have greater physical or mental resources to work with. One worker might have to work twice as hard to have the same effect as another; shouldn't this extra dedication be worth something? Are results all that should matter?

3. Reward for effort. Such concerns have led many to adopt a modified version of the contribution principle in which it is the input of the individual (or group), and not the output, that determines rewards. From an ethical standpoint, we are rewarding what people give of themselves for others, even if chance or the uneven distribution of talent does not always translate this effort into tangible benefits. As a practical matter, this approach has the virtue of providing strong incentives to all members of society to work hard, whether or not their skills are in the most demand. Of course, this virtue is also a vice, since rewarding people for simply trying may not give them enough incentive to apply their energies to the things society places its highest value on. In general, market economies do not generate rewards for effort apart from its role in the ultimate product being produced, so some interference in labor or other markets is required if effort per se is to be recognized.

Here is a conundrum you may want to think about in connection with reward for effort: Suppose there are ten workers working on an assembly line. Each operates a different machine, each operation is equally necessary and each is equally difficult. The line moves at a common pace, so workers can neither increase nor decrease the speed of their work. The output of the line is a flow of products that can be sold for a given amount of money. If reward for contribution is the criterion, each worker should get the same pay. If, on the other hand, the workers are paid in accordance with their effort, the least capable workers will earn the most, since they have to put in more effort to keep up with the pace of the line. Their extra pay will in turn mean lower pay for the most capable, who are, in effect, being punished for having more strength or agility. Is this fair?

4. Equality of opportunity. Perhaps the world is too complex to measure either contribution or effort with any accuracy. There are so many different kinds of effort to compare, and the ways contributions are combined in real-world production systems makes it difficult to tell just who contributed what. Moreover, perhaps both contribution *and* effort should be recognized, although not in any precise combination. In that case we might be drawn to an approach that says, let all start with an equal chance to succeed, and let effort, contribution and luck determine outcomes however they will. Specifically, the criterion of equal opportunity embodies two elements, that there should be a moment in each individual's life (the "starting point") at which equality should reign, and that the rules that govern success should not be biased toward any particular individuals or groups. These are extremely demanding requirements, and it is doubtful that any existing society meets them completely; yet they could serve as goals to be pursued. In practical terms, the first will usually require substantial intervention in market outcomes, since the advantages that children of rich parents would otherwise have need to be offset, but the second is usually thought of as compatible with the way markets should work if they are regulated to be transparent and fair.

There are two large difficulties with equal opportunity as a principle of justice. First, what exactly should be this hypothetical moment of perfect equality—the equal starting line, to use the metaphor of a footrace? Should it be birth? This means that the unequal distribution of luck *before* birth must be counterbalanced, so that those who are congenitally stronger or more clever should be disadvantaged in equal measure. If that doesn't appeal to you, then you perhaps imagine a moment even before birth and before genetic qualities are doled out. But related to this is the problem that, as soon as we are born, we begin to do things or have things done to us that, if not offset, will lead to unequal life chances down the road. The further back we push the moment of equality, the more subsequent inequality we must accept. If opportunities are to be equal at birth, then the advantages that some get in childhood will not count against "equal opportunity". Perhaps you would set a much later age for the "starting point"—say 18. This commits you to much greater intervention to offset all the many pluses and minuses that can accrue by that age, including many that are due to the choices that children make for themselves. At the same time, it can be seen as a bit heartless, since it doesn't allow for second chances. If someone discovers what they truly want at the age of 25 or so, too bad: they missed the moment of equality and they will have to make do with whatever opportunities they are lucky enough to still have. This sort of criticism can be addressed by requiring a multiplicity of "somewhat equal opportunities" that can reappear as one grows older, but then the criterion loses its sharpness: how equal must these second chances be and how many must be offered?

The second large difficulty is that equality of opportunity is compatible with almost any level of general inequality, as we defined it in this chapter. Suppose, for example, that you have a society that works according to this rule: every year a lottery is held with just one winning number. The individual who wins that year gets everything—every last penny of income, all the wealth, the land, everything of value. Everyone else must beg for enough to survive on. The principle of equal opportunity demands only one thing, that the lottery be perfectly fair, so that each person has the same chance to be tycoon-for-a-year, but surely this demand does not go far enough. Can extremely unequal divisions of life's good things be viewed as just simply because the system is fair at the moment just before division?

5. Equality of outcomes. This principle, which we can call egalitarianism for short, does not concern itself with who gets more or how they acquired it; more versus less is itself the problem. The ideal world would be one in which the rewards of our common social and economic life are apportioned perfectly equally. This would presumably be true not at a given moment, such as in equal opportunity, but at all times.

Of course, perfect equality is not really possible. It would take too large a bureaucracy to measure and distribute everything in perfectly equal measure, and we would have the problem of figuring out how much of one sort of good, like security, should be worth another, like income. In practical terms, egalitarianism is an orientation toward more equality of outcomes in preference to less. Thus, to take the case of income distribution, an egalitarian would prefer a more equal distribution (a lower Gini coefficient), all else being equal. It is a preference for equality as a value in itself.

One of the most vexing practical difficulties faced by egalitarians is determining just what it is that should be made more equal. Money income is a logical candidate, but questions arise: Should large families have more income than smaller ones? Should workers with more dangerous or uncomfortable jobs receive extra pay to make up for their hardship? Should people with special needs, for instance due to disabilities, receive the extra income they need to meet them? These are not abstract puzzles in logic; they arise whenever we try to apply egalitarian principles to real human beings.

Another set of problems arises from what egalitarianism is not—not a system that assigns value to contribution or effort. This is an ethical concern, since contribution and effort both make claims on our sense of justice. It is also an issue of great practical importance, since it is very likely that, without the incentives that unequal rewards depend on, people would neither contribute enough work nor be guided to work in the most beneficial ways. To the extent this is true we face what has been called a tradeoff between equity and efficiency, where equity means egalitarianism and efficiency the production of the greatest quantity of economic value. It should be remembered, however, that, while economic incentives are indispensable, they are not the only forces that motivate us, and sometimes they get in the way of more desirable, intrinsic motivators. (See the discussion in Chap. 10.) Thus, the tradeoff between equity and efficiency is real, but not everywhere and always. In any case, it is difficult to claim that egalitarianism should be the only ethical criterion, and that no weight should be given to contribution or effort, particularly since some degree of inequality will persist in any real-world situation.

6. Guaranteed minimum rewards. In the twentieth century there was renewed interest in approaches to justice that emphasize the needs of those at the bottom of the distribution. Perhaps what we should look for, it was reasoned, is not a principle that governs every issue of distribution for everyone, but which focuses on the crucial needs of the worst-off. There are two main variants at the present time, the brainchildren of John Rawls and Amartya Sen.

(a) Rawls: Maximize the minimum well-being. Rawls, perhaps the most influential philosopher in the field of justice in modern times, takes as his starting point two principles, objectivity and risk aversion. Objectivity means that our evaluation of an economic or social order should not depend on our own place in it; it should be the same no matter which role we come to occupy. His device for achieving this was an imaginary "thought experiment": suppose we were about enter a society (through birth, for example), but we first had a chance to put an evaluation on it, prior to knowing who we would come to be, including who our parents would be, what our physical inheritance would be, etc. This evaluation would be ideal, according to Rawls, since it would be based on a perfectly objective analysis.

The second principle is that such an evaluation should be governed by risk minimization. What would weigh most heavily in our judgment would be the potential to be someone who is unhappy or oppressed in a society, which we could identify with having a very low income. If this is the case, we would rank societies on the basis of how well-off the worst off person is. If the total income of the economy were a given, Rawls' theory would dovetail with perfect egalitarianism, since under that rule the worst-off person would be as well-off as possible. Rawls assumes, however, the necessity of economic incentives to motivate production, so that too much equality might well reduce the rewards attainable by the worst-off. The ideal, in his estimation, would be that balance of equality and inequality that maximizes the position of the bottom person in the economic distribution. As a global proposition, this would be difficult to apply, but we might be able to employ it when looking at a particular distributional issue, such as whether the wages for a particular group of workers ought to be raised. Even so, it would be a difficult empirical task to estimate just how much particular distributional adjustments are likely to change economic growth, the extent and direction of innovation, and the like. Toward the end of his life, Rawls retreated from more rigid formulations of his principle.

(b) Sen: Maximize the fulfillment of human capabilities. Amartya Sen follows in the footsteps of Aristotle, who argued that human beings have a common nature and by realizing our potential we can achieve "flourishing". Aristotle in effect advocated the use of social science to observe a variety of societies to see, empirically, under what conditions their members flourished, so that we could replicate the best of these features in our own ideal. In the more than two millennia that have transpired since Aristotle, however, we have learned much more about how to do such observation, and we have a much broader base of human possibility to draw from.

Sen believes that we are in a position today to make an informed judgment along Aristotle's lines, provisional (in the spirit of all science) but with real practical implications. We will look at the details of his approach in the next chapter when we focus on poverty, but for now it is enough to mention the broad outlines. Human beings are said to have capabilities, modes of functioning in the physical, psychological and social universe. Exercising strength, solving problems that interest us, engaging with others—these are the sorts of things we all do, but in different ways in different cultures. Sen, who is a Nobel laureate economist as well as a philosopher, suggests that all societies grant "entitlements" to people to enable them to access the resources that make the exercise of capabilities possible. These entitlements may take the form of income, or they may be social obligations to provide particular goods or opportunities, or they may be distributed politically. However we come by them, we need enough of them and in the right combination to fully exercise our capabilities—to flourish.

Although he has not presented his theory in quite this way, it would be a reasonable deduction from his approach to regard the universal attainment of full human functioning as the primary ethical norm. If this goal were achieved, his system of justice would be indifferent regarding the distribution of the "extra" goods not needed for realizing our capabilities. In this way it could be considered a cousin to Rawls, since it would have the primary effect of raising the well-being of the worst off.

This presentation of Sen's theory of capabilities may appear highly abstract, too abstract to be useful in practical situations. This criticism will be addressed in the following chapter, when we see how it has actually been applied, but it should be conceded that this difficulty has never quite been dispelled. There is disagreement among Sen's followers regarding which capabilities are fundamental and how their fulfillment can be measured. There is also a potential risk in any approach which claims to tell us what we "really" need, since economists and philosophers have their own biases and blindspots. On the other (third?) hand, one of the main things we pay philosophers to do is advise us on what we need and how we should regard ourselves.

To summarize, here we have five principles of just distribution. The first three of them try to do too much, and it would probably be a mistake to apply them in every situation. The last (combining Rawls and Sen) at best does too little, since they tell us only about what is fair for those at the bottom, and not for those in the middle or at the top. The fourth (equal opportunity) is both too demanding in its requirements and also not demanding enough. In short, they all have their flaws.

This brief survey should inspire a measure of humility, since whatever yardstick you adopt you will be vulnerable to counterarguments. Also, as in the other truly difficult problems we have explored in this book, you should be encouraged to be flexible, to be willing to use more than one framework when circumstances seem to call for it.

References

Holzer, H. J., & Hlavac, M. (2012). A very uneven road: U.S. labor markets in the past 30 years. Providence: US2010.

Krueger, A. B. (2012). The rise and consequences of inequality in the United States. Delivered to the Center for American Progress, Jan 12. Accessed at http://www.americanprogress.org/events/2012/01/pdf/krueger.pdf

19 Poverty

As a very first approximation, we could consider the average lifespan of a population to be an indicator of how far it has risen from poverty and economic deprivation. Of course, many things affect how long people can expect to live, such as war, epidemics and natural disasters, but throughout history there has been a rough correlation between longevity and prosperity.

When we think of the great achievements of the ancient civilizations of China, Greece and Rome, it is sobering to bear in mind that in none of these places and times did the life expectancy at birth exceed 30. Even in western Europe as late as 1900, this figure was less than 50. Such numbers speak powerfully about the living standards of the majority of the world's population over time.

What about today? Lifespans have increased dramatically, and not only for the richest segment of the world's population. Still, there are noticeable differences in national averages, as Table 19.1 makes clear.

The ratio of the longest lifespan (Japan) to the shortest (Ethiopia, Nigeria, South Africa) is over three-to-two, which is remarkable considering that these are averages over entire national populations.

Clearly these averages disguise very important life expectancy differences within countries, and this can be seen by looking at the United States. A group of researchers led by health economist Christopher Murray divided up America into eight "countries" based on race and location. Those with the longest lifespans were Asian-Americans (wherever they might live); those with the shortest were Blacks living in inner-city neighborhoods. They calculated life expectancy differences between men and women in each group, and their results emphasize that living standards remain highly unequal in the US. Asian men can expect to live more than 15 years longer than inner-city Black men; the corresponding gap is over 12 years for women. "Middle American Whites", those who live neither in rural north-central areas nor in the southeast, have about a 6-year (men) and over 4-year (women) advantage compared to "Middle American Blacks" (neither inner-city nor rural south). The study also found significant mortality differences in comparisons among Whites, among Blacks, and extending to Native residents of the western states. In general, the disparities found by Murray and his colleagues

P. Dorman, *Microeconomics*, Springer Texts in Business and Economics,
DOI 10.1007/978-3-642-37434-0_19,

Table 19.1 Life expectancy at birth in selected countries, 2009

Country	Life expectancy
Bangladesh	65
Bolivia	68
Brazil	73
China	74
Cuba	78
Egypt	71
Ethiopia	54
France	81
Germany	80
Haiti	62
India	65
Indonesia	68
Japan	83
Kenya	60
Mexico	76
Nigeria	54
Pakistan	63
Philippines	70
Poland	76
Russian Federation	68
South Africa	54
Sweden	81
Thailand	70
Turkey	75
United Kingdom	80
United States	79

Source: World Health Organization Statistical Information System (WHOSIS)

are roughly comparable to those found between rich and poor countries, apart from those, like Nigeria, where health conditions are the bleakest.

We cannot make any direct inferences about poverty from these raw facts concerning life and death, but they do make clear that the most basic necessities all people rely on, that keep them alive to do whatever else they may choose, are still out of reach of many, even in the world's richest countries. In this chapter we will take a closer look at poverty as an economic problem. How is poverty defined and measured? How prevalent is it? What are its causes, and what can be done about it?

19.1 What Is Poverty?

Like unemployment, a concept we will examine in the next volume, poverty took on a new meaning when historical conditions made it possible to imagine a society without it. For most of human history, the poor were simply a part of the whole population, larger in some places and smaller in others, but to all appearances an inevitable fact of nature. If the poor mobilized themselves politically to challenge their place in the world, it was not to escape from poverty (this was not conceivable except in Utopia), but to be treated with justice and sympathy. The demand that poverty itself be eradicated seldom appears in any political program prior to the Industrial Revolution.

Modern definitions of poverty all have the characteristic that they are not inevitable. However defined, it is now within the possibility of existing societies to eliminate poverty from the human condition. From the long historical perspective, this is revolutionary.

Very generally, we can distinguish between two different approaches to defining and measuring poverty, one absolute, the other relative. **Absolute poverty** refers to a lack of a sufficiently high income to purchase what is regarded as a necessary standard of living. Social scientists have drawn up lists of what people in various societies are seen as needing; these items are priced, and individuals are deemed poor if they don't have enough money to buy them. **Relative poverty** occurs when individuals fall below a certain percentage of the average or median income of their population. It is not based on any particular standard of living, but on how far one has fallen relative to the average. As we will see, the capabilities approach of Sen has been used to try to reconcile these two.

Let's take a closer look at absolute poverty. The intuition behind this approach is that we can distinguish between necessities and luxuries, and the poor are those who can't afford the necessities. To make this concept operational, we would need to draw up a list of those necessities and figure out how much they cost. In fact, this is exactly what poverty researchers have done in most countries; the result of their labors is a **poverty line** that sets a minimum income for a family of a given size. If the family receives less than this it is recorded as poor. The method used in the US was developed in the 1960s by Mollie Orshansky, an economist in the US Department of Labor. She found that, on average, a third of all income received by low-income families went to food, so she calculated the cost of the cheapest food basket that would keep a family of four in good nutrition for a month and then multiplied it by three. This determined the poverty line, which could then be adjusted each year based on the changing cost of this food basket. Simple as it is, this approach is still the basis for official calculations of the poverty line in the US, although most poverty researchers regard it as flawed. (It ignores non-cash benefits families receive; it has not been adjusted for the much greater role that non-food expenses, like housing, childcare and medical care, now play in family budgets.)

Ironically, the absolute approach to defining poverty is not so absolute when we need to make international comparisons. What is an absolute necessity in one country turns out to be a luxury in another, or so it seems if the different calculations are all believed. What would it mean to compare poverty rates if the they result from poverty lines based on contradictory assumptions? To get around this, researchers have proposed setting a single global standard, based on a fixed level of daily income per person. Of course, no single number could ever be correct, so the usual practice is to use a range of numbers, making comparisons at each level.

One simple standard is \$1.25 per day, measured using Purchasing Power Parity (PPP) to convert income between different currencies. (PPP is based on comparisons between how much a standard basket of goods costs in different countries.) This cutoff has been promoted by the World Bank in particular as a basis for estimating poverty rates, and it has the advantage of being conservative: it is unlikely that there are many people who would be called poor under this definition who aren't.

Using this yardstick, it is estimated that 1.2 billion people should be regarded as poor as of the last global count in 2010. When one considers how conservative the yardstick is, this number poses a deep ethical challenge. Who are these poor people? Where are they?

The World Bank makes national estimates based on household surveys it conducts around the world. Table 19.2 on the following page shows the household poverty rate for a selection of countries and gives the year the survey data were collected.

Some countries, like Haiti and Nigeria, are predominantly poor, even by the stringent \$1.25 a day measure. Others, like Turkey and Mexico, while certainly containing large populations locally regarded as poor, have few citizens falling under this very low poverty line. In some rapidly developing countries, like China, large gaps in the household poverty rate have opened up between urban and rural populations. We will return to the issue of the poverty-reduction benefits of economic growth later in this chapter.

Clearly a limit of just \$1.25 a day records the most extreme forms of absolute poverty, but what would we find if we increased it to \$2? For the most recent year for which there is evidence, 2010, the numbers are daunting: 2.4 billion people, over a third of the world's population, live below this line. This includes about 67 % of the population of South Asia and 70 % of sub-Saharan Africa, numbers that reflect about a 20 % decline in poverty rates in South Asia but almost no change in sub-Saharan Africa since 1981. On the other hand, in the early 1980s nearly the entire population of China was in poverty according to the \$2-a-day standard, but by 2008 only about 27 % still qualified as poor by this criterion, demonstrating that rapid progress is possible.

The other major approach, relative poverty, is based on the notion that each society has a "normal" standard of living to which everyone aspires (or wishes to surpass). This could be thought of as measured by the income of the average, or median, individual, the one whose income is exactly at the halfway mark in the overall distribution. To be poor, according to this view, is to be very far below this median person—say, at least 50 % below. That is, the technique for establishing a poverty line would be to identify the income of the median individual or household and then divide this by half. Those earning below this line would be regarded as poor. In a society with a relatively equal income distribution (a low Gini

Table 19.2 Percentage of households receiving less than $1.25 PPP per capita per day

Country	Year	Poverty rate
Bangladesh	2010	43.3
Bolivia	2008	15.6
Brazil	2009	6.1
China (rural)	2008	22.3
China (urban)	2008	0.9
Ethiopia	2005	39.0
Guatemala	2006	13.5
Haiti	2001	61.7
India (rural)	2009	34.3
India (urban)	2009	28.9
Indonesia (rural)	2011	15.0
Indonesia (urban)	2011	17.4
Mali	2010	50.4
Mexico	2010	4.0
Nigeria	2009	68.0
Pakistan	2007	21.0
Philippines	2009	18.4
South Africa	2008	13.8
Turkey	2008	0.0
Uganda	2009	38.0

Source: World Bank PovCal Tool

coefficient), this could be a small number; in an unequal society it could be very large, although, obviously, it could never be a majority as absolute poverty could be—and in some places is.

Proponents of the relative poverty approach regard it as far more realistic than absolute measurements. We can understand their discomfort if we look more closely at Table 19.2. Is it credible to say that only about 4 % of all households in Mexico, and hardly any at all in Turkey, are poor? Even a $2 a day standard would result in only about 8 % of Mexicans and 4 % of Turks being considered poor. Yet if we raised the income standard to be more realistic for Mexico, would it become more unrealistic for, say, Mali? Perhaps the only consistent way to measure poverty in both countries would be in relation to their typical, or median, incomes. A resolute defender of an absolute approach to poverty might reply that, yes, only 4 % of Mexicans are subject to the sort of deprivation that almost 70 % of Nigerians face, and this needs to be recognized. Obviously, we are barely scratching the surface of this debate.

Nevertheless, the relative income approach to poverty measurement generally works better for comparisons among more developed countries, where extreme deprivation is uncommon. In Table 19.3 we see how several of the wealthier countries measure up in poverty rates, where the poverty line is set at 50 % of the median income.

Table 19.3 Percentage of population receiving less than 50 % of the median income, 2000

Country	Poverty rate
Canada	11.4
France	8.0
Germany	8.3
Sweden	6.5
United Kingdom	12.4
United States	17.0

Source: Luxembourg Income Study

This clearly demonstrates that it would be a mistake to think that a relative definition of poverty means that high rates of poverty are inevitable; countries can have more equal distributions so that fewer of their citizens fall below half the median income. Poverty in Sweden exemplifies this. In general, English-speaking countries tend to have higher poverty rates, and the United States is a star performer, so to speak, in this respect.

A compromise approach to poverty, which tries to respect both the differences in national norms and the claims of extreme deprivation, has been formulated by Amartya Sen. As discussed in the previous chapter, he takes as his starting point the notion first developed by Aristotle, that it is possible to observe the conditions that make possible a satisfactory life, since all people have common needs. Sen refines this idea by pointing out that, while the needs, or capabilities, may be common, the specific forms they take, and the resources needed to satisfy them, will differ around the world. For instance, mobility is an essential and universal human capability: being able to get to the places we need to go is a necessary part of living a satisfactory life. Yet different societies impose different needs for mobility. In a small, traditional community (the sort that is becoming less common with each passing year) it is enough to get around the village and perhaps to the next village just down the river or over the hill. In a modern city one must be able to get to the essential places for shopping and work. The need is universal, but the manifestation is particular.

By specifying the principal capabilities, researchers can lay the groundwork for national studies of what it takes to exercise them, and the numbers of poor people based on these calculations would indeed be comparable across national borders. The main difficulty, as you would expect, is getting agreement on what the core capabilities consist of and how they should translate into local conditions. In Box 19.1 we present one possible solution to this problem.

Box 19.1: Nussbaum's List of Fundamental Capabilities

Philosopher Martha Nussbaum, a frequent collaborator with Sen, has developed one possible list of basic capabilities in her article "Capabilities as Fundamental Entitlements: Sen and Social Justice" (2003):

1. Life: not having to die prematurely.

(continued)

Box 19.1 (continued)

2. Bodily health: having access to nutrition and shelter, also reproductive health.
3. Bodily integrity: mobility, freedom from physical violation, opportunity for sexual and reproductive choice.
4. Senses, imagination and thought: aesthetic and intellectual opportunity, especially in education; freedom of thought and expression; access to pleasurable experiences.
5. Emotions: the development and exercise of love and attachment, but also grief, desire and justified anger.
6. Practical reason: the freedom and resources to develop a life plan and set of values one deems appropriate.
7. Affiliation: participation in social life, the development and expression of sympathy and compassion, the experience of friendship and justice, being treated with the same respect shown others.
8. Other species: being able to live in relationship to animals, plants and other natural elements, and being able to develop a concern for them.
9. Play: laughing, playing and taking part in recreation.
10. Control over one's environment: the right of political participation, including freedom of speech and organization, and the right to property and equal access to employment opportunities.

One of the striking features of the capabilities approach is its determination to combine economic and social or political criteria that are usually kept apart in discussions of poverty. If Sen and Nussbaum are correct, poor people cannot escape from poverty by giving up religious or political freedom for material gain; if they succeeded at this they would only exchange one form of poverty for another. This is a strong argument against the contrary view, that political and cultural freedoms are luxuries that have no value to those who lack food or housing. But a defender of that view might question whether all the items on Nussbaum's list, assuming we agreed with them, should be given equal status.

A disadvantage of the capabilities approach is that it is inherently less quantitative. It certainly cannot be employed as an algorithm to extract a poverty headcount from census data. This means that we cannot show how it would produce tables like those we saw for the absolute and relative poverty measures. On the other hand, it is highly applicable to policy debates, as we will see later in this chapter.

19.2 Mass Poverty in the Global Economy

As we have already seen, by the most stringent measure of absolute poverty, about a fifth of all those alive today can be said to be poor, and it might be more accurate to describe them as destitute. More flexible measures easily yield two billion or more people in poverty, and the consequences for life expectancy and health, not to mention the opportunity to enjoy the deeper satisfactions that life offers, are beyond doubt. (Happiness research has confirmed this.) Ending this state of affairs is one of the main challenges facing us in this era.

One of the main causes of poverty throughout history transcends economics: war. Wherever there is violent conflict, large numbers of people lose their livelihood, and hunger and disease normally follow. Even in western Europe, which had been the center of production and commerce for centuries, a large portion of the population remained destitute for several years after the end of the Second World War. Today there are regions in which war remains endemic, and in all of them poverty and forced displacement are serious problems: Uganda, Sudan, Colombia, the Philippines. Without peace and reconciliation there are limits to even the best economic policies.

Yet poverty exists on a mass scale even where war is unknown, and here economics has much to say. In this section we will survey some of the debates among economists over what causes poverty and how it can be alleviated.

The most obvious answer, and for some the most important factor, is insufficient economic growth. Average incomes can rise only if the overall economy grows faster than population, and in much of the world such growth has been lacking. It is undeniable that poverty is a far less severe problem in the high-income countries that have experienced decades or even centuries of sufficiently rapid economic growth, and that it is most widespread in sub-Saharan Africa, where population growth generally outstrips economic progress. Until recently, it was the official position of the World Bank, for instance, that measures that promote economic growth should be given priority, even if they have direct costs for the poor. Thus, Bank policy-makers called for an end to food and fuel subsidies and for increased fees for water and education, believing that this would stimulate the economy and lead to eventual reductions in poverty.

In recent years, however, opinion has turned against this strategy. In some parts of the world, particularly in sub-Saharan Africa and Latin America, inequality is so great that families at the bottom end of the income distribution may see no improvement at all from growth and may even fall further behind. Moreover, there is no magic formula for making stagnant economies grow more rapidly. The result is that experts at the World Bank have turned to what they call "pro-poor growth", a combination of growth-oriented measures along with policies that specifically try to help the poorest portion of the population. We will see many examples of this orientation in the next few pages when we turn to issues of human development.

In general, mass poverty in the developing world is accompanied by a number of related problems, such as poor health conditions, inadequate education, lack of access to credit (and economic opportunity more generally) and harmful child labor. These should really be seen as a complex whole, since it is difficult to pull apart the strands of mutual causation. Nevertheless, researchers have tried to isolate some of the particular mechanisms at work, to get a better sense of their relative importance as well as the types of interventions most likely to be effective.

1. Health. We have already seen that poverty is loosely correlated with reduced life expectancy, but the ability of people to enjoy and make use of the years available to them is even more at risk. Many of the conditions that plague poor populations, like diseases from contaminated water supplies or infections like malaria, are largely preventable and seldom occur in regions where people can afford to avoid them. Poverty undermines health, but poor health also reproduces poverty. Unhealthy people are less able to study and work, and when they become sick or disabled their care becomes a burden on their families. When life and health are uncertain people are less motivated to invest in education or other future-oriented commitments.

To tackle ill health in a systematic manner, it is useful to have an idea of what diseases and other health threats are the most important in a given population. The World Health Organization, a branch of the United Nations devoted to improvements in public health, publishes this information in its period reports on the global burden of disease. The measurement it uses is the **Disability Adjusted Life Year,** or DALY. This measures the portion of a year lost due to a disease or injury, where a full year would mean a year of premature death. For instance, losing a limb would be registered as a fraction of a life year; if several people lost a limb, this would be equivalent to one person dying. The weights given to specific disabilities is determined by surveys of health professionals. The DALY is not without problems, but it represents one way to reduce the many forms of injury and disease to a single numerical index.

To see the usefulness of the DALY, consider Table 19.4 on the next page, extracted from the WHO's database on the global burden of disease and injuries; it shows the total DALY's lost worldwide due to various causes.

Many of these problems, such as those relating to childbirth, water quality and the control of communicable diseases, could be greatly reduced by investments in public health. At the same time, the pervasive effects of these threats to health exacerbates poverty and cuts into the resources that could otherwise be available to deal with them.

Other organizations prefer an alternative measure, the QALY, which stands for a **Quality Adjusted Life Year**. This purports to express the loss of health as a percentage of a full year of life based on the effect ill health has on the subjective well-being of its victims. You might think of losing half a QALY as losing half the perceived value of being alive for an additional year. Weights used in calculating QALY's are derived from general population surveys.

Using measurements like QALY's and DALY's, aid organizations have begun to funnel large amounts of money into disease prevention programs in the developing world. The hope is that, by concentrating assistance where it is needed most, these programs will have a bigger effect than those in past years. For instance, there is evidence to indicate that lifting the scourge of malaria from sub-Saharan Africa all by itself could produce a visible increase in economic growth.

Table 19.4 Global disability adjusted life years lost due to selected causes (2004), in millions

Birth complications	97.2
Cancer	75.4
Childbirth (women)	33.6
Depression	67.1
Diarrhea	54.3
Heart diseases	147.9
HIV/AIDS	85.5
Malaria	34.6
Nutritional deficiencies	34.3
Respiratory infections	96.8
Traffic accidents	38.6
Total: 1488.7	

Source: World Health Organization Global Burden of Disease project

2. Education. It would not be an exaggeration to say that those countries which have achieved near-universal success in basic education, and which have also educated many of their inhabitants at a higher level through secondary schools and universities, are the same countries that have undergone prolonged periods of economic growth and have dramatically reduced their rates of poverty. Ever since the first economic studies of education were completed in the 1950s and '60s, showing that the rate of return to investments in teachers and classrooms exceeds most other investments that could be made in developing countries, economists have urged countries to give education the highest priority. Their advice has not changed since then.

On an individual level, the evidence is indisputable that more years of education translate into far higher average future earnings; a reasonable rule of thumb would be 10 % more income per year for each year of additional schooling. This is an extraordinary rate of return. Studies at the national level are less conclusive, but economists are inclined to believe that differences in education explain about a fourth of the international differences in economic progress.

Once we go from generalities to specifics, however, the issue becomes more complicated. It is not enough to build lots of schools and tell parents to send their children there; the schools must be of a high enough quality that actual learning takes place, and this must be visible to parents. This means more teachers and better training for them, but that in turn depends on prior investments in higher education. Schools must be geographically and financially accessible to families, a problem in rural and low-income areas. Thought must be given to setting up curriculum which speaks to the needs of students and their families, and that adapts itself to the particular situation of ethnic minorities, immigrants and other special populations.

3. Credit. Every day ordinary people in the high-income countries take out loans to buy a car or a house, to pay for a college education, or to start a business. They may not be happy with the terms of these loans, but the simple ability to acquire credit is seen as a normal aspect of the economy. In developing countries much of the population has no access to credit at all, or access only on the most unfavorable terms, at interest rates well above 100 % per year. People would borrow at those rates only under the most extreme conditions.

It is worth reflecting for a moment on what this situation means for those who are cut off from credit. Borrowing to open or expand a business is out of the question. Every investment must be paid for out of current income, even those with a very high rate of return, like those for education. Unexpected health care costs may be unaffordable, and treatable health conditions are simply allowed to get worse. Also, interruptions in income due to bad harvests or spells of unemployment mean interruptions in consumption, even in essential nutrition.

In recent years there has been a concerted effort to bring access to modest amounts of credit to low-income households around the world. The pioneer of this movement is Mohammed Yunis, who founded the Grameen Bank in Bangladesh in 1983 and who was awarded the Nobel Peace Prize in 2006. This bank specializes in making what are called micro-loans to very low-income women, using peer pressure among borrowers to ensure repayment. (Borrowers are combined into groups, and if one borrower fails to repay all are penalized.) This bank currently has almost seven million borrowers, and its model has been replicated around the world.

Micro-credit has proved to be a controversial topic among those who study poverty and economic development. Its supporters see it as a crucial first step toward giving the poor the resources to help themselves out of poverty, and they point to the crippling effect that lack of access to credit can have for those at the edge of survival. Critics are less impressed. They claim that the amount of credit involved is rarely enough to lift a family out of poverty, and that the end result may be only that, in addition to all the other burdens of poverty, the poor now find themselves having to pay off loans as well. Both sides may be right to some extent, but the better alternative to micro-loans might be even more access to credit, not less. At the same time, there are limits to the extent to which increased borrowing opportunities can make up for the lack of steady income.

4. Child labor. It is common to think of child labor as a consequence of poverty, but from a long run, multigenerational point of view, it is also a cause. This is an emotional topic for those on all sides of the debate, and there are many misconceptions to be cleared up.

First, not all work by children should be understood as "child labor". The International Labor Organization, a part of the UN system specialized on labor issues, has promulgated a set of agreements (conventions) that specify the ages and types of labor that determine whether children should be counted as laborers. It is the combination of inappropriate work (too demanding or time-consuming) and inappropriate age that makes the difference. No reasonable person is saying that children should never do light work for money, much less normal household chores.

A recent ILO convention singles out the "worst forms" of child labor for immediate action; these include prostitution, soldiering, transporting contraband, coercive (bonded) labor and such dangerous activities as underground mining and working with toxic chemicals and heavy equipment.

In 2013 the ILO published its most recent estimates of the number of child laborers worldwide. It reports that 168 million can be put into this category under the terms of the relevant ILO conventions. Within this group, 85 million were thought to be in hazardous activities and several million more in the "unconditional worst forms" of prostitution, war, contraband and bonded work. These estimates were for the year 2012 and were based on household surveys administered with the assistance of the ILO.

A second misconception is that most child laborers work in factories making goods for sale in the shopping malls of rich countries. Of course, some child labor does take this form, but very little. About two-thirds of all child laborers are involved in agriculture, and the majority work for household enterprises—that is, their own parents. But there are misconceptions within misconceptions. Working in agriculture is not always the "natural", healthy life it is often pictured as, since it can mean working with dangerous equipment and chemicals, large animals and long, back-breaking hours. And parents, while usually well-meaning, can unintentionally expose their children to hazardous conditions due to a lack of sophistication in identifying health risks and a lack of money (credit) to improve work methods. Sadly, the sweatshops conscientious consumers in the rich countries worry about often provide better working conditions than the farms and small workshops most children are found in. (This does not exonerate the sweatshops, of course.)

A third misconception is that child labor is simply the product of poverty, and that it will disappear automatically, so to speak, as incomes rise. There is more than a grain of truth in this view, since child labor is a much greater problem in poor countries than rich ones, but it is also far too simple. The most important problem with this generalization is that countries with similar levels of average income can have very different rates of child labor, depending on the measures they've taken to combat it. We will consider some of these measures shortly. Also, since child labor is a cause of poverty, just as poverty is a cause of child labor, a wait-and-see attitude is not justified. Finally, there continues to be a child labor problem even in the wealthy countries, especially among at-risk groups like immigrants and discriminated-against minorities, so overall economic growth is not a sole answer.

Why does child labor reproduce poverty? The main reason is that it competes with education, which, as we have seen, is one of the most important contributors to economic progress. One has to be careful with this claim, however. Many children both work (even to the point of being child laborers) and go to school. Also, some children neither work nor go to school, so simply prohibiting children from working is not very productive. Sometimes families need the income brought in by some children to provide the resources for their brothers or sisters to get an education. Nevertheless, on average too much work reduces the likelihood of additional schooling, and child laborers tend to get lower grades and learn less when they do attend class. It is above all for this reason that money spent to reduce child labor is an investment that will repay itself many times over.

A second potential negative effect of child labor is on other forms of human capital, especially physical and psychosocial health. Unfortunately, we have little systematic data regarding these impacts and have to rely mostly on impressionistic information. We have too many stories of children suffering muscular-skeletal disorders at an early age, reduced eyesight, respiratory diseases and similar problems to ignore their debilitating consequences. Similarly, too much work too soon can have the effect of narrowing a child's imagination or sense of personal potential, and this can just as surely lead to a lifetime of dull survival. As health and psychological realism become more influential in economics, we can expect more research into these aspects of child labor.

The most powerful intervention to reduce child labor is the payment of **conditional cash transfers** to low-income parents. These funds are intended to replace the earnings or other economic contributions of their children, and they come with a stipulation: children must actually attend school and perform well enough to continue moving through the system. (It is also common to require parents to bring their children to health clinics on a regular basis.) This approach was pioneered in Brazil, where it has had a dramatic impact on both child labor and education outcomes, and Mexico; now many countries in Latin America, Asia and sub-Saharan Africa have programs along similar lines. Expanding them, which is a problem of politics as well as financing, is the most important front in the struggle against child labor.

Meanwhile, the worst forms of child labor require the attention of economists, social workers and activists in local communities. Interventions take many forms, such as information programs for parents, technical and financial assistance to employers so they can make production more adult-oriented, and rehabilitation programs to help children overcome the aftereffects of harmful work. Perhaps the final misconception concerns these types of interventions: contrary to common portrayals in the popular press, policing and punishing employers, while sometimes necessary, is the last rather than the first line of defense. Many of the employers themselves face a difficult battle for survival in the informal economy and are not necessarily happy with the work they ask children to do for them.

Box 19.2: The Millennium Development Goals

A Millennium Declaration was signed by 147 governments at the United Nations Millennium Summit in September, 2000. It sets a 2015 deadline for achieving eight general goals:

1. Eradicate extreme poverty and hunger. Two targets: reduce by half the proportion of people living on less than a dollar a day, and reduce by half the proportion of people who suffer from hunger.
2. Achieve universal primary education. Target: ensure that all boys and girls complete a full course of primary schooling.

(continued)

Box 19.2 (continued)

3. Promote gender equality and empower women. Target: eliminate gender disparity in primary and secondary education preferably by 2005, and at all levels by 2015.
4. Reduce child mortality. Target: reduce by two thirds the mortality rate among children under five.
5. Improve maternal health. Target: reduce by three quarters the maternal mortality ratio.
6. Combat HIV/AIDS, malaria and other diseases. Two targets: halt and begin to reverse the spread of HIV/AIDS, and halt and begin to reverse the incidence of malaria and other major diseases.
7. Ensure environmental sustainability. Three targets: integrate the principles of sustainable development into country policies and programs, reverse loss of environmental resources; reduce by half the proportion of people without sustainable access to safe drinking water; achieve significant improvement in lives of at least 100 million slum dwellers, by 2020.
8. Develop a global partnership for development. Seven targets: transparent and fair trading and financial systems; trade preferences, debt relief and development assistance for the least developed countries; recognize special needs of landlocked and small island states; long-term debt sustainability for all developing countries; decent and productive work for youth; providing access to affordable essential drugs in developing countries; making new technologies, especially in information and communication, more widely available. (Summary)

Are these goals too ambitious or not ambitious enough? Some criticize them for implicitly accepting too much poverty, even as they try to reduce its hardship. (There is no general call for poverty reduction except for the most destitute spending less than a dollar a day.) On the other hand, as of this writing the agreed-upon time allotted for achieving these goals is winding down, and insufficient progress has been made toward several of them.

This brief survey of the main contributors to mass poverty focuses on the economic side of the problem, especially the role of human capital. Just as important, however, is the political side, which has to do with the reasons why effective economic (and other) policies are not always implemented. Here there are two closely-related issues, the quality and character of political institutions and the political influence of the poor. You might think that these matters lie outside the scope of economics, but economists have studied them intensively in recent years, and in any case they are crucial to understanding why such a grave problem has continued to exist for so long.

To a considerable extent, the map of the world that shows us where mass poverty continues to exist coincides with the map of former colonies of the European powers with non-European majorities. Even though decades or even centuries have elapsed since the achievement of independence in these regions, evolution towards democratic and rule-based political institutions has been limited, with too few exceptions. Government has often been what social scientists, borrowing from the lexicon of biology, call predatory: its principle function is to extract resources from society for the benefit of those with access to political power. Elections, when they occur, are frequently seen only as contests between rival groups seeking to benefit from this access. (Aspects of the competition for the spoils of power occur in all existing regimes, of course, but where it is the main activity of government the problem is really serious.) The intermediate levels of the political hierarchy in such systems are marked by relations of clientelism, networks of personal loyalty of underlings to those above them who supply patronage and protection.

It should be obvious that political systems in which patronage and corruption are widespread will not be effective mechanisms for implementing policies to combat poverty. Major areas of expense, like schools and roads, are seen as opportunities for enrichment for those with the right connections, so not enough money makes its way to the teachers and cement-mixers who do the actual work. There is widespread agreement that more resources need to be funneled into activities that promote the development of human capital, but it is not always clear how the money can get safely from those who now have it to those who need it. Unfortunately, the recognition of this problem by those who study development and poverty has not yet had much influence on the ostensibly "honest" governments and corporations in the developed world that continue to do business with, and in many cases intervene in support of, openly predatory regimes in poor countries.

Related to the problem of corruption and government predation is the tendency for political systems in developing countries to be indifferent to the needs of their poorest citizens. This should not come as a surprise, of course, since economic clout is a source of political power everywhere, and the poor by definition have the least. Nevertheless, the situation becomes dramatic when poverty is a mass phenomenon, and the needs of the poor are so vivid. In much of the world it remains the case that, whenever poor people organize for political or economic power, they are at risk of violent repression. Even in more liberal societies the poor generally have little access to communications media or established political parties.

Recognition of these difficulties has led to heightened interest in **NGO's** (non-governmental organizations) in recent years. Those providing money and expertise to development projects often see such voluntary groups as more reliable partners than the governments who are officially in charge of the region or issue. Thus, rather than work with a government forestry department, those promoting sustainable livelihoods for people living in forested areas might work with environmental or social organizations created by the local people themselves. This has had contradictory impacts on these NGO's. On the one hand, the infusion of outside resources, such as money from foreign sponsors, makes it easier to overcome the collective action problem and achieve effective cooperation, for reasons that should be apparent based on the analysis in Chap. 10. On the other, NGO's too can be corrupted by the sudden flow of money in regions where poverty is the norm, coming to resemble the governments to which they were originally an alternative.

Putting the two halves together, there is widespread agreement that addressing the challenge of mass poverty in the developing world requires progress on crafting policies, getting the money to pay for them and fostering democratic and honest social institutions that can administer them. Seeing this as an interconnected problem brings us once again to the capabilities argument laid out by Sen and Nussbaum. It would be tempting to divide Nussbaum's list (Box 19.1) into two groups, the "most urgent" capabilities having to do with life, health and access to credit and employment, and then a second "when we get around to it" group focusing on social and political life. Experience shows, however, that without the second there is little hope for the first. This holistic approach to combating poverty has become the dominant view—but on-the-ground implementation still requires attention to all the details of information-gathering and analysis, and the use of economic and other social science techniques to improve policies and organizational performance.

19.3 Poverty Among Riches

As we saw in Table 19.3, poverty has not disappeared from the upper-income countries. There are large differences in their overall poverty rates, however, and in the poverty trends over time and among particular demographic and social groups—and the purpose for having theories about poverty is to explain these facts and suggest remedies. This is a tall order, one we can only begin to address in the pages to come.

As before, our exemplar will be the United States, which has the highest poverty rates of any wealthy country. Our measurement approach will be absolute poverty, using the much-debated official poverty line developed in the 1960s and since updated. This almost certainly underestimates true US poverty, but it is convenient for our purposes, since the government provides a wealth of data based on it. We can begin with the overall time trend, as presented in Fig. 19.1.

The first big story is the dramatic reduction in poverty between 1959 and 1968, as the economy grew quickly—the 1960s was the best single decade for US economic growth—and as the programs from the "War on Poverty" (a set of government anti-poverty programs) were put into place. Income growth during those years were tilted toward the bottom: those earning least at the end of the 1950s saw their incomes grow faster than those at the top.

The second, less satisfying story, is that progress has essentially ended during the four decades following 1968; in fact, there have been substantial periods in which the rate of poverty has actually increased. Rapid economic growth during the late 1990s was the only bright spot during this long episode. In general, economic growth has tilted away from the poor, and, with a few exceptions we will note briefly, new government programs were not forthcoming.

As for the ethnic and racial composition of poverty, Table 19.5 sends mixed signals:

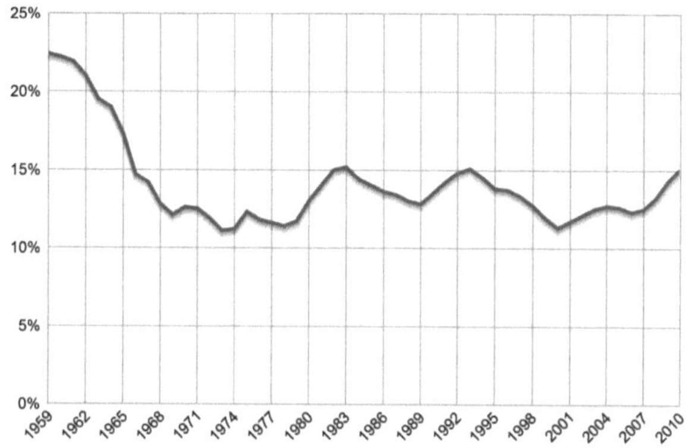

Fig. 19.1 Percent of US population living in poverty, 1959–2010. (*Source*: Economic Policy Institute)

Table 19.5 Hispanic and Black poverty rates as a multiple of White rates, 1973–2010. (US)

	1973	1980	1990	2000	2005	2010
Hispanic/White	2.9	2.8	3.2	2.9	2.6	2.7
Black/White	4.2	3.6	3.6	3.0	3.0	2.8

Source: Economic Policy Institute

On the one hand, there has been noticeable progress in reducing the disparities, especially between Blacks and Whites. On the other, the poverty rate for both minority groups (which are overlapping, since many Hispanics are also classified as Black) remains more than twice as high as for Whites, surely an unacceptable situation. Why these inequalities persist, and what we can do about them, is a major area of disagreement in the study of poverty.

So let's turn to the explanations. There are two major schools of thought in this field. One holds that the main explanation for poverty lies in the characteristics of the poor themselves. If the poor were like the rest of the population, according to this view, poverty would largely disappear. The other is that it is the inequality of the reward structure—too many low-wage or insecure jobs, too much unemployment—that constitutes the true cause of poverty, and that changing this situation, rather than changing the poor, is the key to progress. We will look at each in turn.

1. The poor are the problem. Poor people are not a random cross-section of the population; they are disproportionately less educated, in poorer health, have less job experience, more likely to have children (or be children), and more likely to be single mothers raising families on their own. They are also more likely, as we have seen, to be Black or Hispanic, but a large part of that racial or ethnic effect is actually attributable to these other differences of human capital, position in the labor market and family status. (But it should not be assumed that these "other" differences are not themselves the result of discrimination, as was pointed out in the previous chapter.) If the various social and economic characteristics of the poor could be changed, maybe they would find ways to extricate themselves from poverty.

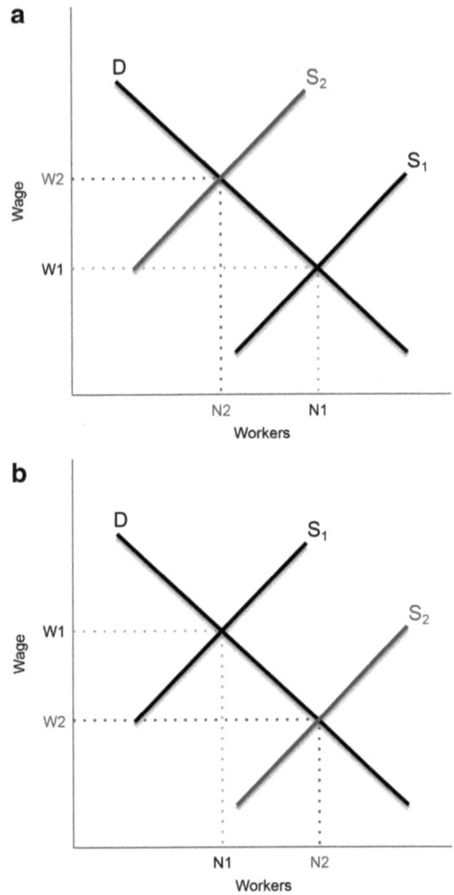

Fig. 19.2 Shifts in wages and employment for low- and high-skill jobs due to shifts in supply. (**a**) In the market for low-skilled jobs, the supply of low-qualified workers declines from S_1 to S_2, leading to fewer jobs (N_1-N_2) at a higher wage (W_2-W_1). (**b**) In the market for high-skilled jobs, the supply of highly-qualified workers increases from S_1 to S_2, leading to more employment (N_2) but at a lower wage (W_2)

There is a logical basis for this hope, drawn from the supply-and-demand model of the labor market. Suppose there are two types of jobs, low-skill and high-skill, and two types of workers, low-qualified and high-qualified. "Qualification" in this context can be thought of as a combination of a good educational background, good health, productive work skills and other attributes that might make the worker a suitable candidate for the high-skill job. Let's see what happens over two time periods. In the first, few workers are highly-qualified; in the second a large number of low-qualification workers are moved into the high-qualification camp. If there is no change in the labor demand curves for the two kinds of jobs, and if supply and demand in the labor market are equalized at an equilibrium wage, Fig. 19.2a, b show us what will happen.

In the market for low-skilled jobs, employment would shrink, while wages would rise. Workers whose qualifications had improved would shift to the market for high-skilled jobs, where employment would increase. While there would be a decline in wages for the higher-skilled workers, workers as a group (high- and low-qualifications combined) would benefit, since more would be working at the better jobs. Depending on how large the wage increase would be in the low-skilled labor market, poverty could be reduced or even eliminated. (Elimination would depend on the rate of unemployment at equilibrium, where the number of unfilled jobs approaches the number of workers looking for jobs, and on the provision of programs to provide benefits to unemployed workers.) As we have already seen in Chap. 16, few economists today regard the simple model behind Fig. 19.2 as an adequate description of how labor markets really work, but some think its main insights are still valid. Even if wages and employment are not quite predictable in this way, surely there must be *some* effect of changes in labor supply along these lines.

Let's take a closer look at some of the characteristics of "low qualification". One of the most important is education. Adults with no more than a high school education are about twice as likely as the more educated portion of the population to be earning low wages that put them at risk of being in poverty. This ratio becomes about three-to-one when we look only at high school dropouts. It makes intuitive sense that, in an economy that has continued to become more technologically sophisticated, those without a strong educational background would be at a disadvantage.

Another factor is health. A recent study found that in 1997, whereas only 6 % of those who reported no disabilities lived in poverty (according to the official poverty line), 12 % of those who said that they had difficulty in at least one area of physical functioning were poor, and this figure rose to 23 % for those who said they couldn't perform at least one such function on their own. This strong relationship between disability and poverty exists despite government programs, like Social Security, that provide income to disabled people. Ill health is also a major determinant of household bankruptcy in the United States.

A set of factors that have attracted increasing attention are combined under the term "social capital"; all of them have to do with the community environments poor people are exposed to. The effects are most apparent in neighborhoods where at least 40 % of the inhabitants are poor. Over one in ten poor people in the United States live in concentrated poverty areas like this; the fraction is almost twice as high for poor Blacks. Similar neighborhoods, where concentrated poverty and racial or ethnic segregation reinforce each other, can be found in other high-income countries, like Britain and France. Negative effects of this situation include:

- Poor schools: these neighborhoods usually have worse schools, despite having higher percentages of students with special needs. Test scores in reading and math are nearly always lower and dropout rates higher.
- Poor social services: essential services like police, fire protection, trash collection and emergency medical care are frequently substandard. The residents of these neighborhoods have less clout with the political and other power centers that decide where resources will be allocated.
- Poor employment options. Because social problems are severe and social services insufficient, businesses are reluctant to locate in such communities.

Often the better job opportunities are far away, and not easily reached by public transportation.

- Poor job networks. A large percentage of jobs are acquired through networks of friends and family. When an entire community is "out of the loop" economically, individuals will have no way to find out where the best opportunities are.
- Lack of role models. People acquire study and work habits largely as a result of the influence of those around them, their reference group. If you don't know people who have benefitted from hard work and a long time horizon, you will be less likely to take on those traits yourself.

Research has found some support for each of these, but we should be careful not to read too much into them. Many superb students emerge from poverty-stricken schools, and most poor people show a capacity for very hard work. (The poor may well work harder than the rich on average.) Moreover, most poor people do not live in areas of high poverty concentration.

The final, and most controversial, factor we will look at is the tendency for many single mothers to end up in poverty. Figure 19.3 on the next page shows the likelihood of single mothers in the US with children under the age of 18 being in poverty as a multiple of the poverty rate for married couples, also with children of this age range.

To interpret this chart, consider how it is calculated. In 1974, for example, 6.0 % of married couples with children were in poverty, but 43.7 % of single mothers were. This gives us a multiple of approximately 7.3, a measure of the relatively greater poverty risk associated with being a woman with children, and not sharing their care and support with a married (male) partner. When put this way, it is clear that both of these characteristics provides an important part of the risk: women earn less than men and bearing the burden of raising children alone is even more difficult.

Figure 19.3 demonstrates that being an unmarried mother is a considerable economic risk, but one that has been slowly declining over the past three decades as discrimination against women in the labor market has diminished and as childcare opportunities have expanded. (The composition of the single mom group has also changed in the direction of those in a better socioeconomic position.) The biggest improvements occurred during the period 1978–1985, however, and progress has largely stalled since then.

For some, the big story is that these women have children and yet are unmarried. In their view, the best anti-poverty policies would be those that discourage childbearing outside of marriage and encourage marriage for those with children. It is not clear how these objectives could be realized, however. It is difficult to regulate sexual behavior, and bad marriages can be more harmful than no marriages at all. Nevertheless, it is the case that many men could do more to support the children they are responsible for, and that efforts to encourage them to take a bigger role should be explored.

For others, the problem is the bind that women with children face in an unsupportive society. As we have seen, despite an encouraging trend, women still

Fig. 19.3 Ratio of the percentage of single mothers to married couples in poverty, both with children under 18, US, 1974–2010. (*Source*: Economic Policy Institute)

earn less than men on average, and the sorts of jobs that many low-income women tend to have—jobs that are predominantly female in composition—pay less, like childcare workers and nursing home attendants. Few jobs, except those for highly-trained managers and professionals, are likely to offer the flexibility that parents need, as children do not get sick only on holidays. Paid childcare, despite the low wages of the child-minding workforce, tends to be expensive. These factors add up to create a great challenge for women raising children alone.

Policy ideas stemming from the overall perspective we have been considering, that the characteristics of the poor are the problem that needs to be addressed, follow from the diagnoses. Some of these are:

- Investments in education. More programs to help at-risk children succeed at school have been called for. Research shows that interventions at an early age, even before first grade, are especially effective. Recent initiatives to withdraw funding from schools with poorly-performing students have been controversial, however.
- Encouraging work. There has been an international trend toward altering benefit programs to push poor recipients into paid employment. This has been most pronounced in the US, where changes in the system during the Clinton administration have cut benefits substantially, with the loss being made up by more hours of work. Some public benefits are now directly tied to work hours, such as the Earned Income Tax Credit.
- Childcare benefits. To make it easier for single mothers in particular to enter the labor force, there is now a trend toward payments to compensate for the cost of paid childcare. The country that has gone the furthest in this direction is France, where public childcare programs are available for the majority of parents, whether male or female, single or in couples.
- Residential desegregation. Neighborhoods with highly concentrated poverty are often the result of racial segregation. Programs that encourage this segregation, such as certain types of zoning and home ownership subsidies, could be cut back. There could be stronger enforcement of laws prohibiting discrimination in housing and bank lending, and low income families could be given vouchers

that they could spend on housing in any location they choose. By breaking up high-poverty neighborhoods, the effects of insufficient social capital could be reduced.

2. The distribution of income and wealth is the problem. Proponents of this view sometimes use the following parable. Consider the children's game, musical chairs, in which a group of children walk around a number of chairs as music is being played. When the music stops the children must find a chair to sit in, but there are fewer chairs than children. Those who are unable to find a chair in time leave the game. A few more chairs are removed, and the next round begins. The game continues until there is just one chair and one winner.

One could imagine that, if the stakes were higher—if significant money or other rewards were involved—programs might be set up to help the children who had the most difficulty getting to a chair. We could improve their reaction times, their ability to see quickly which chairs are empty, their speed at darting to a seat. In this way we could help particular children compete more effectively in musical chairs, but what we couldn't do is change the number of losers in each round, since this is determined by the number of chairs compared to the number of children. The game is set up to systematically exclude players each round, and this is true even if the same children seem to do worse each time the game is played. Those who see only which children are slower or faster and fail to recognize the structure of the game as a whole would be missing the most important factor.

For many observers, this is the story with much of our research and policy concerning poverty in wealthy countries. True, some people are much more likely than others to end up poor, but while their characteristics may explain why they, rather than some others, are the ones who end up on the bottom, they don't explain why the bottom exists in the first place. According to this view, many "anti-poverty programs" serve only to shift poverty from some groups to others.

How reasonable is this position? In its support, we can cite the inequality data we examined in the last chapter. In less regulated economies like the US, as many as a quarter of all available jobs put their holders at risk of being poor; the percentage is much lower in the more regulated economies of western Europe, but even there it is believed to be growing. Unemployment presents a starker picture yet. As we will see in the next volume, policy-makers have been willing to accept unemployment rates far beyond the level that would produce a relatively equal numbers of workers seeking jobs and jobs seeking workers as portrayed by the Beveridge Curve. Whether this is a good idea is something we will explore when we discuss the topic in detail, but for now the point is that, if a particular level of excess unemployment is regarded as acceptable, some people must be in the position of not having work. Unless there are generous public programs to provide other forms of income, they are quite likely to be in poverty. Improving the job-hunting skills of the unemployed will not help much if the unemployment rate as a whole is kept at a high level.

On the other hand, the musical chairs analogy is too extreme. The number of chairs in our economies—the number of jobs that pay wages above the poverty level—is not controlled by some sadistic game director. It is the outcome of millions of decisions by workers, employers, borrowers, lenders and consumers, as well as by policies set by governments and the pressures of civil society organizations. The qualifications of low-income adults are part of this complex system, and if they are changed, the number of good jobs should change too. The model behind Fig. 19.3 may exaggerate this effect, but the effect is not likely to be zero.

From the standpoint of the structural view of poverty, the important question is, what factors tend to promote the shift toward low-wage work? There is a large international body of research on this topic, but the center of attention has been the US, where the shift has been most pronounced. While there is dispute about the precise size of the different influences, most researchers agree on a common set:

- The erosion of minimum wage regulations. The minimum wage set by the Federal Government has not kept up with either inflation or the rise in average wages, so it is possible for the worst-paying jobs to pay that much less. Women workers have been affected by this process to a greater extent than men.
- The declining power of unions. Fewer workers in the US are members of unions, as we saw in Chap. 16, and the bargaining power of unionized workers has steadily diminished. This has removed an important protection at the bottom end of the labor market. The wages of men and especially Black men have been disproportionately affected by this trend.
- Deregulation. Some industries, like trucking and communications, used to be closely regulated by the government and are now largely deregulated. The increased competition has intensified pressure on employers to hold down labor costs, and one result is that more jobs in these sectors pay poverty-level wages.
- Global competition. Workers in the higher-income countries increasingly find themselves in competition with workers in the developing world. One consequence is that employers can use the threat of relocation to increase their bargaining power with their workforce. In addition, many of the jobs that used to pay relatively higher wages to less-qualified workers in the developed world have vanished. (This has been due to changes in technology as well as the global relocation of production.) In a simple supply and demand model, this would be represented by a shift in the labor demand curve for these workers to the left, reducing their wages and employment prospects. Also, immigration may have played a role in heightening competition and lowering wages in some portions of the labor market in developed countries, although this is an area of intense controversy.

Policy, from this perspective, should center on changing the structure of the economy as it results from these and other factors. The goal would be to promote greater equality in wages and incomes, especially at the lower end of the distribution. Indirectly, it is hoped that this will also provide greater incentives for those currently mired in poverty to put more effort into work and school, since the rewards will be seen as worth it. Currently on the agenda are measures such as:

- Living wage ordinances. Proponents feel that the national minimum wage in the US is so far below what is required that local initiatives will be needed to make up the difference. Cities and states have been encouraged to mandate "living wages" linked to the official poverty line; full-time workers at such a wage would no longer be at risk of living in poverty. Sometimes the laws are directed at particular employers, such as those who do business with government or operate in a particular sector, like retail sales.

- Labor law reform. Existing labor laws are viewed by many as putting excessive barriers in front of workers wishing to form unions and providing too little clout if they succeed. Reform measures include simplifying the process by which a majority of a company's workforce chooses a union, allowing union membership on an individual basis (whether or not a majority of coworkers agree), and increasing penalties on employers who violate existing rules.
- **Comparable worth**. This would extend anti-discrimination statutes to require that jobs of comparable economic value pay comparable wages irrespective of whether those who hold them are predominantly male or female. This would particularly improve the earnings of single mothers, but critics fear that administering the law would interfere too much on the prerogatives of employers.
- Managed trade. Various proposals have been put forward to moderate international competition in labor markets. They include the incorporation of labor standards, such as the freedom to join unions, in international trade agreements and measures to prevent highly unbalanced trade, so that job gains and losses from trade are not too unequal.

Both views, that the poor are the problem and that the structure of the economy is the problem, have been presented in rather exaggerated terms, as if one could put all the weight on just one side or the other. Both have to be at least partially true, although the extent and severity of poverty may be due more to one than the other. Since political and economic resources are not infinite, choices have to be made about which factors are the most important, so presenting them as opposite sides of an argument is probably justified.

One last point should also be made: up to now, we have reviewed the various forces that might be responsible for the level of poverty found in the higher-income countries with an eye toward policies that could reduce it. Nevertheless, whatever the level of poverty generated by low wages or unemployment, it is possible to offset it through direct income transfers. These can take the form of progressive taxes which gather more revenues from those earning the highest incomes and public assistance programs that make payments to those at the bottom. These are sometimes seen as an alternative to programs that would reduce poverty generated in the private economy. It should be noted, however, that tax and assistance programs are not without their own effects on markets, and that the cost of these programs depends on the amount of poverty markets generate. Thus, while income transfers can moderate the effect of poverty, they are not a substitute for policies that target the factors that determine how much of this poverty there will be.

The Main Points

1. The simplest measure of poverty is expected years of life. Countries and communities with high levels of poverty have shorter average expected lifespans.
2. There are two main approaches to defining poverty. Relative poverty is defined as income falling below some proportion of the median, for instance incomes less than half the median. Absolute poverty is measured in relation to the cost of a bundle of goods and services believed to constitute a minimum for adequate well-being; those whose income is insufficient to buy this bundle are defined as poor. Absolute poverty is most appropriate for developing countries, where $1.25 and $2.00 per day (in purchasing power parity dollars) are commonly used poverty lines; relative poverty is a better indicator for higher-income countries. The capabilities approach of Sen and Nussbaum combines elements of both absolute and relative indicators.
3. Mass poverty is a fundamental problem across the world, affecting billions of people. It is a product of insufficient economic growth as well as the maldistribution of the gains from growth. Contributing factors include ill-health, lack of education, little access to credit and widespread child labor. The majority of child laborers work in agriculture, in household enterprises; even so, their work often disrupts education and may leave long-lasting physical or psychological scars. In recent years there has been a large increase in the number of countries with income transfer programs under which poor households are given a regular stipend, usually in return for fulfilling education and health obligations toward their children.
4. Much of the effort against extreme poverty is summed up in the Millennium Development Goals, which set numerical targets in eight broad areas, such as health, nutrition, hygiene and education. These goals were selected to achieve a consensus among international organizations, national governments and large NGO's. The deadline is 2015; a few of these goals have already been met and several may be met soon, but others are now out of reach. Planning is under way for a new set of goals for the post-2015 world. At the same time, there is recognition that it is not enough to have a desirable set of goals; the responsiveness and integrity of governments is needed to implement them.
5. Poverty persists in upper-income countries as well, particularly in the United States. Little progress has been made since the "War on Poverty" of the 1960s. There is considerable disagreement among economists who try to explain this. Some see the main barriers resulting from the characteristics and behavior of poor people themselves—their lack of education, generally poorer health, lack of social capital, and the extent of female-headed households. These analysts tend to favor programs such as increased investment in education, changes in how school systems are run, greater financial incentives for accepting low-wage work (or penalties for refusing it), and efforts to break up segregated neighborhoods in order to build social capital among the poor.

6. Others emphasize the effects that changes in the economy have had on those vulnerable to poverty—continuing racial and gender discrimination, the lack of public support for children, and the general increase in the inequality of earnings, particularly as it is reflected in the expansion of the low-wage portion of the labor market. Policies inspired by this view include increases in the minimum wage, changes in labor law to reduce the barriers to unionization, tighter restrictions on discrimination, and measures to moderate the competitive pressures on the labor market stemming from international trade.

▶ Terms to Define

Absolute poverty
Comparable worth
Conditional income transfers
Disability adjusted life year
NGO's
Poverty line
Quality adjusted life year
Relative poverty

Questions to Discuss

1. Try to imagine yourself as a typical person living in ancient Greece or China. How would your way of life be affected by your expected lifespan? In particular, how would this affect the sorts of choices you would be likely to make regarding the age to begin full-time work, the investments you would make in the construction of buildings and tools, and in the other aspects of life we now regard as "economic"?
2. How would you define poverty as it might apply to yourself? That is, on what basis would you decide whether you should be regarded as being poor in the present or at any future time? Do you think a relative or absolute standard is more appropriate for answering this question? Why?
3. Would it be possible to remove any of Martha Nussbaum's ten capabilities without harming the rest? To put the question somewhat differently, is it necessary that all of them be fulfilled concurrently, or might it be possible to put some on a fast track and get to the others at a later time? Why?
4. One of the difficult questions facing global public health policy is how to set priorities for the allocation of limited resources. One could imagine four different criteria: minimizing deaths, minimizing loss of DALY's, minimizing loss of QALY's, and minimizing the negative impacts of poor health on economic growth. Which of these would you favor? Why?
5. Based on the brief survey of factors associated with mass poverty, what is your assessment of the Millennium Development Goals? Do they include targets that are of lesser importance? Do they leave out anything you would view as

essential? What can be done to make it more likely that these goals will actually be achieved?

6. Throughout history, children have always worked at the most demanding jobs they were capable of, at the earliest possible age. Only in recent decades have we come to see child labor as a problem. How would you reconcile these two facts? Was child labor a problem in the past, but unrecognized? Or is it less a problem today than commonly thought? In your answer you should try to be explicit about the opportunity costs of child labor and also the costs of removing children from work.
7. Do the citizens of wealthy countries have an obligation to provide funding to help meet the Millennium and other development goals? On what do you base your answer? If your answer is yes, what would be a reasonable percentage of national income that should be put into development funds? How does this compare to the amounts currently being spent?
8. How much weight would you give to the characteristics-of-the-poor versus the structure-of-the-economy approaches to explaining poverty in the US and other developed countries? Which factors on each side do you regard as most important? Why? Do you have any personal experience or know anyone who has had experience that supports or undermines one of these arguments?

Economics and Ecology 20

Whole classes of animals are mysteriously declining in population and possibly headed to extinction. Take frogs, for example. The Global Amphibian Assessment found in 2004 that, due to mass die-offs and loss of habitat, about a third of all species of frogs, toads and salamanders could soon disappear. That the problem could be worldwide, affecting these creatures in Canada and Madagascar, is particularly disturbing. Recent evidence points to an outbreak of skin fungus as an important factor, itself possibly linked to global climate change, but researchers admit the problem—if it is one problem and not a combination of many problems—is still only dimly understood.

More immediately worrisome for humans is the disappearance of bees. More than a quarter of all bee colonies in the United States have collapsed in the space of a few years, and similar trends have occurred in Europe and Latin America. Bees play an indispensable role in pollinating many of the fruit and vegetable crops that make up a large part of the human diet, so the potential impact on agriculture could be enormous. Pesticides and the outbreak of a deadly virus are possible causes put forward by researchers, but at the moment specialists are far from a consensus on the issue.

These stories exemplify several ominous trends in humanity's changing relationship with nature. Large and potentially very harmful alterations are occurring in the environment. The scale is large, even global. The causes are not fully known, and we have every reason to expect there will be more unpleasant surprises as our knowledge increases. In some areas, like climate change, a huge research effort has clarified the mechanisms that are at work and the tasks that have to be accomplished to avoid greater harm. In many others, however, the complexity of ecological interrelationships leaves us with far more questions than answers.

In this chapter we will look at the uneasy relationship between economics and ecology. The main themes have already been foreshadowed: we will consider the problem that many essentials for life, like bees, frogs and other animal species, have an uncertain status in the modern economy, that the effects of human activities on the environment are often not taken into account, that economies need to be

P. Dorman, *Microeconomics*, Springer Texts in Business and Economics,
DOI 10.1007/978-3-642-37434-0_20,

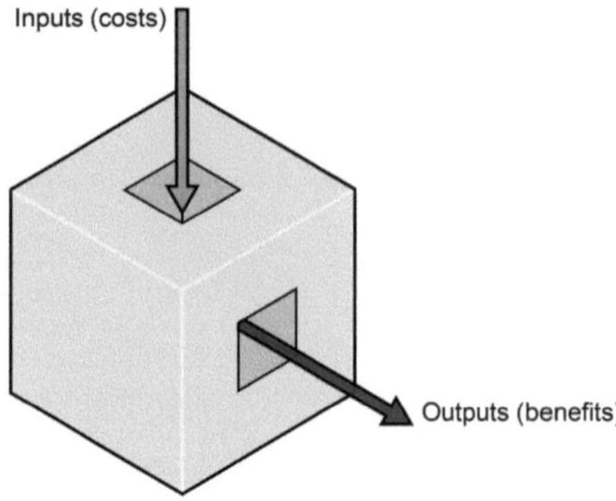

Fig. 20.1 The economy as a machine that transforms inputs into outputs. The economy is seen as taking in inputs such as labor, raw materials and equipment and producing outputs (goods and services) of benefit to consumers

restructured if they are to become sustainable, and that managing complexity and uncertainty will be a large part of the solution.

20.1 Ecology: A Big Omission

Chapter 4 presented the Big Story as traditionally understood by economists. On the first page there appeared Fig. 20.1:

The goal of the economy is to generate net benefits, a value of outputs in excess of the value of inputs, and Fig. 20.1 is intended to express this.

But the Big Story has a Big Hole: where does the input arrow come from, and where does the output arrow go? As presented in the picture, the inputs appear as if by magic, and the outputs disappear in more or less the same way. To be complete, we should pencil in the additional boxes and pipes from which the economy gets its resources and which absorb its products. Much of this would represent what we commonly call "the environment", the physical planet we live on, its web of chemical nutrients and energy, and its vast complexity of plant and animal life. Also on the input side we should recognize the physical and social processes by which human beings are reproduced, raised and cared for, most of which are outside the market economy. Finally, our accumulated social and cultural heritage, including our languages, customs and artistic and scientific insights, are essential contributors to economic progress, and these too ought to be represented in a complete model. While most of this chapter will focus on the natural environment, much of it applies as well to the social and cultural environments within which any economy must function.

20.2 The Environment as a Commons

The words "economics" and "ecology" come from the same Greek root, oikos, which refers to a household, with a further connotation of provision and sustenance. Throughout history thinkers have compared the activities of animals and plants to acquire their nutrients, reproduce themselves and survive as a species to similar human preoccupations. By the same token, we might imagine the economy as we have described it in this book as humanity's use of and adaptation to the environment, seen up close and from the inside. (A bird, if it could write, might produce a textbook on "birdonomics".) Yet this view falls apart in one fundamental respect. The components of the natural environment that have entered our analysis up to this point represent only a tiny fraction of what is actually out there and necessary for our survival. We have considered people and their various abilities ("labor") and land (primarily as space) and certain useful minerals and organisms ("raw materials"), but the vast majority of the environment has made no appearance at all. Where is the energy radiating from the sun, or the atmosphere, the oceans, the global cycles of chemical flows or the genetic resources we call biodiversity? Where, for that matter, are languages, the intellectual legacies passed on through science and literature, and the slowly acquired understanding of how human beings can live and work together, expressed in our cultures through songs, stories and sayings? All of these things are indispensable, but thus far we have simply taken them for granted. Yet, as we saw with the frogs and bees, and as we are learning with climate change, it is all too possible for human economies to undermine the environment we need in order to prosper; there is also reason to think that aspects of our cultural inheritance could be at risk.

At the most basic level, the problem is that modern economies privilege those items, whether they are produced goods or services or natural resources, that are privately owned, but most of the things and systems we depend on aren't. They make up what is often called **the commons**, the set of resources used by human economies which are shared, rather than owned in the conventional sense. A commons may be local, like the fish who make their home in a small stream, or it may be global, like the world's climate system, or it may exist at any level in between. For this reason, it might be more accurate to envision human societies as inhabiting many overlapping commons, adding to the complexity of this already difficult-to-describe dimension of our place in the world.

Box 20.1: "All of Arizona Is Owned by Someone"

Many years ago, I was traveling with my family through a remote part of the Sonoran Desert in Arizona. We drove down small roads until it seemed we had left most traces of civilization behind. On all sides were long vistas of saguaro and other cactuses backed by primitive-looking sandstone formations, a mosaic of brown, green and orange against the bluest of western skies. There were no buildings, no power lines, no farms. Yet suddenly we saw a sign which announced, in stern letters, "Remember, All of Arizona Is Owned by Someone".

On one level, this is certainly true. Every bit of land is legally held either by a private landowner, a tribe or some agency of government, and the sign

(continued)

Box 20.1 (continued)

reminds us that this ownership puts legal restrictions on what visitors, like my family, are permitted to do as we pass through. Yet surely Arizona is more than just an expanse of land. What about the hydrological cycle (the movement of water through precipitation, evaporation and surface and underground flows), which is crucial to the well-being of this hot, dry region? What about the wildlife, like the insects that pollinate the cactuses when they bloom in the spring? What about the history of this state, with its conflicts and accommodation between native peoples and Mexican and Anglo settlers? These too are part of Arizona, but who owns them?

Rather than trying to define a concept like the commons precisely, it is more helpful to look at the sorts of entities people use this term to refer to. Some commons are things, with physical dimensions, like the world's oceans or the continent of Antarctica. We could, if we wanted, put a fence around them, along with a sign like the one I saw in Arizona. Others are physical but take the form of systems, like the global climate system or the genetic diversity of amphibians. Still others are intangible resources like language and other forms of knowledge and culture, or like the broadcast spectrum, a waveform frequency "space" which is occupied by communications systems—radio and television, cellular telephones and other transmissions. Because the elements that would make up a complete list of possible commons is so diverse, it is difficult to say what, if anything, they all have in common. Instead, we can describe some of the features that are typical, but which might not characterize all of them:

1. Absence of private or public ownership. In general, the commons is not owned in the conventional sense of private or public ownership. There is no piece of paper giving a particular individual or organization the right to restrict access, capture the benefits or transfer title to other buyers. Sometimes, however, governments act as if they were owners, by setting rules similar to the ones owners might put in place. For instance, governments do not own the populations of fish that inhabit the coastline, but they often place restrictions on how many fish can be caught in order to prevent these populations from being decimated. Similarly, regulations that prohibit pollution of the water and air can be thought of as the sorts of policies governments might adopt if they were owners of these resources. Nevertheless, government policies tend to be inconsistent in these domains, exactly because governments are not motivated the way true owners would be by threats to the value of their property. (Governments usually take greater care of graffiti on the walls of public buildings than the dumping of toxic substances into lakes and rivers.) We will see later, however, that alternative forms of ownership, neither public nor private in the conventional sense, can have a place in the commons; this is an important frontier of economic institution-building.

2. Unsuitability of private or public ownership. Not only are most commons unowned, they would be difficult to place in conventional ownership. As we have seen, many do not have identifiable boundaries. How could anyone own the hydrological cycle? Everywhere there is water or water vapor, the cycle is present. Every living organism takes in and emits water. If the owner of the hydrological cycle decides to put up a fence, what would be outside it? Another problem is that, even if the resource could be owned, it may be so essential to life and devoid of alternatives that the resulting monopoly power would be too great to bear. It is technically possible for someone to own arithmetic, in the same way that patents are granted for drug formulas. The owner of the arithmetic patent could demand to be paid every time someone performs one of the basic operations (addition, subtraction. . .), and it could be enforced by taking violators to court. Indeed, some higher mathematical algorithms, not different in kind from basic arithmetic functions, *are* patented, and users do have to pay a royalty. There is a debate over whether and to what extent the techniques of mathematics and other scientific fields should be privatized, but all sides agree that the most necessary and widely-used methods ought to remain in the commons.
3. Indispensable services. In 1997 a team of researchers led by Robert Costanza published an estimate of the economic value of the world's ecosystems and other natural resources, which came to about $33 trillion. This sounds like, and is, a lot of money, but it was not much more than the value of the world's total economic production at the time. In other words, according to this study the loss of all of nature would require us to somewhat more than double our human-produced output in order to maintain the same level of overall economic well-being. For all the cleverness these researchers employed in their calculations, their conclusion is clearly false. *There is no substitute for the environment as a whole.* We can damage it a bit more or less, but as an entire system we cannot survive without it. This judgment applies to most individual commons as well. We cannot make do without any of the major nutrient cycles or the hydrological cycle; we cannot function as human beings without our languages and other bases in shared culture; nearly the entire edifice of modern economies rests on the accumulated knowledge of generations of scientists and other scholars. The commons is priceless.
4. Self-reproduction. Most commons survive and prosper to the extent that they are *not* interfered with by human actions. Over timespans that are relevant to human history, the oceans and atmosphere have maintained themselves quite well without human intervention to keep them going. Biodiversity is renewed by the ceaseless pressure of natural selection against a gradually changing natural environment. Languages generally develop and become more sophisticated without the need for official organizations to control how they are spoken and written—although organizations exist in some countries to influence how languages evolve, and on occasion (particularly in the adoption of written scripts) conscious intervention can play a crucial role. It is true that in some of the cultural commons, like science, an infusion of economic resources can propel the rate of growth, and governments and financial interests can influence

which questions scientists investigate, but efforts to prevent scientists from following their research leads or communicating their results ultimate destroy the basis for scientific work altogether. In the great majority of cases, preserving the commons means allowing its intrinsic forces to operate without outside interference. The corollary to this principle is that, if we keep such interference to a minimum, the commons we pass on to future generations will be at least as valuable to them as the commons we inherited from our ancestors was to us, and in the case of the cultural commons, even more so.

The economic analysis of the commons became a matter of great public interest with the publication of the article "The Tragedy of the Commons" by biologist Garrett Hardin in 1968. This short, powerfully argued study presents the exploitation of the commons in a form corresponding to the prisoner's dilemma that has already made several appearances in this book. Consider, proposes Hardin, a community of shepherds who share a common grazing area. (We will take some liberties with his original presentation, but the idea is the same.) This pasture is not owned by anyone, individually or collectively. It provides food for any sheep who graze on it, but too many sheep will destroy its productivity. Even at their most profligate, it would take the sheep of many shepherds to accomplish this. Suppose there are two choices facing each shepherd, to use the pasture with restraint, so that, if all do this, its productivity will be maintained, or to use it excessively, so that, again if all do the same, the pasture will become barren. This first choice can be called cooperation and the second defection. Using our device of referring to any particular shepherd as A and all the others taken together as B, we can set up the payoff matrix on the following page (Fig. 20.2).

To simplify, we express the outcomes for each shepherd with the numbers 1–4, corresponding to how they would be valued by them. The best outcome is 1. In this case, since all the other shepherds are behaving sustainably, and since the overuse by just one shepherd is not enough to destroy the pasture, the sole defector gets the best of both worlds, continuing use of the pasture and the advantage of being able to feed more sheep from it. Second-best is 2. Once again the pasture is maintained, which is of great value to all shepherds, but, compared to the first-best outcome, the individual shepherd takes less advantage from it. Much worse is 3, since now the pasture is destroyed, but even worse than this is 4, since, not only is the pasture useless in the future, the shepherd even loses the temporary benefit of having his sheep overgraze it for a season or two.

As we know from previous encounters with the prisoner's dilemma, there is a strong case that the shepherds will follow the individually rational strategy of choosing D and allowing the pasture to be ruined. They may deeply regret this result, but it is not in any one person's interest to break from the pattern. If this is truly the model that best predicts how a commons, like a common pasturage, will be treated, we are all in a lot of trouble. Hardin felt that there were only two solutions: either establish ownership rights to the pasture so that someone will have the personal incentive to enforce restrictions on access (for instance by charging a fee), or institute government regulations to prevent the shepherds from engaging in overexploitation. The **tragedy of the commons** is the inevitable destruction of

		Shepherd B	
		C	D
Shepherd A	C	A:2, B:2	A:4, B:1
	D	A:1, B:4	A:3, B:3

Fig. 20.2 Payoff matrix for the exploitation of an unowned sheep pasture. If *C* represents sustainable grazing by a shepherd and *D* unsustainable grazing, there is an individual incentive to choose *D*, and the unowned common pasture falls victim to the collective irrationality of a prisoner's dilemma

unowned resources that will occur without these interventions, based on the logic of the prisoner's dilemma.

In 1990, however, political scientist and future Nobel economics prize-winner Elinor Ostrom replied with her influential book, *Governing the Commons: The Evolution of Institutions for Collective Action.* Ostrom points out that, in many instances, real-world herders, such as communities of Swiss farmers sharing common Alpine pastures, managed to avoid the disastrous result predicted by Hardin. The reason, she argued, was that the problem is better understood as a repeated prisoner's dilemma, along the lines we examined in Chap. 10. As we saw, when the game is played a large (and indefinite) number of times, incentives emerge for the players to initiate cooperation and to defect only if others defect. If the rewards to cooperation are large enough (which in the case of a fragile commons they normally would be), and if the players' time horizon is long enough (if their discount rate is low enough), then mutual cooperation rather than mutual defection would be the expected result.

The effect of this argument was to generate new respect for the commons as an economic institution. While private ownership and government regulation both have roles to play, the commons, and the cooperative customs and attitudes that evolve to support it, could be seen as a third basis for human economies. To emphasize this new legitimacy, those who adopt this view often use the phrase **common property resources** to describe what was formerly seen as simply unowned. In most cases, the use of the term "property" in this expression is metaphorical, since property rights in the formal sense do not exist. Nevertheless, the idea is that communities can develop ways of respecting these resources as if they were actually owned in common. The term is also used to make the point that a commons does not have to be defenseless against those who would abuse it. Instead, those commons that are not protected by cooperative institutions are singled out as **open access resources**. Much is made of the argument that common property does not necessarily mean open access. To put this another way, making such a distinction implies that, where we find open access resources, which anyone can exploit without limit, we should try to establish the sorts of cooperative governance measures that characterize better-regulated common property resources.

To some extent, the dispute between these two ways of thinking about the commons is artificial. In many instances the tragedy of the commons is real and urgent, and formal ownership or public regulation offer the only solutions. In others we see just the sort of cooperative arrangements that advocates of common property resources prefer, or at least the possibility of helping them become established. Sometimes all of these factors are in play: cooperation does some of the job but needs to be supplemented by other forms of control. The real world does not conform to any single academic model.

Preserving the commons normally means containing the reach of the private market. A community of shepherds that respects the biological limits of its common pasturage will probably have fewer sheep, or will have to redirect its economy toward other activities that will enable it to purchase more feed from other sources. And these other sources might become more limited or expensive if the common property resources they depend on are respected as well. Ultimately, like our hypothetical shepherds, the overall size and growth of our own economy, as well as the types of activities it extends into, may come into conflict with our need to maintain the various commons whose health is important to us.

This generalization is clear enough when we consider issues like climate change and biodiversity (which requires that many plant and animal habitats be left in a natural state), but a particular flashpoint has been the cultural commons. In recent years there has been a change in the laws governing patents and copyrights, together referred to as **intellectual property rights**. On the one hand, permitting companies and individuals to own a wider range of ideas, like phrases, genetic structures (for life forms) or scientific insights, can serve as a spur to investment in their creation. (We briefly considered the debate over intellectual property rights in Chap. 13.) On the other, each extension of these property rights is also a reduction in the space given to intellectual common property. When scientific ideas are privately owned they are no longer the common heritage of society. When songs and fictional characters remain private property long after they have permeated the general culture, they cannot as easily serve as the raw material for new cultural creation. The broadcast spectrum, which is of enormous economic value, has only recently begun to be auctioned to private companies which earn profits from its use. Just where the line should be drawn between common and private property is a matter for debate, but there is reason to think that, in a world in which private property is widespread and generates powerful incentives for its owners to expand their access to all available resources, and where common property is generally unowned and incentives to safeguard it are weaker, there will probably be a bias in the direction of excessive privatization.

This insight has led to new efforts to develop and institutionalize property forms for common property resources—to turn metaphor into reality. How could communities come to exercise common ownership of at least some portion of the commons? We have already seen, in Chap. 15, how communities with a tie to a particular resource can be given de facto ownership, so that access can be rationed through a market; the example of Japanese coastal regulation illustrates this. Another approach is the creation of trusts which hold formal title to resources and whose statutes legally obligate them to protect their continued value. In many countries there has been a rapid increase in the number of land trusts, for instance. These bodies own parcels of land, but not for purposes of private gain. They are required to ensure that the ecological values of these lands are preserved for future generations and can use them to earn income or provide other benefits only if this primary mission is fulfilled. Other trusts have been established to safeguard cultural treasures, like ancient buildings or the homes of celebrated artists, writers or political leaders.

The question is whether this type of institution can be adapted to provide protection for the most urgently at-risk resources, like the atmosphere (with its concentration of greenhouse gases) and biodiversity. Moving in this direction will require that such trusts operate on a much larger scale, at least national and perhaps international. If common property owners charge for access to their resources (such as carbon fees), a lot of money will be at stake. This suggests that trusts or similar entities may have to be carefully designed and regulated to prevent some combination of large financial temptation and distended organizational structure from undermining their fidelity to the primary mission of resource preservation.

20.3 Natural Resources as Economic Inputs

Up to this point our focus has been on commons as realms to be protected from exploitation, but much of their value, of course, depends on the economic uses they are put to. In this section we will shift the spotlight to the way natural resources ought be used if economies are to make the most of them.

In very broad strokes, we can distinguish between three types of resources, renewable, depletable and nonaugmentable. The first two of these have been the subject of a vast amount of economic theorizing; the third is something of a hybrid.

1. **Renewable resources**. An excellent example of this type of resource is topsoil, the basis for agricultural productivity. The economics of agricultural land were first systematically explored by the brilliant economist David Ricardo at the beginning of the nineteenth century. Ricardo wrote of what he called "the original and indestructible powers of the soil", but he was a city boy (Amsterdam and London, although he later purchased a country estate in England). As any real farmer knows, soil can be built up or eroded away. Good practices leave as much or more productive soil in place for the next season, and bad practices cause erosion and the loss of this valuable natural resource.

Ricardo's theory of land rents was based on the assumption that the productivity of agricultural land is fixed, so that landowners can raise their prices based on the scarcity of land relative to the demand for food. In particular, he examined the consequences if there are differences in productivity across land, or if more labor or other inputs have to be provided in some farms in order to produce enough food to meet the needs of consumers. More recent theories take into account the possibility that land (soil) and other renewable resources can either be drawn down or built up.

The simplest version of the theory puts it this way: a profit-maximizing resource owner will compare the return on investments in a renewable resource to other investments available in the economy, as reflected in the going rate of interest on bonds or other financial assets. For instance, if it will cost extra money to farm in a way that preserves topsoil, the "rational" farmer will compare the return on this cost—more productive land next year—to what could be obtained by putting the extra money into an average investment account. The same analysis, in the opposite direction, applies to cutting production costs and allowing the soil to deplete.

The process can be seen most vividly in another such resource, timber. Consider the situation of a profit-maximizing owner of a timber stand. Suppose her trees grow at a certain rate per year, say 5 %. This means that, by letting the trees stand, she can have 5 % more wood the following year. But she can also cut down the trees, sell them, and invest the proceeds. If the expected return on this financial investment, again approximated by the prevailing interest rate, exceeds 5 %, it is more profitable to cut the trees. In other words, not cutting the trees is equivalent to investing in them and earns a return equal to the growth rate of the trees. Our profit-maximizing timber owner compares this return to the one she could make on her money if she cuts the trees and buys a financial asset. Her choice is determined by whichever return is greater. Since trees grow more slowly as they age, it is typical that, for a period of time there is more money to be made by letting them continue to grow, and then at some point this incentive ends and the trees should be "liquidated" so that they can be replaced by a more profitable asset. Of course, it is also possible for interest rates to change. Very generally, one can say that, as interest rates in the economy rise, it becomes more profitable to draw down the stock of renewable resources like timber and topsoil, and vice versa. This generalization applies to other renewable resources, like harvestable fish.

2. **Depletable resources**. Some extremely important natural resources, like oil and other minerals, are in fixed supply. There is a certain amount available in the earth's crust and that's it. Of course, improvements in technology can make it possible to extract some portion of this resource that was previously unavailable, but there are ultimate limits to how much can be made available to the economy. The original theory of the efficient extraction of such depletable (or nonrenewable) resources was developed by Harold Hotelling, a British mathematician and economist, during the 1920s, and it has been embellished considerably since then.

In the simplest version of Hotelling's model, it is assumed that the resource has a single, profit-maximizing owner. The total amount available for extraction is known with complete certainty, and so also are future demands and interest rates. Finally, it is assumed that there is some other resource or technology which provides a perfect substitute, called a backstop, but at a higher price. If there are no costs of exploration or production, the price of the depletable resource should be exactly equal to that of the backstop at the moment it is exhausted, and it should rise to this level over time at exactly the rate of interest. The reasons are not difficult to fathom. The backstop price should prevail at the moment when the change from one resource to the other occurs, since this would permit the owner of the resource being depleted to sell the very last bit at the highest possible price. The price should rise at the interest rate because otherwise it would be profitable to either extract and sell the resource more quickly (putting the money into an interest-bearing fund) or leave it in the ground (where its price would rise faster than alternative investments), depending on whether the price growth is below or above the interest rate. Finally, if we know where the price has to end up, and if we know how quickly it must rise from one year to the next, and if we also know the demand for the resource—the relationship between price and quantity demanded—as well as how much of the resource lies in the ground to be extracted, we can calculate both the starting price today and the number of years before complete resource exhaustion occurs. In other words, if we feed in enough information, the model can compute the future time path of both prices and production levels right up to the last barrel or ton.

This is an ideal model in some respects, but it relies on many assumptions that have little basis in reality. All the crucial variables—the total amount of the resource to be extracted, future demands, future interest rates, future backstops—are generally unknown. This is the case with oil, for instance. There is tremendous debate over how much oil awaits development, and whether it will be economically feasible to make use of deposits with very high costs of extraction. Some geologists think we are already approaching **peak oil**, where the rate of production reaches its highest possible level, only to decline thereafter; others think the peak still decades away. There is enormous uncertainty over future demand, especially in the context of efforts to stem global climate change. At this point no one can say just which technologies will take the place of oil in transportation and the other uses in which its high energy density is particularly valued.

From a political perspective, the Hotelling analysis also misses an important aspect of the real world: most owners of depletable resources like oil deposits are not profit-maximizing businesses but governments with other objectives and much shorter time horizons. There is no indication that any government of an oil-producing country actually performs a Hotelling-like calculation to decide the rate of extraction, and there is no reason to expect, when all the oil is used up at some future date, that historians looking backward will find that the production decisions along the way had anything to do with maximizing returns. At best, Hotelling's theory provides a normative benchmark for what resource policies should look like, not a prediction of what they will actually be.

One important corollary of the Hotelling model does turn out to be useful, however. In principle, if we leave out the role of production costs, the steady increase in the resource price should reflect its increasing long-run scarcity as deposits are depleted. If production costs also rise over the course of depletion, it is the difference between the price and the cost that reflects scarcity. This difference is what economists refer to as "rent". Suppose one of our social goals is that no generation exploit any later generation for economic gain—that we do not profit at the expense of our children or grandchildren. This would seem to be violated automatically if depletable resources are extracted, because it leaves less for the future. But if the rent portion of the resource price reflects the scarcity that results from depletion, we can set things right by putting this portion aside and saving (investing) it for the benefit of the future. This requirement that rents not be consumed but placed in reserve to make up for our consumption of depletable resources is the **Hartwick Rule**. The clearest example of a country following this rule is Norway, which puts all of its rental earnings from the North Sea oil it sells into a special investment fund. This fund is for the benefit of future generations who will inherit a Norway without these lucrative oil deposits.

Note that the ideal Hotelling and Hartwick visions still involve the complete depletion of all economically useful mineral deposits. Whether this is such a good idea is a question we will return to later in this chapter.

3. **Nonaugmental resources**. Certain natural resources have some of the characteristics of renewable resources and some more typical of depletable resources. Take the case of biodiversity. Like soil and trees, the genetic resources of our planet can be used over and over without causing them to disappear. As long as we harvest species at a rate that permits them to continue to survive, and as long as we maintain sufficient habitat of sufficient quality, we will not suffer a loss of biodiversity. (We could even permit some species to become extinct as long as the rate of extinction does not exceed the rate at which new species are being evolved.) A similar story could be told about wilderness, which is valued for its recreational, spiritual, scientific and cultural attributes. We exploit wilderness by visiting it and trampling it underfoot to some extent, but so long as we don't overdue it we can have the same wilderness to enjoy year after year. On the other hand, if we exploit resources like biodiversity and wilderness too intensively, they decline irreversibly (at least within relevant human time frames). In this second respect they are subject to depletion like mineral deposits.

Economically, the question is whether it is ever appropriate to allow nonaugmentable resources to become depleted. The general answer is yes, since they may not yet be scarce enough to generate rents that offset the economic advantages of heavy exploitation. The problem with this answer, however, is that to have any confidence in it, we would have to be fairly confident of our knowledge of future demands for the resource. If we clearcut or pave over a wilderness area today, for instance, we should not only take into account the current value placed on it but also the value that future generations are likely to express, since these actions are largely irreversible. In practice, most economists are reluctant to see our stock of nonaugmentable resources diminish, mainly because of this uncertainty.

One point that is common to all three types of resources we have considered is that today's uses affect tomorrow's availability. When we measure our economy, the value of goods and services we produce each month or year, too often we fail to take account of the effects our choices have on future supplies of natural resources. If you read in the newspaper that economic growth was 3 % last year, for example, it is highly unlikely that this number was adjusted for the depletion of resource stocks, or possibly the accumulation of new stocks of renewable resources. There is widespread agreement among economists that these adjustments ought to be made, although the technical problems with calculating the changing value of natural resources are demanding. Partial measures of the depreciation of "natural capital" can be found in the World Banks's World Development Indicators, however—possibly a harbinger of still more accurate accounting methods to come.

20.4 Pollution

In Chap. 15 we looked at the theory of externalities, which is the main tool economists use to study pollution. We will briefly review it here in preparation for a larger discussion of the effectiveness of economic analysis in light of the structure of ecological systems.

Recall that the theory takes as its starting point the Market Welfare Model, whose conditions are that the demand curve for goods represents the marginal benefit they provide to society, the supply curve represents the marginal cost to society, and there is a single, market-clearing equilibrium. In this happy state the market price would register both the marginal cost and the marginal benefit to society of producing and consuming one additional unit, and the equilibrium level of production will also maximize the net benefits attainable by society. Into this Eden the snake of externality is introduced. Now (since our interest is pollution) the supply curve can no longer represents social cost; instead, some of the cost is unpaid, and the supply curve is lower than it should be. This situation is summarized in Fig. 20.3 on the next page.

If the market is left to work on its own, it would arrive at the equilibrium quantity Q_e, and the price charged would be P_e. Both of these distort true benefits and costs. At Q_e the level of production is excessive, since some units are being produced whose true social cost, measured by the MSC curve, exceed their social benefit (measured by D). Similarly, P_e does not reflect the true social cost of the last unit produced at Q_e; the amount is understated to the extent of E, which represents the cost of the externality (pollution). An example of this situation might be the burning of coal to generate electricity. There are large effects on the environment from this process that are not included in market costs. The extraction of coal, especially in surface mines, harms land and water resources; burning it pollutes the air, with consequences for human health, acid precipitation and climate change. These externalities are not paid for by coal companies, electricity generating companies or consumers of electrical power. The price per kilowatt-hour does not reflect the true cost of producing this energy, and we have too many power plants burning too much coal.

If Fig. 20.3 is our guide, and if we have perfect information regarding marginal social costs and benefits, two options immediately suggest themselves. First, we could place a tax of E on each unit being produced (assuming E is the marginal cost

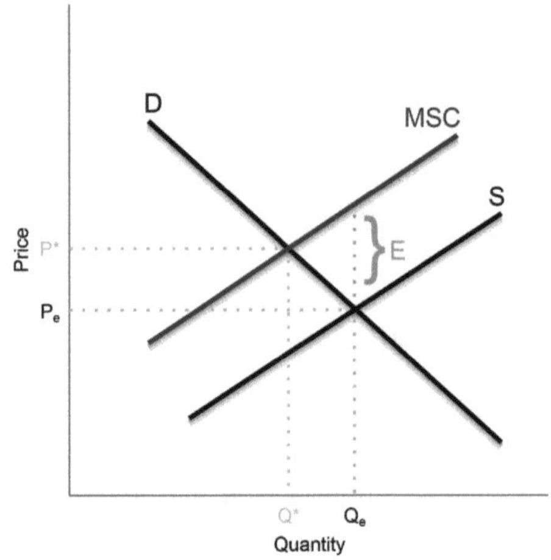

Fig. 20.3 An external cost of production. The Market Welfare Model is assumed to apply to demand but not supply. Q_e is the quantity sold at price P_e in the market equilibrium, but Q*, sold at P*, would maximize net benefits to society. At Q_e the marginal social cost curve MSC is above the market supply curve by the vertical distance E, which represents the external social cost

of the externality at all levels of production). In this way, the supply curve would shift upward and superimpose itself on the MSC curve; Q_e would fall to Q*, P_e would rise to P*, and all would be as it should be. Or a public authority could announce that only the amount of pollution at Q* will be permitted. This amount could be divided into many individual permits, and these permits could be placed on a market. The price of the permit would rise to the point where the total cost of production at Q* was equal to P*, since this is what market demand will support—but no more. Thus, the government can either set a price for pollution and allow the market to determine the quantity (approach 1), or it can set a quantity and allow the market to determine the price (approach 2). In a world of perfect information these are essentially equivalent.

In the real world, of course, information is far from perfect. In the case of coal, for instance, uncertainties include the amount of pollution from different extraction and combustion technologies, the true cost of this pollution, the potential for competing technologies, such as wind generators, to emerge, and the future trend in the demand for electricity—for instance, as other pressures increase for greater conservation and efficiency. The choice between the two approaches then boils down to a question of which risk one would rather take, unpredictable prices or unpredictable quantities. If we set a fixed pollution price, and if this price has long-run credibility, firms have the advantage being able to plan ahead, knowing exactly how much they will have to pay for the polluting production methods. The risk of uncertainty falls on the environment, which may have to absorb less pollution or more, depending on how developments unfold. If we set a fixed quantity of pollution the impact on the environment is more certain, but now producers cannot know in advance what their costs will be. The choice between these two options largely comes down to which risk is more acceptable to those in a position to decide.

Let's take a closer look at the second option. To simplify to some extent, we can say there are also two ways to fix the total amount of pollution through the use of pollution permits. First, these permits can be auctioned off to the highest bidder. If this happens, each firm that wants to buy a permit to produce a good or service will have to pay the market price, which is determined by the number of permits sold and the market demand for the things firms produce. The second approach is to give these permits away to the firms and then let the firms trade amongst each other. Those with more permits than they need will sell to those who have fewer. The market price should once again rise to level of the external cost. There is a big difference between these two approaches. If the permits are sold, firms as a group must pay to pollute; money goes to the government (or perhaps an environmental fund), which can then be spent on another purpose or rebated to the public. This is the idea behind **green taxes**, for instance, which use revenues from selling pollution permits to replace existing taxes, like those on income. If permits are given away and then traded, firms as a group neither lose nor gain, provided other factors remain constant. There is no net revenue for the public. In addition, it is not clear on what basis an initial distribution of permits should be made. Should those who polluted most in the past get the biggest allotment? This is usually how it's done, and it rewards those with the poorest pollution track record. Most economists believe there is a strong case for auctioning pollution permits, but, given the clout businesses have in the political process, it is much easier to pass legislation that gives them away.

Up to this point, we have followed the overall logic of Fig. 20.3, which is based on an adjustment to the Market Welfare Model. The three conditions of this model are assumed to hold except only for the single externality of pollution. In most real-world cases, however, we cannot be so confident of this. There are, after all, many uncompensated externalities, public goods, instances of asymmetric information, less-than-perfect competition and other assumption-violating aspects to economic life. Thus, even if we were to put exactly the right price on the externality in front of us, the result may be far from optimal—including the amount of pollution itself. If the demand curve overstates true social benefit, for instance, then perhaps even less pollution in meeting that demand should be tolerated. Even more troubling is the fundamental doubt that has arisen over the entire approach of the Market Welfare Model due to advances in behavioral economics. As we have seen in previous chapters, the analysis that links choices in the marketplace to the well-being of workers and consumers (and people in their other social roles) has retreated in the face of evidence that people do not act according to the assumptions of economic rationality, and that improvements in human well-being (happiness) do not fit to the rational economic model in any case. Economics is in a state of transition: some economists feel the time has come to jettison the normative apparatus of welfare economics; most, however, are reluctant to give it up. To the extent that one doubts the welfare approach, one also doubts whether it provides a useful basis for deciding how much pollution should continue to be allowed.

So let's follow this second train of thought. In Fig. 20.3 the optimal level of production Q* was determined according to the assumptions that demand represents marginal social benefit and that a proper adjustment to the supply curve would convert it into a measurement of marginal social cost. Suppose we decide that the whole approach is unwarranted, what then? One alternative that is increasingly being employed is to allow pollution limits to be determined by the analyses of public health or ecological scientists rather than economists. For instance, if the main problem with the pollution under consideration is that it harms human health, policy-makers might agree on a maximum health risk the public would be asked to face. The level of pollution that gives us that risk would be the level allowed. Or ecologists might determine that a particular concentration of a pollutant in surface waters would destroy essential fish or other habitat, and the total amount of pollution would be capped so that this concentration is not reached. In either case, we would determine the allowable amount of pollution and the resulting Q* with little or no regard to market demand and supply conditions. The use of permits or pollution taxes would be tailored to achieving this Q*; that is, market mechanisms would be employed to achieve goals that are not market-determined. Of course, in nearly every policy debate, market factors do enter in; consideration is given to the costs to producers and consumers and not only to health or habitat. Nevertheless, in principle the types of pollution control processes we have sketched in this section could be put at the service of goals determined by professionals in other fields.

In Chap. 15 it was pointed out that, rather than trying to regulate the price or quantity of pollution, public policy could take the form of carving out property rights so that a new market in pollution would emerge, and the externality would cease to exist. This is based on Coase's insight that an externality is due simply to the absence of a market in something that should have one. If water pollution is an externality, it is because no one owns the water being polluted or has a clear legal basis to charge a fee to the polluter. We are now in the position to connect a pair of dots, since earlier in this chapter we raised the issue of strengthening property rights in common property resources. It should be clear that this could have an important bearing on pollution policy. If more components of the commons can be vested in institutions whose mission is to preserve them, the burden of determining prices and quantities of pollution can shift from government to a new set of markets. The main advantage of this shift would be political: governments have many motives, and controlling pollution is only one of them. Common property institutions would, in principle, have only the motive of protecting the commons and would decide how much pollution to allow accordingly. Of course, political problems never disappear entirely; in a sense, the problem would shift from how to get governments to value the commons to how to ensure that those charged with exercising common property rights actually adhere to their mission.

20.5 Sustainability

"Sustainable" seems to be a word that makes people feel good. We have sustainable coffee, sustainable furniture and sustainable investing. Sustainability has connotations of solidity, far-sightedness and moral virtue. The closer one looks at the concept, however, the more questions arise: there is no single standard for what constitutes sustainability, nor how it should be measured.

The core idea is straightforward—sort of. Sustainability is based on the underlying value of **intergenerational equity**, the principle that no human generation should spend its accumulated inheritance at such a rate that subsequent generations would be worse off than them. Our children and grandchildren should live at least as well as we do, and the minimum ethical principle is that we should not live without regard for them. Actually, in the wealthier countries the trend has been the opposite: each succeeding generation has lived somewhat better, so the current interest in sustainability indicates that many now fear this trend may be reversed. The reason is that ecological damage is taking place much more rapidly and on a much wider scale than in the past, to the point that it is at least conceivable that the world we will leave our heirs will be severely impoverished.

The main difficulty with sustainability is that it has been given two fundamentally different interpretations, one based on traditional economics, the other on the view that environmental values supercede all others.

The economic interpretation is that living standards should not fall over time, where living standards are seen as the result of both economic wealth and the quality of the environment. This means that deterioration of the environment and the stock of natural resources is entirely compatible with sustainability, provided that increases in human-produced wealth at least compensate. For instance, if we chop down a forest for timber, and invest the earnings in better schools and roads, future generations will be at least as well off as we are if the loss of this forest is made up by the benefit from better schooling and transportation. In the traditional economic view, there is nothing magic about the natural environment: it is one aspect of our overall wealth (natural capital), but so is produced wealth. It is the sum of all wealth, natural and produced, that should matter.

The implication of the economic approach to sustainability is that any exploitation of natural resources, whether by drawing down renewable resources, using up depletable or nonaugmentable ones, or by polluting the environmental commons, that earns its way in financial terms is permissible. If the economic value of pumping oil from the ground and burning it to move cars along highways is greater than the value of leaving the oil in place, it is consistent with sustainability that we pump the oil. Presumably rational decision-makers can be relied on to make this choice where resources are owned; using economically justified regulations to control exploitation is still the remedy where ownership is missing or insufficient.

But one further stipulation must be met to achieve **economic sustainability**: any permanent loss in natural capital has to be offset by a corresponding investment in some other form, whether physical (buildings, machines, infrastructure) or human (education, health). That is, we cannot simply take the revenues from pumping oil and have bigger parties; this would leave future generations with nothing to compensate them for the loss of this valuable resource. Instead, we should sequester the money corresponding to the increased scarcity of oil (due to our pumping it) and make sure it is invested. Since this scarcity is reflected in the portion of the price attributable to rent (the difference between the selling price and the production cost), it is this amount that must be saved. If your short-term memory is in good shape, you will recognize this as the Hartwick Rule, from the section on depletable resources. So the lesson from economic sustainability is this: to be sustainable is simply to do what one should in order to be efficient in general, but also to see to it that all resource rents are funneled into productive investments.

According to the "strong" environmental view of sustainability, the economic approach is a recipe for disaster. It is a mistake, these proponents say, to believe that human-produced capital can take the place of the natural environment. Hydrocarbons like oil, natural gas and coal, for example, also provide the raw material for plastics. The earth's supply took hundreds of millions of years to create and cannot be renewed within a humanly meaningful time frame. If we burn them up for transportation, heating and electricity and leave nothing for our descendants, they will not be able to make use of plastics and other materials, some of which may not yet be invented, that are based on hydrocarbons. No amount of bridges and skyscrapers will compensate them for this. Moreoever, as much as we may worry about completely exhausting the earth's supply of minerals, this is likely to be far less consequential than the potentially catastrophic effect of uncontrolled climate change or other disruptions in the earth's ecological systems. For instance, if our production of greenhouse gases today makes it inevitable that sea levels rise by 25 ft or more over the next century, as they would under some scenarios, then the loss of thousands of years of human habitation and investment along the world's coastlines would dwarf any conceivable capital fund we might set aside as an offset.

If this so-called **strong sustainability** position is adopted, what are the implications for environmental and resource policies? Strictly speaking, they are incapable of being met. They tell us that no human activities should be permitted to damage natural capital: that all renewable resources be maintained at their current levels, that there be no extraction of any depletable resources, and that no nonaugmentable resources, such as wilderness areas and endangered species, be lost to the future. They also imply that no pollution should be permitted if it causes damage that cannot be reversed before future generations appear. This would mean, among other things, that all further emission of greenhouse gases should cease immediately.

Advocates of strong sustainability recognize that, taken literally, this program is out of reach, but they suggest that it can still provide helpful guidelines for policy. Thus, according to this view, we should try as far as we are able to reduce our dependence on depletable mineral resources as soon as possible, and we should place a similar priority on reducing, eventually to zero, our emissions of persistent forms of pollution, like atmospheric carbon. The economic feasibility of these goals has to be taken into account, they say, but the purpose is not economic but ecological, and success should be measured by environmental and resource criteria, not economics.

To some extent, these two positions, economic and strong sustainability, are separated by different value systems; in this sense they can't be bridged. On a practical level, however, much of the disagreement comes down to a single question: how substitutable are natural and human-produced capital? Is it true, as the economic-oriented advocates say, that in nearly every case more of the produced kind can take the place of less of the natural kind? Would we be as happy living in a town with a theater for cultural events instead of a nearby pond that served as a watering hole for migratory birds? (Maybe we drained the pond and sold the land to raise money for the theater, and maybe people in the theater can watch movies about bird migrations.) Or is it the case that such substitution is more the exception than the rule, and that the less visible, but just as significant results of our loss of natural capital, like the larger ecological effects of disrupting bird migrations, are impossible to compensate?

It is impossible to answer such questions at this level of generality. (Attempts to do this are more likely to lead to shouting matches than reasoned discussions.) It may be, however, that the extent of substitution and compensation can be analyzed for particular resources, so that we might choose different criteria for different situations. Climate change probably does not allow for much substitution; perhaps following the Hartwick Rule is sufficient for many of our scarce mineral resources.

One final complication arises from the fact that we have introduced a new form of equity, between generations, but the other, between different people within our own generation, is still a concern. We have seen that living standards are dramatically uneven around the world and within our individual countries. Billions still live in poverty. Do the demands of intergenerational equity come into conflict with those of present-day social justice?

Most advocates of sustainability, whether of the economic or strong variety, are willing to attach a rider to their proposals under which some sort of commitment to present-day equality is affirmed. The problem is that this elides the difficult question of how to proceed if there is a tradeoff between these two types of equity. One solution that has been proposed goes like this: (1) First, calculate the total amount of worldwide resource use that would be consistent with meeting our sustainability goals. This would have to be done individually for each major type of resource. (2) Set a date for achieving sustainability. (3) Estimate the future population of the planet at the time determined in (2). (4) Divide each resource use in (1) by the number of people in (3). The result is a resource use target for each person or, adding them up, each community of persons. This has been called each individual's **equitable sustainable share**. Very roughly, adoption of this approach would require about a 90 % reduction in the use of most natural resources (including via pollution) on the part of the citizens of the wealthy countries if a target date in the mid-twenty-first century is selected.

The attractive aspect of this calculation is that it accommodates the generally accepted philosophical standard of universalism (as laid out by, among others, Kant), that all human beings be treated equally. The world's poorest people are given the same amount of resources to improve their living standards as the world's richest are to sustain them. The approach may be criticized, however, for being based on the assumption that every person will be in a position to actually make use of these resources within the time frame of the calculation. If millions remain in poverty and are cut off from access to resources, the others could conceivably have more than their share. Those who take inspiration from the potential Pareto principle (see Chap. 6) might also argue that giving the most productive societies more access to resources, and then mandating that they share the spoils, might improve the lot of the poorest countries more than a perfectly equal division. But who would make them share? And who would arrange to have resource use limits correspond to equitable sustainable shares?

20.6 Complexity and Uncertainty

Throughout this chapter we have been referring to ecology, but we haven't really said what it is. Since few readers of this book are likely to be familiar with this large and fast-developing field, it is important to say a few words about it.

Ecology is the study of the interrelationships among organisms and between them and their physical environments that determine how they survive and reproduce. It draws on chemistry, biology, geology and other sciences to develop models of the linkages between the living and nonliving components of an ecosystem. The central concepts involve cyclical flows:

- energy flows from sunlight to photosynthesis to food chains to reradiation of heat back into space;
- nutrient flows, such as carbon, nitrogen and phosphorus, between living and nonliving elements;
- the hydrological cycle, which provides water to organisms, draws it from organisms (evapotranspiration) and moves it between atmosphere, land and ocean.

At a more detailed level, ecologists study how particular species or communities of species (like a marsh) function within these flows; for instance, how nutrient flows support or result from the growth and decay of a particular type of marsh grass. Such interrelationships are complicated by the distinctive life histories of organisms—for instance, the role of seed dispersal. Most research in ecology operates between the two levels of specific organisms, which can be collected in the field and analyzed in the laboratory, and the system-level processes within which these organisms function.

At a deep level, ecology is at odds with economics. Economics is about a world of self-contained things and people. The goods and services that trade in markets have thick lines around them, so to speak, establishing a clear distinction between what is owned and what is not. If I buy a chair from you, and we take it from your living room and put it in mine, both of us know quite well what has changed and what has stayed the same. It is not as though some part of the chair has remained behind in its old quarters; what I see in your house is what I get in mine. And we don't expect that your other furniture will suddenly become less stable because they miss their former roommate. The separateness of the chair is what makes it "work" as an item of exchange. Ecology, by training us to see the connectedness of the things it studies, makes us less sure that ownership and exchange are always useful notions.

The problem of complex interaction, which is the subject matter of ecology, can be seen by looking at one example, maintaining spawning habitat for salmon. First the context: salmon are remarkable fish. They are born mostly in the small streams of the colder coastal regions. After feeding in fresh water for a period of time, they swim downstream and enter the ocean, somehow making the adjustment to a saltwater world. For between one and four years, depending on the species, they patrol the oceans, making journeys of hundreds of miles; here they find more food to sustain them, and also sometimes end up as food themselves. Finally they experience an urge to return to their native stream. Salmon have the ability to identify the "taste" of their native water, even though their stream might have been a minor tributary of another minor tributary; and, remarkably, they can do this from their migration route in the ocean, far from the stream they somehow remember. A concentration of native water of no more than a few parts per billion of ocean water is enough to tell them where to go. The salmon then make the reverse adjustment back to fresh water, head up the stream to where they were born (often leaping over rapids so tourists can take pictures of them) and search for a mate. The females dig nests in shallow gravel bottoms by throwing and twisting their bodies; the fish mate and die, leaving the newborn to renew the cycle.

As tremendously competent as these fish are in their age-old tasks, their lifecycle is vulnerable to disruption at many points. Dams or other obstructions can prevent the fish from moving up or downriver; the water may be too warm for salmon to live in; currents may be too swift or too slow, and the eddies may not be right for spawning spots; riverbanks may be stripped of vegetation, denying cover to the fish and removing habitat for the creatures they feed on early in life; gravel beds may be washed away; river flow may be too great or too small or may not match the needs of the fish at different times of the year; competing species may be introduced into salmon streams. This is not even a complete list of hazards, but it gives us the general idea.

What then is the economics of salmon habitat restoration or preservation? There are multiple requirements that have to be met if salmon are to flourish on a particular stream—are these like the "goods" we observe in human economies, except that they are good for fish? If they were, we could put a weight (price) on each one, which would tell us how much more of one requirement, like vegetative cover, is worth how much less of another, like stream flow. But this is not how the fish economy works. First, requirements are not like goods. Below a certain level life cannot be sustained; above a somewhat higher level there is no additional benefit and maybe even a lethal cost. Economic goods are valued from less to more, biological requirements as either within a suitable range (both minimum and maximum levels) or outside it. The second difference is even more difficult to manage: the value of each biological requirement depends on the value of all the others. Stream flow, water temperature, vegetative cover—these all interact to produce a habitat that can or cannot sustain salmon. None can be properly valued in isolation from the rest. By way of contrast, the market value of a chair sitting in your living room does not depend on what other furniture you have. True, its value to you does depend on this, but if it falls below the market price you can sell it, and the chair can find a new owner who values it for at least this amount. (And the chair does not change when you deliver it if you are careful....)

In practical terms, the significance of this discussion is that it is not possible to put an economic price on any particular feature of a functioning salmon stream. Even if we could put a price on the fish themselves (there is debate over whether this is meaningful), we could not say what portion of this value is conferred by planting trees along the bank or preventing dredging at a sensitive part of the river. Economic tools simply don't work for this problem, since we cannot compare the marginal cost of any particular habitat intervention with its marginal benefit. What we can do, however, is estimate the economic cost of providing an entire set of habitat conditions, and we can compare this to the benefits we can expect from doing this. Producing studies like this is useful and important, but it abandons the attempt to put prices on individual activities or their impacts, which is what economics normally tries to do. Of course, one further implication of this insight is that markets in ecological "goods", even if we could fashion them, would not maintain functioning ecosystems, since individual exchanges would fail to incorporate all the complex interrelationships that are responsible for their true value. This is a problem we will return to in the final chapter.

An additional source of complexity in ecosystems stems from their ability, under the right conditions, to recover from stress. A forest can be cut down and turned into farmland; then, generations later, the farms can be abandoned and the same sort of forest will gradually take over. Changes in a streambed might make it impossible for salmon to survive for a few seasons, but restoration of this habitat might enable the salmon to return. Ecologists call this property of ecosystems **resilience**, and it plays a crucial role in our impact on the natural world. Unfortunately, resilience cannot be assumed. If a lake suffers eutrophication (excessive nutrient loading, leading to oxygen-choking algae blooms) beyond a certain point, the organisms necessary to maintaining the interrelationships characteristic of a living lake may disappear, and stopping the harmful inflows may not lead to recovery. The problem is, what is the critical level of stress, such as the nutrient loading that might be caused by fertilizer runoff, at which resilience fails? This is difficult to determine in small, relatively well-understood systems like marshes and ponds, but it is impossible to determine with much confidence on larger scales, such as the earth's climate system.

From our survey of sustainability, it should be clear that knowing how far we can push natural systems before they lose their resilience is a key aspect of achieving a sustainable economy. If we go past the tipping point and leave to future generations an environment that is compromised beyond repair, we have failed the test, particularly if the systems we have ruined are so important that other forms of capital cannot compensate for them. Yet in few cases can we say with certainty just where the tipping point lies. This is a crucial issue in environmental policy, faced across a wide range of problems, from setting allowable concentrations of persistent organic pollutants (like many industrial and agricultural chemicals that have toxic effects and remain in the environment for decades or centuries) to establishing targets for the buildup of carbon in the atmosphere.

Because of the complexity of ecosystems and the difficulty of establishing the limits to resilience, we simply don't understand them very well. There are too many connections to trace, and understanding each individual connection can be someone's life work. Moreover, what one researcher discovers about a small piece of ecosystem functioning can force us to revise what we thought we knew about the other pieces. At this point, what we don't know about ecological processes vastly outweighs what we do. With each new bit of understanding come new surprises. It is a fair generalization to say that, on average, we continue to learn that the linkages between human beings and the rest of the natural world are wider, deeper and tighter than we had previously thought. This is why those who study ecology closely tend to be concerned that what we call "ecological problems" today comprise only a portion of the challenges we will have to face in the future.

These two factors, deep uncertainty about how ecological systems work and suspicion that what we don't know would (if we did) make us take ecological risks even more seriously, have led to attempts to set more stringent rules governing human impacts on the environment. These have crystallized in a set of ideas grouped together as **the precautionary principle**. Originally introduced into German chemical regulation, the precautionary principle has been invoked in a wide variety of environmental laws and treaties, from local ordinances to global agreements. Nevertheless, the term is used rather loosely and means different things to different people. Some of the possible elements of precaution include:

- Standards of evidence. We should not wait until scientists have produced evidence of harm at the level of certainty required in scholarly research. A reasonable suspicion of harm should be sufficient basis for taking action.
- Burden of proof. It should not fall on those worried about environmental impacts to demonstrate the risk of harm; rather, those who want to benefit from activities that threaten the environment should have the burden of demonstrating that the risk is below the level of concern.
- Extent of risk. It is unfair to make those with no say in the matter, such as future generations, bear *any* risk of significant, irreversible harm. Therefore these risks should be reduced to zero as quickly and completely as possible.
- Forward-looking risk assessment. Evaluation of environmental risks should be based, not only on what we know today (which is often very little), but, as far as possible, on what we can reasonably expect to know in the future, as evidence accumulates. In this we can be guided by the historical bias of new discovery: if certain risks have consistently gained in seriousness as we learned more about them, we should assume that they will be seen as even more serious in the future. Environmental policies that have been repeatedly made more stringent as new information appeared were too lenient in the past, before being changed, and are probably too lenient today. (Corresponding to the efficient market hypothesis presented in Chap. 17 is an efficient regulation hypothesis: a regulation that uses information efficiently should have an equal likelihood of being made more or less stringent as new information becomes available.)

The precautionary principle has many detractors, however. Most economists and many other policy analysts regard it as too fuzzy at best and restrictive to the point of paralysis at worst. How would we know whether we are being precautionary or not—what exactly is the test? For instance, in the first element, concerning standards of evidence, we know what scholarly research protocols are for statistical significance; typically they require 95 % confidence with the ready possibility of replication. (See Box 11.2 in Chap. 11.) Advocates of precaution want a lower standard, but what should it be? (One solution is the use of the expected utility formula introduced in Chap. 3: accept any likelihood of harm, however small, that emerges from research, and multiply this likelihood by the estimated amount of harm.) The burden of proof requirement of precaution can be criticized for placing so many barriers in front of businesses and governments that valuable goods and services would never be produced. Demanding that some risks should be reduced to zero would shut down large portions of the world's economy. As for future orientation, maybe the expectation that future knowledge will lead us to put more value on the environment has no basis other than the emotional commitment of environmental scientists and activists to nature—a personal bias no more worthy than someone else's commitment to TV sets and sports cars.

This debate has echoed in international policy disputes, especially over climate change and the role of environmental standards in international trade. For instance, one longstanding disagreement has pitted the United States against Europe on the question of growth hormones in cattle feed. The Europeans think these hormones should be banned under the precautionary principle, and they not only prohibit their own farmers from using them but also ban imports of hormone-laden American beef. The US government has argued that there is no conclusive scientific evidence demonstrating that these hormones are dangerous, and that the European policy is a violation of trade agreements established under the World Trade Organization. In this way a theoretical dispute over precaution has mushroomed into a multi-billion dollar conflict over trade, public health and the environment. Currently there is a temporary agreement under which a limited quantity of US beef, registered as hormone-free, is permitted to be sold in the EU—but this is a truce, not a solution.

The Main Points

1. Seeing the economy as a self-enclosed system is misleading. There are also critical relationships with the natural and social environment: natural resources, ecological processes that sustain life, and the social and cultural mechanisms on which human beings and their abilities depend.
2. Many crucial ecological and cultural resources take the form of a commons, meaning that they are shared in general rather than being owned by any individual or organization. Typically, a commons is unsuitable for formal ownership: it is difficult to delimit and would be very costly to charge access to. Most resources of this type are self-reproducing—not only do they not need economic inputs the way most economic goods do, they maintain themselves best when not interfered with.
3. Exploitation of a commons can generate a "tragedy of the commons". This happens when individual users have an incentive to use up shared resources even though the group as a whole would be better off if the resource were maintained. It is possible to model this process as a prisoner's dilemma. If the community sharing a commons interacts over time, however, it is possible for a

cooperative solution to emerge; in that case economists use the expression "common property resource" to indicate that the shared good is managed in common.

4. An important issue is whether society would be better off if a particular commons is privatized. This can provide an incentive for maintaining the resource in question, but in many circumstances it can degrade it by disrupting the process by which it is sustained. This is a point of dispute in the current debate over intellectual property rights: when does private ownership of an idea or cultural attribute help stimulate more and better culture, and when does it stifle the cultural basis for creative work?
5. It is difficult to find an appropriate institutional form for a commons. One possibility is a trust, an organization whose explicit mission is the preservation of a portion of the shared heritage, like a historical monument or ecologically significant habitat. There are many unresolved issues in the organizational design of trusts.
6. Some natural resources are renewable: they can be replenished indefinitely, but the amount available in the future depends on the amount used today—fisheries, timber resources and topsoil are all examples. Profit-maximizing owners of such resources will compare their rate of growth if not harvested to the interest rate on money earned by harvesting and selling. Thus lower interest rates imply greater conservation.
7. Depletable natural resources have an approximately fixed stock, so any use today comes at the expense of less availability in the future; minerals provide the primary example. (The usable stock of minerals can change as the technology for exploiting them is developed, however.) Ideally, societies that draw down their stock of such resources should compensate future generations by earmarking rents (the difference between selling price and production cost) for investment projects.
8. A third type of natural resource, nonaugmentable, combines elements of the other two. These can be replenished, but if exploited beyond some threshold will be unavailable to future generations; examples include wilderness areas and biodiversity. In principle it may be warranted to use up some nonaugmentable resources if there are large enough gains in doing so, but uncertainty over their future value, and the irreversibility of such decisions, should make us cautious.
9. Pollution is normally analyzed as an external cost of economic activity. This suggests two approaches to policy, setting a price on damages that polluters are required to pay and mandating limits to polluting activities. The first is preferable when we are relatively certain of the marginal cost of pollution: this enables us to put the "right" price on it, and then market responses can determine how this translates into environmental outcomes. The second is preferable when we are relatively more certain what limits need to be respected on environmental damages: we can impose these limits and let the market determine how prices will adjust. To put it differently, priced-based approaches like pollution taxes determine the cost of the policy but accept uncertainty in its

environmental effects, while quantity-based approaches, like pollution permits, determine environmental outcomes but accept uncertainty in the costs individuals and businesses will have to pay.

10. Two meanings have been given to the concept of sustainability. "Strong" sustainability requires that we use natural resources today in such a way that future generations inherit at least as large (or valuable) a stock of such resources in the future. This calls for significant constraints on our harvesting of renewable and nonaugmentable resources and the least possible use of nonrenewable resources. "Economic" sustainability requires that any reduction in the availability of natural resources to future generations be compensated in the form of equally valued increases in produced resources, like infrastructure, equipment, innovations and human capital.
11. Ecosystems are extremely complex and not well understood; the problem of uncertainty is such that in many cases it is not possible to fine-tune regulations or pollution taxes to maximize the net benefits to society. In such situations some economists and environmental advocates would invoke the precautionary principle; this calls for a bias against permitting uncertain environmental or public health damages—in effect, a buffer between the policies that would appear optimal based on current knowledge and the policies we should actually implement. Although widely used, this principle remains controversial among economists.

► Terms to Discuss

Common property resources
Commons
Depletable resources
Ecology
Economic sustainability
Equitable sustainable share
Green taxes
Hartwick Rule
Intellectual property rights
Intergenerational equity
Nonaugmentable resources
Open access resources
Peak oil
Precautionary principle
Renewable resources
Resilience
Strong sustainability
Tragedy of the commons

Questions to Consider

1. What types of commons have played a role in the creation of this textbook? Does the book "use up" any of these common property resources? If you are reading this book as part of a class, is your classroom a commons? If so, are there any actions which have the potential to reduce its value to you and other students?
2. You and I are the recipients of a gift from previous generations, an environmental and cultural commons we can all freely take advantage of. Does this obligate us to make a comparable gift to our descendants?
3. Does global climate change represent a tragedy of the commons? Can you construct a payoff matrix that expresses it as a prisoner's dilemma? Who are the players, and what choices do cooperation and defection represent? Is there any evidence that common management is evolving along the lines predicted by Ostrom?
4. Are you familiar with any trusts along the lines discussed in this chapter? If so, what resources do they protect and how well do they protect them? What methods are used to ensure that they remain loyal to their main purpose?
5. Based on the analyses of renewable and depletable resources, some argue that environmentalists should generally be in favor of lower interest rates. Why would they make this claim? Do you agree? Can you think of any counterarguments, even considering only environmental impacts?
6. Most of the discussion concerning how to minimize climate change has centered on reducing the emission of carbon-containing gases into the atmosphere. Do you favor restricting the total amount of carbon that can be released, by issuing a fixed number of permits, and allowing the price to fluctuate, or setting a price for carbon and allowing the amount of carbon released to fluctuate? Why? If you prefer permits, should these be auctioned or distributed freely?
7. In 1967 the US government abandoned its plan to build a dam that would flood a portion of the Grand Canyon for hydroelectric power and water supply control. Was this decision in the interest of sustainability, against sustainability, or unlikely to matter much one way or the other? In your answer be as precise as possible about the criteria you are using for sustainability, and in particular whether they fall closer to the economic or strong versions of this concept.
8. Do you think that it should be an objective of economic and ecological policy to aim toward an equitable sustainable share of resource use for all people? Why or why not? Are there conditions under which the adoption of these targets would be politically feasible? What are the implications of your answer for sustainability policy?
9. As mentioned at the beginning of the chapter, one of the suspected causes of the decline of bee populations is a class of commonly used pesticides. Studies of the effects of these agricultural chemicals have been inconclusive one way or the other. Would you support invoking the precautionary principle to ban these chemicals while further studies are done? Does your answer depend on the economic benefits farmers get from using them? Does it depend on the balance between studies supporting and failing to find a negative effect on bees? What criteria are you using to answer these questions?

Questions to Consider

Markets as Systems

21

In the first few chapters of this book we presented the fundamental question modern economics was created to answer: can the awesome power unleashed by the industrial revolution be left to the push and pull of the marketplace, or does it need to be steered by the conscious intervention of government or some other institution acting on behalf of society? Adam Smith thought that markets could do most of the job on their own, and subsequent generations of economists have struggled to identify the precise conditions under which Smith's Invisible Hand could be expected to function. Much of what they discovered has been summarized in the Market Welfare Model and the many adjustments and caveats we have examined in our tour of microeconomics.

Up to this point, however, we have looked at markets one at a time, largely in isolation from one another. We have looked at the market for coffee, for instance, as an example of supply and demand and also bargaining power, but separately from the other markets that interact with it, such as the labor markets for workers in the coffee sector and for consumers of coffee, or the markets for equipment used to process and ship each year's harvest. Much can be learned by putting individual markets under a microscope, but much is lost. In this final chapter we will step back to look at the entire system of markets and ask what the invisible hand hypothesis would mean at this level, and whether it would be justified. Our topic is the market economy as a whole.

Markets, we may recall, are simply the result of adding up individual two-sided exchanges. Two parties come to an agreement over a transaction—how much to buy or sell, at what price, and with what stipulations of quality, timing etc.—and their decisions are combined with thousands or millions of others to produce market prices and quantities. The question of whether the market system as a whole functions in the social interest largely boils down to whether desirable social decisions, such as those about what to produce and in what way or how the proceeds should be divided up, can be made by adding up very large numbers of one-on-one agreements.

Without going into the matter more technically, we can see the outlines of a likely debate. On the one side, leaving economic choices to a multitude of

P. Dorman, *Microeconomics*, Springer Texts in Business and Economics,
DOI 10.1007/978-3-642-37434-0_21,

individual agreements has the advantage of decentralization, spreading decision-making to a great many people. This in turn has the potential to draw on their diverse skills, attitudes and sources of information. It also is noncoercive in the sense of relying on negative freedom, as discussed in the appendix to Chap. 6. These are all attractive features, and for many they are appealing enough to make them devotees of "free market economics", no matter what the other drawbacks might be.

On the other side, society is more than just a sum of separate individuals; it has social and political structure, cultural values, shared physical spaces and the other qualities we find in the commons. What guarantee is there that, if people pursue only their personal self-interest, these social factors will be taken into account? Also, isn't it likely that, by not incorporating the indirect consequences of our choices, the sum of individual agreements will be very different from what society as a whole might prefer? We saw a stark example of this in the prisoner's dilemma, where the pursuit of self-interest can lead to worse outcomes for everyone compared to what they could get by making common decisions for the group. Moreover, individuals have highly unequal bargaining power, and the distribution of rewards generated by markets may be incompatible with commonly held standards of justice and fairness. Thus, one might begin this chapter with a deeply-held bias against markets.

In the pages to come we will see what contemporary economics has to add to this debate. It turns out that many of these issues are much better understood now than they were a few decades ago. The controversy over how much economic decision-making can safely be left to markets continues, but at a higher and more constructive level.

We will begin by setting forth a criterion for evaluating economic outcomes that has played a central role in modern social theory, **Pareto optimality**. Next we will turn to a stripped-down version of the economic analysis of markets as a system, which goes under the name **general equilibrium theory**. We will look at it from positive and normative angles, and then consider how it is put into practice in the form of **computable general equilibrium** (CGE) models. After this we will look at the qualifications that have been introduced by modern research: the **General Theory of the Second Best**, the problem of indeterminacy of equilibrium due to false trading, and the positive and normative issues raised by the existence of multiple general equilibria. Only then will we return to the core question of market analysis and the invisible hand for a final summing up.

21.1 Economic Efficiency and the Pareto Principle

In Chap. 6 we looked at the normative side of economics from the vantage point of a single market using the framework of net social benefits. This was the basis for the Market Welfare Model, which sets forth the conditions under which a particular market equilibrium can also be regarded as producing the best possible outcome for society. Unfortunately, this approach cannot be used to analyze an entire system of markets, so we will have to develop another one. Our immediate objective is to produce a formal definition of economic efficiency to serve as our criterion.

Let's begin with a relatively straightforward problem, determining whether a particular production system, such as a steel mill, is efficient. We could say that it meets this standard if it is not possible to produce any more output without using at least some additional inputs. This corresponds to the basis for the Production Possibility Curve presented in Chap. 3. By the same token, we could describe an allocation of goods between two people as efficient if it is not possible, through a reallocation, to improve the utility of one person without reducing the utility of the other. It is really the same idea, but using the production of utility rather than goods as the objective, achieved by rearranging outputs rather than inputs.

It is not difficult to translate this concept into familiar terms; for instance, a particular technology for producing steel may be regarded as efficient because there is no other way to produce as many ingots of the same quality without using more iron, or coal, or labor, or some other input. Similarly, the allocation of meals to two customers at a restaurant is efficient if it is not possible to switch plates so that both are happier with what they're eating. If each is eyeing the other's order and they don't make the switch, there is a loss of potential efficiency in terms of utility.

So the concept of efficiency is clear enough when we are examining small pieces of the economy, but how can it be applied to a world with millions of goods and billions of people; that is, how can we determine whether an entire economy is efficient? To be realistic, we would have to specify two different types of efficiency, static and dynamic, where **static efficiency** refers to how efficiently goods and resources are allocated in an economy at a particular moment in time, and **dynamic efficiency** refers to how well the economy is organized to grow over time. To keep matters as simple as possible in this chapter, we will focus only on the first of these. Our tool will be the concept of Pareto optimality, named for the early twentieth-century Italian sociologist Wilfredo Pareto. The main ideas are summed up in Fig. 21.1 on the following page.

Each axis measures the utility level of an individual in a two-person economy; the points in the quadrant represent economic outcomes: levels of production of goods and their distribution between the two potential consumers. The downward-sloping curve extending from one axis to the other is a **utility possibility frontier**; any point on or within it represents a feasible state of the economy. In particular, we are interested in points A, B, and C—how do they rank?

The principle of **Pareto optimality** states that one allocation is preferred to another if no individual is worse off and at least one individual is better off. Clearly that criterion can be used to show that A is preferable to B, since both individuals have higher utility at A, but what can we say about the ranking of A and C, or even B and C for that matter? In the first case both points are Pareto optimal, and that's the end of the story; neither can be said to be better or worse than the other by this criterion. As for the second, the inability to rank is paradoxical. After all, there is no point on or within the utility possibility frontier that would be Pareto preferred to C,

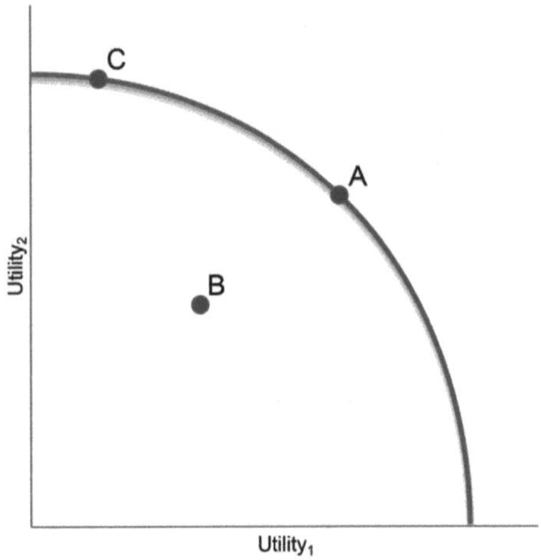

Fig. 21.1 A utility possibility frontier with Pareto rankings. Maximum potential combinations of utility for individuals 1 and 2 are shown by the curved line. Points *C* and *A* are Pareto optimal; neither can be made better off at such a point without reducing the utility of the other. *B* is worse than *A*, but the Pareto principle can't tell us how *C* and *A* or even *C* and *B* compare

since the only way one person could be made better off is by making the other worse off, whereas many points (such as A) would be Pareto preferred to B; nevertheless, C is not Pareto preferred to B, since individual 1 is better off at B than at C. This suggests the fundamental weakness of Pareto optimality as a criterion for normative efficiency: it doesn't supply a ranking over all, or even over a majority, of potential comparisons.

To remedy the situation, economists have advanced a more flexible version in the form of **potential Pareto optimality**. An allocation is potentially Pareto preferred to another if the individuals who gain from the first could fully compensate those who lose from it (so that after compensation they would be no worse off than under the second) and still have some of their gains left over. Suppose, for instance, that the utility depicted in Fig. 21.1 can be measured in dollars, and that each individual has the same dollar-to-utility exchange ratio. The transfer of equal amounts of utility/dollars from person 1 to person 2 or from 2 to 1 would take the form of movement along a line whose slope is -1 (U_1/U_2). Starting from C, for example, it is clear that potential compensation could result in point D, as shown in Fig. 21.2.

The loss of utility experienced by individual 2 due to paying compensating is exactly equal to the gain by individual 1 for receiving it, so both points could be regarded as equally ranked. But now we also have ways to rank A versus C and B versus C: A is potentially Pareto preferred to C since it is preferable to D, and by the same logic C is preferred to B. Allowing for the possibility of compensation has given us a complete ranking of all the points. For this reason, the principle of potential Pareto optimality is far more powerful than its more rigid, compensation-blind cousin. For purposes of practical implementation, economists are usually willing to assume that dollars are a close proxy for utility, so that maximizing the dollar value of an allocation is equivalent to maximizing its ranking according to the potential Pareto principle.

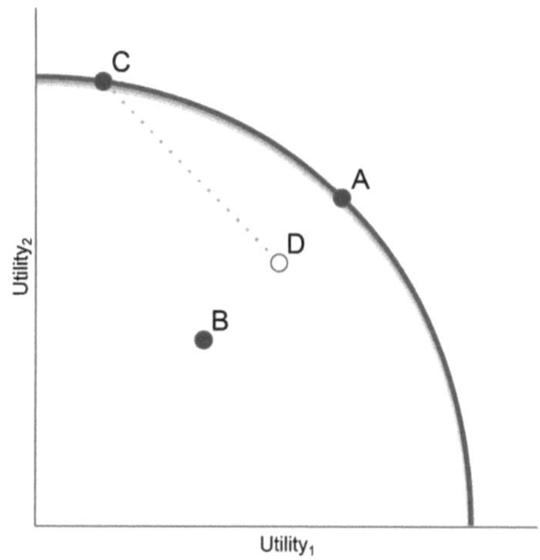

Fig. 21.2 A utility possibility frontier with potential Pareto rankings. The addition of the potential Pareto equality between *C* and *D* makes it possible to rank all four points: *A* best, *C* and *D* equal, *B* worst

It is important to emphasize that the compensation envisioned under the potential Pareto principle is strictly hypothetical. In general, this compensation does not actually get paid; in fact, if it did, potential Pareto optimality would be transformed into Pareto optimality pure and simple. This is because, having received their compensation, those who would otherwise lose from a redistribution would now be at least as well off as they were originally, while those who paid compensation would (if the redistribution were potentially Pareto preferred) be better off. In fact, this is what usually happens in a market transaction. Goods or services are redistributed from one owner to another; in return, compensation is paid. The ability of one side of the transaction to compensate the other suggests that all voluntary transactions are Pareto-improving and do not need the additional boost of the potential Pareto criterion.

To sum up so far: the Pareto principle covers a minority of potential alterations of the economy, but its standard is met in most or all market exchanges. For other possible economic interventions, such as those that might result from nonmarket methods like government regulation, it is necessary to have a comprehensive system of evaluation like the potential Pareto principle. In either case we still encounter all the difficulties with preference theory that we surveyed in Chap. 11, of course. If the general framework of utility analysis, with its assumptions about human behavior and well-being, are incorrect, as they appear to be, the particular techniques of Pareto and potential Pareto analysis have little to add. Nevertheless, since they play a central role in general equilibrium theory and economic approaches to policy analysis, we will keep them in view.

21.2 General Equilibrium

Consider two markets, one for labor and the other for rice. Let's imagine that labor is needed to harvest and process rice and that rice is important for the diet of workers. As the price of labor goes up, it becomes more expensive to produce rice. On the other hand, with higher wages workers will want to buy more rice. If we take just one market into consideration, say rice, it is not difficult to determine what we mean by market equilibrium: it is where the amount of rice people want to buy equals the amount producers want to sell at a common price. We could say something similar about the labor market, assuming that it works along the lines of supply and demand. (Chap. 16 gave us some reasons to doubt this.) But how do we know whether *both* markets could be in equilibrium simultaneously? After all, it may be that the wage that equalizes the supply of and demand for labor produces a cost and a demand for rice at which no equilibrium is possible. On what basis would we presume that the concept of equilibrium could apply to a system of interconnected markets and not just to one market in isolation from the rest?

This question haunted Leon Walras, a French economist of the second half of the nineteenth century. In 1871 he published a treatise setting out the results of his analysis. Walras approached the issue mathematically, expressing each individual market equilibrium as a single equation. In this equation, the quantities supplied and demanded of a good are determined by its price, along with the influences coming from all the other markets. Putting all these equations together, Walras created a system for simultaneously determining all the prices, much in the same way one would solve a system like this:

$$\begin{aligned} x + 2y &= 10 \\ 3x - y &= 9 \end{aligned} \tag{21.1}$$

(Check your math: $x = 4$, $y = 3$.) This system can be solved because there are two equations and two unknowns. Walras' system had an indefinitely large number (n) of equations, but also same number of unknown prices. (Well, almost: the number of independent equations is $n-1$, so Walras can solve only for all the other prices relative to one given price.) Once the prices are calculated, the quantities of each good can be calculated too. The result would be a general equilibrium: the prices would satisfy the requirement that supply equals demand in each market, and they would do this simultaneously for all the markets in the economy.

Or so he thought, but the problem turned out to be more complicated than this. The little two-equation example above can be solved because it is linear; neither x nor y has an exponent, nor are they multiplied by each other. Try to solve, for instance, a different example:

$$\begin{aligned} x^2 + y &= 4 \\ x - y^4 &= 1 \end{aligned} \tag{21.2}$$

Simple methods don't work any more; in particular, one cannot say in advance that there is only one solution for such a system.

A second problem is that supply equals demand only for goods that are produced. Many goods are not produced, either because there is no demand at a price that suppliers would be willing to sell at or because there is no supply at a price that buyers would be willing to pay. In such cases what we have is not an equality (between supply and demand), but an inequality (one more than the other). Therefore, to represent a whole economy, Walras' system must include both equations and inequalities. The mathematics has become more difficult.

These two problems were solved only in the 1930s by mathematicians and economists employing tools that were not available to Walras half a century earlier. Finally, in the 1950s a complete specification, incorporating time, location and the full range of economic goods, produced and unproduced, was published by Kenneth Arrow and Gerard Debreu. It was seen at the time as a major intellectual triumph, one that provided a theoretical foundation for the entire field of economics.

What these theorists produced could be described in several ways. First, they had given a mathematical proof that an entire economy taking the form of a system of markets would have one and only one general equilibrium. This had a powerful implication: if you know the given aspects of an economy—the supply of resources available to it, the preferences of its members, and the initial distribution of resources among these members—you can determine the general equilibrium that should result. In this way the economy can be predicted and explained. To put it somewhat differently, markets, operating through the forces of supply and demand, are capable of fully regulating an economy, determining its precise outcomes over time. This is exactly what Walras had been searching for.

Second, they produced proofs of two normative propositions that have come to be known as the **Fundamental Theorems of Welfare Economics**. These are that, in the absence of market failures, (1) a general equilibrium is always Pareto optimal, and that (2) any possible Pareto optimal state of the economy can be arrived at through a general equilibrium provided that the initial distribution of resources is properly adjusted. It will take a little explanation to make these clear.

First, consider that, in a sense, the deck has already been stacked in favor of Theorem 1 because Pareto optimality rather than some other criterion, such as potential Pareto optimality, has been chosen as the basis for making evaluations. As discussed above, every market exchange is Pareto-improving: the final outcome must be Pareto preferred to the initial situation, otherwise the exchange wouldn't have taken place. Therefore the only additional burden this theorem takes on is demonstrating that *all* such Pareto improvements will occur—that in general equilibrium, and with no market failure, there are no such mutually advantageous exchanges that fail to take place. But, as we will see in slightly more detail in a moment, the model of general equilibrium economists work from assumes exactly what must be assumed in order for this theorem to hold, so it does. As a result, in the narrow but precise terms of the Pareto principle we can say that a system of markets in general equilibrium is economically efficient—again, if there is no market failure.

The second point is more subtle. Suppose in our labor and rice example we arrived at a general equilibrium in which supply equals demand in both markets, but wages are low and workers are hungry. We might prefer some alternative outcome where all workers are well-fed. This might in turn lead us to want to interfere with the market, to require that wages rise or that the price of rice be held down. Such interventions would, of course, mean abandoning the principle of market regulation for some other form of economic control.

The second theorem presents an alternative approach. It notes that there are many potential Pareto optimizing outcomes possible, such as points A and C in Fig. 21.1, depending on the initial distribution of resources in the society. If we can put our finger on one of the outcomes on the utility possibility frontier that we regard as sufficiently equitable, we can arrive at it without interfering with the way markets work, but only by changing the initial distribution. In other words, pick any efficient result and it is possible to use markets to get there, provided you do the right redistributions at the beginning. For many economists, this is an argument against price controls and other forms of public regulation and in favor of progressive taxes and income transfer programs. The advantage of the strategy of redistribution, they argue, is that by letting markets operate freely we can arrive not only at outcomes that have the balance we are looking for, but which are also efficient (as measured by the Pareto principle). In our labor and rice case, for example, this could mean redistributing some money from owners of rice-growing operations to their workers, so that demand for rice would increase, owners would invest in more harvesting equipment, rice workers would become more productive, and then their wage would rise. (This is a purely hypothetical account, and, without knowing the production and consumption responses on all sides, one couldn't say for sure what redistribution would lead to. The Second Theorem tells us there is *some* redistribution that can do the trick, but it doesn't tell us which one.)

But both the positive (single, predictable equilibrium) and normative (fundamental theorems of welfare economics) properties of general equilibrium depend on a large number of assumptions that must hold regarding how markets operate, and this is really the most important point: the general equilibrium theorists have shown us what these conditions are. The list is largely the same as the one that applies at the single market level in order to invoke the Market Welfare Model: no market failures like public goods or missing markets, no asymmetries or other distortions due to information, rational behavior (in the economic sense of Chap. 3) by every participant in the economy, and conditions in every market to achieve a single, market-clearing equilibrium. In other words, general equilibrium comes with no greater guarantee than its single-market relative, and in fact it comes with far less, since these conditions must hold throughout the economy. Since it is inevitable that they won't, practical guidance depends on how much deviation is thought to be "too much" for the positive and normative conclusions to be acceptable.

21.3 Applied General Equilibrium Models

General equilibrium theory is highly abstract, but it has given rise to a new approach to economic prediction in the form of computable general equilibrium modeling. The use of CGE has become widespread in recent years, so it is useful to know how it works.

The theories we have been describing try to represent every market operating in the economy simultaneously. Incorporating every worker and consumer, every owner of every resource, and every good or service produced, strictly applying such theories would be far beyond the calculating power of any computer. To transform this approach into workable applied models, tremendous simplification is required.

To begin with, the economy is reduced to a manageable number of markets. For instance, the most widely used model in international trade, developed by the Global Trade Analysis Project (GTAP) at Purdue University, provides 57 sectors in its most recent incarnation. This simplification is achieved by combining a large number of specific markets into one large aggregate. To take one example, depending on the desired level of detail, a CGE modeler might work with "agriculture" or perhaps a four-way division into "grains", "fruits and vegetables", "meat and dairy" and "fibers" instead of the thousands of agricultural markets that a real economy would have. Resources too must be grouped together: it is common, for instance, to use only four or five categories to incorporate natural resources, capital and different types of labor.

Next, instead of the millions of individuals and households whose decision-making drives real world markets, the model would include a single representative individual for each general role. For instance, in modeling savings decisions, a CGE model might assume that all households are the same, each with an average budget and average savings and consumption inclinations. At most, it would have one such type of household for each major sector or income class of the economy under study, like agriculture or "middle income".

If the model is concerned with international issues like trade and global environmental impacts, location has to be taken into account. This is done by specifying specific countries or groups of countries. The previously mentioned GTAP model, for example, uses 87 countries or other locational groupings.

Finally, the supply and demand factors operating within markets would be greatly simplified. Expectations of future prices, for example, might be held constant, or they might depend on recent and current prices according to some simple mathematical formula. Problems of quality differences among goods, strategic competition between firms and other complexities would mostly be suppressed. Most CGE models depend on a vision of market equilibration that looks little like the rough-and-tumble of normal life; at most they might highlight a market or two for more realistic treatment.

Although it gets ahead of our story somewhat, mention needs to be made of the macroeconomic dimension of CGE models. These include such results as the level of unemployment, the government's budget surplus or deficit and the trade balance of a national economy. Many techniques have been tried, but none are satisfactory at the present time. The most common approach among CGE modelers is to simply exclude macroeconomic effects, so that the outcomes listed above are assumed to remain constant. For instance, in models of international trade the usual approach is to assume that changes in trade policy have no effect on any country's trade balance (the difference between imports and exports), but only on the composition of trade (the particular goods imported or exported). In addition, it is assumed that changes in trade policy will have no effect on the number of workers employed in any country. While assumptions like these can be criticized, and frequently are, they result from the simple supply and demand framework (general equilibrium) the models are based on. The tension between supply and demand analysis and other approaches to the study of macroeconomics will be a thread running through the second volume of this text.

Once the model has been made simple enough, the next step is **calibration**. Each equation has parameters that govern the relationship between key variables, like prices, and outcomes, like quantities bought and sold. These relationships should produce results that look like those in the actual economy. For instance, one such relationship is the elasticity of demand, the percentage change in quantity demanded divided by the percentage change in price. If a particular equation represents the automobile sector, the elasticity of demand in it should correspond to the actual relationship between changes in auto prices and number of vehicles sold. Calibration is the process of setting all these parameters so that the model approximates the real world as much as possible.

The final step is to enter the data that tells the model what the initial state of the economy looks like: the incomes of the households, the production levels for each sector, initial prices and any other variables of interest like investment rates and international trade flows. This sets a starting point for running the model. Now the researcher is in a position to propose a change to one or more of the parameters. Suppose, for instance, that a law is passed that raises production costs in one sector; how will this ricochet through the economy to produce a new general equilibrium? Altering this one factor and recalculating the model will provide an answer.

CGE models have found many uses. They are popular in the analysis of trade policy, such as changes in tariffs or other trade barriers. They are used to estimate the ultimate effect of a tax change, particularly where it might effect one segment of the economy directly but the others indirectly. As you might expect, there have been many CGE analyses of policies to mitigate global climate change, since both the policies, like carbon taxes, and the effects of climate change themselves are likely to have large impacts throughout entire economies. Would increasing the cost of burning hydrocarbons like coal and oil raise or lower the incomes of farmers? How could you find out without doing some form of modeling that takes into account the main direct and indirect linkages between energy and other sectors?

Despite their increasing prominence, CGE models are not viewed favorably by all economists. The simplifications required to make these models tractable inevitably suppress much of the unpredictable dynamics of real events; the future is seldom as much like the past as the models predict. General equilibrium itself is a doubtful proposition given all the conditions that must hold if it is to arise as the models assume, and, as we will see, new questions regarding general equilibrium have emerged since the classic version of the 1950s. Above all, these models have a weak track record. There are few cases where CGE modelers have been able to successfully predict the results of economic policy changes or other shocks, and many of the well-known models have generated predictions that were nearly the opposite of what actually happened. In their defense, proponents of CGE have asked, if not this then what? Models of single markets or other small pieces of the economy make even greater assumptions, since they hold everything else constant, so what other direction is there to go in? Their hope is that, as computing power and modeling sophistication advance, their methods will become more effective. Critics feel that the shortcomings of general equilibrium as a basis for modeling will vitiate any improvement in technique.

21.4 The General Theory of the Second Best

The first significant qualification to general equilibrium theory, although it was not seen this way at the time, appeared in 1956 in the form of an article written by the Canadians R. G. Lipsey and Kelvin Lancaster. It called into question what mathematicians would call the asymptotic properties of general equilibrium—whether the properties of such an equilibrium, like the two Fundamental Theorems, apply more fully the closer one gets to it. This is an important question for any ideal arrangement in the social and natural sciences, because the real world seldom matches an ideal model perfectly, but instead moves closer to or further from it.

Suppose, for instance, a farmer in a dry region wants to know how much irrigation is required for growing a crop like sunflowers. It turns out that a particular amount of water, distributed in a particular way over the season, is optimal and yields the largest, healthiest crop. If water is expensive, however, the farmer might want to settle for a bit less than this. The crucial piece of information would be the relationship between water availability and crop growth as a little less than the optimal amount is used. Normally, we would expect that, if the water is nearly optimal so also will be the crop. If not—if a small decrease in water or some other input could cause a large decrease in the sunflower harvest—this is crucial information to have. It is this issue, transferred to the realm of economics, that is illuminated by the General Theory of the Second Best.

To return for a moment to the perspective of a single market, the Market Welfare Hypothesis presents a vision of the best possible state of affairs, where the marginal benefit to society of producing an extra unit of something is exactly equal to its marginal cost. Moreover, when all the assumptions of the model are adhered to, the equilibrium price, determined solely by the market, will convey both pieces of information, marginal benefit and marginal cost, perfectly. It is almost inconceivable, however, that this will be true for each and every market; surely there will be some which are out of adjustment for some reason, either because the assumptions do not hold (e.g. the presence of external costs or benefits) or the market is unable to reach equilibrium. The theory of market failure tells us that markets with such distortions may need surgery in the form of public intervention. But what about the otherwise undistorted markets connected to it via the linkages of a market system? Suppose the MWM conditions appear to hold for market A, but not for market B to which it is linked. Does this mean that only B needs attention, and that A can be safely ignored?

The general answer is no. It comes to us as The General Theory of the Second Best, which can be stated in this way: if the conditions for optimality are violated in one market, attainment of the second best generally requires that they be violated in at least one other market as well. By second best we mean the best that can be achieved given that the economy-wide conditions for the first best (P = MB = MC) are not attainable. The proof of this proposition requires more math than we can deploy here, but the intuition behind it is surprisingly simple. Consider the following:

Suppose you give me the best possible directions from the Eiffel Tower in Paris to the Coliseum in Rome, and that they take the form of "follow this road 2 miles, then turn right and continue for 8 miles, turn right again and continue for 300 miles" and so on. They are the best instructions in the sense that, if I follow them exactly, I will arrive at the right destination via the shortest possible route. I take these directions and almost follow them perfectly. Unfortunately, instead of turning right on the first turn, I turn left. If I continue to follow each succeeding instruction to the letter I might end up not in Rome but, say, Warsaw. There is a lesson here. Once I made my first mistake I was no longer on the first-best route. Worse, by continuing as if everything were just fine I failed to follow even a second-best (or tenth-best) route. On the contrary, once I had veered from the ideal path, my best course would have been to violate at least one further instruction, so that my itinerary, while not as good as the initial one you gave me, is the best possible given my earlier mistake. This additional adjustment could be as simple as turning around and returning to the original itinerary, or it could entail an entirely different itinerary, but the general point holds: one unprogrammed turn requires another.

So it is with economics. The Market Welfare Hypothesis can be understood as a set of instructions which tell us to arrange each market such that P = MB = MC. If the economy deviates from this prescription in one market, however, it will usually be necessary to make some offsetting change in another market to compensate. Here is a directly relevant example from current economic debates. Suppose that the price of oil is "too low". This might be because environmental externalities (which increase the true social cost of producing and distributing oil) are not taken into account, or because the governments which own most of the world's oil supplies give insufficient attention to potential future scarcities, or perhaps because our grandchildren, who will inherit a world largely depleted of this resource, are not represented in today's markets. If one or more of these factors are at work, the first-best option would be a substantial increase in the price of oil. But this may not be possible, either for political reasons, or because the macroeconomic effect, like recession, would be too severe. That puts us in the situation of searching for the second-best option. One measure that might be taken—in fact, it is a policy that the US government has followed for nearly four decades—would be to mandate, by law, that auto company product lines meet minimum standards for fuel efficiency. Such a policy is obviously an infringement on the freedom of buyers and sellers in the automobile market to pursue the dictates of what they see as their individual rationality.

If we look more closely at the fuel-efficiency policy it becomes apparent why a breakdown in the optimality properties of the oil market might demand an offsetting intervention in the car market. One of the assumptions for the Market Welfare Model to hold is that the demand curve reflect the true marginal social benefit from acquiring another unit of the good under consideration. In our example this means that the amount consumers are willing to pay for different types of cars truly reflect the benefits they provide. But in making their choices, consumers are incorporating in their calculations the price of gas. If gas were priced correctly, internalizing all externalities, this would not be a problem. We are assuming, however, that the price of gas does not reflect its true cost, and so consumers are not giving sufficient weight to fuel efficiency when they choose between cars. Thus they will tend to purchase larger gas guzzlers, imposing on society the costs of too much air pollution and a too-rapid depletion of oil reserves. To put it differently, the mispricing of oil has created a problem not only in the oil market, but in the car market as well. If we are unable to correct the price of oil, the second-best alternative is to compensate by intervening in the car market. (Whether this is best done by fuel efficiency standards, tax incentives on different types of cars, subsidy of public transit, or some other device is another matter entirely.)

Taken literally, the general theory of the second best applies everywhere. This is because there are many markets in which the assumptions of the Market Welfare Hypothesis do not hold, and because, directly or indirectly, all markets in the economy are interconnected; so these distortions are disseminated throughout the entire system. Consider one more example: Everyone knows that the labor market, which sets the price of labor for different types of work, is highly imperfect. We see discrimination by race and gender, barriers to the ability or willingness of workers to move between jobs, lack of compensating wage differentials, excess supply (unemployment) and many other features, discussed in Chap. 16, that suggest that wages do not represent the "true" costs to society (whatever that might mean!) of employing people. But all industries employ workers, and the prices they charge for their products depend in part on what they have to pay the people who produce them. If the wages are not right, neither are the prices of the products.

In practice, a large percentage of economic policy is concerned with second-best-type tinkering. Since so many prices in our economy are out of sync with true marginal benefits and costs, we must do a lot of ad hoc adjustment to minimize the resulting economic irrationality. On the other hand, it is certainly true that in many markets the distortions arising from linkages with the rest of the economy are minor, and the gains to be made by intervening are not worth the potential harm of overriding the market mechanism. Ultimately, where to draw the line—where to say, "This is an urgent problem requiring a policy to achieve the second best", and where to decide that the market works well enough—is a question of values. In our car example, for instance, everything depends on the initial assumption that oil is seriously mispriced. If oil is only slightly mispriced there may be no need to do anything about it. Reasonable people, of course, can disagree about whether a particular price distortion is serious or not.

If there is a single lesson to be learned from the theory of the second best, it is this: to evaluate the case for intervention versus laissez-faire in any market, it is necessary to look at the most closely-linked markets as well. The economy is an interconnected system, not a mere jumble of parts.

Recall also the point raised at the beginning of this section, about the farmer wondering whether or not small deviations from the optimal irrigation policy will lead to correspondingly small changes in the harvest. The General Theory of the Second Best can be seen as giving economic analysts just this sort of information. Any economy can move closer to being optimal in the sense that more markets adhere to pricing based on marginal cost and willingness to pay, but *further* in terms of the value of its outcomes to society, since second best may require more, not fewer, deviations from the marginal cost/benefit principle. Thus, even though a world in which all the assumptions of general equilibrium and perfect competition hold might be best of all, it would be a mistake to think that the more this world is approximated the better off we will be. This is a highly paradoxical result, which says that what works in its pure or perfect form may be a false objective in a world of compromises.

Second best analysis, however, should not be undertaken at such an abstract level, but in relation to the specific distortions that can't be removed in the economy. It is not enough to just invoke the principle every time you want to make an intervention; there has to be a clear connection between the intervention in one market and the distortion in another.

21.5 Out-of-equilibrium Trading and the Indeterminacy of Equilibrium

Real markets are seldom if ever in equilibrium; so the predictive force of theories based on equilibrium depends on the mechanisms that tend to move markets toward their equilibrium state. We have already examined the forces that do this at the level of a single market. If, for instance, the price is initially below its equilibrium level buyers will experience a shortage: the amount supplied will be less than the amount demanded. There will be a tendency for the price to be bid up, thereby stimulating additional production, and this process will continue until an equilibrium is reached. The story would not change a bit if the initial price were very much lower than equilibrium or only slightly lower; the same forces would be at work, but with greater or less intensity, and the same ultimate equilibrium would set the direction to which prices and quantities were heading. If we begin with a price that is too high, a similar mechanism works, except in the other direction: the bidding down of prices, the decrease in production. It does not matter what the initial

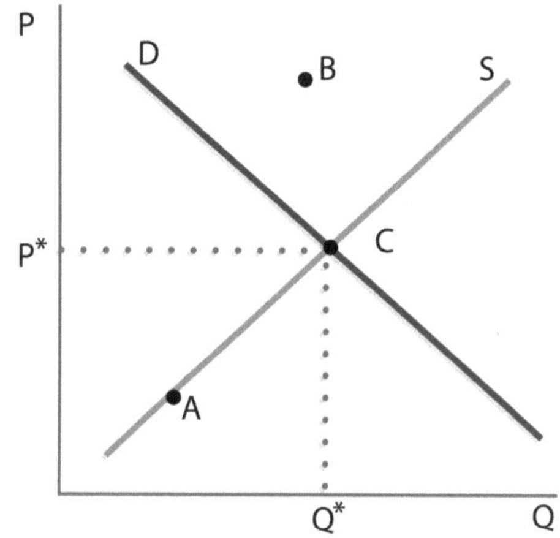

Fig. 21.3 In a single market, the equilibrium doesn't depend on the starting point. Point *C*, where the price is P* and the quantity is Q*, is the equilibrium and eventual destination for the market, whether it begins at point *A*, point *B* or somewhere else

situation is in this analysis of a single market: the equilibrium toward which the market tends is the same. Recall that this characteristic is enshrined in the third condition required for the Market Welfare Model to hold. It is portrayed visually in Fig. 21.3 above.

This property is clearly important for economics, since it establishes that, once we know the supply and demand curves, we know the one and only equilibrium. *This property does not hold in general equilibrium.* On the contrary, the initial out-of-equilibrium state of the economy plays a crucial role in determining which equilibrium the economy as a whole will end up at, as was shown in a series of articles published separately in the 1970s by Gerard Debreu, Rolf Mantel and Hugo Sonnenschein.. The mathematics behind this result are complex, but the idea is straightforward. In the single market case the only out-of-equilibrium possibilities concern prices and quantities that may be too high or too low. There is no reason why these starting points (A and B in Fig. 21.3) should affect the shape or locations of the demand and supply curves since they are not ceteris paribus conditions. The same cannot be said for out-of-equilibrium conditions in the economy as a whole

Suppose, for example, that the price of agricultural products is below equilibrium. This is reflected not only in the market for these goods, but all other markets as well. Farmers, after all, will have less income if their products are underpriced, and this means there will be less demand for the things farmers buy. Farm equipment manufacturers will face a shift in their demand curves, and there will be less demand for other farm-related goods. The ripple effects continue, as the consequences of these second-round effects cycle through the economy. Ultimately, if no other disturbances arise, a general equilibrium would be reached, but it would not be the same equilibrium as the one that would result from, say, an initial situation in which agricultural prices were too high. The curves themselves, and not just the momentary prices and quantities, have been altered.

Simply put, we can contrast single-market and general equilibrium as follows: In a single market, equilibrium is determined by supply and demand only. In general equilibrium, the outcome also depends on the initial and every subsequent out-of-equilibrium state of the economy: which prices are too high, which too low, whose income depends on which prices, and what the preferences are of these individuals. Clearly this presents a problem for both the positive and normative dimensions of economic analysis. On the positive side, the general equilibrium an economy tends toward cannot be predicted from supply and demand only, nor even from the initial state of the economy, since it also depends on continued out-of-equilibrium ("false") trading that may further shift the market conditions on which equilibrium depends. On the normative side, the equilibrium that exerts its gravitational force at any moment in time is only one of a vast number of possible equilibria, each the result of purely arbitrary factors, like the temporary mistakes traders may make. Even if the first two assumptions of the Market Welfare Model hold throughout the economy, so that the demand curves reflect marginal benefits and the supply curves marginal costs, there is no reason to suppose that society is better off under one of these equilibria than another.

How serious is this problem for the effectiveness of the market as an allocative device? It is difficult to say. If these potential equilibria are close together—if, to follow the previous example, the equilibrium resulting from initially high agricultural prices is broadly similar to that resulting from initially low prices—the difficulty is not too great. On the other hand, it is possible to imagine situations in which the effects of out-of-equilibrium adjustment are of great importance. Take the case of the great California Gold Rush of the late 1840s.

One could imagine that, just prior to the gold frenzy, there was an "equilibrium" distribution of Euro-Americans within the US. On the basis of their preferences for where to live, the technologies for transportation available to them and their wealth, a certain number would have chosen to move to California, with the rest moving to other regions or staying put. Then a false gold strike was announced. Based on misinformation, many thousands flocked to the west coast. They didn't find gold, but many found economic opportunities catering to the gold prospectors, as well as all the others catering to the caterers, etc. Once it became apparent that there were no fortunes to be made sifting sediments from California riverbeds, a few '49ers returned home, but most stayed. Some were unable to afford passage home, but most stayed because the new economy spurred by the Gold Rush changed their opportunities: they had now adjusted to a new "equilibrium" set of locations. The result was that the demand to live in California had shifted irreversibly; its effects continue down to the present. Was this ultimately for the better? Does the fact that the course of history was changed as a result of a mass delusion affect your answer?

21.6 Interaction Effects and Multiple Equilibria

The market is an institution that structures and processes human interaction. Workers compete for jobs, and the labor market determines who will be employed and at what wage. Firms compete for consumers, and markets determine which goods earn their producers a profit, and who will end up purchasing them. When we draw demand and supply curves, we are incorporating two types of social interconnections: the making an agreements between buyers and sellers, and competition between buyers or between sellers for the privilege of making such agreements. At the level of a single market, and assuming that these are the only relationships between people that should affect the final outcome, we can infer a single equilibrium.

The situation changes dramatically when individuals affect one another in a variety of ways, only some of which can be channeled through markets. First, as we have already seen, there arises the possibility of external benefits and costs, which directly violate the first two conditions of the Market Welfare Model. But that is not all. Nonmarket interaction, the connections between people or the goods they own that occur outside the boundaries of the marketplace, often give rise to multiple market equilibria.

Here is a simple example at the level of a single market. Suppose we consider the market for storefront space in a shopping mall. The mall owner wants to rent it for as much money as possible, given the demand from those who want to establish retail businesses. The retailers, on the other hand, want to get the best rents they can, also taking into consideration the advantages of location. At first, we might imagine that these interests give rise to the normal downward-sloping market demand curve and upward-sloping market supply curve.

But let us add one additional factor. The desirability of renting any particular property depends on the number of other stores in the mall, since that will affect the amount of foot traffic. No one, after all, wants to be the only store-owner in a "dead" mall. So, if we begin with an empty mall, only a very low rent would attract more than a few retailers to move in. As additional stores open up, however, the location becomes more attractive, and so the mall owner can now raise rents and still find willing buyers. Eventually the pool of retailers looking to relocate is exhausted, so additional inducements must be offered to rent still more space to new individuals and companies. At this level of demand, the demand curve is once again downward-sloping.

The demand relationship discussed in the previous paragraph, combined for simplicity with a perfectly elastic marginal cost curve, appears as in Fig. 21.4 on the next page.

To keep everything as simple as possible, let's assume that the mall owner is "nice" (maybe it is a nonprofit or a government agency) and wants to set the rental price at marginal cost as a perfect competitor would, and not according to the monopoly strategy outlined in Chap. 13. There would then be two possible equilibria. First, if we start at a low level of Q, to the left of the diagram, the equilibrium quantity is Q_1. But if the initial situation is one where many stores already occupy the mall and Q is on the right side of the diagram, Q_2 is the equilibrium. The best strategy for the owner, if the mall is new and initially unoccupied, is to set a rental price below P*, even though it entails a short-term loss. After the number of stores moving in exceeds Q_2, begin to raise the price until it reaches the equilibrium level MC.

Already in this extremely simple example we can see several points that characterize the general theory of interaction effects. First, there is more than one

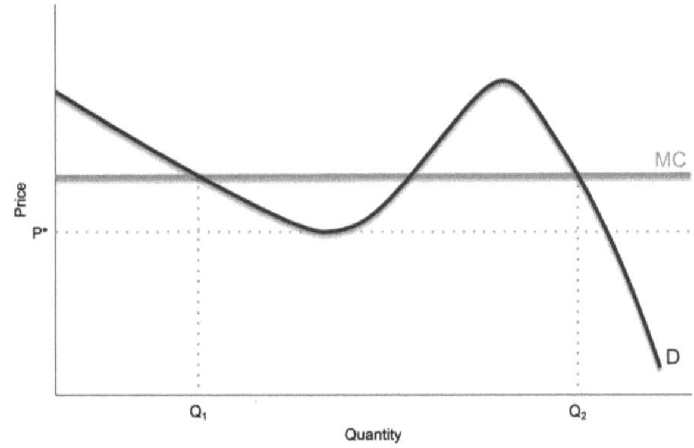

Fig. 21.4 Demand and marginal cost for rental space in a shopping mall. Demand for space at a shopping mall depends on the number of other stores already there. At the same rental price there could be a low demand if the quantity is already low, and a high demand at higher levels of total Q. To set MC = P at the higher level of demand, the mall owner should set a price below P* until Q exceeds Q_2, then raise the price back to MC

equilibrium, in the sense that there is more than one price/quantity combination from which no one would make small deviations. At any starting point in the vicinity Q_1, if buyers and sellers consider small changes in how much they are willing to buy or rent at, they will converge on this amount. The same applies to Q_2. Why do we specify only "small" changes? Because this is how most real-world markets work: each individual participant makes up only a small piece of the market and is able to change quantities demanded or supplied by a only tiny percentage.

Second, if there is more than one equilibrium we can no longer invoke the Market Welfare Model. A single equilibrium is one of the conditions, and the reason should be obvious: there is usually only one optimal allocation, but there are now two which qualify as equilibria. In fact, one of the equilibria in Fig. 21.4 (Q_1) looks pretty dreary, inasmuch as it would leave the mall mostly empty. A useful way to think about this point is that, if there is only one equilibrium in an economy, finding it is very important, but if there are many equilibria it is finding the *right* one that matters.

Third, in the absence of additional information we cannot predict which equilibrium will be chosen by the market. Suppose, for instance, that the mall owner is unable to do more than make very small adjustments in the rent. (Again, this corresponds to the situation in a large market with many participants, where none are able to have much effect.) This means that if the initial situation happens to be on the left side of the diagram, market forces will push it towards Q_1, or to Q_2 for the right side. In this way, the arbitrary force of history, which determines where we "begin" at any moment, makes itself felt. It may be, however, that the mall owner is not willing to leave matters to fate, but instead hires an economist to determine (after a long, expensive study) that, even if the initial situation happens to be the first equilibrium, the owner can do better by getting to the second through the strategy of a temporary price cut. What this means, however, that such a solution to the problem of blind historical inertia succeeds only by replacing the market mechanism with a planning process—replacing incremental adjustments of individual buyers and sellers with a blueprint for an overall, systemic shift.

Finally, note that the source of the problem is that retailers interact not only through the market, but also in the corridors of the mall, in the sense that each retailer's decision to open a store affects the decision of the others by attracting shoppers, and this effect is not directly incorporated in the market. In other words, there is a market in rentals but not in the effect that one rental has on another; this takes the form of a network externality. This is a general point about the relationship between nonmarket interaction and multiple equilibria.

From the standpoint of social theory, we have arrived at an interesting moment in the discussion—toward the end of the nineteenth century, to be exact. In the hundred years following Adam Smith, the notion that individual and collective rationality are reconciled via the invisible hand was the mainstay of educated public opinion in much of Europe and the United States. All social phenomena, it was believed, could be explained by reference to individuals acting in their own personal interest, and if their choices were uncoerced—if markets were free—the case for laissez-faire was self-evident. In the 1880's and '90's, however, a new generation of social scientists emerged to challenge this world view. A society, they said, is more than the sum of its member individuals; it also consists of the interrelationships between them. And not all of these connections occur through the market. On the contrary, Emile Durkheim, often regarded as the founder of modern sociology, felt that individuals are bound together by common intellectual and cultural forces, which they experience as coercive. What I feel, and therefore what I choose, depends on what you feel and, in fact, on what we as a society feel together. Max Weber, the German historian and sociologist from roughly the same period, identified other bonds between people, cemented in the social relations of family, work, government and other institutions. For him, the modern world was less and less an arena of free individual choice, and more a "iron cage" in which the comforts of life are purchased at the cost of massive social regimentation. In both cases, and for other pioneers of the social sciences, individuals were not seen as isolated atoms, bouncing off one another in the frictionless space of free markets; rather they were interconnected in many ways that the market could hardly recognize, much less organize.

The modern social sciences now investigate many systems of nonmarket interaction. There is the kinship system, incorporating family and other relationships of "private" life. There are political systems, in which individuals affect one another through their places in the hierarchies of law and governance. There are the human ecologies of urban life, where geographic proximity becomes the basis for neighborhoods and larger communities. There are cultural and discursive systems, such as the mass media, through which the values and perceptions of individuals are both controlled and given creative force. To this modern economics adds the strategic interaction modeled by game theory: the interplay between principles and agents, cooperators and defectors that people the institutions that make up our economy. And above all there is the natural environment itself, a maze of interconnected systems and cycles, binding together all living and nonliving things in a web of mutual causation, a complex of interaction we considered in the previous chapter. If these perspectives on the interconnectedness of people and things are valid, we would expect to see many instances in which the choices made in the marketplace also trigger significant nonmarket interactions, with the result that market equilibrium is no longer uniquely determined, and factors other than market forces must be taken into account to determine the actual course of events.

Here is a simplified example, which is not intended to represent the full complexity of the issue. Individuals might live predominantly in dense urban areas in which systems of mass transit, such as busses and trains, will best serve their needs. Or most might live in spread-out, more sparsely-populated suburbs for which the private automobile is the vehicle of choice. Each situation may have associated with it a unique equilibrium which reflects the rational decisions of all individuals concerned. If housing becomes a little too decentralized in the first scenario, some people living far from the transit lines may decide to move back into the city, restoring equilibrium. In the second scenario, a family in the suburbs may decide it needs a second car, so that more family members can have access to the places they need to get to. That too may represent movement toward equilibrium. In both cases a system of markets in transportation, housing, and other goods might serve as an efficient mechanism for achieving Pareto superior outcomes, i.e. the best allocation of consumer dollars to housing and transportation in either instance.

But what about the more fundamental question of which scenario we will inhabit? Since each scenario has its own market equilibrium, markets alone cannot do the job of choosing between them. Some other mechanism must be at work. Most likely, it is historical inertia: we will continue to live in the urban/mass transit world if this is what we have inherited from the past, or the suburban/automobile world if this is the initial reality. While real world differences between transportation and residential networks, for instance between parts of Europe and the United States, have more complex causes, the example can serve to illustrate the logic of multiple equilibria under which markets would fall short of both their positive and normative roles. That is, they would not offer a sufficient explanation for the what, how, and for whom of production, nor provide a mechanism for achieving socially rational outcomes. Note that this latter point holds irrespective of which scenario you think conforms to social rationality.

The culprit in this example, responsible for the multiplicity of equilibria, is nonmarket interaction. In fact, there are quite a few candidates for Most Important Nonmarket Interaction in the Field of Urban Development and Transportation. A short list would include the following: obligations (or the lack thereof) to remain close to family members, which can affect and be affected by where people choose to live; the role of neighborhood institutions (social capital), based on stable residential patterns, in making cities more liveable and desirable; and, of course, the effect that housing has on the demand for transit, along with the effect of transportation choices on the demand for housing (the possibility of complementarities). Each of these enter separately into individual market decisions about where to live and what to buy, but the effects they have on one another are not accounted for in markets. The result is a situation in which individuals can exercise individual rationality, but there can be no presumption that the combined outcome is collectively rational.

Economic geography, the field from which the previous example was drawn, has been revolutionized by the use of models incorporating interaction effects and generating multiple equilibria. Another realm in which this approach has become central is the study of financial markets. In an atmosphere of high stakes and great uncertainty, traders are profoundly affected by each others' choices. One very simple case might go like this: each trader might want to follow the lead of the majority in the market; if most of the other traders are bulls, then it is better to be a bull, and otherwise a bear. (Bulls are traders who think the market is headed up; bears think it is headed down.) Why? For one thing, if the trader is working with other people's money there is a great risk of taking a loss, but especially when others are not losing. Then the fund owners might ask, why are you losing when everyone seems to be coming out ahead? The extra cost of being the exceptional loser might outweigh the potential benefit of being a winner when others are losing. If so, it makes sense to go with the crowd. A similar result would occur if each trader is susceptible to being persuaded by the prevailing wisdom simply because it is prevailing. (There is a large literature in social psychology supporting the existence of this tendency.) Going with the crowd, if it becomes the most common strategy, readily creates multiple equilibria. If the crowd thinks the market is moving up, it is in the interest of individual traders to make bets based on moving up. That's one equilibrium. Or the crowd could turn bearish, and each individual trader chooses to go along with that too, creating a second equilibrium. There is quite a bit of evidence that actual financial markets oscillate between multiple equilibria in something like this fashion: that's one reason it's difficult to predict where the markets are headed in advance.

We are now in a position to return to the argument made in the previous chapter regarding complex ecological interaction. Suppose two factories, one making aluminum and the other beer, are located beside a small lake; let's call them A and B for short. Each of them uses the lake to dispose of chemical wastes. This is a problem for the fish who live in the lake, and also for a local sport-fishing resort: the fewer fish the lake can support, the less money will be made by the resort. To make matters very clear, let's suppose that the lake is actually owned by the resort, which has the right to prohibit any form of pollution if it chooses, and that the effects on the resort's profits are the only ones that need to be considered. It would seem we have a perfect setup along the lines of Coase to arrive at a market solution for what would otherwise be an externality. There are no missing markets, and the resort is in a position to compare the marginal cost of each form of pollution at each level to the willingness of each factory to pay for the right to pollute; these bargains should, as we read in Chap. 15, lead to a market equilibrium which is also an efficient allocation of resources—in this case, pollution in paper- and chip-making and water quality for the fish.

Now we will put some numbers to the problem. Each factory has its own effect on the fish based on the tons of waste emitted per week according to Table 21.1, where the effect can be thought of as a financial measure of potential damage to the fish stock as experienced by the resort, for instance in thousands of dollars.

Table 21.1 Separate effects of two factories on lake fish at different pollution levels, measured in tons of waste

Tons of waste	0	1	2	3	4
Factory A	0	1	3	6	10
Factory B	0	2	5	9	14

Table 21.2 Combined effects of pollution from two factories on lake fish (additive)

		Factory B				
		0	1	2	3	4
Factory A	0	0	2	5	9	14
	1	1	3	6	10	15
	2	3	5	8	12	17
	3	6	8	11	15	20
	4	10	12	15	19	24

The rows indicate the possible pollution levels, in tons of waste, from Factory A, the columns the possible pollution levels of Factory B, and the cells reflect the damage to fish resources.

Table 21.3 Marginal costs of pollution from two factories (additive effects)

	0→1	1→2	2→3	3→4
Factory A	1	2	3	4
Factory B	2	3	4	5

What is the combined effect of these two types of pollution? In the simplest case we might just add them together, so that the total cost to the resort would be given in Table 21.2.

Each cell is calculated by adding the sum of the two effects, A + B. For instance, if A emits 2 tons and B emits 3, the highlighted cell shows the sum (3 + 9), the two effects from Table 21.1. The next step is for the resort to calculate the marginal costs of each kind of pollution. This can be determined, as it turns out, directly from Table 21.1, and the calculations are given in Table 21.3.

The marginal cost of one type of pollution is unaffected by the amount of the other in the lake. For instance, if B emits 1 ton, and if A goes from 2 tons to 3, the effect rises from 5 to 8, for a marginal cost of 3. If B is emitting 2 tons and A goes from 2 to 3, the effect rises from 8 to 11—still 3. This means that the resort owner can deal with each source of pollution separately. So let's add the factories' side of the story; this

Table 21.4 Potential social surplus derived from Table 21.2

		Factory A				
		0	1	2	3	4
Factory B	0	−4	−2	−1	−1	−2
	1	−2	0	1	1	0
	2	−1	1	2	2	1
	3	−1	1	2	2	1
	4	−2	0	1	1	0

will provide the basis for bargaining. In the interest of continued simplicity, suppose that the marginal cost of reducing pollution is constant for both factories, 3 for A and 4 for B. That is, it costs A 3 units of money to cut its pollution by one ton per week, no matter how much it is currently emitting, and B's cost per ton is a steady 4.

This means we have all the information we need to describe what economically efficient bargains would look like. Begin with the negotiation between the resort owner and A. To allow the first ton of waste the resort would require a payment of at least 1. This would be in the interest of A, since it would cost 3 to stop it. The next ton would cost the resort an additional 2, so it would still be in the interest of A to offer more than that to continue dumping it. One more ton would just barely pass the test, since now the additional cost of pollution exactly equals the additional cost of abating it. The result is that 3 tons would be emitted, with A paying the resort something between 6 (the continuing damage to the fish) and 12 (the money saved by A for not having to eliminate these tons).

Next would come the negotiation between the resort and B. By the same logic they would arrive at 3 tons as well. The result would be that 15 units of damage to the fish would be allowed, while the factories would save ($3 \times 4 + 4 \times 4 = 28$) in pollution control costs. Is this socially efficient? We can answer that question by constructing a table whose cells reflect the social surplus from each amount of pollution control, defined as the benefit of reducing pollution to that level minus the cost. The benefit we can calculate as 24 (the cost of maximum pollution) minus the damage at each cell in Table 21.2; the cost is the combined cost of pollution control to A and B. This would give us Table 21.4.

It turns out that the pair of agreements does maximize the potential net social benefit from pollution control (although in this example the measurement of pollution is too lumpy to narrow down the range of four optimal possibilities). There is, as in Coase's original analysis, only one social optimum and bargaining between the affected parties arrives at it.

Now let's see what happens when pollution, operating through an ecosystem, is interactive. Again keeping to simplicity, let's change the combined effect of the two forms of pollution to $A \times B$, making it multiplicative rather than additive. This will mean that marginal effect of each type of waste will depend on the level of the other. Table 21.5 gives us the new joint impacts.

From this we can calculate two tables of marginal costs, for A and for B:

Suddenly things have become much more complicated. Each row in Table 21.6 is computed from the corresponding row or column from Table 21.5. For instance, if B is dumping 2 tons per week we are in the column headed "2" in Table 21.4.

Table 21.5 Combined effects of pollution from two factories on lake fish (multiplicative)

		Factory B				
		0	1	2	3	4
Factory A	0	0	0	0	0	0
	1	0	2	5	9	14
	2	0	6	15	27	42
	3	0	12	30	54	84
	4	0	20	50	90	140

Table 21.6 Marginal costs of pollution on lake fish (multiplicative)

		Factory A			
		0→1	1→2	2→3	3→4
Factory B	0	0	0	0	0
	1	2	4	6	12
	2	5	10	15	20
	3	9	18	27	36
	4	14	28	42	56

		Factory B			
		0→1	1→2	2→3	3→4
Factory A	0	0	0	0	0
	1	2	3	4	5
	2	6	9	12	15
	3	12	18	24	30
	4	20	30	40	50

Thus, as A goes from no tons to 1, damage goes from 0 to 5, then from 5 to 15 and so on. The row and column these numbers come from are highlighted.

The first impression we get is that the resort owner's task has become much more complicated. Since each marginal cost depends on the amount of the other pollution, each negotiation now depends on the other. (We can imagine the resort owner running back and forth between two offices where bargaining is taking place.) But the problem is actually more difficult still. Suppose, for instance, that the resort begins discussions with A. A is willing to pay as much as 3 per ton to continue polluting. So the resort owner might think, "Maybe B will be willing to purchase the right to dump 1 ton, so I should consider myself as being in the second row of A's marginal cost table. This means that, at a maximum price of 3 per ton, I should sell the right to dump one ton, since at 2 tons the marginal cost rises to 4, out of A's price range." So the deal is made, and then negotiations between the owner and B begin. If A is emitting just one ton, B will want to buy the right to dump 3 tons. That's a problem, since the agreement with A was based on the assumption that B would be emitting just one; now there is no room for an agreement with A. But if A is forced to end all pollution, the resort can now afford to sell the right to emit all four tons to B, since there is no marginal cost to B's pollution at all. The result is that the three parties would arrive at an equilibrium: no pollution from A and four tons from B. But the very opposite process could also occur. If a preliminary

Table 21.7 Potential social surplus derived from Table 21.5

		Factory B				
		0	1	2	3	4
Factory A	0	112	116	120	124	128
	1	115	117	118	118	117
	2	118	116	111	103	92
	3	121	113	99	79	53
	4	124	108	82	46	0

agreement with A leads to at least two tons of pollution from this source, no pollution by B can be allowed. But then it makes sense to sell all four tons to A and produce a *second* equilibrium: A pollutes four tons and B none.

In short, there are *two* Coase bargaining solutions to this problem, and both are equilibria. Is one equilibrium better than the other? Yes. Consider Table 21.7, which calculates net social benefit from pollution control in the same way Table 21.4 was calculated, except that now 140 rather than 24 is regarded as the maximum pollution cost. This makes the numbers much higher in Table 21.7, but it is the pattern that matters.

As we can see, both highlighted options maximize net social benefits *in the nearby area of the table*. Small movements away from either would reduce this benefit. Nevertheless, having A eliminate all pollution and allowing B to dump away is the better choice, since it is more costly for B to reduce its emissions. Since all of the social benefit is potentially available to the resort, either through a cleaner lake or more payments from the factories, if all of this information is publicly available the resort (after paying an economist a lot of money to sift through it) should choose the better option.

It is not likely, however, that the resort will have access to the factories' cost data. Instead, this will normally be revealed only during the process of negotiation, and, since negotiation must begin somewhere, the initial decision whether to limit primarily one sort of pollution or the other is likely to determine which option finally results. It will take a bit of luck for the resort to choose the right course of action.

Real world environmental issues are, of course, much more complicated than this deliberately simple example. There are often many sources of pollution, and their effects interact more complexly than a formula like A $\times$ B could possibly capture. There is seldom a single owner of a natural asset that needs to be preserved, and severe coordination and transaction cost problems are likely. The result is that potential markets, if we could set them up, face a multitude of equilibria with almost no possibility of selecting the best one. What is needed in such cases is an entity that can take in the entire scope of the problem, identify an overall solution and get all the parties involved to carry it out. Decentralized markets need to give way to centralized plans.

In the end, we should not be surprised by the pattern we've seen in these examples. Markets come to a collective decision by adding up individual choices. If there are important interactions between people or between the goods being exchanged, these will be left out of the process. Markets are thorough but myopic. They scour the economic landscape, looking for every small bit of improvement: possible exchanges that will put a resource in the hands of someone who wants it a little more. They proceed incrementally, however, one exchange at a time. If the situation calls for a coordinated approach, making many changes simultaneously because of the interconnections involved, markets stumble.

In very general terms we can see two types of coordinated action that economies need in addition to markets. One is public intervention—regulation, rule-setting, public enterprise—which was surveyed in Chap. 9. The other is the administrative coordination found in business organizations, and particularly entrepreneurship, the subject of Chap. 8. We don't often think of them as related, and they differ greatly according to which objectives they set for themselves and to whom they are accountable. Nevertheless, from the perspective of the theory of interaction effects, both embody a sort of planning that can span multiple equilibria and make choices among them. Fortunately, both forms are malleable: governments can become more entrepreneurial in style and corporations more responsive to democratic mandates. One of the main trends in modern politics is the search for hybrid economic and political forms that can answer society's need for innovation and coordinated action to respond to the challenge of interdependence in ways that are both democratic and economically efficient.

21.7 A Final Summing Up

We began with the Invisible Hand and we end with it. Adam Smith conjured up this image, but he left it for later generations of thinkers to determine whether it had any validity. Microeconomics as we understand it today is the result of painstaking efforts to identify the precise conditions under which markets could be expected to serve the larger social interest.

In very general terms, we have considered markets under three different sorts of lenses. We have looked at them as social institutions, as a multitude of processes that generate the prices and quantities we see for particular goods and resources, and now as a single interlocking system of allocation.

As social institutions, markets begin in metaphor, seeing all of economic life as an expression of two-sided exchange. An idealized realm of "the market" is culled from the diverse experiences societies have with markets that have evolved in different ways. This idealization sacrifices realism, but in return it offers powerful analytical tools, such as supply and demand analysis and the Market Welfare Model. Markets can also be scrutinized by methods based on other metaphors, like the prisoner's dilemma and bargaining power.

Much of this book is dedicated to a close examination of the way markets function in specific contexts: how shifts in supply or demand affect equilibrium for commodities like coffee, the role of market failure, the social dimension of work, inequality and poverty, and the interplay between economic, political and ecological factors. This has given us a more realistic sense of how markets actually function and what consequences they have. The Invisible Hand reappears as a benchmark in many of these cases, rather than as a force that can be relied on to operate on its own.

Now we have taken a very wide view of markets as they might constitute an entire system. The main message of this chapter is that a market system, unaided by other forms of organization, would be too limited. It would not take interaction effects into account, it would be too vulnerable to the random effects of error and out-of-equilibrium trading, and it would not necessarily function better in closer proximity to the stipulations of the Market Welfare Model than further from them. At this very general level the Invisible Hand simply cannot operate. But this should not surprise us, since no actual economy functions on the basis of markets alone; all depend on the multiple systems of allocation we first examined in Chap. 3. In particular, government and large-scale business are as fundamental to modern economies as markets. What general equilibrium theory offers us is not a challenge to the basic features of modern capitalism, but a basis for seeing more clearly what tasks have to be accomplished and how we should measure success.

The Main Points

1. An economic situation is Pareto optimal if it is not possible to improve one person's utility without reducing someone else's. If it is possible, the reallocation that achieves this is called a Pareto improvement. The problem with Pareto optimality is twofold. First, there is a vast number of allocations that are Pareto optimal (or efficient), and the principle gives no guidance regarding which should be chosen. Second, it is possible that a Pareto nonoptimal allocation could be regarded as preferable to a Pareto optimal one.
2. One remedy for these shortcomings is to adopt the criterion of potential Pareto efficiency. This considers whether, in switching from one allocation to another, it is possible for those who gain to fully compensate those who lose and still experience an improvement. If so, the second allocation is potential Pareto preferred to the first. An allocation is potential Pareto optimal if there is no other allocation potential Pareto preferred to it. One caveat should be borne in mind when thinking about the potential Pareto principle: the compensation it depends on is hypothetical and rarely offered in real life.
3. The various versions of the Pareto principle pertain to the static efficiency of an economy. Dynamic efficiency is about how successful an economy is at growing over time.
4. General equilibrium is a state in which all the markets that constitute an economy are in equilibrium simultaneously with respect to one another. They are linked because price and quantity outcomes in one market are normally factors that will affect outcomes in many other markets. In this way, an

economy can be considered a large, complex, highly interlinked system of individual markets. It is not obvious that such a system would in fact have an overall equilibrium.

5. The problem was framed in the late nineteenth century by Léon Walras, who represented the market system as a set of equations in which participants make offers to buy or sell. General equilibrium occurs when supply equals demand in the entire system of simultaneous equations. Technical difficulties in demonstrating this solution were overcome only in the twentieth century.
6. Given a number of supporting assumptions, theorists have established two fundamental theorems of welfare economics, that (1) a general equilibrium is always Pareto optimal, and that (2) any possible Pareto optimal state of the economy can be arrived at through a general equilibrium provided that the initial distribution of resources is properly adjusted.
7. In recent years there has been a large increase in the use of applied general equilibrium models. These reduce the number of markets and participants to mathematically convenient levels and, by basing equations on real-world data, calculate what general equilibrium ought to arise. Applied general equilibrium models are controversial, however: they require heroic assumptions to be mathematically tractable, and there is little evidence at this point that they improve forecasting.
8. The normative properties of general equilibrium are undermined to some extent by the General Theory of the Second Best. This holds that, if one component of an ideal allocation is violated, at least one other needs to be violated as well in order to arrive at a second-best solution. In practical terms, this implies that, even if a general equilibrium would be the best possible state for the economy, "closer" to this equilibrium is not necessarily better than "further" from it.
9. Modern research into general equilibrium theory has demonstrated that the process of arriving at an equilibrium can alter the equilibrium itself. This means that it is not possible to predict where the economy will end up without knowing its initial, out-of-equilibrium state and having detailed knowledge of the adjustments that will be made between the initial state and the ultimate equilibrium. In practice, this significantly reduces the predictive power of general equilibrium models, including the current generation of applied models.
10. The existence of a single general equilibrium for an economy depends on the assumption that its elements—individual participants and the goods and services they buy and sell—do not interact outside the bounds of the marketplace. If there are such interaction effects, such as social, cultural, political or ecological interconnections, it is likely that there will be multiple potential equilibria. The implications are both positive and normative: it is more difficult to predict where the economy is headed, and additional information would be required to determine whether any particular equilibrium that eventuates is preferred to others that do not.
11. General equilibrium theory is the branch of economics that speaks most directly to the Invisible Hand hypothesis. On the basis of this theory we can

now identify with some precision the assumptions that must hold in order for this hypothesis to be vindicated. Realistically, it is extremely unlikely that all the needed assumptions will be in place for any actual economy, so the question is whether the deviations from Invisible Hand properties are significant enough to warrant corrective action.

▶ Terms to Define

Calibration
Computable general equilibrium
Dynamic efficiency
Fundamental Theorems of Welfare Economics
General equilibrium theory
General Theory of the Second Best
Multiple equilibria
Nonmarket interaction
Out-of-equilibrium trading
Pareto optimality
Potential Pareto optimality
Static efficiency
Utility possibility frontier

Questions to Consider

1. Can an economy with slavery be Pareto optimal? Can it be potentially Pareto optimal? In each case, to answer "yes", what exactly would have to be shown?
2. In this chapter it was asserted that general equilibrium theory presents the modern version of Adam Smith's Invisible Hand hypothesis. Is that entirely true? Does the claim that an ideal market economy has a single general equilibrium that adheres to the Two Fundamental Theorems of Welfare Economics encompass everything Smith meant by his invisible hand metaphor? Be specific, reviewing Smith's argument from earlier in this book.
3. Defenders of CGE modeling argue that the inability of such models to predict the actual effects of policy changes should not matter, since in real life many factors are always changing simultaneously, and not only particular economic policies model-builders are interested in. Do you agree? What should consumers of economic models—those who, like most of us, use them as potential sources of advice—expect them to offer?
4. In every developed country, and in many of the poorer countries as well, the government subsidizes agriculture by making payments to farmers. Economists sometimes criticize these subsidies on the grounds that the revenue farmers get should be determined by the willingness to pay of consumers for their products and nothing more—the logic of the Market Welfare Model. In their view, farmers are being encouraged to oversupply the market. Defenders of these subsidies might argue that they represent a second-best response to mispricing

in other aspects of the economy. Do you agree? If you do, what particular forms of mispricing are entailed, and how might they be offset by farm subsidies. How likely is it that the General Theory of the Second Best actually, and not only potentially, justifies existing agricultural policies?

5. As we saw in Chap. 5, one reason for the coffee crisis of the early 2000's was the rapid increase in supply during the 1990s. Since then, as the price of raw coffee beans plunged, many producers began ripping out their coffee trees and switching to other products; this should eventually cause prices to return to something like their previous level. Does this expansion and then decline of production reflect out-of-equilibrium production decisions by coffee producers? If so, could it have long-lasting effects on the equilibrium size and distribution of the global coffee sector?
6. Suppose workers, when deciding whether to take a job, are strongly influenced by how well that job pays in comparison to the other jobs they know about. Could this lead to more than one equilibrium wage in the labor market? Explain. What form of nonmarket interaction is involved?

Glossary

Absolute poverty A measure of poverty based on a minimum level of consumption. The income equivalent of this consumption establishes a "poverty line", and those below the line are counted as being in poverty.

Administration The process by which one individual or group makes decisions for other individuals or groups. Administration is hierarchical; those who decide (the administrators) have authority over those who receive the decision.

Allocation The use of resources for some purposes or in some ways or for some people rather than others.

Arbitrage Buying goods or assets in one market where they are cheaper and selling them in another where they are more expensive. When enough people engage in arbitrage this tends to equalize prices across the various markets.

Asymmetric information Occurs when one party to a transaction has more information than the other(s). Typically this is information about the party itself or goods it has direct experience with. In an employment negotiation, for instance, the worker has private information about her skills and habits, but the employer has private information about the employment situation, such as prospects for promotion. Both are potential examples of asymmetric information.

Bads Outcomes of production or consumption that have negative effects on others. If there is a market in bads, those who receive them have to be compensated. If they are uncompensated they take the form of negative externalities. Pollution that threatens human health is an example of a bad.

Bear market A market dominated by those who think the prices of the assets traded on it are likely to fall. Selling pressure in such a market will tend to exceed buying pressure, and prices really will fall.

Bears Traders in a market who expect the price to fall. They are eager to sell in order to avoid the financial losses they anticipate.

Beveridge Curve A curve showing the relationship between the number of unemployed workers in the economy and the number of vacant jobs. It is named for an influential British economist of the middle twentieth century.

Book value The value of the assets held by a firm added up individually minus its total liabilities.

Bull market A market dominated by traders who expect prices to rise. This means that buying pressure will exceed selling pressure, and that prices will tend to rise.

P. Dorman, *Microeconomics*, Springer Texts in Business and Economics,
DOI 10.1007/978-3-642-37434-0, © Springer-Verlag Berlin Heidelberg 2014

Bulls Traders who expect prices to rise. They want to buy these assets now in order to benefit from the anticipated price rise.

Calibration Using real-world data to make quantitative predictions from theoretical models. Technically, calibration estimates the parameters of predictive models from existing data in order to specify the relationship between the variables in these models.

Capabilities In Amarya Sen's theory of well-being, the human potentialities which need to be fulfilled in order for people to live desirable lives.

Capital Something that is the product of investment and that generates a flow of services over time. Capital can take many forms—capital goods, financial capital, human capital, social capital, etc.

Capital goods Goods that contribute to production for an extended period of time following their initial acquisition.

Caveat emptor "Let the buyer beware". This is a legal rule that absolves the seller of liability for negative aspects of the goods they sell that careful buyers have the capacity to discover for themselves.

Ceteris paribus "Other things being equal". This is the technique of holding all the factors that determine a particular outcome constant except for one, in order to examine the relationship between the outcome and that one factor.

Coefficient A number that serves as a weight in a regression formula. It tells what effect a change in its associated variable is expected to have on the variable the formula is set up to calculate. Computing coefficients from existing data is the main activity of regression analysis.

Coercion Occurs when someone is dissuaded from making a choice they would otherwise make because of a threat by someone else, when the threatened party is unable to avoid this threat by breaking off contact with the one making it.

Collective organization A decision-making process in which a group of people make a decision that applies only to themselves.

Commodities market Markets in agricultural products, minerals or other goods whose paper claims have acquired the characteristics of financial assets.

Common property resources Goods that are collectively owned or managed by a community of users.

Commons Goods, services or assets that are not owned either by private owners or government. Often commons provide services that are self-reproducing if human beings can be dissuaded from interfering with them.

Comparable worth A nondiscrimination principle according to which workers should be paid equally if their jobs are of equal value to the employer.

Compensating wage differentials Wage differences that offset nonwage differences between jobs. Ideally, people in more difficult, dangerous or unpleasant jobs should be paid more than those in easier, safer or more pleasant ones.

Computable general equilibrium A model of the economy that reduces it to a small number of aggregate markets and solves for the prices and outputs at which all such markets would be in equilibrium simultaneously.

Conditional income transfers Programs that provide money to low-income households in return for meeting certain conditions, such as school attendance by children or visits to health clinics.

Consumer surplus The difference between what consumers would be willing to pay and what they actually pay, i.e. the market price. Graphically, it is the area under the demand curve but above the price.

Cooperation vs defection (in a Prisoners Dilemma) Cooperation is taking an action that benefits other players; defection is taking an action that reduces the payoff to them.

Cost shifting Policies or actions that, rather than (or perhaps in addition to) reducing costs, shift them from some parties to others.

Custom A "process" for making decisions that simply continues making the same decisions that were made in the past.

Default In economics, failure to service debts or other financial obligations. A borrower may default on a loan; a business may enter into default if it cannot generate enough revenue to meet its obligations to workers, suppliers or other creditors.

Demand curve The quantity of a good or service that potential buyers are willing to acquire as a function of the price they expect to pay for it. All other determinants of their demand are assumed to be constant, the "ceteris paribus" assumption.

Demand schedule A table that shows what quantity of a good or service will be demanded at each of many possible prices.

Demographic transition A long-lasting reduction in the rate of population growth due to a restoration of balance between mortality and fertility. When life expectancy first rises, a gap opens between fertility and mortality, resulting in a rapid rate of population growth. The demographic transition is complete when fertility falls to replacement levels, so that population stabilizes. It appears that all countries go through this process, although at different rates and different time periods.

Demography The study of human population, its components and determinants.

Depletable resources Natural resources which, when used, are no longer available for future use. Minerals like petroleum and copper are examples.

Depreciation The reduction in the value of an asset, like a capital good, over time as it is used up.

Disability adjusted life year A measurement that combines years of life lost due to premature death with reductions in the functions people can exercise per year due to injuries or disease. The latter is calculated as a fraction of the former based on the degree of disability.

Discrimination Unequal treatment of equals or equal treatment of unequals.

Disutility Negative utility, the amount of discomfort, anxiety or other harm experienced by an individual.

Dividends Payments made to shareholders that distribute a portion of a firm's profit. Shareholders derive income either from dividends or capital gains, if they can sell their stock for more than they paid for it.

Division of labor Different tasks are divided among different people, rather than everyone doing everything. The main form that division of labor takes in modern society is specialization in the production of different goods and services. A society with no division of labor would be one in which individuals are self-sufficient, producing all the goods they consume to survive.

Dynamic efficiency The extent to which an economy, or some portion of it, innovates in products or methods. This is represented graphically by an outward shift of a production possibility curve.

Ecology The study of the interrelationships between organisms and between them and their physical environment.

Economic behavior Actions that participants in an economy take that affect how that economy works. The study of economic behavior has become a central focus of economic research.

Economic benefits Utility that people acquire from the consumption of goods and services produced in an economy.

Economic costs Opportunity costs and/or disutility resulting from actions taken to produce economic benefits.

Economic efficiency The ratio of economic benefit to economic cost of particular actions, institutions or policies.

Economic institutions Rules or organizations that structure economic activity; these include aspects of firms, markets, government and civil society.

Economic outcomes The results of economic activity, the production and distribution of economic benefits and costs.

Economic sustainability The ability to maintain the existing level of utility across future generations.

Economic vs noneconomic benefits Economic benefits can be given acceptable monetary equivalents, either through markets or appropriate economic analysis; noneconomic benefits are outcomes that are desirable but cannot be given a monetary value.

Economics vs economizing Economics studies the economic benefits and costs of particular policies, institutions or actions; economizing means reducing costs only.

Economics vs the economy Economics is a particular approach to studying how economies work, based on a historically evolving set of concepts, theories and methods; the economy is the realm in which economic life takes place and is only partially represented by economics.

Economies of scale Reductions in the cost per unit of producing something based on the production of a larger quantity of units.

Efficiency wage A wage employers may choose to pay above the market equilibrium in order to gain an added advantage through recruiting higher-quality employees, increasing their motivation, or avoiding the costs of turnover.

Efficient markets Markets that reach equilibrium quickly with a minimum of false trading, that do so with few transaction costs and that, in the process, utilize all available information.

Elastic vs inelastic supply/demand The quantity supplied or demanded is elastic if its percentage change exceeds the percentage change in price; it is inelastic if it is less.

Equilibrium A situation in which all participants are acting according to their decision rules, simultaneously. If what I want to do depends on what you are doing, and if what you want to do depends on what I am doing, an equilibrium occurs when we are both doing what we want in relation to each other at the same time. One characteristic of an equilibrium is that there is no "inner" tendency for the situation to change, since no participant can see an advantage in acting differently. Note that the intersection of a supply and demand curve might be an *example* of an equilibrium, but it also might not, depending on how the underlying market is described and analyzed. An attainable equilibrium also requires a process that brings participants to an equilibrium from whatever initial situation they find themselves in.

Equitable sustainable share The amount of something, typically a nonrenewable resource, that satisfies two equity criteria, equity across people at a point in time and equity across generations over time.

Equity In finance, the surplus of a firm's assets over its liabilities. In ethics, equity is the satisfaction of some principle of distributive justice. Economists often use the equality of income distribution as a criterion for the extent to which a set of outcomes satisfies the criterion of equity.

Event analysis A research technique that uses changes in stock prices or other financial assets after an unanticipated event to infer the economic impact of that event.

Excess demand The surplus of the amount demanded of a particular good at a particular price over the amount supplied at that price.

Excess supply The surplus of the amount supplied of a particular good at a particular price over the amount demanded at that price.

Expected utility The sum of the various possible utility outcomes of a course of action weighted by their probability of occurring. If the action were a game, this is the amount you would be willing to play the game and accept the various possible outcomes if you had no extra like or dislike of risk as such.

Externalities Beneficial effects of actions which recipients do not pay for or costly effects for which those who bear them are not compensated. In short, externalities arise because of a missing market.

Factor markets Markets for goods and services employed in production. The labor market is an especially important factor market.

False trades Transactions between buyers and sellers that take place at out-of-equilibrium prices and that would not take place at all if the market were at an equilibrium. This means that either the buyer's willingness to pay is less than the equilibrium price or the seller's marginal cost is above it.

Financial capital The amount of money invested in a productive activity.

Freedom of contract A legal order in which no one is obligated to undertake any action unless they have agreed to do it via a contract, and in which all commitments made under contract are enforceable. This second stipulation indicates that people are free to make any contracts they wish; their terms will be enforced.

Functional distribution of income Its distribution across groups with different sources of income—wages, interest, rent and profit.

Fundamental Theorems of Welfare Economics (1) A general equilibrium of a perfectly competitive system of markets is Pareto optimal. (2) Any desired Pareto optimum can be arrived at by first imposing a particular reallocation of assets and then permitting the system of perfectly competitive markets to arrive at its corresponding general equilibrium.

Fundamentals approach to financial markets An approach to price forecasting based on the expected future earnings of the asset in question.

General equilibrium Occurs when all the markets that comprise an economy are in equilibrium simultaneously.

General equilibrium theory The branch of economics that studies the characteristics of general equilibrium in models of the economy. It is concerned with topics such as, do these models have a general equilibrium? If so, only one or more? What welfare properties (e.g. Pareto optimality) do these equilibria possess? What is the nature of the adjustment process to equilibrium?

General inequality Inequality across a population as measured by a statistic like the Gini coefficient.

General Theory of the Second Best If an economy is unable to avoid a distortion (price not equal to marginal cost) in one market, it is generally the case that, to achieve second best, it must have a distortion in at least one other market as well, to compensate.

General vs firm-specific human capital General human capital is productive in a wide variety of employment contexts; firm-specific human capital is productive in just a single firm.

Gift exchange A system in which individuals provide goods and services to one another without immediate compensation.

Gini coefficient The ratio of the area between a Lorenz Curve and an equal-distribution (45°) line to the entire area under the equal-distribution line. The closer the Lorenz Curve approximates the equal distribution line, the lower the Gini coefficient. 0 represents perfectly equal distribution, while 1 represents perfectly unequal distribution—one person has everything and everyone else nothing.

Green taxes Taxes on polluting or resource-depleting activities, to generate revenue for the government while reducing environmental harm.

Hartwick Rule Royalties from the extraction of depletable resources (the difference between their selling price and cost of production) should be invested to provide offsetting returns to future generations, to compensate them for having less of these resources.

Human capital Aspects of human productive capacity, like education and health, that can be enhanced by investments and which can generate economic returns over a long period of time.

Ideology Beliefs or mental frameworks that may (if common theories of ideology are correct) have a relationship to the interests or particular life experiences of those who hold them. Ideology is a theory of why people hold particular beliefs, not whether or not those beliefs are justified.

Implicit market A market in which aspects of goods, like their quality or durability, are traded indirectly. Studying such markets makes it possible to assign market prices to characteristics of goods that are bought and sold only as part of larger "packages".

Incentive A personal cost or benefit to taking some course of action. Economists often assume that incentives provide the only source of motivation for individuals in the economy.

Individual vs collective rationality Individual rationality occurs when people choose separately, taking the course of action that provides the largest benefit to them personally; collective rationality occurs when people act as a group, taking the course of action that provides the most benefits to them in the aggregate.

Initial public offering The process by which a privately-held firm is sold to anyone who wishes to buy shares in it. A quantity of shares is auctioned off, with each share representing a portion of the entire equity.

Institution-centered financial systems Systems in which firms are mainly financed by banks or similar institutions rather than relying on stock or bond markets.

Intellectual property rights Legal guarantees for the owners of ideas, images, music and other mental products that allow them to control access and set prices for use.

Intergenerational equity Equality of benefits across generations; not benefitting the current generation at the expense of future generations.

"Internal" freedom Freedom from addiction, convention or routine—a free mental disposition.

Invisible Hand The hypothetical process by which individuals, seeking their own personal benefit, collectively promote the benefit of society.

Labor force participation rate the proportion of working-age individuals who are either employed or seeking paid employment.

Laissez-faire The philosophy that government should regulate business as little as possible, leaving most economic decision-making to market competition.

Law of demand The "law" that the quantity demanded will fall if the market price rises and vice versa.

Liberal The philosophy that government power should be kept to a minimum, in economics but also in other aspects of life.

Libertarianism The philosophy that the only legitimate purpose of government is to prevent greater coercion though the provision of police and an army strictly devoted to national defense.

Liquid assets Assets that can be readily converted to cash.

Lorenz Curve A curve that represents the cumulative proportion of income (or wealth) accruing to different portions of the population—how much to the bottom 10 %, the bottom 20 %, the bottom 50 %, and so on, up to 100 %.

Marginal benefit The additional benefit provided by an additional unit of some good or service.

Marginal consumer The consumer who purchases the additional unit of a good or service when the price falls a small amount or who would just be priced out of the market if the price rose by a small amount.

Marginal cost The additional cost of producing an additional unit of some good or service.

Marginal product The additional output attributable to the employment of an additional unit of some factor of production.

Marginal return on capital The additional profit that can be earned by investing in one additional unit of capital

Marginal time preference The proportion by which an additional good today is preferred relative to the same good at a future point in time, such as 1 year later, by the individual who faces this choice.

Marginal utility The extra utility obtained from one additional unit of a good or service. Algebraically, it is the change in total utility divided by the change in the number of units acquired.

Marginal utility of money The extra utility an individual gets from a small change in how much money he has. It serves as an "exchange rate" between measurement in utility and measurement in money.

Market disequilibrium A condition in which some participants in the market are experiencing disappointment with the results of their choices based on the choices of other participants, such as excess supply and excess demand.

Market equilibrium A condition in which all participants in the market, both buyers and sellers, are making choices consistent with the choices made by everyone else. Typically this means that there is neither excess supply nor excess demand.

Market failure A condition that causes markets to achieve less-than-optimal outcomes. This can result from public goods, externalities, monopoly and asymmetric information.

Market microstructure The specific ways in which market participants acquire information, locate one another, bargain and transact.

Market Welfare Model A framework for analyzing the relationship between market equilibrium and social well-being. It stipulates that if three conditions are met—the supply curve represents marginal social cost, the demand curve represents marginal social benefit, and there is a single, stable equilibrium where they intersect—market equilibrium will maximize net social benefit.

Market-centered financial systems Economic systems in which firms are financed primarily by the stock and bond markets.

Markets Social institutions in which buyers and sellers come together to exchange goods and services, generally for money.

Money vs "real" economic goods and services Money is a measure of value and can be used to purchase valuable goods and services, but it is not valuable in itself. The "real" economy consists of things that are valuable in themselves.

Monopoly Strictly speaking, a single seller that has captured an entire market. It is common to refer to firms with very high but not complete market share, however, as monopolies.

Moral hazard The effect that insurance or other forms of compensation for loss can have, where individuals fail to take all possible precautions against ill events because they are (partially) protected from them.

Movement of vs movement along a curve Movement of a curve occurs when the ceteris paribus conditions on which it is based change; movement along a curve occurs when one of the variables the curve represents (like price or quantity in a market demand or supply curve) changes.

Multiple equilibria Many possible equilibrium outcomes. A market has multiple equilibria, for instance, if there are multiple combinations of price and quantity at which supply equals demand.

Negative vs positive freedom Negative freedom is freedom from coercion; positive freedom is the opportunity to make desired choices. These are often summarized as "freedom from" and "freedom to" respectively.

Net economic benefits Economic benefits minus economic costs.

Net worth The value of an individual or enterprise's assets minus liabilities.

NGO's Nongovernmental organizations.

Nonaugmentable resources Natural resources whose stock can be maintained at current levels but not increased. Such resources can often be depleted by human action, however. Biodiversity is an example of such a resource.

Nonexclusion principle When it is not practical to exclude users of a good or service if they don't pay for it. This is one characteristic of a public good.

Nonmarket interaction A situation in which one person's choices have effects on other people that do not occur via markets. They can occur instead through culture and communication, social networks, physical proximity, etc.

Nonrivalry principle There is zero or near-zero marginal cost of supplying a good or service to an additional user. This is one characteristic of a public good.

On-the-job training When workers acquire productive skills as part of their employment.

Open access resources Natural resources that are available for anyone to use, without paying or obtaining permission from an owner.

Opportunity cost A cost of taking a course of action equal to the value of the best alternative option foreclosed by that choice.

Out-of-equilibrium trading Trades that take place at prices other than the equilibrium price, usually when the market is in the process of arriving at an equilibrium.

Pareto optimality A condition in which it is not possible to make one individual better off without making some other individual worse off.

Paternalism The view that some or all people can be made better off by having choices made for them by better-informed authorities.

Payoff matrix A rectangular array that shows the payoffs to each individual player in a game based on the choices they make and the choices made by the other players.

Peak oil The point at which the maximum amount of oil that will ever be produced is being produced; after this point the level of production will continuously decline. This is based on the assumption that oil production only goes up for a period of time, after which it only goes down.

Positive vs normative statements Positive statements are descriptions, explanations or predictions; normative statements are evaluative (how good is this?) or prescriptive (what should someone do in this situation?).

Potential Pareto optimality A condition in which it is not possible to make one individual better off without making some other individuals worse off, under the proviso that those who benefit from an action fully compensate those who are harmed by it. In effect, potential Pareto optimality sets a cost-benefit test: is the monetary value of the benefit of an action greater than the monetary value of its cost? If so, there is enough "surplus" money in the benefit to compensate those who experience a cost and still leave some money left over.

Poverty line A level of income below which an individual or a household is regarded as being in poverty.

Precautionary principle A framework for decision-making that has one or more of these elements: (a) a reasonable suspicion of harm rather than proof of harm should be a sufficient basis for avoiding certain risks, (b) the burden of proof should fall on those who want to engage in or permit risky activities rather than those who want to prohibit them, (c) those who are not in a position to agree to risks (like future generations) should be protected from them, and (d) decisions about risk should be made on the basis of not only what is currently known but also what we can reasonably anticipate knowing in the future.

Price elasticity of demand The percentage change in the quantity demanded divided by the percentage change in price.

Price-earnings ratio The ratio of the value of a firm's outstanding stock to the level of its current profit. It is one piece of evidence that can suggest whether share prices are over- or undervalued.

Prisoner's Dilemma A social situation involving potential cooperation and defection in which three conditions hold: it is individually beneficial to defect when others cooperate, it is individually harmful to cooperate when others are defecting, and the individual benefits to joint cooperation are greater than to joint defection.

Production possibility frontier A curve that shows the maximum quantity of one good or service that can be produced in an economy given the quantities of other goods or services also being produced. In a two-good model, for instance, this frontier shows how much of the first good can be produced given various levels of the production of the second, and vice versa.

Public goods Goods that have at least one of two characteristics, nonexclusion and nonrivalry.

Purchase value vs replacement value The purchase value of a capital asset is what was paid for it; its replacement value is how much it would cost to buy a new one today.

Quality adjusted life year A unit of measurement that combines years of life lost due to premature death with years of life lived unfavorably due to injury or disease. The proportion of unfavorable years regarded as "lost" is determined by how much utility individuals expect to lose under that condition.

Rational choice Choices that maximize the decision-maker's expected utility.

Relative poverty Poverty defined according to how far below the average (median) income a given household is.

Renewable resources Natural resources that regenerate through natural processes, like the reproduction of an animal population or the formation of new topsoil.

Reservation wage The lowest wage for which a worker will agree to accept employment. This is typically less than the wage actually accepted.

Resilience The ability of a natural system to recover from stress.

Reward effects The effect on overall income inequality of differences between the rewards offered for different positions in the economy.

Risk premium An extra interest rate that must be paid to compensate creditors for accepting a higher level of risk.

Satisficing Setting a minimum level of acceptable quality or a maximum acceptable price and choosing the first good or service that meets this criterion. This is an alternative to rational choice, which requires the decision-maker to maximize expected utility. In other words, it is choice based on "good enough" rather than a more demanding search for the very best.

Selection effects The effect on overall income inequality of differences in the proportion of different groups that attain positions that offer higher rewards.

Signaling (in labor markets) Making choices about education, employment etc. in order to send a message to future employers regarding one's (unobservable) personal qualities. For instance, someone might get a college degree not for the learning it represents, but to signal to future employers that she is the sort of person who works hard to achieve a goal.

Skill-biased technical change The introduction of new methods of production that benefits workers with one set of skills relative to those with another. It provides a possible explanation why some workers' wages are rising while others' are falling.

Social norm Customs, habits or values that are widely shared in a society and that individuals may be penalized in some way for violating.

Solvent/insolvent A firm is solvent if its assets exceed its liabilities; it is insolvent otherwise.

Static efficiency Attaining the most output for a given input, or utilizing the least input to attain a given output. One aspect of this is distributing outputs to those who value them most and costs on those who require the least compensation for accepting them.

Statistical significance The likelihood that a statistical result would not result from pure chance. If a result is significant to the 5 % level, it means that there is no more than a 5 % chance that the claim that the result does *not* occur could be mistakenly rejected due to random fluctuation.

Strong sustainability The principle that future generations should inherit a natural environment, including stocks of natural resources, that are not diminished relative to their current quality and abundance.

Supply curve The quantity of a good or service that sellers wish to supply to a market as a function of the price they expect to be paid for it. All other determinants of their supply are assumed to be constant, the "ceteris paribus" assumption.

Technical approach to financial markets Strategies for buying and selling financial assets based on patterns of price movements that can be found in historical or current data.

Tobin's *q* The ratio of the market value of a firm (the value of its outstanding stock) to its book value.

Tragedy of the commons The depletion of an open-access resource that results from participants overusing it in their own individual interest.

Transaction cost The economic cost of using a market rather than some other method of allocation. This can include search costs, the cost of drawing up contracts, and the legal and other costs that can be anticipated if contracts are violated.

Type I versus Type II error Type I error is believing a hypothesis to be true when it is actually false ("false positives"), while Type II error is believing a hypothesis to be false when it is actually true ("false negatives").

Utilitarianism The philosophy that holds that the best action is that which maximizes the sum of society's net benefits. It denies that there are general rules that ought to be followed irrespective of their anticipated consequences, and it denies that the distribution of costs and benefits across individuals should be allowed to override the calculation of net benefit to society as a whole.

Utility possibility frontier A curve that shows the maximum level of utility one person can have given the level of utility obtained by another. It is assumed to be downward-sloping; that is, if an initial allocation is efficient in the sense that A and B both have the greatest potential utility given the utility of the other, any reallocation that increases A's potential utility must decrease B's.

Value of the marginal product The amount of revenue a firm can expect to receive from selling the marginal product of an additional unit of a factor of production, such as an extra worker.

Willingness to pay The maximum price at which a consumer would still wish to purchase a given good or service. It is generally greater than the amount that must actually be paid (the market price), with the difference constituting consumer surplus.

Index

P. Dorman, *Microeconomics*, Springer Texts in Business and Economics,
DOI 10.1007/978-3-642-37434-0,

MIX
Papier aus verantwortungsvollen Quellen
Paper from responsible sources
FSC® C105338

If you have any concerns about our products,
you can contact us on
ProductSafety@springernature.com

In case Publisher is established outside the EU,
the EU authorized representative is:
Springer Nature Customer Service Center GmbH
Europaplatz 3, 69115 Heidelberg, Germany

Printed by Libri Plureos GmbH
in Hamburg, Germany